APPLYING ECONOMIC PRINCIPLES

Because a solid understanding is still the bottom line.

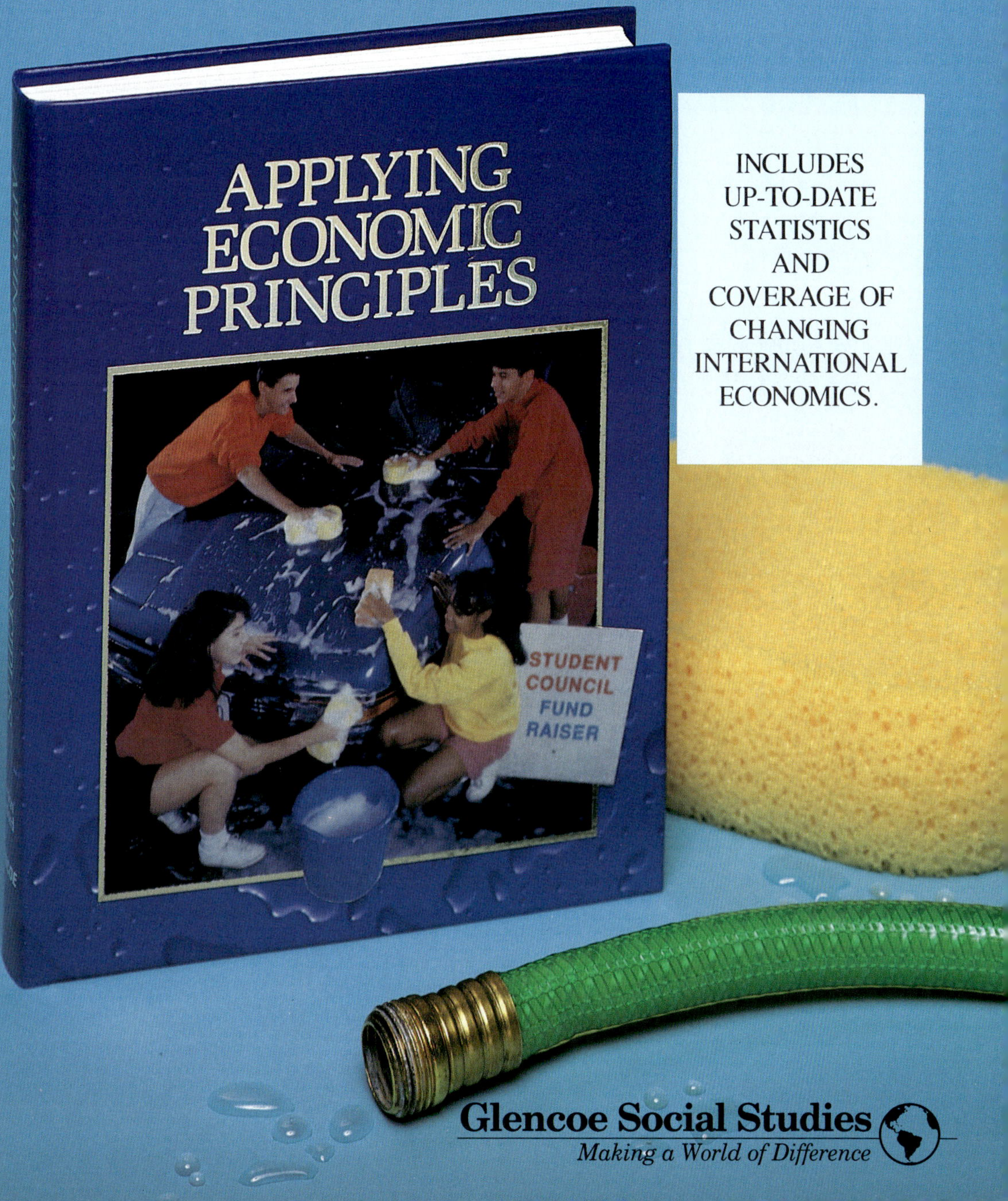

Glencoe Social Studies
Making a World of Difference

Make the language of economic

If your students are going to succeed in the world of "opportunity costs," "diminishing returns," and "business cycles," they're going to need a book that makes these terms clear—and relevant—the first time around.

Glencoe's *Applying Economic Principles* meets that challenge for every student you teach.

It brings a new perspective to such complex issues as the fall of communism, supply, demand, and competition. The words we choose and the way we organize the economic theory and principles puts economics on a level that students can grasp and apply to everyday life.

CHAPTER 12

Government Decisions and Economic Success

Objectives

In the sections of this chapter, you will learn:

A

how the government uses *fiscal policy* to attempt to promote employment, production, and purchasing power, and how Classical economists and Keynesian economists disagree about using fiscal policy;

B

how government price controls and supply-side policies have been used in an attempt to control inflation and unemployment, and why they have met with only limited success;

C

how the ability to regulate our economy is limited by the global nature of our economy; and

D

about programs that are intended to guarantee a minimum level of economic security for all Americans.

Introduction

The Declaration of Independence states that governments are created to secure the rights of "life, liberty and the pursuit of happiness." We believe that our government exists to serve the people. Among other things, our government assures us an opportunity to earn a decent living. To carry out this responsibility the government must be involved in our economic system.

The Laissez-Faire System

In the early days of the United States, the government played a relatively small part in the economic system. The role of the government was limited to protecting property rights, making sure that contracts were carried out, establishing a fair civil code (laws dealing with business transactions), and enforcing general rules for how businesses could operate. In general, the government stayed out of the everyday affairs of individual firms. There was a **laissez-faire** economic policy. This means that the government tried to let the economic system run on its own with as little government involvement as possible.

In a laissez-faire economy (also known as a *free-market* economy) the forces of demand and supply are allowed to make the basic economic decisions of *what, how,* and *for whom.* People who favored this type of

319

Student-friendly organization provides a list of easy-to-understand objectives at the beginning of each chapter and dedicates a separate section to each objective to make topics less overwhelming for students.

Personal Narratives provides engaging real-life anecdotes that relate economic issues to the kinds of situations your students face every day.

216 *Understanding the Economy as a Whole*

Section A What Is the Gross Domestic Product?

This section will introduce the *Gross Domestic Product* and ex
its measurement through the *expenditure* and *income* approac

Personal Narrative

More Is Better, Isn't It?

A door slams, "SMASH," feet run across the floor, "THUD, T
THUD," there is panting in the next room, "WHEEZE, WHEE
Someone is trying to get herself under control. The door slo
opens and your daughter Alison steps gracefully into the ro
"Daddy," (you know you're in trouble) "Can you be a dear
please lend me $20 until next week? I found the most wo
top at the mall and it's on sale for 30 percent off." You kn
chance of her ever paying you back is about as good as
in July. You try to ignore her, but she pokes you in the ri

"You think I'm made of money! Last week it was ne
the week before you had to have a bathing suit. You al
something and your closet is stuffed with things you ne
need to learn a little self control. When I was your age
more than two pairs of jeans to my name!"

Alison starts to pout. "Those old things are out of
wear them. Do you want everyone to laugh at me? I
your stupid jeans. Those were the old days anyhow.
about me at all!" She makes a snuffling noise and l
bor's basset hound.
far. You're angry because
your room an

elevant to your students.

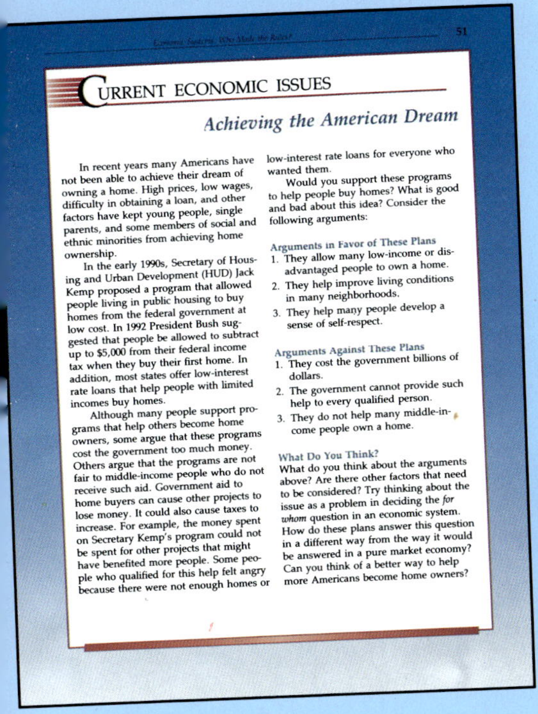

CURRENT ECONOMIC ISSUES

Achieving the American Dream

In recent years many Americans have not been able to achieve their dream of owning a home. High prices, low wages, difficulty in obtaining a loan, and other factors have kept young people, single parents, and some members of social and ethnic minorities from achieving home ownership.

In the early 1990s, Secretary of Housing and Urban Development (HUD) Jack Kemp proposed a program that allowed people living in public housing to buy homes from the federal government at low cost. In 1992 President Bush suggested that people be allowed to subtract up to $5,000 from their federal income tax when they buy their first home. In addition, most states offer low-interest rate loans that help people with limited incomes buy homes.

Although many people support programs that help others become home owners, some argue that these programs cost the government too much money. Others argue that the programs are not fair to middle-income people who do not receive such aid. Government aid to home buyers can cause other projects to lose money. It could also cause taxes to increase. For example, the money spent on Secretary Kemp's program could not be spent for other projects that might have benefited more people. Some people who qualified for this help felt angry because there were not enough homes or low-interest rate loans for everyone who wanted them.

Would you support these programs to help people buy homes? What is good and bad about this idea? Consider the following arguments:

Arguments in Favor of These Plans

1. They allow many low-income or disadvantaged people to own a home.
2. They help improve living conditions in many neighborhoods.
3. They help many people develop a sense of self-respect.

Arguments Against These Plans

1. They cost the government billions of dollars.
2. The government cannot provide such help to every qualified person.
3. They do not help many middle-income people own a home.

What Do You Think?

What do you think about the arguments above? Are there other factors that need to be considered? Try thinking about the issue as a problem in deciding the *for whom* question in an economic system. How do these plans answer this question in a different way from the way it would be answered in a pure market economy? Can you think of a better way to help more Americans become home owners?

Current Economic Issues helps your students develop a solid understanding of the broad national economic issues that affect the lives of U.S. citizens.

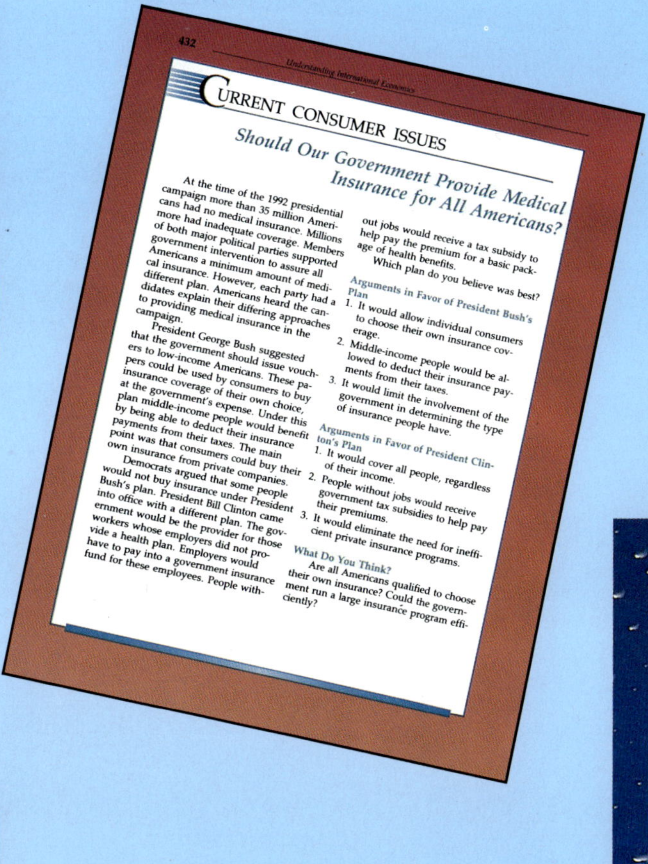

CURRENT CONSUMER ISSUES

Should Our Government Provide Medical Insurance for All Americans?

At the time of the 1992 presidential campaign more than 35 million Americans had no medical insurance. Millions more had inadequate coverage. Members of both major political parties supported government intervention to assure all Americans a minimum amount of medical insurance. However, each party had a different plan. Americans heard the candidates explain their differing approaches to providing medical insurance in the campaign.

President George Bush suggested that the government should issue vouchers to low-income Americans. These papers could be used by consumers to buy insurance coverage of their own choice, at the government's expense. Under this plan middle-income people would benefit by being able to deduct their insurance payments from their taxes. The main point was that consumers could buy their own insurance from private companies.

Democrats argued that some people would not buy insurance under President Bush's plan. President Bill Clinton came into office with a different plan. The government would be the provider for those workers whose employers did not provide a health plan. Employers would have to pay into a government insurance fund for these employees. People without jobs would receive a tax subsidy to help pay the premium for a basic package of health benefits.

Which plan do you believe was best?

Arguments in Favor of President Bush's Plan

1. It would allow individual consumers to choose their own insurance coverage.
2. Middle-income people would be allowed to deduct their insurance payments from their taxes.
3. It would limit the involvement of the government in determining the type of insurance people have.

Arguments in Favor of President Clinton's Plan

1. It would cover all people, regardless of their income.
2. People without jobs would receive government tax subsidies to help pay their premiums.
3. It would eliminate the need for inefficient private insurance programs.

What Do You Think?

Are all Americans qualified to choose their own insurance? Could the government run a large insurance program efficiently?

Current Consumer Issues applies economic principles on a personal level to give students a more solid understanding of economic theory.

Developing Your Economic Skills in each chapter provides real applications to help your students develop their ability to interpret economic data.

Student Edition

There's no better way to us

Just one look. That's all it takes to get in-depth background information, lesson objectives, teaching strategies, extension activities, answers to questions, and much, much more. It's all right here, in our Teacher's Annotated Edition.

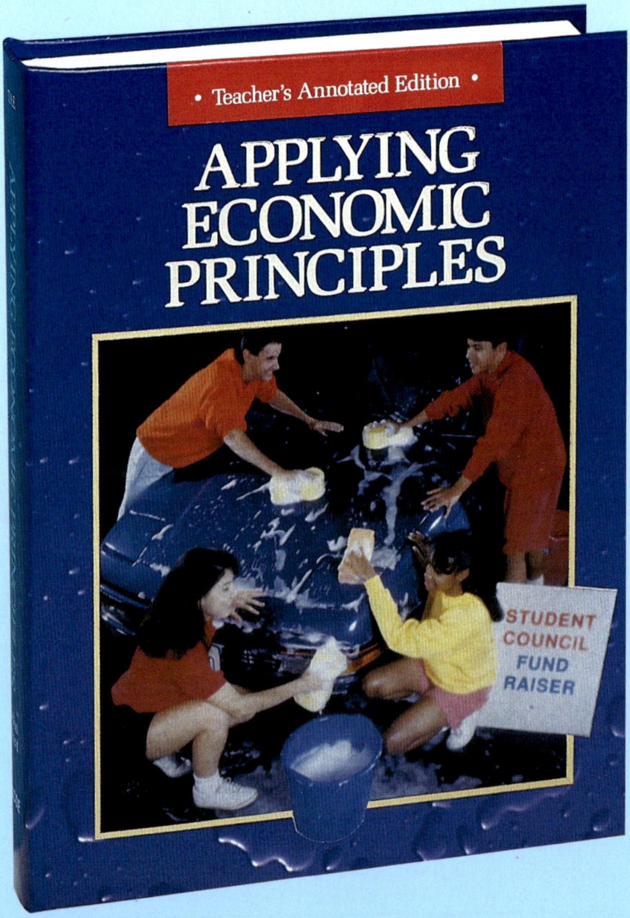

Teacher's Manual is bound into the book to help you pull together multi-dimensional lessons quickly and easily.

Complete Lesson Plans for each chapter provides you with comprehensive teaching suggestions to incorporate guided practice into your classes.

All Teacher's Resource Material is cross-referenced to each section of every chapter, to help you locate blackline masters in seconds.

our time economically.

Note. In the past, payments of interest on the national debt did redistribute income from those who pay taxes to those who own government securities. However, the money stayed within the American economic system. As more of the debt is owned by foreign individuals or organizations, payments on the national debt may redistribute money out of this country.

Example. Ask students if they would rather be in debt $5,000 or $10,000 if they had to choose one or the other. Most will choose $5,000. Then tell them that if they choose $5,000 they are "on their own," but if they go into debt $10,000, you will see that they get a job that pays them $50,000 a year. Let them make the choice again. Most will choose $10,000. The point is that the size of a debt is not as important as the ability to pay the debt.

In the last few years, a large part of the federal debt has been financed through the sale of government bonds to people and businesses in foreign nations. This is a significant change from the past. Until recent years, interest payments on the debt went to Americans or American organizations. Now a significant portion of the interest payment leaves the country.

Is the National Debt Bad?

There are many different points of view concerning the importance of the national debt. Some people are upset by the size of the debt alone. They point out that the debt was over 15 times as large at the end of 1992 as it was in 1945. Other people argue that the debt should be evaluated in terms of our ability to carry or pay on the debt.

Suppose two people were in debt. Mr. *A* owed $20,000 while Ms. *B* owed $50,000. You might think that Ms. *B* was further in debt, but you might be wrong. If Mr. *A* earns $12,000 a year while Ms. *B* earns $100,000 a year, Ms. *B* is in a better position to pay her debt, even though she owes much more money.

The same argument can be made for the United States. In 1945 our debt of 230 billion dollars was more than our entire GDP. In 1991 the debt was about half of the GDP. From this point of view, the debt was less of a burden in 1991 than it was in 1945.

Some economists believe that the trend of the debt is more important than its size. Between 1945 and 1980 the GDP grew more rapidly than the debt. Therefore the debt seemed less important. But between 1980 and 1992 the debt grew more rapidly than GDP. It was therefore becoming more significant.

Part of the national debt represents borrowing from people who have bought savings bonds.

On-page Annotations include Background Notes, Questions for Discussion, Problem Solving Activities, answers, and cross-referenced to the Teacher's Guide.

ull-motion video will add interest for your students.

ll the drama of full-motion video, losely correlated to lessons and accesible in a matter of seconds. That's what ou'll find in the **Video Encyclopedia f the 20th Century,** an extraordinary rogram from CEL Educational esources.

 handy **Barcode User's Guide** has een included to help you access ppropriate images instantly. With the troke of the light pen, the carefully rganized barcodes bring images to the creen, ready to reinforce lessons.

Teacher's Annotated Edition

Get greater returns wit

With ten different types of activities, all on reproducible blackline masters, your most effective classes can get out of the planning stages, and into action.

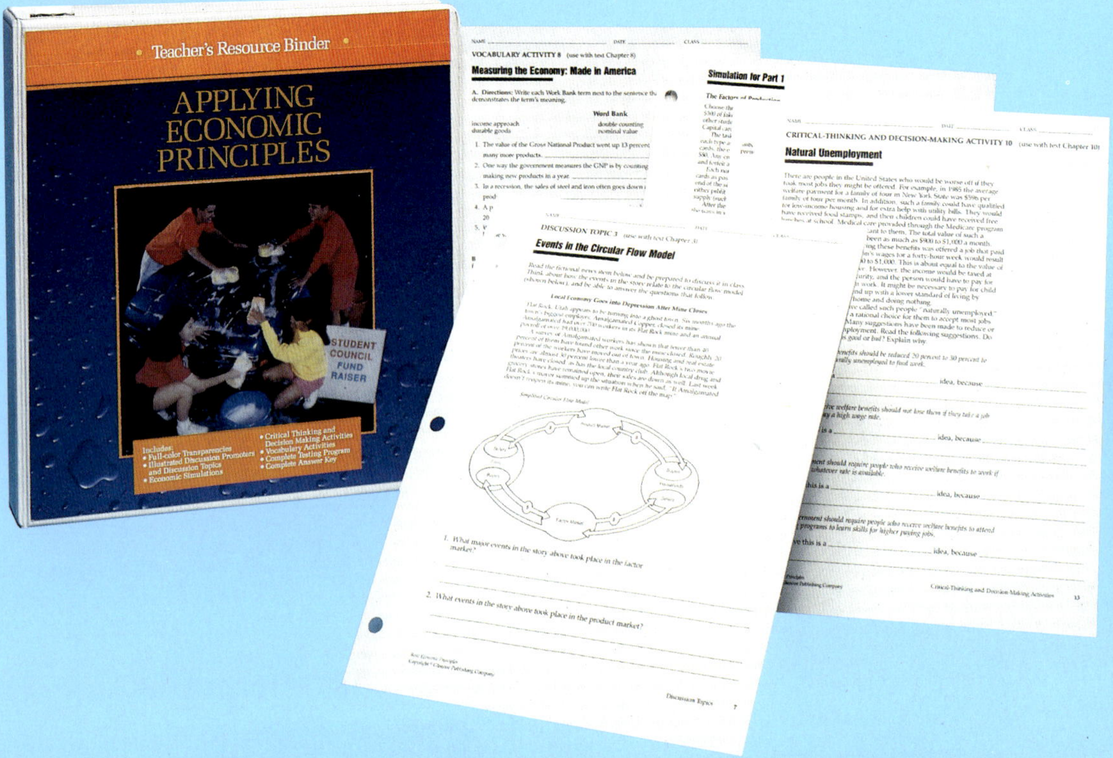

Student Activity Book provides reviews, reinforcement activities, vocabulary exercises, and historical perspectives for every chapter in the text.

Discussion Topics uses a variety of hypothetical situations as a backdrop to help students pinpoint and analyze economic principles at work in everyday life.

Vocabulary Activities, provided for every chapter develops students' proficiency with the new language of economics.

Simulations takes economic principles off the page and into a format students can actually act out in class, to help them develop communication and decision-making skills as they develop a deeper understanding of economic concepts.

Critical Thinking and Decision Making Activities encourage students to uncover key economic concepts as they analyze a number of scenarios, so they can further develop their critical thinking and decision-making skills as they build their comprehension.

ne convenient package.

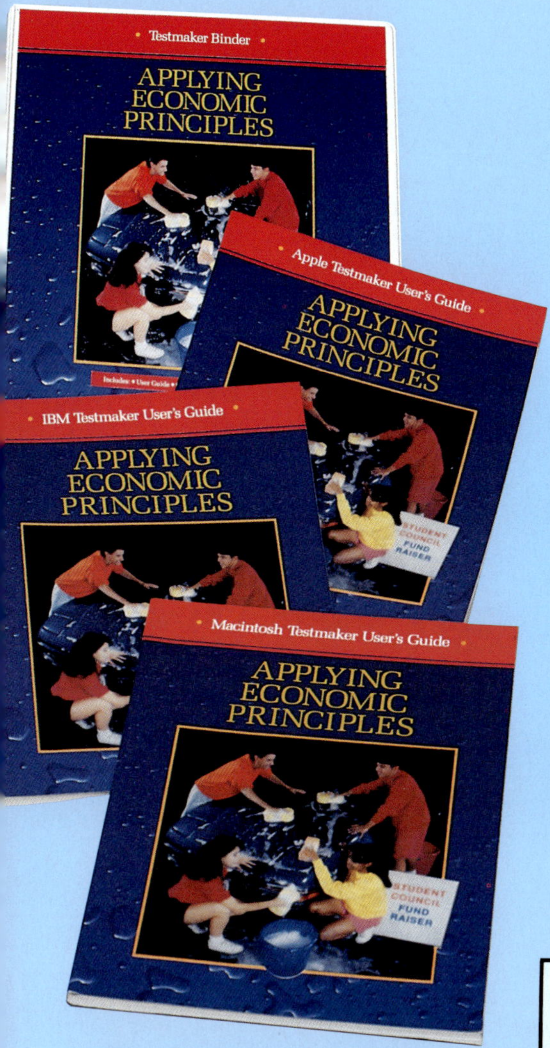

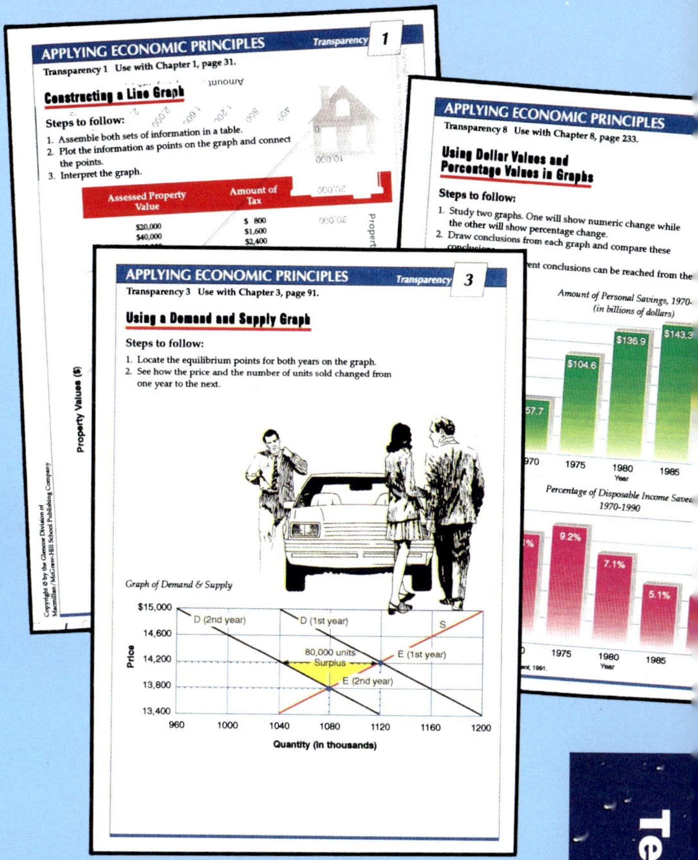

Full-Color Overhead Transparencies provide a high-impact format to help you introduce and reinforce key economic concepts presented in the text.

Testmaker Software... with formats for Apple, IBM, and Macintosh, a variety of questions to choose from, and the opportunity to edit questions or add your own, you can develop tests quickly and easily at the touch of a button.

Nightly Business Report Videotapes
These four videotape programs, produced by the highly acclaimed PBS television program, allow you to present issues in a format students will find relevant to them and easy to understand.

How Wall Street Works Part I
How Wall Street Works Part II
NBR's 1992 Economic Issues
NBR's Guide To Buying Insurance

Teacher's Resource Binder & Additional Resources

Give your students the absolute advantage they need to succeed. Select Glencoe's *Applying Economic Principles*.

With student-friendly language, high-involvement features and a more effective organizatio
the advantages of this program are absolutely clear.

Student Edition	0-02-822711-5
Teacher's Annotated Edition	0-02-822712-3
Teacher's Resource Binder	0-02-822713-1
Student Activity Book	0-02-822714-X
Activity Book Answer Key	0-02-822715-8
Testmaker Software (Apple)	0-02-822716-6
Testmaker Software (IBM)	0-02-822717-4
Testmaker Software (Macintosh)	0-02-822718-2
Nightly Business Report Videotapes	
How Wall Street Works Part I	0-02-822855-3
How Wall Street Works Part II	0-02-822856-1
NBR'S 1992 Economic Issues	0-02-822858-8
NBR'S Guide To Buying Insurance	0-02-822857-X
All 4 Volumes	0-02-822859-6

For more information contact your nearest regional office or call 1-800-334-7344.

1. Northeast Region
GLENCOE
17 Riverside Drive
Nashua, NH 03062
603-880-4701
800-424-3451

2. Mid-Atlantic Region
GLENCOE
5 Terri Lane, Suite 5
Burlington, NJ 08016
609-386-7353
800-553-7515

3. Atlantic-Southeast Region
GLENCOE
Brookside Park
One Harbison Way, Suite 101
Columbia, SC 29212
803-732-2365

4. Southeast Region
GLENCOE
6510 Jimmy Carter Boulevard
Norcross, GA 30071
404-446-7493
800-982-3992

5. Mid-America Region
GLENCOE
4635 Hilton Corporate Drive
Columbus, OH 43232
614-759-6600
800-848-1567

6. Mid-Continent Region
GLENCOE
846 East Algonquin Road
Schaumburg, IL 60173
708-397-8448
800-762-4876

7. Southwest Region
GLENCOE
320 Westway Place, Suite 550
Arlington, TX 76018
817-784-2100
800-828-5096

8. Texas Region
GLENCOE
320 Westway Place, Suite 550
Arlington, TX 76018
817-784-2100
800-828-5096

9. Western Region
GLENCOE
610 East 42nd Street, #102
Boise, ID 83714
208-378-4002
800-452-6126
Includes Alaska

10. California Region
GLENCOE
15319 Chatsworth Street
P.O. Box 9609
Mission Hills, CA 91346
818-898-1391
800-423-9534
Includes Hawaii

Canada
Maxwell Macmillan Canada
1200 Eglinton Avenue, East
Suite 200
Don Mills, Ontario M3C 3N1
Telephone: 416-449-6030
Telefax: 416-449-0068

Overseas
Macmillan/McGraw-Hill International
10 Union Square East
New York, NY 10003
Telephone: 212-353-5700
Telefax: 212-353-5894

Glencoe Catholic School Regio
GLENCOE
25 Crescent Street, 1st Floor
Stamford, CT 06906
203-964-9109
800-551-8766

GLENCOE

Macmillan/McGraw-Hill
P.O. Box 508, Columbus, Ohio 43216

SS90740-3 12-92

APPLYING ECONOMIC PRINCIPLES

Teacher's Annotated Edition

Sanford D. Gordon

Alan D. Stafford

GLENCOE

Macmillan/McGraw-Hill

New York, New York   Columbus, Ohio   Mission Hills, California   Peoria, Illinois

Authors

Alan Stafford earned a Bachelor of Science degree in economics from the honors program at Western Michigan University and Master's degrees in social studies education and business administration from the State University of New York. He served as a Peace Corps volunteer in Micronesia, taught in an urban high school for 12 years, and currently is an associate professor of economics at Niagara County Community College. He has taught courses sponsored by the New York State Department of Education and the New York Developmental Economics Education Program (DEEP). A recipient of 2 first place teaching awards from the New York State Council on Economic Education, he is coauthor of several economics texts.

Sanford D. Gordon earned a Ph.D. in economics from New York University. Active in the economic education movement since 1960, he served as the Executive Director of the New York State Council on Economic Education from 1979 to 1989. He is a recipient of the Calvin Kazanjian Foundation award for innovation in teaching economics and the first winner of the Bessie B. Moore Award for outstanding service and dedication to excellence and innovation in economic education. Dr. Gordon has authored many books on economics and economic education and has been adviser to numerous school districts, the New York State Education Department, banks, and local governments.

Send all inquiries to:
GLENCOE DIVISION
Macmillan/McGraw-Hill
936 Eastwind Drive
Westerville, Ohio 43081

ISBN 0-02-822711-5 (Student Text)
ISBN 0-02-822712-3 (Teacher's Annotated Edition)

2 3 4 5 6 7 8 9 10 11 12 13 14 15 AGH/LP 00 99 98 97 96 95 94

CONTENTS

CONTENTS

AUTHENTIC ASSESSMENT

In response to the growing demand for accountability in the classroom, many educators are advocating new approaches to assessment. One such approach is authentic assessment, which measures student achievement in a more constructive and interactive manner than traditional tests. In general, authentic assessment includes performance-based assessment and portfolios.

Performance tests ask students to effectively and creatively apply the knowledge they have gained. These tests require the application of problem-solving skills rather than mere recall. Instead of using a multiple choice test to assess knowledge of a specific battle, for example, a performance-based test asks students to write a first-person account of the battle. In designing performance-based tests, educators devise tasks that have more than one correct answer and which require more than one step to complete. A key element in scoring such tests is to analyze the *process* the students use to clarify and solve the problem. Scoring involves rating students' performance on multiple factors, resulting in a descriptive profile of performance.

The portfolio approach is often used with performance-based assessment. Portfolios contain samples of students' work collected over a period of time—an entire grading period or even a semester. Students often help choose which items will be included in their portfolios.

Portfolios allow for assessing a broader range of skills than traditional tests. Students can see how much progress they are making by comparing the work that they have completed throughout the course.

Each Part Review in *Applying Economic Principles* includes activities that may be adapted for authentic assessment. See the teacher footnotes in Part Review pages 59, 211, 359, and 438.

AT-RISK STUDENTS

Most educators today agree that the nation's schools are facing an epidemic of students who are at risk of failure. It is difficult to define exactly what constitutes an at-risk student because being at risk is often linked to several environmental causes such as poverty, low self-esteem, substance abuse, or pregnancy. Current educational research has shown that certain teaching methods can help keep at-risk students from dropping out. One method is to maximize time-on-task to help students overcome distracting outside stimuli.

Another method is to establish high expectations and a school climate that supports learning. Many schools actively involve parents in this process so that the expectations for success are not left inside the classroom after school is out.

It is important to build at-risk students' self-esteem. Many teachers give positive feedback at the end of each successfully completed assignment and include awards ceremonies for students who meet expectations.

Rather than emphasizing remedial techniques, many educators believe that at-risk students need to learn at a *faster* rate. Instruction emphasizes assets that at-risk students often bring to the classroom—interest in oral and artistic expression and kinesthetic learning abilities. For example, at-risk students may excel at dramatizations in which they also construct the sets.

INTRODUCTION

Economics, like any subject, can be most successfully taught to students when they recognize what they can gain from the learning. With that in mind, *Applying Economic Principles* has been written to emphasize the relationships between the economic concepts taught in school and the events and challenges that young people experience on a daily basis. *Applying Economic Principles* is designed to reach out to students and draw them into economics. The program makes economics a practical subject, which students can begin to use right now in their own lives.

To motivate students and to make the connection between economic concepts and real-world applications, the concepts taught in *Applying Economic Principles* are introduced with **Personal Narratives**—stories in which the narrator/protagonist is a young person or someone with whom young people can identify. These are not case histories in the common vein. They are dramatically structured narrations that will enable teachers to more easily draw students into discussions of how economic principles have a continual impact on students themselves.

To make economics more accessible to greater numbers of students, the book uses more than one hundred **teaching photographs**, each accompanied by a caption that describes an economic principle using the chapter's vocabulary terms. More than 70 charts, graphs, and tables clarify and enhance the narrative.

In addition to emphasizing student accessibility, *Applying Economic Principles* is also designed to be flexible in meeting the instructor's needs in different teaching situations. Each chapter is divided into short sections that can each be taught separately. This **section-by-section** structure allows teachers to more easily tailor lessons to the needs of individual students.

THE PROGRAM

The *Applying Economic Principles* program includes

- the Student Textbook
- the Teacher's Annotated Edition of the Student Textbook (including this Teacher's Manual)
- the Teacher's Resource Binder
- the Student Activity Book

THE STUDENT TEXTBOOK

The textbook is organized into 4 parts, 15 chapters, and 57 sections.

Parts

Each of the four parts is preceded by a short introduction and followed by a Part Review, which contains a summary of significant economic concepts and a series of exercises and questions that will reinforce student understanding and develop critical-thinking abilities.

Part 1. Understanding the Fundamentals of Economics. In this part students are introduced to the basic concepts and methodology of economics and are given a foundation for the study that follows.

Part 2. Understanding How Individuals and Businesses Make Economic Decisions. This part focuses on microeconomics and the economic decision-making process. Students learn to recognize the basic concepts of capitalism as it functions in our economic system and to understand demand, supply, prices, and the allocation of resources in our economy. This part also describes the basic forms of business organization and examines the decision-making process that businesses use in attempting to maximize profit in perfect and imperfect competition. Finally, this part explains how demand and supply for factors of production determine wage rates, rents, and interest.

Part 3. Understanding the Economy as a Whole. This part provides a macroeconomic overview of how the economy functions and how the government plays a role in the economy. Students are introduced to methods used by economists to measure the performance of our economy and to evaluate the problems of unemployment, inflation, and poverty. Theories of how our economic system works and how it can be controlled are examined. Keynesian economic theory, monetary theory, and supply-side theory are discussed, as well as practical limitations on the effectiveness of each.

Part 4. Understanding International Economics. This part discusses U.S. trade, exchange rates, and problems the United States has had with negative balances of trade and payments. The special problems faced by developing nations are explored. Finally, this part describes the theories, potential, and recent failures of alternative economic systems.

Chapters

Individual chapters are preceded by a list of learning Objectives, which identify the central concepts that will be covered in each section of the chapter. Each chapter ends in a Chapter Review, which includes a summary, *What Have You Learned?*, of important economic concepts from the chapter. Concepts in the summaries are organized in the same order as they were introduced in the chapter, making it easy for students to check their understanding and refer back to the chapter as necessary.

Each chapter summary is followed by a series of activities which may be assigned as a whole or in parts. Each series includes

- A list of important *Words and Terms* from the chapter
- A vocabulary exercise, *Building Your Vocabulary*, which requires students to demonstrate their understanding of economic terms by placing them in sentences
- A comprehension exercise, *Understanding Economics*, which requires students to explain or use economic concepts in situations similar to those in the chapter
- An application exercise, *Thinking Critically About Economics*, which requires students to use economic concepts in new situations
- A group of *Consumer Skills Projects* that suggest enrichment activities that relate chapter material to today's economic decisions

Some activities are most appropriate for students of specific ability levels. The range of activities allows teachers to choose those that are suited to the individual students.

Sections

Chapters are divided into Sections. Each Section presents a limited number of economic concepts and is designed to be completed by most students in one class period or as one homework assignment.

For many reasons, individual teachers may not choose to cover all the economic concepts included in this text. Sections can stand alone to facilitate individualized instruction and to allow teachers to structure their lessons to cover the topics they feel are most significant. More challenging Sections that might not be emphasized for the class as a whole can still be assigned individually to more able students. Also, the ability to use each Section as an independent lesson will help teachers provide work to allow students who have been absent to catch up.

Each Section includes

- A statement of important terms and concepts that will be presented in the Section
- A *Personal Narrative*, which tells the story of a person in a situation that involves

economic concepts of that section. *Personal Narratives* describe events with which students can identify and demonstrate that economic concepts and problems are faced by people similar to students and their friends and relatives

- Textual material that explains and relates the economic concepts that were introduced in the *Personal Narrative*
- A series of *Self-Check* questions that allow students to check their understanding of important points from the Section (and which can also be used by teachers for brief section-by-section evaluation)
- One or two *Applying What You Have Learned* questions, which may be completed for practice or evaluation

Special Features

Three types of special boxed features are integrated in the chapters: *Profiles*, *Current Consumer* or *Economic Issues*, and *Developing Your Economic Skills*.

The nine *Profiles* demonstrate that economists are real people who help make important decisions. Each *Profile* describes an economist's ideas and how those ideas have contributed to the way the world operates. Each *Profile* is positioned in a chapter to correspond to related economic concepts.

One *Current Economic Issue* or *Current Consumer Issue* feature is positioned just before each Chapter Review. These features encourage students to practice critical-thinking skills. Each describes a current issue of economics that concerns young people, providing two lists of arguments that present opposing points of view. After these arguments are considered, students are asked to draw conclusions about the issue and recommend actions that should be taken.

At the end of each chapter is a *Developing Your Economic Skills* feature, which will help students understand and use tables, graphs, and other methods of organizing economic data. Each feature identifies a skill, gives a step-by-step example of how to apply it, and provides a practical exercise.

Vocabulary Treatment

At the beginning of each Section is a statement of the most important terms and concepts that will be covered in the Section. Within the Section, major terms are set in boldface type when they are first discussed. All major terms are listed in the Chapter Review and in the *Glossary*, and in both places the terms are cross-referenced to the specific text pages where they first occur.

Appendixes

Features at the end of the text include a discussion of *Careers and Employment Opportunities* and an economics *Glossary*. The *Careers* section shows students how to evaluate their interests and abilities so that they can choose a career that will be rewarding to them as individuals. Fifteen careers are described as examples. Each of these career choices is explained in terms of the nature of the work, necessary training and education, and the job outlook. The intent of these descriptions is not to focus students' attention on specific careers, but to help students recognize some of the factors that should be taken into account in making career choices.

The *Glossary* includes definitions of all the vocabulary terms from the text. Following each term is a cross-reference to the text page on which the term is first introduced.

THE TEACHER'S ANNOTATED EDITION

In addition to the same material that is found in the student's text, the *Teacher's Annotated Edition* contains

- Annotations that will help you make the best use of the text

- The program description you are reading
- Lesson plans, including student behavioral objectives, teaching suggestions, and strategies for each individual section
- Answers for all section, chapter, and part review material of the textbook

Annotations

You will find annotations on almost every page of the *Teacher's Annotated Edition*, positioned to correspond to specific text material. They have been prepared to help you make the best use of the textbook. Each annotation begins with a key word that identifies the type of information or activity that is being suggested. The following key words are used:

- *Discuss.* Identifies an issue that could be used as the topic for a class discussion
- *Stress.* Identifies information that is of particular importance or that could be easily misunderstood if not carefully explained
- *Question.* Identifies an issue that students could be asked to explain or give opinions on
- *Explain.* Identifies information that students may find more difficult
- *Values.* Identifies issues that involve conflicting values
- *Note.* Provides additional information concerning a topic for teachers. This information may be appropriate for some students but too challenging for others.

Lesson Plans

The *Teacher's Annotated Edition* includes a suggested lesson plan and teaching strategies for each individual section. These plans identify the economic concepts that the sections are designed to teach, and they suggest methods for teaching and reinforcing student knowledge. Each Lesson Plan includes the following features:

Objectives. These student behavioral objectives suggest learning outcomes you can expect students to accomplish when they complete each Section.

Preparation Activities. The first part of this feature suggests a way to introduce the section's primary economic concept(s) to class discussion. The suggestion begins with an aspect of students' lives with which they can all identify, and leads into a connection between that aspect and an economic principle.

The second part of this feature states the economic concept(s) that are demonstrated in the *Personal Narrative* and explains how these also tie in with students' lives.

Teaching Suggestions. Discussion topics are provided to illustrate specific aspects of economic concepts. In addition, creative teaching strategies are suggested, including

- *Student Surveys.* Students gather and evaluate information.
- *Interviews.* Students interview people who have a special need or responsibility within local economies.
- *Values.* Students identify values associated with economic issues and suggest answers to economic problems that would be most acceptable to themselves and to society in general.
- *Simulations.* Students take the roles of individuals who are involved in economic problems.
- *Debates.* Students identify and debate points of view concerning an economic issue.
- *Small Group Activities.* Students are divided into small groups and given specific tasks to accomplish which are related to important economic issues.

Lesson Checkpoint. The Checkpoint provides answers for the *Self-Check* that concludes each text section.

Follow-up Assignments. This section includes answers to the *Applying What You Have Learned* text sections as well as occasional out-of-class assignments.

Section Evaluation. This section provides a reference to the appropriate *Self-Check* sections in the textbook to specific questions in the textbook's Chapter Review. At the end of each chapter's set of lesson plans is a *Teacher's Bibliography* for the chapter, including references on topics in economics and on additional teaching strategies.

Answer Keys

As noted above, answers for *Self-Check* and *Applying What You Have Learned* are included in each Section-by-Section Lesson Plan. Answers for Chapter and Part Reviews occur at the end of the set of lesson plans for each part or chapter.

THE TEACHER'S RESOURCE BINDER

The Teacher's Resource Binder includes a complete testing program and a wide variety of handouts and activities to be used in class or as homework assignments.

Testing Program

The testing materials include a Pretest, Chapter Tests, Part Tests, a Final Examination, and an Answer Key. In addition, Testmaker software (IBM, Apple, or Macintosh) offers a bank of questions that provides the flexibility to modify existing questions or add new ones.

The Pretest covers general knowledge rather than specific economic concepts. Most students should score well on this test, which will help them develop a positive attitude toward economics.

Each chapter test includes a selection of questions associated with a specific level of learning. Listed in ascending order of difficulty, the classifications are:

- *Matching.* Students match economic terms with definitions. (simple recognition)
- *True/False.* Students identify statements as being true or false. (simple recognition)
- *Multiple Choice.* Students choose the correct answer out of four possible answers. (multiple recognition)
- *Fill-in-the-Blank.* Students place economic terms in blanks to complete sentences. (complex recognition)
- *Explanation.* Students answer questions in complete sentences concerning situations from the text, demonstrating their understanding of economic concepts. (complex recall)
- *Application.* Students write a paragraph that answers questions about a situation they have not studied in class. (application)

Questions are provided that test at different learning levels for most important economic concepts. This makes it possible for the teacher to test the whole class for the same concept, while using individualized tests for students with different abilities.

The four Part Tests include questions similar in nature to those of the Chapter Tests. Although the questions test for the same information and understanding as the chapter tests, no question is used twice.

Handouts and Transparencies

Several types of materials are provided for promoting class discussion, demonstrating economic principles through game playing, and illustrating concepts visually for the class as a group. These include

- *Illustrated Discussion Promoters.* These are sketches that illustrate economic concepts.

They are designed especially for introducing lessons and for reinforcement for lower-level students.

- *Discussion Topics.* These are short handouts that students can review in class or take home overnight, most appropriate for in-class review and reinforcement for lower-level students.
- *Simulations.* The simulations provide students the opportunity to act out situations that illustrate the functioning of major economic concepts. Instructions and the necessary blackline masters are provided.
- *Transparencies.* A transparency is provided for illustration and discussion of each of the 15 *Developing Your Economic Skills features.*

Activities

The activities provide an opportunity for reinforcement and review and for encouraging students to apply economic principles to situations of daily life.

- *Vocabulary Activities.* These are fill-in questions with a vocabulary list, appropriate for reinforcement at all levels.
- *Critical-Thinking and Decision-Making Activities.* These are applications of economic concepts to everyday situations. The situations are personal and student-oriented, appropriate for all levels.

THE STUDENT ACTIVITY BOOK

The *Student Activity Book* provides four types of supplementary student activities for each chapter in the *Student Textbook.* Each activity is designed to help students achieve a specific set of goals and type of understanding. The activities include:

- *Vocabulary Exercise.* These activities will reinforce student knowledge of economic terms and their definitions. Activities include crossword puzzles and other types of word puzzles.
- *Factual Recall.* These quizzes allow students to test their learning of the basic economic concepts included in the chapter.
- *Using Data.* These activities will help students understand and evaluate either tabular or graphic data. Tables and graphs parallel but do not duplicate those in the Student Textbook.
- *Historical Perspective.* These are brief essays that describe a situation from U.S. history that demonstrates one or more economic concepts. The essays show students that economic problems have existed throughout our history. They are followed by a series of questions that encourage students to apply economic concepts to the historical situations, and which may be used to evaluate student learning.

PART 1

UNDERSTANDING THE FUNDAMENTALS OF ECONOMICS

CHAPTER 1

Life Is Economics (text pages 4–31)

SECTION A. Unlimited Wants and Limited Resources (text pages 8–10)

Objectives (Lesson Focus)

Upon completion of this section, students will be able to:

- Recognize and explain the economic concept of scarcity.
- Explain how scarcity forces people, businesses, and the government to make choices.

Preparation (Instruction: Pre-teaching—Vocabulary or Activity)

1. Discussion Introduce this section by asking students what single item they would like most to have but which they do not currently own. Ask them why they don't own the item and what they could do to acquire one in the future. Lead the discussion into the concept of scarcity.

2. The Personal Narrative The Personal Narrative for Section A demonstrates how people, businesses, and the government face scarcity. Scarcity affects people in the Narrative in a number of ways. For example, the boy does not have enough money to buy new shoes. Joe can't afford better tools. The boy's mother doesn't have money to buy everything she would like for her family. The city can't keep lions in the zoo anymore.

The Narrative describes situations that will help students become aware of the basic economic problem of scarcity. Students should be encouraged to identify examples of scarcity that they face in their own lives.

Teaching Suggestions (Modeling/Guided Practice)

1. Stress the fact that scarcity necessitates choice. We can't have everything we want, so we are forced to choose what we want most. We usually make choices in terms of how we spend our income.
2. Discuss the difference between the types of scarcity faced by people who are rich and by those who are poor. Poor people sometimes have to choose between heating their homes and having enough to eat. Be sure your students are aware that rich people face scarcity too. If they buy an expensive car, they may not be able to build a new swimming pool.
3. Have your students make lists of at least five things they know their local government does not have enough of. These could include police or fire protection, teachers, parks, roads, or snow plows. Combine the individual lists on the chalkboard. Discuss why the local government does not have these things and what would have to be done to acquire them.

Lesson Checkpoint

Text: Self-Check, text page 10
Answers

1. We can't get everything we want for free.
2. We do not have enough resources to produce enough products to satisfy everyone's wants.

Follow-Up Assignments (Independent Practice/Extension/Homework)

1. Text: Applying What You Have

Learned, text page 10
Answers

a. The person telling the story did not have enough money to buy a new pair of shoes.
b. Joe Rizzo did not have enough money to buy new tools.
c. The brother did not have a job that provides a good income.
d. The man with the suit did not live somewhere with good streets.
e. The city did not have enough money to feed the lions or to fix the roads.
f. The animals in the zoo did not have large cages.

2. Teacher's Resource Binder: Critical Thinking Activity, Chapter 1 (answers in Binder).

Section Evaluation

Self-Check, text page 10
Understanding Economics, question 1 (Chapter 1 Review, text pages 28–30)

SECTION B. Everyone Pays Opportunity Costs (text pages 11–13)

Objectives (Lesson Focus)

Upon completion of this section, students will be able to:

- Identify trade-offs that take place whenever a choice is made.
- Recognize and explain with examples the concept of opportunity cost.

Preparation (Instruction: Pre-teaching—Vocabulary or Activity)

1. Discussion Introduce this section by asking students to identify several items they would consider buying if they were given money for a birthday present. Ask them to rank the items from the one they would want most to the one they would least desire. If they could only afford to buy the first item, their opportunity cost would be the value they placed on their second choice. Stress the fact that all choices involve opportunity cost.

2. The Personal Narrative The Personal Narrative for Section B demonstrates the economic concept of opportunity cost. Opportunity cost is the value of a second choice that is given up when a first choice is taken. The subjects in the Personal Narrative make choices that involve trade-offs. For example, the boyfriend chooses to buy gas for his car rather than a pizza for his girlfriend. To afford gas, he had to give up the company of his girlfriend for at least a period of time.

The Narrative describes a situation that will help students become aware of opportunity costs they pay when they make choices. Students should be encouraged to identify examples of opportunity costs they pay in their own lives.

Teaching Suggestions (Modeling/Guided Practice)

1. Explain the fact that choices are often no better than the information they are based on. If Ted (from the Personal Narrative) had asked his girlfriend about her feelings before he took her to the movie, he would have had more information. What other choices could he have made? How would his opportunity costs have been different?
2. Discuss the opportunity costs paid by young people who choose to join the military. What benefits do these people receive? What costs do they pay? The costs and benefits of being in the military service could also be discussed in this section.

3. Have students keep a list of their personal spending for a week. For each purchase made, ask students to identify their second choice or opportunity cost.

Lesson Checkpoint

Text: Self-Check, text page 13
Answers

1. A trade-off occurs when one thing of value is given up in order to receive something else, usually of greater value.
2. When any choice is made, there is a trade-off. A second choice is given up to take the first choice. The value of the second choice is the opportunity cost.

Follow-up Assignments (Independent Practice/Extension/Homework)

1. Text: Applying What You Have Learned, text page 13
   Answers
   a. She could have stayed home. Her opportunity cost could have been going out with some of her girlfriends or with another boy. She also could have stayed home to do her economics homework.
   b. Ted could have taken his girlfriend to get a pizza and not gone to a movie at all. He could have taken her to a movie she would have liked better. His opportunity cost was related to the value he placed on her goodwill and company.
   c. Ted could have tried to find some other alternative that would have pleased his girlfriend. He could have used half the money for gas and bought her a hamburger. His opportunity cost may have been related to his desire not to let her "push him around."
2. Have students interview an older person who has returned to school (either to high school or to college). The decision to return to school would involve many special costs for an older person. Such a person could be giving up a job and income, time to be with families, or many other things. Ask students to list the opportunity costs being paid by the individual they interview.

Section Evaluation

Self-Check, text page 13
Understanding Economics, questions 2 and 3 (Chapter 1 Review, text pages 28–30)

SECTION C. From Resources to Products (text pages 14–16)

Objective (Lesson Focus)

Upon completion of this section, students will be able to:

- Recognize and explain with examples each of the factors of production.

Preparation (Instruction: Pre-teaching—Vocabulary or Activity)

1. Discussion Introduce this section by asking students to identify all the things that are needed to bake cookies. Classify each item according to the type of factor of production. The oven, bowl, and cookie sheet are capital. The effort of the cook is labor. Bringing the factors together is entrepreneurship. It is likely that no natural resources will be directly used, but they are necessary. For example, the grain for the flour had to be grown on land that was a natural resource.

2. The Personal Narrative The Personal

Narrative for Section C identifies the factors of production. The subject of the Narrative is a boy who assembles the factors necessary to produce a dog house. Stress the fact that examples of each factor of production are necessary to accomplish production.

The Narrative describes a situation that will help students become aware of how factors of production are used to create the goods and services they use in their own lives.

Teaching Suggestions (Modeling/Guided Practice)

1. Discuss the fact that labor implies skills and abilities and not just people. Why do many people choose to go to school? The education and training they receive should increase the value of their labor and their future earnings. Wanting to be a lawyer, a doctor, or a scientist is not enough. People must be trained to have these jobs.
2. Have students complete the following simulation. (Blackline masters for money and factor cards can be found in the TRB):

   Choose three or four students to be entrepreneurs. Give each of them $100 of "fake" money to buy factors of production. Give the other students Natural Resource Cards, Labor Cards, or Capital Cards. The task of each entrepreneur is to buy as many factor cards of each type as possible at the lowest possible cost. For each set of three cards, the entrepreneurs can make one product that can be sold for $50. If they make no products, they go out of business and forfeit all of their money.

   All non-entrepreneurs try to get as much money for their factor cards as possible. If they don't sell their cards, they get nothing. At the end of the simulation, the students may use the money they earned in either profit or from selling factor cards to "buy" some product you supply (whatever reward is appropriate in your school).
3. Have students complete each of the following sentences:
   a. A tree is a natural resource, but lumber is not, because. . .
   b. A hammer and a computer are both capital because. . .
   c. A high school drop-out and a nuclear physicist do not provide the same type of labor because. . .
   d. An entrepreneur is a person who. . .

Lesson Checkpoint

Text: Self-Check, text page 16
Answers

1. Natural resources are only those resources that have not been changed by human labor. Lumber, for example, is capital, not a natural resource, because it has been changed by human labor.
2. The four factors of production are natural resources, labor, capital, and entrepreneurship.

Follow-up Assignments (Independent Practice/Extension/Homework)

Text: Applying What You Have Learned, text page 16
Answers

a. Natural resources were directly used only in terms of space in which to put the dog house. Trees before they were made into lumber, crude oil before it was taken from the ground to make shingles or paint, and iron ore before it was mined to make nails would be examples of natural resources.

b. Labor was provided by both the boy and his neighbor, Ed. The difference in their levels of skill should be pointed out.

c. Capital consisted of the lumber, nails, paint, shingles, and tools that were used to build the dog house. The truck was also capital.

d. Entrepreneurship was provided by the boy when he organized the production of the dog house. He looked up how to build it. He provided the money to pay for its construction. He got his neighbor to provide labor necessary to production.

Section Evaluation

Self-Check, text page 16
Understanding Economics, question 4 (Chapter 1 Review, text pages 28–30)

SECTION D. How Economists Use Models (text pages 17–19)

Objectives (Lesson Focus)

Upon completion of this section, students will be able to:

- Explain what models are and to identify common examples of models used in everyday life.
- Explain why it is necessary for economists to use models in their studies of the economy.

Preparation (Instruction: Pre-teaching—Vocabulary or Activity

1. Discussion Introduce this section by asking students to look at pictures of various people and guess what their personal lives are like. Point out that people do this all the time as they meet new people. Pictures from old school yearbooks can be both humorous and useful.

2. The Personal Narrative The Personal Narrative for Section D demonstrates how people use models. When the speaker in the Narrative meets someone new, an idea of what this person will be like is formed. In a way a model is used to predict the future. People often change first impressions as they gather more information. Economists do the same when they form economic models. Economic models are used to predict the future and are adjusted as additional information becomes available.

The Narrative describes a situation that will help students realize how they form and use models in their own lives.

Teaching Suggestions (Modeling/Guided Practice)

1. Have students identify the sport team they are most interested in. Ask them what factors they would consider in predicting how any team will do in the next season. Explain that these factors are models. You could point out that some people who bet on sporting events use models to predict outcomes.
2. Have your students complete a survey, as follows. Tell students to write each of their ages on a separate sheet of paper, without their names. Collect the papers. Tabulate your students' answers on the board. List the number of students in each age group represented in your class. Find out the total number of students there are at your school in your class's

grade level. Divide the number of students in your class into that total. Project the number of students in each age group for the entire grade level by multiplying the factor you have found times the number of students in each age group from your class. Discuss why this is a model. Do your students believe that its results are valid?

For example, if there are 27 students in your class and the total number is 326, the factor would be 326/27 = 12.07:

Age of Students in Your Class	Number of Students in Age Group	Factor		Projection for Entire Grade Level
16	5	× 12.07	=	60.35
17	18	× 12.07	=	217.26
18	3	× 12.07	=	36.21
19	1	× 12.07	=	12.07
	27			325.89

Lesson Checkpoint

Text: Self-Check, text page 19
Answers

1. Economists must use models because it is impossible to consider every factor that could affect an economic decision.
2. Models do not always result in accurate predictions because they cannot include all factors.

Follow-up Assignments (Independent Practice/Extension/Homework)

Text: Applying What You Have Learned, text page 19
Answer

Students' predictions will vary. You may wish to add other subjects to the list of predictions. Events of local interest to your students can help to develop interest in this activity. Be sure that students' names are on their predictions to reduce the possibility of creative but socially inappropriate predictions.

Section Evaluation

Self-Check, text page 19
Understanding Economics, questions 5 and 6 (Chapter 1 Review, text pages 28–30)

SECTION E. Making Rational Choices (text pages 20–23)

Objectives (Lesson Focus)

Upon completion of this section, students will be able to:

- Explain the meaning of rational choice.
- Recognize and explain the difference between positive and normative statements.

Preparation (Instruction: Pre-teaching—Vocabulary or Activity)

1. Discussion Introduce this section by asking students to list some of the major goals they have set for their own lives. Discuss these goals in class. Why do students feel that their goals are rational choices? Do other students agree? How do different goals reflect different values? How is it possible for a decision to be a rational choice for one person but not for someone else?

2. The Personal Narrative The Personal Narrative for Section E demonstrates how people try to make rational choices. The subject of the Narrative is trying to make a career choice for her future. Her objectives are not the same as those of her mother. She weighs the costs and benefits of various actions and decides to pursue a career in journalism. She believes that the benefits associated with her decision are greater than the costs she must pay.

The Narrative describes a situation that will help students become aware of the choices they have to make in their own lives. Students plan their choices to receive the greatest benefits at the least cost. These choices are rational choices.

Teaching Suggestions (Modeling/Guided Practice)

1. Describe the various historical choices to your students that may or may not have been rational choices. Examples could include the German decision to use hydrogen in the *Hindenburg,* Russia's decision to sell Alaska to the United States in 1867, or the decision of the Senate not to ratify the Treaty of Versailles after World War I. Discuss why the decisions were made and whether or not they were rational choices.
2. Divide your class into teams of three or four students. Tell them to pretend that their school has received a gift of $5,000 from a local foundation. The money must be used to improve the quality of education in their school. Have each team establish and rank a list of four possible uses for the money. Ask them to explain their choices to the rest of the class. Discuss whether or not they have made rational choices.

Lesson Checkpoint

Text: Self-Check, text page 23
Answers

1. Positive statements can either be proven or disproven, but normative statements depend on different people's individual points of view.
2. Each individual has his or her own values, making an individual's rational choice relatively easy to achieve. Groups of people often have different values, and so they often do not all agree on what is the rational choice.

Follow-up Assignments (Independent Practice/Extension/Homework)

1. Text: Applying What You Have Learned, text page 23
   Answers

   Mother's positive statement: "Things are different today. . ." [Statement that women today have more choice in determining their life goals.]
   Mother's normative statement: "You could do something really important. . ." [Statement that being a doctor is more important than being a journalist.]
   Daughter's positive statement: "I get A's in English all the time. . ." [Statement that her English grades are demonstrably higher than her math grades.]
   Daughter's normative statement: "I would be happy writing for a living. . ." [Statement of personal values.]
2. Have your students find articles in local newspapers which describe decisions made by local businesses. Ask students to explain what the costs and benefits of each decision was, or will be. Discuss whether or not your students feel each decision was a rational choice.

Section Evaluation

Self-Check, text page 23
Understanding Economics, questions 8 and 9 (Chapter 1 Review, text pages 28–30)

SECTION F. Using the Production Possibilities Frontier (text pages 24–26)

Objectives (Lesson Focus)

Upon completion of this section, students will be able to:

- Read and plot values on a graph.
- Read and explain the meaning of a production possibilities frontier.
- Draw a production possibilities frontier from data supplied on a table.

Preparation (Instruction: Pre-teaching—Vocabulary or Activity)

1. Discussion Introduce Section F by reviewing graphing skills described in Developing Your Economic Skills for Chapter 1. Be sure students are aware that the horizontal axis is the *x* axis and the vertical axis is the *y* axis. In plotting ordered pairs, the value of the *x* axis is given first and the *y* axis second.

2. The Personal Narrative The Personal Narrative for Section F demonstrates how trade-offs can be represented on a graph called a production possibilities frontier. The subject of the Narrative must choose what combination of cucumbers and tomatoes to grow with her limited resources. She draws a graph to help her decide what choice to make.

The Narrative describes a situation in which an economic decision is shown through a graphic model. It will help students understand how graphs can be used to help solve economic problems.

Teaching Suggestions (Modeling/Guided Practice)

1. Explain that the graph of a production possibilities frontier is a very simplified model. It does not include price or mention alternative products that could be produced from the resources available. It is intended more to show students how graphs can be used to represent an economic choice than to approximate reality.
2. Have students draw a production possibilities frontier that represents the different combinations of loaves of bread or cookies they could make from a five-pound bag of flour. Each loaf of bread requires 1/2 pound of flour. Each batch of 48 cookies requires one pound of flour. The graph should look like this:

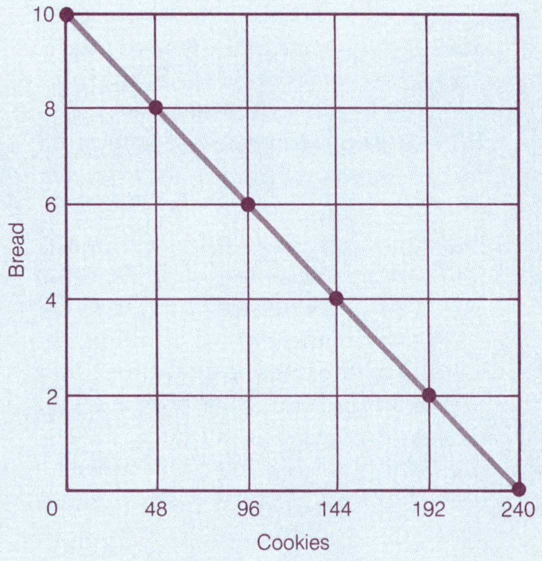

Lesson Checkpoint

Text: Self-Check, text page 26
Answers

1. A production possibilities frontier shows different combinations of two products that could be produced from a given quantity of resources.
2. A production possibilities frontier shows trade-offs as one moves

from one point on the frontier to another. A quantity of one product is given up in order to produce a greater quantity of the other.

Follow-Up Assignments (Independent Practice/Extension/Homework)

Text: Applying What You Have Learned, text page 26
Answers

a. true
b. true
c. false
d. false
e. true

Section Evaluation

Self-Check, text page 26
Understanding Economics, question 7 (Chapter 1 Review, text pages 28–30)

ADDITIONAL MATERIALS FOR CHAPTER 1

Chapter Evaluation

Teacher's Resource Binder: Chapter 1 Quiz

Reteaching and Extension

See the *Teacher's Resource Binder* and the *Student Activity Book* for additional handouts and activities for Chapter 1.

TEACHER'S BIBLIOGRAPHY FOR CHAPTER 1

Economics Sources

Boulding, Kenneth E. *Economics As a Science*, Lanham, Md.: University Press of America, 1988.

Fusfeld, Daniel R. *The Age of the Economist*, 6th ed. Glenview, Illinois: Scott Foresman and Co., 1990.

References for Additional Teaching Strategies

Gordon, Sanford. *Economics USA, a Resource Guide for Teachers*. New York: Joint Council on Economic Education, 1988.

Mansfield, Edwin, and Behravesh, Nariman. *Economics U.S.A.*, 3rd ed. New York: W.W. Norton, 1992, Chapter 1. This text and the previous title are keyed to the telecourse of the same title developed by the Southern California Consortium.

Walstad, William R. and Saunders, Phillip. *The Principles of Economics Course: A Handbook for Instructors*, 11th ed. New York: McGraw-Hill, 1990.

CHAPTER 1 REVIEW ANSWERS

Building Your Vocabulary (text page 29)

1. opportunity cost
2. scarcity
3. economics
4. positive statement
5. natural resources
6. production
7. factors of production
8. production possibilities frontier
9. labor
10. normative statement
11. entrepreneurship
12. rational choice
13. capital
14. model
15. trade-off
16. goods
17. services
18. resources

Understanding Economics (text pages 29–30)

1. a. There is no limit to what people want.
   b. There is a limit to our ability to produce goods and services to satisfy these wants.
2. John's opportunity cost would be the value he placed on the new shirt that he did not buy.
3. When people make trade-offs, they are trying to maximize their satisfaction. In doing this they try to make rational choices such that their benefits exceed their costs.
4. a. A natural resource would be the tree.
   b. The Native Americans' efforts would be the labor.
   c. The tools the Native Americans used would be the capital.
   d. The orders given by the chief would be the entrepreneurship.
5. Models are representations of reality used by economists to simplify economic problems so that they can be more easily understood. They are also used as the basis of predictions of the future.
6. Predictions made by economists are important because they are often used by the government and businesses as the basis for their decisions.
7. The firm would have to give up the production of 50 chairs to make ten more tables.
8. Rational choice is making decisions such that the value of the results exceeds the value of the costs.
9. A positive statement is a statement of fact that can be either proven or disproven. A normative statement involves a value judgment that can neither be proven nor disproven.

Thinking Critically About Economics (text page 30)

1. The student's list of five items should be clearly explained in relation to why these items are of greater value than alternatives that could have been taken.
2. The student's list of the factors of production should be clearly defined. The distinction between capital and natural resources will probably give students the greatest difficulty.
3. The students' opportunity cost should clearly be the value they associated with their second choice that they gave up when they took their first choice.
4. Other models your students might use could be maps of bus routes or subways, diagrams of how products they buy must be put together, or play plans for football teams.
5. Be sure that all statements identified as positive can be either proven or disproven.
6. The point of this question was to evaluate the students' understanding of rational choice. Look for a clear distinction between the students' description of the costs and benefits of the decision that was made.
7.

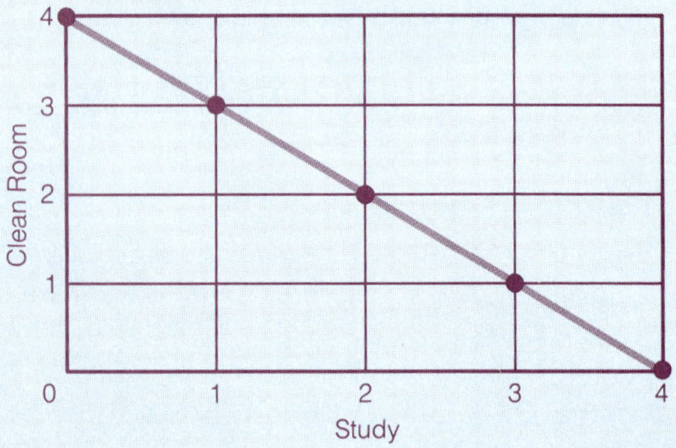

Consumer Skills Projects (text page 30)

1. Student answers are likely to show that adult decisions deal more with family responsibilities than those given by students. Different decisions made by different people may all be rational choices if they have different needs.
2. This bulletin board can help students evaluate the goods and services they consume and to understand how these products are produced. It may be useful to have students find photographs and news articles that relate to the various stages of production of a product manufactured in your area. It may be of particular value for students with limited academic ability.
3. These collages can be useful as topics for a discussion concerning how advertising is used by firms to try to influence what products people feel they need to consume.

CHAPTER 2

Economic Systems: Who Made the Rules? (text pages 32–59)

SECTION A. How Economic Systems Developed (text pages 35–39)

Objectives (Lesson Focus)

Upon completion of this section, students will be able to:

- Explain the basic functions of economic systems.
- Recognize and explain the central characteristics of capitalism.
- Recognize and explain the economic advantages offered by the division of labor and specialization.
- Recognize and explain the relationship between the accumulation of wealth and increased productivity.

Preparation (Instruction: Pre-teaching—Vocabulary or Activity)

1. Discussion Introduce this section by asking students to list five things they own which they feel they could make for themselves *from basic raw materials* if they had to. They may find this list difficult to complete. Then ask them to list five items they own that they could not make. What characteristics can they find that are common to each group of items? Do the items in the second group require specialized tools or labor to produce?

2. The Personal Narrative The Personal Narrative in Section A describes the development of a fictional economic system at the dawn of history. The subject of the Narrative is a native who has the idea of creating a division of labor. His idea succeeds and allows specialization, greater productivity, and the accumulation of wealth.

The Narrative describes a situation that will help students become aware of the function of an economic system in organizing production. It shows examples of the division of labor which can be related to situations that exist in students' lives. Something as simple as having a different teacher with different training for each subject can make this point.

Teaching Suggestions (Modeling/Guided Practice)

1. Try the following simulation: Choose a team of three students. Have them sit at a table with paper, three staplers, three pairs of scissors, and three felt-tip pens. Tell them they are going to manufacture

counting books for first-grade students. They are to fold the paper into fourths, cut it along the folds into four pieces, staple the pages together, and number them from 1 through 8 (one number on each side of each piece of paper). Inform the students that you will not accept inferior or incomplete products. Have your students work individually the first time. Give them four minutes and count their total production.

Discuss how a division of labor could allow them to specialize and increase their production. If one person cuts paper, a second staples, and a third writes numbers, they should be able to produce more books. Try this and see what happens to the number of books they can make in four minutes.

2. Discuss why some people are better at some jobs than others. Are there jobs where it is better to be small? Think of racing jockeys, or a person who assembles electrical components. What types of jobs require strength, special training, or a specialized education? You could lead this discussion into the subject of career choice.
3. The division of labor in a hospital is usually very clear. Either have one of your students interview a nurse, or invite a nurse to speak to your class. Discuss how and why labor is divided in a hospital. What jobs are aides, nurses, and doctors allowed to do? What is the reason for this particular division of labor? What is the "product" a hospital produces? Why is it more difficult to measure the productivity of a hospital than that of a normal business?

Lesson Checkpoint

Text: Self-Check, text page 39
Answers

1. An economic system is a set of rules that governs what goods and services to produce, how to produce them, and for whom they are produced.
2. The division of labor allows specialization of both labor and capital.
3. An economic system must provide wealth in order to grow.

Follow-up Assignments (Independent Practice/Extension/Homework)

1. Text: Applying What You Have Learned, text page 39
   Answer

   Three examples of the division of labor include all of the village's hunting done by Grug, all of the fishing by Thump, and all of the bread making by Buff. This division of labor gave the villagers the time to invest in tools that increased their productivity as well as enabling them to have more time to consider options such as trading with other villages, a possible benefit to enhance their lifestyle and to exchange different skills.
2. Teacher's Resource Binder: Critical Thinking Activity, Chapter 2 (answers in Binder).

Section Evaluation

Self-Check, text page 39
Understanding Economics, questions 1–3 (Chapter 2 Review, text pages 52–54)

SECTION B. The Basic Questions: *What*, *How*, and *For Whom*? (text pages 40–43)

Objectives (Lesson Focus)

Upon completion of this section, students will be able to:

- Recognize the three basic economic questions, *what, how,* and *for whom.*
- Explain how the three basic economic questions are answered in capitalism.

Preparation (Instruction: Pre-teaching—Vocabulary or Activity)

1. Discussion Introduce this section by asking students to identify five personal items their parent (of the same sex) buys that they would not need to buy. Hair coloring, false teeth powder, or arch-supports could be some examples. What would happen to a store that wanted to sell to young people but only offered these products for sale? The students could also make a list of items they would buy that their parents would not. Point out that stores must offer products their customers are willing to buy if they intend to succeed. This is the way the question *What* is answered in a market economy.

2. The Personal Narrative The Personal Narrative for Section B provides an example of how each of the three basic economic questions—*what, how,* and *for whom* is answered in a market economy. The subjects of the Narrative are students and their teacher who meet to discuss the management of a school store. They are concerned over its losses and suggest ways to improve its performance. The idea of offering different products that would sell better is suggested. They discuss how to store the new products. Finally, the question of their compensation is discussed. The teacher makes the point that if they are not able to sell more products, they will either have to take a cut in their pay or close down.

The Narrative demonstrates a situation that will help students realize how people like themselves make basic economic decisions.

Teaching Suggestions (Modeling/Guided Practice)

1. Discuss why many sports stars receive very high salaries. What do they do that justifies earnings in excess of a million dollars a year? How do their earnings help answer the question *for whom?* Remember that it is the people who pay for tickets or buy the products advertised on television that are really paying the salaries. Many people who earn little money cannot afford to go to a game. Should the government limit what a sports star earns to two or three hundred thousand dollars a year and then force ticket prices to be lowered? In what way would such a law change the way the question *for whom* is answered? Would this be consistent with a market economy?
2. Give your students a copy of Discussion Topic 1 from the *Teacher's Resource Binder.* Ask them to describe what the news story shows about the way the basic economic questions *how* and *for whom* are answered in the United States.

Lesson Checkpoint

Text: Self-Check, text page 43
Answers

1. *What* refers to the decision of which goods to produce; *how* refers to the method used to produce them.
2. In a market system, benefits are allocated according to the value of a person's contribution to production.

Follow-up Assignments (Independent Practice/Extension/Homework)

Text: Applying What You Have Learned, text page 43
Answers

What?
1. "We should sell candy bars and potato chips."
2. "How about granola bars?" (There are several other possible answers in the story.)

How?
1. "There's an old one in the basement you could use."
2. ". . . you could have fewer clerks."

For Whom?
1. ". . . we have been paying clerks $4.50 an hour and haven't earned enough money to cover their wages."
2. "You could take a cut in pay to, say, $3.50 an hour. . . ."

Section Evaluation

Self-Check, text page 43
Understanding Economics, question 4 (Chapter 2 Review, text pages 52–54)

SECTION C. The Role of Profits in the Economy (text pages 44–46)

Objectives (Lesson Focus)

Upon completion of this section, students will be able to:

- Explain what a firm in capitalism must do to earn profits.
- Explain the relationship between profits and the allocation of resources in capitalism.

Preparation (Instruction: Pre-teaching—Vocabulary or Activity)

1. Discussion Introduce this section by discussing specific local businesses that have grown. What is it about these firms that have enabled them to acquire the resources necessary to expand? What is the relationship between their ability to earn a profit and their ability to grow? The same idea can be used for firms that have not grown. Do these firms share low profitability? Is their market saturated with many producers?

2. The Personal Narrative The Personal Narrative for Section C demonstrates how a person is motivated to go into business by the expectation of profit, and how profits are related to the allocation of resources. The subject of the Narrative is a young woman who is opening a small hot dog stand on a dock. She believes that retired people who live near the dock will buy her food and make her business profitable. She expects to be able to open similar businesses on other docks in the future. Whether she is able to acquire the necessary resources depends on the success of her first venture.

The Narrative describes a situation that will help students appreciate the relationship between a firm's profitability and its ability to afford additional resources.

Teaching Suggestions (Modeling/Guided Practice)

1. Discuss how much profit is "too much" profit. Few people would complain about a firm making a profit of five to ten percent on its investment. More people would be upset about a firm making a 50 percent return or more. If a firm makes large profits, its customers must be willing to pay its price. Does this fact justify large profits? If not, *how* do your students feel profits should be limited?
2. Explain that in the United States resources are sometimes allocated according to governmental rules *rather*

than profits. For example, the federal government sets a minimum wage. This minimum hourly rate benefits many workers. It may also eliminate some jobs because employers who cannot afford to pay the minimum wage may not hire as many employees or may not go into business at all. Discuss the current minimum wage. Would those who cannot find a job be willing to work for less than the minimum wage?

3. The price of fresh produce in grocery stores fluctuates widely. Assign a student to interview a produce manager about pricing policy. How do they set prices? What do they do if there is a shortage of lettuce or carrots? How do they limit losses from spoilage? How do they know how much of each item to order? To what extent is the manager responsible for profit in his/her department? If the produce department is profitable, will it be expanded? Why or why not?

Lesson Checkpoint

Text: Self-Check, text page 46
Answers

1. To earn a profit, a firm must sell products that customers want at prices they are willing to pay.
2. Profit is the basic method of allocation in capitalism.

Follow-up Assignments (Independent Practice/Extension/Homework)

Text: Applying What You Have Learned, text page 46
Answers

a. Regina used natural resources indirectly. The lumber and paint she used were capital, but they came from trees and crude oil that were natural resources.

b. Regina used her own labor for the most part. If she hired plumbers or electricians, their labor could be included.

c. Regina used the building, tools, kitchen equipment, and the dock itself as capital for her business.

d. Regina's decision and direction of the other factors of production represented entrepreneurship.

Section Evaluation

Self-Check, text page 46
Understanding Economics, questions 5 and 6 (Chapter 2 Review, text pages 52–54)

SECTION D. Economic Decisions in Other Systems (text pages 47–50)

Objectives (Lesson Focus)

Upon completion of this section, students will be able to:

- Recognize and explain the different characteristics of a command economy relative to capitalism.
- Describe how the three basic economic decisions are made in command economies.
- Explain the allocation of resources in a command economy as compared to their allocation in capitalism.

Preparation (Instruction: Pre-teaching—Vocabulary or Activity)

1. Discussion Introduce this section by asking each student to write a brief description of what they would look for in a car they would someday like to own. Ask them how they would feel if they could only choose one type of car and if they might have to wait up to two years to get one. This essentially has been the situation in many command economies.

Governments in these nations determine what products will be produced. They may choose to produce only one type of car. Also point out that resources are allocated in command economies according to government plans rather than profits which result from consumer demand.

2. The Personal Narrative The Personal Narrative for Section D shows how economic decisions are made in command economies. The subject of the Narrative is an American whose great-grandfather came from China. Visiting China, the young woman learns some of the costs and benefits of a command economy. She discovers some of the limitations on people's freedom to make economic choices in China.

The Narrative will help students become aware of alternative methods of answering the basic economic questions of *what, how,* and *for whom.*

Teaching Suggestions (Modeling/Guided Practice)

1. Write the following list on the chalkboard:
   a. 10-speed bicycle
   b. portable TV
   c. desk lamp
   d. ski jacket
   e. pair of sneakers
   f. watch
   g. personal computer
   h. CD player
   i. designer jeans
   j. tickets to a favorite concert

   Select two students who will act as the planning committee in a command economy. Have these students determine how many of each of the above items should be produced. Their economy is only able to produce total units equal to 4 times the number of students in the class. For example, in a class of 25 the planning committee may have 100 items produced. These may be distributed in any priority across the 10 listed items.

   Meanwhile, instruct all the students (including the planners) to rank the four items they would most like to have from the list. Survey the class to find the total number of each item that students said they would like to have. Compare these totals with the number the committee planned to produce. Note that there are shortages of the most desirable goods.

   This exercise is a small version of the problem faced by planning agencies in a planned economy. Help your students draw conclusions about the difficulty of planning in such systems. Ask: How could a planning committee in a command economy better determine priorities for production? (survey consumers, use past records of consumer wants) Ask: What advantage in choosing personal items does the planning committee have? (They know what items may be scarce and also can produce more of what they personally want.)
2. Discuss the fact that schools are much like small command economies. Education is being produced by allocating resources. One job that administrators have is to be sure that all resources (students and other educational materials) are in the right place at the right time. How well does this work in your school? Are students always scheduled into the correct classes? Once scheduling is completed, do all students and other educational materials combine to produce education? Is society getting its money's worth? What difficulties does this demonstrate about command economies?

Lesson Checkpoint

Text: Self-Check, text page 50

Answers

1. In a command economy, the questions *what*, *how*, and *for whom* are answered by the government.
2. Advocates of a command economy believe that running businesses to earn profit results in production of goods intended mainly for the rich, thereby ignoring the poor and unfairly distributing the nation's wealth.

Follow-up Assignments (Independent Practice/Extension/Homework)

Text: Applying What You Have Learned, text page 50

Answers

a. A capitalistic firm that makes a shirt no one wants would have low sales and would probably go out of business.

b. A capitalistic firm that hires too many workers would have high costs of production and therefore low profits. It would likely lose money and be forced out of business.

c. A capitalistic firm that makes poor quality goods would soon find that it has no customers. People would buy from other producers of quality products.

d. A capitalistic firm that pays its workers too little would not be able to attract workers and would either produce little or low-quality products that would force it out of business.

If a firm in a command economy did these same things there would be little effect on the firm. If there were no competition, out-of-style shirts could sell even if they were of low quality. Also, workers would have little choice in where they worked, regardless of the wages. This would mean that inefficient firms could continue to operate and there would be little way to measure how efficient or inefficient they were.

Section Evaluation

Self-Check, text page 50

Understanding Economics, question 7 (Chapter 2 Review, text pages 52–54)

ADDITIONAL MATERIALS FOR CHAPTER 2

Chapter Evaluation

Teacher's Resource Binder: Chapter 2 Quiz

Reteaching and Extension

See the *Teacher's Resource Binder* and the *Student Activity Book* for additional handouts and activities for Chapter 2.

TEACHER'S BIBLIOGRAPHY FOR CHAPTER 2

Economics Sources

Carson, Robert, B. *What Economists Know: An Economic Policy for the 1990s and Beyond.* New York: St. Martin's Press, 1989.

Creedy, John, ed. *Foundations of Economic Thought.* Cambridge, Mass.: Basil Blackwell, 1990.

Eatwell, John et al. *New Palgrave Series: The World of Economics: Essays in the Worldly Philosophy.* New York: W. W. Norton, 1991.

Heilbroner, Robert L. *Behind the Veil of Economics: Essays in the Worldly Philosophy.* New York: W. W. Norton, 1989.

Silk, Leonard. *Economics in Plain English*. New York: Touchstone Books, 1986.

References for Additional Teaching Strategies

Morton, John et al. *High School Economics Courses: Teaching Strategies*. New York: Joint Council on Economic Education, 1985, Chapter 2.

Saunders, Phillip et al. *A Framework For Teaching the Basic Concepts*. New York: Joint Council on Economic Education, 1984, 1993.

Tower, Edward. *Public Choice, Political Economy, Law & War (Economics Reading Lists, Course Outlines, Exams, Puzzles & Problems)*: Vol. 20, Durham, N.C.: Eno River Press, 1990.

CHAPTER 2 REVIEW ANSWERS

Building Your Vocabulary (text page 53)

1. division of labor
2. economic system
3. *for whom?*
4. specialized capital
5. command economy
6. market
7. wealth
8. *how?*
9. capitalism
10. specialization
11. allocation of resources
12. profit
13. traditional economy

Understanding Economics (text page 53)

1. An economic system is a set of rules that governs how the factors of production will be used to produce goods and services and also determines how these goods and services will be distributed.

2. The division of labor is cutting up the job of production into various parts. This allows specialization in that different individuals can learn how to do each part more efficiently. This also allows for the creation of specialized tools that will add to the efficiency of production.

3. Specialized tools increase the efficiency of production. Greater production increases the ability of an economic system to satisfy needs for current consumption and have production left over that can be accumulated as wealth.

4. There are many examples that could be used for this question.

a. The question *what* should be answered through the purchase of some item or service.

b. The question *how* should be answered in terms of cutting cost to improve profitability.

c. The question *for whom* should be answered in terms of income being dependent on the value of a person's contribution to production.

5. To be profitable, a capitalistic firm must offer products or services that people want at prices they are willing and able to pay.

6. In capitalism, firms that are most efficient should be most profitable. Firms that are profitable will be able to afford more resources. Therefore, resources should be allocated to the most efficient firms in capitalism.

7. a. In command economies, the products that are manufactured are determined by the government.

b. In command economies, the method of production is determined by the government.

c. In command economies, the distribution of what is produced is determined by the government.

Thinking Critically About Economics (text pages 53–54)

1. Most of the answers that would be acceptable for this question deal with the greater ability of large schools to serve the diverse needs of many students. Possible answers would include:

   a. ability to afford more science equipment

   b. ability to afford different types of teachers

   c. ability to offer different subjects

   d. ability to afford more tools and machines in shops, etc.

   e. ability to provide more varied points of view

2. The small stores will probably not stock as many specialized items. The reason has to do with turning over inventory. It does not provide as much variety, since it would be poor business to have money tied up in items that do not sell. There is also the possibility of spoilage. It also uses resources and space that could be put to better use.
3. There will be many different salaries offered. Try to draw a correlation between the amount of the salaries and the value of what the worker will contribute to production.
4. There are many possible answers to this question. Try to make it clear that the firm was not answering the questions of *what* or *how* effectively and efficiently.
5. Again, there are many possible answers to this question. Try to show how these firms were more effective and efficient in answering the questions of *what* and *how*.
6. Owners of capitalistic firms in the United States are allowed to

   a. set their own price.

   b. decide what products to make.

   c. decide who to buy from.

   d. decide what to invest in.

   e. decide what to pay workers.

   f. decide how to make their products.

   (There are many other answers that would be just as correct.)

Consumer Skills Projects (text page 54)

1. There are many possible ways to complete this assignment; however, students should demonstrate an understanding of how consumer choices have changed in the past 50 years because of the use of computers in our economy.
2. Student maps and answers should demonstrate an understanding of the value offered to consumers by stores that do business in a convenient location.
3. Students will probably find that there was almost no regulation of consumer products many years ago. You may choose to discuss the costs and benefits demonstrated by the answers reported by students. How do students' beliefs about the costs and benefits of these regulations differ from the beliefs of those interviewed?

PART 1 REVIEW ANSWERS

Understanding Economic Concepts (text pages 56–57)

1. The answer is provided as an example in the text.

2. When we choose to buy the product we want most, we pay an *opportunity cost*, which is the value of the second choice we gave up.
3. The *four factors of production* economists have identified, which are necessary to create goods and services, are: *natural resources*, things in their natural state that have not been changed by people; *labor*, human effort that is applied to natural resources; *capital*, the tools used by labor in making products; and *entrepreneurship*, the organization necessary to bring about production.
4. Economists use *models*, which are theories of how something works, to better understand the past or present and to predict the future.
5. Economists try to make *rational choices* in which they take things of greater value than those which are given up.
6. Economic systems increase the efficiency of production through the *division of labor*, which breaks the process of production into specific tasks and allows *specialization* in which individual workers concentrate their efforts on one specific task. This enables them to become more efficient at their work.
7. All economic systems must answer the four basic economic questions: *What* (what goods and services should be produced?); *How* (how should these goods and services be produced?); *For Whom* (for whom should these goods and services be produced?).
8. The economic system in the United States is mixed, but it is most like *capitalism*. In capitalism the means of production (factors of production) are owned and controlled by individuals or groups.
9. In capitalism firms that are most profitable are best able to purchase additional resources. Therefore, resources are *allocated* to firms according to the *profits* they earn.
10. In a *command economy*, like the one found in China, the means of production are owned and controlled by the government. This means that most basic economic decisions are made by the government.

Writing About Economics (text page 57)

1. Students should show an understanding that they cannot both buy the supplies they need for their math class and go to a movie. This decision will require them to pay an *opportunity cost* when they give up their second choice by taking their first choice.
2. Students should show an understanding that producing and selling letter boxes will require each of the *four factors of production*. The lumber they use was originally a *natural resource* when it was a tree standing in a forest. The student's efforts to make and sell the boxes is *labor*. The hammer and nails they use to put the pieces of wood together are *capital*. Their decision to produce and sell the boxes is *entrepreneurship*.
3. Students should show an understanding that the decision to work together on one job at a time will result in a *division of labor* in which each person will *specialize* in accomplishing one task that is a part of the entire job. This should allow each individual to become more efficient at that task and improve efficiency.
4. Students should show an understanding of the way the three basic economic questions are demonstrated by the problems they have running their appliance store. The good sales of radios and TV's will help them answer the question *What*

they should sell. Hiring a repair person to fix appliances answers the question *How*. Deciding to give, or not give, their employees an increase in salary answers the question *For Whom*.

Discussing Economics (text pages 57–58)

1. Students should identify the issue that the proposal is based on: Is the rationing plan a fair and efficient way to distribute a limited (scarce) supply of gasoline? Students should clearly state whether or not they support the plan for rationing gasoline. They should clearly explain the costs and benefits associated with the plan and explain why their answer is best.
2. Students should identify the issue that the zoning law is based on: Is it fair to limit housing in an area to those people who can afford to buy and build on a one-acre lot? Students should clearly state whether or not they support the law. They should clearly explain the costs and benefits associated with the law and explain why their answer is best.

Problem-Solving in Economics

Chapter 1 (text pages 58–59)

1. Students should clearly describe the problem and the choice that was made, identify the scarce resources that were used, and describe an alternative use of scarce resources. This exercise may be used to demonstrate the economic concepts of *scarcity* and *opportunity cost*.
2. Students should clearly describe each of their four decisions and the alternative choices they could have made, which were the *opportunity costs* they paid in each case.
3. Students should demonstrate an understanding of the factors of production. Be careful with their identification of natural resources. Students often identify things that have been changed by human effort (capital) as natural resources.
4. a. *Positive*—the population of the U.S. in 1990 is a measurable fact.
   b. *Positive*—the unemployment rate in West Virginia and the rest of the U.S. at any given time are measurable facts.
   c. *Normative*—whether the President of the United States is the most powerful person in the world is a matter of one's individual point of view.
   d. *Normative*—whether watching TV is a waste of time is a matter of one's individual point of view.
   e. *Positive*—changes in the price of products are measurable facts.
   f. *Normative*—whether buying Japanese cars is wrong is a matter of one's individual point of view.
5. Lists of assumptions may have included: young people take more risks; young people are less experienced drivers; young people drink excessively more often than older drivers.

   The table shows that fatal accidents per 100,000 drivers ages 16-17 and 18-21 were reduced sharply after the new policy was introduced. Fatal accidents per 100,000 drivers declined less sharply in the other age categories and actually increased in the age 35-44 category.

   Students should demonstrate that they have considered the logic of the assumptions on their list. They should show that they understand the table and that the assumptions are forms of *models*.

6. Students should clearly demonstrate an understanding of *rational choice* by listing and evaluating the costs and benefits associated with the choices they identify.

Chapter 2 (text page 59)

1. Students should show they realize Jerry is having trouble because he is not able to take advantage of the *division of labor*, *specialization*, or *specialized tools*, and that he is unable to *accumulate* much *wealth* because his business is so small and he does most things himself.
2. There are many products students could identify. One example would be movie cameras. Few people would want to buy a movie camera now because they would rather have a portable video camera. Stores must stock *what* their customers want to buy. Most video cameras sold in this country in recent years were manufactured in other countries where costs were lower. This is *how* firms thought they could make the most profit. Firms that produced quality video cameras for personal use made large profits. The owners and their employees received the benefits.

PART 2

UNDERSTANDING HOW INDIVIDUALS AND BUSINESSES MAKE ECONOMIC DECISIONS

CHAPTER 3

Demand and Supply (text pages 62–91)

SECTION A. The Elements of an Economic System (text pages 64–68)

Objectives (Lesson Focus)

Upon completion of this section, students will be able to:

- Explain the flow of money, products, and factors of production when provided with a copy of a circular flow model.
- Identify transactions that would occur in the product market.
- Identify transactions that would occur in the factor market.

Preparation (Instruction: Pre-teaching—Vocabulary or Activity)

1. Discussion Introduce this section by asking each student to list their sources of income and several products they frequently buy. Draw a large circular flow model on the board and place the information from the students' lists in the appropriate places on the chart. It is likely that part or all of their income is the result of their parents' earnings in the factor market rather than their own. This does not change the fact that their spending in the product market depends on earnings in the factor market. Also, wages paid in the factor market depend on sales in the product market. The parts of the model are interdependent just as parts of the real economic system depend on one another.

2. The Personal Narrative The Personal Narrative in Section A (and those in the other sections of Chapter 3) describes how a farm in the Midwest fits into the U.S. economic system in the mid-1970s. The subject of the Narrative is a young man who grew up on the farm. He discusses resources that his family purchased in the factor market and how their earnings were spent in the product market. These activities are placed into the circular flow model in the rest of this section.

The Narrative will help students see how their own spending and earnings are a part of the circular flow model.

Teaching Suggestions (Modeling/Guided Practice)

1. Give your students a copy of Discussion Topic 2 from the *Teacher's Resource Binder.* Ask them to read the news story and discuss how it relates to the circular flow model.
2. Discuss ways people receive income. Although wages are the largest part of the flow of money through the factor market, interest, rents, and profits are also parts of that flow. Point out that money which people deposit in a bank can be loaned to firms to help them produce goods and services. Depositors are paid interest by the bank for the use of their money which they can then spend in the product market. When a farmer rents land to a business, the same type of events occur.
3. Provide students with copies of a local newspaper. Ask them to cut out news articles or advertisements that concern

the transfer of money. These could include "help wanted" ads, food ads, bank ads, articles about new buildings, etc. Ask your students to explain (either orally or in writing) where each transaction would be placed on the circular flow model.

Lesson Checkpoint

Text: Self-Check, text page 66
Answers

1. A sale of crude oil would be found in the factor market.
2. A sale of a TV set would be found in the product market.
3. They are equal in value.

Follow-up Assignments (Independent Practice/Extension/Homework)

Text: Applying What You Have Learned, text page 67
Answers

a. Selling vegetables is part of the product market.
b. Renting land from Mr. Sims is part of the factor market.
c. Hiring extra workers is part of the factor market.
d. Going to a movie is part of the product market.
e. Selling corn to a co-op is part of the product market.
f. Buying seed is part of the factor market.
g. Buying gas to drive to Cedar Rapids is part of the product market.
h. Hiring Mr. Sims is part of the factor market.
i. Buying a pair of jeans is part of the product market.

(It is possible to put some of these transactions in other locations on the flow model. For example, buying gas may be a part of the factor market if it is used to run tractors or to transport seed for planting.)

Section Evaluation

Self-Check, text page 66
Understanding Economics, questions 1 and 2 (Chapter 3 Review, text pages 88–90)

SECTION B. The Law of Demand (text pages 69–72)

Objectives (Lesson Focus)

Upon completion of this section, students will be able to:

- Restate the law of demand.
- Read a demand schedule and a demand curve.
- Draw a demand curve from a demand schedule.
- Identify and explain four determinants of demand: tastes, income, the price of related products, and number of customers.

Preparation (Instruction: Pre-teaching—Vocabulary or Activity)

1. Discussion Introduce this section by asking students what they would do if they inherited $1,000. How would their spending change? Would they simply buy more of what they already buy, or would they purchase different products? Point out the fact that demand is more than a desire to buy something; it is the ability and willingness to actually buy it. Changes in income, tastes, and the other determinants of demand cause people to demand either more or less of a product *if its price does not change.*

2. The Personal Narrative The Personal Narrative in Section B continues the story of the farm in Iowa. It describes how the farm prospered due to the sale of food to the Soviet Union, which increased demand for agricultural products in the 1970s. The father in the Narrative uses his increased income to buy more goods in the product market.

The Narrative demonstrates the fact that demand may change for a variety of reasons: among them, an increase in the number of customers.

Teaching Suggestions (Modeling/Guided Practice)

1. Take a survey of students in your class concerning how many of them would buy ice cream cones at various prices. Use the results to complete a demand schedule similar to the one below. Either plot the data from the demand schedule as a demand curve on the board, or have students draw their own curves at their seats.

Price of Ice Cream Cones	Number Demanded
$1.75	______
$1.50	______
$1.25	______
$1.00	______
$ .75	______
$ .50	______

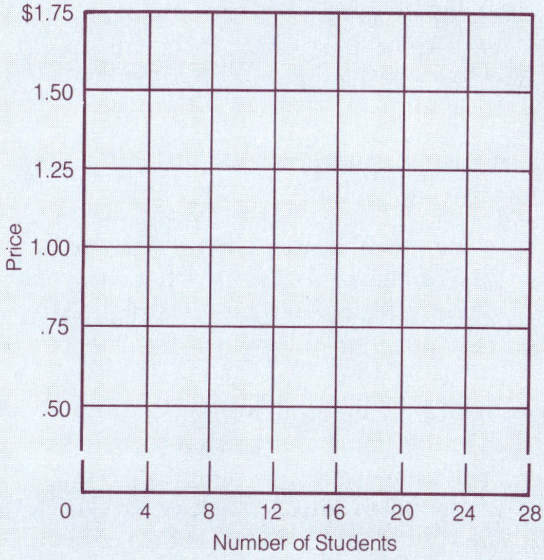

2. Assign students to think of five examples of complementary products and five examples of substitute products. Write some of their examples on the board and discuss how changes in the price of one of the paired items would cause the demand curve for the other to move.
3. Provide students with the list of firms below. Tell them that they have $5,000 to invest in one or more of the firms. They should explain (in writing or orally) why they would or would not want to invest in each type of firm. Point out how future demand is related to the number of customers a firm expects to serve.
   a. a firm that makes equipment for nursing homes
   b. a firm that makes playground equipment for new schools
   c. a firm that makes replacement parts for propellor-driven planes
   d. a firm that makes cloth baby diapers
4. If it is possible in your school, have students sell apples or large cookies outside the school cafeteria during lunch periods. On the first day charge $.50 for each item. On the second day lower the price to $.40. On the third and final day charge $.30. Keep careful records of the number of items sold each day. Your students can use this data to make a demand schedule and to draw a demand curve for their product. Be sure the student body is not aware that the price will fall each day. The expectation of falling prices could change current demand.

Lesson Checkpoint

Text: Self-Check, text page 72
Answers

1. Wanting a new coat becomes demand when the new coat is actually sold.

2. The number of products sold should decrease.
3. Economists call these factors the determinants of demand.

Follow-up Assignments (Independent Practice/Extension/Homework)

Text: Applying What You Have Learned, text page 72
Answer

The bad harvests in Russia from 1971 to 1973 resulted in the American sale of large quantities of grain to the Soviet Union. The number of potential customers was the determinant that resulted in a growth in demand.

Section Evaluation

Self-Check, text page 72
Understanding Economics, questions 3 and 4 (Chapter 3 Review, text pages 88–90)

SECTION C. The Law of Supply (text pages 73–76)

Objectives (Lesson Focus)

Upon completion of this section, students will be able to:

- Restate the law of supply.
- Read a supply schedule and a supply curve.
- Draw a supply curve from a supply schedule.
- Explain how and why changes in the costs of production change supply.

Preparation (Instruction: Pre-teaching—Vocabulary or Activity)

1. Discussion Introduce this section by giving each student a 3-by-5 card. Tell them to describe on the card the job they are expected to do at home that they like *least*. Washing dishes could be an example. On the back of the card, have them write how much they would be willing to pay someone else to do the job for them (if they had an income of $50 a week).

Collect the cards. Read several jobs to the class telling how much the person would be willing to pay. Ask how many students would do the job for the suggested amount and write the number on the board. Increase the amount of pay several times and ask the students each time how many would do the work. By recording their answers, you will create a supply schedule for the service. Use the supply schedule to draw a supply curve.

2. The Personal Narrative The Personal Narrative for Section C continues the story of the farm in Iowa. It describes the growth in supply of agricultural products that occurred in response to increased demand in the 1970s. The subject's father used his increased income and borrowed money to purchase additional resources in the factor market. Other farmers did the same. As a result, the production of farm products surpassed their demand by the early 1980s.

The Narrative demonstrates that a firm's willingness to supply products changes with its costs of production and expectations of being able to sell additional products.

Teaching Suggestions (Modeling/Guided Practice)

1. Invite an admissions counselor from a local college or vocational school to speak to your class about their institution. After their presentation, discuss the value of the service they were selling with your class. How is supplying an education different from supplying food, furniture, or clothing? How much more does it cost the school to educate another student? Why do private training schools tend to

start up in areas with high rates of unemployment? What product are they supplying? How are they responding to a change in demand?

2. Describe the following situation to your class:

    There is a community in the western part of the United States, near a wilderness area that has a river in a deep valley. The area is used by campers, hunters, and by many other people.

    There is a high rate of unemployment in the community. A local business has offered to expand its factory and add 500 jobs if it can be supplied with inexpensive electric power. A dam and hydroelectric project in the wilderness area could provide the power. The project would flood most of the river valley. The state has to decide whether to allow an electric company to build the dam so the factory can grow.

    Ask your students to consider the problem. If the dam is built, what would happen to the firm's willingness to supply products to the market? What would the costs and benefits of the decision be? Do your students feel the dam should be built?

3. Use Discussion Topic 3 from the *Teacher's Resource Binder* to illustrate the use of a supply curve and the effects of changes in the costs of production.

Lesson Checkpoint

Text: Self-Check, text page 76
Answers

1. The number of products for sale will decrease.
2. The cost of additional units of production will increase.
3. The number of products offered for sale will decrease.

Follow-up Assignments (Independent Practice/Extension/Homework)

Text: Applying What You Have Learned, text page 76
Answer

The farmers decided to make the investments necessary to increase production because the price of corn had gone up.

Section Evaluation

Self-Check, text page 76
Understanding Economics, questions 5 and 6 (Chapter 3 Review, text pages 88–90)

SECTION D. Surpluses, Shortages, and Equilibrium (text pages 77–80)

Objectives (Lesson Focus)

Upon completion of this section, students will be able to:

- Identify and explain the meaning of equilibrium.
- Explain how surpluses or shortages tend to force prices to the equilibrium price in a market economy.

Preparation (Instruction: Pre-teaching—Vocabulary or Activity)

1. Discussion Introduce this section by giving students a list of products and asking them to find the current price for each item in advertising supplements from a local newspaper. Items could include specific brands of soap, foods, or personal care items. Your students should find that most stores charge about the same price for similar items (although many stores will have loss-leaders to attract shoppers). Discuss how the forces of demand and supply interact to reach a market price. What would an individual store find if it charged substantially more or less than other stores for the same item?

2. The Personal Narrative The Personal Narrative in Section D continues the story of the farm in Iowa. It describes how the excess supply of agricultural products forced prices down and eventually led to bankruptcy for many farmers. It emphasizes the problem farmers had in repaying loans taken out when prices were high with reduced income earned when prices were low.

The Narrative will help students understand how the forces of demand and supply interact to set prices. It shows that the price a firm can sell its product for may have little to do with the amount the firm paid to make the product.

Teaching Suggestions (Modeling/Guided Practice)

1. Use the Demand and Supply Cards in the simulations section of the *Teacher's Resource Binder*. Hand out copies of the cards to your students. Give about two-thirds of them "Demand Cards" and the rest "Supply Cards." The difference between the cards reflects different tastes and levels of income for consumers, or costs of production for producers.

   Read off the different possible prices in class and ask each person how many products he/she would demand or supply according to his/her card. Tabulate these quantities on the board and make them into a demand and supply schedule. Convert the schedules into a graph of demand and supply. What is the equilibrium price and quantity that has been identified on the graph?
2. Your students may enjoy producing an imitation of the television show "The Price is Right." Choose a panel of four students who will guess the true market price of various items. Those who are closest to the correct price without going over will win the item. Using humorous items, such as fish food or purple hair spray, can help to hold student attention. When they are finished, discuss the idea of equilibrium price as it applies to the items used as prizes.
3. Point out the fact that there are always end-of-season sales in which stores attempt to sell leftover items like summer clothes or snow shovels. Ask your students to explain what is happening to the location of demand curves that causes stores to reduce their prices. Why do changing seasons change the location of the point of equilibrium? What would happen to the store's sales and inventories if it refused to lower its prices as customer demand fell?

Lesson Checkpoint

Text: Self-Check, text page 80
Answers

1. The point of equilibrium is found at the intersection of the supply and demand curves.
2. It must lower its price to eliminate its surplus.
3. If the firm is charging less than the equilibrium price, it will have a shortage of product. This will encourage it to increase its price.

Follow-up Assignments (Independent Practice/Extension/Homework)

Text: Applying What You Have Learned, text page 80
Answer

The price of corn in any year is the result of the interaction of demand and supply. An overall shortage of supply causes an increase in price, and so a farm might make a profit even though crops are poor. An overall surplus of corn causes the market price to fall, and so a farm might make no profit even though crops are good. However, crop failure on a single farm, when all other farms are having a good year, will not produce a shortage in the market, and so will not boost a farm's profits.

Section Evaluation
Self-Check, text page 80

SECTION E. Elasticity (text pages 81–86)

Objectives (Lesson Focus)
Upon completion of this section, students will be able to:

- Identify demand as being price elastic or price inelastic when given appropriate examples.
- Recognize the relationship between percentage changes in price and resulting percentage changes in the quantity sold that demonstrate a product's price elasticity of demand.
- Identify characteristics of products that tend to make their demand either price elastic or price inelastic.
- Identify situations in which a product's price elasticity of demand has economic importance.

Preparation (Instruction: Pre-teaching—Vocabulary or Activity)

1. Discussion Introduce this section by asking students how much they would pay to hear music played by a local group that is not very popular or talented. They would probably be willing to pay a dollar or two, but no more. If the group charged $5.00 for tickets, they would sell few. Explain that the demand for their music is quite elastic. As the price increases, the quantity demanded falls rapidly.

Then ask your students how much they would pay to see a famous national rock star (you supply the name). It is likely that your class, as a group, would buy about the same number of tickets at $10, $15, $20, or even $25. Explain that the demand for music played by famous performers is quite inelastic. A change in price results in relatively little change in the quantity demanded.

2. The Personal Narrative The Personal Narrative in Section E continues the story of the farm in Iowa. It demonstrates the fact that demand for some products is more sensitive to changes in price than demand for other products. The subject of the Narrative comes to realize that people need about the same amount of food each year. If production grows beyond what people need, the product cannot be easily sold and prices will fall rapidly. On the other hand, shortages of food cause prices to increase just as rapidly.

The Narrative will help students understand the difference between elastic demand and inelastic demand. It also shows how price elasticity of demand can affect individual firms.

Teaching Suggestions (Modeling/Guided Practice)

1. Give students Discussion Topic 4 from the *Teacher's Resource Binder,* describing a hypothetical situation about an essential medicine that is too expensive for many people to afford. Help your class identify the issues involved in this question. Divide your class into teams to debate whether or not the government should provide the drug.
2. Ask your students to list five products they believe are necessities and five they believe are luxuries. Have them find the

current market price for these products. Tell them to assume that the price for all of the products just went up by 50 percent. Assign them to write a paper in which they predict the percentage decline in sales that would result from the increase in price for each product. If they believe the sales would be cut by more than half, the demand is elastic. If they believe the sales would be cut by less than half, the demand in inelastic. Your students should find that the demand for necessities is less elastic than the demand for luxuries.

3. Explain that when firms advertise, they are often trying to change the price elasticity of demand for their products. If they can convince their customers that their product is necessary and that no similar product is as good as theirs, they will be able to charge more for their product while losing few customers. They are trying to make the demand for their product more price inelastic. Have students bring in or identify advertisements that are intended to do this.

Lesson Checkpoint

Text: Self-Check, text page 86
Answers

1. Elasticity describes this relationship.
2. The demand is price elastic.
3. The demand is price inelastic.

Follow-up Assignments (Independent Practice/Extension/Homework)

1. Text: Applying What You Have Learned, text page 86
Answers

a. Demand for one brand of toothpaste is elastic because there are many other brands that can be substituted.
b. Demand for trips to Florida in July is elastic because it is warm in most places and there are also other places to go.
c. Demand for heart disease medicine is inelastic because it is very important to its consumers.
d. Demand for tickets to a reading of English poetry probably is very elastic because the students would probably rather not attend.
e. Demand for tickets to a rock concert may be quite inelastic if many people want to attend.
f. Demand for water by people lost in the desert would be very inelastic since its use would keep them alive.

2. Teacher's Resource Binder: Critical Thinking Activity for Chapter 3 (answers in Binder).

Section Evaluation

Self-Check, text page 86
Understanding Economics, question 7 (Chapter 3 Review, text pages 88–90)

ADDITIONAL MATERIALS FOR CHAPTER 3

Chapter Evaluation

Teacher's Resource Binder: Chapter 3 Quiz

Reteaching and Extension

See the *Teacher's Resource Binder* and the *Student Activity Book* for additional handouts and activities for Chapter 3.

TEACHER'S BIBLIOGRAPHY FOR CHAPTER 3

Economics Sources

McConnell, Campbell R. and Brue, Stanley L. *Economics: Principles, Problems, and Policies*, 11th ed. New York: McGraw-Hill, 1990, Chapters 3 and 4.

Miller, Roger LeRoy. *Economics Today*, 7th ed. New York: Harper Collins, 1991, Chapters 3 and 4.

Samuelson, Paul A. and Nordhaus, William D. *Economics*, 14th ed. New York: McGraw-Hill, 1992, Chapters 4 and 5.

References for Additional Teaching Strategies

Maybury, Richard J. *Whatever Happened to Penny Candy? For Students, Business People & Investors: A Fast, Clear & Fun Explanation of the Economics You Need For Success in Your Career, Business and Investments*. Placerville, Calif.: Bluestocking Press, 1989.

Mansfield, Edwin, and Behravesh, Nariman. *Economics U.S.A.*, 3rd ed. New York: W. W. Norton, 1992, Chapters 2 and 16. Keyed to Southern California Consortium's telecourse of the same title.

Morton, John et al. *High School Economics Courses: Teaching Strategies*. New York: Joint Council on Economic Education, 1985, Lessons 5, 6, 7, and 10.

CHAPTER 3 REVIEW ANSWERS

Building Your Vocabulary (text page 89)

1. supply
2. demand
3. product market
4. factor market
5. price inelastic demand
6. price elastic demand
7. demand schedule
8. supply curve
9. diminishing returns
10. circular flow model
11. supply schedule
12. demand curve
13. complementary goods
14. substitute goods
15. surplus
16. law of demand
17. shortage
18. elasticity
19. point of equilibrium
20. determinants of demand
21. law of supply

Understanding Economics (text page 90)

1. Three of the many possible transactions that could take place in the product market include:

a. the purchase of a meal at a restaurant
b. the purchase of a bus ticket
c. the purchase of a pair of socks

All purchases in the product market involve consumer goods and services that are used to directly satisfy human wants.

2. Three of the many transactions that could take place in the factor market include:

a. paying a clerk in your store
b. buying supplies for your restaurant
c. paying for land on which to build a factory

All purchases in the factor market involve goods or services that will be used to produce something else that will eventually satisfy human wants.

3. If you want or need something, it will do a firm and the economy little good if you cannot also buy it. There is no profit to be made from a product people want but don't buy.
4. a. A blizzard would increase the demand for snow tires by changing tastes and preferences.
   b. The demand for tea would decrease when the price of coffee falls, because tea and coffee are substitutes.
   c. The demand for specialty food decreases in a recession because people have lower incomes and do not buy as many luxury items.
   d. The demand for housing increases when people move to avoid crime because of a change in tastes and preferences.
5. Diminishing productivity occurs when, as more factors of production are added to the production of a product, the resulting increase in production keeps getting smaller. This happens because (a) there is a limit to how many workers can be used efficiently in a factory, and (b) there is also a limit to the number of machines that can be placed in a factory without causing overcrowding.
6. a. The supply would increase if the cost of a product's basic raw material went down.
   b. The supply would decrease if the wages paid to workers increased.
   c. The supply would increase if a new machine reduced waste.
   d. The supply would increase if a firm converted to gas from electricity. The only reason to convert would be to reduce costs of production.
7. a. If the demand for a product is price elastic, a change in price will cause a greater percent change in the number sold.
   b. One would expect the price elasticity for medicine to be inelastic if there were few substitutes for such important products.
   c. If a firm raises the price of its brand of dish soap by 10 percent, one would expect a larger than 10 percent drop in sales because there are many other brands of soap consumers could buy.

Thinking Critically About Economics (text page 90)

1. Virtually any job could be used. The students should make it clear that they understand that labor supplied to a firm in the factor market allows people to buy goods and services in the product market.
2. Any changes that would affect the determinants of demand would be acceptable. Be sure not to accept a change in price that *would not* change demand. Three possible answers are:
   a. Advertise to convince people your shoes are superior.
   b. Move your store to a town where people have higher incomes.
   c. Stock a larger supply of different types of shoes.
3. If the items listed are important, the probability is that many of them will have price inelastic demand. Many of these will end up being a "judgment call." For example, the demand for a hamburger is elastic for most people, but some people may really prefer one particular product. Be sure to note that although an individual may have product loyalty, this would not be true of large groups.

Consumer Skills Projects (text page 90)

1. Student posters should demonstrate their understanding of the determinants of demand.
2. Student suggestions will vary but should demonstrate their understanding of factors that could cause consumers to own television sets. People who own televisions are also likely to subscribe to cable services or may own satellite dish antennas.

CHAPTER 4

The Consumer and the Economy: Getting What You Pay For (text pages 92–113)

SECTION A. How We Make Spending Decisions (text pages 94–97)

Objectives (Lesson Focus)

Upon completion of this section, students will be able to:

- Define the principle of diminishing marginal utility and recognize situations that demonstrate this principle.
- Explain how the slope of a demand curve demonstrates the principle of diminishing marginal utility.

Preparation (Instruction: Pre-teaching—Vocabulary or Activity)

1. Discussion Introduce this section by assigning students to identify the one item they feel they most need now, and to explain why they need it. Ask your students to describe how much they would want a second unit of the item if they were given the first unit. Ask them why a second unit might not be as important to them as the first was. Would they want something else instead?

Explain how the fact that most students would not find a second unit to be worth as much as the first demonstrates the principle of diminishing marginal utility.

It is possible to complete this exercise by giving students a fictional amount of money to spend. They will probably choose to distribute their spending among many items.

2. The Personal Narrative The Personal Narrative for Section A describes a person who wants to own classic sports cars to the point of obsession. The subject of the Narrative gives up as many other goods and services as possible to save for a car. The point is made that the average person does not behave this way. People usually distribute their spending among many items to maximize the utility they obtain from their income.

The Narrative describes a situation that will help students understand the principle of diminishing marginal utility and how it affects the way they spend their money.

Teaching Suggestions (Modeling/Guided Practice)

1. Ask your students to count the number of television sets they have in their homes and put the number on a piece of paper. Collect the papers and tabulate the results on the chalkboard. Discuss why some families have many more sets than others. What might explain the difference? Could it show a difference in individual values? Point out that diminishing marginal utility does not mean everyone has the same values. One person might feel one television was enough while another might want three or four.
2. Many stores offer discounts for large quantity purchases. However, many customers choose to buy small quantities that cost more per amount. An example might be ice cream that costs $3.59 per

half gallon or $1.19 per pint. The half gallon is four times as large as a pint, but only costs three times as much. Still, many people buy pints of ice cream. Ask students to explain what this has to do with the principle of diminishing marginal utility.

3. Ask your students to predict the ending to the following story which demonstrates diminishing marginal utility:

   Johnny entered a contest in his newspaper and won. He was thrilled because the prize was being able to ride a roller-coaster as often as he wanted to at a local amusement park. He got to the park at 9:00 AM so that he would be able to ride it as many times as possible. At the start of the day he felt very happy. By 10:00 AM, he . . .

Lesson Checkpoint

Text: Self-Check, text page 97
Answers

1. The second television set would be of less value.
2. After a person has a few of them, additional ones become less important.

Follow-up Assignments (Independent Practice/Extension/Homework)

Text: Applying What You Have Learned, text page 97
Answers

Student answers will vary. It is probable that some of your students will find that some of the items they buy in small quantity are the most important to them. For example, students would not buy more than one calculator, but having one is very important if they are taking math. This would demonstrate the principle of diminishing marginal utility. The first one would be very important, but there would be little point (utility) in having more than one.

Section Evaluation

Self-Check, text page 97
Thinking Critically About Economics, question 1 (Chapter 4 Review, text pages 109–111)

SECTION B. Consumer Sovereignty (text pages 98–101)

Objectives (Lesson Focus)

Upon completion of this section, students will be able to:

- Explain the meaning of the term, "consumer sovereignty," and its relationship to the way the basic economic question, *what*, is answered in capitalism.
- Explain the meaning of the term *invisible hand* and its relationship to maintaining competition in price and quality in capitalism.

Preparation (Instruction: Pre-teaching—Vocabulary or Activity)

1. Discussion Introduce this section by giving students a copy of a clothing advertisement taken from a newspaper that is five to ten years old (most libraries can help you make a copy of such an advertisement). Be sure to choose one that shows clothing that is currently out of style. Ask your students to write a brief essay in which they describe what would happen to a store that tried to sell these clothes now. Have several students read their essays in class and discuss what they had to say. In general, students will recognize the problem a store would have in selling dated styles. The discussion can then be led into the topics of consumer sovereignty and the invisible hand.

2. The Personal Narrative The Personal Narrative in Section B describes a situation that demonstrates the idea of consumer sovereignty and the invisible hand. The subject of the Narrative is a young woman who owns a boutique that specializes in selling fashionable clothing at reduced prices. To succeed in her business, she is forced to offer products that her customers want to buy. She earns her profit by working very hard to provide products her customers want at low prices. By looking out for her own interests, she also serves those of her customers.

The Narrative will help students appreciate the limited freedom businesses have in a competitive market economy. In many ways they are forced to make decisions by their customers and by competition.

Teaching Suggestions (Modeling/Guided Practice)

1. In most areas there are one or two radio stations that young people listen to more than others. There are other stations that appeal to older people. The types of advertising heard on these stations is likely to be very different. The radio stations are in business to sell air-time to advertisers. Discuss factors that make a radio station successful with your class. How does the fact that it is hard to find stations that play "classical" music in many areas relate to consumer sovereignty?
2. Hand out copies of Discussion Topic 6 from the *Teacher's Resource Binder*. Discuss how the story is related to the ideas of consumer sovereignty and the invisible hand.
3. If there is a local farmer's market, assign several students to survey the prices charged by different farmers for the same types of produce. They should find that all the farmers charge almost the exact same price for produce of equal quality. Ask your students to explain why the farmers do this, and how it demonstrates the idea of the invisible hand.

Lesson Checkpoint

Text: Self-Check, text page 101
Answers

1. To sell products, producers must meet consumer needs. This is consumer sovereignty.
2. The "invisible hand" means that producers will serve the interests of society when they attempt to serve their own interests.

Follow-up Assignments (Independent Practice/Extension/Homework)

Text: Applying What You Have Learned, text page 101
Answers

The determination of how many pink polka dot dresses and baggy pants will be manufactured in the next year will be based on the items' previous desirability by consumers. If these items sold well and are still considered popular by the consumer, they will likely be a manufacturing priority again. If not, manufacturers will likely limit or discontinue the items altogether.

Section Evaluation

Self-Check, text page 101
Understanding Economics, questions 1 and 2 (Chapter 4 Review, text pages 109–111)

SECTION C. Individual Freedom and Consumer Protection (text pages 102–105)

Objectives (Lesson Focus)

Upon completion of this section, students will be able to:

- Describe why there has been a growing need for government consumer protection as the economy has grown over the past 200 years.
- Identify and explain several of the trade-offs that are made when the government undertakes consumer protection.

Preparation (Instruction: Pre-teaching—Vocabulary or Activity)

1. **Discussion** Introduce this section by asking students to make a list of at least five ways in which they are affected by government regulations intended to protect them. The warning on cigarettes, seatbelt laws, drinking ages, being required to attend school, and speed limits are some examples. Ask them to explain the reasoning behind each rule and to give their opinion of the need for the rule. Do they feel that their parents would have the same opinions they have? Why or why not?

2. **The Personal Narrative** The Personal Narrative for Section C tells the story of a man who wants the government to stay out of his life, at least most of the time. The subject of the Narrative is a young person whose uncle is offended by the government's regulations which are intended to protect consumers. He resents warnings on cigarette packages and seatbelt laws. However, he expects the government to help him when he feels he has been cheated.

The Narrative demonstrates the trade-off between the costs and benefits of government consumer protection.

Teaching Suggestions (Modeling/Guided Practice)

1. Many states have passed "lemon laws" that make auto dealers responsible for making repairs to used cars they sell. Dealers have argued that such laws force them to charge much more for used cars. They say the law causes many people to buy used cars that are defective from private individuals who are not covered by the law. They suggest that poor people will be hurt by the law because they won't be able to afford decent transportation. Other people argue that poor people will benefit because they won't be sold "junk" cars by dishonest dealers.

   Organize a debate in your class based on this topic. Do students believe the law is a good or bad idea? Is it a reasonable type of consumer protection? Should these laws be extended to other products?
2. Use Discussion Topic 7 from the *Teacher's Resource Binder* to discuss an issue relating to consumer protection, government regulation, and First Amendment rights.
3. The government requires specific information on all labels, including a list of each ingredient and breakdowns on nutritional information such as fats, proteins, and carbohydrates. Have your students cut out "ingredients labels" from foods they eat and bring them to class. Discuss whether or not the labels provide useful information, and whether people really pay attention to them.

Lesson Checkpoint

Text: Self-Check, text page 105
Answers

1. Products are much more complicated today.
2. Additional money must be spent

to meet regulations, and this cost is passed on to the consumers.

3. Trade-offs include reduced competition and a slower acceptance of new ideas.

Follow-up Assignments (Independent Practice/Extension/Homework)

Text: Applying What You Have Learned, text page 105
Answers

1. The answers in this exercise will depend on the students' individual values. Their explanations should be clear. Class discussions of these points can lead to important understandings of why people have different opinions and values.
2. Included in the picture are the following government-regulated activities:
   a. traffic signals and regulations
   b. taxi service
   c. telephone service
   d. billboards (size restrictions in some cities)
   e. lighting (government-regulated utility)

Section Evaluation

Self-Check, text page 205
Understanding Economics, questions 3 and 4 (Chapter 4 Review, text pages 109–111)

SECTION D. Advertising and Consumer Demand (text pages 106–108)

Objective (Lesson Focus)

Upon completion of this section, students will be able to:

- Identify and explain the difference between advertising that is intended to inform and advertising that is intended to persuade.

Preparation (Instruction: Pre-teaching—Vocabulary or Activity)

1. Discussion Introduce this section by asking students to make a list of specific advertisements they find obnoxious or of little value, and a second list they feel are valuable to them. These lists may be done either by individual students or in groups. Ask the students to explain what there is about each ad that makes it good or bad from the point of view of the consumer. Why do some firms use advertisements that are clearly obnoxious?

2. The Personal Narrative The Personal Narrative for Section D concerns a young woman and how she is affected by advertising. Although the subject of the Narrative professes to see no value in advertising, she repeatedly is influenced by it. She uses advertising to remind herself of things she needs to do, as a source on information so she can make better decisions, and ultimately as a source of personal income.

The Narrative shows students how advertising affects people like themselves. It demonstrates the difference between advertising that is intended to persuade and that which is intended to inform.

Teaching Suggestions (Modeling/Guided Practice)

1. Many states have outlawed advertising on major interstate highways to make them more attractive. They feel travelers would rather look at the scenery than at a collection of billboards. The owners of businesses often say this reduces their sales and does not serve the interests of travelers. When someone is looking for a

place to stay or eat, they don't know where to stop. They may have to keep getting off the road to ask or they may miss good places. Ask your students to discuss this issue and see if they can reach a consensus on what limits should be placed on highway advertising.

2. Choose several products your students are likely to purchase and assign each student to write two newspaper ads for one of the products. Their first advertisement should be informative. The second should be intended to persuade. Have them read their ads in class and discuss the factors that make them likely to succeed. Remember the purpose of the advertisement is to alter consumer demand, not just to entertain.
3. Assign students to interview local businesspeople about their use of advertising. Students should ask questions about how the firm decides what sort of advertising to use, where and when to advertise, how much to spend on advertising, and how they measure the success of their advertising. Students should report their findings to the class. Help your students find common factors among the various firms.

Lesson Checkpoint

Text: Self-Check, text page 108
Answers

1. Firms advertise to increase demand for their products.
2. Informative advertising gives actual differences between products. Persuasive advertising attempts to change the customer's tastes or preferences.
3. One reason that persuasive advertising is sometimes considered harmful to consumers is that such advertising can convince people—especially children—to buy products that are not healthy for them.

Follow-up Assignments (Independent Practice/Extension/Homework)

1. Text: Applying What You Have Learned, text page 108
   Answers
   a. Sherry looked at want ads in the paper. *inform*
   b. Sherry found out about a shoe sale. *inform*
   c. Sherry was reminded of Mother's Day. *inform*
   d. Sherry found out about a new play. *persuade*
   e. Sherry heard of an inexpensive diet program. *inform*
2. Teacher's Resource Binder: Critical Thinking Activity, Chapter 4 (answers in Binder)

Section Evaluation

Self-Check, text page 108
Understanding Economics, questions 5 and 6 (Chapter 4 Review, text pages 109–111)

ADDITIONAL MATERIALS FOR CHAPTER 4

Chapter Evaluation

Teacher's Resource Binder: Chapter 4 Quiz

Reteaching and Extension

See the *Teacher's Resource Binder* and the *Student Activity Book* for additional handouts and activities for Chapter 4.

TEACHER'S BIBLIOGRAPHY FOR CHAPTER 4

Economics Sources

Carson, Robert B. *Economic Issues Today: Alternative Approaches.* New York: St. Martin's Press, 1987.

Council on Economic Priorities. *Shopping For a Better World.* New York: Ballantine, 1991.

Galbraith, John Kenneth. "Economics and Advertising: Exercise in Denial." *Advertising Age,* November 9, 1988, pp. 80–87.

Gordon, Sanford D. and Dawson, George G. *Introductory Economics,* 7th ed. Lexington, Mass.: D.C. Heath Inc., 1991.

Heilbroner, Robert. *The Making of Economic Society.* Englewood Cliffs, N.J.: Prentice Hall, 1985.

Leet, Don R. and Driggers, Joann. *Economic Decisions for Consumers,* 2nd ed. New York: Macmillan, 1990.

Mansfield, Edwin, and Behravesh, Nariman. *Telecourse Study Guide for Economics USA,* New York: Norton, 1992, Chapter 20. Text provides exercises for and is keyed to the television course *Economics USA,* developed by the Southern California Consortium.

Miller, Roger LeRoy, and Stafford, Alan D. *Economic Issues for Consumers,* 7th ed. St. Paul, Minn.: West, 1993.

References for Additional Teaching Strategies

Ristau, Robert et al. *Basic Business and Consumer Education.* New York: Joint Council on Economic Education, 1985.

CHAPTER 4 REVIEW ANSWERS

Building Your Vocabulary (text page 110)

1. persuasive advertising
2. consumer protection
3. consumer sovereignty
4. informative advertising
5. invisible hand
6. diminishing marginal utility

Understanding Economics (text page 111)

1. A firm that sells wooden wagon wheels will have difficulty staying in business because there is very little demand for this product.
2. To earn a profit, producers in competition must sell products of similar quality and price or their customers will buy elsewhere. If Joe is charging an excessive price for inferior tires, few people would buy from him. It is as if there were an "invisible hand" forcing him to do what his competition does.
3. Most people believe the government should regulate the production and distribution of chemicals and similar products because few consumers have the knowledge to make these decisions for themselves.
4. The trade-off is between environmental safety and additional production. The chemical could increase crop yields but would make people ill at the same time.
5. The advertisements used by the students should include specific information that would help consumers make rational choices in how they spend their money.
6. The advertisements used by the students should be misleading and intended to convince consumers to do something that could be harmful to them.

Thinking Critically About Economics (text page 111)

1. The price a consumer is willing to pay for a product is a measure of the value or utility that it would provide to the con-

sumer. If John would pay $50 for his first jacket but only $20 for a second one, the second one is of less value to him. This demonstrates the principle of diminishing marginal utility.

2. Today few people would buy sack dresses. A store that tried to sell them would do poorly. This demonstrates the idea of consumer sovereignty: Firms must sell what consumers are willing to buy.
3. If a firm offers inferior products at higher prices than other firms charge in competition, they will sell few products, make little profit, and probably go out of business. This is the idea behind the invisible hand.
4. Providing information about the nutritive value of all food offered in a restaurant would be very costly. Servings would have to be measured for uniformity and nutritive values. This would have to be done by specialists and would cost a great deal of money. It would also prevent the business from offering new dishes. The price of the food would be forced up and the number of choices on the menu would be reduced.
5. The students' advertisements should be clearly informative and persuasive. Real ads are often mixed, but in this artificial situation you can require them to be all one or the other.

Consumer Skills Projects (text page 111)

1. You will probably find that most of your students feel the ban is justified. This may be the result of having grown up with various forms of public smoking restrictions. If the same survey were taken among their parents, there might be a different result. You would likely find stronger reactions to outlawing public smoking.
2. Your students will find that the prices are much the same in similar stores if no sale is being offered. Stores of different size and location will have different prices because they are offering something other than just the product. They may be closer to home, or open longer hours.

CHAPTER 5

Business and the Economy (text pages 114–139)

SECTION A. Forms of Business Organization (text pages 116–121)

Objectives (Lesson Focus)
Upon completion of this section, students will be able to:

- Identify and describe the basic characteristics of single proprietorships, partnerships, and corporations.
- Identify and explain the advantages of corporations which have allowed them to dominate production in the U.S. economy.

Preparation (Instruction: Pre-teaching—Vocabulary or Activity)

1. Discussion Introduce this section by reviewing the factors of production. Ask students how these factors can be brought together to create goods and services. Point out that owners must have money to finance new businesses. The form of business organization chosen depends at least in part on the amount of money that is needed.

A second important point is that all businesses involve an element of risk. New businesses usually have more risk than older, more established firms. People may be hesitant to invest in a firm unless there is a way to limit their exposure to risk.

A final consideration is the degree to which individuals want to be involved in the management of a firm. This may determine the type of organization they choose to invest in. Many people would like to benefit from the success of a business but have little interest or skill in running a firm. Others want to help make decisions and manage the firm. These people would probably choose to invest in different types of business organizations. Having discussed these points, identify and explain the advantages and disadvantages of the three basic forms of business organization which appear on Table 5–1 in the text.

2. The Personal Narrative The Personal Narrative for Section A (and for the following Narratives in this chapter as well) concern Rita and Joshua, a married couple, who open a restaurant. This Narrative demonstrates how they identify and solve the problems of organizing a new business. At first, they decide a partnership with Rita's father offers the best trade-off between costs and benefits for the type of business they want to run. Eventually they form a corporation to allow their business to grow.

The Narrative demonstrates the types of decisions that must be made when a new business is organized.

Teaching Suggestions (Modeling/Guided Practice)

1. Identify several types of businesses that can be found in your community. Ask students, either as individuals or in groups, to choose the type of business organization that is more appropriate for each firm and to explain why.
2. Use Discussion Topic 7 from the *Teacher's Resource Binder* which asks students how they would organize a business to market a wonderful food combination they've discovered.

Lesson Checkpoint

Text: Self-Check, text page 120
Answers

1. Unlimited liability: the owners' personal property can be taken to satisfy debts of the business. Limited liability: the individual owners cannot lose more than they have invested in the firm.
2. Partnerships can raise more money to establish the business; they can share certain kinds of expensive capital and services.
3. Corporations can raise money through the sale of stocks and bonds, have limited liability, and have unlimited life.

Follow-up Assignments (Independent Practice/Extension/Homework)

Text: Applying What You Have Learned, text page 121

One possible ending: Joshua and Rita began to look for additional locations, but the shareholders did not agree with them on their choices. Eventually a compromise was reached, settling on locations that Joshua and Rita did not really want. Two of the new locations failed, and profits for the entire company were very low.

Joshua and Rita could keep control of the corporation by retaining at least 51 percent of the shares, but this would bring in less money from the investors. Joshua and Rita would have to either supply more of the money themselves—increasing their risk if the venture should fail—or else restrict their expansion.

Section Evaluation

Self-Check, text page 120
Understanding Economics, question 1
(Chapter 5 Review, text pages 135–137)

SECTION B. The Costs of Production (text pages 122–124)

Objective (Lesson Focus)

Upon completion of this section, students will be able to:

- Identify, define, give examples of, and explain the difference between fixed and variable costs.

Preparation (Introduction: Pre-teaching—Vocabulary or Activity)

1. Discussion Introduce this section by giving each student a red card and a green card. Tell them that you are going to read a list of different costs of production for a firm that manufactures tennis shoes. If the cost will not change when more shoes are produced (fixed costs), they should hold up the red card. If the costs will change when more shoes are produced (variable costs), they should hold up the green card. You may want to count to three and have them all do it at once to avoid having students just copy one another. This exercise will encourage participation by all students. Explain the differences between the costs as you go along.

Costs of Production for a Tennis Shoe Manufacturer

wages for production line workers	(variable)
salary of the firm's president	(fixed)
rubber for the soles	(variable)
cost of electricity to run machines	(variable)
property taxes on the factory	(fixed)
canvas for tops	(variable)
television advertising	(fixed)
mortgage payment on the factory	(fixed)
shipping for finished shoes	(variable)
wages for security guard	(fixed)

2. The Personal Narrative The Personal Narrative for Section B continues the story of Rita and Joshua. The specific costs of production are identified in the Narrative. The fact that Rita and Joshua still have personal expenses to pay while they are starting their business is made.

The Narrative demonstrates the difference between fixed and variable costs.

Teaching Suggestions (Modeling/Guided Practice)

1. Use Discussion Topic 8 from the *Teacher's Resource Binder* to discuss the significance of fixed costs when sales decline.
2. Ask your students to identify the fixed and variable costs of running their households.
3. Most students either own, or would like to own, an automobile. Help your class list the costs of having a car and to identify each cost as a fixed or variable cost.

Lesson Checkpoint

Text: Self-Check, text page 124
Answers

1. Fixed costs must be paid regardless of how many products the firm manufactures. Variable costs change with the number of products made.
2. Fixed costs are most often underestimated.
3. Increasing the number of products sold is one way to reduce fixed costs.

Follow-up Assignments (Independent Practice/Extension/Homework)

Text: Applying What You Have Learned, text page 124
Answers

1. Kitchen equipment—once purchased would be a fixed cost
2. Dishes & utensils—once purchased would be a fixed cost
3. Rent for six months—would be a fixed cost
4. Insurance—would be a fixed cost
5. Paper products—would be a variable cost
6. Utilities—would be a variable cost (except for minimum monthly payment)
7. Furniture—would be a fixed cost
8. Wiring and plumbing—would be a fixed cost
9. License & fees—would be a fixed cost
10. Food and inventory—would be a variable cost
11. Cash register—would be a fixed cost
12. Advertising—once contracted would be a fixed cost

Section Evaluation

Self-Check, text page 124
Understanding Economics, question 2 (Chapter 5 Review, text pages 135–137)

SECTION C. Reducing Average Fixed Costs (text pages 125–128)

Objective (Lesson Focus)

Upon completion of this section, students will be able to:

- Define average fixed cost and explain the advantages that are often the result of diversification.

Preparation (Instruction: Pre-teaching—Vocabulary or Activity)

1. **Discussion** Introduce this section by asking students how they would react to school being open year round (if your district does this already, you could ask students how it has worked out). In some districts, schools run the entire year. Students are assigned to attend school in two of three yearly semesters. Some students have winters off, while others have most of the fall or spring.

Explain why this has been done. It reduces the district's fixed costs per student. Fifty percent more students can be educated in the same buildings when they are run all year. Businesses do the same when they run a night shift. Can your students think of any other advantages or disadvantages of the idea?

2. **The Personal Narrative** The Personal Narrative in Section C continues the story of Rita and Joshua. In this section they attempt to reduce average fixed costs by offering different items for sale. They also choose to stay open for longer hours. In this way they are able to distribute their fixed costs among more items and reduce the amount of fixed cost per item.

The Narrative demonstrates why many businesses have chosen to diversify into different markets.

Teaching Suggestions (Modeling/Guided Practice)

1. In Section B of this chapter, students were asked to identify the fixed and variable costs of running a household. A variation on this idea is to ask them to explain how much more it costs to have a large family than a small one. Which costs do not increase with the size of the family? How can a family reduce its average fixed cost per member?
2. Use Discussion Topic 8 from the *Teacher's Resource Binder* to show the significance of reducing average fixed costs.
3. Assign your students to survey local gro-

cery stores to find non-food-related products for sale. Combine the lists on the board in class. Discuss why grocery stores stock so many non-food items.

Lesson Checkpoint

Text: Self-Check, text page 128
Answers

1. Firms can make a larger profit if they reduce average fixed costs.
2. The average fixed cost would be two dollars.
3. Selling different types of merchandise is one way of reducing average fixed costs.

Follow-Up Assignments (Independent Practice/Extension/Homework)

Text: Applying What You Have Learned, text page 128
Answers

Rita and Joshua did a number of things to reduce their average fixed costs. These include:

- expanding their menu to sell more products
- selling snack foods to children on their way home from school
- staying open for longer hours so they could sell more items

Section Evaluation

Self-Check, text page 128
Understanding Economics, question 3
(Chapter 5 Review, text pages 135–137)

SECTION D. Rent, Interest, and How Businesses Obtain Money (text pages 129–133)

Objectives (Lesson Focus)

Upon completion of this section, students will be able to:

- Define the terms *rent, interest, profit, bond, stock, dividend,* and *capital gain.*
- Explain how each of these terms relates to the ability firms have to acquire factors of production.
- Explain how the forces of demand and supply set the price of stock on a stock exchange.

Preparation (Instruction: Pre-teaching—Vocabulary or Activity)

1. Discussion Introduce this section by listing the amounts of money necessary to start various franchise businesses. The following were advertised in the *Wall Street Journal* on 3/19/92.

Type of Franchise	*Minimum Investment*
tutoring service	$ 50,700
muffler business	$ 70,000
printing business	$ 95,000
seafood restaurant	$170,000
recycling business	$185,000
industrial equipment repair business	$300,000

Ask your students how they would go about raising the money necessary to go into these or other businesses.

2. The Personal Narrative The Personal Narrative in Section D continues the story of Rita and Joshua. In this section the couple decide to expand their business but experience difficulty in raising the necessary money. They do not have sufficient funds of their own, Rita's father is unwilling to lend them more, and they are turned down for a large enough loan by a bank. Eventually they agree to form a corporation and sell a controlling interest in their business to other people.

The Narrative demonstrates the financial limitations of single proprietorships and partnerships. It also shows the ability of the corporate form of business organization to gather money through the sale of stock and bonds.

Teaching Suggestions (Modeling/Guided Practice)

1. Tell your students to assume that they are loan officers for a local bank. Assign them to write two paragraphs.
   a. In the first paragraph they should choose a local business that they would be willing to lend $500,000. They should explain three different reasons that cause them to believe that the firm is worthy of the loan.
   b. In the second paragraph they should choose a different local business that they would not be willing to lend $500,000. They should explain three different reasons that cause them to believe the firm is not worthy of the loan.
2. Many businesses choose to rent equipment rather than buy it. Discuss the advantages and disadvantages of renting an expensive computer. These would include:

   Advantages

   a. lower monthly payments
   b. can't get "stuck" owning out-of-date equipment
   c. allows firm to use its money for other things

   Disadvantages

   a. don't own equipment at end of rental period.
   b. may not have the same tax advantages
   c. may cost more in the long run
3. Discuss the advantages and disadvantages of allowing a controlling interest of a privately held corporation, or a proprietorship or partnership to be bought by others. How much is it worth to be able to make business decisions for yourself? How much freedom does any business really have, considering the ideas of the invisible hand and consumer sovereignty?

Lesson Checkpoint

Text: Self-Check, text page 133
Answers

1. Rent and interest are both payments for the use of resources that are owned by someone else.
2. Larger, established businesses are considered to have a lower risk than smaller, newer businesses.
3. When the price of a type of stock goes up, this indicates a situation in which more people want to own the stock and fewer people want to sell it.

Follow-up Assignments (Independent Practice/Extension/Homework)

1. Text: Applying What You Have Learned, text page 133
   Answers

   Rita and Joshua considered borrowing money from a bank (or from Paul, Rita's father) or by forming a corporation and selling stock. They wanted more money so they could buy additional factors of production to expand their business. They were particularly interested in obtaining more capital (tools, equipment, etc.), and labor (workers for new restaurants).
2. Teacher's Resource Binder: Critical Thinking Activity, Chapter 5 (answers in Binder).

Section Evaluation

Self-Check, text page 133
Understanding Economics, questions 4–6 (Chapter 5 Review, text pages 135–137)

ADDITIONAL MATERIALS FOR CHAPTER 5

Chapter Evaluation

Teacher's Resource Binder: Chapter 5 Quiz

Reteaching and Extension

See the *Teacher's Resource Binder* and the *Student Activity Book* for additional handouts and activities for Chapter 5.

TEACHER'S BIBLIOGRAPHY FOR CHAPTER 5

Economics Sources

Armstrong, Fred C. *The Business of Economics.* St. Paul, Minn.: West, 1986.

Heilbroner, Robert L., and Galbraith, James K., II. *The Economic Problem.* Englewood Cliffs, N.J.: Prentice-Hall, Inc., 1987.

Love, John F. *McDonald's: Behind the Arches.* New York: Bantam, 1986.

Sobel, Robert, and Sicilia, David B. *The Entrepreneurs: an American Adventure.* Boston: Houghton Mifflin, 1986.

References for Additional Teaching Strategies

Economics and Entrepreneurship: Master Curriculum Guide. New York: Joint Council on Economic Education, 1991, Lesson 13.

How a Business Operates. Four film strips with cassettes, worksheets, and a study guide. Social Studies School Service, P. O. Box 802, Culver City, CA 90230-9983.

Young People's Introduction to the World of Wall Street. Albuquerque, N.M.: Institute for Economic and Financial Research, 1987.

Tower, Edward. *Economics Reading Lists, Course Outlines, Exams, Puzzles & Problems,* Volume 20. Durham, N.C.: Eno River Press, 1990.

Niss, James; Brenneke, Judith; and Clow, John. *Basic Business and Consumer Education.* New York: Joint Council on Economic Education, 1979. Lesson 6 for costs, prices, and profits; Lesson 7 on production costs; Lesson 8 on the role of advertising.

CHAPTER 5 REVIEW ANSWERS

Building Your Vocabulary (text page 136)

1. variable costs
2. stock
3. limited life
4. single proprietorship
5. corporation
6. partnership
7. dividend
8. limited liability
9. unlimited life
10. fixed costs
11. rent
12. capital gain
13. average fixed cost
14. interest
15. bond
16. prime rate
17. unlimited liability

Understanding Economics (text page 136)

1. a. Corporations offer limited liability. Owners of stock risk no more than the value of their investment in the stock.
   b. Corporations are better able to raise funds through the sale of stock and bonds.
   c. Corporations have unlimited life: if an

individual stock owner dies, the firm will continue to function.

2. Students could choose any number of different firms. Their lists should demonstrate a knowledge of the difference between fixed and variable costs.
3. The average cost of raising a child in a large family could be lower than the cost for raising only one child because the same items of furniture and clothing can be used more than just one time.
4. Corporations must pay interest on their bonds regardless of whether the firm earns a profit. Also, if the firm fails, bondholders have access to the assets of the firm before any of the stockholders.
5. A rich person might choose to buy stock instead of a bond because he or she is better able to afford a risk. If the firm does well, the value of its stock could increase and it could pay large dividends.
6. Very profitable firms are the best credit risks and therefore are best able to borrow money at the lower interest rate.

Thinking Critically About Economics
(text pages 136–137)

1. *Firm A* should be a partnership because the lawyers would benefit from sharing the costs of a law library, computer, secretary, and assistants. It would be difficult to sell stock in such a firm. *Firm B* should be a corporation because it will require large investments that could only be made by many owners. *Firm C* should be a single proprietorship because it will not require large investments and the owner will take responsibility for its operation.
2. If John sells camping equipment as well, he would be able to distribute the cost of his rent to more products. This would lower his average fixed cost per item and increase his profit per item sold.
3. I sell 10 bicycles a day for $110 each so I have a total revenue of $1,100 a day. My costs are now $50 in fixed costs and $80 in variable costs for each of the 10 bicycles. This totals $850. I am making $250 a day in profit now.

   If I lowered my price to $100, I would sell 20 bicycles a day to take in $2,000 in total revenue. My costs would be the $50 in fixed costs plus $80 multiplied by 20 bicycles in variable costs for a total of $1,650. I would then earn a profit of $350. Therefore, I should lower my price.
4. a. Sharon could try to borrow the money she needs from a bank. Banks, however, may be unwilling to make large loans to such a small firm.

   b. Sharon could try to find private investors who would either loan her the money or become partners. This would be relatively difficult to accomplish and could dilute her control.

   c. Sharon could form a corporation and sell stock. This would be a relatively difficult process and one for which she might need legal help. It could also require her to give up control of the firm if she sold more than fifty percent of the stock to other people.
5. If the firm Barbara has invested in continues to grow rapidly, it may earn large profits in the future. This should increase the number of people who want to own its stock. The price of the stock would then go up and Barbara could sell her stock for a capital gain.

Consumer Skills Projects (text page 137)

1. Student charts will vary but should show how characteristics of the three forms of business organization can affect consumers they serve.
2. Student answers will vary but should

demonstrate their understanding of the costs of running a business. They should also realize that cutting costs and prices may not be good for consumers if the result is lower quality goods or services.

3. Student answers will vary but should show that the value of a corporation's stock is likely to be directly related to its profitability and therefore to how well it serves its customers.

CHAPTER 6

Perfect and Imperfect Competition (text pages 140–171)

SECTION A. Perfect Competition (text pages 143–146)

Objectives (Lesson Focus)

Upon completion of this section, students will be able to:

- Recognize and explain the characteristics of perfect competition.
- Explain how the market acts as a regulator of the economy through its competitive forces.
- Explain possible advantages offered by diversification in a competitive market.
- Identify possible dangers of having too much competition.

Preparation (Instruction: Pre-teaching—Vocabulary or Activity)

1. Discussion Introduce this section by asking your students what it is like to try to get a date with the most popular boy/girl in school. In effect they would be in competition with many other students who have the same idea. They would have to be nicer, more attractive, or have a better car to succeed. If they said something wrong, they might never get another chance.

Explain that running a business in a competitive market is much the same. Like popular students, customers have their choice. They may patronize many different firms who all want their business. Firms must offer the best service, quality products, and lower prices. Even if a customer buys from a store once, there is no guarantee that he/she will buy there again in the future. Running a business in a competitive market is not easy.

2. The Personal Narrative The Personal Narrative in Section A describes a business in a market that is close to perfect competition. The subject of the Narrative owns a filling station and convenience store on a busy highway near many other stores that sell similar products. His customers shop largely according to prices, which he must therefore keep low. He has diversified into other types of products and cut his costs in an attempt to improve his profits.

The Narrative demonstrates the difficulty of running a firm in a competitive market and the benefits of competition for the consumer.

Teaching Suggestions (Modeling/Guided Practice)

1. Ask your students to identify a type of business that they think they could actually start and own by themselves. List several of these on the board. You should find that most of them are in markets that are quite competitive. Point this out to your students. Firms that individuals can start tend to be quite small and require limited financial resources. Therefore, many people who want to go into business will go into these types of businesses. This causes strong competition, forcing firms to charge low prices and earn small profits. Most business failures

occur among small businesses in competitive markets.

2. Use Discussion Topic 9 from the *Teacher's Resource Binder* to show some of the effects of high profits in a competitive economy.
3. Most fast-food restaurants are very competitive. Assign your students to survey prices at different local hamburger or pizza restaurants. They should find that the prices are almost the same. Discuss their findings in class. Can they explain any differences in price in terms of quality, location, or advertising?

Lesson Checkpoint

Text: Self-Check, text page 146
Answers

1. Customers look for the firms that offer the lowest prices.
2. Diversification can add products for which there is less competition and can also reduce average fixed costs.
3. Too much competition can reduce firms' abilities to accumulate enough wealth to invest in research and new technology and may also reduce firms' abilities to survive a downturn in the economy.

Follow-up Assignments (Independent Practice/Extension/Homework)

Text: Applying What You Have Learned, text page 146
Answers

a. If it costs little to start a particular type of business, there can be many of them which will increase competition.
b. If it takes limited skill and training to run a business, then many people would be able to operate such firms which will increase competition.
c. If it requires few employees to run a business, then it would require less money to operate such businesses, thus allowing more firms to be in competition.
d. If it is easy to buy necessary resources for a business, then many people would be able to run such businesses which would increase competition.

Section Evaluation

Self-Check, text page 146
Understanding Economics, questions 1 and 2 (Chapter 6 Review, text pages 168–170)

SECTION B. Monopolies (text pages 147–151)

Objectives (Lesson Focus)

Upon completion of this section, students will be able to:

- Identify and explain the basic characteristics of perfect monopoly, monopolistic competition, oligopoly, and natural monopoly.
- Recognize and explain the relationship between monopoly-like powers and the four-firm concentration ratio.

Preparation (Instruction: Pre-teaching—Vocabulary or Activity)

1. Discussion Introduce this section by telling your students the following story:

> Once upon a time in a faraway land, a starving artist named Raphael lived in great poverty. Although he was very poor, he was happy because he liked to

paint. He was sure he would succeed if he kept trying.

One day he met a beautiful young princess who fell in love with him because he was pure and honest. The people of the kingdom loved the princess, and because she loved Raphael they bought his paintings, although they were really quite awful. Raphael, however, misunderstood the situation. He thought he had been "discovered" at last. He believed that it was he who the people loved. He raised his prices and spent the money on himself. He acted like he was the king. Soon the princess realized that Raphael had become conceited and greedy so she went away. No one wanted to buy his paintings anymore. Raphael could not pay his bills and died in a debtors' prison.

Help your students understand how the story of Raphael relates to the characteristics of a monopoly. When the princess loved Raphael, he had a monopoly because no one else could paint pictures and be loved by the princess too. He was able to raise prices and make large profits. However, there was a limit to how much he could charge. When he showed himself to be greedy, the princess—and then his customers—decided to do without him and his paintings.

Firms with monopoly-like power can set their own prices and often earn large profits. But if they charge too much, they invite either competition or the substitution of other products by their customers. There are limits to a monopoly's power.

2. The Personal Narrative The Personal Narrative in Section B describes a business in a market that is almost a pure monopoly. The subject of the Narrative owns the only filling station within 20 miles of a small town in Nebraska. His customers have no realistic alternative to buying his products. As a result, he is able to charge a higher price than more competitive firms in other locations. On the other hand, he is afraid of encouraging competition and does not exploit his market power excessively. He is careful to provide quality service and to keep up with new innovations.

The Narrative demonstrates the advantages of running a firm that has monopoly-like power. It also shows that there are limits on monopoly powers and that customers can benefit from these powers in some ways.

Teaching Suggestions (Modeling/Guided Practice)

1. Many people believe that the telephone company has or had a pure monopoly. This is not quite true. The telephone is only one of many ways to communicate over a distance. Ask your students to help you make a list of other ways to communicate. Alternatives include telegrams, the mail, carrier pigeons, driving there, ham radio, computers, etc. Although the telephone company did not have a pure monopoly, it could have set very high prices if the government had allowed this. Ask your students why this is so. Are any of the alternatives to the telephone as quick and easy? Do the alternatives to the telephone represent meaningful competition? Why are government regulations of telephone rates necessary?
2. Most school cafeterias have a form of monopoly. Students usually must either buy food in the cafeteria or bring their lunch from home. Ask your students to take a survey among themselves and their friends:

   How many eat cafeteria food for their lunch?
   How many would eat their lunch elsewhere if they had a choice?

How much do they feel the cafeteria food is really worth?
What do they believe the cafeteria would do if it had any real competition?

Discuss the results of the survey in class. You should point out that most school cafeterias are supported in part from taxes and therefore charge less than private restaurants can afford to charge.

3. Assign your students to cut out advertisements from newspapers that try to convince them to buy a product *without mentioning price*. Discuss the ads in class and classify them as having been placed by firms that are in competition, monopolistic competition, oligopoly, or natural monopoly. It is likely that the majority will be from firms in monopolistic competition. Explain this is because these firms are trying to make a distinction in the minds of the consumer between their products and similar products.

Lesson Checkpoint

Text: Self-Check, text page 151
Answers

1. The factors include the possibility that high prices will cause low sales and an increased fixed cost per item; high prices may also encourage competition or the substitution of other products by the consumer.
2. An imperfect market exists when businesses are large enough to have some, but not complete, control over the prices they can charge customers.
3. Three types of imperfect markets are monopolistic competition, oligopoly, and natural monopoly.

Follow-up Assignments (Independent Practice/Extension/Homework)

Text: Applying What You Have Learned, text page 151
Answers

a. Property values and services provided by the government in rural areas are smaller. Therefore, property taxes tend to be lower.
b. Insurance would be less costly because there is usually less crime in rural areas.
c. It may be easier to find people who are willing to work for lower wages in a rural area because the cost of living is also likely to be lower.
d. The original building will be less costly in a rural area because of lower wage rates for construction and lower property values for the land on which it is located.

Section Evaluation

Self-Check, text page 151
Understanding Economics, questions 3, 4 and 5 (Chapter 6 Review, text pages 168–170)

SECTION C. Combinations and Big Business (text pages 153–157)

Objectives (Lesson Focus)

Upon completion of this section, students will be able to:

- Explain the difference between horizontal and vertical combinations.
- Explain the respective advantages offered by horizontal and vertical combinations.
- Describe how large firms are able to either help or harm their customers' interests.

Preparation (Instruction: Pre-teaching—Vocabulary or Activity)

1. Discussion Introduce this section by asking your students to list all the reasons they might choose to shop at one store instead of another. Possible reasons would include price, selection, quality, friendly service, availability of repairs, and reputation.

Then help your students identify specific stores that compete in the area of their school. Be sure that some are locally owned, and others are parts of large chains.

Are some of the reasons identified by your students more often associated with large chain stores, while others are associated with local firms? What effect do your students believe competition between the large and small firms has on the owners of the small firms?

2. The Personal Narrative The Personal Narrative in Section C describes how the owner of a small independent store is affected by competition with a much larger chain store. The subject of the Narrative owns a hardware store and prides himself on providing quality products and service. However, he is unable to match the low prices of a new discount store.

The Narrative shows students the problems that can result for the owners of small firms when they compete with larger firms. It emphasizes the fact that low prices are not the only benefits firms can offer their customers.

Teaching Suggestions (Modeling/Guided Practice)

1. Explain that many small stores have joined associations which are able to provide advantages similar to those of larger firms. These associations can advertise more efficiently, distribute goods quickly, and buy products in quantity to cut costs. One example of this is the Independent Grocer's Association, which is made up of many small grocery stores. What other businesses can your students identify that have done the same? Others include independent drug stores, hardware stores, and auto parts stores. These organizations offer advantages that are similar to those of a horizontal combination.
2. Some of your students may have part-time jobs in large chain stores. Ask them to explain what they do if a customer brings back a product that does not work. Do they feel that they are qualified to explain many of the products they sell? Ask them about the rate with which employees come and go at their store. Is the store able to keep good people? What do the answers to these questions mean to the quality of customer service and satisfaction at a large chain store? If other students work in a small local store, ask them the same questions and see how their answers compare with the answers of the students who work in chain stores.
3. Emphasize the fact that big is not necessarily bad. Large firms may be much more efficient than similar smaller firms. This efficiency may result in lower prices and high quality. If large firms offered no advantages, people would realize it and stop buying from them. The fact that many people continue to buy from large businesses supports the idea that they are making an important contribution to our economic success.
4. Assign your students to survey the prices of several products at local hardware stores and at large chain discount stores. Have them report their findings to the class. How significant is the difference in prices? Help your students find the average percentage difference. Would your students choose to shop at the small local store or at the discount store?

Lesson Checkpoint

Text: Self-Check, text page 157
Answers

1. When one type of business grows, there is a good chance that some other type of business will shrink or fail.
2. A horizontal combination is a joining of firms that do the same thing.
3. Vertical combinations are often able to sell their products for less because they can control most of their costs of production.

Follow-up Assignments (Independent Practice/Extension/Homework)

Text: Applying What You Have Learned, text page 157
Answers

1. Possible answers include:
   a. There could be no one to repair many products.
   b. There could be less competition so the other store could increase price.
   c. There could be a further decline in the quality offered by the discount store.
   d. There could be less choice in the type of products people could buy.
   e. There could be a reduction in the number of good jobs offered in the community.
2. The advertisements should include reference to things like:
   a. quality service
   b. convenient hours
   c. quick repairs
   d. wide choice in products

Section Evaluation

Self-Check, text page 157
Understanding Economics, question 6
(Chapter 6 Review, text pages 168–170)

SECTION D. Advantages and Disadvantages of Big Business (text pages 158–161)

Objectives (Lesson Focus)

Upon completion of this section, students will be able to:

- Identify and explain several examples of economies of scale.
- Identify and explain several examples of diseconomies of scale.

Preparation (Instruction: Pre-teaching—Vocabulary or Activity)

1. Discussion Introduce this section by showing students a copy of a mail-order catalog from a large retailer like Sears or Penney's. Ask them why they would or would not like to shop from such a catalog. Point out that people who lived in rural areas 50 to 70 years ago often did most of their shopping from mail-order catalogs because there were few stores near their homes. Local stores they could go to stocked few items and often had higher prices. Help your students list reasons that allowed the mail-order firms to offer more selection and lower prices than local firms. Ask your students what dangers there may have been in shopping from mail-order catalogs.

Most of the differences your students identify will be related to the size of each firm's market. A large firm can stock more items and sell at lower prices because it sells many more products. It can also afford to try new ideas that smaller firms could not risk. On the other hand, the local firm can provide more personal service. If a product is defective, it does not have to be returned through the mail.

Point out that many of these same characteristics are associated with large and small firms today. Economists call them economies and diseconomies of scale.

2. The Personal Narrative The Personal Narrative in Section D describes how an individual customer is affected by competition between a small independent store and a much larger chain store. The subject of the Narrative used to shop at a small local hardware store where he received personal service but felt prices were high. He now frequents a large chain discount store where he pays lower prices but receives less personal service.

The Narrative shows students the trade-offs customers make when they choose to shop at different stores. It emphasizes the fact that low prices are only one of many things firms can offer their customers.

Teaching Suggestions (Modeling/Guided Practice)

1. Organize a debate in your class. Select one group of students who will represent a large drug chain that wants to open a new store in your neighborhood. A second group will represent the owners of a small, locally owned drugstore. The question to be debated is whether or not the city council should rezone a vacant lot from residential to commercial so the chain store will have a place to build. Students should center their arguments on what the store has to offer their community, and what it will cost the community and the owners of the local store. What are the advantages and disadvantages of the large store to the community?
2. Point out that many new innovations are very expensive. One example is diagnostic electronic devices that are used to find and analyze problems in cars. These machines cost many thousands of dollars and take special training to be used properly. Today's cars have become so complicated that many problems cannot be repaired without such machines. Although large service centers have diagnostic devices, many small private garages cannot afford to buy them or to train people to use them. Discuss why expensive innovations may lead to small firms either being put out of business, or forced to grow, or to merge with other firms.
3. Assign your students to ask their parents and other adults how they have been affected by the breakup of the phone company. Also have them ask how many long-distance calls each person makes. Combine the results of the surveys on the chalkboard and try to draw conclusions concerning how people feel about the dissolution of the phone company. Can your students find a difference between the opinions of business owners and of people who only have home phones? People who make many long distance calls should have benefited from lower long distance rates.

Lesson Checkpoint

Text: Self-Check, text page 161
Answers

1. The importance of economies of scale is evidenced by so many firms growing larger.
2. Rockefeller said that Standard Oil's profits were the result of efficiency.
3. The courts divided Standard Oil into several smaller companies in 1914.

Follow-up Assignments (Independent Practice/Extension/Homework)

1. Text: Applying What You Have Learned, text page 161
   Answers

   Possible answers include:

   a. lack of choice or lower quality
   b. no service department to repair products
   c. no knowledgeable salespeople
   d. impersonal service

2. Teacher's Resource Binder: Critical Thinking Activity, Chapter 6 (answers in Binder).

Section Evaluation

Self-Check, text page 161
Understanding Economics, question 7 (Chapter 6 Review, text pages 168–170)

SECTION E. The Government's Role in Competition (text pages 162–166)

Objectives (Lesson Focus)

Upon completion of this section, students will be able to:

- Define and explain the significance of workable competition.
- Describe how government antitrust policy tries to achieve workable competition.

Preparation (Instruction: Pre-teaching—Vocabulary or Activity)

1. Discussion Introduce this section by asking students if they would rather attend a large or small college or vocational school after they graduate from high school. There are some state-sponsored schools with as many as 50,000 students. Some private schools have 250 or fewer students. What advantages and disadvantages are associated with the size of a school?

Large schools may offer more specialized classes and equipment. Small schools may provide more individualized instruction. One responsibility of state education authorities is to see that their colleges do not become too large to provide quality education.

Explain that many of the advantages and disadvantages of size in schools are also applicable to businesses. It is the responsibility of the government's antitrust division to protect the interests of the people by balancing the advantages of bigness with the dangers of monopoly power. Any time a decision is made, there is a trade-off between the costs and benefits of size.

2. The Personal Narrative The Personal Narrative in Section E describes the effect of government-approved dissolutions and mergers on consumers. The subject of the Narrative has received a seven-page phone bill that he does not understand. The point is made that the break-up of the phone company was accomplished with government oversight. Similar events in the airline industry and in military contracting are mentioned.

The Narrative shows students that there is a trade-off when the government allows dissolutions or mergers. In many cases some people gain while others lose. Making the best choice for all is a difficult task.

Teaching Suggestions (Modeling/Guided Practice)

1. In 1986 and 1987 there was a rapid increase in the number of near misses between aircraft. The rate increased by almost 30 percent in the first six months of 1987 alone. Some people said deregulation of the airline industry led to this problem. Discuss this issue in the context of what has happened since 1987. Was

deregulation a good idea? Has it led to too many flights and lax controls? What have the costs and benefits been in terms of passenger safety?

2. Tell your students the following story. This story is not far from that of the Lockheed Corporation in the early 1970s. In that case the government did guarantee a billion-dollar bank loan that saved the firm from bankruptcy.

   There is a very large firm that is in danger of going bankrupt. The firm's problems are largely the result of poor planning and management. It has also been suggested that some of the firm's workers have been paid too much and have been lazy.

   The firm employs over 60,000 workers. It has an annual payroll of almost $2 billion. The firm's employees pay over $700 million in taxes to federal, state, and local governments each year. If the firm closed, these taxes would not be paid and former workers would receive many millions of dollars in benefits from the government.

   The firm is a major supplier of government military equipment. If it failed, important military projects would be slowed down. Failure would also reduce competition within the military equipment industry.

   The firm has asked the government to help it get a $1 billion bank loan. The owners of many small firms have protested, claiming that if they had been poor managers the government would not have helped them.

   Should the government help the firm get the loan? What do your students believe should be done?

Lesson Checkpoint

Text: Self-Check, text page 166
Answers

1. Such a balance is called workable competition.
2. A firm that is found guilty of violating antitrust laws can be fined or broken up into smaller companies.
3. AT&T was accused of monopolizing telephone service.

Follow-up Assignments (Independent Practice/Extension/Homework)

Text: Applying What You Have Learned, text page 166
Answers

The answer to this question will be related to the values of each individual student. Their answers should reflect a reasonable level of thought and logic. There is a trade-off between more government control and individual freedom to run a business. The students' explanations should show an awareness of these trade-offs.

Section Evaluation

Self-Check, text page 166

ADDITIONAL MATERIALS FOR CHAPTER 6

Chapter Evaluation

Teacher's Resource Binder: Chapter Quiz

Reteaching and Extension

See the *Teacher's Resource Binder* and the *Student Activity Book* for additional handouts and activities for Chapter 6.

TEACHER'S BIBLIOGRAPHY FOR CHAPTER 6

Economics Sources

Carson, Robert B. *Economic Issues: Alternative Approaches*, 5th ed. New York: St. Martin's Press, 1990.

Edgmand, Michael R. et al. *Economics and Contemporary Issues.* Hinsdale, Ill.: Dryden Press, 1991.

Miller, Roger LeRoy. *Economics Today*, 7th ed. New York: HarperCollins, 1991, Chapters 23-26.

Samuelson, Paul A. and Nordhaus, William D. *Economics,* 14th ed. New York: McGraw-Hill, 1992, Chapters 9-11.

References for Additional Teaching Strategies

Mansfield, Edwin, and Behravesh, Nariman. *Telecourse Study Guide for Economics USA,* New York: Norton, 1992, Chapters 18-20. Text provides exercises for and is keyed to *Economics USA,* a television course developed by Southern California Consortium.

Morton, John et al. *High School Economics Courses.* New York: Joint Council on Economic Education, 1985, Lesson 12, "When There Isn't Pure Competition."

Tower, Edward. *Economics Reading Lists, Course Outlines, Exams, Puzzles & Problems.* Vol. 20, Durham, N.C.: Eno River Press, 1990.

CHAPTER 6 REVIEW ANSWERS

Building Your Vocabulary (text page 169)

1. regulatory agency
2. vertical combination
3. perfect competition
4. workable competition
5. oligopoly
6. antitrust policy
7. economies of scale
8. monopolistic competition
9. diversification
10. horizontal combination
11. perfect monopoly
12. diseconomy of scale
13. natural monopoly
14. imperfect competition

Understanding Economics (text pages 169–170)

1. Small stores often earn small profits because they often have low sales. This means that their fixed costs per item are rather high. To be competitive with larger firms they can be forced to accept a smaller profit margin.

2. Many stores, small stores included, have diversified into selling other types of products. By selling more items, they can reduce their average fixed cost per item sold and improve profits.

3. If a store made very high profits, it would encourage other people to open up similar stores in the area. This would result in competition, which would eventually force prices and profits down.

4. Possible answers include:

a. *Soap.* Advertisers try to convince consumers that there will be more meaning in their lives if they use their particular brand of soap.

b. *Hair color.* Advertisers try to convince consumers that by coloring their hair with the firm's product they will look younger or more beautiful.

c. *Pain relievers.* Advertisers try to convince consumers that doctors would really choose the advertised brand of aspirin over some other product if they were lost in the woods.

5. The cost of building a utility can run into the billions of dollars. It would make no sense to spend this amount of money twice to service the same area. No amount of competition could justify such spending.
6. To make a hamburger chain a vertical combination, it would be necessary to join a beef farmer, wheat farmer, potato farmer, baker, dairy, pickle producer, paper product manufacturer, and many other firms that supply hamburger stands.
7. The following are possible answers:

   a. GM could buy natural resources at lower costs.
   b. GM could advertise and distribute more efficiently.
   c. GM could borrow at lower interest rates.

Thinking Critically About Economics (text page 170)

1. The following are possible answers:

   a. I could hire a famous person to visit my store and wear my clothes.
   b. I could advertise on TV or on radio.
   c. I could expand my product line to include jewelry and accessories.

2. These three firms illustrate an oligopoly, in that they all operate in the same market and sell the same basic product. Their costs of production are about the same and many of their employees have worked for more than one of the firms. It is not surprising to find them all performing more or less the same functions.
3. Breaking up electric companies into smaller firms would be inefficient because:

   a. the new firms would have to invest in similar equipment.
   b. much of the equipment would be underutilized.
   c. the new firms would have to hire many new workers to service the new equipment.

4. Possible answers showing the advantage of the larger farms include:

   a. The merged farms have the ability to borrow money at lower cost.
   b. The merged farms can afford to buy new, more expensive equipment.
   c. The merged farms should be able to distribute product more efficiently.

Consumer Skills Projects (text page 170)

1. Student lists should show that most stores now sell many different types of products that are not related to their original markets. This may benefit consumers by reducing the number of stores they visit when they shop.
2. Students will probably find that many air fares are lower than they were in the past. The lower fares may be the result of greater competition that resulted from deregulation.

CHAPTER 7

Labor and the Economy: "I Built a Railroad,. . ."(text pages 172–211)

SECTION A. How Wages are Set (text pages 175–181)

Objectives (Lesson Focus)

Upon completion of this section, students will be able to:

- Place the labor market as part of the factor market in the circular flow model.
- Explain why the demand for labor, or other factors of production, is a derived demand.
- Identify examples of diminishing marginal productivity.
- Recognize a definition of the labor force participation rate, and explain the relationship between changes in wage rates and the willingness of people to look for work.
- Recognize how the forces of demand and supply for labor result in an equilibrium wage rate.
- Explain the difference between nominal wages and real wages that have been adjusted for inflation.

Preparation (Instruction: Pre-teaching—Vocabulary or Activity)

1. Discussion Introduce this section by using Discussion Topic 10 from the *Teacher's Resource Binder* to draw a supply curve for labor based on responses from your students.

2. The Personal Narrative The Personal Narrative in Section A describes an individual worker who is affected by a decline in his employer's sales. The subject of the Narrative has been laid off due to greater competition in the product market. His employer has suggested that he could have his job back if he and other union members are willing to accept reduced wages. He is faced with the prospect of being forced to take a job that pays less than his old job.

The Narrative demonstrates the relationship between a firm's ability to sell its product and the number of workers it will choose to hire. It shows how workers and employers are affected by diminishing marginal productivity.

Teaching Suggestions (Modeling/Guided Practice)

1. Ask your students to read the *help wanted* advertisements from a local newspaper. Tell them to find five different jobs that are frequently advertised. List the jobs they identify on the chalkboard. Can any generalizations be made about the level of skill and training necessary for the jobs listed? Are low- or high-skill workers more in demand?
2. Use Discussion Topic 11 from the *Teacher's Resource Binder* to reinforce the principle of diminishing marginal productivity.
3. Discuss the following with your students: There is a limited number of people who know how to shoe horses. Ask your students what would happen to the demand for the labor of blacksmiths, and their resultant earnings, if horseback riding became very popular. Discuss how these events would fit into the circular flow model. If the earnings of blacksmiths increased rapidly, what should happen to the number of people who choose to learn this skill? What should happen to the higher earnings of blacksmiths over time?

Lesson Checkpoint

Text: Self-Check, text page 181
Answers

1. Natural resources, labor, capital, and entrepreneurship are sold in the factor market.
2. Diminishing marginal productivity refers to the point where adding more workers results in fewer additional products being produced.

3. At a higher product price, a firm will be willing to hire more workers at the same wage rate.
4. As wage rates increase, more people should want to work.

Follow-up Assignments (Independent Practice/Extension/Homework)

Text: Applying What You Have Learned, text page 181
Answers

a. At a wage rate of $250, 600 workers would want jobs.
b. At a wage rate of $250, 300 jobs would be available.
c. At a wage rate of $250, there would be a surplus of workers.
d. At a wage rate of $250, there would be a surplus of 300 workers.
e. The equilibrium wage rate in this example is $200.

Section Evaluation

Self-Check, text page 181
Understanding Economics, questions 1 and 2 (Chapter 7 Review, text pages 198–201)

SECTION B. Labor Unions in the Economy (text pages 182–187)

Objectives (Lesson Focus)

Upon completion of this section, students will be able to:

- Describe what a labor union is and explain how it attempts to serve its members through collective action.
- Recognize, define, and explain the differences between industrial and craft unions.
- Describe the significance of labor laws, including: The Sherman Antitrust Act of 1890, The Clayton Act of 1914, The National Labor Relations Act of 1935, and The Taft-Hartley Act of 1947.

Preparation (Instruction: Pre-teaching—Vocabulary or Activity)

1. Discussion Introduce this section by dividing your class into two groups, one representing the workers at a firm that makes bowling balls, the other representing the owners. Then give the students copies of the story in Discussion Topic 12 from the *Teacher's Resource Binder.*

The group of students representing workers should develop a set of arguments to convince workers to form a union. The group representing the owners should develop a set of reasons why workers should not form a union. The arguments should then be presented to the class as a whole.

2. The Personal Narrative The Personal Narrative in Section B describes the problems that individual workers could have that might lead them to form unions. The subject of the Narrative works in a cannery to support her family. She feel that her earnings are too low and that her work is dull and dangerous. She has mixed feelings about the possibility of forming a union. On one side, she feels exploited by her employer. On the other, she is afraid a union could cost her the job she needs to support her family.

The Narrative describes the trade-off between costs and benefits that workers consider when they decide whether to organize a union.

Teaching Suggestions (Modeling/Guided Practice)

Choose two local firms. One should be a large successful firm that employs skilled workers. A pharmaceutical or computer services firm could be a good example. The other firm should be a grocery store or a fast-food restaurant that does not employ highly skilled workers or have a large profit margin. Discuss why workers at the firm firm would probably be more successful in negotiating raises and improved working conditions than those at the second firm. Point out that the workers at the first firm would be more difficult to replace and that the demand for the firm's product is probably relatively inelastic (if the firm raises its price, its sales will not go down much).

Lesson Checkpoint

Text: Self-Check, text page 187
Answers

1. The two basic types of labor unions are craft unions and industrial unions.
2. In accordance with the NLRB, management must negotiate with any union that has organized more than half of the firm's workers.
3. Union membership has fallen since 1960.

Follow-up Assignments (Independent Practice/Extension/Homework)

Text: Applying What You Have Learned, text page 187
Answers

1. A union might be able to prevent
   a. people being fired the first time they fall asleep.
   b. the firm from hiring new workers.
   c. unsafe working conditions.
   d. low wages.
   e. inadequate benefits for workers who are hurt on the job.
2. The following are possible answers:
   Management might believe that
   a. people should be fired if they fall asleep and cause waste or damage to equipment.
   b. they should be able to hire other workers who are willing to work for relatively low wages.
   c. working conditions are safe if workers take reasonable care in their jobs.
   d. the wages are as much as the firm can afford to pay.
   e. more insurance could only be afforded if workers would accept lower pay.

Section Evaluation

Self-Check, text page 187
Understanding Economics, questions 3 and 4 (Chapter 7 Review, text pages 198–201)

SECTION C. Labor-Management Relations (text pages 188–192)

Objectives (Lesson Focus)

Upon completion of this section, students will be able to:

- Define and explain possible steps the government can take to help resolve labor disputes, including mediation, fact-finding, voluntary arbitration, and compulsory arbitration.
- Define terms, including union shop, agency shop, slowdown, boycott, secondary boycott, sit-down strike, strike, picket line, union label, political action committee, lockout, strikebreaker, and relocation.

Preparation (Instruction: Pre-teaching—Vocabulary or Activity)

1. Discussion Introduce this section by asking your students to rank each of the following considerations according to their importance. Which ones do your students feel they would be most likely to go on strike for if they were ten years older and had a family to support? (You may want to be more specific about the demands. Suggestions are made in parentheses.)

1. Higher pay ______ (a 10 percent raise)
2. Greater job security ______ (a no layoff guarantee)
3. Better health care ______ (full coverage of all medical bills)
4. Safer working conditions ______ (removal of toxic chemicals from the workplace)
5. Better retirement benefits ______ (full retirement after 30 years regardless of age)

After discussing these demands from a worker's point of view, consider them once more from the owner's point of view. Which ones would the owner be most likely to agree to? Which would be resisted the most?

Discuss how this exercise shows that union-management negotiations may be an adversarial rather than a cooperative process.

2. The Personal Narrative The Personal Narrative for Section C describes the 1984–1990 BASF lockout from the point of view of one worker and his family. The subject of the Narrative is a young man whose father was locked out by BASF. The Narrative explains factors which support the workers' position and the company's point of view.

The Narrative demonstrates the conflict between the needs of a firm's workers and its desire to remain competitive and earn a profit. It shows that compromise may be an alternative to confrontation.

Teaching Suggestions (Modeling/Guided Practice)

1. Tell your students to imagine they are the chairpersons of the board of a large corporation (you may want to identify a specific firm for your class). They have just agreed to give their workers a 10 percent wage increase. In the long run they feel the increase is in the best interest of the firm and its stockholders. There will be no strike to interfere with business this year. The firm's sales have been good and profits have been high so they can afford to pay the increase. They also believe about 20 percent of the workers can be eliminated over the next few years through the purchase of new equipment. However, the firm's profits will be smaller next year because of the agreement.

   Each student should write a letter to the stockholders in which they explain the firm's reasoning behind the settlement. Read several of the better letters in class and discuss their reasoning. (You can do the same exercise with the firm refusing to give the workers a 10 percent increase, thus precipitating a strike.)
2. Discuss why politicians do not like major strikes. Strikes are bad for the country's economy and for people who hold elective offices. Voters may feel their leaders are responsible for problems that result from strikes. Inflation, shortages, layoffs of nonstriking workers, picket-line violence, plant closings, loss of tax revenue, extra government spending for social programs, and loss of foreign markets can all result from major strikes. Students should be aware of the implications of labor unrest for government leaders.

Lesson Checkpoint

Text: Self-Check, text page 192
Answers

1. Right-to-work laws say that workers cannot be required to join or pay a fee to a union if they don't want to.
2. Unions and management negoti-

ate through the process of collective bargaining.

3. Workers lose wages, management loses profits, government loses tax revenues, and consumers lose the use and benefits of products.

Follow-up Assignments (Independent Practice/Extension/Homework)

1. Text: Applying What You Have Learned, text page 192
Answers

Student evaluations of these two arguments depend on their individual values. Their answers should be graded according to how well they are supported with logic and reason.

Possible arguments from the union's point of view:

a. They helped the firms through hard times; now their help should be rewarded.
b. Many firms have returned to profitability and can afford to pay higher wages.

Possible arguments from the management's point of view:

a. Current profits should be invested in new equipment, not in higher wages.
b. The return to profits will disappear if wages go back up.

2. Teacher's Resource Binder: Critical Thinking Activity, Chapter 7 (answers in Binder).

Section Evaluation

Self-Check, text page 192
Understanding Economics, question 5 (Chapter 7 Review, text pages 198–201)

SECTION D. Minimum Wages and Employment (text pages 193–196)

Objectives (Lesson Focus)

Upon completion of this section, students will be able to:

- Discuss the purposes and possible effects of minimum wage laws.
- Define the term *marginal worker*.

Preparation (Instruction: Pre-teaching—Vocabulary or Activity)

1. Discussion Introduce this section by asking students to help make a list of benefits they might receive from a first job. This list could include wages, experience, training, good references, or a chance to work their way into a better job. Ask your students to explain which of these benefits is most important to a young person in the long run. Would they be willing to accept a job that paid poorly if it gave them training in a field they are interested in? Why or why not?

2. The Personal Narrative The Personal Narrative in Section D describes the effects of changes in the minimum wage on workers who hold low paying jobs. The subject of the Narrative is a woman who believes an increase in the minimum wage would not increase her earnings but instead would only bring other workers up to the wage rate she worked years to achieve. She resents workers who receive higher wages and better benefits because they belong to unions. She wishes the minimum wage was high enough to make a substantial difference in her own compensation.

The Narrative demonstrates the problems experienced by workers who hold low-, or minimum-wage jobs. It shows how difficult it would be to support a family on such wages.

Teaching Suggestions (Modeling/Guided Practice)

1. Choose a local business that pays the minimum wage to most of its workers. Ask your students to write a brief essay or discuss in class what they believe the firm would do if the minimum wage was increased by 50 cents an hour. Point out the list of possible reactions in their text on pages 194–195. Read and discuss several of the essays in class.
2. Most workers who earn the minimum wage do not belong to unions. Discuss possible reasons for this lack of organization. Are marginal workers too easy to replace? Do they change jobs too often? Is it because they lack specialized skills? Does it have anything to do with the type of firms they work for? Does organized labor see little point in trying to organize these workers?

   If these workers do not belong to unions, why do unions support higher minimum wages?

Lesson Checkpoint

Text: Self-Check, text page 196
Answers

1. Firms that pay wages that are already higher than the minimum wage are not directly affected by increases in the minimum wage.
2. People who earn the minimum wage and who also have another means of support are called marginal workers.
3. Some people believe the minimum wage helps to protect workers from exploitation, while others believe the minimum wage reduces employment opportunities for the poor.

Follow-up Assignments (Independent Practice/Extension/Homework)

Text: Applying What You Have Learned, text page 196
Answers

1. If the minimum wage were increased to $5 the following would be possible results:
   a. fewer jobs that pay minimum wage
   b. more investment in labor-saving machines
   c. firms that had employed low-skilled workers could go out of business
   d. workers could be expected to do more work
2. Students' answers will vary, but they should provide adequate explanation for their three choices. Possible answers include that the firm could accept a smaller profit; increase prices to their customers; pay no more than minimum wage; lay off some workers; purchase labor-saving equipment; replace low-skill workers with higher-skilled, more productive workers; move the firm or some of its production to a low-wage country; or simply close down.

Section Evaluation

Self-Check, text page 196
Thinking Critically About Economics, question 6 (Chapter 7 Review, text pages 198–201)

ADDITIONAL MATERIALS FOR CHAPTER 7

Chapter Evaluation

Teacher's Resource Binder: Chapter Quiz

Reteaching and Extension

See the *Teacher's Resource Binder* and the *Student Activity Book* for additional handouts and activities for Chapter 7.

TEACHER'S BIBLIOGRAPHY FOR CHAPTER 7

Economics Sources

Brown, C. V. and Jackson, P. M. *Education, Unemployment & the Labor Market.* New York: Taylor and Francis, 1991.

Busman, Gloria, ed. *Union Strategies for a High Tech Era.* Los Angeles: University of California Institute of Industrial Relations, 1989.

Douglas, Sara U. *Labor's New Voice: Unions & the Mass Media.* Voigt, Melvin J., ed. Norwood, N.J.: Ablex Publications, 1986.

Howland, Marie. *Plant Closings & Worker Displacement: The Regional Issues.* Kalamazoo, Mich.: W.E. Upjohn, Institute for Employment Research, 1988.

McConnell, Campbell R., and Brue, Stanley L. *Contemporary Labor Economics,* 2nd ed. New York: McGraw-Hill, 1989.

Montgomery, David. *The Fall of the House of Labor: The Workplace, the State & American Labor Activism.* New York: Cambridge University Press, 1987.

Ross, Myron H. *A Gale of Creative Destruction: The Coming Electronic Boom.* Westport, Conn.: Greenwood, 1989.

Samuelson, Paul A. and Nordhaus, William D. *Economics,* 14th ed. New York: McGraw-Hill, 1992, Chapters 14 and 15.

Thurow, Lester C. *Dangerous Currents: The State of Economics.* New York: Random House, 1984.

References for Additional Teaching Strategies

Braud, Patricia. "What Workers Want," in *American Demographics.* August, 1992, Vol. 14, no. 8. Includes surveys of workers' opinions on job characteristics.

Economics and Entrepreneurship: Master Curriculum Guide, New York: Joint Council on Economic Education, 1991, Lesson 16.

Mansfield, Edwin and Behravesh, Nariman. *Telecourse Study Guide for Economics USA,* New York: Norton, 1991, Chapter 22. This text provides for and is keyed to *Economics USA,* a telecourse developed by the Southern California Consortium.

Walstad, William R. and Saunders, Phillip. *The Principles of Economics Course: A Handbook for Instructors,* 11th ed. New York: McGraw-Hill, 1990.

Employment and Earnings. Washington, D.C.: United States Bureau of Labor Statistics, monthly government publication.

CHAPTER 7 REVIEW ANSWERS

Building Your Vocabulary (text pages 199–200)

Sections A & B

1. injunction
2. diminishing marginal productivity
3. closed shop
4. National Labor Relations Act
5. craft union
6. industrial union
7. equilibrium wage rate
8. Clayton Act
9. right-to-work law
10. derived demand
11. Taft-Hartley Act
12. marginal physical product
13. labor force participation rate
14. money wages
15. real wages
16. diminishing returns
17. labor unions

Sections C & D

18. lockout
19. strike
20. compulsory arbitration
21. Fair Labor Standards Act
22. sit-down strike
23. relocation
24. mediation
25. voluntary arbitration
26. agency shop
27. political action committee
28. marginal workers
29. wildcat strike
30. slowdown
31. picket line
32. union label
33. strikebreaker
34. minimum wage
35. union ship
36. collective bargaining
37. boycott

Understanding Economics (text pages 200–201)

1. If the saw only requires two workers to operate it, a third worker will only give the two current workers a chance to rest. This will increase production but only by a limited amount. The third worker did not add as much to production as the second worker did. This demonstrates the principle of diminishing marginal productivity.
2. If a firm is suddenly able to charge more for its product, it will find that its workers are worth more and the firm will be willing to not only hire additional workers but also pay them a higher wage.
3. Workers in a car wash are probably low skilled and easy to replace. Aircraft engineers are high-skilled workers and difficult to replace. The aircraft firm is probably more profitable than the car wash. The aircraft workers are therefore in a better position to demand and receive higher wages.
4. If there was an extended rail strike that was harming the national interests, the President could request an injunction from a federal court that would require the workers to return to work for up to 80 days. During this time the federal government would attempt to help the parties reach a settlement through mediation.
5. Facts that I as mediator would want to know before suggesting a solution would include:
   a. what similar workers are paid elsewhere
   b. what fringe benefits the workers receive
   c. what profit the firm makes
   d. what the rate of inflation has been
   e. if the firm could raise its prices
   f. if the workers have been or could be more productive
   g. what investments in new machinery have been or could be made
   h. what wage increases have been given to workers in past contracts

Thinking Critically About Economics (text page 201)

1. Workers who would be harmed by the new equipment would include:
   a. production workers who lost their jobs
   b. people who had maintained the old equipment
   c. workers at firms that sold to the workers who lost their jobs

Workers who would benefit from the new equipment would include:

a. workers who build the new equipment
b. workers who maintain the new equipment
c. workers who sell to the people who gain jobs from the new equipment

2. Reasons to accept concessionary contracts could include:

a. greater job security
b. opportunity for firm to invest in new equipment
c. chance to receive greater income at some future time

3. A right-to-work law could make it more difficult for a union to organize workers for the following possible reasons:

a. Some workers might choose not to join or support the union.
b. Some workers might be afraid that the union could not protect them.
c. There might be more arguments between workers who joined the union and those who did not join.

4. Possible reasons for union membership decline include the following:

a. Many low-skill union jobs have been eliminated by automation.
b. Many new jobs are in non-union service industries.
c. Some workers may feel unions have been unresponsive to their needs.

5. Owners might use a lockout if they felt that wage concessions could be won by doing so. When sales are low, owners have less to lose by closing down. In a recession, workers may not have enough savings to stay off work for very long.
6. *In Favor:* A lower minimum wage would allow more young workers the opportunity to gain experience so that they could get a better job some time in the future. *Against:* A lower minimum wage would only allow employers to take advantage of young workers and to hire fewer older workers.

Consumer Skills Projects (text page 201)

1. The results of student surveys will vary widely. Help your students draw correlations between people's attitudes toward buying union-made products and their economic situations.
2. Lead a discussion in class that concerns how many of the union leaders' statements about the importance of buying union-made products to consumers are normative and how many are positive in nature. Do your students agree with the accuracy of the normative statements?
3. Do students believe the business owners' answers are concerned with benefits to consumers or do they more closely relate to the ability to earn a profit?

PART 2 REVIEW ANSWERS

Understanding Economic Concepts (text pages 205–206)

1. The answer is provided as an example in the text.
2. The number of products a firm sells should increase if the price of similar products goes up. Customers will *substitute* the firm's product for the similar one that is more expensive. This change in one of the *determinants of demand* will cause demand for the firm's product to increase.
3. If a firm pays its workers a higher wage it will have higher *costs of production,* which will cause it to *supply* fewer products if it

is not able to increase the price it charges.

4. If a firm produces more products than it can sell at its current price, it will have a *surplus* of its product. It will probably lower its price to the *equilibrium price*, where the quantity of the product that is demanded will be equal to the quantity the firm is willing to supply. At this lower price, the surplus will be eliminated.
5. Consumers distribute their spending among many different types of products because of *diminishing marginal utility*. As they acquire additional items of a particular type, each one has less value. They are able to receive greater value by buying other types of products.
6. In capitalism firms produce products that consumers buy because it is impossible to earn a profit from producing a product no one wants. The idea that consumers determine what products are produced and offered for sale is called *consumer sovereignty*.
7. The need for the government to provide *consumer protection* has grown over the years because our economic system and the products we buy have become much more complex.
8. Most large firms are corporations because they are able to raise the large amounts of money they need through the sale of *stocks* and *bonds*. Single proprietorships and partnerships are not able to gather money in these ways.
9. Many firms would like to increase the number of products they manufacture or sell to reduce their *average fixed cost*. This practice should reduce their cost per item produced and improve their chance of earning a profit.
10. The owner of corporate stock may earn money when the firm pays a part of its profits to the stockholders in *dividends*. Money may also be earned from a *capital gain* when the value of the stock increases and the owner sells the stock for more than the purchase price.
11. Many large firms have been formed from small firms being joined together. When firms that produce the same product join together, it is called a *horizontal combination*. When firms that provide different steps in the process of producing a single product join together, it is called a *vertical combination*.
12. Some firms require such large capital investments that it would be inefficient to have more than one in any area. These firms are called *natural monopolies*. Public utilities are examples of such firms and are usually regulated by an agency of the government so they cannot take advantage of their customers.
13. The government of the United States uses its antitrust policy to try to create *workable competition*, an attempt to achieve the best trade-off between the advantages of industrial size and those of competition.
14. As firms hire additional workers they will reach a point where extra workers add progressively smaller amounts to production. This fact is called *diminishing marginal productivity*, and it results from the limited resources available for additional workers to use.
15. The government has frequently become involved in labor/management negotiations or the collective bargaining process. This involvement has taken several forms. In *mediation* the government provides a neutral party who listens to both sides and suggests a solution. In *voluntary arbitration* the two sides allow the

neutral party to set the contract or conditions of employment. When there is *compulsory arbitration*, the two sides are required by law to allow the neutral party to set the contract.

Writing About Economics (text pages 206–207)

1. Students should understand the need firms have to reduce their *average fixed costs* by increasing the number of items they sell. One way this can be accomplished is by providing customers with additional information through *informative advertising*. This advertising may increase the demand for the firm's product by changing customer tastes (a determinant of demand) for the product.
2. Students should understand how *persuasive advertising* may be used to influence consumer tastes. They should demonstrate an appreciation of the trade-offs between freedom of choice and *consumer protection* that are made when the government regulates advertising. Students should finally address the idea of the *invisible hand*, which suggests that a firm which does not charge reasonable prices for quality products will eventually lose its customers and fail.
3. Students should understand the firm's need to convince its customers that its product is superior to other similar goods. If the firm accomplishes this distinction through *informative advertising*, it will be an example of a firm in *monopolistic competition*, because the firm will possess a monopoly over its name and reputation rather than over its type of product.
4. Students should understand the trade-offs that must be made in implementing *antitrust policy*. When *horizontal combinations* are created, the new, larger firms may be able to take advantage of *economies of scale* and become more efficient. However, they might abuse their economic power. The government tries to create *workable competition*, in which the best features of size and competition are achieved.

Discussing Economics (text pages 207–208)

1. Students should identify the issue(s) that are involved in a law that would require the use of motorcycle helmets. One possible issue is the trade-off between personal freedom and public responsibility to care for individuals who are injured in motorcycle accidents. Students should clearly state whether or not they would support such a law. They should clearly explain the costs and benefits associated with such a law and explain why they believe their point of view is correct.
2. Students should identify the issue(s) that are involved in passing the cost of unfinished nuclear power projects on to customers. One possible issue is the fairness of requiring the individual stockholders of the power company to pay the cost through reduced dividends or the possible failure of the firm. Other possible issues relate to what degree and in what way the owners of government-regulated, natural monopolies should be accountable for their business decisions.

   Students should clearly state whether or not they would support forcing electric customers to pay for the power plants. Students should clearly explain the costs and benefits associated with forcing electric customers to pay for the power plants and explain why they feel their point of view is correct.

3. Students should identify the issue(s) that are involved in making it against the law for public employees to go on strike. One possible issue is the fairness of allowing private but not public employees to strike. Students should clearly state whether or not they would support a law against public employees going on strike. Students should clearly explain the costs and benefits associated with making public employee strikes illegal and explain why they feel their point of view is correct.

Problem-Solving with Economics

Chapter 3 (text pages 208–209)

1. a. An increase in taxes would reduce consumer income and *decrease* demand for all products.
   b. A baby boom would *increase* the demand for diapers by increasing the number of customers.
   c. The demand for snow shovels would *increase* at the start of December because of a change in tastes as winter started.
   d. The demand for popcorn would *increase* if the price of peanuts went up, because customers would substitute popcorn for peanuts.
   e. The demand for hospital beds would *increase* if people lived longer because there would be more old people in hospitals.
   f. The demand for all products would *increase* if people got better jobs because customers would have more income to spend.
   g. The demand for fish nets would *increase* at the start of a salmon run because of a change in tastes or possibly the number of customers.
   h. The demand for canvas shoes would *increase* when leather becomes very expensive because customers would substitute canvas shoes for leather shoes they could no longer afford.
2. a. If the firm's workers are paid 10 percent more it will *increase* their costs of production and cause their supply curve to move to the *left*.
   b. If the firm has to pay more for heat it will *increase* their costs of production and cause their supply curve to move to the *left*.
   c. If the firm buys more efficient trucks it will *decrease* their costs of production and cause their supply curve to move to the *right*.
   d. If the firm installs pollution controls it will *increase* their costs of production and cause their supply curve to move to the *left*.
   e. If the firm buys a computer system it will *decrease* their costs of production and cause their supply curve to move to the *right*.
   f. If the firm spends money on training it will *decrease* their costs of production and cause their supply curve to move to the *right*.
3. a. At $5.00 30 toys would be offered for sale.
   b. At $4.00 20 toys would be offered for sale.
   c. If the price went from $3.00 to $5.00, more toys would be offered for sale.
   d. If the price went from $3.00 to $5.00, 20 more toys would be offered for sale.
   e. At $2.00 no toys would be supplied.
4. a. An increase in consumer income would cause the demand curve to move to the right and *increase* the equilibrium price.

b. A 10 percent increase in labor cost would cause the supply curve to move to the left and *increase* the equilibrium price.
c. A decrease in the cost of raw materials would cause the supply curve to move to the right and *decrease* the equilibrium price.
d. An increase in the popularity of the product would cause the demand curve to move to the right and *increase* the equilibrium price.
e. A government report that a product caused cancer would cause its demand curve to move to the left and *decrease* the equilibrium price.
f. If the raw materials become less expensive, the equilibrium price would *decrease*.
g. An increase in the price of a substitute would cause the demand curve to move to the right and *increase* the equilibrium price.
h. A decrease in exports of the product would cause the demand curve to move to the left and *decrease* the equilibrium price.

Chapter 4 (text page 209)

1. Students' lists of things they would take should include many different items. This exercise can be used to point out that no one would take more than one of any particular item. This demonstrates *diminishing marginal utility*. The first item is important but second items of the same type do not have as much value.
2. The things that students identify should be intended to shift demand, probably by affecting consumer tastes. Things like autograph sessions, or a chance to meet the players would be good ideas. Be sure to point out that giving expensive gifts away is really little different from lowering the price of the tickets.
3. The table shows that advertisers shifted their spending from newspapers to television between 1950 and 1989. This represents a change in their demand because of a change in their tastes.

Chapter 5 (text pages 209–210)

1. The businesses identified by your students should demonstrate the following characteristics:
   - The single proprietorship should be small and require relatively little capital to start. It probably will have many competitors.
   - The partnership should be formed among entrepreneurs who need to share an item or service that is relatively costly. Doctors sharing the cost of a laboratory or nurse would be a good example.
   - The corporation should be relatively large and require large investments in capital. The need for limited liability or professional management could also be brought out.
2. Possible fixed cost students might identify include: property taxes, mortgage payment, fire insurance, a lease on the firm's truck, weekly newspaper advertisements.

   Possible variable costs include: wages of people who set up bikes, cost of replacement parts, cost of power to run tools, cost of gas to deliver bikes, cost of ordering new bicycles.
3. There are many fixed costs associated with running a school. The costs of a library or science lab are good examples. A library costs little more to run if it has 20 or 200 students using it each day. The

costs of such facilities can be spread out among more students in large schools.

4. These firms must pay their workers whether they work or not. This means their salaries are fixed costs. It might be less expensive for these firms to produce products at a loss than to pay workers for doing nothing.

5. a. Owners of firms that want to encourage savers to invest in their business must offer a return equal to or greater than the interest banks pay. In 1990 banks paid only 7.52 percent, so businesses could attract investment by offering relatively low dividends. However, in 1981 people could deposit their savings in a bank and earn almost 16 percent interest so businesses had to pay more too.
   b. Having to pay high dividends or interest would discourage firms from making investments in new equipment.
   c. The need to pay high interest or dividends could discourage firms from renting equipment. This would cause rent paid for the use of resources to fall because of the reduced demand.

Chapter 6 (text pages 210–211)

1. a. Farms or businesses that supply basic raw materials are the best examples of pure competition. A farmer who grows corn cannot charge more than other farmers, because if he did his customers would choose to not buy his product but that of his competitors.
   b. If all firms in a competitive industry try to produce more products, the industry's total supply will increase and the equilibrium price will fall.
   c. If competitive firms try to earn more money by producing and selling more products, they may force the price of their product down, causing them to earn even less income.

2. The following are possible answers:
   a. Americans buy fresh fruits and vegetables from competitive firms.
   b. Americans buy beauty products and pain relievers from firms in monopolistic competition.
   c. Americans buy automobiles and tires from firms in oligopoly.
   d. Americans buy electric power and natural gas from firms that are natural monopolies.

3. Students should demonstrate an understanding of economies and diseconomies of scale. Possible advantages (economies of scale) include (1) raw materials (cheaper when bought in quantity); (2) lower rates of interest; (3) ability to afford new machinery; (4) more efficient use of advertising.

   Possible disadvantages (diseconomies of scale) include (1) more difficult control; (2) less personal relationship with customers; (3) possibly more government controls; (4) possibly more labor problems.

4. Students should demonstrate that they have considered the costs and benefits of government ownership and have reached their decision through reason and logic.

5. a. The number of workers would increase, because each firm would need its own production, distribution, and management employees.
   b. The total cost of distribution and advertising would increase, because

there would be so many firms and products to sell.

c. There would be many new soft drinks on the market.

d. The market price of soft drinks might go up if the costs of production increased enough.

e. The quantity of soft drinks sold might go down if prices increased.

Chapter 7 (text page 211)

1. a. The entry of many new, young workers into the labor force would lower wages because there would be more people competing for each job.

b. An increase in the imports of inexpensive products from other countries would lower wages because there would be fewer jobs for Americans to compete for.

c. Inflation would increase wages because fewer people would be willing to work if their wages could buy less.

d. An increase in government aid to the poor would increase wages because it would be harder for employers to attract employees who would now find it easier to not work.

2. Students should demonstrate that they have considered the merits of each of these contradictory arguments. Their decisions should be based on logic and reason.

3. Students should demonstrate that they have considered the merits of the "weapons" of labor and management. Their decisions should be based on logic and reason.

4. Two possible arguments in favor are that a lower minimum wage for young people would make it easier for them to find jobs and that a lower minimum wage for young people would give them experience.

Two possible arguments against are that a lower minimum wage for young people would result in their exploitation and that a lower minimum wage for young people would hurt older workers' chances of getting a job.

PART 3

UNDERSTANDING THE ECONOMY AS A WHOLE

CHAPTER 8

Measuring the Economy: Made in America (text pages 214–233)

SECTION A. What Is the Gross Domestic Product? (text pages 216–220)

Objectives (Lesson Focus)

Upon completion of this section, students will be able to:

- Define the term *Gross Domestic Product.*
- Describe two methods used for measuring the gross domestic product: the expenditure approach and the income approach.
- Identify and explain various difficulties in measuring the gross domestic product accurately, including double counting and the underground economy.

Preparation (Instruction: Pre-teaching—Vocabulary or Activity)

1. Discussion Introduce this section by asking your students how large their yearly income would have to be to satisfy their wants and needs if they were adults with a family to support. Caution them to be reasonable and at least somewhat realistic. List these amounts on the chalkboard and figure an average for the class.

Tell your students how much the average yearly income for Americans is. It is likely that on an average your students will want a larger yearly income.

Ask your students what would happen if everyone in the country was given as much money as they would like. They should recognize that an increase in people's incomes would not increase the number of goods and services that are being produced and offered for sale. An increase in income would lead to an increase in demand, and then in prices. Emphasize the fact that as a group, our standard of living is limited not by the amount of money we earn but by the quantity of goods and services we produce.

2. The Personal Narrative The Personal Narrative in Section A demonstrates our desire for more and better goods and services. The subject of the Narrative is a young woman who wants to buy a piece of new clothing. Her father feels she wants too many things. He recognizes a difference between what he provides to his daughter and what he was able to have when he was her age. He feels that there is a better use for his limited income.

The Narrative reminds students of the problem of scarcity and the fact that our demand exceeds our ability to produce goods and services. It shows that our limited GDP determines our ability to satisfy demand.

Teaching Suggestions (Modeling/Guided Practice)

1. Ask your students what mistake was made in the following story:

> Marty repairs cars for a living. Last week he fixed the brakes on my car. He turned the disks, put on new pads, and replace the master cylinder. When he finished he charged me $283.49. I figure he added $283.49 to the Gross Domestic Product.

The problem is double counting. The value of the new pads, the new master cylinder, and any other parts Marty used were added by some other firm. Only the value added by Marty's labor is part of GDP. Point out the difficulty of avoiding double counting in measuring GDP.

2. Take a survey of your students. Ask them if they earn money that they do not report to the government (outside of their own family). This could be babysitting, cutting grass, etc. This income is part of the underground economy. There are slightly over 3,000,000 high school seniors in the country. If each one earns this amount of unreported income, how much production is going unreported and untaxed (assume that all of this income would be taxed at a 15 percent rate)?
3. Explain that changes in our life-styles make it difficult to compare GDP statistics over long periods of time. For example, 50 years ago most women did not hold jobs outside of their homes. They often did work that they were not paid for, like making clothing and cleaning their house.

   Many women no longer perform these tasks but hold outside jobs instead. They buy ready-made clothes and hire services to clean their homes. Housework done by women in the past was not counted as part of GDP because it was not paid for. But work in outside jobs is compensated and is counted as part of our GDP. Why does this fact make comparisons between past and present GDP values difficult?

Lesson Checkpoint

Text: Self-Check, text page 220
Answers

1. The Gross Domestic Product is the retail market value of everything produced in the nation in a year.
2. The two methods used to measure GDP are the expenditure and the income approach.
3. The underground economy represents production that is not reported to the government.

Follow-up Assignments (Independent Practice/Extension/Homework)

Text: Applying What You Have Learned, text page 220
Answers

1. a. would
   b. would
   c. would not
   d. would
   e. would not
   f. would not
   g. would (it is part of his/her job)
   h. would not
2. There is an almost unlimited number of goods that could be listed by your students. You might also discuss what their parents have that their grandparents did not have, or what they expect their children to have that they will not have.

Section Evaluation

Self-Check, text page 220
Understanding Economics, questions 1–5
(Chapter 8 Review, text pages 230–232)

SECTION B. What GDP Really Means (text pages 221–224)

Objectives (Lesson Focus)

Upon completion of this section, students will be able to:

- Explain the difference between real and nominal values.
- Explain the difficulties that are experienced in attempting to equate the GDP to the quality of life.

Preparation (Instruction: Pre-teaching—Vocabulary or Activity)

1. Discussion Introduce this section by giving students a copy of an advertising supplement from a newspaper that is 10 or 20 years old (most libraries can help you make a copy of such an advertisement). Be sure the supplement lists many different types of items. Ask students if they feel prices were low then. Then ask what *low* means. Is a price of 40 cents for a quart of milk low if you only earn $90 a week? Point out that there are also differences in quality. A television set that was new 20 years ago is not the same as a new television today. What types of information would be necessary to talk about the standard of living 10 or 20 years ago?

2. The Personal Narrative The Personal Narrative in Section B describes changes in a family's standard of living that resulted from their growing needs and inflation. The subject of the Narrative is a young person whose father works as a draftsman. The father has become more productive by completing special training. However, his income has not kept up with his family's needs and inflation. Many things they could afford in the past are now too expensive.

The Narrative compares the difficulties experienced by this family with those of other people who have greater or lesser problems. It shows the difference between changes in real and nominal GDP, and how people are affected differently by these changes.

Teaching Suggestions (Modeling/Guided Practice)

1. Use Discussion Topic 14 from the *Teacher's Resource Binder* to discuss how various products do or do not add to the quality of life.
2. Explain that although there has been an increase in real personal income in recent years, this increase has not been evenly distributed. Roughly 12 percent of the U.S. population lived in poverty in 1991. Ask your students if they would be willing to have their families pay higher taxes to support enough aid to the poor to help eliminate poverty. Why or why not?

Lesson Checkpoint

Text: Self-Check, text page 224
Answers

1. Nominal and real values differ in that real values have been adjusted for inflation but nominal values have not.
2. Real GDP *per person* includes adjustments for changes in the population.
3. The real GDP per person does not tell us the type of products that were produced, and this can have an effect on people's standards of living.

Follow-up Assignments (Independent Practice/Extension/Homework)

Text: Applying What You Have Learned, text page 224
Answers

1. All of these are opinion answers. Many students will believe that

additional production of these items adds little to the quality of life.

2. Things that enhance the quality of life without involving money are likely to include family relationships, religion, enjoying the outdoors, and friendship.

Section Evaluation

Self-Check, text page 224
Understanding Economics, questions 6 and 7 (Chapter 8 Review, text pages 230–232)

SECTION C. Life Within the Business Cycle (text pages 225–228)

Objectives (Lesson Focus)

Upon completion of this section, students will be able to:

- Describe the four sections of the business cycle: expansion, peak, contraction, and trough.
- Identify durable and nondurable goods and explain why the sales and production of durable goods are more affected by the business cycle than nondurable goods.
- Identify and explain several leading indicators.

Preparation (Instruction: Pre-teaching—Vocabulary or Activity)

1. Discussion Introduce this section by asking your students which of the following decisions they would make if they were ten years older and believed that there was a good chance they might soon lose their jobs in a recession.

Which of the following would you decide to do?

- save more money
- buy a new car
- put off buying a swimming pool
- continue buying food
- drive your car less
- put an addition on your house
- take an expensive vacation
- buy your kids new shoes for school
- skip going to the doctor when you get sick
- register for night classes at a business college

Discuss your students' answers to these questions. How would their actions affect the economy? Would they tend to make a recession worse or not as bad? Point out that not all types of production would be affected equally. People would continue to eat even if they expected a recession.

2. The Personal Narrative The Personal Narrative in Section C describes a family that suffers from a recession. The subject of the Narrative is a young man whose father is laid off from a truck factory when sales fall during a recession. He realizes that part of the problem is caused by high truck prices and the fact that individuals and businesses are less likely to borrow money to buy expensive goods in a recession.

The Narrative demonstrates problems that result from recessions and points out that these problems are not equally distributed throughout the economy.

Teaching Suggestions (Modeling/Guided Practice)

Use Discussion Topic 15 from the *Teacher's Resource Binder* to illustrate the significance of the leading economic indicators. Read and discuss some of the better answers with your class.

Lesson Checkpoint

Text: Self-Check, text page 228
Answers

1. The four phases of the business cycle are expansion, peak, contraction, and trough.
2. A *durable* good has a life span of several years and is likely to be expensive. *Nondurable* goods—such as food and clothing—are intended for immediate use and are likely to be less expensive.
3. Leading indicators help businesses decide whether to make additional investments.

Follow-up Assignments (Independent Practice/Extension/Homework)

1. Text: Applying What You Have Learned, text page 228
   Answers
   a. A refrigerator is a durable good.
   b. Shampoo is a nondurable good.
   c. Gasoline is a nondurable good.
   d. Shoes are nondurable goods.
   e. A television set is a durable good.
   f. Radio batteries are nondurable goods.
2. Teacher's Resource Binder: Critical Thinking Activity, Chapter 8 (answers in Binder).

Section Evaluation

Self-Check, text page 228
Understanding Economics, questions 8 and 9 (Chapter 8 Review, text pages 230–232)

ADDITIONAL MATERIALS FOR CHAPTER 8

Chapter Evaluation

Teacher's Resource Binder: Chapter 8 Quiz

Reteaching and Extension

See the *Teacher's Resource Binder* and the *Student Activity Book* for additional handouts and activities for Chapter 8.

TEACHER'S BIBLIOGRAPHY FOR CHAPTER 8

Economics Sources

Cash, Adam. *Getting Started in the Underground Economy.* Port Townsend, Wash.: Loompanics, 1987.

Gordon, Sanford D. and Dawson, George G. *Introductory Economics,* 7th ed. Lexington, Mass.: D.C. Heath, Inc., 1991. Chapter 11 provides a simple introduction to macroeconomics. Chapter 12 is a good source for the theory of income determination.

McConnell, Campbell R. and Brue, Stanley L. *Economics Principles, Problems, and Policies,* 11th ed. New York: McGraw-Hill, 1990. Chapter 9.

Miller, Roger LeRoy. *Economics Today,* 7th ed. New York: HarperCollins, 1991. Chapter 8.

Moore, Geoffrey H. *Leading Indicators for the 1990s.* Homewood, Ill.: Irwin, 1989.

Survey of Current Business, Washington, D.C.: U.S. Department of Commerce, published monthly.

References for Additional Teaching Strategies

Econ/GNP (also available as Huntington I Simulation Programs). Digital Equipment Corporation, 146 Main Street, Maynard MA 07154. A computer-assisted game that simulates the U.S. economy.

Mansfield, Edwin, and Behravesh, Nariman. *Telecourse Study Guide for Economics USA.* New York: Norton, 1992, Chapters 3 and 4. Text provides exercises for and is keyed to *Economics USA,* a television course developed by the Southern California Consortium.

Wolfson, Mary, and Buranelli, Vincent. *In the Long Run We Are All Dead: A Macroeconomics Murder Mystery,* 2nd ed. New York: St. Martin's Press, 1989.

CHAPTER 8 REVIEW ANSWERS

Building Your Vocabulary (text page 231)

1. underground economy
2. nominal values
3. real values
4. leading indicator
5. income approach
6. business cycle
7. expenditure approach
8. gross domestic product
9. durable goods
10. nondurable goods
11. real hourly wage
12. double counting

Understanding Economics (text page 231)

1. The new machine is part of current production (thus a part of GDP) while a used car was produced in some previous year.
2. The types of spending included in the expenditure approach to measuring GDP value are:
   a. consumption spending by individuals
   b. investment spending by businesses
   c. government spending
   d. spending by people from other countries
3. The types of earning included in the income approach to measuring GDP value are:
   a. wages
   b. profits
   c. rent
   d. interest
   e. some taxes
   f. wear out
4. Any example of double counting that shows the same contribution to GDP being counted more than once would be acceptable.
5. As expenditures and income in the underground economy go unreported, the job of measuring the GDP becomes more difficult. Reported GDP is smaller than actual GDP. This also means that those people who report their income pay more than their fair share to support the government in taxes.
6. A wage of $60,000 a year in 2008 means little until we know what has happened to the cost of living between the present and then.
7. An increase in real GDP could be taken up by population growth, by additional government spending, or could be distributed unequally.
8. During a recession, people and businesses are often afraid to borrow money to buy expensive durable goods. They might believe that they would not be able to repay the loan.
9. If the leading indicators have been down for five months, it would be a sign that the economy is going into a recession. Few people or businesses would invest or grow during such a time.

Thinking Critically About Economics
(text page 232)

1. Possible answers for why GDP is not a perfect measure of the quality of life include:
   a. We would need to know about inflation.
   b. We would need to know how the GDP is distributed.
   c. We would need to know what products are being produced.
   d. We would need to know what has happened to population growth.
2. Before you could make any judgments about the $0.25 minimum wage in 1935, it would be necessary to know what goods that $0.25 could buy in that year.
3. Included in the underground economy would be:
   a. cutting your neighbor's grass and not reporting the income
   b. babysitting and not reporting the income
   c. a farmer not reporting income from a roadside stand
4. If this spending actually reduces the use of drugs in this country, it could
   a. increase spending for other goods and services
   b. reduce crime
   c. improve the productivity of people who previously used drugs
5. Car sales fell during the recession because they are expensive, durable goods. Because milk is a nondurable good, milk sales increased as the population grew.
6. a. Falling inventories show that products are being sold and will have to be replaced with new production.
   b. An increase in the hours worked reveals that workers will have more money to spend.
   c. An increase in building permits shows that there will soon be more jobs in construction.

Consumer Skills Projects (text page 232)

1. Your students may need help explaining what these GDP figures show. You might consider talking about them in class before you have your students write about them.
2. Your students should find that their parents' first jobs had very different levels of pay from current entry-level jobs. When these wage rates are adjusted for inflation they will be much closer to each other. This should help your students understand the difference between real and nominal values.
3. It is possible that some of your students will come from families that underwent major economic changes because of the recession of 1991–1992. Firsthand knowledge of such events can add relevance to your discussion of the business cycle and what it means to people's lives.

CHAPTER 9

Government's Role in the Economy (text pages 234–263)

SECTION A. Public Goods and Services (text pages 237–242)

Objectives (Lesson Focus)

Upon completion of this section, students will be able to:

- Recognize, define, and give examples of public goods and services.

- Describe reasons for our growing need for public goods and services.
- Define and give examples of negative externalities.
- Explain the function of the government in reducing or eliminating negative externalities.
- Explain reasons for government redistribution of income.
- Explain the difference between transfer payments and transfers in kind and give examples of each.

Preparation (Instruction: Pre-teaching—Vocabulary or Activity)

1. Discussion Introduce this section by asking your students to help you make a list on the chalkboard of public goods and services from which they benefit. Help your students explain how each item on the list is paid for. Are the people who pay to support the public goods or services the same as those who benefit from them? Do your students feel there is a fair distribution of costs and benefits from the items on their list? Ask them to explain why or why not.

A second topic that could be discussed is how your students would be affected if the items on their list were not provided by the government.

2. The Personal Narrative The Personal Narrative in Section A describes public goods and services provided by the government. The subject of the Narrative is a young man who attends a public high school. The Narrative traces the events in a typical day of his life. It demonstrates how he—or his relatives and friends—benefit from public goods and services of which they may not even be aware.

The Narrative demonstrates the trade-off between the costs and benefits of public goods and services. It also shows that these costs and benefits are not equally distributed among all people.

Teaching Suggestions (Modeling/Guided Practice)

1. Many older people do not feel that they should be expected to support public schools. They often vote against increases in school taxes when they are given an opportunity. Ask each of your students to prepare a list of ways in which older people benefit from the taxes they pay to support public schools. Combine the lists on the chalkboard and discuss them.

   How do your students feel about the prospect of paying Social Security taxes to support older retired people? Can they see any similarity between older people paying school taxes, and their own feelings regarding Social Security support?
2. Point out the fact that there are thousands of tons of radioactive waste in this country that have been produced over the years. This waste must be disposed of in one way or another. Use Discussion Topic 16 from the *Teacher's Resource Binder* to demonstrate the problem.
3. Many Americans believe that government transfers are received only by the poor. Explain that this is not the case. Virtually all Americans either currently or in the future will receive some benefit from government social programs. For example, most Americans will qualify for Social Security benefits and belong to the government's Medicare program when they retire. Children of wealthy families may be given lunches at school that are partially supported by the government. It could also be argued that stockholders in firms which received government financial assistance have in effect received a

type of transfer payment. For example, the stockholders of the Chrysler Corporation would not have done well without the government's loan guarantee in 1979.

Lesson Checkpoint

Text: Self-Check, text page 242
Answers

1. Unlike public goods, private goods are owned by individuals and are subject to the principle of exclusion.
2. Continued growth and increasing specialization in the United States have increased the need for public goods and services.
3. A negative externality occurs when someone who is neither the producer nor the consumer of a product pays a cost associated with the product.

Follow-up Assignments (Independent Practice/Extension/Homework)

Text: Applying What You Have Learned, text page 242
Answers

Ten public goods or services mentioned in the Personal Narrative include:

a. a school bus
b. sewers
c. a traffic court
d. police
e. a school lunch program
f. roads
g. a waste treatment plant
h. a school
i. a traffic light
j. a municipal arena

(There are several other acceptable answers.)

Section Evaluation

Self-Check, text page 242
Understanding Economics, questions 1 and 2 (Chapter 9 Review, text pages 260–262)

SECTION B. Taxes and the Economy (text pages 243–247)

Objectives (Lesson Focus)

Upon completion of this section, students will be able to:

- Identify and explain four principles of taxation: the benefits received principle, the ability-to-pay principle, the productivity principle, and the least-likely-to-offend principle.
- Define and identify examples of progressive, regressive, and proportional taxes.

Preparation (Instruction: Pre-teaching—Vocabulary or Activity)

1. Discussion Introduce this section by asking your class to help you list different taxes that are paid in this country. Review the types of taxes that are defined in the text on page 244. Then try to categorize each tax you have listed as an *ability-to-pay* tax, a *benefits received* tax, a *productivity* tax, or a *least-likely-to-offend* tax. The list compiled by you and your students, separated into types of taxes, should resemble the one provided below. It could be argued that several of these taxes do not clearly fall into one category only. Which taxes do your students believe are most and least fair?

Property tax is supposed to be an ability-to-pay tax but does not always work as such because property owners may not have much income. Property tax is usually regressive.

Income tax is an ability-to-pay tax; as taxable income goes up, so does the tax rate. Income tax is often progressive.

Sales tax is a least-likely-to-offend tax. It is paid in small amounts and is regressive.

Gasoline tax is a benefits received tax. Those who drive pay the tax which in turn pays for the roads. This tax is regressive.

Cigarette tax is a least-likely-to-offend tax. It is paid by smokers in small amounts and is very regressive.

Social Security tax is a benefits received tax. Those who pay by having money withheld from their paychecks throughout the years will eventually receive benefits from the program. This tax is somewhat regressive.

Tariffs are productivity taxes. By making imports more expensive, tariffs encourage people to buy American rather than foreign products. Tariffs are somewhat regressive.

Estate tax is intended to be an ability-to-pay tax. Those who inherit wealth should be able to pay the tax. Problems often occur, however, when property is inherited. Estate tax is somewhat progressive.

Corporate income tax is an ability-to-pay tax. Corporations that earn profits should be able to afford taxes. This tax is somewhat progressive.

2. The Personal Narrative The Personal Narrative in Section B demonstrates how taxes reduce our disposable income. The subject of the Narrative is a young woman who has just received her first paycheck. She is surprised by the number of ways in which her income is taxed. She feels that too much of her small income is taken by the government. She is less aware of the benefits she has received from the government that are paid for by taxes.

The Narrative demonstrates the ways in which governments collect revenue from the people. It shows that there is a trade-off between the value a taxpayer could receive from spending income on private goods and the benefits of public goods and services that are supported through taxes.

Teaching Suggestions (Modeling/Guided Practice)

1. Ask your students to imagine they are running for a seat in their state legislature. It is clear that the state needs more money and taxes will have to be raised. There are four types of taxes listed below that could be increased. Each student should write a speech in which they identify which taxes would and would *not* increase, and explain why. Tell them to remember they are trying to be elected.

   They could be in favor of, or opposed to, increasing: (a) state income tax by two percent, (b) state sales tax by one percent, (c) state gasoline tax by five cents a gallon, (d) state cigarette tax by twenty-five cents a pack.
2. There is almost always an argument about local taxes. Review the budgetary process of your local government with your students. List the sources of revenue. Discuss controversial issues that have resulted in tax increases. Do your students feel the increases were justified?

Lesson Checkpoint

Text: Self-Check, text page 247

Answers

1. The two basic principles of taxation are the *benefits received* principle and the *ability-to-pay* principle.
2. In *progressive* taxation, people with higher incomes pay a higher per-

centage of tax on their income than do people with lower incomes. In *regressive* taxation, people earning lower incomes pay a higher percentage of tax on their income than do people with higher earnings.

3. Income tax is the most important source of tax revenue for the federal government; sales tax for the state government; and property tax for local government.

Follow-up Assignments (Independent Practice/Extension/Homework)

1. Text: Applying What You Have Learned, text page 247
Answers
   a. The $2.94 state income tax withheld from paycheck was a progressive tax.
   b. The 8 percent sales tax on the dress purchase was a regressive tax.
   c. Social Security taxes are proportional until earnings reach a limit, beyond which additional earnings are no longer taxed.
   d. The toll and parking fees were based on the benefits received principle.
   e. The $5.56 federal withholding tax from paycheck was based on the ability-to-pay principle.

2. Ask your students to survey their adult relatives concerning taxes. Students should ask the following questions and report their findings to the class. Discuss the results of the survey in class.
   a. Roughly what part of your income do you pay in taxes?
   b. Which tax do you believe is the most reasonable?
   c. Which tax do you believe is the least reasonable?
   d. How well do you believe the government uses your tax money?
   e. What is your opinion of someone who cheats to avoid paying taxes?

Section Evaluation

Self-Check, text page 247
Understanding Economics, questions 3 and 4 (Chapter 9 Review, text pages 260–262)

SECTION C. Government Spending (text pages 248–252)

Objectives (Lesson Focus)

Upon completion of this section, students will be able to:

- Explain the difference between the decision-making process in government and in business.
- Describe the process of preparing the federal budget, including the possibility of pork barrel legislation.

Preparation (Instruction: Pre-teaching—Vocabulary or Activity)

1. Discussion Introduce this section by asking students to review the list of public goods and services they made in Section A. Ask them to classify each item on their list as either (1) indispensable, (2) important, (3) useful, (4) of little value, or (5) a waste of money.

Combine the student lists on the chalkboard and discuss their rankings. Try to reach a consensus on what your students feel the government should and should not spend money on. Point out that it is possible to believe that the government should support a particular program without approving of the way the program is currently being run.

2. The Personal Narrative The Personal Narrative in Section C describes possible uses of and limitations on government revenues. The subject of the Narrative is a young man who lives in a southern city. He has suffered from cuts in government programs but recognizes the greater needs of other people. He is surprised by the limited number of areas in which government spending cuts can be made. He concludes that more federal aid would be one answer to local problems.

The Narrative demonstrates that government resources are limited by scarcity. It shows that a call for federal aid is a common reaction to local shortages. Many people make a distinction between money spent from local taxes and that which is supported through federal revenues.

Teaching Suggestions (Modeling/Guided Practice)

1. Ask your students to imagine that the army has been buying a particular type of weapon for the past 20 years. Each weapon costs $30,000. The government now has 15,000 of them. These weapons, however, are out-of-date, fairly inaccurate, and quite vulnerable to attack. The army would like to stop buying them. Do your students think this would be a good idea?

   Now have your students imagine they are members of the House of Representatives and that the weapon is made in their elective district. More than 2,300 people are employed making the weapon in their district, and unemployment there is already high. The students must run for office again next year. Do they think it would be a good idea for the army to stop buying the weapon under these circumstances?

   Discuss the conflict of interests demonstrated in this situation between what is good for the nation as a whole and what is good for one local area.
2. There is almost always a "controversial" project that has been undertaken by a local government. Identify such a project for your class and discuss various points of view concerning the value of the project. Do your students feel that their tax dollars are being well spent? Is there some other type of spending they would support more?
3. Before the Social Security Act of 1935, the federal government offered little or no aid to individuals who suffered economic hardship. Today there are many programs supported with federal money that are intended to help people who are in financial difficulty.

   Some people believe that it has become too easy to get along without a job in the United States. They argue that many people choose to be unemployed because they know the government will give them enough to "get by" on. Discuss this idea with your students. In their opinion, does our government do too much or too little for people who are out of work?

Lesson Checkpoint

Text: Self-Check, text page 252

Answers

1. Businesses make decisions to earn a profit; public decisions are made to directly benefit the people.
2. The preparation/writing of the federal budget is the responsibility of the President.
3. Both houses of Congress must approve the federal budget.
4. Payments to individuals is the most important type of spending performed by the federal government; educational spending is

most important for both the state and local governments.

Follow-up Assignments (Independent Practice/Extension/Homework)

Text: Applying What You Have Learned, text page 252
Answers

In the postsecondary school at the center of the photograph, students should easily recognize a number of facilities typically funded by the government (as part of a school or other public works). Most obvious are the recreational facilities: running track, tennis courts, swimming pool, baseball diamond. The postsecondary school itself is likely supported at least in part by government funds. Other items of government spending include the city streets and the traffic signals, lighting, and landscaping that accompany them. The housing tract requires sewer and water services, often a function of city government. Students may also suggest that some of the unidentified buildings may be hospitals or libraries.

Section Evaluation

Self-Check, text page 252
Understanding Economics, question 5 (Chapter 9 Review, text pages 260–262)

SECTION D. The Problem of the National Debt (text pages 253–258)

Objectives (Lesson Focus)

Upon completion of this section, students will be able to:

- Identify the four sources for most federal government borrowing before the 1980s: people, the banking system, businesses, and government trust funds.
- Explain that since 1980 more of this debt has been financed by sales of government securities to individuals and organizations in foreign countries.
- Describe different points of view concerning the importance of the national debt.

Preparation (Instruction: Pre-teaching—Vocabulary or Activity)

1. Discussion Introduce this section to the students by posing the following question: Which of the items below would you be willing to borrow money to obtain?

- a home
- a new car
- college tuition fees
- vacation expenses
- a new television

Point out that these items are really not all the same. Borrowing to pay for a trip to Florida is different from borrowing to go to college or to buy a car you need to get to work. Borrowing for college tuition or for a car would increase your future income; the trip to Florida would not. Ask your students what other factors they would need to consider. For example, their income and other financial responsibilities are related to the amount of money they should borrow.

Now ask students which of the following things they believe the federal government should be willing to go into debt to support:

- defense spending by the military
- more aid for colleges and universities
- environmental protection projects
- a new office building for the Senate
- rebuilding the nation's roads and waterways.

Discuss why your students would or would not support government borrowing to pay for each of these programs. Which of these programs should increase future income (production) in this country?

2. The Personal Narrative The Personal Narrative in Section D describes events that concern an individual's debt. The subject of the Narrative is a young man whose neighbor has borrowed more money than he is able to repay. The neighbor reacts to his situation by denying that the problem is his own fault. He blames both the institutions that lent him money and the people who have laid him off from his job. When he compares his borrowing to that of the federal government he sees a double standard. He does not understand why he should be in trouble for going into debt when the government borrows billions of dollars every year.

The Narrative highlights issues that concern the importance of the national debt. It asks if there is, or should be, a different set of standards for individuals and government borrowing.

Teaching Suggestions (Modeling/Guided Practice)

1. Explain that in 1991 the federal government was in debt about $18,000 for each man, woman, and child in the country. The amount of the per-person debt grew by almost $1,200 in fiscal 1991-1992 alone. The burden of this debt will be carried by future generations.

   Discuss the costs and benefits of this debt with your students. Point out that they as well as future generations will benefit in some ways from programs supported through government borrowing. Roads, airports, and buildings paid for with borrowed funds will still be here in the future for others to use. On the other hand, borrowing to support current social programs will do relatively little for future generations.

2. Discuss whether allowing foreign interests to buy U.S. securities is a good idea. Some people oppose this practice because future interest payments will send money out of the country. They also feel allowing foreign interests to buy our securities gives them too much influence in our economy.

   On the other hand, if we did not allow foreign purchases of our securities, our government would probably have to pay higher interest rates to borrow money. This could cause interest rates to increase, which would be bad for businesses and consumers.

   Can your students think of any other reasons why foreign sales of U.S. securities is a good or bad idea?

Lesson Checkpoint

Text: Self-Check, text page 258
Answers

1. Until recently, four frequently used sources of government borrowing included: (a) people buying savings bonds, (b) banks and the Federal Reserve System buying bonds, (c) businesses buying bonds, and (d) government trust funds buying bonds.
2. The government has recently borrowed more money by selling securities to foreign interests than it has in the past.
3. There is little consensus of opinion regarding the importance of the national debt.

Follow-up Assignments (Independent Practice/Extension/Homework)

1. Text: Applying What You Have Learned, text page 258
   Answers

(1) Two additional ways in which George's debt and the national debt differ include the following possible answers:

a. The government can use taxation in order to obtain money to repay the national debt; George does not have this resource.

b. George's property can be seized to satisfy his debts; such an action would not happen to the government.

(2) The seven different points of view concerning the national debt are presented on pages 255–256 of the student text. Student answers should include restatements of any four of these points of view. Look for logic and reason in the explanations for their four choices.

2. Ask your students to survey their parents about their concern for the size of the national debt. Have students ask the following questions and report their findings to the class.

a. Do you believe the federal government should spend no more than it collects in taxes?

b. Is there a difference between the government going into debt and an ordinary person borrowing money? If so, what is the difference?

c. Do you believe the federal debt is too large and will cause trouble for our country in the future?

d. Would you be willing to pay higher taxes to balance the budget?

e. What government spending program would you cut first to help balance the budget?

3. Teacher's Resource Binder: Critical Thinking Activity, Chapter 9 (answers in Binder).

Section Evaluation

Self-Check, text page 258
Understanding Economics, question 6 (Chapter 9 Review, text pages 260–262)

ADDITIONAL MATERIALS FOR CHAPTER 9

Chapter Evaluation

Teacher's Resource Binder: Chapter 9 Quiz

Reteaching and Extension

See the *Teacher's Resource Binder* and the *Student Activity Book* for additional handouts and activities for Chapter 9.

TEACHER'S BIBLIOGRAPHY FOR CHAPTER 9

Economics Sources

Butler, Willem. *Principles of Budgetary and Financial Policy*. Cambridge, Mass.: MIT Press, 1990.

Cantor, Jeffrey A. and Stabile, Donald R. *History of the Bureau of the Public Debt, 1940-1990, with Historical Highlights from 1789-1939*. Washington, D.C.: United States Government Printing Office, 1990.

Carson, Robert B. *Economic Issues Today: Alternative Approaches*. New York: St. Martin's Press, 1987. See Issue 5, "Government Regulation of Business: Has Deregulation Worked?"

Gregory, Paul R. *Essentials of Economics*, 2nd ed. Glenview, Ill.: Scott Foresman/Little Brown, 1990. Chapter 16.

Eatwell, John et al. *New Palgrave Series: The*

World of Economics. New York: Norton, W. W., & Co, Inc., 1991.

Peckman, Joseph A. *Who Paid the Taxes, 1966-1985?* Washington, D.C.: Brookings Institution, 1985.

Samuelson, Paul A. and Nordhaus, William D. *Economics,* 14th ed. New York: McGraw-Hill, 1992. Chapters 18 and 19.

References for Additional Teaching Strategies

Tax Whys: Understanding Taxes. Agency for Instructional Technology, Box A, Bloomington, IN 47402. Six 15-minute video programs.

Taxes and You. Agency for Instructional Technology, Box A, Bloomington, IN 47402. Two video programs and computer-aided instruction that concern the economics of taxation and tax preparation.

CHAPTER 9 REVIEW ANSWERS

Building Your Vocabulary (text page 261)

1. principle of exclusion
2. productivity principle
3. benefits received principle
4. least-likely-to-offend principle
5. ability-to-pay principle
6. public goods
7. private goods
8. pork barrel legislation
9. progressive taxes
10. regressive taxes
11. proportional taxes
12. redistribution of income
13. negative externality
14. transfer payments; transfers in kind
15. deficit; national debt
16. intergovernmental revenue
17. social insurance tax
18. personal income tax
19. corporate income tax
20. sales tax
21. property tax

Understanding Economics (text page 262)

1. Public goods are available to all citizens on an equal basis, while private goods are not and are subject to the principle of exclusion.
2. Examples of negative externality will probably deal with local cases of pollution.
3. The following would be acceptable examples of each of the four principles of taxation:
   a. Progressive income taxes are an ability-to-pay principle tax because the percent of income paid increases with taxable income.
   b. The gas tax is a benefits received principle tax because the money collected is used to maintain the roads.
   c. The cigarette tax is a least-likely-to-offend principle tax because it is collected a little at a time as cigarettes are sold.
   d. Giving firms property tax cuts if they build in certain areas of many cities is an example of a productivity principle tax. If the firm invests, its taxes go down.
4. We would need to know how much money Joe and Phil earn and what type of tax is being paid before determining if the taxes are progressive, regressive, or proportional.
5. Decisions made by the government are often intended to help particular people or to keep a politician in office. Profit or economic efficiency often has little to do

with these decisions. In business, decisions are made to increase profits and are based on achieving economic efficiency.

6. Before 1980, the four most important sources of borrowed money for the federal government were:

   a. people who bought savings bonds
   b. banks and other financial institutions
   c. businesses
   d. government trust funds

   After 1980, foreign sources of borrowing became more important to the U.S. government.

Thinking Critically About Economics
(text page 262)

1. Most public goods mentioned by students could not be purchased by most individuals. Most of your students would have to do without these things if they were not provided by the government.
2. By requiring pollution-control devices on cars the government forced car prices up but reduced the danger to the public health that had been posed by automobile pollution. The cost was paid by the customer and the producer instead of by third parties that had nothing to do with the production or use of the cars.
3. Answers to be based on graphs in Figures 9-2 and 9-3 in text:
   a. Federal—personal income tax; State—sales tax; Local—property tax
   b. Federal—payments to individuals; State—education; Local—education
4. A cut in taxes will not help just one part of the country and therefore just one politician. A new port would be in just one location and could therefore help one particular politician.
5. If the debt is held by foreign people, future interest payments will send money out of this country.
6. Between 1945 and 1980, the national debt fell as a percent of GDP. After 1980 the national debt increased as a percent of GDP.

Consumer Skills Projects (text page 262)

1. Your students will probably find that people will not generally agree upon where spending cuts should be made. The personal interests of students and adults may affect their decisions about the cuts. Because people have differing opinions about the value of each of these government programs, cutting the budget is difficult for government.
2. Items for your bulletin board may include goods and services such as sanitation, education, transportation, and police and fire protection—things individuals cannot easily provide for themselves.

CHAPTER 10

Inflation, Unemployment, and the Distribution of Income (text pages 264–287)

SECTION A. The Costs of Unemployment (text pages 267–270)

Objectives (Lesson Focus)

Upon completion of this section, students will be able to:

- Define, identify examples of, and explain frictional, seasonal, cyclical, and structural unemployment.
- Explain the meaning of the term *discouraged worker*.

Preparation (Instruction: Pre-teaching—Vocabulary or Activity)

1. Discussion Introduce this section by identifying the largest single employer in the area of your school. Ask your students to describe what would happen in your community if this firm closed down. People who had worked for the firm would be affected first but soon others would be too. Former employees would not be able to spend as much money, so local businesses and their employees would suffer. Banks would be hurt if people could not pay back loans. The local government would collect less money in sales taxes and might have to lay off some workers. Make the point that unemployment would strike those who worked for the firm first but that its effects would eventually spread to the entire community.

2. The Personal Narrative The Personal Narrative in Section A is a conversation between people who are waiting in line to receive unemployment compensation checks. Each of the subjects of the Narrative is unemployed for a different reason and demonstrates a different type of unemployment.

The Narrative demonstrates four basic types of unemployment and describes problems associated with each. It shows different reasons for unemployment and demonstrates how unemployment affects people in different ways.

Teaching Suggestions (Modeling/Guided Practice)

1. Ask each student to identify the specific job they would like to hold in ten years. Then have them explain, either orally or in writing, how they believe this job would or would not be affected by a future recession in the economy. You may want to use their answers to lead into a discussion of career choice.
2. Invite a person who does hiring for a local firm to come to talk to your class. Ask this person to talk about what he or she looks for when interviewing a potential employee. You could also ask the speaker to discuss possible causes for a current employee to be fired. Use this information to start a discussion of how students can prepare themselves to find the job they want.

Lesson Checkpoint

Text: Self-Check, text page 270
Answers

1. Because of frictional unemployment—people moving within the work force—there will always be at least 4 to 5 percent unemployment.
2. Structural unemployment is considered to be the most serious type because to remedy it requires training, which is a long and costly process for both the individual and the economy as a whole.
3. The government classifies discouraged workers as those who have given up in their search for employment.

Follow-up Assignments (Independent Practice/Extension/Homework)

1. Text: Applying What You Have Learned, text page 270
Answers

(1) a. Jerry represented structural unemployment.
b. Tina represented frictional unemployment.
c. Shawn represented seasonal unemployment.
d. James represented cyclical unemployment.

(2) Students could (a) develop good math and reading skills, which would help them move from one type of job to another if it became necessary, (b) broaden their knowledge to include many different things that would help them in the labor market, and (c) train for jobs that will always be necessary, such as in the health care industry.

2. Almost all students know an adult who has changed jobs, either through choice or necessity. Assign your students to interview at least one such adult. Have them ask the following questions and report their findings to the class:

a. What was your previous job and why did you leave it?
b. What is your current job and how long did it take you to find it?
c. Do you believe your new job is better or worse than your old job? Why do you believe this?
d. Did you suffer any economic hardship when you changed jobs? If so, describe the hardship.
e. Did you need any special training to qualify for your new job that you did not need for your previous job?

Help your students identify the type of unemployment involved in each job change reported. Were all people affected in the same ways by their job change?

3. Teacher's Resource Binder: Critical Thinking Activity, Chapter 10 (answers in Binder).

Section Evaluation

Self-Check, text page 270
Understanding Economics, questions 1 and 2 (Chapter 10 Review, text pages 284–286)

SECTION B. Life with Inflation (text pages 271–276)

Objectives (Lesson Focus)

Upon completion of this section, students will be able to:

- Explain how the consumer price index is determined and used.
- Explain the difference between demand-pull inflation and cost-push inflation and recognize examples of each.
- Describe the effects of inflation and explain why it does not affect all people equally.

Preparation (Instruction: Pre-teaching—Vocabulary or Activity)

1. Discussion Introduce this section by asking each student to list five items they frequently buy. Ask them to explain what they would do if the price of these items doubled. Point out that although prices have not recently doubled in the United States, they did increase slightly over 100 percent between 1971 and 1980. Discuss different ways in which people react to higher prices. They can

a. decide not to buy as many items.
b. buy the same items and save less for the future.
c. demand higher wages or profits.
d. buy lower quality, less expensive goods instead.
e. take a second job to earn more money.

Point out that not all people are equally able to do these things. A person who is retired and lives on a fixed income is not in a position to demand higher wages. He or she may also be too sick or weak to take a job and thus may be forced to do without needed goods or services. A person who is young, healthy, and holds a good job is less likely to be harmed by inflation.

2. The Personal Narrative The Personal Narrative in Section B describes how people are affected by inflation. The subjects of the Narrative are several young men who have gone to a movie where they find the price of admission has been increased. This forces them to choose between either paying the higher price and giving up other things they would have liked to buy or not going to the movie.

The Narrative discusses several possible causes of inflation and different ways in which people react to it. The Narrative also shows that people are not equally affected by inflation.

Teaching Suggestions (Modeling/Guided Practice)

1. Tell your students to imagine that they have asked one of their parents for ten dollars to help pay for a date. Instead of the money, they receive a speech about their parent's first job in 1967, which only paid $1.40 an hour. Assign them to write an essay in which they logically explain why the amount that could be earned in 1967 has little to do with the present.
2. Explain that one of the most important causes of inflation is the *expectation* of inflation. Ask your students to describe what they would do in each of the following situations if they honestly believed prices would increase 12 percent next year.

   a. They are negotiating for a wage increase for next year.
   b. They are deciding what price to charge for their product.
   c. They are deciding how much interest they will accept from someone who wants to borrow money from them.
   d. They are deciding how much more they want for a piece of property they have decided to sell.
   e. They are considering whether or not to take a job that pays the minimum wage.

   Point out that in each of these cases the expectation of inflation will encourage people to make decisions that will tend to cause inflation. The expectation of inflation is a self-fulfilling prophecy. If we all believe there will be inflation, it will probably take place.
3. Not all items are affected equally by inflation. The value of some items tends to increase with an increase in prices, while the value of other items does not. Explain that many people try to "hedge" against inflation by investing in different ways. Ask your students which of the following they would rather have if prices were increasing at 8 percent:

   a. $10,000 in cash
   b. $10,000 deposited in a bank that pays 6 percent interest
   c. $10,000 invested in the stock of a utility that pays an 8 percent dividend
   d. $10,000 invested in land near a place where the state is thinking of building an important highway
   e. $10,000 invested in gold and silver coins

   Point out that the possibility of a higher return is associated with greater amounts of risk. Investing in gold coins may have a high potential for return, but it also has substantial risk. There is the possibility that the price of gold will go down or that its increase in value will not keep up with inflation. People who have no money to invest, of course, are not in a position to hedge against inflation and may be hurt the most.

Lesson Checkpoint

Text: Self-Check, text page 276
Answers

1. The CPI (Consumer Price Index) is found through a survey of several hundred goods and services. The prices for the goods and services are totaled and compared with their levels at the base year.
2. Cost-push inflation is associated with a movement of the supply curve to the left.
3. Demand-pull inflation is associated with a movement of the demand curve to the right.

Follow-up Assignments (Independent Practice/Extension/Homework)

Text: Applying What You Have Learned, text page 276
Answer

In the situation presented in the Personal Narrative, increases in the rental price of the property where the theater was located and in the wages paid to theater employees contributed to increases in theater ticket and concession prices.

Section Evaluation

Self-Check, text page 276
Understanding Economics, questions 3–6 (Chapter 10 Review, text pages 284–286)

SECTION C. The Distribution of Wealth and Income (text pages 277–282)

Objectives (Lesson Focus)

Upon completion of this section, students will be able to:

- Explain why poverty is not the same in all countries.
- Explain the difference between income and wealth.
- Read a Lorenz Curve.

Preparation (Instruction: Pre-teaching—Vocabulary or Activity)

1. Discussion Introduce this section by asking your students how much income they would have to earn to feel that they were rich. Remind them that it is not really the income that they care about but what the income will buy. As long as we can produce a limited supply of goods and services, there can only be a limited number of rich people.

Ask them what characteristics of a person's standard of living would indicate that he was poor. Is poverty not having a place to live and food to eat, or is it not owning a car or a new television set? Does poverty have anything to do with how people feel about themselves? Could a person live in a log cabin in a forest, eating only what he grew and gathered for himself, and not be poor?

Try to help your students reach a consensus about what makes a person rich or poor. Ask them to what degree they feel society has a responsibility to aid poor people.

2. The Personal Narrative The Personal Narrative in Section C describes how one person is aware of differences in the distribution of income and wealth. The subject of the Narrative is a young man who sees a world in which some people are very wealthy while others are in need. He does not understand why there is such inequity in a country that has so much wealth.

The Narrative points out problems that are related to the unequal distribution of income and wealth in the United States. It concludes with a common assumption that giving poor people more income would solve their problems. The remainder of the section will show that this is not necessarily a correct assumption.

Teaching Suggestions (Modeling/Guided Practice)

Explain that there is disagreement among government leaders over whether new technology will reduce or increase poverty. Some people say new machines will produce more goods which will allow more people to have a better standard of living. Others argue that new machines will take low-skill jobs from poor people while they earn greater profits for the wealthy. They believe that new technology will make the difference between the rich and the poor even larger than it is now.

Discuss this question with your students: What will new technology do to the distribution of income and wealth? Point out that to remain competitive in the world economy, the United States is almost compelled to invest in new technology. Can we afford to be inefficient in order to protect jobs for some people?

Lesson Checkpoint

Text: Self-Check, text page 282
Answers

1. The federal government's definition of poverty is based on studies that provide an estimate of what is necessary to supply an adequate diet for a family of four living in a city.
2. Income is a flow of value; wealth is an accumulation of value.
3. A Lorenz Curve is used to show the distribution of income.

Follow-up Assignments (Independent Practice/Extension/Homework)

1. Text: Applying What You Have Learned, text page 282
   Answers

   Although there are many possible answers, students should recognize that people who live in poverty have many problems beyond a lack of money. Many poor people may not know how to use sudden, large amounts of money to make permanent improvements in their standard of living. They might use it for things that have no permanent value, instead of investing in improving their skills and education.
2. Have each of your students survey five adults and report their findings to the class. They should ask each adult the following questions:
   a. What does poverty mean in the United States?
   b. Do you feel there are more or fewer poor people in this country now than there were five years ago?
   c. What reasons can you give for any change in the number of poor people over the past five years?
   d. Do you expect the number of poor people to increase or decrease over the next five years?
   e. Would you be willing to pay higher taxes so the government could give more aid to poor people?

Section Evaluation

Self-Check, text page 282
Understanding Economics, questions 7 and 8 (Chapter 10 Review, text pages 284–286)

ADDITIONAL MATERIALS FOR CHAPTER 10

Chapter Evaluation

Teacher's Resource Binder: Chapter 10 Quiz

Reteaching and Extension

See the *Teacher's Resource Binder* and the *Student Activity Book* for additional handouts and activities for Chapter 10.

TEACHER'S BIBLIOGRAPHY FOR CHAPTER 10

Economics Sources

Bloom, Howard S. *Back to Work: Testing Reemployment Services for Displaced Workers.* Kalamazoo, Mich.: Upjohn, W. E., Institute for Employment Research, 1990.

Brown, C. V. and Jackson, P. M. *Education, Unemployment & the Labor Market.* New York: Taylor and Francis, 1991.

Chesshyre, Robert. *Cost of Living.* New York: Aperture, 1991.

Geographic Profile of Employment & Unemployment, 1989. Labor Statistics Bureau Bulletin Series: No. 2361, Department of Labor, Washington, D.C., 1990.

Miller, Roger LeRoy. *Economics Today,* 7th ed. New York: HarperCollins, 1991, Chapter 7.

A Primer on Inflation. The Federal Reserve Bank of New York, 33 Liberty Street, New York, NY 10045, 1984.

Thurow, Lester C. *Dangerous Currents: The State of Economics.* New York: Random House, 1984.

References for Additional Teaching Strategies

Gordon, Sanford. *Economics USA, a Resource Guide for Teachers.* New York: Joint Council on Economic Education, 1988.

Mansfield, Edwin, and Behravesh, Nariman. *Telecourse Study Guide for Economics USA.* New York: Norton, 1992. Chapters 4 and 7. This text and the previous reference provide exercises for and are keyed to *Economics USA,* a television course developed by the Southern California Consortium.

Miller, Roger LeRoy, and Shannon, Russell. *The Economics of Macro Issues.* St. Paul, Minn.: West, 1989, Chapters 17, 18, 19, and 20.

Morton, John et al. *High School Economics Courses.* New York: Joint Council on Current Issues, Educational Publications, Close Up Foundation, 1235 Jefferson Davis Highway, Arlington, VA 22202. Yearly publication of critical economic, political, and social issues.

CHAPTER 10 REVIEW ANSWERS

Building Your Vocabulary (text page 285)

1. inflation
2. consumer price index
3. cost-push inflation
4. demand-pull inflation
5. income; wealth
6. base year
7. frictional unemployment
8. structural unemployment
9. cyclical unemployment
10. discouraged workers
11. seasonal unemployment
12. Lorenz Curve
13. poverty

Understanding Economics (text page 285)

1. Student examples should be:

   a. someone who is unemployed short term and is between jobs

   b. someone who loses employment during a particular time of each year

   c. someone who has lost employment due to a recession

   d. someone who has lost employment and will require retraining

2. A person who is designated as unemployed by the government is actively looking for work while a discouraged worker has given up trying to find work.

3. Factors that could cause the supply curve to shift to the left include an increase in the cost of labor or of raw materials. This would cause cost-push inflation.

4. Factors that could cause the demand curve to shift to the right include an increase in consumer income or an increase in government spending. This would cause demand-pull inflation.
5. The consumer price index is found by surveying several hundred items in several thousand outlets each month. Some items are counted more often than others because consumers buy them more often. The total for each month is compared to the total from some base time. Changes are expressed as percentage changes of this base time.
6. People that lend money can be hurt by inflation if it makes the purchasing power of the money they are paid back less than the money they lent out.
7. Poverty is measured in relation to what other people in the communities have. Most poor people in the United States are not starving and most have a place to live. In many other countries this is not the case. In many parts of Africa, for example, poverty means starvation.
8. Income is a flow of value while wealth is an accumulation of value.

Thinking Critically About Economics
(text page 286)

1. Structural unemployment is the worst type of unemployment for both the economy and the individual because it requires retraining. This is a long expensive process. During this retraining period, the worker will add little value to production or to the support of his or her family.
2. Possible reasons for becoming a discouraged worker include:
   a. lack of an adequate education
   b. lack of job experience
   c. lack of success in job hunting
   d. poor health
   e. old age
3. Possible reasons for the different rates of employment include:
   a. discrimination in hiring
   b. different quality of education available to different groups
   c. different socioeconomic backgrounds
4. The increase in the price of crude oil caused cost-push inflation because crude oil is a basic raw material for many types of products. This increase in the cost of production was passed on to customers in the form of higher prices.
5. Four possible answers illustrating how inflation hurts people are:
   a. reducing the value of their savings
   b. reducing their ability to buy goods and services
   c. forcing interest rates up
   d. making it harder to sell products to other countries
6. If everyone had the same standard of living, there would be little reason to work hard to produce goods and services. The number of products manufactured would probably fall.
7. Student answers should make it clear that they understand poverty is defined in terms of community standards and not by absolutes.

Consumer Skills Projects (text page 286)

1. Your students will probably find that people who have been unemployed for an extended period of time have a differ-

ent outlook on life than people who have never experienced such economic hardship. Some may react by becoming very cautious; others may have a more "live-for-today" attitude.

2. Your students will probably find that the prices of some items have changed very little over the past ten years, while others have increased a great deal. Help them to understand why there has not been uniform inflation. What does this tell them about the relative demand and supply for these different items?
3. It may be hard to measure changes, but there should be a small trend to a less equal distribution of income. If this trend can be found, discuss what causes there may have been for the change and what it shows about changes in the U.S. society as well as the economy.

Chapter 11

Money and the Economy (text pages 288–317)

SECTION A. What Money Is and Where It Came From (text pages 291–296)

Objectives (Lesson Focus)

Upon completion of this section, students will be able to:

- Explain what money is in economic terms.
- Identify the functions and characteristics of money.
- Explain the relationship between changes in the money supply, changes in the quantity of products offered for sale, and changes in price levels.

Preparation (Instruction: Pre-teaching—Vocabulary or Activity)

1. Discussion Introduce this section by describing a society in which there is no money. All transactions are made through barter. Ask your students to explain why each of the following transactions would be difficult in such a society. Identify the function or characteristic of money demonstrated in each situation.

a. You own a cow that you want to trade for a pig and a new tent. The pig belongs to one person, while someone else owns the tent you want. *(money must be divisible)*

b. You want to trade some chickens for a new cooking pot. The person who makes cooking pots does not want any chickens. *(money must be accepted)*

c. You want to save up for a new house. You grow fresh fruit for a living. *(money is a store of value)*

d. You want to trade your goat for eight chickens, but the owner of the chickens will only give you six of them in exchange for your goat. *(money is a measure of value)*

e. You make stone corn grinders for a living. You have to pay a large debt to someone who lives 50 miles away. *(money must be portable)*

Discuss the fact that all advanced economic systems require a form of money that possesses the characteristics listed in the text, so that it can perform the functions of money in the economy.

2. The Personal Narrative The Personal Narrative in Section A illustrates that something which has value does not necessarily have to be money. The subject of the Narrative is a young man who has inherited a gold watch from his grandfather. He recognizes that the watch has value but that it would be difficult to use its value to buy anything else without first selling the watch. The watch is not money for many reasons, which include the fact that people do not agree on the amount of value it has and that its value is not divisible.

Teaching Suggestions (Modeling/Guided Practice)

1. Ask students how they would feel if an uncle had left them $1 million. They would probably be happy about the money although they might not be happy with the death of their uncle. Ask them to identify several items they would buy with the money.

   Extend the example by telling the students that the uncle was very rich and left everyone in the United States a million dollars. How much better off would the students be if everyone had the same amount of additional money? Would they be able to buy the items they identified above?

   Simply because people had more money to spend would not mean additional products would be available to buy. The extra money would force prices up. Each individual would end up being able to buy about the same amount of goods and services as before. Remind your students that money is not important: it is what you can buy with money that people care about. Discuss how this example relates to Figure 11-1 in the text.
2. Use Discussion Topic 17 from the *Teacher's Resource Binder* to reinforce the nature of money and the significance of the money supply.

Lesson Checkpoint

Text: Self-Check, text page 296
Answers

1. Economists define *money* as a claim on something that possesses value; in other words, money represents value but rarely has any intrinsic value of its own.
2. The three functions of money identified in this section included: money as a medium of exchange, as a measure of value, and as a store of value.
3. When the availability of money grows more rapidly than the amount of goods and services offered for sale, prices go up and inflation exists.

Follow-up Assignments (Independent Practice/Extension/Homework)

1. Text: Applying What You Have Learned, text page 296
   Answers

   Possible problems the young man could have encountered in trying to use his watch as money include:

   a. The watch lacked a clear definition of value.
   b. The watch would not have been universally accepted.
   c. The value of the watch was not easily divisible.
   d. There was no way to determine if the value of the watch would remain the same in the future.
2. Some adults do not understand the relationship between prices and the amount of money in circulation. Ask students to

survey five adults who do not work at their school. They should ask this single question: "What would happen if the government simply printed the money it needs to pay its bills?" Have students individually report the results of their surveys to the class as a whole. What percentage of adults surveyed realized such a policy would cause inflation?

Section Evaluation

Self-Check, text page 296
Understanding Economics, questions 1 and 2 (Chapter 11 Review, text pages 314–316)

SECTION B. Checks, Money, and the Economy (text pages 297–301)

Objectives (Lesson Focus)

Upon completion of this section, students will be able to:

- Follow the flow of a check through the economy using the chart provided in this text.
- Explain what the term "reserve requirement" means.
- Explain how money can be expanded through checking accounts by the banking system.
- Recognize the meaning, and explain the use of, the expansion multiplier.

Preparation (Instruction: Pre-teaching—Vocabulary or Activity)

1. Discussion Introduce this section by asking students to list three of the most important financial transactions they ever expect to make. They will probably identify such transactions as buying a house or a car, paying college tuition, starting a business, or paying for an expensive vacation.

Consolidate the individual lists on the chalkboard. Ask your students if there are any transactions on the list that they would expect to make in cash. Point out the fact that almost all large transactions are carried out with demand deposits or checks. This means that the government must control the checking system if it wants to control spending in the economy.

2. The Personal Narrative The Personal Narrative in Section B describes how one family uses demand deposits to pay its bills and how the checking system is part of the money supply in our economy. The subject of the Narrative is a young woman whose father uses checks to pay the family's bills. She describes how she came to understand how checks work when she got a job. She also realizes that if the government wants to control the money supply, it must first control the checking system.

The Narrative demonstrates how checks are used in our economic system and why they are such an important part of our money supply.

Teaching Suggestions (Modeling/Guided Practice)

1. Ask your students to sit in a large circle. Hand one student 200 fake one dollar bills and a numbered sheet of paper for tabulation. (The money must be entirely in ones; using larger bills for this exercise would be confusing.) Tell the first student to write $200 on the paper after number 1. Then tell the student to keep twenty of the dollars and to pass the remaining $180 and the tabulation paper to the next student. This student writes $180 on the sheet, keeps $18, and passes the remaining money and the tabulation paper on to the next student. The pro-

cess is repeated until all students have done it, keeping 10 percent of the money (rounded to the nearest full dollar) and passing on the rest. When all students have completed the process, total the amounts on the tabulation paper.

Explain how this exercise is similar to the expansion of an original $200 deposit through the banking system when there is a 10 percent reserve requirement. Each time money is passed from one student to another, they are to assume that a bank has made a loan, the money has been spent, and redeposited into the banking system. Each successive student represents another bank that must keep 10 percent of the deposit on reserve. The remaining 90 percent can be loaned out as the next step in the process.

The table below indicates how much each student should pass on.

Student/Amount	Student/Amount
1/$180	16/$37
2/$162	17/$33
3/$146	18/$30
4/$131	19/$27
5/$118	20/$24
6/$106	21/$22
7/$ 96	22/$20
8/$ 86	23/$18
9/$ 77	24/$16
10/$ 70	25/$14
11/$ 63	26/$13
12/$ 56	27/$12
13/$ 51	28/$10
14/$ 46	29/$ 9
15/$ 41	30/$ 8

2. Repeat the same process as above, but this time use a reserve requirement of 12 percent. Note the difference in the expansion of the original $200. Again, the amounts in the table below have been rounded to the nearest full dollar, and are what should be passed on.

Student/Amount	Student/Amount
1/$176	16/$26
2/$155	17/$23
3/$136	18/$20
4/$120	19/$18
5/$106	20/$16
6/$ 93	21/$14
7/$ 82	22/$12
8/$ 72	23/$11
9/$ 63	24/$ 9
10/$ 56	25/$ 8
11/$ 49	26/$ 7
12/$ 43	27/$ 6
13/$ 38	28/$ 6
14/$ 33	29/$ 5
15/$ 29	30/$ 4

Compare the total expansion with the two differing reserve requirements of 12 percent and 10 percent. Point out how powerful a change in the reserve requirement would be when the entire economy is considered. A one-percent change in the reserve requirement would change the money supply by many billions of dollars.

Lesson Checkpoint

Text: Self-Check, text page 301
Answers

1. More than half of all spending is done with checks.
2. The reserve requirement is the percentage of the deposit that the law says a bank must keep on reserve.
3. Banks normally keep more money in reserve than is required, and some people hold onto cash rather than depositing it in banks.

Follow-up Assignments (Independent Practice/Extension/Homework)

1. Text: Applying What You Have Learned, text page 301
Answers

Advantages of checks include:

a. They are safer to use than cash.

b. They are easier to carry than large amounts of cash.

c. They provide a record of transactions.

d. They can only be used by the person to whom they are written.

2. Ask your students to survey their parents concerning what part of their total spending is done with checks. Students should also ask their parents to identify the types of payments they make with checks. Have the students report their findings to the class. Students should discover that many adults do most of their spending with checks. Are there any generalizations that can be made about the kind of spending carried out with checks?

Section Evaluation

Self-Check, text page 301

Understanding Economics, questions 3–5 (Chapter 11 Review, text pages 314–316)

SECTION C. Banks Are in Business to Make a Profit (text pages 302–305)

Objectives (Lesson Focus)

Upon completion of this section, students will be able to:

- Explain why banks would follow procyclical policies if this were permitted by the Federal Reserve System.
- Explain the function and importance of the Federal Deposit Insurance Corporation.
- Identify a cause of S&L failures.

Preparation (Instruction: Pre-teaching—Vocabulary or Activity)

1. Discussion Introduce this section by asking each student to think of their best friend. Then tell them to imagine that this person asked to borrow $500 (they should also imagine they had the money to lend if they wanted to). Ask your students to make a list of reasons that might cause them to make the loan. Also ask them to make a second list of reasons that could cause them to deny the loan. Ask them which of their reasons would be important to a bank and which would not. Point out that although friendship may be an important reason for them, it would have little to do with the decision of a bank. Remind them that banks are businesses that intend to make a profit.

2. The Personal Narrative The Personal Narrative in Section C describes how an individual business can be hurt by a downturn in the local economy and how these problems can be aggravated by the actions of banks. The subject of the Narrative is a young man whose father works as a gardener. When there is a water shortage, many of his customers are not allowed to use his services. Because his business is not doing well, his bank is unwilling to loan him the money he needs.

The Narrative demonstrates that banks are in business to make a profit. The decisions they make are based on economic conditions and their perception of risk. Banks will not loan money unless they believe it will be repaid.

Teaching Suggestions (Modeling/Guided Practice)

1. Invite a loan officer from a bank to talk to your students. The topic of the interview should be the importance of a good

credit rating and how a young person can establish such a credit rating. (If you can't find a loan officer who is willing to meet with your class, it may be possible to find one who will agree to be interviewed by a student.) Whether you send a student to interview a loan officer or have one visit your class, take the time to prepare good questions. You do not want your guest to think the interview is a waste of time. A list of possible questions appears below:

a. What are the advantages of having a good credit rating?
b. What can a young person do to develop a good credit rating?
c. If a bank turns you down when you ask for a loan, what rights do you have?
d. If a person feels he or she has been unjustly denied credit, what can he or she do?
e. How does a bank decide how much money it is willing to loan to a person or to a business?
f. If a person fails to make payments on a loan, what actions will a bank take?
g. Why are there different interest rates for different types of loans?
h. What is the effect of getting married or divorced on a person's credit rating?

2. The following list of items often appears on a bank's balance sheet. Help your class determine where each item would appear— on the left side with assets or on the right side with liabilities. Assets are property and cash (capital) and credits that a bank has with customers. Liabilities are credits that depositors or investors have at the bank.

a. a one-year certificate of deposit (right side)
b. a car loan it has made (left side)
c. a deposit in a checking account (right side)
d. a loan it has received from another bank (right side)
e. rolls of coins (left side)
f. its office building (left side)
g. its stockholders' equity (right side)
h. money it has borrowed from the Federal Reserve System (right side)
i. government securities it has purchased (left side)

3. Emphasize the importance of the Federal Deposit Insurance Corporation. Ask your students if they would be willing to deposit their savings in a bank that did not belong to the FDIC. Remind them that prior to 1935 there was no FDIC; if banks failed, depositors often lost part or all of their savings. Help your students appreciate the fact that without the FDIC our banking system could not work as well as it does. Many people would not deposit their money into banks. This would reduce the effectiveness of the expansion of money.

Lesson Checkpoint

Text: Self-Check, text page 305
Answers

1. Banks earn a profit by charging their borrowers a higher interest rate than they pay their depositors.
2. *Pro-cyclical* refers to policies that would increase any existing economic trends.
3. The FDIC insures deposits in order to maintain public confidence in banks.

Follow-up Assignments (Independent Practice/Extension/Homework)

1. Text: Applying What You Have Learned, text page 305
Answers

Students will likely include the following three factors to explain why the bank considered the man in the Personal Narrative to be a poor credit risk for a loan.

a. His debts and other obligations exceeded his financial capacity to repay them in a timely manner.
b. His cyclical employment as a gardener created an unstable demand for his services; therefore, his employment record was insecure.
c. He had few assets to pledge as collateral for a loan, and little value had been built up in his residence.

2. Teacher's Resource Binder: Critical Thinking Activity, Chapter 11 (answers in Binder).

Section Evaluation

Self-Check, text page 305
Understanding Economics, questions 6 and 7 (Chapter 11 Review, text pages 314–316)

SECTION D. What the Federal Reserve System Does (text pages 306–311)

Objectives (Lesson Focus)

Upon completion of this section, students will be able to:

- Describe the conditions that resulted in the creation of the Federal Reserve System.
- Define monetary policy and explain the basic tools of monetary policy used by the Federal Reserve System: adjusting the reserve requirement, discount rate, and open market operations.
- Describe several examples of uses the Federal Reserve has made of its monetary powers.

Preparation (Instruction: Pre-teaching—Vocabulary or Activity)

1. Discussion Introduce this section by asking students to pretend they are in business and are considering five potential investments. Remind them that they are in business to make a profit. They would only borrow money if they expected to earn more than the cost of the loan. Their firm would have to borrow money to pay for any of the projects they are considering. The table below indicates the expected rate of return (profit) from each possible investment.

Investment	Expected Return	Cost
1. a new truck to make quicker deliveries	8.1%	$ 20,000
2. a new machine for the assembly line	10.1%	$ 70,000
3. a new computer to control inventory	12.1%	$ 50,000
4. an expansion of the factory	9.1%	$250,000
5. insulation to reduce heating costs	11.1%	$ 80,000

Help your students figure out how much money the firm would borrow at each of the possible interest rates listed below (answers are provided in the second column):

Interest Rate	Amount Borrowed
8%	$470,000
9%	$450,000
10%	$200,000
11%	$130,000
12%	$50,000
13%	$0

Use this exercise to show your students how important interest rates are to business spending and therefore to employment and earnings in the economy as a whole.

2. The Personal Narrative The Personal Narrative in Section D demonstrates the importance of Federal Reserve policies to the economy. The subject of the Narrative is a young man whose father is an architect. The family's income is sensitive to changes in interest rates. When interest rates grow, there is often less construction and consequently less work for his father. When interest rates fall, there is often more contruction and work for his father. The young man realizes that interest rates are affected by decisions made by the Federal Reserve System. He sees that there is a relationship between his father's success and the actions of the Federal Reserve System, but he doesn't understand how the relationship works.

The Narrative shows students that decisions made by the Federal Reserve System are important both to the economy as a whole and to each individual.

Teaching Suggestions (Modeling/Guided Practice)

1. Ask your students to pretend they have all become members of the Federal Reserve's Board of Governors. They have agreed that too many loans are being made. Businesses are spending far too much money and are trying to hire more workers than there are people looking for work. People are also borrowing and spending large amounts of money. Although the situation is not yet totally out of control, the rate of inflation is clearly increasing. There have been three suggestions made on what should be done. Ask your students which of the following suggestions should or should not be put into action. Help them explain and evaluate each suggestion, either in writing or orally.

   Suggestion 1: Increase the reserve requirement on demand deposits from 10 to 12 percent.

   Suggestion 2: Increase the discount rate from 5 percent to 6 percent.

   Suggestion 3: Sell $1 billion worth of government securities.

2. Divide your students into groups of three to five students. For each describe one of the following situations. Ask each group to either (a) agree on the best policy for the Federal Reserve to follow in their situation *or* (b) explain why a policy change by the Fed would not solve the problem. If you feel that these situations are too challenging for your students, you could choose to discuss them together in class. (For your reference, the desired student responses to each individual situation are included here as well. Suggested responses are italicized and parenthesized directly following each respective situation.)

   Situation 1

   The economy is in a very deep depression. Individuals and businesses seem afraid to borrow money no matter what the interest rates are. *(If individuals and businesses are really afraid to borrow money, there may be little the Fed can do to get the economy moving. People could simply ignore extra money that was put into circulation.)*

   Situation 2

   The economy has had a high rate of inflation over the past year, largely because the cost of imported goods and raw materials has increased by over 35 percent. *(If the inflation is caused by increased prices for imports, there is probably little the Fed can do to solve the problem. People in other countries who sell to the United States often do not care what interest rates are in this country.)*

Situation 3

There has been a large decline in new housing construction because people who want to buy homes have found it difficult to borrow money or don't want to pay high interest rates. *The Fed would probably buy government securities to increase the money in circulation and to reduce interest rates. It would be less likely to lower the discount rate or the reserve requirement.)*

Situation 4

Interest rates are a little lower than the Fed would like them to be for all types of loans. *(The Fed would probably sell a few government securities to decrease the money in circulation and to increase interest rates. It would be less likely to increase the discount rate or the reserve requirement.)*

Situation 5

The Treasury has been borrowing large amounts of money by selling government securities. This has resulted in a temporary shortage of money for banks to loan to other people and in higher interest rates. *(The Fed might ignore what the Treasury is doing or it could choose to buy more government securities to supply more money and keep interest rates down. This policy could lead to higher rates of inflation.)*

Lesson Checkpoint

Text: Self-Check, text page 311
Answers

1. The most important job of the Federal Reserve is to maintain a stable supply of money.
2. Changes in the reserve requirement have a very large effect on the economy; therefore, the Board of Governors initiates such changes as infrequently as possible.
3. The Fed uses monetary policy to stabilize the economy.

Follow-up Assignments (Independent Practice/Extension/Homework)

1. Text: Applying What You Have Learned, text page 311
Answers

a. If the Fed increases the discount rate, banks will be less likely to borrow from the Fed and the money in circulation will decrease.
b. If the Fed lowers the reserve requirement, banks will have to keep less money in reserve, loans will increase, and the money in circulation will also increase.
c. If the Fed buys government securities, bank deposits will go up as the bonds are paid for and the money in circulation will also increase.
d. If the Fed sells government securities, bank deposits will go down to pay for the bonds and the money in circulation will also decrease.

e. If the Fed raises the reserve requirement, banks will have to keep more money on reserve, loans will decrease, and the money in circulation will also decrease.

f. If the Fed lowers the discount rate, banks will be more likely to borrow from the Fed and the amount of money in circulation will increase.

2. Ask your students to take a survey of five adults. They should ask each person what the Federal Reserve System does. Then they should ask how much the person would care if interest rates for consumer loans went up 5 percent. Ask students to report the results of their survey to the class. It would not be surprising to find that many people who believe interest rates are important know little about the Federal Reserve System.

Section Evaluation

Self-Check, text page 311

Understanding Economics, questions 9–10 (Chapter 11 Review, text pages 314–316)

ADDITIONAL MATERIALS FOR CHAPTER 11

Chapter Evaluation

Teacher's Resource Binder: Chapter 11 Quiz

Reteaching and Extension

See the *Teacher's Resource Binder* and the *Student Activity Book* for additional handouts and activities for Chapter 11.

TEACHER'S BIBLIOGRAPHY FOR CHAPTER 11

Economics Sources

Clark, Simon. *Keynesianism, Monetarism, & the Crisis of the State.* Brookfield, Vt.: Gower Publishing Co., 1988.

Galbraith, John Kenneth. *Money: Whence It Came, Where It Went.* Boston: Houghton Mifflin, 1975.

McConnell, Campbell R. and Brue, Stanley L. *Economics Principles, Problems, and Policies.* 12th ed., New York: McGraw Hill, 1993. Chapters 15, 16, and 17.

Mishkin, Frederic S. *The Economics of Money, Banking and Financial Markets*, 3rd ed., New York: HarperCollins, 1992.

Open Market Operations. Federal Reserve Bank of New York, 1985.

References for Additional Teaching Strategies

See the Federal Reserve Systems, *Public Information Materials*, Federal Reserve Bank of New York, 33 Liberty Street, New York, NY 10045, for a comprehensive guide to materials available from the entire system.

Gordon, Sanford. *Economics USA, a Resource Guide for Teachers.* New York: Joint Council on Economic Education, 1988.

Mansfield, Edwin, and Behravesh, Nariman. *Telecourse Study Guide for Economics USA.* New York: Norton, 1992. Chapters 8, 9, and 13. This text and the previous reference provide exercises for and are keyed to *Economics USA*, a television course developed by the Southern California Consortium.

Miller, Roger LeRoy, and Shannon, Russell. *The Economics of Macro Issues*, St. Paul, Minn.: West, 1986, Chapters 22 and 23.

Morton, John et al. *High School Economics Courses.* New York: Joint Council on Economic Education, 1985, Lesson 18.

Spiselman, David. *A Teenager's Guide to Money, Banking & Finance.* Englewood Cliffs, N.J.: Messner, Division of Silver Burdett Press, Simon & Schuster, Inc., 1988.

You're Accountable. New York State Banking Department and Cornell University. A videotape with instructor's workbook on saving, spending, and borrowing.

CHAPTER 11 REVIEW ANSWERS

Building Your Vocabulary (text page 315)

1. FDIC
2. savings and loan associations
3. inflation
4. expansion of money
5. money
6. functions of money
7. characteristics of money
8. deflation
9. fiat money
10. reserve requirement
11. discount rate
12. Federal Reserve System
13. pro-cyclical
14. countercyclical
15. monetary policy
16. open market operations
17. money supply

Understanding Economics (text page 316)

1. A gold ring would not work well as money because it would not have a uniformly agreed-upon value; it would not be accepted by all people; and we do not know how much it will be worth in the future.

2. If the money supply increased by 50 percent, prices would also go up because there would be more dollars trying to buy about the same number of goods and services.

3. If a person put $100 in a checking account, the bank would be required to keep $10 on reserve. It could lend out the remaining $90.

4. If the bank loaned out the $90, this money would be spent and eventually redeposited into the banking system. This deposit would then become the basis for additional loans, spending, and deposits. This is called the expansion of money.

5. The expansion process can be controlled by the Fed by changing the reserve requirement on checking deposits or by changing the amount of money available for new deposits.

6. If banks were not regulated by the Fed, they would act in a pro-cyclical way. In a recession, they would be able to make few loans. In an expansion, they would make many loans. This would make both the recessions and expansions larger than they would have been.

7. The FDIC insures deposits in banks. If the bank fails and is unable to repay depositors, the FDIC will. In 1992, for example, the FDIC could repay depositors up to $100,000. This encourages people to put their savings into banks where it can be loaned to other people.

8. The decision-making body within the Federal Reserve System is the Board of Governors.

9. The Fed can carry out monetary policy by

a. changing the reserve requirement or the percentage of deposits that banks must keep on reserve.

b. changing the discount rate or the percentage of interest banks pay when they borrow from the Fed.

c. buying or selling government securities in open market operations, which regulates the amount of money banks have in order to expand.

Thinking Critically About Economics (text page 316)

1. It would be hard to use the land as the basis for paying for school unless it was sold and converted into cash. The land does not have a universally agreed upon value. Not everyone would want the land, and there is no way to determine its future worth.
2. Drawings should clearly demonstrate the students' understanding of the relationship between the amount of money in circulation, the quantity of products offered for sale, and the price levels.
3. The $500 deposit in a checking account can be expanded because the bank will have to keep 10 percent on reserve. The other 90 percent can be loaned out. Loans would be spend and money redeposited in the banking system. This would permit other banks to make additional loans which would support still more spending and deposits. The process would continue until total deposits had grown by several thousand dollars.
4. If the reserve requirement was increased to 12 percent, banks would have to keep larger reserves so each step in the expansion process would be smaller. The total amount of money put into circulation by the process would also be smaller.
5. If there were no FDIC, many people would be afraid to deposit their money into banks. This would reduce both the ability of banks to make loans and the amount of money in circulation.
6. If the discount rate was increased by 2½ percent, fewer banks would choose to borrow from the Fed. This would reduce the amount of money in circulation.

Consumer Skills Projects (text page 316)

1. Your students will discover that the interest rates do not differ greatly from one bank to the next. Those banks that offer higher rates are often those that are new to an area, are trying to grow, or have been in financial difficulty and have to pay higher rates to attract deposits. Likewise, rates for loans will probably be similar at different banks. A lower rate at any bank may indicate that it has more money available to lend.
2. If you can arrange for a loan officer of a bank to speak to your students, it would be both educational and helpful to their own financial future.

CHAPTER 12

Government Decisions and Economic Success (text pages 318–355)

SECTION A. Government Spending and Jobs (text pages 322–330)

Objectives (Lesson Focus)

Upon completion of this section, students will be able to:

- Recognize and explain the basic beliefs of the Classical economic theory.
- Describe how government involvement in the economic system increased after the Great Depression of the 1930s.
- Contrast the ideas of John Maynard Keynes with those of John Baptiste Say.
- Define and explain the meaning of fiscal policy.
- Define, give examples of, and explain

both automatic and discretionary fiscal policy.

- Describe various weaknesses in Keynesian economic policy; in particular, the crowding-out effect and the difficulty of dealing with inflation and unemployment at the same time.

Preparation (Instruction: Pre-teaching—Vocabulary or Activity)

1. Discussion Introduce this section by reading the following quotation from the Employment Act of 1946:

> [the federal government should] use all practical means . . . to promote maximum employment, production, and purchasing power.

Explain that although this quotation shows the law sets an objective for government policy, it *does not* require the government to find a job for everyone who wants to work.

Ask your students if they feel the government should guarantee a job to everyone who wants to work. How much would it cost to provide more than 6 million jobs (the number of unemployed people in 1991)? Would this force taxes up too much? If everyone was guaranteed a job, would people feel less pressure to work hard? Try to reach a consensus among your students over what the proper role for the government should be in providing jobs to people who are out of work.

Another related question that could be discussed is whether or not everyone who receives government aid and is able to work should be required to work, and if so, how much choice should a person have in the type of work they choose to do?

2. The Personal Narrative The Personal Narrative for Section A describes how one family benefited from a job training program provided by the federal government. The subject of the Narrative is a young woman whose widowed mother supported a family of five by working in a shirt factory until it closed. The family lived on welfare benefits for years. Finally the mother found a job working for a government training program. Although the woman's family was helped through the program, she doubts that it will accomplish its objectives for many other people.

The Narrative demonstrates accomplishments and problems that may result from government programs intended to help the poor.

Teaching Suggestions (Modeling/Guided Practice)

1. Ask your students to pretend they own a factory that makes chairs. It costs them $15 to make a chair. They would like to sell the chairs for $25. There is a major recession in the nation's economy and sales have been very poor. The firm lowered the price of its chairs to $20, but sales did not pick up much. It has been determined by market research that the firm could sell all of its chairs at $14 each. Ask your students whether they would sell their chairs at $14, or close down the factory, store the chairs they have, and wait for prices to go up.

   Next, ask your students to imagine that they worked for the same business under the same conditions. They have a contract that entitles them to a wage of $8.50 an hour. Their manager asks them to accept $6.50 per hour. Remind them that they have mortgage payments to make, children to feed, and need a new car. Ask your students if they would be willing to take a cut in pay.

With the discussion of this situation in mind, ask your students to explain why Say's law didn't work at the beginning of the Great Depression.

2. Ask your students what would happen in each of the following cases (the correct answers, according to J. M. Keynes, have been underlined):

   a. People become convinced that a major recession is about to happen so they decide to save (more or less) out of their current income.
   b. Because of this, they spend (more or less) than they otherwise would have.
   c. Total business sales therefore go (up or down).
   d. Business inventories start to (increase or decrease).
   e. This causes businesses to (lay off or hire more) workers.
   f. As a result, total income for all workers goes (up or down).
   g. The workers who have lost their jobs are unable to save anything, so total savings for all workers goes (up or down).
   h. By trying to save more, workers as a group have actually ended up saving (more or less) and national income has gone (up or down).

   Explain that Keynes called this idea the "Paradox of Thrift." When society as a whole tried to save more, it ended up saving less, because sales would go down, people would be laid off, and would not be able to save at all. Keynes said the government should increase its spending when people become worried and spend less. He claimed that this would keep total spending and employment at a steady rate and would reduce the effects of a recession.

3. To illustrate a limitation on Keynesian policy, ask students to complete the story in Discussion Topic 18 from the *Teacher's Resource Binder*. Read some of the better papers in class and discuss them.

   After your students discuss their paragraphs, point out that this is essentially what happened in the United States from 1982 to 1983. The economist Milton Friedman said that it took so long for the government to act that the country would be better off if Congress didn't try to carry out discretionary fiscal policy. By the time jobs were created by the new tax, the economy was already on the road to recovery.

Lesson Checkpoint

Text: Self-Check, text page 330
Answers

1. Classical economists believed the market economy would end a recession by lowering prices, interest rates, and wages.
2. Keynes believed that in a recession, the government should help the market along by spending more money than it took in from tax revenues.
3. Discretionary policy requires a choice of specific action to go into effect, whereas automatic fiscal policy does not.
4. The action chosen may take place too long after the economic event, thus rendering the remedial action ineffective.

Follow-up Assignments (Independent Practice/Extension/Homework)

Text: Applying What You Have Learned, text page 330
Answers

Strengths of Government-Sponsored Job Training Program

1. These programs offer job training whereby formerly unemployed workers can acquire skills to help their future employability.
2. These programs decrease government spending and taxes to support welfare and unemployment compensation programs.

Weaknesses of Government-Sponsored Job Training Program

1. The job-training programs offered to workers are impractical if work in that field does not exist in their local area.
2. Government spending that is required to fund these programs may conflict with attempts to fight inflation and high interest rates.

Section Evaluation

Self-Check, text page 330
Understanding Economics, questions 1–4 (Chapter 12 Review, text pages 352–354)

SECTION B. Government Policies and Inflation (text pages 332–337)

Objectives (Lesson Focus)

Upon completion of this section, students will be able to:

- Describe attempts by the federal government to regulate prices and/or wages.
- Explain why government price controls may cause shortages.
- Explain how supply-side economists believe it is possible to fight inflation and unemployment at the same time.

Preparation (Instruction: Pre-teaching—Vocabulary or Activity)

1. Discussion Introduce this section by asking students how they would react to a ten-percent rate of inflation if they lived on a fixed income of $745 a month and had the following expenses. Give each student a copy of the list in Discussion Topic 18 from the *Teacher's Resource Binder* and ask them where they would, or could, cut back.

Point out that even if students stop setting aside money for savings, they still would need an income next year of $770 a month just to buy the same things they are buying now. Ask your students where they would be forced to cut back. If the inflation went on year after year while their income remained unchanged, what would eventually happen? Use this exercise to demonstrate the importance of controlling inflation for people on a fixed income.

2. The Personal Narrative The Personal Narrative in Section B describes how various people are affected by inflation. The subject of the Narrative is a young woman whose grandmother is adversely affected by inflation because she lives on a fixed income. The young woman is planning to attend a junior college and faces increased transportation, tuition, and book expenses. Her father discovers that his property taxes are about to be increased. All of these people wonder why the government has not been able to limit inflation.

The Narrative demonstrates the need that many people feel for more effective government control over inflation.

Teaching Suggestions (Modeling/Guided Practice)

1. Ask your students to pretend they trap lobsters for a living. Lobster fishermen

have dangerous jobs and work hard. They expect to earn a good income. Lobsters have recently been selling for $7 a pound, and their price has gone up about 10 percent per year. Even so, many lobster fishermen have given up their jobs for other employment in recent years.

Suppose the government passed a law that said lobsters could not be sold for more than $5 a pound. This would make it impossible for lobster fishermen to earn more than $20,000 a year after they had paid all of their expenses. Ask your students how they would answer each of the following questions under such conditions:

a. What would happen to the number of lobster fishermen who would consider looking for other work?
b. What would happen to the number of lobster fishermen who would choose to invest in new boats and equipment?
c. What would happen to the supply of lobsters offered for sale over the next year or two?
d. What would happen to the number of people who would want to buy lobsters when the government forced fishermen to lower their prices to $5 per pound?
e. What problem would be caused by the government price control?

Use this example to discuss why government price controls have often led to shortages of products.

2. Discuss whether special tax breaks for elderly people are fair. Many local governments allow older people to reduce the assessed value of their property by a specified amount when they figure their property tax. Bus fares and other public services are often reduced for elderly people. They receive special consideration when they pay their income taxes. In addition to these special considerations, older people receive substantial aid from the government that is paid for by other taxpayers. Do your students support giving elderly people special treatment if it means higher taxes for other people? Why or why not?
3. The rates that public utilities are allowed to charge for electricity are set by state regulatory agencies. Such utilities operate with what is essentially a form of government price control. Many people would like to see rate requests turned down or limited. Discuss how a public utility could react to a lack of rate increases when its costs had increased. Which of the following possibilities do your students feel would be most likely? How would customers be affected by each of the following possible actions?

a. Stop paying interest on loans and dividends to stockholders. (A utility that did not pay interest could be forced into bankruptcy by its creditors. The mere possibility of such a decision would cause a utility to pay higher interest rates for money it needs to borrow. This could cause a need for even higher rates in the future.)
b. Spend less on service to its customers.
c. Spend less on investing in new equipment and replacing equipment that wears out.
d. Reduce employee salaries and benefits.
e. Reduce the number of employees.

Point out that the long-range effect of many of these decisions would hurt customers. Reducing employees could reduce service. If the utility did not invest to maintain equipment, it could face costly replacements. There could be a shortage of electrical power in the future that could cost people their jobs and hurt the area's economy.

Lesson Checkpoint

Text: Self-Check, text page 337
Answers

1. Most economists consider fiscal policy to be more effective in the control of demand-pull inflation.
2. Government price regulation has often resulted in product shortages.
3. Pressure on the government to regulate prices has lessened in recent years.

Follow-up Assignments (Independent Practice/Extension/Homework)

Text: Applying What You Have Learned, text page 337
Answers

There are many possible answers that could be given by students. Each answer should be graded according to the logic and basis of support provided. Three potential problems created by the enactment of a law that would limit prices charged to the elderly could include:

1. People under 65 could be forced to pay more to make up for those over 65 who pay less.
2. Fewer goods and services might be ordered for those over 65.
3. The government would have to spend more money to enforce the law.

Section Evaluation

Self-Check, text page 337
Understanding Economics, questions 5–7 (Chapter 12 Review, text pages 352–354)

SECTION C. Government Policy in a Global Economy (text pages 338–342)

Objectives

Upon completion of this section, students will be able to:

- Identify and explain several examples of events that have happened in the global economy that impacted the U.S. economy.
- Explain why the economic results of these events could not be effectively controlled by either U.S. government fiscal or monetary policy.
- Explain why our government is likely to have even less control over our economic system in the future.

Preparation (Instruction: Pre-teaching—Vocabulary or Activity)

1. Discussion Introduce this section by asking students to identify ways that the United States benefits from the global nature of our economic system. Examples could include any of the following:

- Our ability to buy products manufactured in other countries
- Our ability to sell products we manufacture to other countries
- Our ability to buy resources we do not possess from other countries
- Foreign competition encouraging U.S. businesses to become more efficient
- Our ability to borrow funds from other countries

Follow up this discussion by asking students to identify costs we pay as the result of the global nature of our economy. They are likely to mention the loss of U.S. jobs, our indebtedness to foreign nations, or our dependence on imported goods. They are not likely to mention the limitations placed on the effectiveness of our economic policy. Ask students the following questions:

1. If you were the leader of a country in the Middle East and you were at war with a neighboring country, would you care about the effect the war had on interest rates or taxes in the United States?
2. If you were a farmer in France, would you grow less food because your crops might force prices down for U.S. farmers?
3. If you were a citizen of Germany, would you buy a U.S. government bond that paid less interest than a bond offered for sale by your own government?
4. If you were a Japanese investor and you had just lost millions of yen in your stock market, would you care whether U.S. firms were having a hard time raising money to fund expansion?

Point out why the answers to these questions have an important impact on the U.S. economy and the ability of our government to implement economic policy. If we were not part of a global economy, the answers to these questions would not be very important to our nation.

2. The Personal Narrative The Personal Narrative in Section C describes how a young worker in a U.S. factory was affected by the increase in the cost of crude oil in the summer of 1990. The subject of the Narrative did not believe that the invasion of Kuwait by Iraq would have any impact on his personal life. He found that he was wrong, because the increased cost of oil caused his employer to lay him off and probably encouraged investment in cost-reducing equipment. Although he eventually found another job selling shoes, the subject suffered a reduction in his income and standard of living. Through this process there was little our government could have done with either monetary or fiscal policy that would have kept the price of oil down or protected the American economy from the impact of increased costs.

The Narrative demonstrates the limitations on the ability of U.S. economic policy to deal with problems that are the result of the global nature of our economy. In your discussion of this Narrative you should point out that some Americans did benefit from the increased cost of oil. Businesses and workers in oil-producing states received more income. Also when the subject's employer invested in labor-saving devices, the prices of the counter tops were kept lower than they otherwise would have been. This made the business more competitive.

Teaching Suggestions (Modeling/Guided Practice)

Ask your students how they would be affected by each of the following events, and what, if anything, they believe that government could do to help them with monetary or fiscal policy.

- They own a firm that roasts and sells 100 percent Colombian coffee to gourmet shops. There is a freeze in Colombia that kills many coffee trees, causing the cost of coffee beans to double.
- They own a farm in California where they grow oranges that they sell in Japan. The government of Japan reduces the number of oranges it will allow to be imported by 50 percent.

- They own a firm with factories in Mexico that supply parts which are assembled into finished products in the United States. The Mexican government passes a law that requires all firms to pay for medical care for workers in Mexico.

Point out how all of these events would impact the American economy and why there is little that could be done through either fiscal or monetary policy to change the effects of these events.

Lesson Checkpoint

Text: Self-Check, text page 342

Answers

1. More than half the oil we consume is imported.
2. To compete with Germans for borrowed money, we need to pay similar interest rates.
3. If stock prices fall in London, it may worry American investors and cause them to sell their stock, forcing down prices of American stock.

Follow-up Assignments (Independent Practice/Extension/Homework)

Text: Applying What You Have Learned, text page 342

Answer

An example might be an investment made by a foreign firm in an American industry that created more jobs in this country.

Section Evaluation

Self-Check, text page 342

Understanding Economics, question 9 (Chapter 12 Review, text pages 352–354)

SECTION D. Government Social Programs (text pages 343–348)

Objectives (Lesson Focus)

Upon completion of this section, students will be able to:

- Explain the need for government social programs.
- Describe the basic characteristics of government social programs, including Social Security, unemployment compensation, and welfare.

Preparation (Instruction: Pre-teaching—Vocabulary or Activity)

1. Discussion Introduce this section by giving each student a 3-by-5 card. Tell them not to put their names on the cards. Students should imagine that they are currently thirty years old, have a family with three children, and earn roughly $30,000 a year of which they pay $7,200 in all types of taxes. Ask them to answer each of the following questions:

a. Would you support greater aid for the nation's poor?

b. Would you be willing to pay more taxes to help the poor?

c. How much of your income would you contribute each year to help the poor?

d. What do you believe is the single most important thing the government could do to help reduce poverty?

Discuss your students' answers. Why would some students support greater aid while others would not? What suggestions were made to reduce poverty? Were they realistic?

2. The Personal Narrative The Personal Narrative in Section D describes a young man's reaction to his first personal contact with people who live in poverty. The subject of the Narrative lives in an affluent suburb but has volunteered to cook and deliver food to a city mission in a poor urban area. He is surprised to find that people who use the mission come from many backgrounds. He recognizes his good fortune in having been born in a family that has income and wealth and wonders why more has not been done to help poor people.

The Narrative describes different groups that often experience poverty in the United States and raises the question of determining society's degree of responsibility to these people.

Teaching Suggestions (Modeling/Guided Practice)

1. Discuss whether your students believe unemployment compensation and welfare should be run by the federal government—as with Social Security—instead of by each state. Help your students make one list of advantages that could result from putting these programs under federal control and a second list of problems that could be caused by federal control. Possible items for each list are found below.

Possible Advantages of Federal Control

(1) There would be equal benefits throughout the country.

(2) Tax burdens would be better equalized.

(3) There would be less reason for poor people to move to different areas to obtain more benefits.

(4) It would reduce the possibility of local political patronage in these programs.

Possible Disadvantages of Federal Control

(1) There would be equal benefits regardless of differences in the cost of living.

(2) Money would be taken from areas that were successful and sent to less successful areas.

(3) There would be a reason for poor people to move to areas with low costs of living.

(4) It would provide even greater political power to the federal government.

2. Some people have suggested institutionalizing people who are unable to take care of themselves because of mental, emotional, or other problems. They believe people who have no home should be placed in shelters and cared for regardless of their individual wishes. Others believe that society should not take personal freedoms from people simply because they live on the street. If the government required institutionalization for such people, it would cost billions of dollars every year. Discuss this issue with your students. Do they feel this idea would be morally correct and/or economically possible? Can they think of alternative plans to solve the problem of our nation's homeless?

Lesson Checkpoint

Text: Self-Check, text page 348
Answers

1. The Social Security Act of 1935 created programs for retirement benefits, unemployment insurance, and welfare.

2. The trends toward smaller families and longer life expectancy have put pressures on the Social Security system.

3. State-administered programs include unemployment insurance and welfare. Federally-administered programs include Social Security and Medicare.

Follow-up Assignments (Independent Practice/Extension/Homework)

1. Text: Applying What You Have Learned, text page 348
   Answers
   a. Relatively few welfare recipients could work for their benefits. Whether or not those recipients who are able to work should be required to do so is a value judgment.
   b. Cuts in welfare benefits would probably increase the number of recipients who are looking for work; however, many would not be able to work under any conditions because they are too young, too old, or disabled.
   c. The people who would be most hurt by a cut in benefits are those who could not support themselves. Many of these people would be young, old, or disabled.
2. People of different age groups often have varying opinions on Social Security taxes. Assign each of your students to ask the following question to at least one working person in each of the following age groups: 20 to 25, 30 to 35, 40 to 45, and 50 to 55. Tell them to report their findings to the class. Discuss possible reasons for any differences between the answers provided by the age groups. Question:
   "Would you support increasing the Social Security tax to guarantee that Social Security benefits are kept at their present level?"
3. Teacher's Resource Binder: Critical Thinking Activity, Chapter 12 (answers in Binder).

Section Evaluation

Self-Check, text page 348
Understanding Economics, questions 10 and 11 (Chapter 12 Review, text pages 352–354)

ADDITIONAL MATERIALS FOR CHAPTER 12

Chapter Evaluation

Teacher's Resource Binder: Chapter 12 Quiz

Reteaching and Extension

See the *Teacher's Resource Binder* and the *Student Activity Book* for additional handouts and activities for Chapter 12.

TEACHER'S BIBLIOGRAPHY FOR CHAPTER 12

Economics Sources

Biven, W. Carl. *Who Killed John Maynard Keynes? Conflicts in the Evolution of Economic Policy*. Homewood, Ill.: Irwin, 1989.

Cairncross, Alec. *Economics and Economic Policy*. Cambridge, Mass.: Basil Blackwell, 1987.

Hailstones, Thomas J. *A Guide to Supply-Side Economics*. Englewood Cliffs, N.J.: Prentice-Hall, Inc., 1983.

Ross, Myron H. *A Gale of Creative Destruction: The Coming Economic Boom*. Westport, Conn.: Greenwood, 1989.

Schiller, Bradley, R. *The Economics of Poverty and Discrimination*, 5th ed. Englewood Cliffs, N.J.: Prentice-Hall, Inc., 1989.

References for Additional Teaching Strategies

Gordon, Sanford. *Economics USA, a Resource Guide for Teachers*. New York: Joint Council on Economic Education, 1988. This text provides exercises for and is keyed to *Economics USA*, a television course developed by the Southern California Consortium.

Miller, Roger LeRoy, and Russell, Shannon. *The Economics of Macro Issues*. St. Paul, Minn.: West, 1986. Chapters 24–27.

Morton, John et al. *High School Economics Courses*. New York: Joint Council on Economic Education, 1985. Lessons 14, 15, and 19.

CHAPTER 12 REVIEW ANSWERS

Building Your Vocabulary (text page 353)

1. crowding-out effect
2. AFDC
3. Social Security Act
4. indexed
5. laissez-faire
6. John Baptiste Say
7. John Maynard Keynes
8. Phase II
9. productivity
10. fiscal policy
11. Classical economics
12. individual retirement account
13. supply-side economics
14. automatic stabilization
15. discretionary fiscal policy
16. Employment Act of 1946

Understanding Economics (text pages 353–354)

1. Classical economists believed that in a recession prices, wages, and interest rates would fall, which would bring the recession to an end.
2. Keynes identified spending that supported personal consumption, business investment, and the government.
3. During a recession, according to Keynes, the government could bring about higher spending levels by either increasing government spending without increasing taxes or by cutting taxes without cutting government spending.
4. Automatic fiscal policy, such as unemployment compensation, requires no new or special action by the government to go into effect. In contrast, discretionary fiscal policy does require new action by the government. Increases in federal tax on gasoline is an example of discretionary fiscal policy.
5. Increased spending by the government to fight unemployment could contribute to higher rates of inflation.
6. Decreased spending by the government to fight inflation could contribute to higher rates of unemployment.
7. Many people felt that President Nixon's Phase II regulations were an unnecessary intrusion by the government into the free market. They often argued that the policy would result in the misallocation of resources.
8. According to supply-side economists, if firms produce more goods and services, there will be more jobs and less need to increase prices.
9. As long as the United States imports half of the oil we use, monetary and fiscal policy cannot control the cost of oil.
10. The benefits paid for welfare and unemployment compensation are different in each state. It is possible that people have chosen to move to states that have relatively higher payments. This may have created a concentration of less affluent people in these states.
11. Private programs are limited to the ability and willingness of people to give. In areas where there are many poor people, there will probably be fewer people who

are able and willing to help them than in areas that are more affluent.

Thinking Critically About Economics
(text page 354)

1. The following three factors, or circumstances, have changed to increase the role of the government in the economy:
   a. The products sold now are much more complicated.
   b. The size of businesses now are much larger.
   c. The number of goods consumers now have to deal with is much larger.
2. In a recession, a Classical economist would want the government to run a balanced budget and wait for the economy to adjust itself. A Keynesian economist would want the government to increase its spending or cut taxes to increase the amount of total spending and create more jobs. A supply-side economist would want the government to reduce taxes to provide firms with more money to invest in increasing their productivity.
3. This event shows that it often takes a long time to carry out discretionary fiscal policy. The additional spending was needed in 1981–1982, but it did not actually take place until the end of 1983. By that time, the economy was already recovering. A tax cut would probably have taken almost as much time to put into effect. The only part that might have taken less time would have been the time needed for people to spend the money after their taxes had been cut.
4. Additional government borrowing could force interest rates up from what they otherwise would have been. Higher interest rates will discourage people and businesses from borrowing and spending. Therefore, the additional government spending could result in less personal consumption spending and business investment.

Consumer Skills Project (text page 354)

Your students will probably find that the welfare forms require a fairly high degree of sophistication and understanding to complete. They will also find that the forms ask for a significant amount of personal information that some people might not want to provide.

PART 3 REVIEW ANSWERS

Understanding Economic Concepts
(text pages 357–358)

1. The answer is provided as an example in the text.
2. It is difficult to measure the GDP accurately because many goods and services are produced and not reported to the government in the *underground economy*.
3. *Durable goods* are products that last a long time and tend to be expensive. Firms that produce these goods are hurt more than other firms in an economic downturn because they are expensive and customers often put off buying these items in a recession.
4. The government publishes a list of *leading indicators* each month, made up of factors that tend to change before the rest of the economy. By studying these indicators businesses are often able to make accurate predictions of economic trends in the near future.
5. Many important products would be too expensive for people to afford individually if they were not provided as *public*

goods and services by the government. Examples include roads, schools, and national defense.

6. A *negative externality* occurs when a third party who is not the producer or consumer of a product pays a cost associated with the production of that product. Pollution of our water is a common example of this. When the government forces a firm to stop polluting a river, it is attempting to correct a negative externality.
7. A *benefits-received* tax is placed on those who use the public good or service that is supported by the tax they pay. An *ability-to-pay* tax is placed on those who are most able to support public goods and services.
8. *Pork barrel legislation* is government spending that is intended to help elected government officials keep their offices by supporting projects which benefit people in their elective districts.
9. Federal income taxes are *progressive* because people who have larger taxable incomes pay a larger percentage of their income in taxes than those with smaller taxable incomes. Most state and local taxes are *regressive* because people who have larger incomes often pay a smaller percentage of their income in taxes than those with smaller incomes.
10. *Frictional unemployment* is made up of people who have been out of work for only a short time.

    Seasonal unemployment is made up of people who have been laid off because their jobs only exist during one part of the year.

    Cyclical unemployment is made up of people who have been laid off because of a recession or a downturn in the economy.

    Structural unemployment is made up of people who have been laid off because their skills or abilities are no longer in demand.
11. There are two basic types of inflation. *Demand-pull inflation* occurs when people try to buy more goods than there are goods offered for sale. The resulting shortage forces prices up. *Cost-push inflation* occurs when firms try to pass increased costs of production on to customers in the form of higher prices.
12. *Poverty* is a relative term and is defined by comparing what most people in a group have with the smaller amount that those who live in poverty have. In the United States, people who are unemployed often suffer from poverty and this situation may be made worse by inflation.
13. The three functions of money are to serve as a:

    - *medium of exchange*, providing units of value which allow transactions to take place.
    - *measure of value*, providing a method of comparing the value of different products offered for sale.
    - *store of value*, providing a method of accumulating or saving value at one time to be used in the future.
14. When banks receive new deposits of cash, they are required by law to keep a set percentage of the deposit on hand in reserve. They may loan out the remainder, which will be borrowed, spent, and redeposited in the banking system. This new deposit becomes the basis of repeated loans, spending, and deposits. Economists call these transactions the *expansion process*.
15. Federal Reserve System steps to regulate the money supply that are intended to

stabilize the economic system make up what is called *monetary policy*.

16. To regulate the money supply and carry out monetary policy the Federal Reserve System may:
    - change the *reserve requirement* or percentage of deposits banks are required to keep on hand.
    - change the *discount rate* or percentage of interest charged to banks that borrow funds from the Federal Reserve System.
    - buy or sell government securities in *open market operations*, which will adjust the level of deposits in banks.
17. If banks were not regulated by the Fed they would probably follow *pro-cyclical* policies. In recessions, they would find it difficult to make many loans, causing the recession to be deeper. In an expansion, they would be able to make many loans, making the expansion greater.
18. The *Federal Deposit Insurance Corporation* was established in the Great Depression to insure deposits and restore confidence in the nation's banking system.
19. *Keynesian economic theory* suggests that it is possible to stabilize the economic system by adjusting the government's taxing, spending, and budget deficit to create enough total spending to supply jobs for all people who want to work.
20. The global nature of our economy makes it difficult for monetary and fiscal policies to regulate the economy because other nations' economic conditions affect decisions that are made by the U.S. government.

Writing About Economics (text pages 358–359)

1. Students' answers should reflect an understanding of the meaning of the *gross domestic product* and the two methods of measuring the GDP: the *income approach* and the *expenditure approach*.
2. Students' answers should reflect an understanding of the three economic concepts identified in the question by explaining the costs and benefits associated with each of the three possible plans. The first plan relates most closely to the *productivity principle* of taxation in that it is intended to encourage business growth and an expansion of production. The second plan relates to the *ability-to-pay-principle* of taxation in that it would reduce taxes for those who own property. Allowing the firms to bury waste on public land would probably result in *negative externalities*.
3. Students' answers should reflect an understanding of the costs and benefits associated with implementing *supply-side economic* policies. People who are relatively well-off would benefit most directly from the reduced taxes. People who are relatively poor would be hurt most directly by reduced government services.

Discussing Economics (text pages 359–360)

1. Students should identify the issue(s) involved in limiting the government's ability to tax and should clearly state whether or not they support the idea. Students should clearly explain the costs and benefits associated with the plan and why they believe their answer is best.
2. Students should identify the issue(s) involved in simply giving people who

live in poverty enough money to bring them above the poverty level and should clearly state whether or not they support the idea. Students should clearly explain the costs and benefits associated with the plan and why they believe their answer is best.

3. Students should identify the issue(s) involved in requiring banks to make a share of their loans to minority-owned businesses and should clearly state whether or not they support the idea. Students should clearly explain the costs and benefits associated with the plan and why they believe their answer is best.

Problem-Solving in Economics

Chapter 8 (text page 360)

1. Items listed by students may be things that did not exist when their parents were young or things their parents could not afford.
2. Items listed by students that do not involve money are likely to be related to their family, friendships, or to nature.
3. Student answers will reflect their individual values and should be given credit as long as they are explained in a logical way.
4. a. A decrease in new building permits indicates a downturn in construction.
   b. Lower interest rates should encourage borrowing and spending.
   c. Working longer hours indicates greater production and income, which should bring about greater spending.
   d. Slower deliveries indicates more customers and steady employment.
   e. Reduced saving rates reflect greater spending and probably consumer confidence in the economy.
   f. Few new businesses being started indicates reduced confidence in the future and probably a slower creation of new jobs.

Chapter 9 (text page 361)

1. These are only some of many possible correct answers.
   a. A person who owns land on the river might support the idea because it should increase the value of his property.
   b. A person who owns a farm on the other side of town would probably oppose the idea because he would receive little benefit from it.
   c. A person who owns a bait shop would probably support the idea because it should increase the number of customers he has.
   d. A person who owns a house on the river and likes peace and quiet would probably oppose the idea because it would increase the traffic on the river.
   e. A person who owns a factory along the river would probably oppose the idea because he would not benefit directly from it, and it could increase public pressure to reduce any pollution the factory might be creating.
2. Answers that are reasonably close to those below should be accepted.
   a. Roughly 33 percent of federal spending went to payments to individuals in 1970.
   b. Roughly 48 percent of federal spending went to payments to individuals in 1990.
   c. Roughly 41 percent of federal spend-

ing went to national defense in 1970.

d. Roughly 25 percent of federal spending went to national defense in 1990.

e. The proportion of federal spending for payments to individuals grew by about 15 percent of total spending, while spending for defense fell by about 15 percent of total spending.

f. The part of the federal budget that went to pay interest on the national debt almost doubled between 1970 and 1990.

Chapter 10 (text page 362)

1. a. Joe is cyclically unemployed because he was laid off when his employer's sales went down.

b. Max is frictionally unemployed because he is moving between jobs with the expectation of finding a better job soon.

c. Jan is seasonally unemployed because she was laid off after the Christmas season.

d. Sue is structurally unemployed because her employer no longer needs her skill. A computer is doing her work instead.

e. Ted is structurally unemployed because he does not have the skills possessed by the college graduate.

2. Students' answers will vary. Most of their answers will probably involve interpersonal relations, families, and self-respect.

3. Students' answers will vary. Their explanations should demonstrate logical thinking and a consideration of the costs and benefits of each alternative.

4. Students' answers will vary. Their suggestions and explanations should demonstrate logical thinking.

Chapter 11 (text pages 362–363)

1. a. When money is saved, it is a store of value.

b. When money is used to buy something, it is a medium of exchange.

c. When you shop where prices are lowest, money is used as a measure of value.

d. Money that is borrowed has been saved by someone and is therefore a store of value. When a loan is paid back, the money will have value, which shows that it has reasonably stable value over time.

2. a. If the Fed lowers the reserve requirement to 10 percent, it will increase the amount of money in circulation because banks will not have to keep as much money on hand and will be able to make more loans.

b. Reducing the money supply means the same as decreasing the amount of money in circulation.

c. If people hold less cash and make more deposits, banks will have more money to lend. This will increase the amount of money in circulation.

d. If banks decide to hold more cash, they will be able to make fewer loans. This will decrease the amount of money in circulation.

e. Increasing the money supply means the same as increasing the amount of money in circulation.

f. If the Fed raises the reserve requirement to 14 percent, banks will have to keep more money on hand and will be able to make fewer loans, which will reduce the amount of money in circulation.

3. Student answers will vary. They should demonstrate an understanding of the factors that determine the risk associated with lending money. These could include the person's credit history, income, assets they own, and other financial responsibilities.
4. a. In inflation, the Fed is likely to decrease the amount (or rate of growth) of money in circulation.
   b. If there is unemployment, the Fed is likely to increase the amount (or rate of growth) of money in circulation.
   c. It is hard for the Fed to deal with both inflation and unemployment at the same time because it cannot increase and decrease the amount of money in circulation at the same time.
   d. If prices go up because the cost of imported raw materials go up, there is little the Fed can do about it because foreign producers are little affected by the money supply or interest rates in the United States.
   e. If people and businesses are worried about the future, they may choose not to borrow, regardless of how low interest rates are.
   f. It is difficult for the Fed to deal with the problems of (1) inflation and unemployment at the same time because it can't increase and decrease the money supply at the same time; (2) increased prices of imports because foreign suppliers are not affected by changes in the money supply or interest rates in this country; (3) bad recessions because people and businesses may choose not to borrow and spend money, regardless of how low interest rates are.

Chapter 12 (text page 363)

1. Students' answers will vary. They should address all parts of the question and demonstrate careful thought and the use of logic.
2. Students' answers should address the problems this firm will have in staying in business if it does not increase its prices by more than 4 percent. Students should make use of the facts provided in the question.
3. If there were no programs to help the poor, in a recession:
   a. The poor would have to cut back more on the number of items they purchase than they would have if these programs existed.
   b. The number of foreclosures and repossessions would increase more than they would have if these programs existed.
   c. There would be fewer jobs than there would have been if these existed.
   d. Programs to help the poor also help those people who are not poor or unemployed because they allow the poor to continue spending.

PART 4

UNDERSTANDING INTERNATIONAL ECONOMICS

CHAPTER 13

Why Countries Trade (text pages 366–389)

SECTION A. The Benefits of Trade (text pages 369–376)

Objectives (Lesson Focus)

Upon completion of this section, students will be able to:

- Identify the theories of absolute and comparative advantage, and describe the conclusions that can be drawn from them concerning international trade.
- Describe possible reasons for establishing tariffs, quotas, or other barriers including: the infant industry argument, the national security argument, the protection of domestic jobs argument, and the maintaining economic stability argument.
- Explain why countries generally benefit from a positive balance of trade and how they may be harmed by a negative balance of trade.

Preparation (Instruction: Pre-teaching—Vocabulary or Activity)

1. Discussion Introduce this section by asking students how they would react if they were assigned to do tasks with which they were unfamiliar. For example, you could ask some students what they would say if they were required to participate in a motorcycle race. Or you could ask other students what they would do if they had to bake a cake. Mention tasks that you believe some students in your class will know how to perform.

Remind your students about the terms *specialization* and *division of labor* presented in Section A of Chapter 2. Point out that if students were able to decide who would do each task, they would be able to accomplish the tasks more efficiently, since students could perform the tasks to which they were best suited. The tasks could be completed more quickly and all the students would gain.

Explain that the same concepts can be applied to countries. When countries specialize in making products, they produce more efficiently and only trade for products they do not produce as well. Production becomes more efficient and all nations are better off.

2. The Personal Narrative The Personal Narrative in Section A describes the benefits that some individuals have received from international trade and compares them with the cost paid by other individuals. The subject of the Narrative is a young man whose father sells imported cars for a living. Many of his friends believe there is something un-American about his father's job. He describes arguments his father uses to answer people who feel selling imports is wrong.

The Narrative demonstrates the tradeoffs between the costs and benefits of international trade. It also shows that the people who receive the benefits may not be the same people who pay the costs.

Teaching Suggestions (Modeling/Guided Practice)

Describe the difference between tariffs that were used to raise revenue for our government in the early 1800s and those which have been used, or suggested, more recently to protect American manufacturers. In the early part of our history there was no income tax to support the federal government. Most federal tax revenue came from tariffs and excise taxes. We taxed imports to support the government more often than to control trade. Today tariff revenues are less than 3 percent of the federal budget and are used primarily to regulate trade.

Ask your students what would happen to trade if the government tried to balance the budget by raising tariffs. Remember that our 1990 budget deficit was roughly $160 billion while we imported $727 billion in foreign products that year. Tariffs high enough to balance the budget would so drastically reduce trade that little money would be collected.

Lesson Checkpoint

Text: Self-Check, text page 376

Answers

1. According to the theories of absolute advantage and comparative advantage, nations should specialize in making the products they are most effective at, and they should trade for their least efficiently produced items.
2. A tariff is a tax on an import; a quota is a limit on the amount of a product a nation will allow to be imported. Voluntary export restraints may prevent other nations from setting up barriers to a country's exports.
3. The infant industry argument suggests that tariffs be used to protect a developing nation's new industries.
4. Countries with a positive balance of trade are likely to have more jobs, more profitable businesses, and economic growth. The most likely problem is inflation. Having a negative balance of trade causes the opposite situation with fewer jobs, and less profit and growth.
5. American trade policy has changed most often in terms of the rate at which tariffs have been charged. In good economic times tariffs have tended to fall. They have been increased in times of economic problems.

Follow-up Assignments (Independent Practice/Extension/Homework)

Text: Applying What You Have Learned text page 376

Answers

1. The *infant industry argument* states that new firms should be protected from more advanced foreign competition with tariffs until they have a chance to grow and become more efficient.
2. The *national security argument* states that we should produce products that are important to our national defense even if they can be purchased for less from other countries. We do not want to be dependent on other countries for things we really need.
3. The *protection of domestic jobs argument* states that we should restrict imports so that American workers will be employed.
4. The *maintaining economic stability argument* states that we should diversify into areas where we are not as efficient as other nations

because we do not want to be too dependent on a relatively low number of products.

Section Evaluation

Self-Check, text page 376
Understanding Economics, questions 1–3 (Chapter 13 Review, text pages 385–387)

SECTION B. The Value of the Dollar and Trade (text pages 377–380)

Objectives (Lesson Focus)

Upon completion of this section, students will be able to:

- Describe the importance of the value of the U.S. dollar to our ability to import and/or export products.
- Define the terms appreciation and depreciation and explain how exchange rates are set.
- Describe how economic conditions and the value of the U.S. dollar are related to each other.
- Identify and explain factors that caused the value of the U.S. dollar to appreciate after 1980 and to depreciate after 1985.

Preparation (Instruction: Pre-teaching—Vocabulary or Activity)

1. **Discussion** Introduce this section by asking students to imagine that they had visited Germany in May of 1992 when the U.S. dollar was worth 1.64 marks. Help them figure out how much each of the following items would have cost in dollars at that time. Do this by dividing the price in marks by 1.64. Then figure the same prices at the 1985 exchange rate of 2.84 marks to the dollar. Discuss how much difference the change in exchange rate made in the apparent price of German products to American tourists.

Product	Price in marks	Price in 1992 dollars	Price in 1985 dollars
Camera	M 750	$457	$264
Hotel room	M 150	$ 91	$ 53
Restaurant meal	M 60	$ 37	$ 21
Theater ticket	M 20	$ 12	$ 7

This difference in price made all German products less expensive to Americans in 1985 than they were in 1992. It would have also made U.S. products more expensive to Germans in 1985. Similar situations concerning exchange rates existed between the United States and most other countries at this time. This contributed to the growth of our negative balance of trade in the mid-1980s.

2. **The Personal Narrative** The Personal Narrative in Section B describes events surrounding the operation of Mert's Machine Parts. The subject of the Narrative is the son of an employee of Mert's. He explains how his father's income changed over the years depending on the ability of his employer to sell products in foreign nations. In years when the value of the U.S. dollar had appreciated, sales were low and workers' hours were cut back. In other years the value of the U.S. dollar was lower and Mert's foreign sales were good. In these years employees worked more hours. The point is made that the central factor in the firm's success was the

value of the dollar: a factor over which the firm had no control.

The Narrative emphasizes the importance of exchange rates in determining the ability of American firms to compete internationally. It also describes how this ability impacts American workers.

Teaching Suggestions (Modeling/Guided Practice)

1. The United States imports many products (such as television picture tubes) in large quantities from other countries. Point out that if the value of the dollar falls rapidly, making foreign imports more expensive, we would initially pay the higher prices and send even more money out of the country. This is because dependence on foreign manufacturers has prevented the nation from investing in factories necessary to make these products. Therefore, a decline in the value of the dollar might not lead to a quick reduction in our balance of trade deficit.
2. Many people do not understand how the United States can sell many more products to other countries without eliminating our negative balance of trade. Work through the following example in class to provide students with one explanation.

   Suppose the U.S. dollar was worth 200 yen in 1985 (this number is used to simplify the math). If the Japanese bought oranges for 10 cents each, they would need to exchange 20 yen to pay for an orange, or you could say that the United States earned 20 yen for each orange sold. Now imagine that the exchange rate for yen changed to 100 to the dollar in 1993. It would then cost the Japanese 10 yen for each 10 cent orange. To earn the same 20 yen that was received for one orange in 1985, Americans would have to produce and sell two oranges in 1993. If the same situation was true of all American products, we could produce and sell many more products without earning a larger number of yen because of the lower value of the dollar.

Follow-up Assignments (Independent Practice/Extension/Homework)

Text: Applying What You Have Learned, text page 380

Answers

a. It would have cost fewer dollars in 1985 when the U.S. dollar was worth 238.5 yen than in 1992 when it was only worth 133 yen.

b. It would have been less expensive to buy the Italian shoes in 1989 when the dollar could be exchanged for 1372 lira.

c. If the value of Swiss francs continues to fall, the longer Americans wait to buy Swiss products, the less expensive they will be.

Section Evaluation

Self-Check, text page 380

Understanding Economics, questions 4–7 (Chapter 13 Review, text pages 385–387)

SECTION C. Multinational Corporations (text pages 381–384)

Objectives (Lesson Focus)

Upon completing this section, students will be able to:

- Explain what multinational corporations are and how they may be organized.
- Identify and explain costs and benefits commonly associated with multinational corporations.

- Explain steps that have been or could be taken to limit the economic and political power of multinational corporations.

Preparation (Instruction: Pre-teaching—Vocabulary or Activity)

1. **Discussion** Introduce this section by showing students examples or pictures of products that were produced by multinational corporations. Examples could include pictures of a Honda automobile, Nestle's candy bars, or Norelco shavers. Ask them if the fact that these and many other products are made by businesses that are owned and controlled by people in many countries is important to them or to other Americans. Spend some time explaining what a multinational firm is.

   Provide students with a more specific example. How would they feel if they worked for a multinational firm like Delco Auto Parts which was building many factories in developing nations that have low wages? Would they be afraid of losing their jobs? How would they feel if they lived in Ohio near the new Honda automobile factory? Lead into a discussion of whether businesses have a moral obligation to protect the economic interests of people in nations where they do business.

2. **The Personal Narrative** The Personal Narrative in Section C describes the difficulty of determining what an American product is and of determining the costs and benefits of multinationals. The subject of the Narrative is a student whose father sells imported cars at a U.S. manufacturer's dealership and whose uncle works for Honda in Ohio. He learns that these firms are multinational corporations and that multinationals have become important in the world economy. He recognizes costs and benefits associated with multinationals, but he remains confused about how he should think of these firms and their products.

Teaching Suggestions (Modeling/Guided Practice)

1. Multinationals have been accused of not paying their fair share of taxes in all countries where they do business. Work through the following example to demonstrate how this may happen.

   Imagine Multinational XYZ does business in Germany, Ireland, and the United States. It manufactures parts for a kitchen mixer in Germany that costs $40 to make. These parts are sold by its German branch to its Irish subsidiary for $40, so it earns no profit in Germany and pays no tax. The parts are assembled in Ireland at a cost of $20 and sold to the firm's American business for $100. Taxes are low in Ireland, so the firm only pays about $5 on the $40 profit it earned there. The American branch sells the mixer to retail stores in the United States for $100. It pays no tax, because it earns no profit in the United States. Firm XYZ ends up only paying taxes in the country with the lowest rates.

   The point of this example is that multinational corporations are able to use accounting methods to make it appear that more of their profits are earned in countries with lower tax rates. Do students believe this is fair? What could be done about this situation?

2. Business lobbies are accepted in the U.S. and other nations as part of the political process. Some nations regard multinational lobbying as interference in their internal political affairs. Ask students to discuss why it may be easier for a multina-

tional corporation to influence the government of a developing nation and why this type of influence is likely to cause resentment.

Lesson Checkpoint

Text: Self-Check, text page 383

Answers

1. Companies have become multinationals to take advantage of opportunities in other countries and to maintain their competitive position in the world economy.
2. Multinationals often create additional jobs and make investments in new capital in host countries.
3. Developing countries may fear multinationals because they think these firms may exert too much political and economic power in their system.

Follow-up Assignments (Independent Practice/Extension Homework)

1. Text: Applying What You Have Learned, text page 383
   Answers
   a. Most people think of an American company as one that started in this country and that maintains its world headquarters in the United States.
   b. American consumers benefit from having a wider selection of products and lower prices. People in developing nations benefit from more jobs and capital investments.
2. Teacher's Resource Binder: Critical Thinking Activity, Chapter 13 (answers in Binder).

Section Evaluation

Self-Check, text page 383

Understanding Economics, questions 8 and 9 (Chapter 13 Review, text pages 385–387)

ADDITIONAL MATERIALS FOR CHAPTER 13

Chapter Evaluation

Teacher's Resource Binder: Chapter 13 Quiz

Reteaching and Extension

See the *Teacher's Resource Binder* and the *Student Activity Book* for additional handouts and activities for Chapter 13.

TEACHER'S BIBLIOGRAPHY FOR CHAPTER 13

Economics Sources

Annual Report on Exchange Arrangements and Exchange Restrictions. Washington, D.C.: International Monetary Fund, 1990.

Burger, Albert E., ed. *U.S. Trade Deficit: Causes, Consequences, and Cures.* Norwell, Mass.: Kluwer Academic Press, 1989.

Elfstrom, Gerard. *Moral Issues and Multinational Corporations.* New York: St. Martin's Press, 1991.

Pomfret, Richard. *International Trade: An Introduction to Theory and Policy.* Cambridge, Mass.: Basil Blackwell, 1991.

References for Additional Teaching Strategies

The Development Book and Teaching Guide. Washington, D.C.: The World Bank, 1989.

Mansfield, Edwin, and Behravesh, Nariman. *Telecourse Study Guide for Economics USA.* New York: Norton, 1992, Chapters 27 and 28.

Morton, John et al. *High School Economics Courses.* New York: Joint Council on Economic Education, 1985, Lessons 21 and 22.

Wild About Trade. Federal Reserve Bank of San Francisco. A 15-minute tape on trade and foreign exchange rates.

CHAPTER 13 REVIEW ANSWERS

Building Your Vocabulary (text page 386)

1. appreciation
2. depreciation
3. tariff
4. comparative advantage
5. absolute advantage
6. quota
7. protective tariff
8. protection of domestic jobs
9. national security
10. infant industry
11. maintaining economic stability
12. restrictive tariff
13. multinational corporation
14. exchange rate
15. positive balance of trade
16. negative balance of trade
17. dumping
18. revenue tariff

Understanding Economics (text pages 386–387)

1. To follow the theories of absolute and comparative advantage, countries should specialize in producing products that they make most efficiently and trade for the items that they are not able to produce efficiently. This will improve their productivity because they won't be allocating resources to the types of production at which they are least efficient.
2. Countries that are not economically advanced often place high tariffs on imports to increase the price of these imports and to encourage their people to buy products made in their own country.
3. These countries do not want to be dependent on other countries for products they need to defend themselves.
4. A country that has a positive balance of trade can expect to have greater employment, more profitable firms, more growth, and a larger tax base.
5. People who might have produced these products in the United States may have not been able to find work. Thus, the cost of these imported goods is not evenly distributed.
6. People who produce oil in the United States found their income declining with the price of oil in 1985 and 1986.
7. The voluntary limits on the export of cars from Japan increased the price of these cars in the United States and saved over 40,000 jobs in the U.S. auto industry.
8. To say that the value of the dollar appreciated 40 percent means that the dollar could buy 40 percent more units of other types of currency after this happened. Therefore, the price of foreign goods appeared to be lower to U.S. consumers.
9. Three nontrade-related reasons for the appreciation of the U.S. dollar in the early 1980s include:
   a. high interest rate in the U.S. leading foreigners to invest here
   b. instability in other countries leading foreigners to invest here
   c. the early recovery from recession causing foreigners to invest here
10. The U.S. dollar decreased in value from 1985 because U.S. interest rates fell, and the economy was not growing as rapidly as other nations' economies.
11. Corporations become multinationals to take advantage of opportunities and to maintain their competitive positions in world markets. They may harm the interests of host nations.

12. Host nations benefit from the jobs and capital investments that multinationals bring. They may be harmed by abuses of economic and political power of the multinationals.

Thinking Critically About Economics
(text page 387)

1. Higher tariffs would please workers and businesses that had been hurt by imported goods; however, higher tariffs would displease other people who have to pay higher prices as a result and those who might be hurt by tariffs put on our exports by other countries.
2. Student answers will vary according to their individual points of view. Their answers should be graded relative to the logic on which they are based.
3. It is the result of a compromise. It provides protection for some businesses, while encouraging investments that will make them more competitive in the future.
4. If a country sells products to other countries for less than it sells them to its own people, it could be both creating jobs and reducing unemployment. Dumping would also contribute to a positive balance of trade and of payments.
5. If interest rates go down in the United States, foreigners will be less interested in depositing their money in our banks. This would reduce the demand for the dollar as well as reduce its value.
6. Many products we buy are made from parts that are manufactured in different countries. Foreign multinationals both help and hurt different parts of the U.S. economy. Individual businesses and workers may be harmed by foreign competition, while multinational businesses may provide lower prices, better quality, and greater productivity.

Consumer Skills Projects (text page 387)

1. It might be interesting to investigate the possibility of a change in the perception that people have of American goods over the past five to ten years. Do people now have a higher or lower opinion of U.S. quality? What might have caused any changes?
2. The value does not usually change dramatically in the short term. The dollar may be going up in relation to one currency and down in relation to another.

CHAPTER 14

Developing Nations, Growth, and Population (text pages 390–413)

SECTION A. The Problems of Developing Nations (text pages 393–397)

Objectives (Lesson Focus)

Upon completion of this section, students will be able to:

- Identify and describe problems that are common to many developing nations, including traditional economies and a lack of infrastructure.
- Identify and describe difficulties developing nations face in overcoming economic problems.

Preparation (Instruction: Pre-teaching—Vocabulary or Activity)

1. Discussion Introduce this section by asking each student to identify one task that requires some basic technical skill that they were taught to do by a parent or guardian. Using a VCR, running a dishwasher, repairing a car, or changing a light bulb would be good examples. List these tasks on the chalkboard.

Tell your students to imagine what their lives would have been like if no one they knew could teach them how to do these things, that they didn't know how to read, and there were no schools. Stress the difficulty of acquiring new knowledge if you have no base of understanding from which to build. The more you know, the easier learning becomes. Emphasize that this problem is common in developing nations. In such a situation, how much good would it do to send people a new tractor, electric generator, or water pump?

2. The Personal Narrative The Personal Narrative in Section A describes the steps taken by individuals in the United States to help people in Africa. The subject of the Narrative is a young African American woman who becomes aware of starvation and other problems of some countries in Africa from watching television news reports. She wonders why the problems occurred and what she could do to help.

The Narrative shows that although many Americans are willing to give help to developing nations, we often do not understand the nature of these problems or their causes.

Teaching Suggestions (Modeling/Guided Practice)

1. Ask your students to identify as many examples as possible of infrastructure used by a manufacturing firm in their local area. For each provided example of infrastructure, discuss what different course of action would have been required by the firm in order to continue production had this type of infrastructure not existed in their community. (Students might pose the following example as a basis for discussion: "How could a firm that produces machine tools operate if there were no electricity?") Point out that developing nations face similar difficulties in efficiently producing goods, since no developed infrastructure is present.
2. Ask your students to pretend they are twenty-three years old and have recently graduated with college degrees. They are offered two different jobs (for ease of discussion, hereafter identified as *Job 1* and *Job 2*). Job 1 is local, thus allowing them to remain close to family and friends. Job 1 requires employees to work 48 hours a week, earning $10,000 annually with few fringe benefits. Furthermore, the firm's equipment is technologically outdated. Job 2, in contrast, would require a move to another state. Employees have a 40-hour work week, and earn an annual income of $32,000. In addition, extensive fringe benefits are offered by the firm, and workers are provided with quality, up-to-date equipment.

   Ask your students to choose either Job 1 or Job 2. Point out that this is the type of "choice" encountered by many educated people from developing nations when they choose to work in their own countries or move to more developed nations. They must weigh the costs and benefits carefully. What other costs and benefits can your students suggest that would likely be involved in this decision?

3. Ask your students to identify potential problems that could result from an attempt to form a new country comprised of Alaska, the eastern region of Russia, and Japan. Although these areas are geographically close to one another, their respective people, languages, social values, and economic systems are very different. Governing such a nation would be virtually impossible. Explain that comparable problems often occur in developing nations that are made up of diverse social and ethnic groups.
4. Governments of developing nations have to make difficult choices in determining the use of available financial resources. Among the most serious needs of developing nations are medical care, safe drinking water, education, roads, and improvement of agriculture. Ask students to suppose they were a committee of high officials of a developing nation with the task of determining the government's budget for the upcoming year. By what priorities would they rank these needs? Have each student rank these needs from one to five, most serious to least. Then have some students explain why they chose a particular need as number one. Try to arrive at a class consensus, so that a set of government budget priorities can be determined. The exercise should point out how difficult it is to sacrifice any serious need for another priority.

Lesson Checkpoint

Text: Self-Check, text page 397
Answers

1. This type of economy is very slow to change because people gain most of the knowledge they have from other family members who also lack technological skills.
2. For developing nations to grow they need training, capital, management, and stable government.
3. Countries in South Asia have grown most rapidly, while those in Sub-Saharan Africa and Latin America have had the slowest growth.

Follow-up Assignments (Independent Practice/Extension/Homework)

Text: Applying What You Have Learned, text page 397
Answers

Student answers will vary but should consider education, infrastructure, farming, and basic industry needs.

Section Evaluation

Self-Check, text page 397
Understanding Economics, questions 1–3 (Chapter 14 Review, text pages 409–411)

SECTION B. The Relationship Between "Have" and "Have Not" Nations (text pages 399–403)

Objectives (Lesson Focus)

Upon completion of this section, students will be able to:

- Describe the aid given by the United States in relation to that given by other developed nations.
- Describe the importance of multinational corporations to developing nations.
- Explain difficulties experienced in deciding what sort of aid to extend that could be best used by developing nations.

Preparation (Instruction: Pre-teaching—Vocabulary or Activity)

1. Discussion Introduce this section by holding a discussion similar to the one in the Personal Narrative. List on the chalkboard the points of view expressed in the Narrative. Then ask the students to explain *their* opinions of each. Can your students think of any other points of view concerning foreign aid? Can a distinction be made between humanitarian considerations and those that are political or economic in nature?

2. The Personal Narrative The Personal Narrative in Section B presents various points of view on the issue of United States extension of aid to developing nations and further speculates that, if such aid is warranted, the amount and type of aid must still be considered.

The Narrative demonstrates the diversity of public opinion that exists within the United States regarding the issue of foreign aid.

Teaching Suggestions (Modeling/Guided Practice)

1. Dramatic social and economic changes swept through Eastern Europe beginning in 1989. New, more democratic governments emerged and almost immediately appealed to the United States and other developed nations for economic aid that would ensure the permanence of these changes. This came at a time when the United States had been slashing its total foreign aid package as a means to help reduce its own federal deficits. Latin American nations, scheduled to receive major assistance from the United States, worried that much of U.S. aid would be siphoned off to Eastern Europe. Japan stepped in to help out, giving $300 million in aid to Panama alone.

   Illustrate the foreign aid situation by listing the main players on the chalkboard: Areas of developing nations seeking aid: Eastern Europe, Asia, Africa, and Latin America; Industrialized nations and groups providing most aid: Japan, the United States, and Western Europe. Discuss the following questions with students: Should the United States provide more foreign aid as its military assistance to other countries decreases? Should developed nations that are geographically closer to developing nations be more responsible for aid in their own areas? A corporate Japanese offer to pay Brazil's entire foreign debt in exchange for gold mining rights in the Amazon region fell through. If you were the head of a developing nation, would you accept this kind of offer? Why or why not?
2. Ask your students if they consider it reasonable to expect developing nations to do what we want them to, or to show gratitude when we send them aid. As an analogy, point out that all—or nearly all—students have received help in one form or another from their parents. Ask students if they always show appreciation to their parents for this assistance, or if they always do what their parents want them to do. If not, have them explain the reasons for their contrary actions.

   Now ask your students to share their reactions to this comparison of U.S. assistance to foreign nations to parental aid to children. Do they consider this to be a reasonable comparison? Do countries (*should* they) behave like people? When a United States–aided foreign nation does something we consider undesirable, how and to what degree should our government react?
3. Use Discussion Topic 20 from the *Teacher's Resource Binder* regarding one of the problems with some types of aid to devel-

oping nations. Your students should realize that providing fabric to the developing nation will destroy its newly developing domestic textile industry. These new firms cannot compete with free goods provided by developed nations. This situation demonstrates the potential problem of giving aid that both benefits and harms the receiving nation.

Lesson Checkpoint

Text: Self-Check, text page 403
Answers

1. The United States's share of total aid has become smaller in the past 40 years.
2. A larger part of aid now takes the form of bank loans and investments by businesses in developing nations.
3. The debt crisis was caused by a drop in prices that developing nations received for their exports at the same time that the value of the U.S. dollar was increasing.

Follow-up Assignments (Independent Practice/Extension/Homework)

1. Text: Applying What You Have Learned, text page 403
   Answers

   Student answers will vary but should consider the effect a decrease in aid would have on the receiving country and the problem continuing aid would have on the U.S. economy.

2. Ask your students to survey their parents or other adult relatives concerning the value of foreign aid. Have students ask each of the following questions and report their findings to the class. Discuss the results of the survey. Can any conclusions be drawn about the kind of people who would or would not want the government to give aid?
   a. Do you feel that your family has enough income to maintain an adequate standard of living?
   b. Do you expect your standard of living to improve, stay about the same, or become worse in the next two years?
   c. Do you, or any person who lives with you, receive support from the government? (social security, unemployment compensation, welfare, food stamps, etc.)
   d. Do you believe government aid to developing nations is spent effectively?
   e. Do you believe government aid to developing nations should be increased, remain the same, be reduced, or be completely eliminated?

Section Evaluation

Self-Check, text page 403
Understanding Economics, questions 4 and 5 (Chapter 14 Review, text pages 409–411)

SECTION C. The Population Explosion (text pages 404–407)

Objective (Lesson Focus)

Upon completion of this section, students will be able to:

- Describe problems related to population growth that are faced by many developing nations.

Preparation (Instruction: Pre-teaching—Vocabulary or Activity)

1. Discussion Introduce this section by asking your students how many people are in their families. Since each may have a different understanding of "family," it may be easier to simply ask them how many people they live with. Ask them to discuss and decide what constitutes a "large" family. They will probably agree that "large" begins with approximately five or six family members. Having established this, ask students to identify several advantages and disadvantages of living in a large family. Many of the disadvantages are likely to be economic, while the advantages will probably be more social in nature.

Discuss how large families provide both advantages and disadvantages for people who live in developing nations. Why have many people suggested that government social programs would help reduce population growth in developing nations?

2. The Personal Narrative The Personal Narrative in Section C describes problems that result from population growth. The subject of the Narrative is a young man who doesn't understand why people continue to have children they will be unable to support or to care for. He sees reports on the news that show masses of poor people in developing nations. His reaction is to blame the parents in these countries for having too many children.

The Narrative demonstrates that such a point of view concerning population growth in developing nations is held by many people.

Teaching Suggestions (Modeling/Guided Practice)

1. Explain that increased food production within some developing nations has led to increased population growth as well. With an increased food supply, parents are able to provide better nutrition for their children, thus resulting in a decreased child mortality rate. Do your students view this as a favorable or unfavorable result? Ask them to identify other possible results of an increase in food production. Point out that such an increase—by eliminating the need to import food—would allow the nation to spend its money on machines, job training, and other needed goods and services, which in turn would increase the nation's own production capacity.
2. Discuss the costs of raising a child in the United States. (Be sure to include the cost of an education.) Then compare this cost to that of raising a child in a developing nation. Your students are likely to assume that there would be less expenses required in the developing country; point out, however, that this is probably *not* the case. Although Americans may spend a larger quantity of money on their children, the necessary expenses—as a percentage of their overall income—are probably less, particularly if educational costs are included. Many developing nations do not provide public education. Families in these countries can educate their children only by making great personal sacrifices.
3. The population growth in developing nations can in part be attributed to an overall increase in people's lifespans. The elderly—whether they live in rich or poor nations—require more care than members of most other age groups. Have students discuss any sacrifices that have been made by their families in order to care for an elderly relative. Ask your students if they think such sacrifices would constitute a greater or lesser problem in developing nations. (Be sure to have them explain the reasons for their responses to this question.)

   Re-emphasize the point that the *least* economically advantaged family unit—

whose subsistence level is barely adequate—is *most* likely to be adversely affected by one of its own family members who is unable to "pull his or her own weight."

Lesson Checkpoint

Text: Self-Check, text page 407
Answers

1. People in developing nations often desire large families in the anticipation that they will need their offspring to provide economic support when they grow old and unable to work.
2. A reduced mortality rate has resulted in people living longer, thus adding to, rather than helping to eliminate, population problems.
3. A high birthrate results in more children to provide for and educate. In addition, at least for the first few years of their lives, children do not contribute to the enhancement of the nation's economy through production.

Follow-up Assignments (Independent Practice/Extension/Homework)

1. Text: Applying What You Have Learned, text page 407
Answers

The students' lists of advantages and disadvantages may include other acceptable answers that are not provided here; in addition, the degree of importance placed on these "pro" and "con" factors—to a developing nation as compared to the United States—may *greatly* vary. The rankings given by each student will in part reflect his or her priorities and values. They should be graded according to the logic presented in supporting their answers.

Advantages of a large family in the United States include

a. *lower income taxes.* In most developing nations, taxes are less important, since they are not reduced for large families.
b. *more government aid if you are poor.* In a developing nation such aid is so minimal—if it exists at all—that having extra children would add nothing to a family's standard of living.
c. *more family members to help one another.* This is considered a particularly important asset in a poor, developing nation, where often the only support offered to the elderly is that provided by their offspring.

Disadvantages of a large family in the United States include

a. *greater overall living expenses in raising a large family.* Increased expenses is an equal—if not greater—problem in many developing nations, where the most serious population problems exist.
b. *lack of ability to provide advanced education for all children.* In many developing nations, a large family can prevent the children from obtaining *any* education.

c. *inadequate nutrition for all children.* This is a particularly common occurrence in many developing nations, where the percentage of large families with many children far exceeds such U.S. families.

2. Teacher's Resource Binder: Critical Thinking Activity, Chapter 14 (answers in Binder).

Section Evaluation

Self-Check, text page 407
Understanding Economics, questions 6 and 7 (Chapter 14 Review, text pages 409–411)

ADDITIONAL MATERIALS FOR CHAPTER 14

Chapter Evaluation

Teacher's Resource Binder: Chapter 14 Quiz

Reteaching and Extension

See the *Teacher's Resource Binder* and the *Student Activity Book* for additional handouts and activities for Chapter 14.

TEACHER'S BIBLIOGRAPHY FOR CHAPTER 14

Economics Sources

Dell, Sidney. *International Development Policies: Perspectives for Industrial Countries.* Durham, N.C.: Duke University Press, 1991.

Orr, Robert M. *Japan: Its Changing Foreign Aid Policy.* New York: Columbia University Press, 1990.

Perkins, Dwight H., and Roemen, Michael, eds. *Reforming Economic Systems in Developing Countries.* Boston: Harvard University Press, 1991.

Sorensen, George. *Democracy, Dictatorship, and Development.* New York: St. Martin's Press, 1991.

Todaro, Michael P. *Economic Development in the Third World,* 3rd ed. New York: Longman, 1989. A good reference work, particularly on foreign aid and investment.

Williams, Marc. *Third World Cooperation.* New York: St. Martin's Press, 1991.

World Bank Staff. *World Development Report, 1990.* Washington, D.C.: World Bank Publication Service, Oxford University Press, 1990.

References for Additional Teaching Strategies

The Development Book and Teaching Guide. Washington, D.C.: The World Bank, 1988.

Mansfield, Edwin, and Behravesh, Nariman. *Telecourse Study Guide for Economics USA.* New York: Norton, 1992, Chapter 25. This text provides exercises for and is keyed to *Economics USA,* a television course developed by the Southern California Consortium.

CHAPTER 14 REVIEW ANSWERS

Building Your Vocabulary (text page 410)

1. developed nations
2. newly developed nations
3. traditional economy
4. mortality rate
5. infrastructure
6. developing nations

Understanding Economics (text page 410)

1. In a traditional economic system, people learn how to produce goods and services from their families. There is often no formalized system of education and therefore no established vehicle for introducing new ideas or for bringing about change.
2. A lack of infrastructure increases the costs of production. Without adequate roads, power, and water, it is difficult to produce and transport goods and services efficiently.
3. There were several reasons for the debt crisis in developing nations. First, the value of developing nations' exports fell sharply. Second, the value of the U.S. dollar was increasing, making it more difficult to pay back loans. Third, economic growth slowed, making it difficult to increase exports. Finally, inflation contributed to increasing the size of the debt compared to developing nations' GDP.
4. A tool is no more useful than the ability of the person who uses it. Sending tools to people who do not know how to use them will not help these people to become more productive.
5. Multinational corporations have the money to invest in developing nations. They can be helpful in developing resources, employing people, and training management. On the other hand, multinationals may attempt to get profits from the developing nations without contributing much to their economy. They may also exercise too much power and influence in developing nations, causing resentment.
6. Countries with high rates of population growth often have difficulty in achieving economic growth because the additional production they achieve is largely taken up supporting the increased population.
7. Many people in developing nations value large families for a variety of reasons. To reduce the rate of population growth, it is necessary to either convince them or force them to have fewer children. In either case, these people have to be taught how to limit their family size, a tremendous national reorientation that could only be effective under a well-organized government.

Thinking Critically About Economics (text pages 410–411)

1. Student lists will vary with their individual family backgrounds.
2. The people in the various countries of Africa are very different from one another. They have different languages, religions, and social systems. To have them join together would be an open invitation to political, social, and economic discord.
3. Opening a factory in any location requires the four factors of production. The needed raw materials might be easily available in the form of trees. A skilled labor force, however, would be very difficult to obtain in the middle of a tropical rain forest. The necessary capital, or tools, would also be difficult to build there. Finally, managers would be needed to run the factory. Attracting qualified managers to live in a tropical rain forest would also be a problem. It would be doubtful that a paper factory could be a success in any such location, South American or otherwise. (This was in fact attempted in the mid-1970s in Brazil. The project failed.)
4. It is likely that your students will emphasize vocational training. Be careful of attempts to make everyone Ph.D.s. There should be a reasonable chance that

these people would be able to realistically use their education.

5. The aid payments had to be spent in the United States to prevent a flow of dollars out of this country and to provide jobs and business for American workers and firms.
6. Student answers will vary with their personal points of view and values. Their answers should be graded according to the logic used to support them.
7. Any steps that are to be taken must either address the rate of population growth and/or the rate of economic growth. Steps should limit population or increase production.

Consumer Skills Projects (text page 411)

1. Your students will probably find that adults are often against sending more aid to developing nations but are willing to send tools. This probably reflects their desire to see people in developing nations learn to support themselves.
2. Your students will discover that their neighborhoods are absolutely full of examples of infrastructure. You could try to place some sort of value on these things. Why would it be hard for a developing nation to compete with firms that exist in a nation that already has a developed infrastructure?
3. Your students will probably find that families are smaller now than they were in the past. Students frequently enjoy discussing why many people have chosen to have fewer children and whether this is a wise choice. What does this show about changing values in this country?

CHAPTER 15

Alternative Economic Systems (text pages 413–436)

SECTION A. A Variety of Economic Systems (text pages 414–420)

Objectives (Lesson Focus)

Upon completion of this section, students will be able to:

- Describe differences between various economic theories and the reality of economic systems that exist in the world.
- Explain why all economic systems must answer the basic economic questions *what, how,* and *for whom.*
- Explain why all countries have mixed economic systems that combine characteristics of command and market economies.
- Identify and describe three methods that have been used to place different economic systems on a range between pure command and market economies.

Preparation

(Instruction: Pre-teaching—Vocabulary or Activity)

1. Discussion Introduce this section by reviewing the general principles of how a command economy works. Ask your students to help you compile a list of decisions that American business owners make that managers of government-owned-and-operated firms would not be able to make in a command economy. Items that could appear on the list include:

What product to make
Where to produce the product
How to make the product

Who to buy raw materials from
How many workers to hire
How much to pay the workers
What price to charge for the product
How to market the product
What equipment to invest in
What to do with leftover funds (profits)

All of these decisions are made by government planning agencies in command economies. Discuss possible reasons why workers in planning agencies would be more likely to make bad choices than the owners of capitalist firms. What may these reasons have had to do with the shift from command economies to more market-oriented economies that happened in many nations in the late 1980s and 1990s?

2. The Personal Narrative The Personal Narrative in Section A describes a young man who went to live and work on a kibbutz in Israel for a summer. While in Israel he found that the kibbutz was run as a small command economy. Most of the basic economic decisions were made by an elected central authority. Members worked for the benefit of all, receiving little personal reward. They gave up much of their economic freedom and privacy for greater security and a sense of community. Although the young man was invited to return to the kibbutz, he decided to stay in the United States where he could work for his individual benefit and have the use of private possessions.

The Narrative demonstrates different trade-offs people make between personal freedom and security in different economic systems.

Teaching Suggestions
(Modeling/Guided Practice)

1. Tell your students the following story: Imagine that you are all in the same English class. Your teacher announces that there will be a major unit test next week but that it will be graded differently than other tests. The individual scores from all the tests will be averaged together and each student will receive the class average as a grade, instead of the score that was placed on his or her own paper.

   Ask your students if they believe this would be a good plan. Would they study more or less if grades were determined in this way? Point out the similarity between this situation and those found in a command economy. If students think of their individual scores as income, how do they feel about sharing their "income" with other students who did not study as much? Would this system give them an incentive to do their best?

2. Remind your students that there are many features of the American economy that make it a mixed capitalistic system. Social Security, established in the 1930s during the Depression, provides income to people who are no longer working to contribute to production. Other government programs and policies that are socialist in nature include public ownership of utilities, progressive income taxes, welfare, unemployment compensation, public schools, Medicaid, and Medicare. Ask your students to identify and discuss costs and benefits that might result from eliminating these policies and programs. Lead this discussion to show that the United States needs a mixed economic system, although there is debate over what mixture is best.

3. Tell your students to imagine they have jobs that they cannot be fired from unless they do something really terrible. If their work is slow and they make minor mistakes little will happen to them, although their fellow workers will not respect

them. On the other hand, if they try hard and do exceptional work their income will not increase very much, although their fellow workers will have a high opinion of them.

Ask your students to describe the effort they would put into a job under these circumstances. Point out that these are essentially the conditions under which many Japanese employees who are guaranteed jobs work. Do your students believe many American employees would do their best work under this system? What may account for differences in factors that motivate Japanese and American workers?

Lesson Checkpoint

Text: Self-Check, text page 420

Answers

1. A kibbutz is an example of a command economy and should be placed far to the left on the range in Figure 15–1.
2. Countries have mixed economic systems because neither pure market nor pure command economies work efficiently. Too many mistakes and too little incentive exist in a pure command economy, while a pure market economy could result in some people starving to death.
3. Nations that have central control over most of the basic economic decisions generally need strong political powers to enforce their decisions.

Follow-up Assignments (Independent Practice/Extension/Homework)

1. Text: Applying What You Have Learned, text page 420

   Answers

   Student answers will vary depending on the debate over government spending that is identified and discussed. Students' statements should demonstrate their understanding that greater government spending requires greater taxation and therefore a larger role for the government in the economy. They should associate greater government spending with movement to the left on the range in Figure 15-1 toward a system with more characteristics of a command economy.
2. Teacher's Resource Binder: Critical Thinking Activity, Chapter 15 (answers in Binder).

Section Evaluation

Self-Check, text page 420

Understanding Economics, questions 1-4 (Chapter 15 Review, text page 434)

SECTION B. Economic Theory vs. Economic Reality (text pages 421–426)

Objectives (Lesson Focus)

Upon completion of this section, students will be able to:

- Explain the basic theory of communism and why Karl Marx believed it would replace capitalism as the most common type of economic system.
- Describe problems that developed in countries that had various forms of communist systems.
- Identify advantages and disadvantages of the socialistic economic systems found in the nations of Western Europe and Scandinavia.

- Identify and describe characteristics of socialism that exist in the mixed economic system of the United States.
- Explain reasons for the recent shift from socialism to more market-oriented economies in many nations.

Preparation (Instruction: Pre-teaching—Vocabulary or Activity)

1. Discussion Two possible courses of action—present in the form of alternatives—are offered for each of the following entries. Each question is intended to stimulate thinking in regard to the advantages and disadvantages among alternative economic systems and the trade-offs that may be made within these systems. Keeping these objectives in mind, introduce this section by asking students to choose one of the alternatives presented for each entry. Then discuss differing student choices with the class as a whole.

Question: Which is more important to you?

a. being told where you will live and having low housing costs *or* being able to choose where you want to live at a higher cost?
b. being guaranteed a job with a wage that will allow you to just pay your bills *or* having the right to start a business of your own that may succeed or fail?
c. receiving just enough income to pay for your needs regardless of what you do *or* receiving income based on the value of your labor?
d. having low prices for products you need but that are often out of stock *or* being able to buy these products when you need them but at higher prices?
e. paying higher taxes so everyone has health care provided by the government *or* having lower taxes with all people responsible for providing their own health care?
f. having free higher education provided only to those who are able to pass tests *or* having higher education available to those who are able to pay for it?
g. paying taxes throughout your life to support a government retirement program *or* having each individual responsible for paying for his or her own retirement?

Explain that all of these questions involve trade-offs that are made in different ways by different countries depending on the mix of command and market economies they have. The first alternative in each case is associated with systems that are more like command economies. These nations give up a degree of personal freedom in exchange for greater security. The second alternatives are found in nations that rely more on the market system. They offer more individual choice but less security. Discuss the choices your students make. Do they place more value on personal security or on individual freedom? Point out that this listing only compares economic differences between these systems, not political or social ones.

2. The Personal Narrative. The Personal Narrative in Section B describes the experiences of a student who sees a movie of an interview from 1960 with Gus Hall in her high school economics class. She is surprised to hear him say that many problems in the United States were caused by our capitalist economic system. Although she doubted Mr. Hall was right, she was convinced that he believed what he was saying. When she tries to talk about the movie at home, her father tells her that communism failed because it didn't give people a reason to work hard. Stating that more people in the former Soviet Union were poor while a few communist political leaders lived very well, her father says he does not want to hear any more about Gus Hall or what he said.

The Narrative demonstrates differences between the theory of communism as stated by Mr. Hall, and the economic and political reality that existed in countries that used this system.

Teaching Suggestions (Modeling/Guided Practice)

1. Find a newspaper article about a local person who has become a successful entrepreneur. Discuss what factors made this person a success and how his or her efforts have benefited other people in your community. What functions did the profit motive and private property play in this person's life? Ask your students to imagine how this person's life would have been different if he or she had lived in a country that had a command economy. Would other people in such a country have been able to benefit from this person's efforts?
2. Use Discussion Topic 21 from the *Teacher's Resource Binder* to illustrate one of the problems with incentives in a socialist economy.

   Your students should recognize that Chen would have less incentive to build the machine, because he would receive little personal reward and could certainly cause problems by causing 50 workers to lose their jobs.

Lesson Checkpoint

Text: Self-Check, text page 426
Answers

1. A government planning agency in the former Soviet Union decided what products would be produced, how they would be made, and to whom they would be distributed based on its understanding of what was best for that nation.
2. Our Social Security and welfare programs, progressive income taxes, and government regulation of utilities are socialist in nature.
3. Many nations have chosen to use less socialism in their economic systems in recent years to try to increase their people's incentive to work and be more productive.

Follow-up Assignments (Independent Practice/Extension/Homework)

Text: Applying What You Have Learned, text page 426
Answers

Student answers will vary depending on the politicians they choose to investigate. Their answers should demonstrate an understanding of the relationship between socialist characteristics and programs that require greater government spending and involvement in our economic system.

Section Evaluation

Self-Check, text page 426
Understanding Economics, questions 5-7 (Chapter 15 Review, text pages 433–436)

SECTION C. Different Kinds of Capitalism (text pages 428–432)

Objectives (Lesson Focus)

Upon completion of this section, students will be able to:

- Describe differences between the two types of capitalist economic systems that exist in the United States and Japan.
- Identify possible reasons for the rapid growth of the Japanese economy since the end of World War II.

- Explain why the Japanese economy is an example of industrial capitalism.
- Identify and explain problems that may exist with the Japanese economic system.

Preparation (Instruction: Pre-teaching—Vocabulary or Activity

1. Discussion Introduce this section by asking students to describe the feeling they believe working adults may have toward the businesses they work for. Do they think of this organization as an extension of their family? Do they feel a sense of loyalty to their employer? Would they make personal sacrifices to help other workers or the owners of this business? How do they regard their managers? Do they believe their opinions or ideas are wanted or respected? Can they talk to managers as equals? After discussing student answers to these questions describe the type of relationship that exists between workers and many businesses in Japan. Do your students believe such a relationship could ever exist in the United States? What factors in our values and personalities would help or hinder such a system?

After completing the discussion described above, ask students to predict how typical American firms and Japanese firms would react to a drop of 10% in their sales. Which firms would be best able to adjust to lower demands? Ask students to explain their opinions.

2. The Personal Narrative The Personal Narrative in Section C describes a discussion in a class led by a student who has recently returned from living in Japan for a year. He describes an experience he had visiting a Japanese factory. He was particularly impressed with the apparently close relationship between Japanese workers and their employers. Students in the class react to the presentation by feeling both envious and worried. On the following day a different speaker describes some shortcomings of the Japanese system to the same class. Although this talk makes them feel a little better, they are left with a sense of concern about the competition between Japanese and American businesses.

The Narrative demonstrates differences between the types of capitalism that are used in Japan and the United States. It shows how these differences have contributed to the rapid economic growth in Japan and identifies some possible problems in the Japanese system.

Teaching Suggestions (Modeling/Guided Practice)

1. Ask your students if they feel most people who are about 21 years old would be ready or able to choose the firm they should work for during the rest of their lives. Although many Americans think having a guaranteed job for life is a good idea, they often forget that this is a two-way agreement. The employee also makes a commitment to the firm. No other firm is likely to hire an employee who quits such a guaranteed job to take a similar position. A worker who finds he or she does not like his or her employer is left with few employment alternatives. Also, does a firm benefit from having employees who are dissatisfied in their work? Use these ideas to discuss problems that the Japanese system may experience.
2. Remind students that people who save a larger share of their disposable income spend less. This means that the higher rate of saving in Japan is associated with a lower rate of spending. Discuss how this contributes to the need of the Japanese economy to export many goods to other countries. A major objective of

American policy is to encourage the Japanese to consume more. Discuss how this could help solve part of our trade problems with Japan.

3. Although Japan is technologically more advanced than the United States in some types of production, many Japanese students still choose to attend colleges in the United States. Ask your students to identify possible reasons for this choice. Do they feel allowing Japanese students to study in the United States is beneficial to this country? Some possible reasons are listed below. Japanese students choose to study in the United States because:
    a. they will learn our language and customs and be better able to sell to us in the future.
    b. they may not have been accepted at a good college in Japan or they may find Japanese colleges stifle their creativity.
    c. they may want to be involved in U.S. research and development.
    d. they may want to live here in the future.

Lesson Checkpoint

Text: Self-Check, text page 431
Answers

1. Two possible advantages of working for a Japanese firm are greater job security and relatively good wages. Two possible disadvantages of working for a Japanese firm are fewer opportunities to be creative and less chance to change your job if you are dissatisfied.
2. The economies of both the United States and Japan are capitalist because they have private ownership of the means of production, and because their governments spend a much smaller part of national income than the more socialistic economies of Scandinavian countries.
3. Some Japanese firms are identified by their government to receive low-interest rate loans, research grants, and special aid in marketing their goods in other countries that may give them an unfair advantage over American firms they compete with.

Follow-up Assignments (Independent Practice/Extension/Homework)

Text: Applying What You Have Learned, text page 431
Answers

Student answers will vary but should demonstrate their understanding that if the Japanese produced less and consumed more they would have fewer products for export. This would help the United States's balance of trade. It is not consistent with the principles of economics because decreasing the supply of goods and increasing demand would cause higher prices. Japan's products would become less competitive, and consumers in both nations would pay more.

Section Evaluation

Self-Check, text page 430
Understanding Economics, questions 8 and 9 (Chapter 15 Review, text page 435)

ADDITIONAL MATERIALS FOR CHAPTER 15

Chapter Evaluation

Teacher's Resource Binder: Chapter 15 Quiz

Reteaching and Extension

See the *Teacher's Resource Binder* and the *Student Activity Book* for additional handouts and activities for Chapter 15.

TEACHER'S BIBLIOGRAPHY FOR CHAPTER 15

Economics Sources

Adler, Mortimer J. *Haves Without Have Nots: Six Essays on Democracy and Socialism.* New York: Macmillan, 1991.

Bertsch, Gary K. *Reform and Revolution in Communism, Capitalism, and Democracy.* Westport, Conn.: Greenwood Press, 1991.

Sik, Ota, ed. *Socialism Today: The Changing Meaning of Socialism.* New York: St. Martin's Press, 1991.

Trager, Oliver. *Communism: The Final Crisis?* New York: Facts on File, 1990.

Turner, Charles G. *Japan's Dynamic Efficiency in the Global Market, Trade, Investment and Economic Growth.* Westport, Conn.: Greenwood Press, 1991.

CHAPTER 15 REVIEW ANSWERS

Building Your Vocabulary (text page 434)

1. communism
2. incentive
3. profit motive
4. welfare capitalism
5. decentralized
6. kibbutz
7. industrial capitalism
8. socialism

Understanding Economics (text pages 434–435)

1. Social acceptance and self-respect for helping the community are often used as incentives in command economies.
2. The economic systems of all countries include some characteristics of both command and market economies.
3. Countries that have governments that are taking and spending a greater share of income are becoming more socialist.
4. Socialist governments are found in nations with strong central control over their economic systems.
5. Workers would revolt because they received lower and lower wages and conditions would become intolerable.
6. Workers received low wages and had little incentive to work hard. Low production made goods scarce. Government became oppressive.
7. Nations have reduced the amount of socialism in order to encourage more productivity.
8. Three measures that may indicate whether a nation's economy is capitalistic include who owns the means of production, whether resources are allocated according to profit or by the government, and the percentage of national product that the government spends.
9. The Japanese government provides low-interest rate loans, research grants, and marketing assistance to some of its firms.
10. Among the reasons for the rapid growth of the Japanese economy may be low-interest rate loans and other help from the government to business, the rate of saving and investing, the share of income devoted to education, social values of Japanese culture, and smaller expenditures for national defense.

Thinking Critically About Economics (page 435)

1. Student answers will vary but should demonstrate their use of reason and logic

and an understanding of relevant information from this chapter. Possible answers are:

a. In a capitalist economy, like the United States, people who contribute little to production receive little income.

b. Advertising increases demand for products that creates more production and jobs for workers.

c. Resources that are not allocated for schools are available for other uses that society may benefit from.

d. Competition does not mean that people can't get along with each other, particularly when it creates a higher standard of living for most people.

2. Student questions will vary but should be related to the command economic system that exists in a kibbutz.

3. Student answers will vary but should demonstrate their understanding of ways that our government limits the rights of business owners to make free economic choices. Possible answers are:

a. They would have to meet requirements of building codes.

b. They would have to pay Social Security taxes for their workers.

c. They would have to have equal employment opportunities for different workers.

d. They would have to meet safety standards for their workers.

This shows that while the business is operated by a private company for profit, it is regulated by the government to benefit society.

4. Firms in the former Soviet Union could have low-quality production year after year because they had little or no competition. Consumers were forced to buy their products or do without.

5. When people in nations with welfare capitalism realized that a decent standard of living would be provided to them by their government regardless of whether they worked hard or not, some of them chose to do little work.

6. Japanese managers may choose to work hard to achieve a feeling of self-respect and also the respect of other people they live and work with. They may have a greater sense of community.

Consumer Skills Projects (text page 435)

1. Your students will probably find that many adults do not understand the reasons for the changes that have taken place in Eastern Europe and the former Soviet Union. You might discuss why this lack of knowledge exists in the United States. Do your students believe many adults understand how their own economic system works? How may Americans suffer from their limited knowledge of economic systems?

2. Students should complete this project in a way that demonstrates their ability to investigate economic systems in other countries and to use the information they find to place these countries on the range in Figure 15–1.

PART 4 REVIEW ANSWERS

Understanding Economic Concepts

1. The answer is provided as an example in the text.

2. Countries may create barriers to trade by imposing tariffs or taxes in imported goods, they may limit imports with quotas, or set standards that are difficult for imported goods to meet.

3. According to the infant industry argument, developing nations should establish tariffs to protect their developing industries from competition from more developed industries in other countries.
4. Countries would rather have a positive balance of trade because they are more likely to have full employment, economic growth, and a large tax base if they do.
5. One of the most important reasons for the U.S. negative balance of trade in the early 1980s was the high exchange rate for the U.S. dollar. Many foreigners found that they had to trade too many of their units of money to get the dollars they needed to buy American products. It was less expensive for them to buy products they needed from other countries.
6. Multinational corporations that operate in many different nations may help their host countries by providing jobs and investments, but they may also exert too much influence on governments and may pay less than their fair share of taxes.
7. Many developing countries have traditional economies in which most people learn what they know and their values from their families. These countries usually have no developed educational system. This makes it difficult for them to bring about change.
8. Many developing countries lack basic infrastructure, the capital improvements such as roads and electric power necessary to allow their industries to produce goods efficiently. This lack makes it difficult for them to compete with industries in more developed nations that have an advanced infrastructure.
9. Just sending tools and other types of capital to developing countries usually does little good because the people in these nations often do not know how to use them. Because of the inadequate education systems that exist in many of these countries, the capital may be wasted.
10. Advances in medical care have reduced the mortality rates in many developing nations. This has frequently increased the population growth rates in these countries.
11. In command economies like communism and socialism a central government authority answers the basic economic questions *what*, *how*, and *for whom*. It also determines the allocation of resources.
12. In many formerly communist countries workers had little reason or incentive to work hard because their income and standard of living were often not related to the quality of their work.
13. The Japanese economy has been called industrial capitalism because the Japanese government intervenes in the economy to allocate resources and help businesses that they believe will be most successful in achieving greater productivity and are able to export goods.

Writing About Economics

1. Student answers should reflect an understanding of the issues involved in each of the identified terms. Their questions on the protecting domestic jobs argument should demonstrate an awareness of the trade-offs lower tariffs would bring in the job market. Their questions on dumping should show that they understand why exporters might choose to sell products below the price they charge customers in their own country. Their questions on the negative balance of trade should demonstrate their understanding of the economic impact of a negative balance of trade on an economy.

2. Student answers should demonstrate an understanding of the problems in achieving economic growth in developing nations, which result from the traditional economic systems and inadequate infrastructures that often exist in these countries.
3. Student answers should demonstrate an understanding of important differences between the Japanese and American economies. A discussion of help that the Japanese government provides to Japanese firms should be included to show their understanding of industrial capitalism.

Discussing Economics

1. Students should identify issues that are related to the proposed legislation to require all automobiles sold in the United States to be made at least 80 percent from parts made in this country. Students should state whether or not they support the proposed legislation and explain the costs and benefits associated with the legislation and why they believe their answer is best.
2. Students should identify issues that are related to preventing American banks from making loans to developing nations and should state whether or not they support the proposed law. Students should explain the costs and benefits associated with the law and why they believe their answer is best.

Problem-Solving with Economics

Chapter 13

1. Student answers will vary according to their individual values and points of view. Their explanations should show that they logically considered issues such as prices, quality, and buying American products to help the domestic economy.
2. a. Limits on imports could increase employment in industries that produce these products, but could also lead to inflation or retaliatory trade barriers by countries that export the products.
   b. Higher tariffs could increase employment in industries that produce goods that compete with imported goods, but could lead to inflation or retaliatory trade barriers by countries that export taxed goods.
   c. Paying unemployment compensation for two years could help people who are hurt by imports but could also result in higher taxes and costs of production for other U.S. firms.
   d. Providing government retraining programs for workers who lose their jobs due to imports would help these workers but could result in higher taxes and costs of production for other U.S. firms.
   e. Providing government jobs for all workers who lose their jobs due to imports would help these workers, but would increase government spending and probably increase taxes, which would increase the costs of production for other U.S. firms.

Chapter 14

1. Student answers will vary according to their individual points of view. However, all answers should reflect an understanding of the multiple problems faced by developing nations.

2. Student answers will vary according to their individual points of view.

   a. Bringing foreign students to the United States would only help if they returned to their homes and had the tools and other factors of production needed to increase production.

   b. Business investment in less developed nations would only help if people were trained to work in the factories built and there was a market for the goods produced.

   c. Sending U.S. citizens to developing nations would only help if they had the tools and other capital necessary to help people increase their productivity.

3. Student answers will vary according to their individual values and points of view. Their answers should demonstrate careful consideration of the conflicting values and points of view concerning the issue of population growth.

Chapter 15

1. Student answers will vary but should demonstrate a knowledge of the differences between the way command and market economies work.

2. Student answers will vary but should demonstrate an awareness of the different types of personal characteristics that make individuals good managers or electable leaders. They should make it clear that they understand the inherent contradictions between these characteristics and why these contradictions may make it difficult for systems that are both socialistic and democratic to work efficiently.

APPLYING ECONOMIC PRINCIPLES

Teacher's Annotated Edition

Sanford D. Gordon

Alan D. Stafford

GLENCOE

Macmillan/McGraw-Hill

New York, New York   Columbus, Ohio   Mission Hills, California   Peoria, Illinois

Authors

Alan Stafford earned a Bachelor of Science degree in economics from the honors program at Western Michigan State University and Master's degrees in social studies education and business administration from the State University of New York. He served as a Peace Corps volunteer in Micronesia, taught in an urban high school for 12 years, and currently is an associate professor of economics at Niagara County Community College. He has taught courses sponsored by the New York State Department of Education and the New York Developmental Economics Education Program (DEEP). A recipient of 2 first place teaching awards from the New York State Council on Economic Education, he is coauthor of several economics texts.

Sanford D. Gordon earned a Ph.D. in economics from New York University. Active in the economic education movement since 1960, he served as the Executive Director of the New York State Council on Economic Education from 1979 to 1989. He is a recipient of the Calvin Kazanjian Foundation award for innovation in teaching economics and the first winner of the Bessie B. Moore Award for outstanding service and dedication to excellence and innovations in economic education. Dr. Gordon has authored many books on economics and economic education and has been adviser to numerous school districts, the New York State Education Department, banks, and local governments.

Reviewers and Consultants

Christine A. Blumberg
Social Studies Teacher
Burnt Hills—Ballston Lake Senior High School
Burnt Hills, New York

Randolph J. Pachuta
Curriculum Specialist—Social Studies
The School Board of Broward County
Lauderdale Lakes, Florida

Peter Pitard
Department Chairperson, Learning Handicapped
Grossmont High School
La Mesa, California

Harvey L. Prokop
Program Manager, Social Studies
Educational Services Division, San Diego City Schools
San Diego, California

Delores Marie Robinson
Curriculum Specialist, Mentor Teacher
Roosevelt High School
Fresno, California

Joseph Weintraub
Regional Administrator, New York City Developmental Education Program
Adjunct Professor of Economics
Nassau Community College
Garden City, New York

James H. Wimberly
Social Studies Curriculum Director/Secondary
Bibb County Board of Education
Macon, Georgia

Send all inquiries to:
GLENCOE DIVISION
Macmillan/McGraw-Hill
936 Eastwind Drive
Westerville, Ohio 43081

ISBN 0-02-822711-5 (Student Text)
ISBN 0-02-822712-3 (Teacher's Annotated Edition)

4 5 6 7 8 9 10 11 12 13 14 15 AGH/LP 00 99 98 97 96 95 94

CONTENTS

CONTENTS

CONTENTS

CONTENTS

CONTENTS

CONTENTS

CONTENTS

CONTENTS

Howard's
GIFTS & YARNS
·IRISH IMPORTS
·KNITTING MACHINES
·SWEATERS
723

CONTENTS

CONTENTS

Ethanol's Good fo
Economy and Envir

CONTENTS

CONTENTS

CONTENTS

CONTENTS

CONTENTS

CONTENTS

CONTENTS

WSYX6 First Weather
Afternoon
Evening
Tonight
First Weather

FEATURES

Current Consumer Issues

Current Economic Issues

Developing Your Economic Skills

Profiles

FIGURES AND TABLES

FIGURES

FIGURES AND TABLES

TABLES

TO THE STUDENT

Why Study Economics?

Economics has become an increasingly important high school course in recent years. This is partly because many people believe America as a nation will be better off if we all understand how our economy works. Another reason is this: If you understand how the economy works, you personally will be better off too.

All of us live in the economy, and we all must make economic choices. You will soon discover that you have been making economic choices all your life—even when you haven't thought of them as such. As you study economics, you will learn to make these decisions using logic and common sense. This does not have to be difficult, and it can be very interesting. It can also be profitable. The more you know about economics, the better equipped you will be to make choices that bring you the most satisfaction for your time and money.

How to Use This Book

This book will help you understand how economics and your life fit together. It is designed to do this in a way you will find easy to understand. The following features are especially important in using this book.

The Personal Narrative

Each chapter is divided into sections that begin with a Personal Narrative. The Personal Narratives are made-up stories that describe people who are roughly your age. The people in these stories experience problems that could be real. As you read the Personal Narratives, you will discover that principles of economics are at work in important events in the lives of these people. The same principles of economics also affect important events in your life.

Following each Personal Narrative is a section of text that explains the concepts that were demonstrated in the Personal Narrative. Together, the text and the Personal Narratives show how economics is a part of your everyday life. You'll find that the study of economics will help you understand what is happening in the world around you and will assist you in making better decisions.

Section-by Section Organization

This textbook is organized in sections, to enable you to concentrate on important individual principles. The list of Objectives at the beginning of each chapter shows the main principles to look for in each section. At the end of each section, the Self-Check questions help you briefly review what you have learned. The Applying What You Have Learned questions give you an opportunity to reexamine the Personal Narrative and other real-world situations.

Current Economic and Consumer Issues

Near the end of each chapter, you will find either a Current Economic Issue or a Current Consumer Issue. Current Economic Issues deal with economic questions that face the nation. As elected officials address each issue, their decisions will affect every American. Current Consumer Issues will likely affect you directly as you participate in making consumer choices. As you study such issues, you will discover that many problems of economics involve social and political values. That is one reason why people often disagree over what should be done to solve economic problems.

Developing Your Economic Skills

At the very end of each chapter, you will find a Developing Your Economic Skills feature. Each of these features gives step-by-step instructions on how to use a particular kind of skill that is important in economics. For example, one skills feature will show you how to read a table; another will show you how to interpret a bar graph. Each feature has a Skill explanation, an Application, and a Practice to give you hands-on experience in using the skill. Your teacher may ask you to study a particular skills feature when you first read the chapter or as a reference to review that particular skill.

Photographs and Figures

There are many photographs, tables, and graphs in this book. Each was included to illustrate one or more economic concepts. You have heard the saying, "one picture is worth a thousand words." The same is true of these figures. They provide information that would often take many written pages to communicate.

Each photograph is accompanied by a caption that explains a concept of economics. Each figure is explained in nearby text. Take the time to read these captions and explanations. They will make your work much easier in this course and in many other situations in the future.

Highlighted Vocabulary Terms

At the beginning of each section is a short statement of important terms and concepts that you will find in the section. Within the section itself, you will see that some terms are set in a heavy, dark type—these are the most important vocabulary terms. These terms are defined in the Glossary at the end of the book and are reviewed in each Chapter Review. As you read the text, if you forget exactly what a particular economic term means, look it up in the Glossary. The Glossary will define the term, and give you a page number where you can read more about it in the text.

Review Activities

Each chapter and part of the text is followed by a series of activities. All of these Activities will help you check your understanding of economic concepts. Many provide you with additional information. Some give you a chance to apply what you have learned about economics to new situations. Your teacher will probably assign some of these activities as classwork or homework. Don't be surprised if sometimes different students are assigned different activities. There is a wide selection of things to do, and your teacher has been trained to decide which are best for each student.

You may know little about economics right now. If you make a reasonable effort, that statement will not be true in a few months. You will discover that there is a logic about economics that tells you much about the way people behave and about the way things happen in the world. In learning those things, you will learn much that is valuable to you in your everyday life.

APPLYING ECONOMIC PRINCIPLES

BENI .R.
OP

PART

1

Understanding the Fundamentals of Economics

Part 1 lays the foundation for your understanding of economics. It provides you with the meanings of many essential economic terms and concepts. You will learn what the basic economic questions are and how these questions are answered in different economic systems. You will examine the process through which resources are combined to create production and how products are distributed. And perhaps most importantly, you will learn how economists solve problems.

CHAPTER 1

Life Is Economics

Objectives

In the sections of this chapter, you will learn:

A

why *scarcity* is the central economic problem;

B

how the choices we make cause us to pay *opportunity costs*;

C

how the *factors of production* combine to produce goods and services;

D

how economists use *models* to evaluate economic conditions and make predictions;

E

why people do not always agree in selecting the *rational choice;* and

F

how to interpret a graph that shows a *production possibilities frontier.*

Introduction

All your life, you will be dealing with economics. You have no choice: being born, living, and dying all involve economics. One way to define **economics** is to say that it is *the study of the decisions involved in producing, distributing, and consuming goods and services.*

In this chapter you will begin your study of economics by understanding the term *scarcity.* You will learn why we must make economic decisions and how each choice involves a trade-off of alternatives. And you will study the four factors necessary to produce goods and services.

Everyone in the United States consumes goods and services. Goods and services are things that satisfy human wants and needs. **Goods** are *tangible*—meaning that they are physical, touchable objects. **Services** are *intangible*—they are things that people do, not objects that can be touched.

Study the photograph on page 6. How many different goods and services can you identify in the photograph? Many of the people shown are working to produce products or to provide services that other people are buying. How many occupations can you identify? The people who are working are not only producing things for other people to buy, they are also earning money so they can buy products too.

Explain. There are other definitions for economics. This one is relatively simple and therefore appropriate for an introductory text.

The people in this street scene are producing goods and providing services—and also are buying the goods and services produced by other people.

Explain. There are important differences between goods and services. For example, goods can be accumulated while services cannot. The photograph provides examples of each.

Discuss. What is society's responsibility to those who are mentally handicapped? How much of our resources can we (should we) allocate to helping such people?

You have studied a photograph of many people. Now look at the person in the top photograph on page 7. What sort of goods and services would this person want the most? What responsibilities does society have toward him? Do we owe him a basic income if he can't take care of himself?

Now look at the second photograph. What goods and services do children require? What is society's responsibility in providing for them? Do children deserve better treatment than adults? Should society treat a family that lives in poverty differently than the man in the preceding picture? How would you explain your feelings about this to someone else?

The third photograph shows individuals who are employed to make a product. What sort of help should be provided to them if they become unemployed? Do you believe that the unemployed should be treated differently from people who have never worked?

Discuss. What methods do we have for becoming wealthy? Is individual wealth the result of luck, good fortune, hard work, or dishonesty?

The final photograph is of a person who appears to be wealthy. Why do some people have many more things than others? Would you like to live like the man in this picture? What sort of choices might you have to make to be like him?

You have been asked many questions and given few answers in this introduction. There is an important reason for this: many economic issues concern *value judgments.* People often disagree over what is the "best" answer to an economic question. You

Economic decisions affect people who are living in many different kinds of circumstances. This is one reason why economic choices for a society may sometimes be difficult to make.

Stress. Your students often think in economic terms even when they are not aware of it. They have an understanding of the value of money, how to earn it, and of the value of products they can buy. These are learned skills, and the study of economics can improve them.

may feel one way about an issue while other people hold different points of view. This does not prove that you are right while others are wrong. It shows that there are different and conflicting ideas concerning economics. Still, decisions have to be made. It is important that we consider everyone's point of view when we decide what to do.

The best economic decisions are those that do the most good at the least cost. One reason for you to study economics is that by learning more you will have a better chance of making good decisions.

Section A Unlimited Wants and Limited Resources

This section introduces the concept of *scarcity* and explains why consumers, businesses, and governments must all make choices.

Personal Narrative

I Don't Have Enough

There's a hole in my right shoe. It's not a big hole, but it lets water in when it rains. Then I walk down the hall at school going "squish, squash." Everyone laughs as I go by. I really need a new pair of shoes.

I've only got $20 now. That's not enough. On Saturday I'll get paid $30 when I clean out Joe Rizzo's garage. Then I'll be able to afford a decent pair of shoes.

Joe Rizzo runs a garage where he fixes dents and paints cars. He works hard, but he doesn't do a very good job. He says he would do better work if he could afford new tools. Joe dreams a lot and buys lottery tickets. Joe's okay, but I don't want to end up like him.

I know what I want. I want to be able to just walk into a store and buy what I like. I'm tired of having to ask my mom for money that I know she really needs herself. Dad loads trucks for a living. The pay isn't very good, but it's all he can find. There never seems to be enough money by the end of the week.

Discuss. What are the local job opportunities for students who did and did not graduate from high school? Why are there differences?

Next year I'm going to graduate from high school. I hope I can find a good job, but I'm not sure that I will. My older brother graduated two years ago. He joined the Army because he couldn't find a decent job around here.

Sometimes I walk downtown just to look in the stores. I see people buying expensive things. Last week I watched a man buy a suit that cost $350. It doesn't bother me that he spent so much money; I would just like to be able to do it too.

Values. Do your students see any conflict in values when a person able to afford expensive clothes stands in a city street full of holes? Does this show the best allocation of resources for society?

Something happened to the man with the expensive suit that was kind of funny. It was raining when he left the store. A bus hit a pothole just when he got to the curb. It splashed him with muddy water. He may have had an expensive suit, but he was just as wet as I was.

There's a big park with a zoo downtown. On nice days I go in and watch the animals. I feel sorry for them because their cages are so small. On the other hand, they get fed every day. If they could choose, I wonder if they would take freedom or regular meals. There used to be lions in the zoo, but they were sold. It cost too much to feed them. Even the city can't afford to pay for everything.

Yesterday our landlord said that he is raising our rent by $30 next month. "Property tax went up," he said. Maybe it did, but I don't see them fixing the potholes, and the lions aren't back in the zoo.

It's almost three o'clock, time to go home. I still have a hole in my shoe and it looks like rain.

Unlimited Wants and Limited Resources

Scarcity is the economic term that describes a situation where there are not enough products available to satisfy people's needs or wants. Scarcity is based on two ideas. First, there is no limit to what we want. Second, there is a limit to our ability to produce goods and services that will satisfy our wants. This means that scarcity *always* exists. No matter how much we make, someone will always want more.

Explain. Wealth and money are not the same. Money represents wealth only in terms of what it can buy. Scarcity is not the result of a shortage of money, it is the result of our limited ability to produce goods and services to satisfy our wants.

Consumers Must Choose

If we can't have everything we want, then we have to choose what we want the most. We usually make these choices when we decide how to spend our money. If you spend your money on a pair of shoes, that must be what you want most. Anything you pay for is scarce because you are giving up something of value to get it.

Businesses Must Choose

Businesses face the problem of scarcity too. If Joe Rizzo bought fewer lottery tickets he might be able to afford more tools. He can't pay for both.

The Government Must Choose

Discuss. Consumers make choices to meet personal needs and to gain personal satisfaction. Business choices are intended to maximize profits. On what basis do your students believe the government makes choices?

The government also is confronted with scarcity, and must make choices. Even if taxes go up, the government still has to decide what needs to be done. If resources are used to fix the roads, there may not be money left to hire as many teachers.

One example of government choice was the strategic defense initiative (SDI) or "star wars" program. In March 1983, Ronald Reagan announced a plan to develop weapons that would destroy attacking missiles before they could reach American cities or military installations. Spending continued on this program even after the breakup of the Soviet Union in the early 1990s. Today people disagree over whether SDI was a wise use for the nation's resources. It resulted in the development of the Patriot missile that helped protect American soldiers in the 1991 Persian Gulf War. Some people, however, believe the money could have been used in other ways that would have benefited more people.

Because resources are scarce, we must all make choices on how to use what we have. The SDI program was an economic choice on the government level, at a cost of many billions of dollars.

People, businesses, and the government are forced to choose. Part of this book will be devoted to showing you how these choices are made, and to helping you make good choices in your own life.

Self-Check
1. We can't get everything we want for free.
2. We do not have enough resources to produce enough products to satisfy everyone's wants.

Self-Check

1. Why must we all make economic choices?
2. Why does scarcity always exist?

Applying What You Have Learned
See Lesson Plans for Chapter 1, Section A, page T7.

Applying What You Have Learned

Below you will find a list of people or organizations that were mentioned in the Personal Narrative. There was at least one thing that each didn't have enough of. Identify what each found to be scarce.

a. the person telling the story
b. Joe Rizzo
c. the brother
d. the man with the suit
e. the city
f. the animals in the zoo

Section B Everyone Pays Opportunity Costs

This section will explain how every choice involves *trade-offs* and *opportunity costs.*

Personal Narrative

If I Buy You a Pizza, I Can't Put Gas in My Car

Ted used to be my boyfriend. If I told you what I think of him now, they wouldn't print it. Last Friday Ted took me to a movie about some war hero. I didn't want to go, but he was all excited about it. I went with him to make him happy. I don't remember much about the movie. There were lots of guns and explosions. It was boring!

I was really starved when we got out of the theater around nine o'clock. Ted said, "Let's go to your place and see what your mom's got in the refrigerator." Understand, at home there would be nothing to do but watch television. That's boring! My two little brothers would have been screaming at each other and my mother would have been on the phone in the kitchen. Home was the last place on earth I wanted to be.

Discuss. Choices are no better than the information they are based on. How could Ted and his girlfriend have avoided their problems by providing each other with more information? Why is complete and accurate information important in making economic decisions?

I told Ted I wanted to go to Eddy's Pizza to sit and talk. He said, "I've only got 15 dollars to last me until next payday. If I buy you a pizza I can't put gas in my car." Well, I was really mad. I told him that I only sat through his stupid movie because I was looking forward to going out for a pizza afterwards. He said I was selfish. I said he was cheap. Ted got me home in time to see the news. No one even noticed when I came in. I wonder what I'll do next Friday night.

Opportunity Costs

In the story above, Ted and his girlfriend both made choices. Economists call these kinds of choices **trade-offs,** meaning that you choose to give up one thing so that you can have something else instead. In making these choices, Ted and his girlfriend both paid what economists would call **opportunity cost.** Opportunity cost is a term used to describe the value of a second choice that you give up when you take your first choice. Ted refused to buy his girlfriend a pizza. She decided to tell him off. He took her home early. In each case the person got one thing but gave up something else in exchange. Ted, for example, will be able to drive to school next week, but when he gets there his girlfriend probably won't speak to him. Ted must have wanted the gas for his car most. He gave up his girlfriend's company. Ted's opportunity cost was the value he placed on his girlfriend's company.

Stress. Many students will require emphasis that opportunity cost is the value of the second choice that was given up, not the value of the thing that was chosen.

Everyone pays opportunity costs. Each time you spend money you make a choice. You buy what you want most. When you do this, you give up the chance to buy something else instead.

Opportunity cost can also be paid in terms of time. If you take a job after school, you may have to give up the chance to join the basketball team.

Businesses Pay Opportunity Costs

Businesses must pay opportunity costs too. Many firms have invested in factories in Mexico. Money that has been spent there

The nation pays opportunity costs when it makes choices. The money spent on defense cannot at the same time be spent on health services, money spent on health services cannot at the same time be spent on education, and so on. When we pay the opportunity cost that goes with any choice, it means that we give up the value of the thing not chosen.

is money that won't be spent in the United States. Machines sent to Mexico are machines that can't be used here. Jobs for Mexican workers are jobs that American workers won't have. Businesses will receive earnings from their investments in Mexico, but they will give up the earnings they could have made from investments in the United States.

Governments Pay Opportunity Costs

Opportunity cost is also paid by the government. If the President asks for $30 billion for additional defense spending and Congress agrees, that $30 billion worth of resources will be unavailable for education or other purposes. At the same time, the money spent for education will be unavailable for the nation's defense, new housing, or health services. There is no way to be sure which type of government spending has the most value for the most people. Still, the choices must be made. And every time the government spends money an opportunity cost is paid, because the value of something else the government could have done is given up.

Everyone Makes Trade-Offs

Explain. Many trade-offs—for example, the effects of pollution—may not be immediately apparent, and failure to recognize the choice that is being made can be costly.

Life is made up of a series of trade-offs in which we give up one thing in order to gain something else that we feel has greater value. We must make choices all of the time. So do businesses and governments. We all try to make decisions that give us the most value. Sometimes we succeed, sometimes we don't, but we have to go right on making choices and paying our opportunity costs.

Self-Check
1. One thing of value is given up in order to receive something else, usually of greater value.
2. When any choice is made, there is a trade-off. A second choice is given up to take the first choice. The value of the second choice is opportunity cost.

Self-Check

1. What is a trade-off?
2. Why does every choice involve an opportunity cost?

Applying What You Have Learned
See Lesson Plans for Chapter 1, Section B, page T9.

Applying What You Have Learned

In the Personal Narrative, the people made many choices. You will find some of these choices listed below. Explain why you think each choice was made. Describe the opportunity cost that was paid for each choice.

a. The girl's choice to go to a movie she didn't really want to see
b. Ted's choice to go to a movie when he was short on money
c. Ted's choice to take his girlfriend home early

Section C From Resources to Products

This section will explain how four factors—*natural resources, labor, capital,* and *entrepreneurship*—make production possible.

Personal Narrative

I Built a Dog House

I wish you could see my dog Washington: He's a pure-bred Afghan. My uncle gave him to me when he was just a puppy. I named him Washington because when I comb his hair he looks just like the picture on a one-dollar bill.

Washington and I had a problem. My mother said he was a "one-dog disaster area." He tracked dirt all over the house and his hair was on all of the furniture. My mom was mad when I first got the dog. She finally said I had to keep him outside or get rid of him. It doesn't get cold here, but it rains a lot. I decided that the only thing to do was to build Washington a dog house.

Discuss. Ask your students about home improvement projects they have been involved in. Help your class identify the factors of production that were used in these projects.

I went to the library and found a book that told me what I needed and how to do it. I borrowed $75 from my father. We went to the lumber yard to buy plywood, some two-by-fours, nails, shingles and paint. My father brought my supplies home in his truck.

A real problem was that I don't know how to use tools very well. The last time I had picked up a saw I ended up in the emergency room at the hospital. I made a deal with my neighbor Ed. In exchange for cutting his lawn for free, he said he'd help me build my dog house.

We worked on the job all last weekend. Sunday night I painted Washington's house. I don't think he likes it very much. He sits on the porch and whines, but Mom says he'll get used to it. Maybe he will, but I'm not sure.

From Resources to Products

In the story above, Washington's owner decided to build a dog house. Building the dog house is one example of **production,** which is the creation of any kind of good or service. To build the dog house, Washington's owner needed certain resources. **Resources** are all the things that are necessary for production. Washington's owner needed lumber, nails, shingles, and paint. He had to get help from someone who knew how to use tools. He got plans from the library and borrowed money to pay for his supplies. Finally he had to decide where to put the dog house when it was finished. All of these resources would then be called

factors of production by an economist. They are all necessary to produce goods and services.

The Four Factors of Production

Economists classify factors of production in four types (as shown in Figure 1–1). They are:

Stress. Emphasize the distinction between natural resources, which have not been changed by man, and capital, which has.

Explain. Labor implies skills and abilities, not just people. Also, a person's skills and abilities must be in demand if they are to be employed.

Explain. Private ownership is not the only type of entrepreneurship possible. Other nations use alternative methods.

1. **Natural Resources**—things that are in their natural state and have not been changed by people. Examples would be crude oil in the ground, or trees before they are cut down to make lumber.
2. **Labor**—human effort that is applied to natural resources in producing goods and services.
3. **Capital**—the tools that are used by labor in making products. Capital can also be raw materials after they have been processed into various other forms. Money itself is not capital, but it can be considered capital when it is used to buy factories, machines, or anything else in the production process.
4. **Entrepreneurship**—the organization that is necessary to bring production about. This includes the owner or manager of a

Figure 1–1 *The Four Factors of Production*

The construction of the Atlantis *space shuttle required the use of the four factors of production: natural resources, labor, capital, and entrepreneurship.*

firm who organizes the other factors of production and takes the risks associated with running a business.

All four of these factors are necessary to achieve production.

Self-Check

1. Are all resources considered *natural* resources? Explain.
2. What are the four factors of production?

Applying What You Have Learned

The Personal Narrative contains examples of all four factors of production. From the story, make four lists:

a. examples of natural resources
b. examples of labor
c. examples of capital
d. examples of entrepreneurship

Self-Check

1. Natural resources are only those resources that have not been changed by human labor. Lumber, for example, is capital, not a natural resource, because it has been changed by human labor.
2. The four factors of production are natural resources, labor, capital, and entrepreneurship.

Applying What You Have Learned

See Lesson Plans for Chapter 1, Section C, page T10.

Section D How Economists Use Models

This section explains how people and economists all use *models* to understand how things work.

Personal Narrative

How Do You Talk to Someone You Don't Know?

Last summer we bought a house in the suburbs. Before we'd always rented, but Mom and Dad figured it was a good time to buy.

Before we moved in, my dad and I did a lot of work around the house. We ended up with a giant mound of trash. We set it all out just as the garbage truck arrived. It was such a hot day that we asked the two sanitation workers if they wanted a glass of some lemonade we had brought with us.

They accepted, so I poured them each a glass. But I couldn't think of anything to say. I always worry when I first meet someone new. I don't know what they're like. I'm afraid I'll say something foolish. My mom tells me to just look at them and talk about something I think they would be interested in. That's easy for her to say, but not for me to do.

As it turned out, it didn't matter, because they couldn't take time to stay and talk. They just drank the lemonade in two quick gulps and hurried on to finish their work.

I wonder what we would have talked about if they had been able to stay longer.

Using Models

Discuss. Show pictures of various people and ask your students to guess what each person is like. The results can illustrate differences in student perceptions.

What do you think of the situation described above? When you first meet someone, do you always know what to say? Do you know what things the person might be interested in and like to talk about? You might know what someone does for a living, but is there any way to guess other things about the person?

Although you could guess, there is no way for you to actually know what he is like without more information. Still, we all make judgments about other people without knowing very much about them. We often judge people based on our first impressions. If we later find that our first impressions were wrong, we just change our minds. It's not hard, people do it all the time.

Why do we try to guess what people are like when we don't know much about them? We do it because we want to know how to act. We feel safer if we know what to expect. An economist might say that when we do this we are making a **model.**

Like economists, weather forecasters use models to help predict some of the things that might happen in the future.

Explain. Many of your students will be interested in local or professional sports teams. When students make predictions of how the teams will do this year, they are using models.

A model is a theory or an idea of what something is like or how something works. Models are made from incomplete information. We make models about people. Economists make models about how the economy works.

Models Are Based on Assumptions

If you want to predict what will happen to the price of gasoline, you study the factors that you think are the most important.

A list of all the things that might cause the price of gasoline to go up would be very long. No one could think of all the possible reasons at one time.

You would use a model because you know you will not have complete information when you make your prediction.

When we make models we often make assumptions. Assumptions are things that we take for granted as true. We use them as facts even though we can't be sure that they are. For example, I might assume that fancy restaurants are expensive. I might not even try a restaurant if I don't have much money. I would assume that I can't afford it. But I might be wrong. The prices at the restaurant might be quite reasonable. The quality of a model is no better than the assumptions that it is based on.

Models Can Be Revised

Economists use models to better understand the past or present and to predict the future. If an economic model results in a prediction that turns out to be right, the model can be used again. If the prediction is wrong, the model might be changed to make better predictions the next time.

Economists predict how much prices will change. They predict employment, or the number of cars that will be sold next year. They could make predictions about the effects of a tax cut. Sometimes economists' predictions turn out to be wrong, but they keep trying. We study these predictions because they help us make decisions about our own future.

Economic Predictions Affect Us All

Economists' predictions are more important than our own in at least one big way. Their predictions are used by the government and businesses when decisions are made that affect us all. Economic models and predictions are important to everyone. Many of the things you will study in this book concern economic models and how predictions are made.

Self-Check
1. Economists must use models because it is impossible to consider every factor that could affect an economic decision.
2. Models do not always result in accurate predictions because they cannot include all factors.

Applying What You Have Learned
See Lesson Plans for Chapter 1, Section D, page T12.

Self-Check

1. Why do economists use models?
2. Do models always produce accurate predictions? Why not?

Applying What You Have Learned

In this section you have read about how economists and people in general try to make predictions so that they will know what to do in the future. Make some predictions of your own about the future of things you are familiar with. Below is a list of topics. Try to guess what will happen to each of them by the end of this semester. Put your name on your predictions. Seal them in an envelope and give the envelope to your teacher. Your class can open all the envelopes at the end of this semester and see how close you were. Think about things you could do to improve your chances of being right. Your teacher may want you to add other predictions to the list.

a. How much will a gallon of gasoline cost?
b. Who will have the #1 record on the top ten?
c. How many students will earn a *B* or better in this class?
d. How many students will have a job?

Section E Making Rational Choices

This section discusses how people try to make *rational choices* using *positive* and *normative statements.*

Personal Narrative

Careers. What goals have your students set for their own lives? What costs will your students have to pay to achieve their goals? What benefits do they expect to gain? Do their goals represent rational choices?

My Mother Wants Me to be a Doctor

When my mother was a little girl, she had a dream about growing up to be a doctor. What she really did was get married at 17 and have five children in eight years. She never even finished high school. Twenty years later she still has her dream. She knows it won't ever come true for her, so now she wants it for me. The problem is I don't want to be a doctor.

What I like to do is write stories. That's what I'm good at. I get *A's* in English all the time. My math grades are bad and my science grades are worse. I was lucky to pass General Science last year. I tell my mom that it doesn't make any sense for someone who is lousy at math and science to try to be a doctor. She doesn't listen to me at all. She says, "Things are different today. Now a woman can be anything she wants to be. When I was a girl, everyone just expected women to be housewives. Think how much a doctor can earn. You could do something really important. You could save lives and be famous." When I tell her no one gets into medical school unless they have *A's* in science and math, she ignores me. She doesn't want to hear.

I have a lot of thinking to do about my career plans. I know that I can write well. I could go to college to learn how to be a reporter for a newspaper. I think there are lots of jobs in journalism. I'm sure that I would be happy writing for a living. The right choice for me is to study journalism and to forget about being a doctor.

Making Rational Choices

Like the young woman in the story, economists must often decide what is the right or *rational* choice. You have already learned in this chapter that economists study how decisions are made. Every time a choice is made something is given up. The woman in the story recognizes that she must choose between alternatives for her career. **Rational choice** is taking the things with greater value and giving up those with lesser values. That's the rational thing to do.

But which things have greater value? If everyone felt the same about what they did and did not want, it would be easy to decide how to use our resources. The problem is that we don't

Decisions about career goals are some of the more important rational choices that people must make. Like many other choices, they can involve both positive statements (which are based on fact and can be proven) and normative statements (which reflect personal values and will vary from one person to another).

all agree on what is best. When you make a decision just for yourself, it doesn't make much difference how others feel. But many of your decisions will affect other people who may not share your ideas. Making the best choices for groups of people is hard to do.

Positive Statements

Stress. Just because something is in print does not necessarily mean it is true. The headline from 1948 announcing President Truman's defeat by Dewey is a good example.

Some things are facts. Last year's rate of inflation can be measured. We can count how many people were employed over the past year, or past five, or past ten years. And we know it is very likely that if nothing else changes, higher prices will cause lower sales. Economists call these things **positive statements** because they can be proven.

Normative Statements

There are other things that can be just as important as facts. These include things that cannot be proven and over which we may disagree. You might believe you deserve an *A* on your English report when your teacher only gave you a *C*−. The person who owns the hardware store might think that property taxes are already too high when the city council wants to increase them. The President might argue for less money for housing development and more for transportation, while Congress might see it entirely differently. These are areas where there is no "right" answer. What each person believes should be done depends on his or her individual values. Economists call these **normative statements.** Many of the things we will study in this book will be normative, and so will have no single answer upon which everyone can agree.

Social Values and Choices

Economic systems exist within social systems that are made up of traditions and values. Social values—such as equality, justice, and freedom—help determine the goals we set for our businesses. Differences of opinion concerning these "socio-economic" goals often result in conflicting normative statements.

Making rational choices about normative statements is a very difficult job. No matter what you do, some people will end up being better off while others will feel that they are worse off. What we try to do is make decisions that help more people than they harm. When you consider the fact that most people don't agree on what is best, you can see why this is hard to do.

Putting Rational Choices to a Test

Most governments have the right of eminent domain. This means that they may force people to sell private property for public use. In many cities, entire neighborhoods have been torn

In the process of redevelopment, many cities face choices between low-cost housing and new office buildings for businesses. These choices involve trade-offs. The costs and benefits of such choices are not always borne by all people equally.

down and replaced with new buildings. Sometimes people are forced to sell their homes so businesses can move into urban areas. Is this a rational choice for society? What is the role of value judgments in such a decision?

Self-Check
1. Positive statements can either be proven or disproven, but normative statements depend on different people's individual points of view.
2. Each individual has his or her own values, making an individual's rational choice relatively easy to achieve. Groups of people often have different values, and so they often do not all agree on what is the rational choice.

Applying What You have Learned
See Lesson Plans for Chapter 1, Section E, page T13.

Self-Check

1. How are positive statements different from normative statements?
2. Why is it easier to make a rational choice just for yourself than to make one that affects many people?

Applying What You Have Learned

In the Personal Narrative, the young woman deals with both positive and normative statements in choosing a career path. Look back at the story and find

a. one positive and one normative statement made by the mother, and
b. one positive and one normative statement made by the young woman.

Section F Using the Production Possibilities Frontier

This section introduces the idea of a *production possibilities frontier*.

Personal Narrative

Should I Grow More Cucumbers or More Tomatoes?

My name is Ruth. My husband Dave and I own two acres of land just outside of town. Dave doesn't have much free time because he works in a local factory and studies economics in night school. I do most of the housework and take care of our two children. We are often short on money, so I raise vegetables and sell them at a roadside stand. Over the years I have found that tomatoes and cucumbers grow and sell well. Last year I decided growing anything else is too much work. My problem was to decide how much of each crop I should grow.

I kept track of what I grew last year and decided we own enough land to grow either 400 tomato or 200 cucumber plants. I could also grow some of each. An extra cucumber plant means two fewer tomato plants. In August I expect to harvest an average of ten tomatoes or five cucumbers per plant. Therefore, if I grew only tomatoes, I could harvest 4,000 a day in August.

Explain. The graph of a production possibility frontier *is not reality,* but only a model. It is used to demonstrate how a limited choice could be made. Reality is much more complicated. All the variables in reality cannot be included in a graphic representation.

400 plants x 10 each = 4,000 a day

If I grew only cucumbers I could harvest 1,000 a day.

200 plants x 5 each = 1,000 a day

I have drawn the graph below to help me decide what to do.

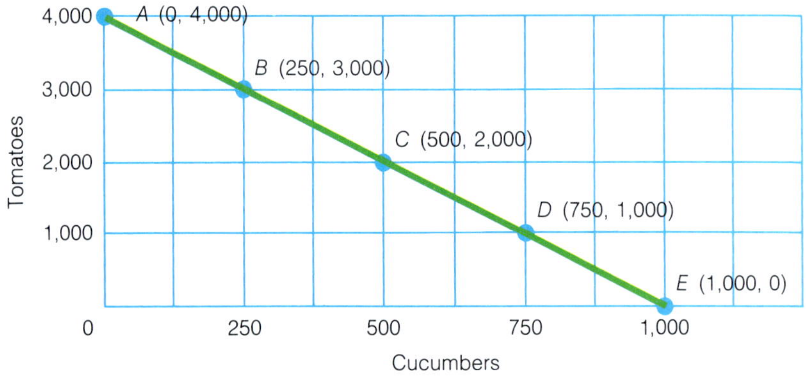

All graphs have two axes, a *y* or vertical axis, and an *x* or horizontal axis. In this case the *y* axis represents tomatoes I could grow while the *x* axis represents cucumbers. Each of the lettered points on the graph stands for a combination of the two crops I could produce. The amounts are shown in parentheses next to the lettered points. The first amount in parentheses is always the *x* axis (cucumbers) and the second amount is always the *y* axis (tomatoes).

If I could sell tomatoes for a higher price than cucumbers, I might choose to grow 4,000 tomatoes and no cucumbers (represented by point *A* on the graph). But I have found that I can't sell more than 2,000 tomatoes a day, so I have chosen to produce 2,000 tomatoes and 500 cucumbers (represented by point *C* on the graph). I have traded the production of 2,000 tomatoes for 500 cucumbers. This trade can be seen as movement from point *A* (0, 4,000) to point *C* (500, 2,000) on the graph.

I have drawn a line connecting points *A* through *E* on the graph. This line represents the different combinations of the two crops I could grow. I understand that economists would call this line a production possibilities frontier.

The Production Possibilities Frontier

A **production possibilities frontier** is a graph that shows the different combinations of two products that can be produced from a given quantity of the four factors of production. Each product is represented by an axis. Amounts of the products that could be produced are plotted along these axes. Suppose that a factory could produce either radios or TV sets. The table below could

The owners of this stand must decide how much of which products to grow and sell. A production possibilities frontier can be used in making such a decision.

Note. The production possibility frontier examples in the text have a fixed trade-off between the two products. In reality, some resources are better suited to producing one of the products, while others are better for the other product. This means the trade-off between the two products would vary, causing the frontier to bend away (in either direction) from the corner of the graph.

represent the combinations of these two products that could be produced from the firm's resources *if* the firm is using its resources most efficiently.

Production Combinations

Combination	Radios	TV Sets
A	600	0
B	400	50
C	200	100
D	0	150

Each combination can be represented by a point on a graph:

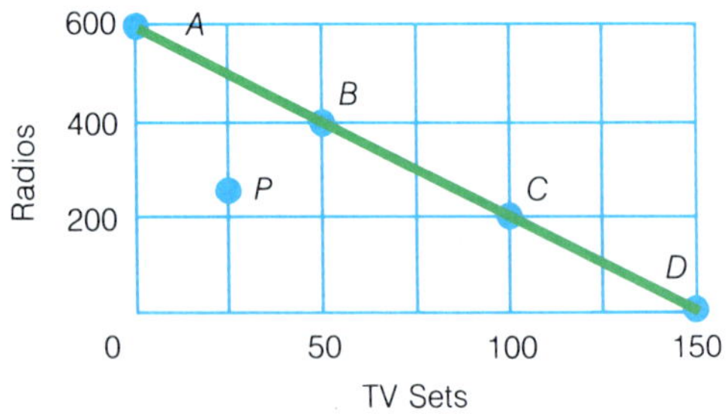

If a firm's actual amount of production appears *inside* the production possibilities frontier (see point *P*), the firm either is not using all its factors of production or else is using them inefficiently.

Self-Check
1. A production possibilities frontier shows different combinations of two products that could be produced from a given quantity of resources.
2. A production possibilities frontier shows trade-offs as one moves from one point on the frontier to another. A quantity of one product is given up in order to produce a greater quantity of the other.

Self-Check

1. What does a production possibilities frontier mean?
2. How does a production possibilities frontier show trade-offs?

Applying What You Have Learned

Applying What You Have Learned
See Lesson Plans for Chapter 1, Section F, page T15.

Production possibility frontiers are economic models. They represent reality. They are not reality itself. Which of the following would be true regarding production possibility frontiers?

a. They don't tell you the price of the products.
b. They can only be used for two products at a time.
c. They don't provide any useful information.
d. They don't tell you how much of one product would have to be given up to get an additional unit of the other product.
e. They assume that there is no problem shifting production from one product to another.

CURRENT CONSUMER ISSUES

Should High School Graduates Come With a Guarantee?

Many Americans believe our high schools are graduating young people who have limited academic ability and few skills. Employers complain that they must often train new employees to read, write, and do simple math. The Los Angeles Unified School District in California has announced steps to try to reduce this problem.

Starting in 1994, graduates of Los Angeles high schools will receive a diploma and a written warranty. The warranty guarantees future employers that graduates have basic skills in reading, mathematics, and effective communications. It also guarantees that students have acquired thinking skills, such as problem solving and reasoning, as well as personal qualities, like self-management and responsibility.

Any employer who finds a 1994 (or later) graduate lacking in any of these areas may request remedial classes for the employee from the school district at no cost. The firm must continue to employ the worker to obtain this help.

Many community leaders and teachers doubt that the program will work. They suggest that if the schools provided an adequate education in the first place, a guarantee would not be necessary. Leaders of the teachers' union called it "smoke and mirrors" to take public attention away from other problems facing the schools. They pointed out that the board of education asked teachers to take a 3 percent pay cut to help reduce the district's budget problems two days after the warranty program was announced.

Do you believe warranties for graduates is a good idea?

Arguments in Favor of the Plan

1. It might make some students and teachers work harder.
2. It would assure employers that new employees would be able to complete certain tasks or they would receive free training.
3. It could make it easier for new graduates to find jobs.

Arguments Against the Plan

1. It would cost a great deal of money to carry out properly.
2. It requires even greater spending for future remedial programs.
3. It takes attention away from the real problems faced by schools.

What Do You Think?

If you were a taxpayer in Los Angeles, would you support this program? If you were a student? An employer? How does this situation relate to scarcity and opportunity costs?

Chapter 1 Review

What Have You Learned?

In this chapter you have learned the following important principles of economics:

- The central problem in economics is *scarcity*—the inability to produce enough goods and services to satisfy all of our wants.
- Scarcity exists because people will always want more than they can have.
- Because of scarcity, people, businesses, and the government must all make *trade-offs* in choosing the products they want the most.
- When a choice is made, an *opportunity cost* is paid. Opportunity cost is the value of the choice given up when the first choice is taken.
- Production—the creation of goods and services—requires four factors. The *four factors of production* are *natural resources, labor, capital,* and *entrepreneurship.* These factors exist in limited quantities, and therefore it is impossible for us to produce all the products we would like to have.
- To understand how the factors of production operate in the economy, we sometimes use *models.* Models are representations of reality, not the reality itself, and although they are not perfect, they do help us try to understand what will happen next in the economy.
- In making economic decisions we try to make the *rational choice.* This means that we try to make the choice that has the greatest amount of benefits compared to costs.
- Decisions may involve both *positive* and *normative* statements. Positive statements are statements of fact; normative statements are statements that express our values.
- Economic choices can often be illustrated with tables or graphs. One such graph—the *production possibilities frontier*—shows the different combinations of two products that can be produced from a fixed quantity of the four factors of production. It also shows what a firm (or nation) is capable of producing if it is using all of its resources efficiently.

Words and Terms

economics (p. 5)
goods (p. 5)
services (p. 5)
scarcity (p. 9)
trade-offs (p. 11)
opportunity cost (p. 11)
production (p. 14)
resources (p. 14)
factors of production (p. 15)
natural resources (p. 15)
labor (p. 15)
capital (p. 15)
entrepreneurship (p. 15)
model (p. 17)
rational choice (p. 20)
positive statements (p. 21)
normative statements (p. 22)
production possibilities frontier (p. 25)

See Chapter 1 Review Answers, page T15.

Building Your Vocabulary

On a separate piece of paper, write the vocabulary word or term that best completes each of the following statements.

1. The value of your second choice that you give up when you take your first choice is ______.
2. The central problem in economics is ______.
3. ______ is the study of the production, distribution and consumption of goods and services.
4. An expression of fact is called a ______.
5. Raw materials that have not been processed are ______.
6. The creation of goods and services is called ______.
7. The resources necessary for production are classified as the four ______.
8. A graph showing the combinations of two products that could be made from a fixed set of resources is called a ______.
9. ______ is human effort that is applied to natural resources to produce goods and services.
10. An expression of a value judgment can be called a ______.
11. A factor that initiates and supervises production is called ______.
12. ______ ______ means making decisions such that the benefits to society are greater than the costs.
13. The tools that are used by labor in making products are ______.
14. A theory of reality used to make predictions is called a ______.
15. When you give up one thing for another, you are making a ______.
16. Tangible things that satisfy human wants and needs are ______.
17. Intangible things that satisfy human wants and needs are ______.
18. ______ are all the things necessary to produce goods and services.

Understanding Economics

Answer each of the following on a separate piece of paper.

1. What are the two ideas upon which *scarcity* is based?
2. Identify the *opportunity cost* John paid when he spent his $20 on a new pair of gloves instead of a new shirt.
3. Explain what people try to achieve when they make decisions or *trade-offs.*
4. Suppose a Native American chief told his people to cut down a tree with axes to make a canoe. Each of the *four factors of production* (natural resources, labor, capital, and entrepreneurship) would be used in making the boat. Identify the specific example of each from this situation.
5. Describe what models are and how they are used by economists.
6. Explain why the predictions made by economists can be more important than predictions we might make as private individuals.
7. According to the *production possibilities frontier* below, how many chairs would the firm have to give up to produce ten more tables?

Production Possibilities Frontier, Al's Furniture

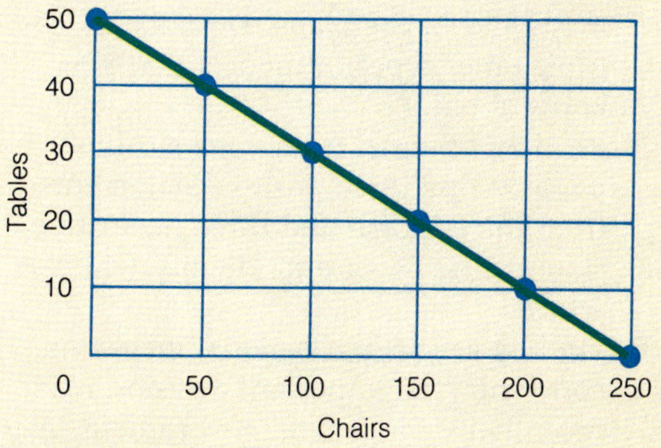

Chapter 1 Review

8. Describe the purpose of making a *rational choice.*
9. Explain the difference between *normative* and *positive statements.*

Thinking Critically About Economics

1. Suppose you won a contest and your prize was a free shopping spree at your local discount store. You could keep anything you carried out in three minutes. Make a list of at least five different products you would take. Explain why you would take each product.
2. Choose a product that you use frequently. Identify each of the four factors of production that were used to make it.
   a. What natural resources were used?
   b. What type of skills did the workers need?
   c. What type of tools were used?
   d. Describe the firm that made the product. Is it large? What else does it make?
3. Describe an important decision that you have made. Explain the opportunity cost you paid when you made this decision.
4. There are many types of models other than economic models. Two are weather maps and house plans. Describe at least three other types of models that you know about.
5. Read an editorial from your local newspaper. Copy three positive statements from the editorial and three normative statements. Be sure to identify which is which.
6. Find an article in a national magazine concerning an important decision made recently by the federal government. Answer each of the following:
   a. Describe the decision that was made.
   b. Identify a particular person or group of people who will be better off because of this decision. In what way will they benefit?
   c. Identify a particular person or group of people who will be worse off because of this decision. In what way will they be hurt?
7. You have four hours to clean your room and/or study for a math test. Draw a production possibility frontier showing the different ways you could use your time.

Consumer Skills Projects

1. Take a survey of students in your class, asking what they would do if they won $50 in a contest. Ask several adults the same question. Describe differences between the kinds of consumer choices these people would make. Suggest reasons why different people make different trade-offs when they make consumer decisions. Why can different decisions be examples of rational choices for different people?
2. Make a bulletin board for your classroom showing the factors of production that are combined into different consumer products you or other members of your family buy. The figure on page 15 in the text may give you some ideas of how to do this.
3. Make one collage of statements cut from newspaper advertisements that are normative and another of statements that are positive. Explain which statements would be most useful in helping people make rational consumer decisions.

Thinking Critically About Economics
(1) identifying alternatives; (2) analyzing cause and effect; (3) evaluating alternatives; (4) making analogies; (5) distinguishing fact from opinion; (6) predicting probable consequences; (7) evaluating alternatives.

Developing Your Economic Skills

Constructing a Line Graph

Skill: In this lesson you'll review how to read and construct a line graph (you already encountered line graphs on pages 24–26). A line graph is used to show the relationship between two sets of information. One set of information is represented by values on the horizontal or *x* axis. The other is represented by values on the vertical or *y* axis. To complete a line graph, you'll follow these three steps:

1. Assemble both sets of information in a table.
2. Plot the information as points on the graph and connect the points.
3. Interpret the graph.

Application: Suppose there is a $40 tax on property for each $1,000 of assessed value in your school district. To construct a graph of the relationship between property values and the amount of tax paid, you would first organize information in a table similar to the one below. This table has two columns. The left column is for assessed property values and the right is for the amount of tax.

Assessed Property Value	Amount of Tax
$20,000	$ 800
$40,000	$1,600
$60,000	$2,400
$80,000	$3,200

The information on the table can now be used to construct a graph. Let the vertical axis represent the assessed property value. The values on the vertical axis must go up from zero to the maximum assessed property value of $80,000. The axis is divided into equal units, each representing an additional $10,000.

Let the horizontal axis represent property taxes. The values on this axis must reach the maximum tax of $3,200. This axis is divided into equal units of $400 each.

Points are then plotted to represent combinations of values on the table. For example, point *A* represents a tax of $800 on property with an assessed value of $20,000. Point *B* represents a tax of $1,600 on property with an assessed value of $40,000. The rest of the points represent other combinations of taxes and assessed values from the table. A graph may be drawn by connecting the points that have been plotted.

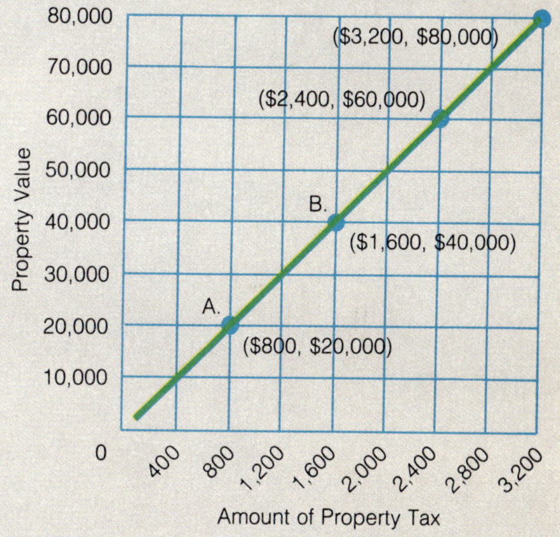

This graph shows there is a *positive* relationship (meaning that as one goes up, so does the other) between property values and the amount of tax owners must pay.

Practice: Graph the relationship between property values and the amount of tax paid in your community.

DETECTO
Red onions
50¢ lb
Yello onions
40¢
3 lb 1.00
White Potatos
40¢
3 lb 1.00
Small white Potatos
60¢ lb
Red Potatos
.50 lb

CHAPTER 2

Economic Systems: Who Made the Rules?

Objectives

In the sections of this chapter, you will learn:

A

why economic systems developed and how the *division of labor* made *specialization*, and *wealth*, possible;

B

how *capitalism* deals with the economic questions *what*, *how*, and *for whom;*

C

how *profits* affect *allocation of resources* in capitalism; and

D

how a *command economy* functions.

Introduction

Who organized the first economic system? Did a cave man walk out of the jungle one day and say, "I think I'll open a taco stand"? The answer to the question is, "Of course not!" Still, someone did start the first economic system.

An **economic system** is a set of rules that governs what goods and services to produce, how to produce them, and for whom they are produced. People organize production in such a system to be more efficient in their use of resources. Improved productivity allows them to have more things and to live better lives. Before there were economic systems, individuals worked just for themselves or for their own families. No one became very skilled at anything because everyone had to do so many different jobs.

Economic systems allow specialization. People can do the things they are best at and trade for goods or services that others provide. When people specialize in the things they do well, total production is greater and people end up being better off.

In this chapter you will learn about different types of economic systems that exist or have existed in the world. You will find that each system has advantages and disadvantages. The system that is best for a country depends on the values and beliefs

Explain. Students already know and follow many economic rules. For example, they know it is wrong to take something that belongs to someone else.

of the people it serves. People are not all the same. Because people are not all the same, there is no one economic system that is best for all countries.

Most of this chapter will be devoted to the American economic system, which is called **capitalism.** Capitalism is an economic system in which the means of production are owned and controlled by private individuals or groups. Governments play a limited role in capitalism. Most economic decisions are made in **markets** that exist when individuals buy and sell goods and services. This is why capitalism is sometimes called a *market* economy.

In the United States, economic decisions begin with consumers. This is not the case in many other countries. Some countries have **traditional** economic systems, in which economic decisions are based mostly on customs. You will learn more about traditional economies in Chapter 14.

At one time there were many countries that had **command** economies. Today there are few. In these countries most economic decisions are made by government authorities. Individuals have little choice in how these economic systems run. (You will learn more about command economies in Chapter 15.)

Although we refer to some economies as command economies and to others as capitalism, no economy is purely one kind or the other. All are *mixed*—meaning that even the most capitalistic economy will incorporate some aspects of a command economy, and even the most extreme command economy will incorporate some aspects of capitalism.

Discuss. There is sometimes a trade-off between personal freedom and the good of the community. What would your students be willing to sacrifice to help others?

The American economy has matured and grown over the past two hundred years. The goods and services we produce and consume have changed. Some of our values are different from what they used to be. Most Americans feel a sense of responsibility for each other. We recognize the rights of individuals, but we also see a need to aid those who are unable to care for themselves. We are willing to give up some of our freedom and property for the good of the community.

As you read this chapter, you will realize that we do not have pure capitalism in the United States. You will learn how economic decisions are usually made in this country. Sometimes you will know of cases where our system does not work the way it is described in the text. Don't let this confuse you. Remember, we are studying how most of the American economy works most of the time. This chapter will teach you the basic ideas of capitalism. Later in the book you will learn why there are exceptions to the rules.

Section A How Economic Systems Developed

This section introduces the ideas of *specialization*, the *division of labor*, and *wealth*.

Personal Narrative

Note. The assumption that there was no trade between the family groups is not realistic, but it makes the idea of specialization more clear. Some of your students may ask about this.

Question. Can your students identify tasks they are expected to do because of their sex or age that they are not good at, or would rather not do?

Discuss. Explain the importance of taking time to make important decisions. Are decisions that are made on the "spur of the moment" likely to be the best ones possible? For example, is there really such a thing as "love at first sight"?

From Yesterday to Tomorrow

Thousands of years ago, on the banks of a small river, Grug (a cave dweller) lived with his relatives. Grug's family and other families grouped together as a unit, but each family took care of itself. Each family fished, hunted, gathered grain, made bread, and performed all of the other jobs necessary to their way of life. Although the family groups met socially at dances, they never traded the things that they made.

Poor Grug! He was most unhappy. You see, Grug was the best hunter that had ever been. He could sling stones two hundred paces and never miss his target. In an hour he could kill all the meat his family needed for a week. Grug loved to hunt.

The problem was that he was expected to do all the other "manly tasks" too. When he went fishing, he usually slipped and fell in the river. When he gathered grain, he got bored. If he tried to bake bread, he burnt his fingers. The only job he liked was hunting.

One day Grug decided to do nothing but hunt. From dawn to dusk he spent all his time hunting. He killed more animals than he could use, so he just left them lying around. Before long the village began to smell. People got angry with Grug. His wife scolded him for never fishing or gathering grain. The chief threatened to throw him into the river if he did not stop. Grug was in despair.

Then Grug had a wonderful idea. He remembered that his cousin Thump was a good fisher, his sister-in-law Buff made the best bread in the village, and his nephew Gerg could gather more grain than anyone else. When he thought about it, Grug realized that each person in the village was best at one particular job.

Grug asked the chief to call a meeting of the villagers. He promised to solve all of their problems. The chief agreed, but said if he didn't like what he heard, Grug would be useful as lion bait. At the meeting, Grug suggested that all the people do only the jobs they were good at and trade for the other things they needed. The villagers immediately saw the wisdom of his idea. They could each spend their time doing the things they liked to do best. Grug was saved from being lion bait.

As Grug's idea was put into practice, people found that they were better off than they had ever been before. Not only were people doing the jobs they liked best, but they were getting better at their jobs because they had more practice. They found that they could produce as many things as they needed in half the time. They had time left to sit in the sun and talk.

Some of this talk was about ways to improve production. The villagers built a dam to store water for the dry season, they discovered how to make bows and arrows, and they even discussed the possibility of traveling to the next village up the river to trade their furs for clay pots that were made there.

When the old chief died, Grug became the new leader. He lived a long and prosperous life in peace and happiness.

The Division of Labor

Of course the story of Grug never happened, but the economic concepts in the story are important and real. Grug lived in a traditional economy. What people did, and how they produced goods and services, was largely determined by customs. When Grug introduced new ways of doing things, he replaced old traditions with new ideas. Economists call his idea the **division of labor.** This means dividing the process of production into specific tasks. Each task is completed by the person who is best suited to that job. Workers become more efficient because each has a chance to practice his or her task.

Specialization Increases Productivity

Discuss. There is specialization in most households. Different individuals often have the responsibility to cook, wash, clean, earn money, etc. How and why have your students' families divided household responsibilities?

The division of labor allows *specialization* of labor. **Specialization** occurs when individual workers concentrate their labor on single tasks, enabling each worker to become more efficient and productive. In Grug's village each person specialized in the task he or she liked best, and their productivity increased.

The division of labor also allows the development of **specialized capital.** In the first chapter of this text you learned that capital is one of the four factors of production. One example of capital is tools that are designed to increase the efficiency of a particular task in production. The dam and the bows and arrows that Grug's villagers made are examples of specialized capital. When everyone worked only for their own family, no one had the time to make these tools. The division of labor gave the villagers the time to invest in tools that increased their productivity and standard of living. They also had the time to consider trading with other villages, which could improve their lives by taking advantage of the skills of other people in other places.

Wealth Permits Investment

Questions. What items of wealth have your students chosen to save for? Would they choose the same items ten years from now?

The tools and products that are accumulated in an economic system are called **wealth** by economists. For an economic system to grow, it must produce enough goods and services so that some people do not need to be involved in production for current consumption. They can build factories or machines that will make it easier to produce more goods and services. In Grug's village the division of labor gave the people enough time to build specialized tools that became the basis for increased production and wealth in the future.

Over time Grug's village could have grown into a city and then a nation. What started out as a traditional agricultural economy could have become a market or command economy. At some time the traditional values and customs might have been changed into a set of rules. A government would have developed that could formalize methods for changing these rules. The rules might have been written down as laws. Grug's ideas would then have become the basis of the nation's economic system.

In different parts of the world other people could have had other leaders and other ideas. They could have developed different economic systems to suit their own needs and beliefs. Still, all economic systems have some factors in common. They all concern the division of labor, specialization, and the accumulation of wealth. In the following sections you will learn about other things that economic systems have in common.

Examples of Increased Productivity

One of the best examples of the advantages offered by the division of labor and specialization is the introduction of the assembly line into automobile manufacturing by Henry Ford. This process cut the time necessary to assemble a car from a day and a half to 93 minutes. It also cut the price of a new car by over 50 percent. The assembly line itself is an example of specialized capital made possible through the accumulation of wealth. Its result was a major improvement in productivity.

Discuss. Many types of capital are intended to increase productivity in schools (a public address system, computers, movie projectors, calculators, duplicators, and tape recorders). How would education be different if these things did not exist?

Another example of the changes that can result from specialized tools can be seen in American agriculture. In 1910 it took over 13 million farmers to feed the United States population of just over 90 million people. Today fewer than 2.8 million farmers

Henry Ford's assembly line introduced division of labor and specialization—assigning a single task to each worker—into automobile production. The process greatly increased production and cut the price of new cars.

can feed a population that is more than two and a half times as large as it was in 1910. Table 2–1 shows how this change has taken place since 1910. This increased production is possible because of the improved tools farmers use today.

Table 2–1
Farm Employment and Production, 1910 through 1990
(values times 1,000)

Year	Acres Farmed	Farmers (full- and part-time)	Production Index (1977 = 100)	Total U.S. Population
1910	879,000	13,555	29	92,400
1930	987,000	12,497	34	123,200
1950	1,202,000	9,926	48	151,700
1970	1,102,000	4,523	66	205,100
1990	988,000	2,772	160	249,600

Source: *Statistical Abstract of the United States,* 1991; *Historical Abstract of the United States,* 1959.

The transition from the horse-drawn plow has been possible because the division of labor gives people the time necessary to create more efficient tools.

Self-Check
1. An economic system is a set of rules that governs what goods and services to produce, how to produce them, and for whom they are produced.
2. The division of labor allows specialization of both labor and capital.
3. An economic system must provide wealth in order to grow.

Applying What You Have Learned
See Lesson Plans for Chapter 2, Section A, page T18.

Self-Check

1. What is an economic system?
2. How does the division of labor improve productivity?
3. What must an economic system provide in order to grow?

Applying What You Have Learned

Look back at the story about Grug and find at least three examples of the division of labor. Name at least two benefits that come about from the division of labor.

Section B The Basic Questions: *What, How,* and *For Whom?*

This section will introduce the basic economic questions of *what, how,* and *for whom.*

Personal Narrative

Should We Sell Yogurt in the School Store?

The school bookstore is in danger of going broke. Lina, the student manager, has called a staff meeting to discuss the problem. She is huddled with the student clerks and their advisor, Mr. Berkley, trying to think of a solution. The conversation begins:

Note. Most school stores do not pay wages to student workers. However, the assumption that these students are paid makes this limited example similar to the decisions a real firm would make.

Mike: So what's the problem, Lina? Haven't we sold enough pencils?

Lina: Oh be quiet! The problem is we've been paying clerks $4.50 an hour and we haven't earned enough money to cover their wages.

Mark: Why not just increase our prices? We could charge 25 cents for pencils and a dollar for pens.

Sharon: Yeah, and no one would buy anything at all. They would just do without or buy it at the discount store after school.

Ralph: We should sell candy bars and potato chips. We'd make a fortune!

Mr. B: We can't sell junk food, Ralph. The principal would close us down. She'll only allow us to sell school supplies and what she calls "nourishing snacks."

Sharon: So what's a nourishing snack? Tofu?

Mark: Don't be stupid! She means things like raisins, sunflower seeds and trail mix.

Ralph: No one's gonna buy that stuff. We may as well forget food. It's too bad; we could make a lot of money from candy.

Question. What other products would your students suggest for the store to sell?

Lina: Well, how about yogurt? The teachers would buy that.

Mark: How can we sell yogurt? We don't have a refrigerator to store it in.

Mr. B: There's an old one in my basement you could use. I think it still works.

Sharon: How about granola bars? They're healthy. You can get them with chocolate chips, honey and everything!

Ralph: Great idea! And we could sell popcorn. That's healthy too.

Mr. B: Slow down. The granola bars and yogurt may be okay, but there's no chance for popcorn. You know, there is another alternative.

Mark: What?

Mr. B: You could take a cut in pay to, say, $3.50 an hour, or you could have fewer clerks. Most of you just stand around as it is. You're not using your resources wisely.

Ralph: Oh, come on, Mr. B. We need the pay. For most of us it's the only spending money we get.

Mr. B: You may think you need the money, but you aren't earning it. Unless you can cut your costs or increase your income, the store will be closed, and then you will earn nothing. The decision is yours to make.

Answering the Basic Economic Questions

These students may not realize it, but their problems are the same ones all economic systems face. They are trying to decide *what* to sell, *how* to sell it and *who* should receive the benefits from what is sold. All economic systems must solve similar problems:

1. **What** goods and services should be produced?
2. **How** should these goods and services be produced?
3. **For whom** is the benefit of these goods and services being produced?

In capitalistic economic systems these decisions are made by people or by groups of people.

What?

Note. Some consumer decisions are influenced by advertising, but that does not contradict the point made here. Stores may earn a profit only if they offer products customers are willing to buy, even if the customer buys the product because of advertising.

The question *what* is answered every time people buy goods or services. When sales are made, stores usually order additional products to replace those that were sold. Manufacturers receive these orders and set their production schedules. They allocate resources to products that sell. Products that do not sell are not ordered and are not produced. In a market economy consumers determine what products will be made when they buy things.

How?

Explain. There are many ways in which most products can be made. The method chosen will be the one expected to result in the lowest unit cost and therefore the greatest profit.

The question *how* is answered by producers according to what will yield the greatest profits. Capitalistic firms are in business to make money. One way to improve profits is to find the least expensive means of production. The least expensive way is also the most efficient way. Customers determine what will be made in capitalism, but entrepreneurs decide how to make it.

For Whom?

The question *for whom* refers to who will receive the benefits produced by the economic system. The question is answered ac-

Every economic system must answer three questions: what will be produced, how will it be produced, and who will receive the benefits of the production. When you buy something in capitalism, you are helping determine what will be produced. When you receive a paycheck, you are receiving some of the benefits of production.

Stress. The U.S. economy is a mixed economy. The rules explained in this section apply to an economic system that is perfect capitalism. Our system often, *but not always,* works this way.

cording to the value of a person's contribution to production. People work and earn money. The amount they earn usually depends on the value of their labor. A research chemist might earn $50,000 a year, while a janitor could earn only $14,000. Economists would explain much of the difference in their pay by pointing out the difference in the value of what they do. The chemist's labor contributes more to the final value of the product than that of the janitor. In capitalism, income usually determines how much people can buy. People who make more valuable contributions to production are paid better and usually receive more of what is produced.

Question. Ask your students to identify products that have been extremely successful for their producers. Are there any similarities between these products?

Everyone knows about a person who has "made it." In capitalism, people who do well usually are those who are best able to answer the questions *what* and *how*. If you can do this, the *for whom* often turns out to be good for you.

For example, the "hula hoop" craze swept the nation in 1958. Suddenly it seemed that everyone was trying to spin a piece of colored plastic around his or her body without letting it fall to the ground. Doctors said it was bad for the back. Some people said it was a waste of time and money. But for the Wham-O company the product was a gold mine. This firm offered a product people wanted at a price they were willing to pay. They sold millions in only a few months. Eventually people got bored with the "hula hoop" and stopped buying it, but for a time Wham-O did very well.

The table below shows that some occupations command higher wages than others. Think about why this is the case. What does this have to do with the workers' contributions to production?

Table 2–2

Average Hourly Wages by Industry, 1991

Industry	Average Hourly Wage
Manufacturing	$11.22
Mining	$14.31
Construction	$14.01
Transportation/Utilities	$13.26
Wholesale Trade	$11.14
Retail Trade	$ 7.03
Finance, Insurance & Real Estate	$10.40
Services	$10.25

Source: *Employment and Earnings*, U.S. Department of Labor, Oct. 1991 (July data).

Self-Check
1. *What* refers to the decision of which goods to produce; *how* refers to the method used to produce them.
2. In a market system, benefits are allocated according to the value of a person's contribution to production.

Applying What You Have Learned
See Lesson Plans for Chapter 2, Section B, page T20.

Self-Check

1. What do the questions *what* and *how* mean to economists?
2. How does a market (or capitalistic) economy decide who will receive the benefits from what is produced and sold?

Applying What You Have Learned

Look back to the story of Lina and her co-workers in the school store. They were trying to answer the questions of *what* and *how* so that the *for whom* could be for them. Study the conversation and find two statements that deal with *what*, two with *how*, and two with *for whom*.

Section C The Role of Profits in the Economy

This section will explain the relationship between *profits* and the *allocation of resources.*

Personal Narrative

If I Make It Big, I Can Retire When I'm 30

Discuss. Ask your students what sort of businesses they would want to run. What factors could motivate them other than profit?

My name's Regina. I'm going to try running my own business. When I was about three my mother took me to see the boats at the dock one hot summer evening. She had promised to buy me a hot dog but the stand had gone out of business. I can still see all those people staring at me while I screamed because she couldn't buy what I wanted. I remember their faces a lot better than I remember the boats. Ever since that day I've had the idea that I could open up that hot dog stand and get rich. I saved my money and rented the stand. Next week I'm going to try.

I've worked for over a month cleaning and painting. It's been 20 years since the stand was used. I bought a new grill and a freezer. I had new wiring and plumbing put in. I ordered hot dogs, buns, ice cream bars and all the other things I need. The health department has been here to inspect my store. I even bought an insurance policy. I've spent over $10,000, and I haven't sold anything yet, but I'm not worried.

Problem Solving. Regina does not know if hot dogs will sell on the dock. Ask your students to describe how she could have surveyed customers to find out what they want before she opened her store.

Every evening retired people come here from the village to fish and watch the sun go down. There are hundreds of them. There isn't a restaurant or fast-food store within a mile. Many of them bring sacks of food and sit on the dock to eat. They must be uncomfortable. I've bought 8 aluminum tables and 32 chairs. I'm sure those people will buy my food and sit at my tables. After I get this store going I can take my profits and start other stands on other docks all up and down the coast. I could retire when I'm 30!

Profits Allocate Resources

The young woman in the story above is going into business in a capitalistic economic system. Her purpose is to make a profit.

Profits Are an Incentive

Profit is the incentive (reason) for starting a business in capitalism. Any firm that makes a profit must be selling products customers want at prices they are willing to pay. The firm's cost of production must also be less than its selling price. Regina

Like Regina, the owner of this food stand is in business to make a profit.

thinks she knows what the people in her community want, but is she right?

Explain. If Regina's store is successful, it will be easier for her to borrow money, enabling her to acquire more resources.

Let's assume that Regina's stand is successful, and she makes a large profit. What would she do with it? She has stated that her plan is to expand her business. She would use her profits to buy more resources and start new hot dog stands. Her profits would enable her to allocate more resources to her business.

Profits Allocate Resources

The **allocation of resources** is a problem that must be solved in all economic systems. In capitalism, profitable firms are better able to afford scarce resources. Firms that are not profitable rarely have the money to buy scarce resources. Successful firms are profitable because they make products people want and sell them for prices people are willing to pay. These are the firms we would like to see grow, and in capitalism they do. The allocation of resources in capitalism is efficient because resources tend to be attracted to the most profitable firms.

The vast expansion of McDonald's would not have been possible if its early hamburger stands had not been profitable.

Note. Profit must exceed the interest paid by banks to encourage investment in businesses. If a bank pays 8 percent, there would be little reason to invest in a firm that only earns 5 percent on your investment.

Explain. Low prices and high sales do not guarantee profitability. Unit price must exceed average unit cost to earn a profit.

Self-Check
1. To earn a profit, a firm must sell products customers want at prices they are willing to pay.
2. Profit is the basic method of allocation in capitalism.

Applying What You Have Learned
See Lesson Plans for Chapter 2, Section C, page T21.

Profit is the basic incentive in capitalism, and it is also the basic method of allocation.

One example of a firm that was able to grow as a result of its profitability is the McDonald's Corporation. When the first McDonald's hamburger stand was opened in the 1950s, the price of a bag of french fries was 12 cents, hamburgers were 15 cents, and soft drinks cost 10 cents. Even in the 1950s these were low prices. People bought McDonald's products and the firm was a great success. Today there are McDonalds stores in every state and in many foreign nations. What did profits and the allocation of resources have to do with the success of this business?

Self-Check

1. What must a firm do to earn a profit in capitalism?
2. What do profits have to do with the allocation of resources in capitalism?

Applying What You Have Learned

In starting her business Regina plans to use various factors of production. Identify specific examples of each of the following:

a. Natural Resources
b. Labor
c. Capital
d. Entrepreneurship

Section D Economic Decisions in Other Systems

This section discusses how the basic economic decisions are made in *command economies.*

Personal Narrative

A Visit Home

My name is Mayling Wang. My great-grandfather came to the United States to build railroads in California in 1880. Although he had expected to return to China, he never went home. He later bought land here and grew vegetables that he sold to earn his living. Eventually he opened a store and became quite wealthy. Grampa Wang died before I was born, but a picture of him and his vegetable store hangs on the wall of our living room. When I was growing up I felt that in some way he was watching over me. I have always wanted to go to China to see the area where our family came from. A few years ago I took the trip back to China that my great-grandfather was never able to make.

I booked my trip through an American travel agency. However, when I reached China my travels were controlled by representatives of a Chinese government tourist organization. The hotels I stayed in were run by the government. The railroads I traveled on were owned and operated by the government. Even the tour guides who went with me were employed by the government. As I traveled I saw steel mills, clothing factories, and coal mines that were government owned and operated. One guide told me that Chinese doctors work for the government and that the hospitals are free because they are paid for by the government. I could tell that the guide was very proud of her country and its accomplishments.

Explain. Personal success in a command economy may be the result of political affiliation rather than of economic contribution.

Before going to China I read about the Chinese people's desire for less government control over their lives. On my visit I learned that during the 1980s people in China had been given some economic freedom. Many farms and small businesses were allowed to operate under private ownership. While this freedom increased the economic choices ordinary people could make, it did not change the basic character of the Chinese economy. Most businesses and resources remained in the hands of the government.

I visited my ancestors' hometown while I was in China. It is located along the banks of the Lijang River near Guilin. The countryside was very beautiful and the farmers seemed happy and successful. Many of them worked their own farms and decided what to grow for themselves. I have come to the conclusion that the people of China have more economic freedom than they had ten years earlier, but that their lives are very different from ours in the United States. I enjoyed my visit, but I don't think that I could adjust to a country where the people have so few freedoms and such limited opportunities.

Other Ways to Decide *What, How,* and *For Whom*

Mayling visited a country that doesn't have a capitalistic economic system. In 1992 in the People's Republic of China and a few other countries, the economic questions *what, how,* and *for whom* were mainly answered by the government.

Capitalism Compared to Command Economies

Discuss. How would our lives be changed under a command economic system? What choices do we make that Chinese citizens are not able to make?

In capitalism people have the right to start businesses on their own. They decide what products to make according to what they expect to sell. They produce goods and services in the way they believe will earn the most profit. People receive income depending on the value of their contribution to production. Their income determines what they are able to buy. This is not how the economic system in China worked in 1992.

People in China live in a command economy. Such an economy attempts to make trade-offs between economic security and personal freedom.

Decisions in a Command Economy

In 1992 in the Chinese economy ordinary citizens did not help make most of the basic economic decisions. Instead, an agency of the government or a central planning authority made these decisions.

Discuss. Ask your students to relate some of their experiences with government decisions. Do you think the decisions would have been different if done by business? Why? What does this show about the way command economies work?

The people who set up this economic system believed that government officials would be better able to decide "what" products should be made. They argued that businesses in capitalism would make products for the rich and ignore the poor. They felt that their government would know what products were really needed.

They also believed that their government would be best able to decide how to make products. In deciding "how" to make goods and services they would consider what sort and number of jobs people needed. They would not allow unemployment because they would not be concerned about making a profit.

Finally, they felt their government would do a better job of deciding "for whom" products should be made. From their point of view, capitalism would cause some people to be very rich while others would be very poor. They were in favor of distributing products according to need.

It may be easier for you to understand how command economies work by considering the chart in Figure 2-1. The chart shows how goods and services and the factors of production move within a command economy. (A chart that portrays the

Figure 2-1 *Flowchart for a Command Economy*

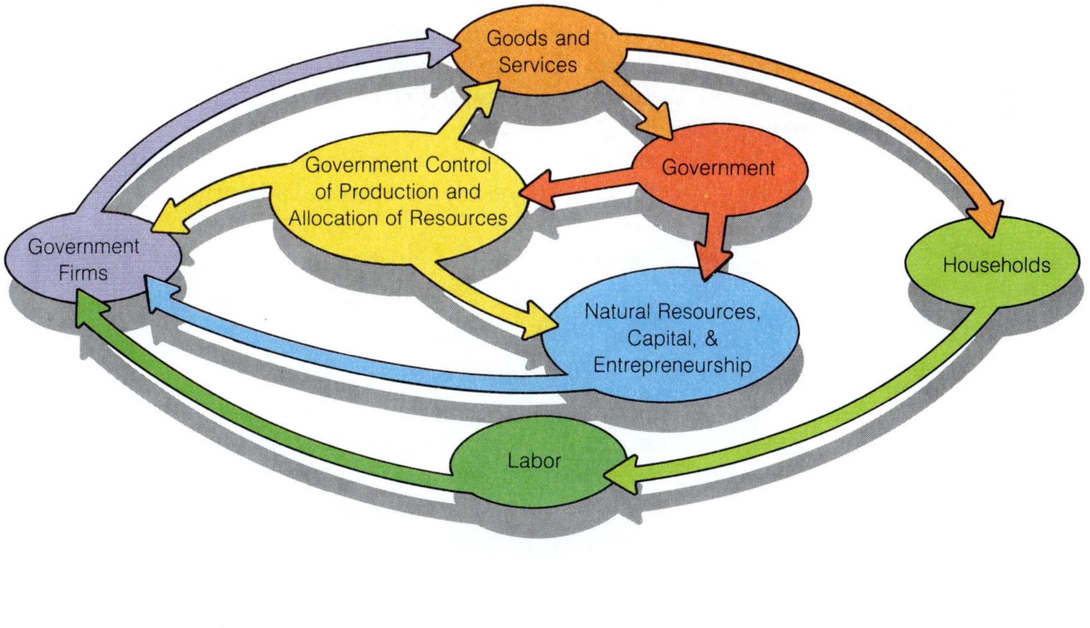

capitalistic economic system will be presented in Chapter 3.) You will notice that most of the factors of production on this chart are controlled by the government.

On the lower half of the chart, resources flow to the firms to be used for the production of goods and services. Only labor comes from households. Natural resources, capital, and entrepreneurship are supplied by the government. These factors are not bought and sold as they would be in the United States. They are allocated by the government, which also owns them.

On the top half of the chart, goods and services flow to the people and the government. The type and number of products that are produced are controlled by the government. The only choice people really have is whether or not to buy the products.

In Chapter 15 you will learn more about alternative economic systems that have government ownership and control over the means of production.

Explain. The power to make economic decisions in a command economy is very centralized. It is difficult to make rapid changes because there are many people with vested interests in the status quo.

Self-Check

1. How are the decisions of *what, how,* and *for whom* made in a command economy?
2. Why do people who believe in command economies think running businesses to earn a profit is a bad thing for most people?

Self-Check
1. In a command economy, the questions *what, how,* and *for whom* are answered by the government.
2. Advocates of a command economy believe that running businesses to earn profits results in production of goods intended mainly for the rich, thereby ignoring the poor and unfairly distributing the nation's wealth.

Applying What You Have Learned

In capitalism it is easy to tell how efficient competitive firms are by finding out how much profit they make. Profitable businesses are efficient businesses. When firms are owned by the government, as explained above, it is much harder to tell whether a firm is efficient or not. They are not in business to make a profit. If a firm only follows government plans, how can you know if it is being efficient?

Below you will find a list of mistakes that a business could make. Describe a likely result for a capitalistic firm if it made each mistake.

a. A firm is making a style of shirt that no one wants.
b. A firm has hired more workers than it needs.
c. A firm is making poor quality products.
d. A firm has trouble finding good workers because it pays too little.

Now consider what would happen if these same things happened to a firm that was owned and told what to do by its government. Why would it be difficult to tell whether such a firm is producing efficiently or not?

Applying What You Have Learned
See Lesson Plans for Chapter 2, Section D, page T23.

CURRENT ECONOMIC ISSUES

Achieving the American Dream

In recent years many Americans have not been able to achieve their dream of owning a home. High prices, low wages, difficulty in obtaining a loan, and other factors have kept young people, single parents, and some members of social and ethnic minorities from achieving home ownership.

In the early 1990s, Secretary of Housing and Urban Development (HUD) Jack Kemp proposed a program that allowed people living in public housing to buy homes from the federal government at low cost. In 1992 President Bush suggested that people be allowed to subtract up to $5,000 from their federal income tax when they buy their first home. In addition, most states offer low-interest rate loans that help people with limited incomes buy homes.

Although many people support programs that help others become home owners, some argue that these programs cost the government too much money. Others argue that the programs are not fair to middle-income people who do not receive such aid. Government aid to home buyers can cause other projects to lose money. It could also cause taxes to increase. For example, the money spent on Secretary Kemp's program could not be spent for other projects that might have benefited more people. Some people who qualified for this help felt angry because there were not enough homes or low-interest rate loans for everyone who wanted them.

Would you support these programs to help people buy homes? What is good and bad about this idea? Consider the following arguments:

Arguments in Favor of These Plans

1. They allow many low-income or disadvantaged people to own a home.
2. They help improve living conditions in many neighborhoods.
3. They help many people develop a sense of self-respect.

Arguments Against These Plans

1. They cost the government billions of dollars.
2. The government cannot provide such help to every qualified person.
3. They do not help many middle-income people own a home.

What Do You Think?

What do you think about the arguments above? Are there other factors that need to be considered? Try thinking about the issue as a problem in deciding the *for whom* question in an economic system. How do these plans answer this question in a different way from the way it would be answered in a pure market economy? Can you think of a better way to help more Americans become home owners?

Chapter 2 Review

What Have You Learned?

In this chapter you've learned the following important principles of economics:

- *Economic systems* organize production by establishing and enforcing rules.
- Economic systems increase the efficiency of production by creating a *division of labor,* which allows *specialization* of labor and capital. This also provides a method of accumulating *wealth.*
- Although there are many different types of economic systems, they all must answer the three basic economic questions, *what, how,* and *for whom.*
- *Capitalism* is an economic system in which the means of production are owned by individual people (not by the government) and the basic economic questions are answered through individual decisions.
- In capitalism, the question *what* is answered by the choices of consumers, *how* is answered according to the lowest cost of production, and the answer to *for whom* depends on the value of a person's contribution to production.
- The basic reason to run a business in capitalism is the desire to make a *profit.*
- Resources in a capitalistic economic system are *allocated* to the firms that make the most profit.
- In *command economies,* the means of production are owned by the government which also makes the basic economic decisions.
- All economic systems in the world today are *mixed.* They are mixtures of both capitalism and command economies.

Words and Terms

economic system (p. 33)
capitalism (p. 34)
market (p. 34)
traditional economy (p. 34)
command economy (p. 34)
specialization (p. 36)
specialized capital (p. 36)
division of labor (p. 36)
wealth (p. 37)
what? (p. 41)
how? (p. 41)
for whom? (p. 41)
profits (p. 44)
allocation of resources (p. 45)

See Chapter 2 Review Answers, page T24.

Building Your Vocabulary

On a separate piece of paper, write the vocabulary word or term that best completes each of the following statements.

1. Splitting up the process of production into specific tasks is called the ______.
2. An ______ is a set of rules through which production is organized.
3. In capitalism, the question ______ is decided according to the value of a person's contribution to production.
4. Greater efficiency in production allows some people to produce ______ instead of making goods for current consumption.
5. In a ______ the three basic economic questions are answered by the government.
6. In a ______ economy, the question *what* is decided according to what is purchased.
7. ______ is an accumulation of products that have been produced.
8. In capitalism, the question ______ is decided according to the firm's costs of production and profits.
9. ______ is an economic system in which the basic economic questions are answered by individuals and not the government.
10. When people do one particular task and buy other things they need, there is ______.
11. In capitalism the ______ is decided according to the profits firms can make.
12. The desire to earn a ______ is the reason for starting a business in capitalism.
13. In a ______ the basic economic decisions are made according to traditions.

Understanding Economics

1. Explain what an economic system is.
2. Define the meaning of the division of labor and explain how it improves the efficiency of production.
3. Explain how specialized tools contribute to the creation of wealth.
4. Describe examples that show the way in which the three basic economic questions, *what, how,* and *for whom,* are answered in a capitalistic economic system. Be sure to provide a different example for each question.
5. Cite two things a firm must do in capitalism to be profitable.
6. Describe the relationship between profits and the allocation of resources in a capitalistic economic system.
7. Describe three differences between a command economy and capitalism.

Thinking Critically About Economics

1. Many communities used to have one-room schools where the teacher taught every subject to each grade level. Almost all of these schools have been replaced with large schools that employ many teachers who often teach several different classes in the same subject. Make a list of at least five different things that can be done better or more efficiently in larger schools than in the old one-room schools.
2. Choose a small independent local grocery store. Which of the following items does it sell? Explain why the store does or does not stock each of these items.

Thinking Critically About Economics
(1) comparison/contrast; (2) analyzing cause and effect;

Chapter 2 Review

   a. Chinese noodles
   b. frozen TV dinners
   c. goldfish food
   d. fresh pineapples
   e. fresh spinach
   f. Russian caviar
3. Look up and make a list of salaries that are being offered for at least five different jobs being advertised in a "help wanted" section of your local newspaper. Explain why each of these jobs commands a different salary.
4. Choose a local business that has closed down recently. Answer the following questions concerning this firm.
   a. What products did the firm sell?
   b. Why did the firm close?
   c. What do you believe the owners could have done to save their business?
5. Choose a local business that is successful. Answer the following questions concerning this firm.
   a. What products does the firm sell?
   b. What factors have made the firm successful?
   c. What do you feel are the most important differences between this successful firm and the one you described in question 4?
6. List at least six different things that can be done by the owner of a capitalistic firm in the United States that could not be done by the director of a firm in a command economy.

Consumer Skills Projects

1. Write a story or draw a picture that demonstrates differences in how computers (a specialized tool) have changed the way we make consumer choices in the past 50 years.
2. Draw a map of your neighborhood including the stores where you shop. Explain what the location of these stores has to do with your choice to buy goods or services from them. How much more could these stores charge before you would shop somewhere else?
3. Interview an elderly person about changes in government regulations of consumer products that have taken place in his or her lifetime. Does this person believe these changes have been helpful or harmful for most people?

Thinking Critically About Economics (cont.)
(3) information from written sources; (4) analyzing cause and effect; (5) analyzing cause and effect; (6) comparison/contrast.

Developing Your Economic Skills

Interpreting a Table

Skill: This lesson shows you how to read a table to find data and answer questions about numeric relationships (*numeric* means *dealing with numbers*). To interpret the table, follow these steps:

1. Read the table title to identify the subject matter of the table.
2. Examine the categories in the table to determine the types of information the table provides.
3. Examine the data of the table to interpret any relationships between the categories.

Application: How valuable is an education? In capitalism, greater education should cause the value of a person's contribution to production to increase—and the person's income should increase accordingly. Study the table below, which provides information that relates educational achievement with earnings for two different groups.

Earnings by Education Level and Sex, 1988
(average for adults 25 and older)

	Sex	
Years of School Completed	**Men**	**Women**
8 years or less	$18,903	$11,710
1 to 3 years of high school	$22,430	$13,834
4 years of high school	$27,139	$17,336
1 to 3 years of college	$31,543	$21,310
4 or more years of college	$40,415	$25,674

Source: *Statistical Abstract of the United States, 1991.*

The title of this table tells you that its topic is *earnings,* and that the table's data will be arranged according to *educational level* and *sex.* The title also tells you that the information was valid for the year 1988, and that the earnings shown are the averages for adults 25 and older.

Now look at the categories of the table. At the far left is the list of vertical (up and down) categories, under the heading "Years of School Completed." At the top of the table is the list of horizontal (across) categories, under the heading "Sex."

To use the table, you will pick a specific vertical category and a specific horizontal category, and find the amount of earnings that corresponds to *both* categories. It's even easier than it sounds. Try these questions:

1. How much more did the average man with four or more years of college earn than the average man with four years of high school? (To answer this question, find the appropriate levels of education on the vertical axis. Read across to find the average earnings for men at those levels. Calculate the difference between the two levels.)
2. How much more did the average man with 1 to 3 years of college earn than the average woman with the same level of education? (To answer this question, find 1 to 3 years of college on the vertical axis. Read across to find the average earnings for men and for women. Calculate the difference between the two levels of earnings.)

This table allows you to answer questions about differences in income that are related to education and sex. It does not explain *why* there are differences. Tables can provide information, show relationships, and suggest areas for additional study.

Practice: Write a paragraph that examines and interprets information on a table found in your local newspaper.

See Part 1 Review Answers, page T25.

Part 1 Review

Summary of Major Economic Concepts

In Part 1 you have learned the following basic economic principles, which will become the foundation for your learning in the next three parts of this book:

- The central problem for all economic systems is *scarcity*, which forces people, businesses and governments to make choices in which *opportunity costs* are paid.
- The *production* of goods and services requires each of the scarce *factors of production: natural resources, labor, capital*, and *entrepreneurship.*
- *Models* are used to help us understand economic relationships and predict the future.
- Economists try to make *rational choices* in which the benefits of a decision are greater than its costs. Rational choices are more difficult to make when they involve *normative* statements (values) rather than *positive* statements (facts).
- Economic relationships are often demonstrated through the use of tables and graphs.
- *Economic systems* organize production by establishing rules that result in greater efficiency through *specialization* and a *division of labor.*
- Although there are many economic systems, they all answer the basic economic questions of *what, how,* and *for whom.*
- *Capitalism* is an economic system in which the means of production are owned by people and the basic economic questions are answered through individual decisions.
- In capitalism, businesses are run to make a *profit*, which allows firms to have more resources allocated to them.
- In *command economies* the means of production are owned by the government, which also makes the basic economic decisions.
- All economic systems in the world today are *mixed.*

Understanding Economic Concepts

Each of the following questions emphasizes one or more of the important economic concepts you have learned in Part 1. An important concept is listed in parentheses after each question. Answer each question in complete sentences that *show you understand the meaning* of the concept. The first question has been answered for you as an example.

1. Why can't we all have everything that we want? (discuss *scarcity*)
   (*Answer:* We can't all have everything we want because we do not have enough resources to produce all the goods and services we would like.)
2. When we choose to buy the product we want the most, what are we giving up? (discuss *opportunity cost*)
3. What types of resources are necessary to create goods and services? (discuss the *four factors of production*)
4. What tools do economists use to help them predict the future? (discuss *economic models*)
5. How do economists try to make decisions? (discuss *rational choice*)
6. How do economic systems increase the efficiency of production? (discuss *specialization* and the *division of labor*)

7. What basic questions must all economic systems answer? (discuss *what, how,* and *for whom*)
8. In general, what type of economic system does the United States have? (discuss *capitalism*)
9. In capitalism, how do we decide which firms will receive more resources? (discuss *profit* and *allocation*)
10. In general, what type of economic system does China have? (discuss *command economy*)

Writing About Economics

Each of the questions below requires you to write a brief essay. Be sure to include each of the following in your answer:

- Demonstrate your understanding of the identified economic concept(s) in your essay.
- Explain how the economic concept(s) is involved in the situation.
- Describe how you would resolve the situation and on what basis you would make your decision.

1. Your mother gave you $5 to buy school supplies you need for your math class. As you are walking to the store you pass a movie theater that is showing a new horror show you really want to see. Tickets to the movie cost $5. You have no other money to spend. Do you buy the math supplies or go to the movie? (discuss *opportunity cost*)
2. You can't find a summer job, so you are considering going into business for yourself. You received an *A* on a wooden letterbox you made in your shop class. You think you could sell them door-to-door for about $5 each. You are going to make a list of the things you need before you actually decide whether to try making and selling the boxes. Do you think you would go into the letterbox business? (discuss *natural resources, labor, capital,* and *entrepreneurship*)
3. You have started a business with three of your friends, cutting grass and doing gardening in your neighborhood. You have so many customers that you are having trouble getting all the work done. At the present, each of you goes to a different house and does all the work. One of your friends has suggested that all of you go to the same house at the same time to get the work done in a hurry. Another wants to buy some electric hedge trimmers and a weedcutter. Do you believe these are good ideas? (discuss *specialization* and the *division of labor*)
4. You own an appliance store. Your business has not been doing well lately. Although sales of radios and TV's have been good, you have sold few washing machines and refrigerators. It has taken too long to have appliances fixed by sending them back to the factory. You are thinking of hiring someone to fix them in your store. Finally, your four employees have demanded an increase in their salary, which you really can't afford. What would you do about each of these problems? (discuss the basic economic questions, *what, how,* and *for whom*)

Discussing Economics

The following paragraphs describe economic proposals that have been the topic of recent public debate. For each, decide whether you support or do not support the proposal, and think about how you would present your opinion to the rest of the class. When you present your opinion to the class, follow these steps:

Writing About Economics
(1) evaluating alternatives; (2) decision-making; (3) testing hypotheses; (4) identifying alternatives.

Part 1 Review

- Identify and describe the controversial issues of the proposal.
- Clearly state the decision you have reached.
- Explain why you think your choice is the best one.

1. It has been suggested that rationing should be used if there is ever another gasoline shortage such as the one that occurred in 1973. One plan would give coupons to licensed drivers that would allow each driver to buy ten gallons of gasoline each week. Drivers not using their coupons would be allowed to sell them to other people for whatever price they could get.

   What would be the costs and benefits of such a plan? Who would be affected? Would you support the plan?
2. Many towns pass zoning laws that limit the use of land within their communities. Some types of zoning laws limit the height of new construction. Others deal with commercial vs. residential use, and others may deal with maintaining public access to coastlines and beaches.

   In one type of zoning law, new residents must have at least an acre of land to build on, and new multiple-unit construction (such as apartment buildings) is not allowed. What purposes do you think such a restriction might have? What are the costs and benefits, and who is affected by the rule? Would you support this zoning law?

Problem-Solving in Economics

Chapter 1

1. Look at a recent copy of a local newspaper. Find examples of choices that were made by a person, by a business, and by the government. For each:
   a. Describe the choice that was made.
   b. Identify what scarce resources were used.
   c. Describe an alternative choice that could have been made.
2. Make a list of four different decisions you have recently made. Explain why you made each decision and what opportunity cost(s) you paid for each.
3. Choose a product that you use every day. Identify as many factors as you can that were used in making the product. Classify each factor as a natural resource, labor, capital or entrepreneurship.
4. Below you will find a list of six statements. Explain why each one is a positive or a normative statement.
   a. There were about 250,000,000 people living in the United States in 1990.
   b. The unemployment rate in the state of West Virginia declined from 1985 to 1989.
   c. The President of the United States is the most important man in the world.
   d. Watching television is a waste of time.
   e. Most prices went up in 1992.
   f. It is wrong for Americans to buy Japanese cars.

Discussing Economics
(1) predicting probable consequences; (2) assessing costs and benefits.

Problem-Solving in Economics
Chapter 1
(1) information from written sources; (2) decision-making; (3) classification; (4) identifying assumptions; (5) identifying assumptions;
(6) evaluating alternatives.

Fatal Traffic Accidents Involving Alcohol

Ages		16–17	18–21	22–24	25–34	35–44	45–54	55–65	65+
Accidents per	(1983)	19.45	31.50	26.40	18.16	7.82	7.59	4.26	2.67
100,000 drivers	(1989)	13.70	26.21	23.64	15.58	9.26	6.42	4.03	2.60

5. In 1985 the federal government threatened to reduce highway aid to any state that did not increase its legal drinking age to 21. This policy was based on many assumptions concerning automobile accidents and the ability of young adults to use alcoholic beverages responsibly. Make a list of the assumptions you believe this rule was based on. Do you believe that these assumptions were a reliable way to predict the future? Explain why you do or do not believe 21 to be a reasonable legal drinking age. The table above should help you.
6. As you near graduation from high school, you need to think about what you will do next. You might try to find a job. You could go on to college or to a vocational school. Think of at least two alternatives for what you would like to do after high school. Make a list of reasons for and against each alternative, and decide which of the alternatives represents the most rational choice. Explain why you prefer that alternative.

Chapter 2

1. Jerry is doing very poorly. Jerry used to sell many orders of hamburgers and fries in his little restaurant. Last year a fast-food chain opened a store down the street. They sell their hamburgers and fries for less than Jerry can possibly charge, and they have orders ready in seconds while Jerry only cooks to order. Explain what Jerry's problems have to do with (1) the division of labor, (2) specialization, (3) specialized tools and (4) the accumulation of wealth. What would Jerry probably have to say about his new competition? What would Jerry's customers say? If you were Jerry, what would you do?
2. Think of a product that was used five to ten years ago that people don't want any more. What might have happened to the firm that made this product? On a separate sheet of paper, write the name of the product. Then describe what may have happened to the producer. Be sure to explain how the questions *what, how* and *for whom* are related to your description.

Chapter 2
(1) analyzing cause and effect; (2) analyzing cause and effect.

Problem-Solving Chapter 1 activities 2 and 6 may be an appropriate method of authentic assessment and may be placed in students' portfolios.

THE CUSTOM SHOP
THE SHARPER IMAGE
B.Dalton
Information

P A R T

2

Understanding How Individuals and Businesses Make Economic Decisions

Part 2 shows how the decisions of individual consumers and businesses affect a capitalistic economy. Economists call this the study of *microeconomics,* meaning that it focuses on specific elements within the economy.

In this part you will learn how spending and production decisions by consumers and businesses relate to the laws of demand and supply. You will explore the effects of competition in the economy. And you will look at the roles of workers and labor organizations in a market economy.

RYAN WALSH

CHAPTER 3

Demand and Supply

Objectives

This chapter discusses how demand and supply function in a market economy. In the sections of this chapter, you will learn:

A

how the movement of elements in the economy can be demonstrated using a *circular flow model;*

B

why people buy more or less of a product (the *determinants of demand*) and what the *law of demand* means to a market economy;

C

how the principle of *diminishing returns* and the *law of supply* affect the economy;

D

how the market adjusts to *surpluses* and *shortages* and tends to move toward a *point of equilibrium;*

E

how *elasticity* of demand affects prices.

Introduction

It's Monday morning, your third week in Economics. Your teacher calls on you and asks, "How much is a granola bar worth? Would you pay a dollar for one?"

Your answer, "It depends."

"It depends on what?"

"Well . . . it depends on how big it is."

"What else?"

"It depends on how hungry I am, or how much money I've got, or whether it's a type that I like."

"Anything else?"

"It depends on whether or not you'll call on someone else if I buy your granola bar!"

In this chapter you will learn how we decide what things are worth. In some ways it is a very easy problem. A product is worth as much as someone is willing to pay for it. But that answer is really too easy. There are many different factors that affect how much customers are willing to pay.

Economists have organized these factors into what they call the theories of demand and supply. When these two theories are studied together, they explain the way prices are set and how firms decide which goods and services to produce.

Explain. The examples in this chapter illustrate general principles, and so are simpler than most real situations.

Section A The Elements of an Economic System

This section introduces the *circular flow model,* the *factor market,* and the *product market.*

Personal Narrative

My Father Was a Farmer

My name is Brad. For as long as I can remember, my family lived on a farm in Iowa. My great-great-grandfather settled here in the 1870s. With every generation we bought more land and grew more food. I thought we had the best possible life. We lived and worked together and in most years we were pretty well off.

Note. Although the personal narrative is fiction, similar events have happened. The data concerning production and prices throughout this chapter is accurate.

By 1980 we owned nearly a thousand acres and rented about five hundred more from our neighbor, Mr. Sims. He had retired from full-time farming. Sometimes we hired him when things got busy in the spring or fall.

We grew corn on most of our land. We also raised hogs and kept a vegetable garden to supply us with produce for a roadside stand. Our corn was sold through the local co-op to a firm in Davenport. Some of it was shipped down the Mississippi River and sent to other countries. We also bought our seed and fertilizer through the co-op.

Our busiest time each year was during the harvest season. There was no way that our family members alone could handle everything that had to be done. So each September we would hire workers to help just during the harvest.

We did most of our shopping in Cedar Rapids, which was about twenty miles south of our farm. I liked going to the city because there was always something to see or do. You might not believe 110,000 people is much of a city, but if you almost never saw more than a hundred people at a time you would think otherwise. My father would drop my brother and me at a mall and give us $25 to spend. At the time we thought it was great. We would buy a shirt or a pair of jeans and go to a movie.

Life on the farm was not easy. It seemed like there was always too much to do and not enough time to do it. But we lost the farm in 1985, and now when I look back, those seem like the best times of my life.

The Circular Flow Model

Explain. Students may not understand the circular flow model without help. A copy in the *Teacher's Resource Binder* may be used to make a transparency for class presentation.

Note. It is easier to measure flows of money than flows of products and factors of production. Since these flows have equal values, economic activity is often measured by studying flows of money.

In the story at the left, Brad described his life on a farm, and he explained part of the role farms play in the American economy. Following this section, you'll look at the economics of Brad's farm using what economists call the **circular flow model.**

The circular flow model is a chart that economists use to show how economic systems work and how firms and people fit into these systems. Figure 3–1 shows one of these charts.[1]

The circular flow model is made up of four boxes, which are connected in a circle by two sets of arrows that point in opposite directions. The box on the left side represents all businesses. The box on the right side represents all households. The top box is for the **product market,** where all sales of consumer products take place. The bottom box is for the **factor market,** where all sales of the factors of production (natural resources, labor, capital, and entrepreneurship) take place.

The arrows of the inside circle are labeled with dollar signs ($). They represent the flow of money through the economy. The arrows of the outside circle represent the flow of goods and services and the flow of factors of production.

Figure 3–1 *Simplified Circular Flow Model*

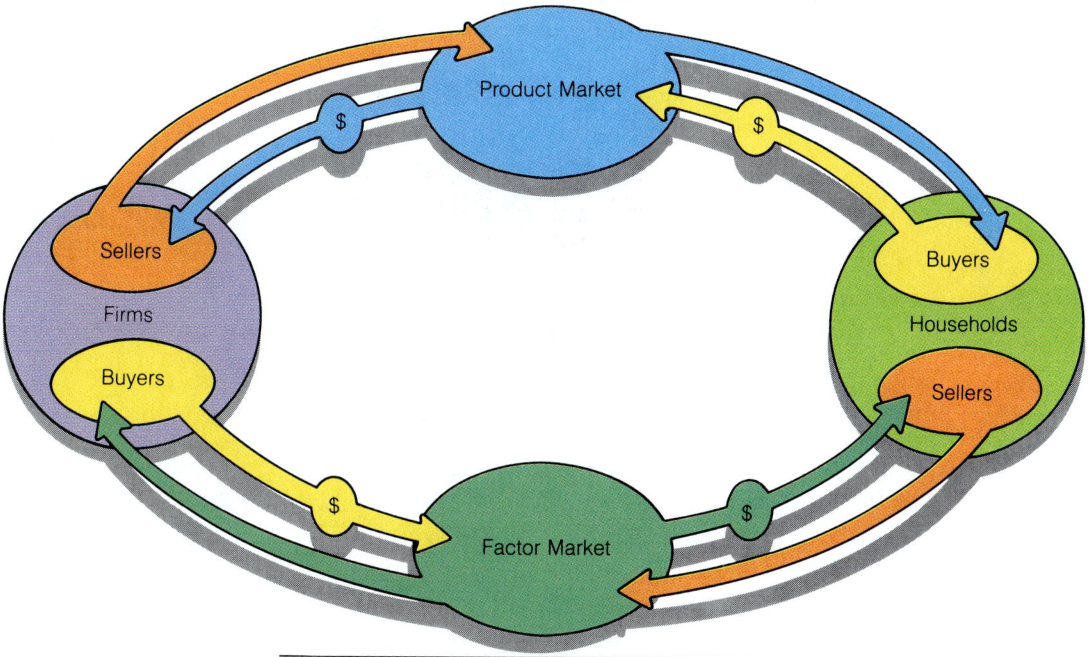

[1]Note that this chart is similar to Figure 2–1 in Chapter 2.

The top part of the model shows what happens when a household consumer buys a product. Suppose that you (like Brad in the story) buy a new pair of jeans. Money would flow from you (the buyer on the right-hand side of the model) through the product market (at the top of the model) to the firm that made the jeans (the seller on the left-hand side of the model). This is across the top part of the model from right to left. In return, a pair of jeans flows across the top of the model from left to right. The jeans go from the firm through the product market to you (a household buyer).

Households provide factors of production to firms in the form of labor they sell, natural resources they own, or in savings they invest. For these factors they are paid wages, rent, and interest.

The bottom part of the model shows what happens when a firm buys any of the factors of production. Suppose that you take a job in a clothing store. You are "selling" your labor to the store. Labor moves from you (the seller on the right-hand side of the model) to the firm. In return, you receive wages from the firm (the buyer on the left-hand side of the model). Money (in the form of wages) flows from left to right through the factor market. Labor and other factors of production flow from right to left through the factor market.

The value of money flowing through the model in a counterclockwise direction is exactly equal to the value of goods and services and factors of production that flow in a clockwise direction.

All transactions can be placed in a circular flow model. This shows that they are all related to each other, just as all parts of the economy are related to each other.

This is a *simplified* circular flow model. It does not include the government or the banking system. It does give us a foundation to build on. We will refer back to this model in the chapters that follow.

Self-Check
1. A sale of crude oil would be found in the factor market.
2. A sale of a TV set would be found in the product market.
3. They are equal in value.

Self-Check

1. In what part of the circular flow model would the sale of crude oil to a refinery take place?
2. In what part of the circular flow model would the sale of a color television set take place?
3. What can be said about the value of products and factors of production that flow through the model in a clockwise direction and the value of money that flows in a counterclockwise direction?

Applying What You Have Learned

See Lesson Plans for Chapter 3, Section A, page T30.

Applying What You Have Learned

In the Personal Narrative, Brad described events that included the following transactions. Show where each fits in the circular flow model by placing its letter in the correct location on the circular flow model you have been given by your teacher. (You may be asked to sketch one yourself.)

a. selling vegetables at a roadside stand
b. renting land from Mr. Sims
c. hiring extra workers during harvest
d. going to a movie
e. selling corn to a co-op
f. buying seed
g. buying gas to drive to Cedar Rapids
h. hiring Mr. Sims
i. buying a pair of jeans

Like Brad living on the farm, most of us fit into the circular flow model in many ways.

PROFILE

Adam Smith
(1723–1790)

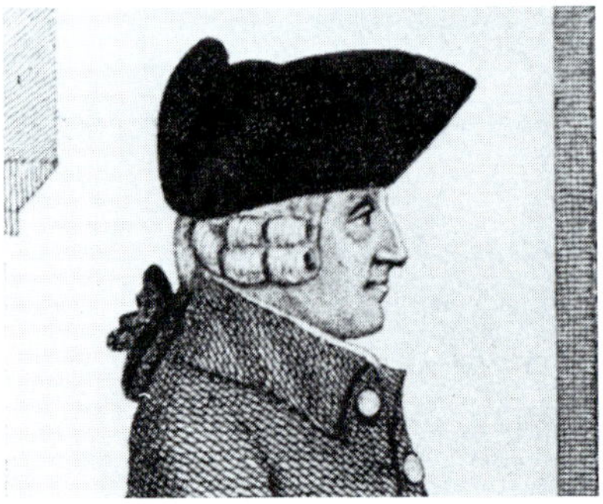

To many economists, Adam Smith was the most important contributor to the development of the theory of capitalism. He is remembered for his famous book, *The Wealth of Nations,* which was published in 1776, the year of the American Declaration of Independence. In this book, he asked and explained how capitalism answered the basic questions of *what, how* and *for whom.*

Smith believed that consumers were the starting point of production. They made their wishes known in the market place through what they bought. Businesses profited if they supplied what consumers demanded. If the government allowed the forces of demand and supply to operate without interfering, consumers would find the best goods at the lowest prices. Businesses, following their own self-interest, would try to produce the best goods at the lowest prices so that they could make the most profits. As if guided by an "invisible hand," consumers, producers, and the factors of production would be brought together, helping them all get the largest part possible of what they wanted.

Smith said that the economy would function best if government would practice *laissez faire,* or a hands-off policy toward the market. He believed competition in free markets—the laws of supply and demand—would ensure good quality products at fair prices.

Smith also believed in the division of labor. He encouraged everyone to specialize in what they produced best and to exchange their products for what others produced. If this was done, he said, everyone would have more goods and services.

Born in Scotland, Smith became a professor of moral philosophy at Glasgow College. A brilliant lecturer, he was also absentminded, timid, and never married. When he became older, he was given the highly paid position of customs collector. Smith's theory of capitalism greatly influenced the development of the American economic system.

Section B The Law of Demand

This section will introduce *demand,* the *law of demand,* the *demand schedule,* the *demand curve,* and the *determinants of demand.* The section will also introduce the terms *substitute goods* and *complementary goods.*

Personal Narrative

Explain. It takes farmers a long time to adjust production to changes in demand. When demand increases, farmers cannot quickly buy more resources and produce more food.

Discuss. Do your students feel it was right for the United States to sell grain to the Soviet Union, which had an economic and political system that most Americans opposed at that time?

He Used to Say, "Everyone's Got to Eat"

I think I was about four years old when I realized that our farm was a business and not just the place we lived. I remember my father talking about the weather and the corn wilting in our fields. It was 1972 and there was a drought in Iowa. Our corn production was down by about ten percent. In the whole country it was only down about one percent, but that didn't do us any good. We thought things looked really bad. But life never works out the way you expect. 1972 turned out to be one of our best years.

That was the year of the Russian grain deal. President Nixon agreed to sell millions of bushels of grain to the Soviet Union. Our crop may have been smaller, but the price we got for our corn went up. We got $1.08 per bushel in 1971. In 1972 the price reached $1.57. We earned almost a third more from our crops that year. The price we were paid for our hogs went up about 15 percent too.

1973 was even a better year. By then the export of U.S. grain to Russia was in full swing. They had a bad harvest. Our crops weren't all that great either, but the price of corn reached $2.37 per bushel. That was more than twice what we got two years before. Our costs had stayed almost the same. We earned more money than we had ever made before.

I was just five years old in 1973, so I didn't really understand, but I do remember my father saying, "Everyone's got to eat, and I don't care if they're a Russian or an American."

Demand

Economists would say that Brad's family's farm did well in 1972 and 1973 because of a growth in demand. **Demand** is a willingness to buy a product at a particular price. Demand occurs when a product is actually sold. Just wanting or needing something is not demand unless you buy the product too. There is a **law of demand,** which states that people will buy more of a product at a lower price than they will buy at a higher price, if nothing else changes.

Demand Schedule

Explain. Although demand schedules are projected from market surveys and are subject to error, the alternative is to use nothing at all.

It is possible to make a table that shows how many products could be sold at different prices. Economists call these tables **demand schedules.** An example of a demand schedule is shown in Figure 3–2. The schedule shows how many of "Joe's Picnic Tables" can be sold at various prices. Joe can sell more tables at a low price than he can at a high price. This demonstrates the law of demand.

Demand Curve

Note. The demand curves used in this chapter are straight lines. Real demand curves bend toward the corner of the graph, because the utility of additional products does not diminish at a constant rate. (See Chapter 4, Section A.)

To the right of the table is a graph that shows a **demand curve.** It is drawn from the information shown on the table. A demand curve shows what quantities will be in demand at various prices. Its vertical (up and down) axis represents price. Its horizontal (across) axis is for the quantity demanded. All normal demand curves slope from the upper left-hand corner of the graph to the lower right-hand corner. This is a *negative slope.* A negative slope shows that if one of the values goes up, the other will go down. (The demand curves used as examples in this chapter are straight lines because this makes them easier to read and understand. Real demand curves usually bend toward the corner of the graph. In Section A of Chapter 4 you will study a demand curve that does bend.)

Figure 3–2
Demand Schedule for Joe's Picnic Tables

Price	Number of Tables Sold
$70	10
$60	20
$50	30
$40	40
$30	50

Demand Curve for Joe's Picnic Tables

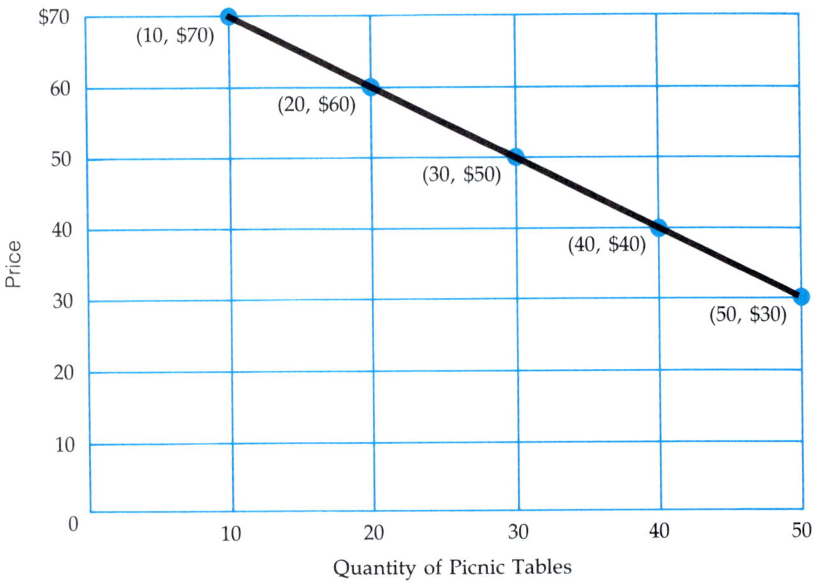

Explain. Many students find it difficult to make the distinction between a change in *demand* and a change in the *quantity demanded*. It should be made clear that a change in demand is a result of a change in the *determinants of demand*, but a change in the quantity demanded is a result of a change in *price*.

Discuss. Ask students to bring photographs of their parents when they were in high school. They can serve as the basis for a discussion of changing tastes.

Explain. Complementary products can be illustrated with analogies to various sports. For example, ask students what would happen to the demand for baseballs or tennis balls if baseball gloves and tennis rackets became very expensive.

Changes in Demand

Demand does not always stay the same. There are a number of factors that will cause demand to either increase or decrease. Economists call these the **determinants of demand.** This name sounds much harder than the idea is. The determinants of demand are listed below.

1. *Tastes:* Consumers don't always want the same things. Items that are popular now may not sell in the future. Thirty years ago many students carried slide rules to school. Now they use pocket calculators instead of slide rules. The demand for calculators has increased. The demand for slide rules has decreased.
2. *Income:* If income increases, people can afford to buy more products. As a result, demand will grow. On the other hand, if income goes down, demand will decrease. There is a direct relationship between income and demand.
3. *The price of related products:* Many products can be substituted for each other. If the price of butter went up, more people would buy margarine instead. The demand for margarine would increase. If the price of hot dogs at the ballpark went down while the price of hamburgers stayed the same, many fans would buy hot dogs instead of hamburgers. The demand for hamburgers would decrease. Economists call these products **substitute goods** because they can be used *in place of each other.*

Demand for American corn has been increasing due to an increase in the number of potential customers (one of the determinants of demand).

Note. Foreign sales accounted for 14 percent of U.S. food production in 1971, 23 percent in 1972, and 21 percent in 1973. Without exports there would have been surpluses of food in the United States, and lower prices.

Other products are **complementary goods.** These products are used *with each other.* Gasoline and automobiles are an example. If the price of gasoline went up to five dollars a gallon, fewer people would drive cars. The demand for cars would decrease because of the increase in the price of a complementary good, gasoline.

4. *Number of potential customers:* If the number of people either increases or decreases in an area, it will change demand in that area. In the 1980s houses in California were in great demand because so many people moved there. At the same time demand for houses in parts of the Northeast fell as people moved to other parts of the country.

If demand for a product increases, its demand curve will move to the right on the graph. If demand for a product decreases, its demand curve will move to the left.

In 1972 and 1973, demand for American corn increased. The biggest reason was our large exports to other parts of the world, particularly to the Soviet Union. The number of our customers and size of their orders increased and so did the demand. Table 3–1 shows our corn exports for 1971–73.

Note. The years 1971 through 1982 were chosen for this chapter because they most clearly demonstrate the laws of supply and demand. Later years are affected by fluctuations in the value of the dollar.

Table 3–1

Exports of U.S. Corn, 1971–1973

(in millions of bushels)

Year	Amount Exported	Total Production
1971	796	5,641
1972	1,258	5,573
1973	1,200	5,643

Source: *Statistical Abstract of the United States*, 1975.

Self-Check
1. Wanting a new coat becomes demand when the new coat is actually sold.
2. It should decrease.
3. Economists call these the determinants of demand.

Self-Check

1. When does wanting a new coat become demand?
2. If the price of a product increases, what should happen to the number sold?
3. Factors such as tastes, income, the price of related products, and the number of customers can all change demand. What is the name economists have given these things?

Applying What You Have Learned
See Lesson Plans for Chapter 3, Section B, page T32.

Applying What You Have Learned

In this section you've learned about four determinants of demand. What event can you find in the Personal Narrative that caused a change in one of the determinants? Which determinant changed, and what was the effect on demand?

Section C The Law of Supply

This section will introduce the ideas of *supply, law of supply,* a *supply schedule,* a *supply curve,* and *diminishing returns.*

Personal Narrative

Many Other People Thought the Same

The 1970s were the "golden years" for our farm. We grew more and more corn and the price kept going up. By 1979 we were getting $2.52 per bushel and our production was up 40 percent from 1973. When the price hit $3.10 a bushel in 1980, we began to think we were going to be like the Rockefellers. The same was true of many other farmers in the country.

Note. Expenses taken on by farmers were long-term and required fixed payments over time, while the decisions to purchase new land and equipment were based on short-term market conditions.

Of course it cost us money to increase our production. We bought 200 more acres of land and started renting from Mr. Sims. We bought new tractors and lots of other equipment. The price of fertilizer went up too. In 1980 we had to pay almost three times as much as we did in 1973, because of the increase in the price of oil.

We borrowed most of the money we needed to expand our production. In 1973 our farm was almost free and clear. By 1980 our debt was over $900,000. We had to pay 12 percent interest on the loan, but our income was up. We thought we had nothing to worry about. We didn't really understand what was happening to farming all over the world.

After 1980 our problems never seemed to end. In 1981 U.S. exports to other countries began to fall. Scientists invented "miracle seeds" that started the "Green Revolution." Countries that had been our customers grew all the food they needed for themselves. Some of them even started to export grain to compete with us. Not only was our production up, but the production of all U.S. farms had increased by about 40 percent. There was more food available than there were people who could afford to buy it. Supplies had been greatly increased while demand had stayed almost the same.

Discuss. Should we have helped developing nations become more self-sufficient, or did this hurt our farmers too much?

Supply

Economists would say that Brad's family was in the business of *supplying* food. **Supply** is the term given to the quantity of products that a firm is willing to sell at a particular price.

When firms first start production, they find the cost per unit goes down as they make more products. However, after they reach a certain level of production, the cost of producing additional items increases. This can be the result of paying overtime, of hiring less skilled workers, or simply the result of overcrowding. Economists call this **diminishing returns.**

Note. A firm's willingness to supply products depends on the price it can charge and its cost of production. Firms often know their costs, but are not as able to predict market prices.

The law of supply states that at higher prices, producers will offer more products for sale. When the price of corn went up, American farmers made the investments necessary to increase production. But at the same time, food production was also increasing in some of the nations that had been customers for U.S. grain.

When costs of production grow, firms require higher prices to produce more products. Higher prices make up for their higher costs. Therefore, at higher prices producers offer more products for sale than they would be willing to offer at lower prices. This is called the **law of supply.**

Supply Schedule

It is possible to make a table that shows how many products would be supplied at different prices. Economists call these tables **supply schedules.** You can see a supply schedule for Joe's picnic tables in Figure 3–3. Joe will be willing to sell more tables if he is able to charge higher prices.

Joe builds picnic tables on his weekends. If he builds more tables, he has to give up more of his free time. He is willing to give up more of his free time if he can sell the tables at higher prices. The price of tables determines how many Joe will make. This demonstrates the law of supply.

Supply Curve

To the right of the table is a graph that is called a **supply curve.** It is drawn from the values on the table. Its vertical (up and down) axis represents price. Its horizontal (across) axis is for the quantity supplied. These are the same values that appeared on the graph in the preceding section on demand.

Figure 3–3

Supply Schedule for Joe's Picnic Tables

Price	Number of Tables Supplied
$70	50
$60	40
$50	30
$40	20
$30	10

Supply Curve for Joe's Picnic Tables

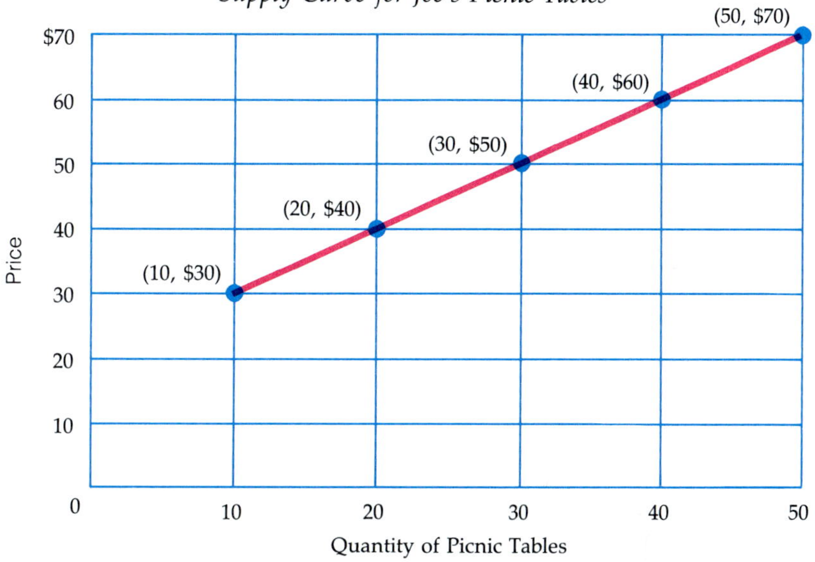

All normal supply curves slope from the lower left-hand corner of the graph to the upper right-hand corner. This is a positive slope. A positive slope shows that if one of the values goes up, the other will go up too.

Note. Many students find it difficult to distinguish between a change in *supply* and change in the *quantity supplied*. It should be made clear that a change in supply is a result of changes in the *costs of production*, but a change in the quantity supplied is a result of a change in *price*.

Changes in Supply

The number of items a firm is willing to supply does not always stay the same. Suppose that the price a firm is able to charge does not change when its cost of production goes up. This increase in cost would cause the firm to offer fewer products for sale at the current price. The firm's supply curve would move to the left on the graph.

On the other hand, if the firm's cost of production fell, it would be willing to offer more products for sale at the current price. In this case the firm's supply curve would move to the right on the graph.

The prices firms are able to charge for their products are often set by powers that are beyond their control. This is usually the case with farmers. There are so many farmers that none of them has the power to set the price alone. The number of products that farmers produce depends on their cost of production and the price they expect to receive when they harvest and sell their crops.

In the late 1970s and early 1980s, higher prices caused farmers to produce more corn. Table 3–2 shows this growth. (1980 was an exception because of a drought.)

Table 3–2
U.S. Corn Production, 1977–1982
(in millions of bushels)

Year	Total Production
1977	6,505
1978	7,268
1979	7,928
1980	6,639
1981	8,119
1982	8,235

Source: *Statistical Abstract of the United States, 1979–1987.*

Self-Check
1. The number will decrease.
2. The cost will increase.
3. The number will decrease.

Applying What You Have Learned
See Lesson Plans for Chapter 3, Section C, page T33.

Self-Check

1. According to the law of supply, what will happen to the number of products a firm offers for sale when prices go down?
2. What will happen to the cost of additional units of production when a firm starts having diminishing returns?
3. What will happen to the number of products a firm will offer for sale if its cost of production increases while prices remain the same?

Applying What You Have Learned

In the Personal Narrative at the beginning of this section, why did the farmers decide to make the investments necessary to increase production?

Section D Surpluses, Shortages, and Equilibrium

Discuss. What happens to prices when there is a shortage? "Scalping" tickets is often a good topic for this discussion.

This section will introduce the ideas of *equilibrium, surpluses,* and *shortages*.

Personal Narrative

Some Years Were Good, and Some Years Were Bad

When we planted our crops in the spring, we never knew what we would be paid when we harvested them in the fall. Prices were high for a while and then they were low. I didn't know why. My father told me it had something to do with how much grain the United States sold to other countries and how big the harvest was, but at the time I didn't understand.

I did know that our business worked in a strange way. Some years we had very poor crops. There was too much rain, or too little rain, or winter would set in too early. My mother would get all worried. Many of those years turned out to be good, because the price for the corn we did harvest was high.

In other years the crop was wonderful. We could produce as much as 115 bushels per acre. But in many of those years the prices were low and we actually ended up losing money. Every time I thought I understood, something new would happen to make me confused. In the end I decided to let my father worry about it.

In the 1970s and early 1980s farm prices went up almost every year. In 1984 they turned around and started going down. In 1985 the price fell to $2.54 a bushel. You might think that was a pretty good price. After all, in 1973 we had been excited about $2.37 a bushel. What you need to remember is inflation. Between 1973 and 1985 the prices of things we had to buy to run our farm more than doubled. What was even worse was the interest on our debt. When we borrowed money in the 1970s, the interest rate was only about 10 percent. By 1983 we had to pay 20 percent or more on some of our loans. Do you know how much 20 percent is when you're in debt almost a million dollars? It works out to be close to $200,000 a year. There was no way we could pay our bills. In 1985 the bank took our farm and sold it for a song. We got almost nothing at the auction because many other farmers were in the same situation. More farms were being sold than there were people to buy them.

Note. The price of farms fell because the supply exceeded the demand.

The price for corn changed from year to year because of changes in its demand and supply. In the 1970s and early 1980s the

Question. Why is it difficult for farmers to organize to control their prices?

demand for corn grew more rapidly than its supply. The result was higher prices. After 1983 the supply of corn exceeded its demand and prices fell. No individual farmer could do anything about it.

Determining Equilibrium

Economists demonstrate what happened to Brad's family through the use of a combined demand and supply schedule, and by drawing demand and supply curves on the same graph. You can see a graph and a demand and supply schedule for picnic tables in Figure 3–4.

These are the same demand and supply schedules and curves that you studied in Sections B and C of this chapter. On the graph, you can see that the demand and supply curves intersect at a point that has been labeled *E*. Economists call this the **point of equilibrium.**

Figure 3–4

Demand and Supply Schedule for Joe's Picnic Tables

Price	Number of Tables Demanded	Number of Tables Supplied	Surplus or Shortage
$70	10	50	+40
$60	20	40	+20
$50	30	30	0
$40	40	20	−20
$30	50	10	−40

Demand and Supply Curves for Joe's Picnic Tables

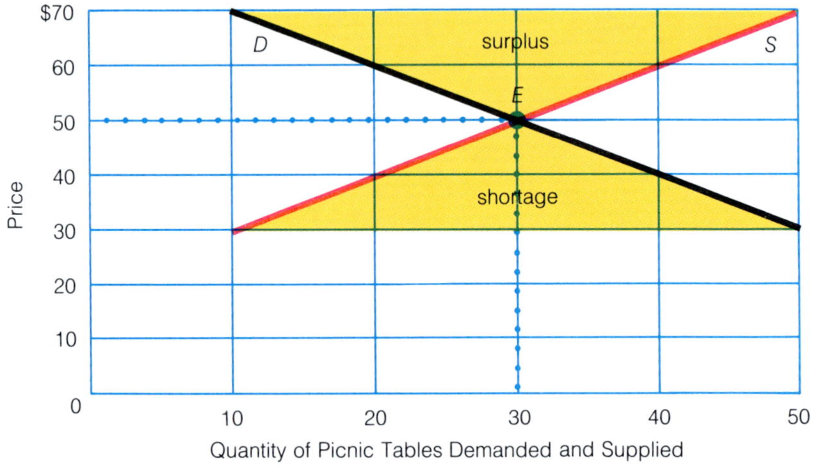

On this graph, the point corresponds to a price of $50 and a quantity of 30. (The colored dots show you how to find these numbers. Read straight across to find the number on one axis and straight down to find the number on the other axis.) This means that at a price of $50, consumers are willing to buy 30 picnic tables *and* Joe is willing to supply 30 tables. The demand and supply schedule shows the same information for the row corresponding to $50. At this price, the quantity demanded is equal to the quantity supplied. When demand and supply are the same, the economic system is said to be at equilibrium.

Discuss. When pocket calculators were first introduced in the early 1970s, their price was over $100. A similar calculator costs only a few dollars today. What must have happened to the supply curve for calculators to have made the equilibrium price fall so far?

In economic theory, the point of equilibrium indicates the price and quantity at which a product will be sold in a competitive market economy.

Suppose Joe thinks he can sell all of his picnic tables at a price of $70 each. This makes it worth his while to produce 50 tables. But the demand curve shows that he would only sell 10 tables at that price. There would be a **surplus** of 40 tables. A surplus is the amount of a product that a firm offers for sale in excess of the quantity customers are willing to buy. The surplus is shown as the upper shaded portion on the graph. Joe would be forced to lower his price to eliminate his surplus. The market price would fall to the equilibrium price.

If Joe thought the equilibrium price was $30, he would only make 10 tables, but he would find he had 50 customers who wanted to buy them. There would be a **shortage** of tables. A shortage is the amount of a product customers want to buy in excess of the quantity a firm offers for sale. This shortage is shown as the lower shaded portion on the graph. Joe would be encouraged to raise his price and produce more tables until the number of tables he was willing to supply was equal to the number his customers wanted to buy. The market price would increase to the equilibrium price.

You can see that market prices tend to move *toward* the equilibrium point. When surpluses exist, prices fall. When shortages exist, prices rise. Given a reasonable amount of time, the market price should become the same as the equilibrium price.

In Brad's story you saw how these forces work. The price of corn in any year is the result of the interaction of demand and supply. Figure 3–5 shows a graph and a table of corn prices for the years 1972–1982. If there is a large increase in demand, the result will be a shortage and an increase in price. If there is a large increase in supply, there will be a surplus and a decrease in price. No single farmer is big enough to have any power over price. All farmers are forced to accept the price the market gives them.

Figure 3–5
Price of Corn per Bushel, 1972–1982

Year	Price per Bushel
1972	$1.57
1973	$2.37
1974	$3.03
1975	$2.54
1976	$2.15
1977	$2.02
1978	$2.25
1979	$2.52
1980	$3.10
1981	$2.50
1982	$2.68

Line Graph of Price of Corn per Bushel, 1972–1982

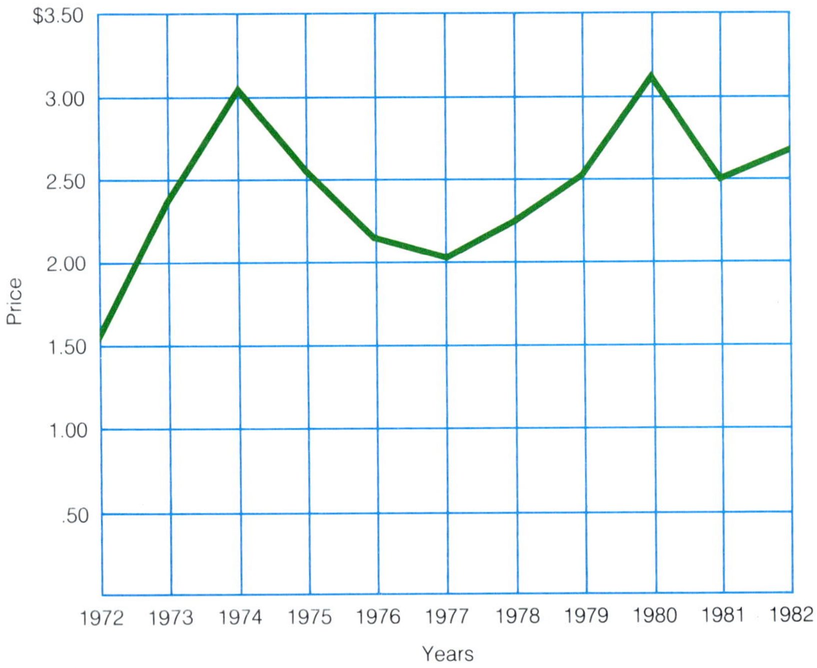

Source: *Statistical Abstract of the United States*, 1975–1987.

Self-Check
1. The point of equilibrium is found at the intersection of the supply and demand curves.
2. It must do so to eliminate its surplus.
3. It would find that it has a shortage, and so would be encouraged to increase prices to the level of consumer demand.

Applying What You Have Learned
See Lesson Plans for Chapter 3, Section D, page T34.

Self-Check

1. Where would you find the point of equilibrium on a graph of a product's demand and supply?
2. If a firm charges a price above the equilibrium price, why will it eventually be forced to lower its price?
3. If a firm charges a price below the equilibrium price, why will it probably increase its price?

Applying What You Have Learned

In the Personal Narrative for this section, Brad described how in some years the farm made good profits even though crops were poor, and in some years the farm made no profit even though crops were good. Explain how this could have been so, based on what you have learned about shortages and surpluses. Suppose that in a particular year Brad's family's farm produced a poor crop (say, because of a single batch of bad seed), but all the other farmers had good crops. Would this affect the farm's profits in the same way as a shortage due to all the farmers having poor crops?

Section E Elasticity

This section will introduce the concepts of *elasticity, price elastic demand,* and *price inelastic demand.*

Personal Narrative

Every Time We Grew More Food, the Price Went Down

A few years ago I finally understood why we had so much trouble on our farm. One of my teachers explained it to me. The problem was that people all over the world need to eat about the same amount of food every year. The price doesn't make much difference; if people can afford to buy food, they will eat.

When there is a bad year for crops, prices go up because people are trying to buy the same amount of food even though there is a shortage. If there is a good harvest, the opposite happens. There is a surplus, and prices fall.

In the 1970s crops were bad in many other countries, particularly in the Soviet Union and Africa. Demand for American food grew throughout the world. Food prices went up rapidly. This encouraged farmers to plant and harvest more crops everywhere.

It takes farmers a long time to adjust their production. If prices are high in September, you can't just go out and grow more corn. It takes years to clear new land and buy new machinery. With prices high, production gradually kept growing until there was more food than people wanted to buy. There was a surplus and prices fell.

A problem farmers faced was that food prices were almost the only prices that fell. The things farmers had to buy kept getting more expensive. The biggest problem for many American farmers was that they had gone so far into debt. They still had their payments to make when their income went down. Many of them simply could not pay their bills, so they lost their farms.

You might say that we were good farmers but poor business-people. My father thought that the government should have helped us out. I'm not really sure what should have been done, but I know we paid a price.

Elasticity of Demand

The problem Brad described is called **elasticity** by economists. It refers to the effect that a change in price has on demand. If people want about the same amount of a product no matter what its price, economists say the demand for the product is **price inelastic.**

Note. The method of finding the price elasticity of demand is to divide the percentage change in the quantity demanded by the percentage change in price. If the resulting value is greater than one, the demand is price elastic; if it is less than one, the demand is price inelastic.

Question. What other products have elastic or inelastic demand?

The demand for some foods is inelastic. For example, the price of salt has little effect on the amount consumers will buy. There are two major reasons why the quantity of salt demanded does not change very much when its price changes. First, even if the price of salt tripled, it still would cost the average family less than a few pennies a day to satisfy their total demand. Second, there is no good substitute for salt. For these reasons, the demand for salt is very inelastic. Basic staples (products that consumers cannot do without) such as bread and milk have inelastic demands. They are viewed as necessities. However, steak, expensive chocolates, and artichokes are luxuries, high-priced and easily substituted. They have **price elastic** demands. When their prices go up, sales fall rapidly.

We can study what happens to staple food prices through the use of a series of graphs.

1. Figure 3–6 shows the world demand (the *D* curve) and supply (the *S* curve) for food in 1971, before the price of food went up. Notice that the demand curve is steeply sloped. This shows that people want about the same amount regardless of price. (On the graph, *P* and *Q* represent the equilibrium price and the amount of sales.)

Figure 3–6

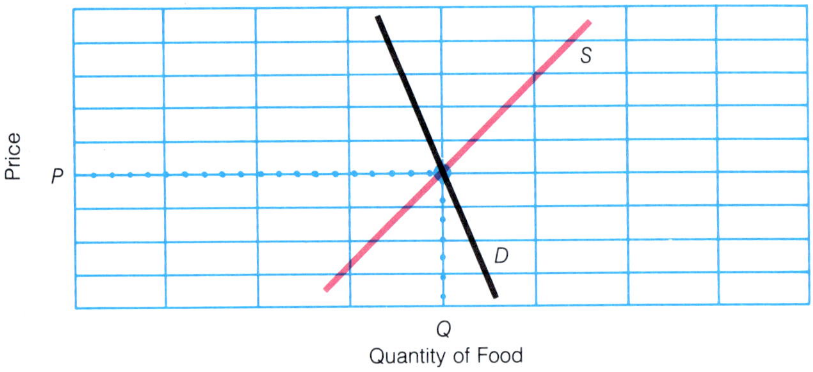

2. Figure 3–7 shows the supply curve moving to the left when many countries had poor crops in 1972 and thereafter. On the graph, P^1 and Q^1 represent the equilibrium price and sales for 1971; P^2 and Q^2 represent the same factors for 1972. There is a significantly higher equilibrium price in 1972 (from P^1 to P^2) but the amount of food sold is down only a little (from Q^1 to Q^2).

Figure 3–7

3. Figure 3–8 shows the supply curve shifting out to the right (from S^2 to S^3). This is the growth in world food production that had occurred by the mid-1980s. There is a lower equilibrium price. Notice that the amount of food sold has stayed almost the same in all of these graphs.

Figure 3–8

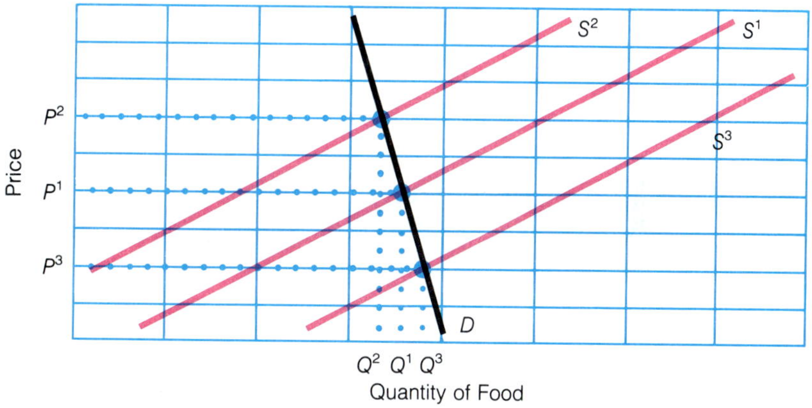

Although the demand for most foods is inelastic, there are many products whose demand is price elastic. For these products a small change in price brings about a larger relative change in the amount of the product that is bought. Elastic demand curves tend to be more horizontal than inelastic demand curves. Study the graphs for a type of granola bar in Figures 3–9, 10, and 11.

Figure 3–9

Figure 3–10

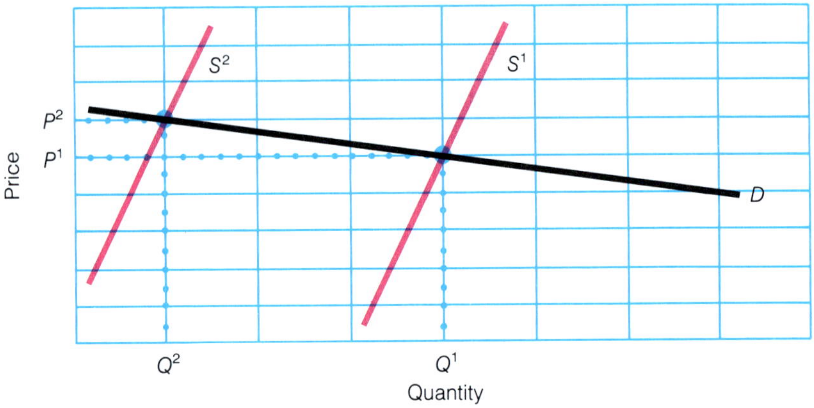

Figure 3–11

1. The demand curve for "Nutty" granola bars is quite elastic. Figure 3–9 shows its demand and supply, and the current equilibrium price *(P)* and sales *(Q)*.
2. If the firm's workers got a wage increase, the supply curve would shift to the left (Figure 3–10) because the cost of production would rise. There would be a higher equilibrium price. The number of granola bars sold would fall rapidly because people would substitute some other type of snack.
3. If the firm bought new machines to replace its workers, it could shift its supply curve to the right (Figure 3–11). There would be a lower equilibrium price and the number of granola bars sold would increase rapidly.

Note. The relatively low price for oil in the mid-1980s discouraged nations from finding alternative sources of energy. The demand for imported oil became more price inelastic. Some American economists worried that the United States would become more vulnerable to future price increases by petroleum exporting nations.

The effect of elasticity can be seen in the Arab–Israeli war of 1973. This war led to an increase in the price of crude oil from about \$2.60 to \$11.00 for every 40-gallon barrel. That price was more than four times greater than it had been. Even with this large increase in price, the importation of oil into the United States fell by less than one tenth. However, the high price did encourage exploration for more oil in other parts of the world. It also encouraged conservation in all countries. By the mid-1980s there was a surplus of oil and its price fell to as low as \$7.00 a barrel.

Medicines are price inelastic. Because they are necessary and are used only to meet specific needs, consumers will want about the same amount of medicines, regardless of the price.

Cosmetics are generally price elastic. Because consumers can do without them if necessary, sales of cosmetics are likely to fall if their prices go up.

Self-Check
1. *Elasticity* describes this relationship.
2. The demand is price elastic.
3. The demand is price inelastic.

Applying What You Have Learned
See Lesson Plans for Chapter 3, Section E, page T36.

Self-Check

1. What is the term that describes the relationship between a change in price and the resulting change in the number sold?
2. When a small change in price results in a relatively larger change in the number demanded, is the demand considered price elastic or price inelastic?
3. Will products that are very important to us and that have no close substitutes have demand that is price elastic or price inelastic?

Applying What You Have Learned

In the Personal Narrative that begins this section, you read about a product—corn—for which demand is price inelastic. Below you will find a list of products. Using the criteria you've learned in this section, decide for each whether the demand is likely to be price elastic or price inelastic.

a. the demand for one brand of toothpaste
b. the demand for trips to Florida in July
c. the demand for a heart disease medicine
d. student demand for tickets to a reading of early English poetry by your teacher
e. the demand for tickets to a concert put on by the most popular rock group in the country
f. the demand for water by people lost in a desert

CURRENT CONSUMER ISSUES

What Value Is There In Designer Clothing?

How much would you be willing to pay for clothes that have been designed by a famous person? Every year American consumers spend billions of dollars for designer fashions that can cost twice as much as similar (but less well-known) garments.

Consumers give different reasons why they choose to buy designer clothes. One common reason is that a famous designer would have his or her name placed only on a quality product. However, this may not be the case. Although a famous person designs these clothes, some garments may be poorly constructed or made from inferior materials.

Other consumers may pay for designer clothing because they like the way these garments look on models in advertisements. They seem to believe that they will also look like the models, or be more popular if they wear these clothes. A problem is that professional models work constantly to keep their weight and appearance at an acceptable level to get assignments. Their income depends on maintaining a professional model's appearance. They also have the advantage of make-up artists and current photographic technology.

One thing consumers can be sure of is that they will pay more for designer clothing than other garments. When famous people design clothing they receive royalties (a percent of sales) for the right to use their names. This forces the businesses to charge higher prices to pay for their higher production costs.

Is buying designer clothes a wise choice for most consumers?

Arguments in Favor of Buying Designer

1. They may have better quality than other garments.
2. They may help people appear to be more attractive.
3. They may help people to be more popular.

Arguments Against Buying Designer

1. They may not have superior quality.
2. They are not likely to make people appear more attractive or make them more popular than they already are.
3. They will cost more than other similar garments.

What Do You Think?

Think about the clothing you own. How much of it is made up of designer clothing? Do you believe the money spent to buy such garments represents a rational choice for most consumers? How do firms that offer designer fashions try to influence the determinant of demand: *tastes?* Would you choose to buy designer clothing if you could afford to?

Chapter 3 Review

What Have You Learned?

In this chapter you've learned the following important principles of economics:

- Money, goods and services, and factors of production flow through the economy. Economists use a chart called the *circular flow model* to demonstrate this flow.
- *Demand* refers to the amount of a product that is sold at a particular price. The *law of demand* states that if nothing else changes, more products will be sold at lower prices than at higher prices. This relationship can be shown on a *demand schedule* or on a graph called a *demand curve.*
- Factors called the *determinants of demand* can change demand. They include tastes, consumer income, the price of related goods, and the number of customers.
- *Supply* is the number of products a firm is willing to sell at a particular price. The number of goods and services a firm is willing to supply in capitalism depends on the price its managers believe they will be able to charge and their expectations of earning a profit.
- As a firm increases its production, it experiences *diminishing returns.* This term describes situations where the cost of production per item increases as the number of products manufactured goes up. Due to diminishing returns, after a certain level of production businesses require higher prices to produce greater quantities of a product.
- The *law of supply* states that if nothing else changes, more products will be supplied at higher prices than at lower prices. This relationship can be shown on a *supply schedule* or on a *supply curve.*
- Changes in the costs of production will change the number of items a firm is willing to supply at a particular price.
- A product's demand and supply curves intersect at a point that is called the *point of equilibrium.* This point indicates the product's market price and the quantity that will be sold. Any price above this price would result in a *surplus* that would force the price down. Any price below this price would result in a *shortage* that would force the price up.
- The sensitivity of the quantity demanded to a change in price is called *elasticity.* When a change in price causes a greater percentage change in the quantity sold, the demand is *price elastic.* If a change in price causes a smaller percentage change in the quantity sold, the demand is *price inelastic.*
- Products with price elastic demand tend to be those that are less important to the consumer and easily substituted. Items with price inelastic demand are often those that are important and difficult to replace or do without.

See Chapter 3 Review Answers, page T37.

Words and Terms

circular flow model (p. 65)
product market (p. 65)
factor market (p. 65)
demand (p. 69)
law of demand (p. 69)
demand schedule (p. 70)
demand curve (p. 70)
determinants of demand (p. 71)
substitute goods (p. 71)
complementary goods (p. 72)
supply (p. 73)
diminishing returns (p. 73)
law of supply (p. 74)
supply schedule (p. 74)
supply curve (p. 75)
point of equilibrium (p. 78)
surplus (p. 79)
shortage (p. 79)
elasticity (p. 81)
price inelastic demand (p. 81)
price elastic demand (p. 82)

Building Your Vocabulary

On a separate piece of paper, write the vocabulary word or term that best completes each of the following statements.

1. The number of products that a firm is willing to sell is also known as the number it is willing to ______.
2. ______ is when a good or service is actually sold.
3. Consumer goods and services are sold in the ______.
4. The four factors of production are sold in the ______.
5. If a change in price results in a smaller relative change in the quantity sold, the product involved probably has ______.
6. If a change in price results in a larger relative change in the quantity sold, the product involved probably has ______.
7. A table that shows the number of items that could be sold at various prices is called a ______.
8. A graph that shows the number of items a firm would be willing to sell at various prices is called a ______.
9. The fact that after a point the costs of production per item increase as the number produced grows shows ______.
10. A chart that shows the flow of money, goods and services, and the four factors of production is called a ______.
11. A table that shows the number of items a firm would be willing to sell at various prices is called a ______.
12. A graph that shows the number of items that would be sold at various prices is called a ______.
13. Two goods that are used together are called ______.
14. Two goods that can be used in place of each other are ______.
15. A market price above the equilibrium price will result in a ______ of the product.
16. The principle that says people will buy more of a product at a lower price than they will at a higher price (if nothing else changes) is the ______.
17. A market price below the equilibrium price will result in a ______ of the product.
18. The relationship between a change in price and a change in the quantity sold is called ______.
19. A product's supply and demand curves will intersect at a ______.
20. Factors that can cause a demand curve to move to the left or right are called ______.
21. The principle of economics that states that at higher prices producers will be willing to offer more products for sale than at lower prices is called the ______.

Chapter 3 Review

Understanding Economics

1. Describe three different transactions that would take place in the product market.
2. Describe three different transactions that would take place in the factor market.
3. Explain why just wanting or needing a good or service is not the same as the demand for the product.
4. In each case below, identify the specific determinant of demand that is causing demand to change.
   a. The demand for snow tires in Chicago increases when a weather forecast predicts a blizzard.
   b. The demand for tea decreases when the price of coffee falls.
   c. The demand for specialty foods decreases in a recession.
   d. The demand for housing increases in the suburbs of a city that is having a crime wave.
5. Explain two reasons for the principle of diminishing returns.
6. Indicate whether supply would increase or decrease in each of the following situations.
   a. The cost of a product's basic raw material goes down.
   b. The workers who produce a product receive a 10 percent wage increase.
   c. A new machine is purchased that cuts raw material waste in half.
   d. The firm converts its electric furnace to natural gas.
7. Answer each of the following questions in relation to elasticity.
   a. If the demand for a product is price elastic, will a change in price cause a larger or smaller relative change in the number sold?
   b. Would you expect the demand for medicine to be price elastic or price inelastic? Explain.
   c. If a firm raised the price of its brand of dish soap, would you expect the relative change in the quantity sold to be greater or smaller?

Thinking Critically About Economics

1. Describe how either you or a relative of yours who has a job fits into the circular flow model. Be sure to discuss both the factor and product markets.
2. Suppose that you own a store that sells women's shoes. Describe three different things you could do to try to increase the demand for your product (hint—cutting price is not one).
3. List three items you buy that are important to you. For each, explain why your demand for the product is either price elastic or price inelastic.

Consumer Skills Projects

1. Make a poster with examples of how changes in each determinant of demand could change a consumer's decision to buy a new car.
2. Take a poll of the number of television sets students have. Suggest possible reasons why different families have made different decisions concerning the number of sets to own. What other consumer decisions do people often make when they own television sets?

Thinking Critically About Economics
(1) using models; (2) predicting consequences;
(3) comparison/contrast.

Developing Your Economic Skills

Using a Demand and Supply Graph

Skill: This lesson will show you how to use a graph of demand and supply that shows a change in market conditions from one year to the next. You will follow these steps:

1. Locate the equilibrium points for both years on the graph.
2. See how price and number of units sold changed from one year to the next.

Application: Imagine that a major American car manufacturer experienced a surplus, and took actions to correct the problem. A graph of demand and supply can be used to show what happened.

In the first year the equilibrium price for the firm's cars was $14,200, and at that price 1,120,000 cars were sold. Because of a recession in the following year, demand fell. However, the firm continued to produce at the same rate, resulting in surplus product. These events are shown on the graph.

The first year's demand has been plotted on the graph. It intersects with the firm's supply curve at the equilibrium price of $14,200 (labeled *E 1st year* on the graph). At this price, the firm sold all 1,120,000 units of its production. In the following year, a recession caused demand to shift to the left (this shift appears as movement from *D 1st year* to *D 2nd year* on the graph). The firm was not aware of this change, and its costs of production were still the same as in the first year. The firm produced another 1,120,000 units of its product and tried to sell them for the same price of $14,200.

The firm discovered it could only sell 1,040,000 units of its product at the old price. It had a surplus of 80,000 units. This surplus is labeled on the graph, and it is the difference between 1,120,000 (the quantity sold in the first year) and 1,040,000 (the quantity sold in the second year). To eliminate the surplus, the firm offered lower prices and reduced its level of production. Eventually the firm found that at an equilibrium price of $13,800 it could sell all of the 1,080,000 products it could supply.

Practice: Write a paragraph that summarizes how to use a graph of demand and supply.

Graph of Demand & Supply, 1978–1979

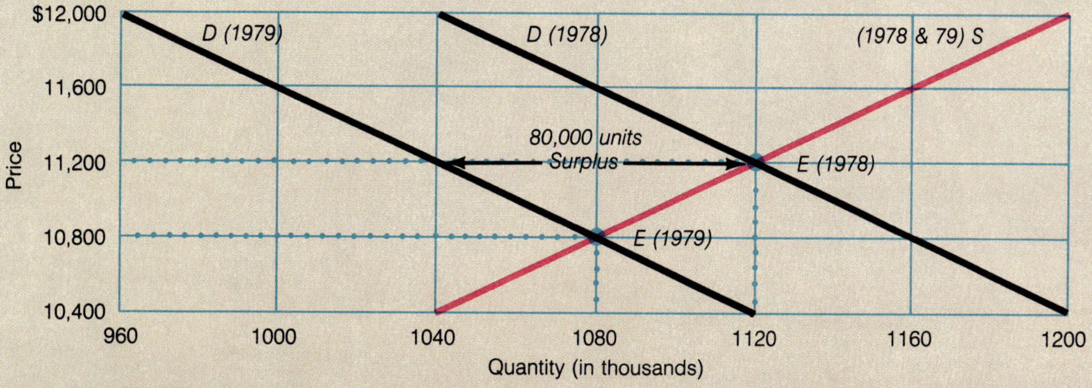

Source: *Facts on File*, 1979.

Coca-Cola
Castro
convertibles
REGAL

CHAPTER 4

The Consumer and the Economy: Getting What You Pay For

Objectives

In the sections of this chapter, you will learn:

A

how the principle of *diminishing marginal utility* causes people to buy many different products rather than only a few;

B

how *consumer sovereignty* and the "*invisible hand*" influence producers' decisions on what to make and sell;

C

the need for *consumer protection* and the trade-offs involved;

D

how businesses attempt to influence consumer demand through marketing.

You may use the *Nightly Business Report* videotape "Buying Insurance" with this chapter.

Introduction

You have been told that we have a free market economy. But is it really true? Do Americans have the power to make the decisions of *what, how,* and *for whom?*

We all know that sometimes there is a difference between what is supposed to happen and what does happen. In this chapter you will learn about economic decisions people make and about limitations on their rights to make these decisions.

In our mixed capitalistic system, the government has a responsibility to protect consumers from unfair business practices and from inferior or dangerous products. To do this, the government limits or influences the decisions consumers make.

In the United States, businesses try to influence consumer decisions. Economists may say that consumers control the economy, but businesses try to affect what their customers do. Business policies that influence both the government and people limit consumer freedom.

American consumers do have a strong voice in controlling our economic system, but they don't have total control. Both the government and businesses limit their economic freedom. In many cases this is to the consumer's advantage. In some cases it may not be. Often there is a trade-off between freedom of choice and consumer protection.

Section A How We Make Spending Decisions

This section introduces the principle of *diminishing marginal utility.*

Personal Narrative

Discuss. What items would your students save for? After they acquired the first item, would they be willing to make the same sacrifices to get a second one? How does this show diminishing marginal utility?

What Should I Do With My Pay?

Harry's whole life is his restored classic sports car. He polishes it and waxes it and cleans it and tunes its engine. About the only time he doesn't spend with his car is when he is at work or asleep.

It took Harry almost five years to save enough money to buy his car. He started when he was only 14 by delivering papers. When he reached 16 he got a job cleaning cars for a used car dealer. At 18 he started selling the used cars. Harry never earned much money, but he saved every penny he could.

Harry doesn't have much of a social life. He almost never dates because it costs too much money. Most of his clothing comes from secondhand stores. Last week he invited a girl out, but when she found that he only wanted her to help him wash his car, she went home.

Harry is 19 years old now. Last week his younger brother asked him what he does with the money he earns. Harry said, "I'm saving for another car!"

Diminishing Marginal Utility

Problem Solving. Pose the following hypothetical situation to illustrate diminishing marginal utility. Suppose the school's freezer broke, so ice cream bars were sold for 5 cents each to get rid of them before they melted. How many bars would each student buy? (They have to eat them right away.)

Most people wouldn't want to live like Harry. We all try to get the greatest possible enjoyment from our lives. This usually means that we do many different things with our time and buy many different products with our money. Harry is different from most people. He is only interested in one thing, his car.

If you really like something, why don't you spend all of your money buying just that product? Economists call the reason **diminishing marginal utility.** Diminishing marginal utility means that each additional unit of a product is less useful to you than the one that came before it.

If you had no shoes, your first pair would be worth a lot to you. The second pair you buy might also be important, but it would not be as desirable as the first. Each additional pair of shoes would have less value to you.

Harry spent all his savings to buy one thing—a classic car. Will he spend all his future savings to buy a second car, and then a third? The principle of diminishing marginal utility says no. When you already have one car (or any other product), each additional unit is less valuable than the one that came before it.

Diminishing marginal utility is why an individual's demand curve for products slopes down from the upper left-hand corner of a graph to the lower right-hand corner. Suppose the demand schedule and curve in Figure 4–1 belong to you.

Figure 4–1
Demand Schedule

Price of Shoes	Number You Would Buy
$70	1
$65	1
$60	2
$55	3
$50	4
$45	5
$40	6
$35	8

Your Demand Curve *for Pairs of Shoes*

Note. Have the students look at the graphs in Section E of Chapter 3. How quickly does the utility diminish for products with price elastic demand? For products with price-inelastic demand?

One of the best measures of a product's value is the amount people are willing to pay for it. In the demand schedule in Figure 4–1, notice that you are willing to pay $70 for the first pair of shoes. You are not willing to buy a second pair until the price falls to $60. The second pair is not worth as much to you as the first. When the price reaches $55, you are willing to buy a third pair, which is worth even less to you.

The graph of your demand curve shows the same principle. As the price goes down, you will be willing to buy more pairs of shoes. This is why the graph slopes down from left to right. The graph and demand schedule demonstrate the principle of diminishing marginal utility.

The end of World War II reduced our demand for certain types of weapons. Although the military continued to use some of these weapons, many that had been built for the war were sold for scrap. They no longer provided enough utility to justify the cost of keeping them in service.

Question. If your doctor says you need one pill to stay alive, you would pay almost anything for that pill. How much would an unnecessary second pill be worth to you? How does this show diminishing marginal utility?

Discuss. Do your students believe it would be worth paying to have a police officer on every street corner? Why or why not? What does this have to do with diminishing marginal utility?

Think back to the question, "If you really like something, why don't you spend all your money buying just that product?" The answer is that after you have a few of them, they aren't so important to you any more. You will spend your remaining money on other products that have greater value to you now.

Even Harry may get tired of classic sports cars after he has two or three. He might become interested in other products then.

Businesses and governments also are subject to diminishing marginal utility. For example, the defense budget for the United States totaled $290.2 billion in 1988. That amount was broken down into the specific types of spending listed in Table 4–1. Why does the Defense Department distribute its spending in so many different programs? If a weapon is successful, why doesn't the government buy great numbers of just that one weapon? What does this have to do with diminishing marginal utility?

Table 4–1
Defense Spending, 1988
(billions of dollars)

Purpose	Amount	Purpose	Amount
General Purpose (largely pay)	$114.9	Training, medical	$37.3
Strategic Forces	$ 19.8	Supply & Maintenance	$24.9
Research & Development	$ 28.4	Intelligence & Communication	$28.3
Guard and Reserve	$ 16.9	Air & Sealift	$ 4.4
Administration	$ 6.7	Support to other nations	$ .8

Source: *Statistical Abstract of the United States*, 1991.

Self-Check
1. The second set would be of less value.
2. After a person has a few of them, additional ones become less important.

Self-Check

1. According to the principle of diminishing marginal utility, why would customers be willing to pay more for their first television set than they would pay for a second television?
2. If you really like a product, why don't you spend all of your money buying just that product?

Applying What You Have Learned
See Lesson Plans For Chapter 4, Section A, page T40.

Applying What You Have Learned

Make a list of five different items that you actually spend money on. Rank them according to their importance to you, most important first and so on. Estimate the number of each item you buy in a year. Does the importance of the items and the number you buy match up? Why or why not? What does this tell you about diminishing marginal utility and the price you are willing to pay for a product?

Section B Consumer Sovereignty

This section introduces the ideas of *consumer sovereignty* and the *invisible hand.*

Personal Narrative

Discuss. How do students decide what clothes they should wear and where to shop? Why do stores sometimes sell at low prices clothes that were once expensive?

Baggy Pants Are Out This Year

"The trick to making money in the fashion industry is knowing what people want to buy before they do." That's a quote from one of my college instructors. Although I didn't say it first, I believe in it completely.

I graduated ten years ago with a degree in merchandising. After working in different women's clothing stores for several years, I opened "JoAnn's Cheap Boutique." I sell the latest fashions at a discount price. Most of my customers are young working women who want to look up-to-date but can't afford to spend much money. Every year I go to shows in New York to see what the expensive stores will be selling. Then I take a trip to the West Coast and buy imitations of the same styles—made in Hong Kong, Singapore, Taiwan or someplace else in East Asia. I can sell clothing for about half the name-brand price.

There are some dangers in this business. Quality can be a problem. Sometimes the garments just fall apart, but that doesn't happen very often.

A real danger is buying products that no one wants. It happens from time to time. There's just no way to avoid it. Last year I ordered a dozen cocktail dresses of blue silk with big pink polka dots. I thought they were striking. My customers didn't agree. I almost had to give them away. I sold one to someone who wanted to wear it to a costume party.

Most of the time I guess right about what will sell. I have a friend who owns a store on the other side of town. She ordered hundreds of pairs of baggy pants. I told her they would be out of style this year but she didn't believe me. I was right. Now she has to figure out some way to unload them.

This is a high-risk business, but the profits are good when you guess right.

Consumer Sovereignty

Firms that are profitable sell products people want at a price they are willing to pay. At least most of the time, customers are in control of what is made in a competitive economic system. They also have a strong impact on both quality and market price. Economists call this idea **consumer sovereignty.**

The principle of consumer sovereignty says that in a competitive economy, customers determine what is made by choosing what they will buy. To stay in business, a clothing manufacturer must make the goods people want and must sell them at competitive prices.

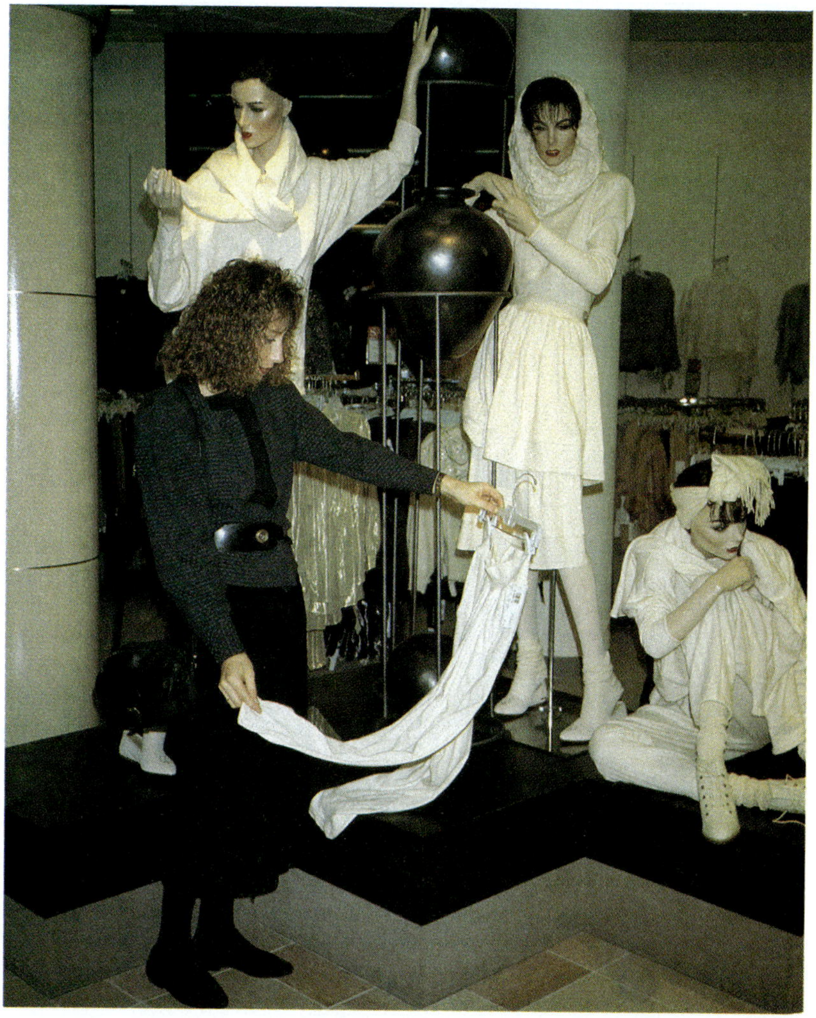

The word *sovereign* means "ruler" or "one who is in charge." Consumer sovereignty means that the consumer is in charge of the economy. Manufacturers must make what customers want to buy if they expect to remain in business.

Discuss. Why can some colleges charge high tuition and still attract qualified students? Is their product different from that of a less costly college?

However, it is not enough to produce goods and services people want. The quality of the products must also be satisfactory. Inferior quality will lead customers to return merchandise and eventually to stop patronizing a business entirely.

Businesses must charge competitive prices even if they are selling quality products people want. When "a better mouse trap" is made, the world will not beat a path to the inventor's door if the price is one hundred dollars per trap.

According to the principle of the "invisible hand," businesses in a market economy must offer products consumers want, and at the lowest possible prices. In this sense, business owners must serve the interests of society if they are to serve their own interests.

The Invisible Hand

Discuss. Students, like business owners, work to protect their own self interests. The desire for good grades can be like an invisible hand, forcing students to do their best work.

Adam Smith (see the Profile in Chapter 3) wrote about the "invisible hand" and what it had to do with competition. In a market economy, owners run businesses to make a profit. To earn profits firms must provide products people want at competitive prices. This serves the interests of society. Therefore, by attempting to serve their own self-interest (to earn a profit) business owners supply products customers want at the lowest possible prices. To Smith, the **"invisible hand"** was the self-regulating market that controlled profit, products, and prices. Consumer choices ruled the market.

In the story at the beginning of this section, JoAnn is able to make a good profit because she sells products her customers want at a price that is lower than her competition. When she makes a mistake and buys low quality garments or products that don't sell, she pays for her mistake through reduced profits. If she made too many mistakes, she would lose her business. Firms can only make a limited number of errors before they fail.

Note. The decline in U.S. steel production reflects lower U.S. demand for steel and an increase in steel imports. Steel mills, once built, are expensive whether they operate or not. Lower levels of sales reduce income more than costs.

Note. The American steel industry took steps to improve its efficiency and rebounded to be a major world competitor in the early 1990s.

Every year both large and small businesses get into financial trouble. One example involved a large steel firm. On July 17, 1986, the second largest steel producer in the United States, the LTV Corporation, filed for bankruptcy. Its last profitable year had been 1981. The firm estimated that it had lost roughly one billion dollars in the preceding two years. Its failure was the result of reduced demand and lower prices for its primary product, steel. An attempt to move into oil production in the 1970s had contributed to the firm's problems by increasing debt and reducing its cash reserves.

Table 4–2 shows that at least part of LTV's problems may have been the result of both a smaller total market and more foreign competition.

Table 4–2

U.S. Steel Production & Imports (in millions of tons)
and
Imports as a Percentage of U.S. Production, 1979–1985

Year	U.S. Production	Imports	Imports as a Percentage of Total U.S. Production
1979	136.3	17.5	12.8%
1980	111.8	15.5	13.9%
1981	120.8	19.9	16.5%
1982	74.6	16.7	22.4%
1983	84.6	17.1	20.2%
1984	92.5	17.2	18.6%
1985	88.3	24.3	27.5%

Source: *Statistical Abstract of the United States*, 1987, 1991.

Self-Check
1. To sell products, producers must meet consumer needs. This is consumer sovereignty.
2. The "invisible hand" means that producers will serve the interests of society when they attempt to serve their own interests.

Applying What You Have Learned
See Lesson Plans For Chapter 4, Section B, page T41.

Self-Check

1. Why do firms have to sell products customers want in order to earn a profit?
2. What is the relationship between the "invisible hand" and the intention of business owners to earn a profit?

Applying What You Have Learned

In the Personal Narrative for this section are two examples of fashion products that consumers didn't want. Explain how the principle of consumer sovereignty will affect how many pink polka dot dresses and baggy pants will be manufactured in the next year.

Section C Individual Freedom and Consumer Protection

This section introduces issues related to *consumer protection.*

Personal Narrative

My Uncle Smokes a Pack a Day

My uncle calls himself an "individualist." He can't stand having other people tell him what to do. He seems to feel that rules were made for him to break. Most of the things he gets upset about are silly and not very important. He does things like walking in the "out" door at the supermarket. Somehow it makes him feel important or independent or something. I never could understand what he thinks he's proving.

Some of the things he does are dangerous and not very smart. He refuses to wear a seat belt. It's not because he doesn't think they make driving safer, it's because the law says he is supposed to wear one. He wore them occasionally before the law was passed. Now he won't put them on "out of principle."

I think the thing that bothers him most is the Surgeon General's cancer warning on cigarette packs. He must have told me a thousand times that this rule is an "infringement on his personal freedom to choose how to lead his life." He thinks the decision to not allow tobacco advertising on TV is "unAmerican." He smokes a pack a day. I sometimes wonder if he will die in an auto accident or of cancer.

Question. Ask students why they believe people smoke and if they think health warnings have an effect on a person's decision to smoke or not smoke.

Last year my uncle bought a used car. It was a 1989 model and he thought he got a really good deal. His exact words were, "Man, did I take him for a ride!" After about a week, things started to go wrong with the car. The radio stopped working and the brakes started to pull to the left. Worst of all, the transmission began to smoke. It cost him over $1,800 to get everything fixed.

He tried to get the dealership to pay for the work, but they refused. It was something about the "as is" clause on the bill of sale. My uncle called the state Attorney General's office to complain. They said there was nothing they could do. It was a legal contract and my uncle had signed it. Although it's been over a year since this happened, I can still count on him to gripe about the "useless government" at least once a day. I guess my uncle is an "individualist" until it concerns his wallet.

Problem Solving. Assign students to find copies of legal documents and ask them to explain what they mean. Should lawyers be required to write legal documents in a manner most people can comprehend?

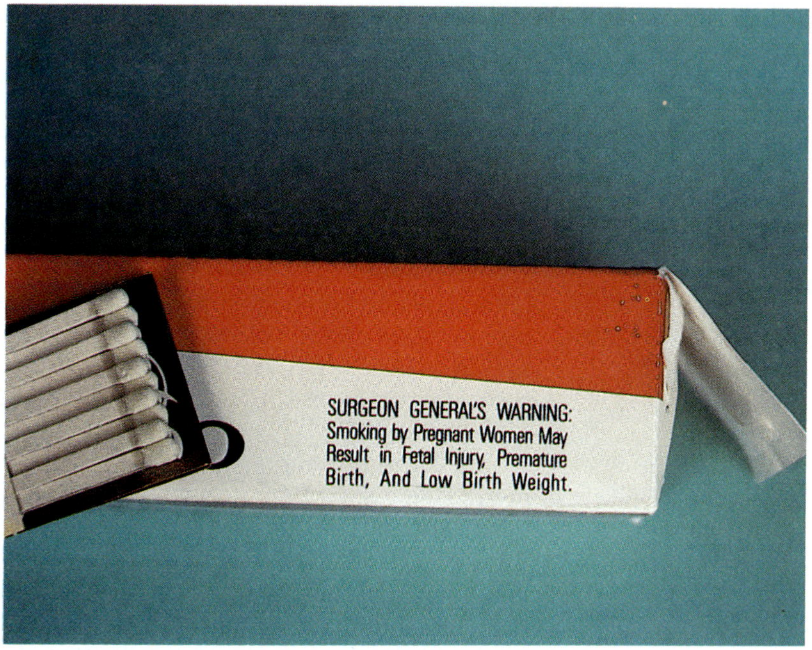

Consumer protection takes many forms. Since 1964, the U.S. government has required that cigarette manufacturers put health warnings on their products.

Why Consumer Protection?

For a competitive market economy to work efficiently, both buyers and sellers must understand the product that is being sold and the conditions under which the exchange takes place. Two hundred years ago most products were fairly easy to understand. When Joe sold Fred a wagon in 1790, they probably both knew what was being exchanged.

Discuss. How can a person who is not trained in medicine know whether he or she is receiving proper medical treatment?

Now products are much more complicated. The average consumer does not know how a TV set really works, or understand microchips, or realize the possible side-effects of various medications. Few people can read legal contracts and know exactly what they mean. If this is the case, does the government have a responsibility to protect us from unscrupulous producers and potentially harmful products? Most people would say the answer to this question is "Yes." The real problem is to decide how much protection is enough.

The U.S. government has a long history of **consumer protection**. In 1964, cigarette manufacturers were forced to put a health warning on their products. The "Truth-in-Lending Act" of 1968 requires businesses to tell customers the actual interest rate they will be paying on installment purchases. The Food and Drug Administration assures extensive testing before new medications can be prescribed in this country. Automobile manufacturers have been required to meet federally mandated pollution, safety, and fuel efficiency standards.

What Are The Trade-Offs?

Consumer protection is a very complicated issue. Although consumers benefit from these rules, they also pay a cost. In meeting federal regulations, businesses are forced to spend additional money. This added cost is passed on to customers in the form of higher prices. It has been estimated that the safety and pollution control equipment on the average 1990 automobile added about $1200 to its price.

Note. Until the mid-1980s, pregnant women could take a drug named Benedectin for morning sickness. Although this drug helped many women, it was thought to increase the possibility of birth defects. The drug was *never* banned by the Food and Drug Administration, but the possibility of being sued caused its manufacturer to stop production. Now there is no medication available for women who suffer from morning sickness. The fear of litigation in this instance has reduced consumers' freedom of choice.

Government regulations may reduce competition. Government rules are often very expensive to follow. This makes it harder for new firms to get started, or for small firms to stay in business. If only large firms can afford to meet government regulations, the result could be fewer firms in each industry, resulting in less competition and higher prices.

Government regulations can slow down the acceptance of new ideas and reduce this nation's ability to compete in the world market. Extensive testing of new products not only costs money, but also takes time. People who could benefit from new medicines or products are forced to do without while they are being approved. This process can go on for years. Some other countries have few requirements. Their firms can provide new products much more quickly. This gives them an advantage in establishing control over new markets throughout the world.

Consumer protection is a trade-off. There is no one right answer to the question, "How much protection is enough protection?" There are value judgments for answers.

A case where government protection was necessary occurred in the late 1950s when thalidomide, a drug that was intended to help people sleep, was marketed. It was first used in West Germany and eventually in the United States. After several years of use, it was found to cause deformities in children whose mothers had used the drug in their first three months of pregnancy. Before the drug was recalled in 1961, it was estimated to have caused the malformation of about 8,000 children throughout the world. The drug had been approved by various government agencies in different countries. Who should be responsible for the costs of caring for the people who were harmed by thalidomide?

Problem Solving. Ask students to follow consumer protection columns printed in many newspapers. Students should report on and evaluate specific consumer issues.

Self-Check
1. Products are much more complicated today.
2. Additional money must be spent to meet regulations, and this cost is passed on to the consumers.
3. Trade-offs include reduced competition and a slower acceptance of new ideas.

Applying What You Have Learned
See Lesson Plans For Chapter 4, Section C, page T43.

Self-Check

1. Why is consumer protection more necessary today than it was two hundred years ago?
2. Why can increased consumer protection cause higher prices?
3. What is one trade-off made for greater consumer protection that *does not directly involve prices or money?*

Applying What You Have Learned

1. At the beginning of this section you read about the reaction of the narrator's uncle to the federal government's health warning on cigarette packages. What do you think of the following federal regulations? Explain why you think each is either justified or unjustified.
   a. The health warning on cigarettes
   b. The list of ingredients on breakfast cereal
   c. The pollution control equipment on cars
   d. The truth-in-lending rules for credit purchases
2. Below you will find a picture of a street in some major city. There are several different products or activities in the picture that are regulated by the government. Identify as many of them as you can, and describe why you think the regulation is or is not necessary.

How many regulated products and activities can you find in this scene?

Section D Advertising and Consumer Demand

This section will introduce issues related to *advertising*.

Personal Narrative

The Man on TV Said I Should Buy It

Sherry is home alone, watching TV. Outside, the wind screams around the house while rain beats against her window. Lightning strikes nearby, there's a crash of thunder and the lights flicker. On the screen, a form gradually appears in a brown uniform and starts to sing, "Aren't you hungry? . . ." It's just another ad. Sherry tries to ignore it. Soon they'll have the "Late Night Fright Show" back on and she can see the rest of "The Fungus That Ate Chicago."

Problem Solving. Ask students to complete a poll of the most misleading advertisements. Do your students believe the ads accomplished what they were intended to do?

Sherry thinks, "There seems to be advertising everywhere you go. Get on a bus, you see advertising. Take a ride in the country, you see advertising. Go to the movies, you see advertising. What's the point? No one pays any attention to it. Advertising is just a waste of money."

The next morning, Sherry takes the morning paper as she leaves for work. She notices that her favorite store has shoes on sale for half price and makes a mental note to stop to buy a pair on her lunch hour.

Sitting on the bus, she glances through the help-wanted section. Sherry's sick of her job but she can't afford to quit before she finds something better. There's nothing new today so she turns to the theater section. A new play has just opened. There is an ad in the newspaper, with quotations from different reviewers. She decides to get her boyfriend Ken to take her to it.

Riding along with nothing particular on her mind, Sherry passes a florist's shop that has a big sign in the window, "Don't Forget Mother's Day." She thinks, "Oh good grief! I've got to send Mom some flowers or she won't forgive me for a year."

She overhears two women talking behind her, ". . . and then I asked her how she got so thin? and she said 'Well, I saw this ad on TV for the *Stay Thin Fat Reduction Plan* and they had memberships for half price all this month, so I just went down and joined and they worked it all off me before I really knew what happened. It really was so easy. Why, I'm down to just 180 now, and I'll bet I can fit into a size 16 before long.' "

Finally Sherry reaches her desk. Her secretary knocks on the door and hands her a letter. She thanks him and opens it quickly. It's from her boss, John Fuller Grey III. He is offering her the job of assistant to the vice president of advertising if she wants it.

Increasing Demand

Discuss. In 1991 it cost $1,000,000 for a 30-second spot of advertising during the Super Bowl. Still, it was impossible to supply time to all the firms that wanted to buy it. Why would a firm want to pay almost $34,000 a second for advertising time?

The two major types of advertising are informative advertising and persuasive advertising.

Advertising is very much a part of the American economy. In 1991 over 120 billion dollars were spent nationwide on different types of advertising. That was over 2 percent of all spending in the country that year. You could also think of it as about $480 for every man, woman, and child in the United States.

Firms advertise because they want to increase the demand for their products. They hope this will increase their sales and profitability. There are essentially two types of advertising. They are:

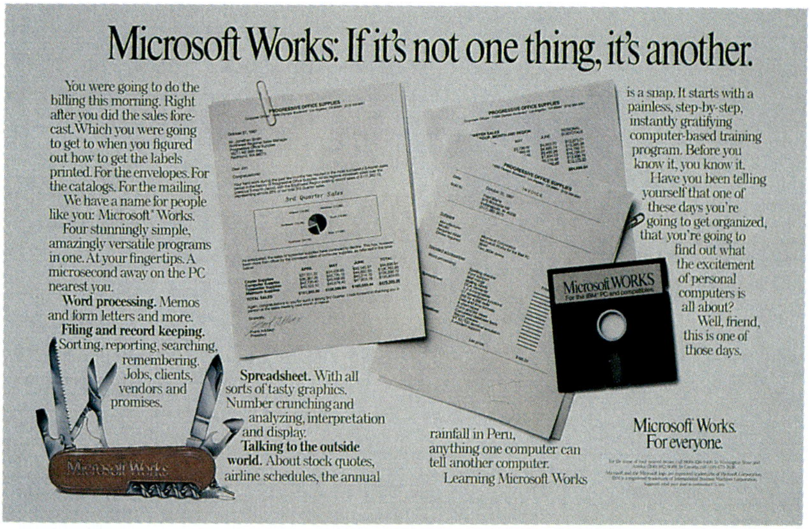

- **advertising that is intended to inform**
  Such advertising tells customers of price or quality differences. This improves their knowledge and should increase their demand for the products that have a price or quality advantage.
- **advertising that is intended to influence or persuade**
  Such advertising attempts to change the customer's tastes or preference for the product being promoted.

Clearly, advertising that is intended to inform is beneficial to the customer in particular and the economy in general. It assists consumers in getting better prices for quality products. It also helps efficient firms earn a profit.

A problem is the possibility that some advertising is either false or misleading. With this possibility in mind, the Federal Trade Commission was given the responsibility of preventing "false and deceptive advertising of goods, drugs, curative devices, and cosmetics." It is against the law to knowingly make false claims about a product.

Note. There is a theory that advertising intended to persuade can help consumers if it allows a firm to grow and become more efficient.

Another debated issue is the value of advertising that is intended to influence or persuade. For example, it has been suggested that advertising on Saturday morning cartoon shows has convinced America's children to demand breakfast cereals that have too much sugar and too little nutritive value. Some countries have made it against the law to use children in any advertising or to direct advertising to an audience made up largely of children.

Discuss. Ask students to bring "junk mail" to class. Making a bulletin board from such advertising often attracts student attention.

Self-Check

1. Why do firms advertise their products?
2. What is the difference between advertising that is intended to inform, and advertising that is intended to persuade?
3. Why do some people feel advertising that is intended to persuade can hurt consumers?

Self-Check
1. Firms advertise to increase demand for their products.
2. Informative advertising gives actual differences between products. Persuasive advertising attempts to change the customer's tastes or preferences.
3. One reason is that such advertising can convince people—especially children—to buy products that are not healthy for them.

Applying What You Have Learned

Although Sherry did not think much of advertising, she used and benefited from it in many ways. Give five specific examples of advertising from the story and identify each example as an attempt to inform or to persuade.

Applying What You Have Learned
See Lesson Plan for Chapter 4, Section D, page T44.

CURRENT CONSUMER ISSUES

How Should We Regulate Cigarette Advertising?

After the government outlawed cigarette advertising on television and radio in the 1970s, tobacco companies concentrated their advertising in the print media and on billboards. RJR Nabisco created one of the most successful advertising campaigns for Camel cigarettes in 1989 based on "Old Joe," a cartoon camel. Many people believe RJR Nabisco's ads persuaded the nation's youth to ignore health warnings and take up smoking.

In 1992 Dr. Joseph R. DiFranza stated he hoped that information he had helped gather would lead to a complete ban on cigarette advertising. Dr. DiFranza had helped carry out one of three studies completed in 1991 by the American Medical Association that found the Camel ads were very successful in reaching children. One study found that a group of six-year-olds were almost as likely to recognize "Old Joe" as they were Mickey Mouse.

The Surgeon General of the United States, Antonia Novello, called on magazines and retailers to voluntarily refuse to accept advertising or to sell products with the likeness of "Old Joe." She called such advertising "deplorable" and declared, "It's time that we invite 'Old Joe' Camel himself to take a hike."

RJR Nabisco claimed that its ads were directed to fun-loving and sophisticated adults. However, its estimated share of the under-18 market increased from less than 1 percent in 1989 to 33 percent in 1992. RJR Nabisco argued that to force it to eliminate the ads would deprive the firm of its constitutional right of free speech.

Do you think RJR Nabisco should have been forced to stop using "Old Joe" advertisements to protect young people?

Arguments in Favor of Banning the Ads

1. It could have reduced the number of young people who smoke.
2. It could have reduced the costs of medical care for people who became ill from smoking.
3. It could have caused other tobacco firms to direct less advertising to young people.

Arguments Against Banning the Ads

1. It would limit the right of RJR Nabisco to free speech and to earn a profit.
2. There is no absolute proof that "Old Joe" ads did cause more young people to smoke.
3. It would have limited the rights of consumer choice.

What Do You Think?

Consider the arguments for and against banning the "Old Joe" advertisements. Could a friendly-faced cartoon camel influence your decision to smoke or not? Do you support the original ban on television and radio advertising of tobacco products?

See Chapter 4 Review Answers, page T45.

Chapter 4 Review

What Have You Learned?

In this chapter you've learned the following important principles of economics:

- Consumers distribute their spending between many different products because of the principle of *diminishing marginal utility.* This principle tells us that as consumers buy more units of a particular product, each additional unit is less valuable to them. Therefore, consumers receive more value when they purchase many different goods and services.
- In capitalism, firms must sell products people want to buy at prices they are willing to pay. Consumers control the goods and services that are produced through what they purchase. This idea is called *consumer sovereignty.*
- In capitalism, firms are in business to make a profit. To do this they must offer products consumers want at competitive prices. By working to protect their own interests, firms serve the interests of the consumer. This idea is called the *invisible hand.*
- As the American economy has become more complex over the past two hundred years, our need for government involvement and *consumer protection* has grown. Although consumers benefit from government protection, they also pay for additional costs that result from government regulation and reduced competition.
- We can often see competition between businesses in advertising. Advertising can be divided into two general classifications. *Informative advertising* provides consumers with additional information to help them make rational choices in how they spend their money. *Persuasive advertising* attempts to convince consumers that they need a particular product.

Words and Terms

diminishing marginal utility (p. 94)
consumer sovereignty (p. 98)
invisible hand (p. 100)
consumer protection (p. 103)
informative advertising (p. 108)
persuasive advertising (p. 108)

Building Your Vocabulary

On a separate piece of paper, write the vocabulary word or term that best completes each of the following statements.

1. When a firm pays a famous person to promote its product, it is using ______.
2. When the government regulates the type and quality of products that can be advertised and sold, it is involved in ______.
3. The idea that firms must produce the products that sell is called ______.
4. When a firm prints the contents of its product on posters in large red letters, it is using ______.
5. An example of the ______ happens when a business owner's self-interest causes the firm to offer products for sale that are similar in price and quality to those of competitors.
6. I don't care about my third hamburger as much as I did my first because of ______.

Understanding Economics

1. Explain why a firm that sold wooden wagon wheels would have difficulty staying in business.
2. Joe wants to earn a profit in his tire business. There are many other tire stores in town. Explain what the "invisible hand" will force him to do.
3. Explain why most people believe the government should regulate the kind of chemicals that can be sprayed on plants that will be used for food.
4. Describe the trade-off that is made when the government tells farmers not to use a chemical that would kill insects that eat their crops.
5. Describe two different advertisements that you believe are helpful to consumers. Include an explanation of how you think they benefit the consumers.
6. Describe two different advertisements that you believe could be harmful to consumers. Include an explanation of how you think they hurt the consumers.

Thinking Critically About Economics

1. John just bought a new jacket for $60. Although he likes his new jacket, he would not be willing to pay more than $30 for a second one. Explain how this situation demonstrates diminishing marginal utility.
2. In the mid-1960s a popular style of dress was called the "sack." This garment looked very much like a potato sack. It was difficult to tell what someone who wore one looked like. Describe what you feel the result would be if a store tried to sell "sack" dresses now. Explain what this has to do with consumer sovereignty.
3. Imagine a store that tried to sell new automobile tires for five hundred dollars each. Also assume that many of these tires failed after several thousand miles of use. Clearly such a firm could not stay in business for very long. Explain what this has to do with the invisible hand.
4. If the government passed a law that required all restaurants to have the nutritive value of the food they served analyzed and printed, it might help consumers follow their diets or to eat more nourishing food. However, consumers would also pay a cost for this form of protection. Describe three specific costs that would have to be paid.
5. Write an advertisement that informs the consumer about a specific product. Write a second advertisement for the same product that is intended to persuade.

Consumer Skills Projects

1. Most states have laws that limit smoking in all public places. Take a survey of the students in your class concerning such laws. Do they feel that these laws are justified or not? Ask them to complete the same survey among their parents or other adult relatives. Do adult opinions differ from those of your fellow students? You could ask them to identify the adults interviewed as smokers or nonsmokers to see how their answers varied.
2. Choose five products that are sold in many stores in your area. Survey the price charged for the exact same products in as many stores as possible. Are the prices more or less the same? Are there any other factors that affect the quality of the product? Describe how your results relate to the idea of a competitive market.

Thinking Critically About Economics
(1) establishing priorities; (2) predicting probable consequences; (3) recognizing cause and effect; (4) predicting probable consequences; (5) recognizing propaganda.

Developing Your Economic Skills

Using Line Graphs to Compare Data

Skill: In this lesson you will learn how two different sets of data can be compared on the same line graph. To complete this lesson, you will follow these steps:

1. Study the data in the table to determine the type of information it provides.
2. Examine the line graph to see the relationship between two sets of data.
3. Consider the possible causes of the relationship between the two sets of data.

Application: Is there a direct relationship between the money automobile producers spend on advertising and the number of cars they are able to sell?

When automobile manufacturers suffer from low car sales there are a number of ways they may react. They could reduce their costs by cutting advertising budgets. This policy, however, might result in even fewer sales and greater losses. Another alternative would be to keep their advertising budgets unchanged and hope that their sales would soon pick up. The third alternative would be to increase their advertising spending to try to encourage more sales.

The data in the table below and on the following graph will show you which of these three strategies was taken by automobile manufacturers during the 1980s and the degree to which their policy succeeded. The table below shows us the advertising budget for print media (magazines and newspapers) of American automobile manufacturers from 1984 through 1989. It also indicates sales of American cars in these years. By examining the table you will see that spending for advertising grew in each year during this period of time (at an average rate of 11.2 percent per year). Car sales, however, showed little relationship to the amount of advertising spending. In some years sales fell even though advertising grew.

The data in the table has been used to create the graph that follows. Study the graph. The horizontal axis indicates the years from 1984 through 1989. Because the amount of money spent and the number of cars sold cannot both be shown on the same axis, two vertical axes are used. The left-hand axis shows spending for advertising in millions of dollars. The right-hand axis shows the number of cars sold in thousands. The two lines on the graph demonstrate that there appears to be little relationship between advertising spending and car sales. There may, however, be other factors such as broadcast advertising or foreign automaker advertising that affect car sales. What other explanations could be offered for declining sales? What other types of data could be investigated in order to provide a clearer picture of the relationship between advertising and sales?

Spending for Print Media Advertising by U.S. Automobile Producers, 1984–1989

Year	1984	1985	1986	1987	1988	1989
Advertising Spending (in $ millions, adjusted for inflation)	$473	$525	$550	$612	$694	$734
Sales of U.S.-Made Cars (in thousands)	7,621	8,002	7,516	7,085	7,105	6,807

Advertising and Sales of U.S. Cars, 1984–1989

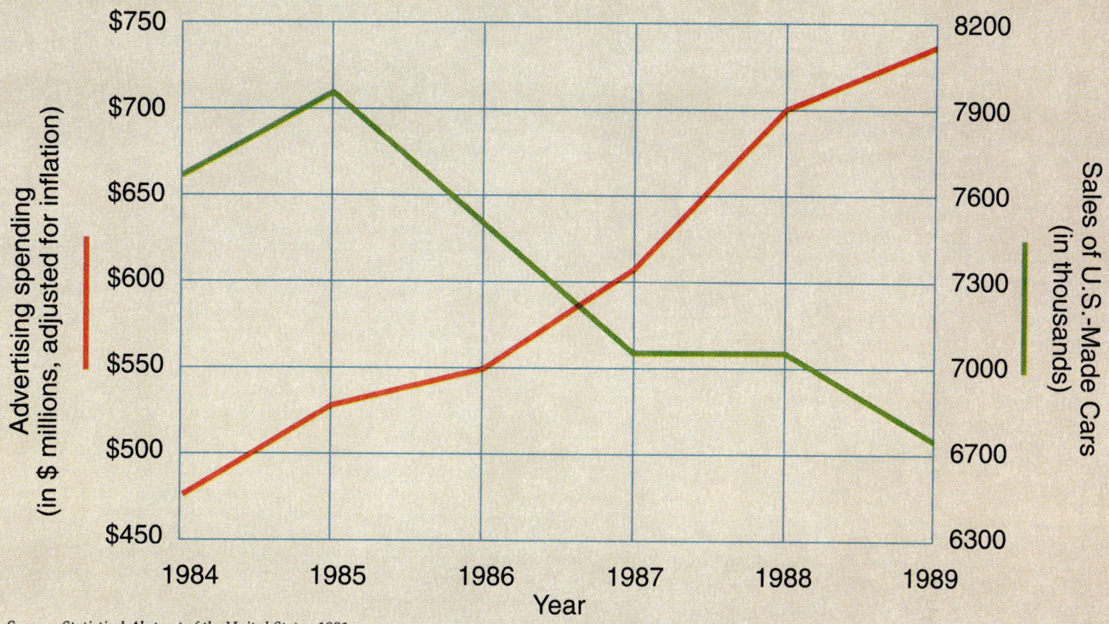

Source: *Statistical Abstract of the United States*, 1991.

Practice: Graphs can be used to show relationships between many kinds of data. Think of events and situations that may have cause/effect relationships that change over a period of time, collect the data, and build a graph similar to the graph above. Time units along the bottom of the graph may be in hours, days, months, etc. For example, is there a relationship between the number of minutes or hours you study for tests and your test scores over a period of weeks? Is there a relationship between the number of students in your economics class who bought lunch in the school cafeteria each day of the week and the number of students in the class who ate breakfast each day?

Howard's
GIFTS & YARNS
·IRISH IMPORTS
·KNITTING MACHINES
·SWEATERS
723

CHAPTER 5

Business and the Economy

Objectives

In the sections of this chapter, you will learn:

A

how businesses can be organized as *sole proprietorships*, *partnerships*, or *corporations*;

B

how *fixed* and *variable costs* are involved in the operation of a business;

C

how *average fixed costs* affect profits; and

D

how businesses obtain and pay for the resources they need.

You may use the *Nightly Business Report* videotapes "How Wall Street Works, I and II" with this chapter.

Introduction

It is one thing to dream about running your own business but it is something quite different to actually do it. Many people think of business ownership in terms of independence, freedom and profits. They tend to overlook competition, responsibility, and the possibility of failure.

In this chapter you will study the different types of business organizations that are common in the American economy. You will discover that each type of business organization has advantages and disadvantages in different situations.

In the second and third sections of the chapter you will investigate how businesses make decisions. The costs of production are particularly important to the profitability of businesses. By controlling these costs firms are able to improve their return. All business decisions are related to the costs of production.

Most businesses require an outside source of money to operate. In many cases this source may be found in the banking community. Corporations, however, are able to raise money through the sale of stocks and bonds. These and other sources of money will be presented in the last section of this chapter.

Stress. Emphasize the distinction between price and cost: price is what a customer pays, while costs are paid by the producer for the factors of production.

Section A Forms of Business Organization

This section introduces the basic forms of business organization in the United States: the *single proprietorship,* the *partnership,* and the *corporation.* It introduces the terms *limited* and *unlimited liability* and *limited life,* and explains the function of *stocks* and *corporate bonds.*

Personal Narrative

I Want to Be the Boss: How Should I Begin?

Rita and Joshua worked together at Sal's Diner for almost five years before they got married. He cooked and she waited on tables. They had talked about going on a honeymoon to Hawaii, but they used the money to open their own restaurant instead.

Discuss. Rita and Joshua gave up current consumption for the possibility of greater income in the future. How does this show opportunity cost and trade-offs?

The place wasn't much of a restaurant at the start. Actually it was an old bookstore, 15 feet wide and 40 feet deep. After they put in a small kitchen, there was room for only six tables and a few chairs at the counter. They chose the location because it was cheap and it was right in front of a bus stop. Every morning and evening hundreds of people would wait outside their door for the bus. They thought some of those people would come inside and buy food.

Rita and Joshua were both right and wrong about their location. Many people did wait for a bus in front of their business, but few came in. One day Rita talked with some of the waiting people. She asked them if they had ever thought of going in to eat. She found that many wanted to buy food but were afraid of missing their bus if they went inside.

Question. Could Rita and Joshua have reduced the risk of their business? Should they have done a market survey? What costly mistakes could they have avoided?

Rita thought she had an idea to solve the problem. She told Joshua that they needed to move the kitchen to the front of the store, put in a window, and sell hot dogs and hamburgers like a fast-food restaurant. Joshua said, "Great, so where do we get the money to do it with? Did you win the lottery or something?"

There was a real problem: Rita and Joshua didn't have any money left. Finally Rita's father, Paul, helped them out. He was retired and had saved for his old age. Rita convinced him to become a partner in the business. They gave him a one-third interest in exchange for $20,000. He didn't have to work; he just had to put in his money. Paul's lawyer drew up the necessary papers and they all signed them.

With a quick-service window in the front of the store, business grew rapidly. Soon they took out the tables and counter so they could expand their kitchen. They sold complete take-home meals.

Discuss. Ask students to name the costs and benefits they believe are associated with owning a business. Classify these costs and benefits into those that are economic and those that concern personal or social values.

They specialized in Mexican and American food. In the morning they sold coffee, rolls, and breakfasts-to-go. At the end of their second year they had paid off all of their debts and even had a few thousand dollars put away in a bank.

Question. Many people who own businesses don't consider the value of their time. If you work 80 hours a week to make $400 "profit," how much are you earning per hour for your labor? ($5)

Rita and Joshua decided it was time to expand. If they could make a good profit in front of their bus stop, why not in front of other bus stops too? Joshua found three other locations that looked promising. Rita, Joshua, and Paul estimated that they needed at least $130,000 to set up the other locations and another $20,000 for inventory. Paul's lawyer suggested they form a corporation. He said that he knew of a number of people who would want to invest in such a successful business. Rita, Joshua, and Paul received 10,000 shares valued at $10 each for their existing business. The lawyer and his friends bought 15,000 shares for $150,000 providing the money necessary for expansion.

Discuss. Many businesses are successful when they are small, but experience difficulties when they grow. What special talents are necessary to run a large business as compared to a small one?

Eventually professional managers were hired to run the other stores. The chain became very successful. Rita and Joshua work at their original store, but they also receive dividends from the income made at the other locations. They no longer control the business, but they are content to collect their share of the profit. Next year they are going to take a fifth anniversary trip to Hawaii.

Forms of Business Organization

The three basic forms of business organization in the United States are the **single proprietorship,** the **partnership,** and the **corporation.** Each form has both advantages and disadvantages.

Note. A franchise is another way to start a business, although it is not a form of business organization. When a person buys a franchise, he or she purchases the right to use an established firm's name and method of production. Franchises may be organized as proprietorships, partnerships, or corporations. The McDonald's store shown on page 46 is an example of a franchise.

Single Proprietorship

The single proprietorship is the easiest type of business to organize. This partially explains why it is the most common form of business organization. Proprietorships place full responsibility on the single owner. This gives individual owners the power to make decisions, but it also prevents them from sharing their responsibilities with others. Proprietors are personally accountable for all financial obligations of their firm. Their personal property can be taken by the courts to satisfy claims on the firm. This is called **unlimited liability.** In addition, proprietorships can have difficulty raising funds because they are limited to the financial resources of the individual owner. Finally, proprietorships have **limited life**—when the owner dies, the business must be reorganized. Completing this process can take a long time and can hurt the firm's competitive position in its market.

The single proprietorship is the most common form of business organization. A partnership—a legal joining of two or more individuals—is the least common form. Corporations are a less common form of organization than single proprietorships, but they generate by far the larger amount of receipts.

Partnership

Partnerships are a legal joining of two or more individuals in a business. This is the least common form of business organization. There are two important advantages of partnerships over proprietorships. First, partnerships can raise more money because they have the financial resources of more than one person to call on. Second, they allow individuals to share expensive capital or services necessary to particular types of business. For example, doctors often become partners so that they can share the costs of a nurse or a lab.

Individuals who join as partners must be very careful because they are financially responsible for personal as well as business debts of their partners (except for those debts specifically exempted in the contract under which their partnership was formed). Like proprietorships, partnerships have unlimited liability and limited life. If one partner leaves, other partners are required to pay his or her debts. The courts can take a partner's personal property to satisfy debts of other partners. If a partner dies the firm must be reorganized.

Corporation

Note. Although corporations have limited liability, it is common for banks and other financial institutions to require the owners of small corporations to pledge their homes or other assets as collateral for loans.

Question. What types of information should people have before they invest in the stock or bonds of a newly formed corporation? Why do such investments involve more risk than investments in established corporations?

Note. Firms can go into bankruptcy to protect their assets. In 1987, Texaco filed for bankruptcy after a court ordered the firm to pay $11 billion to the Pennzoil Corporation.

The corporation is the most difficult form of business organization to establish. However, it offers a number of important advantages over other forms of business organization. Corporations are able to raise money through the sale of either *stock* or *corporate bonds.* Corporate *stock* is a unit of ownership in the firm. It entitles the owner to share in the profits the firm makes. A *corporate bond* is a loan to the firm. Interest must be paid on the loan for some specified time, after which the loan must be repaid.

A corporation is recognized as a legal person before the law. This means that if a corporation is sued or fails, individual owners cannot lose more than they have invested in the firm. This is called **limited liability.**

Legal control of a corporation is determined through a majority of the *voted* stock. If an owner dies or fails to vote his or her stock, the firm will continue to operate. This gives the corporation the advantage of **unlimited life.**

Table 5–1 organizes the characteristics of the three forms of business in a format that will help you remember them. Table 5–2 compares the three forms in terms of how many businesses of each kind exist and the amount of receipts each kind generates. Notice that although sole proprietorships are the most numerous form of business organization, corporations generate by far the greater receipts.

Table 5–1
Characteristics of Business Organizations, Compared

	Single Proprietorship	Partnership	Corporation
Ease of organization	Easiest	Moderately difficult	Most difficult
Capital generally available for operation	Least	Intermediate	Most (best able to raise capital)
Responsibility	Centered in one person	Spread among partners	Policy set by directors; president supervises day-to-day operation
Incentive to succeed	Centered in one person	Spread among partners	Spread among many people
Flexibility	Greatest	Intermediate	Least
Ability to perform varied functions (production or purchasing, accounting, selling, etc.)	Dependent on one individual's versatility	Dependent on capabilities of two or more individuals	Best able to employ individuals with different capabilities
Possibility of conflict among those in control	None	Most prone to conflict, especially if partners have equal interest in business	Chain of command reduces internal conflict; wide ownership minimizes disagreement
Taxation	No corporate income tax	No corporate income tax	Corporate income tax
Distribution of profits or losses	All to proprietor	Distributed to partners in accordance with terms of partnership agreement	Profits retained or to stockholders as dividends; losses reduce price of stock
Liability for debts in event of failure	Unlimited	Unlimited, but spread among partners	Limited to each stockholder's investment
Length of life	Limited by one individual's life span (or until he goes out of business)	Limited (partnership is reorganized upon death or withdrawal of any partner)	Unlimited (with ownership of shares readily transferable)

Source: Adapted, with permission, from Conover, Berlye, and Gordon, *Business Dynamics* (Mission Hills: Glencoe Publishing, 1989), p. 479.

Self-Check
See Lesson Plans for Chapter 5, Section A.

Self-Check

1. What is the difference between the unlimited liability of proprietorships and partnerships, and the limited liability of corporations?
2. Why do doctors or lawyers often become partners?
3. Name at least two advantages of corporations.

Table 5–2
Forms of Business Organization by Number, Receipts, and Percentage of Total, 1960–1987
(number in thousands)
(receipts in billions of $)

	1960	1970	1980	1987
Proprietorship				
number	9,090	9,400	12,702	13,091
% of total	81%	78%	76%	71%
receipts	171	238	506	611
% of total	16%	11%	7%	6%
Partnership				
number	941	936	1,380	1,648
% of total	8%	8%	8%	9%
receipts	74	93	292	411
% of total	7%	5%	4%	4%
Corporation				
number	1,141	1,665	2,711	3,612
% of total	11%	14%	16%	20%
receipts	849	1,751	6,361	9,186
% of total	77%	84%	89%	90%

(The figures for receipts include the value of mergers and other assets that are sold from one firm to another. This explains why receipts are so large. Nevertheless, it is an indication of business activity.)

Source: *Statistical Abstract of the United States*, 1991.

Applying What You Have Learned
See Lesson Plans for Chapter 5, Section A, page T47.

Applying What You Have Learned

Rita and Joshua chose to allow their firm to become a corporation. Although they kept partial ownership, they lost control of the firm because they did not hold more than 50 percent of the stock. Write a new end to the story, starting when Joshua began to look for other locations. What might happen if other shareholders disagree with him? How might Rita and Joshua keep control of the firm themselves? Could they accomplish their expansion and keep control? What danger might there be in this course of action? Include the answers to these questions in your ending.

Section B The Costs of Production

This section will introduce the ideas of *fixed* and *variable costs.*

Personal Narrative

Stress. Emphasize the importance of forecasting costs. People who have made a few items at home often underestimate the costs of going into large-scale production. They may overlook such things as fringe benefits for employees or the need for cash to keep the business going.

How Much Does It Cost To Run a Business?

When Rita and Joshua went into business, they had no idea how much it was going to cost. They knew about the equipment and supplies they had to buy, but the costs of a license from the city to run a restaurant and many other expenses were a surprise. It seemed that there was a new surprise that cost them money every time they turned around. Their biggest unexpected cost was for an insurance policy. They paid $583 a month for liability protection. Their agent said it was because people had gone "sue crazy." The reason did not make them feel any better about spending more money.

Rita and Joshua started with $35,000. Before they opened their door they had spent almost all of it. Joshua made the following list of costs to help keep track of where the money went.

Kitchen equipment	$4,542	Furniture	$2,232
Dishes & utensils	$2,627	Wiring & plumbing	$2,769
Rent for six months	$3,920	License & fees	$ 520
Insurance, 1/2 year	$3,500	Food inventory	$3,434
Paper products	$1,356	Cash register	$ 862
Utilities	$ 792	Advertising	$ 550
		Total	$27,104

Problem Solving. Assign students to itemize the costs of supporting their family for a week. If they were forced to cut costs, where would they do it?

These were only expenses that were related to their business. There were also personal costs they had to pay. When they left Sal's Diner they lost their medical insurance, retirement plan, and paid vacation. They had to take care of their living expenses while they got the restaurant ready to go. All of these things either had to be paid for or done without. Medical insurance alone cost them $387 a month.

The day they sold their first fried egg they were down to less than $500. It is not surprising that Joshua didn't see how they could move the kitchen to the front of the store and start selling fast food. Without additional funds they couldn't afford it.

Costs

Economists have divided the costs of production into two groups, *fixed costs* and *variable costs.*

Mortgage payments on a building are an example of fixed costs. Such costs are paid regardless of how many (or how few) products are made. The raw goods delivered by the truck are variable costs. Such costs vary according to how many products the company decides to make.

Note. In the long run, there are no fixed costs for corporations. Firms can always close down to end their financial responsibilities.

Fixed Costs

Fixed costs are expenses that must be paid no matter how many products the firm manufactures. Mortgage payments and property taxes are two examples of fixed costs. Banks and the city government don't care how many products a firm makes or sells. If a firm owes them money they expect to be paid.

Variable Costs

Variable costs are expenses that change with the number of products produced. Wages and raw materials, such as eggs, are examples of variable costs. These expenses will increase as production grows.

Controlling Costs

Many people who are first starting businesses underestimate their fixed costs. This frequently causes them to charge too little for their product and to overestimate their ability to make profits. They think, "The meat in a hamburger costs twenty cents. The bun and condiments add another six cents. I can sell it for fifty cents and make almost a quarter profit." Reasoning like this ignores the cost of insurance, rent and other fixed costs. It probably costs more than fifty cents to make a hamburger.

Note. The increase in corporate debt between 1980 and 1987 exceeded the rate of inflation in those years by over 90 percent. This increase in indebtedness happened as interest rates went down. Lower interest rates probably encouraged more borrowing.

One way to reduce the importance of fixed costs is to increase the number of products you sell. For example, if your store has fixed costs of $100 and you sell 100 items, there is one dollar of fixed cost per item. However, if you can increase your sales to 1,000 items, the fixed cost per item will go down to just ten cents. The more items sold, the lower the fixed cost per item. This is one reason that high volume stores like McDonald's Restaurants can afford to have lower prices than low volume stores. You could say that Rita and Joshua's restaurant became a high volume store when they put in their quick-service window.

According to tax returns filed with the Internal Revenue Service, the debt of all corporations in the United States grew from $2,034 billion in 1980 to $4,286 billion in 1987. This was an increase of over 110 percent in seven years. During the same period of time, the interest paid by these corporations grew from $345 billion to $500 billion, for an increase of only 71 percent. The increase in interest paid was smaller because interest rates fell during these years. Consider what these lower interest rates did to the firms' cost of borrowing. Can they be sure these rates will remain low in the future?

Study Table 5–3. What happened to profit as a percentage of sales between 1979 and 1989? Why might this have happened?

Table 5–3

Sales and Profits of Manufacturing Corporations, 1979–1989

(in billions of dollars)

	1979	1981	1983	1985	1987	1989
Sales	$1,742	$2,145	$2,114	$2,331	$2,378	$2,745
Profits before taxes	$154	$159	$133	$137	$159	$182
Profits as a percentage of sales	8.8%	7.4%	6.3%	5.9%	6.9%	6.6%

Self-Check
1. Fixed costs must be paid regardless of how many products the firm manufactures. Variable costs change with the number of products made.
2. Fixed costs are most often underestimated.
3. Increasing the number of products sold is one way to reduce fixed costs.

Self-Check

1. What is the difference between fixed and variable costs?
2. Do people who are first starting businesses more frequently underestimate fixed or variable costs?
3. What is one way to reduce fixed costs per item?

Applying What You Have Learned
See Lesson Plans for Chapter 5, Section B, page T48.

Applying What You Have Learned

Joshua listed various costs that he and Rita paid in the story above. On a separate piece of paper, list the 12 expenses and identify each as a fixed or variable cost.

Section C Reducing Average Fixed Costs

This section will discuss the idea of *average fixed costs.*

Personal Narrative

I Could Earn a Bigger Profit if I Sold Popcorn Too

When Rita and Joshua first opened their restaurant, they had a very limited menu. They sold hot dogs, hamburgers, french fries, soft drinks, coffee, and very little else. Their store was so small that they couldn't sell many things. They studied the people who waited for the bus in front of their store. Most of them were lower middle income workers. Rita and Joshua sold food that they considered "safe," instead of more varied and interesting items.

Stress. People who are thinking of going into business should always sample their intended market to determine their chance for success.

After they changed to quick service and take-out food, they had space for a bigger kitchen. Rita wanted to cook Mexican food. Joshua thought they would do better by opening early to sell breakfasts and by stocking snack food. He wanted to sell popcorn. There was a park across the street where children and old men fed pigeons. He said they would buy lots of popcorn. Rita and Joshua compromised. They did both.

Actually, Paul convinced them that expanding their menu was a good idea. He pointed out that a large part of their expenses were fixed costs. They had to pay rent, insurance, license fees and heat whether the store was open one or twenty hours a day. "How much more would it cost to come in early and cook breakfasts?" he asked. "Would it be expensive to stock candy bars, ice cream and other snack food for children on their way home from school?" Paul said they should try to keep their store busy all of the time.

Explain. It is possible to stock too many products. Inventory takes money and space. A store should only stock items it can justify in terms of return on investment.

It turned out that they sold much more Mexican and snack food than anything else. Rita was a good cook. Her tortillas sold as quickly as she made them. A local newspaper did a story about their business. After that they had more customers than they could handle. It was about this time that Joshua began thinking of expansion.

Reducing Average Fixed Costs

Businesses often find that they can make a larger profit when they stay open for longer hours or sell more things. This can be the result of reducing *average fixed costs.* Fixed costs—such as rent, property tax, and fire insurance—must be paid no matter how many products are made or sold. The **average fixed cost** is the total of the fixed costs of operating the business, divided by the number of units produced or sold.

This restaurant can reduce its average fixed costs by staying open for longer hours and adding items to the menu. The fixed costs do not change, but the number of products sold should go up.

Suppose a store sells shirts for $30 each and has fixed costs of $100 a day. If it sells 10 shirts a day, it would have an average fixed cost of $10 per shirt.

$100 in fixed costs ÷ 10 shirts = $10 per shirt

A business can reduce its average fixed costs if it sells more items. When this store stocks hardware as well as groceries, the additional items do not increase the fixed costs, but they do increase the number of products the store can sell.

If the store could increase its sales to 20 shirts a day by lowering its price to $28 each, it could reduce its average fixed costs per shirt to $5.

\$100 in fixed costs ÷ 20 shirts = \$5 per shirt

The store owners would discover that by lowering their price they could both reduce their average fixed cost per item and increase their profits. Here's how it would work:

Suppose the store had a variable cost of $12 for every shirt it sold. When it sold 10 shirts, it would have made $8 profit per shirt.

price	$30
variable cost	− 12
average fixed cost	− 10
profit per item	$ 8

The store would have made a total profit of $80 a day.

shirts sold	10
times profit per shirt	× $8
total profit	$80

If the store could sell 20 shirts a day by lowering its price to $28 it would increase its profit.

price	$28
variable cost	− 12
average fixed cost	− 5
profit per item	$11

The store would make a total profit of $220 a day.

shirts sold	20
times profit per shirt	× $11
total profit	$220

The store could accomplish the same result by selling other products. If it sold ties and gloves, it could reduce the average fixed cost per item. This explains, at least in part, why stores often choose to sell many different types of merchandise.

Large businesses are often better able than smaller firms to reduce their average fixed costs through volume selling. This is one reason that large discount stores can afford to have lower prices than small neighborhood stores.

Note. These ideas are related to economies and diseconomies of scale, which are presented in Chapter 6.

It is possible for firms to become too large to operate efficiently. However, in most cases large firms are more efficient than small ones. You will learn about the advantages and disadvantages of large firms in Chapter 6.

Self-Check

Self-Check
1. Firms can make a larger profit if they reduce average fixed costs.
2. The average fixed cost would be two dollars.
3. Selling different types of merchandise is one way of reducing average fixed costs.

1. Why do firms often try to reduce their average fixed costs?
2. If a firm has an average fixed cost per item of $8 when it sells 200 items a day, what would its average fixed cost per item be if it sold 800 items a day?
3. What reason, mentioned in this section, do firms have for selling many different types of merchandise?

Applying What You Have Learned

Applying What You Have Learned
See Lesson Plans for Chapter 5, Section C, page T50.

In the story at the beginning of this section, find two things that Rita and Joshua did to reduce their average fixed costs. What effect, if any, did these actions have on the *fixed* costs? What effect did they have on the amount of products sold?

Section D Rent, Interest and How Businesses Obtain Money

This section explains how businesses obtain money to pay for the factors of production. New terms include *rent, interest, profit, prime rate, bond, stock, dividend, capital gain,* and *shareholder.*

Personal Narrative

Discuss. At highway interchanges there are often many restaurants that sell almost the same food. Why do firms locate so close to their competition? How important is location to a firm's success?

Discuss. Students are likely to fault banks for not making loans to young people. But banks have a responsibility to stockholders to protect their investments and to earn a profit. If a bank makes risky loans, is it fulfilling this responsibility?

Stress. Emphasize the importance of getting a lawyer's opinion before signing important legal papers.

Stress. Emphasize the importance of diversification in personal investment. People should not put all of their savings into one investment. If Paul put all of his savings into the business and it failed, he would have nothing to fall back on.

If I Borrow $50,000 I Can Open Up Another Store

After their first location became a success, Joshua wanted to open up new stores as rapidly as possible. He was afraid other people would imitate their idea after the newspaper article was published. Joshua found three locations that looked promising. They were all at bus stops and near office buildings. After careful study, Rita and Joshua decided that they needed at least $50,000 for each new store. The problem was where to get the money.

They had almost all of their own money tied up in the first store. Paul was unwilling to "put all his eggs in one basket" by giving them the rest of his retirement savings. Besides, it would not have been enough. They discovered that they would have to find an outside source for the needed funds.

The banks were their first stop, but they had little luck. The loan officers all said about the same thing. They were very happy that Rita and Joshua were successful, but they still didn't think they were a good risk. They had only been in business a year and a half. Restaurants are more likely to fail than most other types of business. There was little market for their used restaurant equipment. Rita and Joshua had nothing else to pledge for collateral. The most they could borrow from a bank would be about $30,000 and they would have to pay 14 percent interest. This just wasn't good enough.

When Rita and Joshua told Paul about their problem, he suggested they see his lawyer. They made an appointment and described the situation to the attorney. He was very interested and helpful. He told them about the possibility of forming a corporation. He liked their business and said he would be willing to invest $10,000 in it himself. He said he could also find other investors.

Rita asked how much of the stock Paul and they would receive. The lawyer suggested 40 percent. He agreed that 40 percent was not a controlling interest, but he pointed out the fact that their total investment so far was less than $50,000. He also reminded them that they lacked managerial training and the legal knowledge to run all four stores at once. Eventually they agreed. The lawyer drew up the necessary papers. Six months later they had four locations open.

Obtaining Resources

To run a business it is often necessary to use resources that belong to other people. Rita and Joshua didn't own any buildings. They had a lease to *rent* from someone else. One definition for **rent** is payment for the use of a resource that belongs to someone else. Rent may be paid on natural resources (such as land) or on capital (such as a building, or a truck, or money). One way of renting capital is to borrow money.

Loans

Explain. Emphasize the distinction between consumer and business loans. Businesses borrow to buy factors of production that will increase their earnings. Consumer loans trade current consumption for future consumption.

Borrowed money is really a borrowed claim on resources. Rita and Joshua wanted to borrow $150,000 to open three new stores. They would have used someone else's money to buy the resources they needed. To use someone else's money they would have had to pay *interest*. **Interest** is payment for the current use of someone else's money.

The amount of interest that must be paid depends on several factors: the risk for repayment of the loan, the demand and supply for loanable funds, the length of time for repayment, the cost of administering the loan, and the competition in the market.

Explain. There is a limit to the money banks can lend. When businesses or the government borrow more, there may be less for individual consumers to borrow.

In this presentation we will concentrate on the market—that is, the demand and supply of money. It is possible to draw a demand and supply graph for loanable funds, like the one in Figure 5–1, which shows the interest rate that banks charge to large corporations that have low risk. The price of money (interest rate) is on the vertical axis. The amount or quantity of money that is loaned out is on the horizontal axis.

Figure 5–1 *Demand and Supply for Loanable Funds*

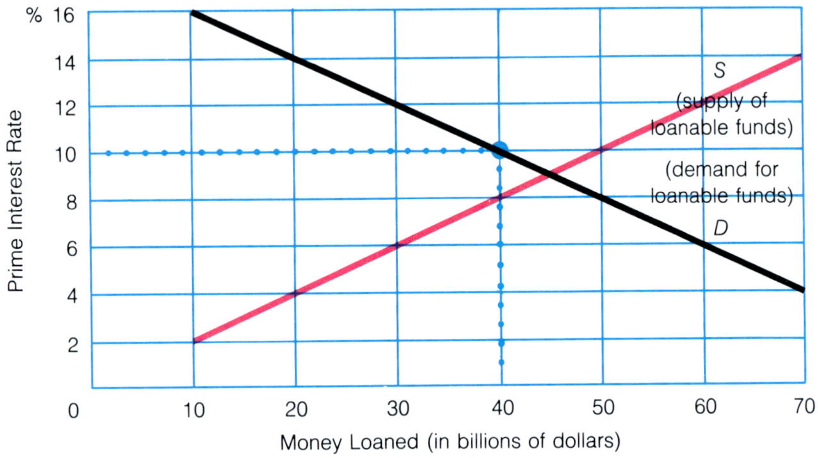

One way to obtain the use of resources is to borrow money from a bank. When you do this, you pay interest. The interest rate that banks charge their best customers is called the prime rate.

In this case the equilibrium interest rate would be 10 percent and 40 billion dollars would be loaned at that rate. But if the loans involved greater risk, the lenders would require higher interest rates, and so the equilibrium interest rate would be higher. Rita and Joshua's loan would have been a high-risk loan, which explains why the bank wanted 12 percent interest to lend them money. If a large, low-risk company such as General Electric wants to borrow money, it would pay the **prime rate.** This is the lowest rate banks charge to their best customers (the 8 percent equilibrium rate in this case). Look at Table 5–4, below, and con-

Table 5–4
Average Prime Interest Rate, 1981–1990

Year	Prime
1981	18.87%
1982	14.86%
1983	10.79%
1984	11.51%
1985	9.93%
1986	8.33%
1987	8.21%
1988	9.32%
1989	10.87%
1990	10.01%

sider what must have happened to the demand and supply of loanable money between 1981 and 1990.

Bonds

Corporations can also raise money by selling bonds. A **bond** is an I.O.U. that a firm sells. The purchaser of a bond is in effect making a loan to the corporation. A bond requires the firm to make interest payments over a specific period of time to the owner of the bond, and to repay the original amount of the loan, or principle, on a specific date in the future. Bonds usually have longer terms, which means they do not have to be repaid as quickly as loans from banks. Although the firm that issues a bond will not cash it in until the date that it is due, bonds can be sold to other people. If bonds could not be sold, few people would buy them in the first place. Few people would be willing to give up access to their money for such long periods of time.

Note. With the exception of savings bonds, government securities cannot be "cashed in" early with the Treasury. However, they can be sold to others in the secondary bond market.

Large corporations often borrow money by selling bonds. Small firms can't do this as easily because they are not as well known or widely trusted. Purchasers of the bonds could find it difficult to sell their bonds to someone else. Therefore, they would be unlikely to buy the bonds in the first place.

Stock

Rita and Joshua finally got the money they needed by forming a corporation and selling stock. A share of **stock** is a unit of ownership in the corporation. People who invest in stock give up the use of their money in exchange for a share of ownership in the firm and a portion of future earnings the corporation might make.

Any investment in a corporation involves some risk. The firm could fail, causing the stock owners to lose their investments. To take such a risk, stock owners must expect to earn more from their stock than they could from a bank, where there is little or no risk.

It is possible to earn a profit from stock in two ways—from *dividends* or from a *capital gain*. **Dividends** are a share of the corporation's profit. They must be approved by a vote of the stockholders. A **capital gain** occurs when stock can be sold for more than it originally cost to buy. The value of stock will go up if the firm does well or if investors believe that it will do well in the future. This will cause more people to want the stock and fewer people to sell it. The value of stock is determined by demand and supply. The following example shows how demand and supply affected the value of stock in Archer Communications, Inc., an electronics company.

In 1988 stock in Archer Communications, Inc., sold for 50 cents a share. By 1990, it had climbed to $20 a share. However, Archer Communications' sales were only $2 million in 1989, and the firm had lost $17.5 million since it was organized. Some may ask why anyone would pay $20 a share for a firm that was losing money. The answer is that many people thought Archer Communications was going to make large profits in the future.

Managers of Archer Communications said the firm had a new type of sound system (called Qsound) that was superior to any other method of reproducing sound. Coca-Cola and the Nintendo Company were interested in using Qsound in advertisements and video games. Recording companies announced their interest. Many people tried to buy Archer stock, but those who owned the firm's stock did not want to sell. The value of the stock rose rapidly.

Note. The value of a share of stock depends more on what owners and potential owners believe will happen in the future than on what has happened in the past. A firm that made a good profit last year could lose money next year. The expectations of future loss would discourage people from buying (reduce demand) and encourage owners to sell (increase supply). This would force the price of the stock down.

In 1990 disaster struck. The sound system was not successful when used in advertisements. Potential customers began to back out of agreements, stating that they would reconsider buying the product after its quality had been tested. By then, most of Archer's stock owners wanted to sell, but no one wanted to buy. The total value of all of the firm's stock fell to $75,000 or less than half a cent per share.

Changes in sales or profits, rumors of a possible take-over, news of a technological breakthrough, or changes in dividends, all can change the demand and supply for a firm's stock and therefore its price. Even the best market analysts have difficulty explaining changes in stock prices on all occasions.

Self-Check

1. Rent and interest are both payments for the use of resources that are owned by someone else.
2. Larger, established businesses are considered to have a lower risk than smaller, newer businesses.
3. When the price of a stock goes up, more people must want to own the stock and fewer to sell it.

Self-Check

1. What is one way in which rent and interest payments are similar to each other?
2. Why are large, established businesses often able to borrow money at lower interest rates than small, new businesses?
3. If the price of a type of stock goes up, what does this suggest about the quantity of that stock being demanded and the quantity being supplied?

Applying What You Have Learned

See Lesson Plans for Chapter 5, Section D, page T51.

Applying What You Have Learned

To expand their business, what two methods of raising money did Rita and Joshua consider? In so doing, which of the four factors of production were they attempting to obtain?

CURRENT ECONOMIC ISSUES

The Fixed Cost of Medical Equipment

During the 1980s and early 1990s the cost of medical care in the United States increased at about twice the rate of other prices. One of the biggest causes for this rapid price increase was the cost of new types of medical devices. Magnetic resonance imaging machines (MRIs), for example, were purchased by many hospitals and private clinics in the 1980s at a cost of roughly $3 million each. MRIs allow doctors to take a series of pictures of the insides of patients to see what is happening to their bodies. This procedure is particularly valuable for people who suffer from various forms of cancer or who have had strokes.

The typical fee for one series of MRI pictures is between $800 and $1,200. Some patients have had a series completed every few weeks over many months. It has been suggested that some MRI sessions have not been necessary but were completed to help pay for the cost of the MRI machines. When a hospital buys one of these machines it has a very large fixed cost it must pay. The actual cost of using the machine is about $200 for each session. The rest of the fee can be used to pay off the cost of the machine. Hospitals can pay for their machines more rapidly by serving many patients.

One possible solution to this problem would be to allow fewer hospitals to purchase expensive medical devices. Many doctors argue that their patients would either have to be moved from one hospital to another for different treatments they need, or do without them. They believe the extra quality care is worth the cost.

Would you support a plan that limits hospital spending on expensive equipment?

Arguments in Favor of the Plan

1. It would probably reduce the cost of medical care.
2. Hospitals and doctors would have less reason to prescribe unnecessary treatments.
3. Patients might have more money left over for other purposes.

Arguments Against the Plan

1. Many patients might not receive the best treatment possible.
2. Patients might have to be moved to another hospital risking their health and causing discomfort.
3. Medical devices would be even more expensive to buy if fewer of them were produced and sold.

What Do You Think?

Should the government regulate the number of expensive medical devices that could be purchased in any area of the country? What would happen to the fixed cost of buying and using these machines if such a plan was started?

Chapter 5 Review

What Have You Learned?

In this chapter you've learned the following important principles of economics:

- There are three principle forms of business organization in the United States: the *single proprietorship, partnership,* and *corporation.* Each form has advantages and disadvantages. Of the three, there are more single proprietorships in this country, but the corporation dominates production.
- All firms must consider both *fixed* and *variable* costs of production. Fixed costs remain the same regardless of the level of production, while variable costs increase with the level of production.
- Firms may try to control the effect of fixed costs by increasing their level of production. This will spread out their fixed costs among more products and reduce the *average fixed cost* per item.
- Most businesses need to use other people's capital from time to time. They may pay other people *rent* to use their buildings, machines, or money.
- Many businesses borrow money to buy the resources they need. When they do, they pay *interest* for the use of someone else's money. The amount of interest that must be paid depends on the risk associated with the loan, the length of time over which the loan must be repaid, and the demand and supply of loanable funds.
- Corporations may raise money by selling *stock.* A share of stock is a unit of ownership in a corporation. It entitles the owner to share in the corporation's earnings. Corporate profits paid to stockholders are called *dividends.* Stockholders may also benefit from a *capital gain,* which occurs when they sell their stock for more than the original purchase price.
- Corporations often raise money by selling *bonds.* A bond is a form of loan through which the firm is required to pay interest to the owner of the bond and to repay the bond on some specific future date. The owner of a corporate bond does not own part of the corporation.
- Firms that are profitable are best able to raise additional money. These firms are able to buy more resources, grow, and become more important to our economic system.

Words and Terms

single proprietorship (p. 117)
partnership (p. 117)
corporation (p. 117)
unlimited liability (p. 117)
limited life (p. 117)
limited liability (p. 119)
unlimited life (p. 119)
fixed costs (p. 123)
variable costs (p. 123)
average fixed cost (p. 125)
rent (p. 130)
interest (p. 130)
prime rate (p. 131)
bond (p. 132)
stock (p. 132)
dividend (p. 132)
capital gain (p. 132)

See Chapter 5 Review Answers, page T52.

Chapter 5 Review

Building Your Vocabulary

On a separate piece of paper, write the vocabulary word or term that best completes each of the following statements.

1. Payments for labor, natural resources, and capital are usually examples of _______ of production.
2. _______ is a unit of ownership in a corporation.
3. _______ means that when one of the owners dies, the firm must be reorganized.
4. The most common form of business organization in the United States is the _______.
5. The form of business organization that has the greatest total sales in the United States is the _______.
6. The least common form of business organization in the United States is the _______.
7. A share of the profit paid by a corporation to its shareholders is a _______.
8. People who own stock in a corporation enjoy _______ because they can't lose more than the value of their investment.
9. If the owner of stock dies, the corporation will continue to function because it has _______.
10. Property taxes, rent and insurance are examples of _______ of production.
11. Payment for the use of someone else's resources can be called _______.
12. One way to earn a profit from owning stock is to sell it for more than it cost. This is called a _______.
13. The fixed cost per unit of production is called the _______.
14. Payment for borrowed money is called _______.
15. An obligation to pay interest over a period of time and to repay a loan, sold by corporations is called a _______.
16. The interest charged to a bank's best customers is the _______.
17. _______ means that the owners are personally liable for the debts of the firm.

Understanding Economics

1. Describe three different advantages that the corporate form of business organization has over either a single proprietorship or a partnership.
2. Identify a local business. Make a list of fixed costs this business would have to pay. Make a second list of its variable costs.
3. Explain why it might be less expensive *on an average* to raise a child in a large family instead of as an *only child.*
4. If you had $2,000 and wanted to make a safe investment in a firm, explain why you might choose to buy a corporate bond instead of buying the firm's stock.
5. Suppose someone else was quite wealthy. Explain why that person might be interested in buying stock in the firm instead of a bond.
6. Explain why the most profitable firms are the ones that will also probably pay the lowest interest rates and tend to grow more than less profitable firms.

Thinking Critically About Economics

1. Three different firms are being organized. Below you will find basic informa-

Thinking Critically About Economics
(1) evaluating alternatives; (2) predicting probable consequences; (3) evaluating alternatives; (4) identifying alternatives; (5) comparison/contrast.

tion about each. Choose the form of business organization that would be best for each firm. Explain your answers.

Firm A is being formed by a group of lawyers. They need to rent a large office, buy a law library that will cost thousands of dollars, hire secretaries and assistants, and rent an expensive computer.

Firm B is being formed to manufacture home appliances. This firm will require a large factory and many expensive machines. It will be in competition with many other firms and will need to spend large amounts of money on advertising and distribution to break into its target market.

Firm C will sell snack food near a local park. The store will not be large but it will be open long hours. The person who runs the store will be responsible for both preparing the food and keeping financial records.

2. John rents a large store where he sells sporting goods. His rent is $1,000 a month. Although business has been good, John has found that he really has more space than he needs. On the other hand, he does not want to move because of his excellent location. John has considered selling camping equipment in his store too. Explain how this could help his business by *lowering average fixed costs per item sold.*
3. I sell bicycles in my store for $110 each. My fixed costs are $50 a day. It costs me $80 to buy and put together a bicycle. I sell an average of 10 bicycles a day. What is my total profit each day now? Should I lower my price to $100 if I could then sell 20 bicycles a day?
4. Sharon owns a proprietorship that makes straw hats. She employs five workers and has sales of about $180,000 a year. She recently received an order from a mail-order firm for $500,000 worth of hats. Sharon must expand her business and she will have to use someone else's money to do it. Describe three different ways she might raise the money she needs.
5. Mark bought stock in a corporation that has a history of paying large dividends. Barbara bought stock in a different firm that makes good profits but pays almost no dividends. This firm invests its profits back in its business. As a result, it has grown very rapidly. Explain how Barbara could make as much money from her stock as Mark does from his.

Consumer Skills Projects

1. Make a chart that includes possible advantages and disadvantages for consumers who seek medical services from a doctor who is: A. a single proprietor; B. a partner; C. an employee of a corporation.
2. Identify a business from which you often purchase goods or services. Make a list of steps the owners of this firm could take to reduce their costs and allow them to lower the price they charge consumers. Would all of these steps be good for consumers?
3. Identify a major corporation that produces products you often buy. Graph the value of this firm's stock over several months. Write an essay that describes how changes in the value of this firm's stock may have been influenced by how well it serves its customers.

Developing Your Economic Skills

Using Tables to Help Make Decisions

Skill: In this lesson you'll learn how data can be analyzed through the use of tables to help make economic decisions. To complete this lesson you'll follow these steps:

1. Study the firm's costs of production and sales as they currently exist.
2. Study the projection of the costs of production and sales as they would be after an expansion.
3. Compare the data from the two tables to determine whether the firm should expand.

Application: Based on your analysis, should your business grow?

Suppose you owned a florist shop. Your business has done well. Sales totaled $280,000 last year. You have wondered if you should open another store on the other side of town. To make your decision you need to compare your costs and earnings as they are now with what you believe they would be with a new store. The first table will help you by providing a list of your current costs. The total cost is listed at the bottom of the table along with the firm's sales. The firm's profit can be found by subtracting the cost of production from its sales.

You did not pay yourself a salary but you keep the profit.

If you open the new store, you expect that its sales would be about $252,000. You expect that 10 percent of your current customers would buy from the new store because they live closer to its location; as a result, sales at the old store would fall slightly, and would also be about $252,000.

Current Costs of Production and Sales

Rent	$ 9,600
Labor (3 workers @ $15,000 each including all fringe benefits)	$ 45,000
Utilities (electricity, heat, water)	$ 6,200
Insurance	$ 1,800
Payment on bank loan for store equipment	$ 5,300
Inventory for sale (flowers, pots, etc.)	$130,000
Advertising	$ 15,000
Delivery trucks	$ 20,000
All other costs	$ 3,100
total cost now	$236,000
total sales now	$280,000
current profit	$ 44,000

You believe most of the costs would double if you open a new store but you know that some would not. For example, advertising would cost you no more because you could advertise for both stores at the same time. The cost of inventory for each store would fall by 10 percent to $117,000. You believe that you could use the same delivery trucks for both stores, but the total cost would increase to $30,000 because of extra driving. You would require four workers at the new store because you could not work at both locations yourself. All other costs would be the same at the new store as they are at the old.

Projected Costs and Sales for Both Stores

	Old Store Before Expansion	Both Stores After Expansion: Old Store	Both Stores After Expansion: New Store
Rent	$ 9,600	$ 9,600	$ 9,600
Labor (3 + 4 workers at $15,000 each)	$ 45,000	$ 45,000	$ 60,000
Utilities (electricity, heat, water)	$ 6,200	$ 6,200	$ 6,200
Insurance	$ 1,800	$ 1,800	$ 1,800
Payment on bank loan for store equipment	$ 5,300	$ 5,300	$ 5,300
Inventory for sale (flowers, pots, etc.)	$130,000	$117,000	$117,000
Advertising	$ 15,000	$ 7,500	$ 7,500
Delivery truck	$ 20,000	$ 15,000	$ 15,000
All other costs	$ 3,100	$ 3,100	$ 3,100
cost		$210,500	$225,500
total cost	$236,000		$436,000
sales		$252,000	$252,000
total sales	$280,000		$504,000
total profit	$ 44,000		$ 68,000

How can you consider all of these ideas at once to make the right decision? One answer is to compare all these amounts on the same table.

The left column will list the same costs of production as those in the first table. The two columns to the right list the projected costs of the old and new stores. By adding the totals for the two right-hand columns together, you can find the total cost of both stores after an expansion. You have estimated that each store will have sales of $252,000 for a total sales of $504,000. The table tells you your total cost will be $436,000. Therefore, you project your profit to be $68,000 if you open the new store. $68,000 is better than $44,000 so you decide to open the new store. The tables have helped you organize data to make a decision.

Practice: Determine what effect opening a third florist store would have on profits.

CHAPTER 6

Perfect and Imperfect Competition

Objectives

In the sections of this chapter, you will learn:

A

how businesses operate in *perfect* and in *imperfect competition;*

B

how various kinds of *monopolies* can exist;

C

how *horizontal* and *vertical combinations* are formed;

D

how there are *economies* and *diseconomies of scale* in having a large business;

E

how the government tries to maintain *workable competition.*

Introduction

There is a popular belief that big businesses usually make big profits. This is often not the case. Remember that profit needs to be looked at in terms of what was done to earn it. If I invest $10,000 and earn $2,000 a year in profit, I am doing very well. The $2,000 is 20 percent of my investment. However, if I invest $100,000 and earn the same $2,000 in profit, I am only earning 2 percent on my investment. I would not be very happy. I could have done better by putting my money in a bank.

A firm's profitability often depends more on the type of market it sells in than on its size. Firms that provide products consumers want with little competition are more likely to make profits than firms in highly competitive markets.

In this chapter you will learn about the differences between firms that operate under perfect competition and those that do business in imperfect markets. The costs and benefits of each type of market to the economic system will be explained. If there were no advantages to monopolistic firms, there would be less of a problem in getting rid of them. The fact is, like so many economic problems, large firms that operate in imperfect markets have both a good side and a bad side.

Discuss. What is a reasonable return for time spent working to earn a profit? A $50 profit is a good return for one hour of work. It is not good for a week's work.

Some businesses, like these stands in a farmer's market, are engaged in near perfect competition. Other businesses, such as electric utility companies, operate in conditions of imperfect competition. Perfect and imperfect competition both have advantages and disadvantages for the economic system as a whole.

The government of the United States tries to prevent firms from getting so large and powerful that they can take advantage of the consumer. You will learn about government antitrust policy in this chapter. You will find that there is widespread disagreement over what role the government should play in maintaining competition.

Section A Perfect Competition

This section will introduce the ideas of *perfect competition, diversification,* and *the market as a regulator of the economy.*

One in a Million

My name is Ron. I run a filling station and convenience food store. My business is located on a major highway that leads into a big city. There are discount stores, fast-food restaurants, and other filling stations all around my store. Once last year I tried to count all the filling stations within a mile of my location. I stopped after I got to thirty. As you might guess, my business is very competitive.

My customers care about one thing, the price I charge. I don't service cars. I have nothing to offer but a low price. At least once a day I drive around my neighborhood to be sure that no one is charging less than I am. I want my customers to know that they will always get the lowest price from me.

In recent months my profit margin has been getting smaller. With the fall in the price of crude oil and gasoline in early 1986, competition between filling stations became fierce. It seemed that prices went down every day. My customers were thrilled, but I was not so happy.

Note. In 1991 petroleum prices fell almost 50 percent after the Persian Gulf War ended. Gas wars broke out among filling stations.

I have already tried to cut costs by installing self-service pumps. I have diversified into selling soft drinks and groceries. On a hot day I actually earn more from selling ice than from gasoline. I'm not getting rich, but I am getting by. I feel that if I can hang on, other firms will eventually go under and I will be able to charge a higher price. I have great hopes for the future.

Perfect Competition

Ron runs his business in a market that is close to **perfect competition.** In perfect competition (as in Ron's business) customers don't care very much whose product they buy. They look for the lowest price. Ron is forced to sell his product at the same or a lower price than his competition. If he tries to charge more than his competition his customers will buy from someone else. Firms in perfect competition are called "price takers" because they have no control over the price they can charge.

Note. The sales of commodities occur in markets that approximate perfect competition. A column in *The Wall Street Journal* entitled "Futures Prices" lists contract prices for products such as grain, livestock, metals, and oil.

A firm in perfect competition can increase its profit only by cutting its costs of production or by increasing its sales. That is probably why Ron installed self-service pumps. The new pumps cut his labor cost and increased the number of customers he could serve.

A firm in perfect competition will lose customers if it raises its prices above those of the competition. Therefore, firms in perfect competition can increase profits only by cutting costs of production or by increasing sales. Diversification—such as selling both gasoline and groceries—is a common way of increasing sales in competitive markets. It also reduces the average fixed cost per item sold.

Diversification

A common step taken by competitive firms is to sell additional types of products. Economists call this **diversification.** There are at least two advantages to this action. First, the additional types of products might encounter less competition, and so could earn a larger profit. Second, diversification should reduce the average fixed cost per item sold. For example, if you have to be in your store to collect money for gas, you might as well collect for dairy foods, groceries, and magazines, too. It wouldn't cost much more to stock these items and they could add to profitability. This is why many self-service gas stations are also convenience food stores.

The Market as a Regulator

Explain. Firms in competitive markets often earn different profits because they are not equally efficient.

If there are too many firms in a competitive market, profits will be low. This should cause some of the less efficient firms to close. This would reduce the supply of the product and increase its price. Ron hopes this will happen. If other filling stations close, he may be able to charge more for his product.

Explain. The number of firms in a competitive market often changes with the number of customers in that market. Between 1972 and 1988, more Americans chose to eat out, which encouraged people to open more restaurants. At the same time, sales of gasoline dropped, reducing the number of gas stations.

If there are only a few firms in a competitive market, profits are more likely to be high. This encourages additional firms to enter the market. The additional firms increase the supply of the product and reduce its price. Through demand and supply the market helps to regulate the number of firms serving the consumer.

Customers in a perfect competitive market should benefit from low prices. One possible danger is that in attempting to reduce costs competitive firms may cut services or reduce quality. Many filling stations no longer service cars. They believe that the cost of providing service is greater than the return they could earn.

Figure 6–1 shows a graph concerning some industries that are quite competitive. The graph shows the numbers of these firms that existed in 1972 and 1988. Why do you suppose some grew in number while others fell?

It has been suggested that there can be too much competition. If there are many competitive firms in an industry, it is unlikely that any will be able to make a large profit or accumulate

Figure 6–1 *Retail Stores in 1972 and 1988*

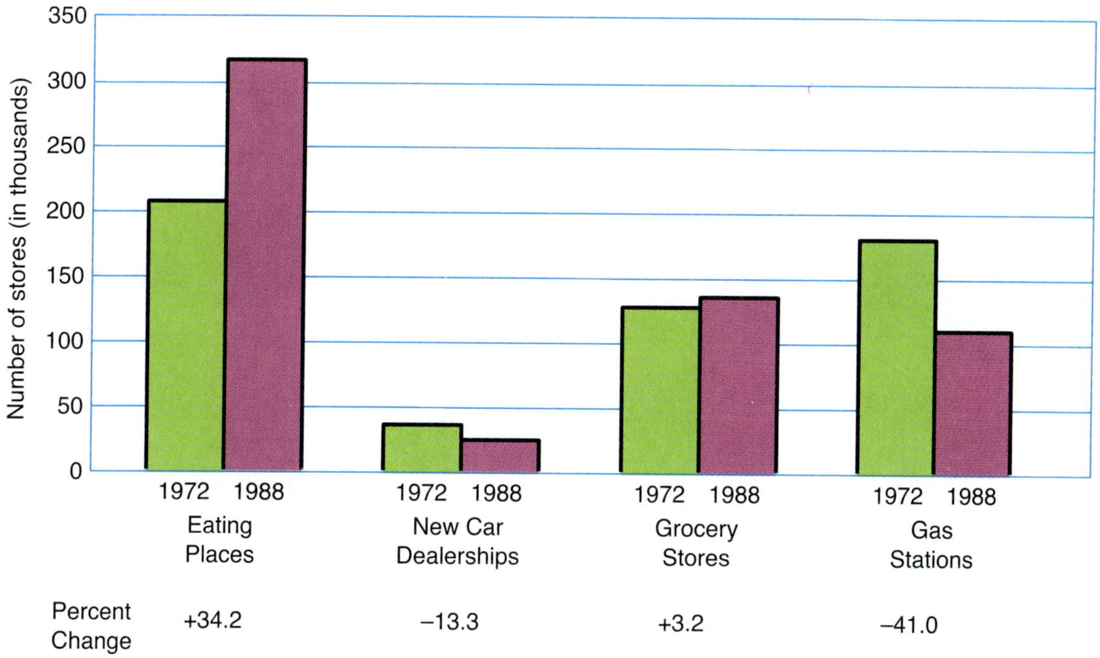

Source: *Statistical Abstract of the United States*, 1981, 1987, 1991.

When the market is competitive, customers should benefit from lower prices. But there can also be drawbacks to such competition, which could include lower quality products or services.

Discuss. Some people feel there may be too many construction firms in the United States. It is quite easy to start a construction business. When there is a recession many of these firms fail, which is not good for the owners or for the economy in general. What, if anything, should the government try to do about this?

large amounts of wealth. This could reduce their ability to invest in research and new technology that would lower production costs or improve quality. It might also reduce their ability to ride out a downturn in the economy. The problems experienced on many farms in the early 1990s are an example of this.

Self-Check

1. How do customers of competitive firms decide where to make their purchases?
2. Why have many firms in competitive markets chosen to diversify?
3. Why do some people believe that there can be too much competition?

Self-Check
1. They look for the lowest price.
2. Diversification can add products for which there is less competition, and can also reduce average fixed costs.
3. Too much competition can reduce firms' abilities to accumulate enough wealth to invest in research and new technology, and may also reduce a firm's ability to survive a downturn in the economy.

Applying What You Have Learned

The types of businesses people can start for themselves are almost always very competitive. There are many reasons for this fact. Below you will find a list of characteristics. Explain why each is common among competitive firms.

a. low initial investment
b. limited skill and training necessary
c. not many employees
d. easy to buy necessary resources

Applying What You Have Learned
See Lesson Plans for Chapter 6, Section A, page T55.

Section B Monopolies

This section will discuss aspects of *imperfect competition,* including *perfect monopoly, monopolistic competition, oligopoly,* and *natural monopoly.*

Personal Narrative

One of a Kind

My name is Gary. I own a filling station and garage in a small town in Nebraska. There isn't another filling station within 20 miles of my business. Most of my customers are local people and farmers. Now and then I get a tourist who is lost. I have no competition worth considering.

Explain. Rural businesses do have some justification for their higher prices. Their inventory turn-over is often slow, so their profit margin per item must be higher. Part of the value of their product is in its location. Gary's customers would not be happy if he closed and they had to drive 20 miles to buy gasoline.

I charge about ten cents more per gallon for gasoline than stations in the big city. My customers have no real choice. They would use more time and gas driving to another filling station than they could possibly save. Sometimes people complain, but I always point out that I wash their windows and check their oil for free.

Another difference between my business and big city filling stations is the fact that I don't have as many customers. If I am going to make as much profit, I have to make more from each one.

Actually, I am very careful to treat my regular customers well. I often go out to farms to work on tractors and farm equipment. I only charge $25 an hour for my work, although I know many big city garages charge $40 or more. If any of my repairs aren't done right, I fix them for free. I try to buy up-to-date equipment for my shop. Without a good profit, the quality of my service would be lower.

Once I got really worried. The state considered putting a major highway through this town. If that had happened, new filling stations would have been opened and I would have had competition. The highway was finally built 20 miles to the north, but I learned a lesson. I decided to do whatever I could to prevent competition. For example, I keep my prices reasonable. I am afraid high prices might encourage someone else to go into competition with me.

Imperfect Competition

Discuss. Teachers of required courses in effect have a monopoly on their product. Students cannot substitute industrial arts for economics if economics is required for graduation.

Gary's business is almost a perfect monopoly. A **perfect monopoly** is a firm that is the only supplier of a product that has no close substitutes. Consumers either have to buy the product from the monopoly or do without. Monopoly power has been called the power to set prices. Monopolists can charge high prices without worrying about the competition. This fact tends to increase the profitability of monopolistic firms.

Monopolistic competition *means that there are many firms producing products that are almost the same. Such firms rely heavily on advertising to convince customers that there is a difference and that their products are better. If successful, they are able to charge a higher price and make more profit.*

There are several factors, however, that limit how high a wise monopolist would raise his or her price. One problem is that high prices will reduce the number of people who are able to afford the product. High prices and low sales cause the fixed cost per item to be large. A monopolist might choose to have lower prices and greater volume to reduce fixed cost per item.

A second danger is that high prices will encourage competition or the substitution of other products by the consumer. For example, it has been suggested that some of the aluminum industry's problems today are the result of their high prices in the past. High aluminum prices encouraged other firms to enter the market and consumers found ways to use substitutes, such as plastic, instead.

There are very few perfect monopolies, but there are many industries that have some of the characteristics of monopolies. Businesses in these industries operate in **imperfect competition.** Imperfect competition exists when businesses are large enough to have some, but not complete, control over the prices they can charge their customers. Industries that sell in such imperfect markets can be divided into three groups—*monopolistic competition, oligopoly*, and *natural monopoly*.

Oligopoly *refers to a situation where there are only a* few *producers of products that are similar, with a high degree of interdependence between them. American automobile manufacturers have been oligopolies, but in recent years foreign competition has reduced their market power.*

Problem Solving. Firms in monopolistic competition most often use advertising that is intended to persuade rather than inform. Ask your students to find and evaluate examples of advertising by firms in monopolistic competition.

Note. Firms in oligopolistic markets often practice "price leadership." When one firm raises its price, others do the same. If they competed in price, firms would match the lowest price, reducing profits for all firms. With price leadership, firms tend to act together as if they were one monopoly.

Monopolistic competition occurs when there are many producers of products that are almost the same. Firms in such a market try to make customers believe that the similar products are actually different. Each producer uses advertising to convince the customer that his brand is superior. Firms that are successful have a monopoly on their name and reputation more than on their product. Customers are willing to pay more for the product because they associate its name with quality or value. Many beauty products, soaps, household cleaners, and over-the-counter medicines fall into this group.

Oligopoly occurs when there are a few suppliers of the same product in the market. Because there are so few, the acts of any supplier may affect prices, production, or sales in the industry as a whole. Generally oligopolists avoid price competition, focusing instead on the differences of their products and advertising brand names. If a few large firms attempt to set prices or to divide up the market among themselves, the law may impose heavy fines or even prison sentences.

Look at Table 6–1. It shows the percentage of total U.S. production supplied by the four largest firms in different industries. This value is given a special name: *The Four-Firm Concentration Ratio*. What conclusions can you draw from this information concerning which types of businesses were monopolistic?

Table 6–1

Four-Firm Concentration Ratios

Note. These concentration ratios do not include imports. If imported cars were included, the Motor Vehicle ratio would have been roughly 70 percent instead of 94 percent.

Industry	Percentage of U. S. Production Supplied by Four Largest Firms
1. Motor Vehicles	94%
2. Chewing Gum	93%
3. Window Glass	89%
4. Sewing Machines	31%
5. Household Detergent	80%
6. Tires	71%
7. Canned Beer	66%

Source: Department of Commerce, *Annual Report*.

In today's world economy, the concentration ratios above are not the threat to the consumer they used to be. For example, in 1990 imported cars accounted for over 25 percent of all auto sales in our country. Competition has helped protect the consumer.

Natural monopoly occurs when a product or service requires such large capital investments (fixed costs) that it would be inefficient to have more than one firm in the area. Utilities such as natural gas and electricity suppliers are good examples of such firms. The cost of producing and delivering electricity or natural gas is so high that it would be terribly wasteful to have more than one firm supply these products in any location. These firms have to be monopolies.

Note. When prices are regulated by government agencies, it becomes difficult to measure efficiency because there is no competition. Regulated industries have many of the same problems associated with command economies, which are discussed in Chapter 15.

The local, state, or federal government has power to grant a permit, certificate, or franchise to a public utility. Most public utilities in the United States are privately owned. Local governments do own and operate airports, transit systems, sewage disposal systems, and water systems. Public utilities are a major factor in the United States economy. Altogether as natural monopolies they rank second between financial institutions and manufacturers in total assets.

The government in each state has established **regulatory agencies** to set rates that natural monopolies can charge. These agencies are boards appointed by the executives of the states. They are responsible for protecting the public from the abuse of market power by natural monopolies.

Natural gas producers tend to be natural monopolies. The fixed costs of such firms are so great that it would be inefficient to have more than one in an area. Natural monopolies are allowed to operate only under licensing and regulation by the government.

Self-Check
1. The factors include the possibility that high prices will cause low sales and an increased fixed cost per item; high prices may also encourage competition or the substitution of other products by the consumer.
2. It exists when businesses are large enough to have some, but not complete control over the prices they can charge customers.
3. Three types of imperfect markets are monopolistic competition, oligopoly, and natural monopoly.

Applying What You Have Learned
See Lesson Plans for Chapter 6, Section B, page T57.

Self-Check

1. What are two factors mentioned in this section that limit how high monopolists will raise their prices?
2. What characteristic tells you that a market has imperfect competition?
3. What three types of imperfect markets were mentioned in this section?

Applying What You Have Learned

In the story on page 147, Gary has a number of advantages over similar firms in a city. Most of these advantages concern lower costs. Explain why Gary would have to pay less for each of the following.

a. property tax
b. insurance
c. hired help
d. cost of original building

PROFILE

Joan Robinson
(1903–1983)

Joan Robinson was one of the most important economists of the 20th century. She is best known for her work on monopolistic competition. Her work, and that of John Maynard Keynes (see Chapter 12), was influenced by Alfred Marshall at Cambridge University in England. During the forty years that she taught at Cambridge, Robinson came to different conclusions concerning competition than Marshall. She explained these ideas in her book, *The Economics of Imperfect Competition.*

Alfred Marshall had believed that the natural condition of markets was competition. He felt competition would keep prices close to business costs, and profits would be held to a reasonable level. He said firms would easily enter or leave markets as demand changed. However, Robinson asked, "Is that the way the world is? No!" It is more likely, she said, to have monopoly-like conditions. Frequently a few large firms, oligopolies, dominate the market. They usually control enough sales to be able to affect prices. This allows these firms to make large profits. With this money they can try to control larger parts of the market and have even more influence over prices.

These ideas led Robinson to the possibility of monopolistic competition. She reasoned that even in cases when many firms were selling in a market, each one would try to gain some control over price. If firms could make their product appear to be different and more desirable than that of their competition, they would be able to charge a higher price to earn a greater profit.

In later years, Robinson became a critic of capitalism and of the economics profession. She believed important problems, such as the way in which wages are set outside of the market, and the impact of world trade on competition, were being ignored. Some might call Joan Robinson the conscience of the economics profession.

Section C Combinations and Big Business

This section discusses how large businesses have developed, and introduces the ideas of *horizontal* and *vertical combinations.*

Personal Narrative

A Discount Store Opened Up In Town and I May Lose My Business

Explain. Many small hardware or grocery stores have formed groups. The Independent Grocer's Association (IGA) allows small grocers to have economies of scale.

I've run a hardware store in a small town for over 20 years. Most of my customers rely on me for minor repairs and personal service. I fix screens and broken windows. When a lock is broken, I replace it. I never charge a high price for my services. A lot of people in this area are retired and can't afford to pay too much. I have been able to make a decent profit by selling lawn mowers, tools and other items at about a 50 percent mark-up. I have found that as a result of stocking many replacement parts, the turnover of my inventory is very slow. That means I have a lot of money tied up in merchandise that takes a long time to turn into cash. I know my prices are a little higher than some of the big stores. On the other hand, I make up for higher prices with quality service.

Until recently I had no effective competition. Customers had to drive eight miles to get to another hardware store. But last year a big discount store opened up in town. They sell lawn mowers that were made in Hong Kong, for almost one hundred dollars less than my price. Their tools are less expensive than mine, but many of them are low quality. In general they don't service any of the products they sell.

Question. Ask students who hold jobs in local stores if they are able to provide quality service to their customers. What do they do if they are asked a question they are not able to answer?

Most of their employees are kids just out of school. The store pays minimum wage. This saves them money, but their clerks don't know anything about the products they sell. If a customer asks a question, no one can answer it. They won't fix screens or broken windows. When something they sold breaks, it gets sent back to the factory. The customer won't see it for weeks.

People keep bringing me things from the discount store to fix. I don't stock parts for the brands they sell. I often can't repair them at all. If I can, I have to send for parts, which takes time. I charge extra for my trouble. Some of my customers are angry with me because they think I charge too much.

My biggest problem is that people just keep buying things at the discount store. I charge $89.99 for a ceiling fan that works and which I could fix if necessary. They charge $49.99 for one that looks about the same. All the customers see is the price. They think they can save $40, so they buy the cheaper product. It often breaks after a month or two. This doesn't change the fact that my sales are down at least 40 percent from last year.

I'm afraid that I won't be able to make ends meet if things don't get better. I still have to pay the rent. If my store does close, many of my customers will lose too. Next time they need a window fixed, there won't be anyone to call.

Small Business—Big Business

When one type of business grows, there is a good chance that some other type of business will shrink or fail. Change involves a trade-off between what was and what will be. It is important to remember that a firm is not just a business. A firm is a source of income for both its owners and its employees. Businesses provide services to customers. Even when a business fails, there were probably some customers who would have wanted to continue buying that firm's products. Businesses pay taxes. When businesses in an area close, it is more difficult to provide government services there.

There are advantages and disadvantages to the economy from both small and large businesses.

Large businesses may be able to offer lower prices and a wider selection than smaller businesses. Smaller businesses, on the other hand, may be able to develop closer relationships with the consumer—and may provide better service.

The growth of big business in the United States led to either the failure or takeover of many small firms. Smaller businesses often could not match the price of larger firms with more capital. Customers often gained in terms of price, but may have lost in other important ways.

Large firms have been accused of being cold and impersonal. It is more difficult to develop a close relationship with customers when a firm has thousands of them to serve. Many people believe that small firms provide better service than large businesses.

The possibility of monopolization is also a danger. If large firms eliminate small firms, they may eventually gain monopoly power and raise prices. Monopolies probably have less reason to provide quality service than competitive firms.

The Emergence of a Monopoly

Two ways in which firms sometimes join together are *horizontal* and *vertical combinations* (Figure 6–2). The growth of Standard Oil in the late 1800s provides an example of both.

Figure 6–2 *Horizontal and Vertical Combinations*

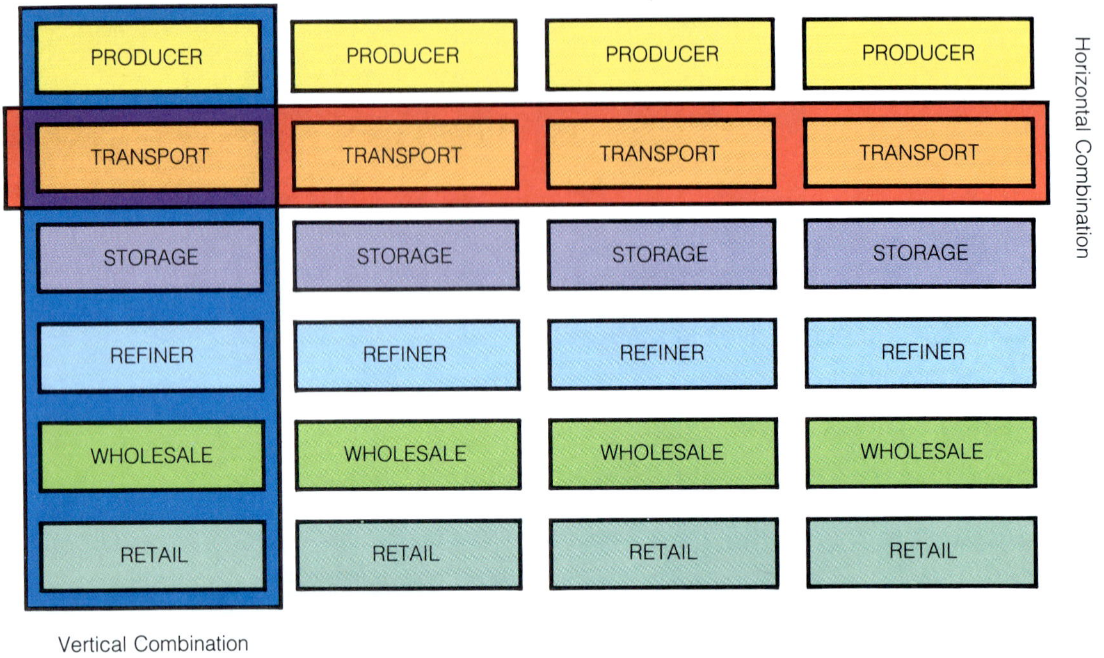

The bar that runs from left to right shows a horizontal combination—*in which firms that do the same thing (in this case transport) join together. The bar that runs up and down shows a* vertical combination—*in which firms that perform different steps in producing a product join together.*

Explain. Standard Oil formed a horizontal combination in the 1870s, and so was able to afford more efficient machines. The high cost of these machines prevented smaller refiners from buying them. Standard Oil drove smaller, less efficient firms out of business.

A Horizontal Combination

In 1865 the firm of Rockefeller and Andrews (eventually to become Standard Oil) was only one of many oil producers in this country. In the late 1860s and early 1870s, this firm bought out and merged with many other firms that took oil from the ground. In doing so, Standard Oil became a **horizontal combination.** Horizontal combinations are formed when firms that do the same thing join together. The combination's greater capital then allows it to become more efficient and sell its products for a lower price than its competition.

A Vertical Combination

In the late 1870s, Standard Oil joined with firms that performed different steps in the process of converting crude oil into finished products. Standard Oil became a **vertical combination.** A vertical combination is formed when firms that perform differ-

Standard Oil began as an oil producer, taking oil from the ground. It bought out firms that did the same thing (forming a horizontal combination), and later merged with firms that performed other steps in the process (forming a vertical combination).

Note. When steps in the process of producing a product are performed by different firms, the final price to the customer is likely to be higher than if the product was produced from beginning to end by only one firm (a vertical combination). Each of the separate firms would be intent on maximizing its profit by charging higher prices to the firm that completed the next step in the process. The result would be a final price that could be undercut by a vertical combination that supplies its own needs.

Self-Check

1. When one type of business grows, there is a good chance that some other type of business will shrink or fail.
2. A horizontal combination is a joining of firms that do the same thing.
3. Vertical combinations are often able to sell their products for less because they control most of their cost of production.

ent steps in producing a product join together. By 1880, Standard Oil was able to take oil from the ground and process it to sell to the final customer without the need of any other firm. It controlled most of its costs of production. Standard Oil was able to sell its final product for less than its competition. Soon it had little competition. By 1880 it provided over 90 percent of the oil products sold in this country.

What do you think would be the costs and benefits of such a monopolistic firm to the economy as a whole?

Self-Check

1. When one type of business grows, what is likely to happen to some other type of business?
2. How is a horizontal combination formed?
3. Why were vertical combinations often able to sell their products for less than their competition?

Applying What You Have Learned

1. Make a list of five specific problems that could develop for customers or the community if the hardware store in the story above went out of business. Identify who would pay the cost.
2. Write an advertisement that the owner of the hardware store could have printed in a local newspaper, designed to convince customers to buy at his store instead of at the discount store. Include at least four specific reasons.

Applying What You Have Learned
See Lesson Plans for Chapter 6, Section C, page T59.

Section D Advantages and Disadvantages of Big Business

This section introduces the ideas of *economies* and *diseconomies of scale*.

Personal Narrative

A Discount Store Opened Up In Town and I Can Buy For Less

I've lived in the same small town for 20 years. I used to deliver milk for a living, but I'm retired now. I live off a small pension and Social Security. I do okay, but I have to be careful how I spend my money.

For years I've had to shop at the local hardware store whenever I needed some nails or a hammer. I always felt I was paying too much, but I had no alternative. Last year a discount store opened up in town. They sell their products for at least 20 percent less than the hardware store. I think it's great!

Explain. Large discount stores are possible because of automobiles. When transportation was more difficult, people were forced to shop locally. Now they can drive many miles to shop.

The best example I can think of is my new lawn mower. I checked the price at the hardware store just to be sure. He wanted $219 for his. The discount store sold me one for just $139. So far I haven't had any trouble with it, and I've had it almost a year.

I wasn't so lucky with the ceiling fan I bought. I got a good price. It was only $49.99, but it broke after I had it for just three months. They boxed it up and sent it back to the factory. I was supposed to get it back in four weeks. That was two months ago and I still haven't seen my fan. The other problem is I had to put it up, take it down, and eventually I will have to put it up again. I don't like working on a stepladder very much, but I don't have any choice. I can't afford to have anyone else do it.

Discuss. In the 1800s, many families had live-in help. This is no longer common. What has caused this change? Is the government responsible for the change by enforcing minimum wages and requiring fringe benefits? Do we have less need for such help today?

Last week my dog Muffy tried to chase a cat by running through a screen door that was locked. He chased the cat, but the screen got a dog-size hole in it. I took it to the hardware store to get it fixed. He charged me twenty dollars. While he was taking my money he complained about how much the discount store had cut into his business. He said they only stocked commonly purchased items and did not service what they sold. He suggested that he might have to do the same to stay in business. He might be right, but I don't feel too sorry for him.

Economies and Diseconomies of Scale

As businesses grow larger they often have advantages over small businesses. Economists call things that make a large firm more efficient than a small firm **economies of scale.** Some examples of economies of scale are:

- the ability to buy resources or products in quantity at lower cost
- the ability to afford more efficient tools and have workers specialize so they can be more efficient
- the ability to distribute fixed costs among more products*
- the ability to afford more research and development

The importance of economies of scale is demonstrated by the fact that so many firms have grown larger. Firms are in business to make a profit. If they could not be more efficient and make larger profits by growing, they would stay small.

It is possible for firms to become too large. A firm that has grown too large or too quickly suffers from **diseconomies of scale.** A diseconomy of scale is anything that causes an increase in the costs of production per unit made when a firm grows. Some examples of diseconomies of scale are:

- inability to coordinate large scale production
- less personal service for the customer
- less personal commitment to the firm by employees
- greater difficulty in meeting the specialized needs of different customers

*You learned about this problem in Section C of Chapter 5.

This large automobile firm has several important advantages over smaller firms. The things that tend to make a larger firm more efficient than a smaller one are called economies of scale.

Although there are diseconomies of scale, they are often not as important as economies of scale. If this were not true, most firms would not want to grow.

Costs and Benefits from a Monopoly

In the late 1800s, Standard Oil and other monopolistic firms were accused of taking advantage of consumers to make unreasonably large profits. John D. Rockefeller denied these claims and stated that consumers had benefited from Standard Oil's market power.

Rockefeller agreed that Standard Oil was able to make significant profits. However, he suggested that these profits were the result of efficiency and not monopoly power. According to him,

It's possible for an increase in size to have disadvantages for a firm. For example, if this small, specialized automobile firm were to expand too rapidly, it might run into difficulty in coordinating large scale production. This would be a diseconomy of scale.

profits earned were largely used to invest in more efficient production, more careful control of quality, and in research and development. Rockefeller argued that as a result of Standard Oil's market power, prices were lower than before the company had come to dominate the oil industry. He believed that he was not exploiting customers but helping them.

Rockefeller's arguments were not accepted by the courts. Standard Oil was forced to break up into several smaller companies in 1914. What is clear is that because of Standard Oil's growth, many small firms were eliminated, and in the process many individuals had been hurt. Whether this was good or bad for the country as a whole was a matter of one's point of view. As usual there was a trade-off between costs and benefits.

Discuss. Does society owe anything to the owners of firms put out of business by large competitors? Can we afford to help small, comparatively inefficient firms stay in business?

Table 6–2 provides the price of oil in this country between 1870 and 1920. It also contains information about prices in general. What other information would help you decide whether or not Rockefeller's point of view was correct?

Note. The drop in the price of crude oil between 1870 and 1920 does not prove Rockefeller's point. The price might have gone down more if Standard Oil had not had monopoly power.

Table 6–2

Oil Prices, 1870-1920

Year	Price of Oil per Barrel	Percent Change From 1870	Inflation for All Products from 1870
1870	$3.86	—	—
1880	$ .94	−76%	−12%
1890	$ .77	−80%	−14%
1900	$1.19	−69%	−12%
1910	$ .61	−86%	+ 6%
1920	$3.07	−20%	+120%

Source: *Historical Abstract of the United States, 1957.*

Self-Check

1. How has the importance of economies of scale been demonstrated?
2. What reasons did John D. Rockefeller give for Standard Oil's ability to earn large profits?
3. What did the courts do to Standard Oil in 1914?

Self-Check
1. The importance of economies of scale is evidenced by so many firms growing larger.
2. Rockefeller said that Standard Oil's profits were the result of efficiency.
3. The courts divided Standard Oil into several smaller companies in 1914.

Applying What You Have Learned

Make a list of four different problems that might occur for a customer who bought from a large discount store instead of a local hardware store.

Applying What You Have Learned
See Lesson Plans for Chapter 6, Section D, page T61.

Section E The Government's Role in Competition

This section will discuss the role government plays in maintaining competition in our economic system and the ideas of *workable competition* and *antitrust policy.*

Personal Narrative

I Can't Understand My Phone Bill

Note. Telephone billing has become even more complex with the introduction of portable phones. These telephones are billed separately but are linked with other phone companies.

I got my phone bill yesterday. It was seven pages long. There was a page for the total bill, and one each for long-distance out-of-state, long-distance within-the-state, long-distance itemization, local billing, local itemization, and a final page to explain what the rest of it said. I'd need a college degree to understand it. I just pay it and don't ask questions.

A few years ago I could understand my bill. It was only two pages long. There was one page for long-distance and another for everything else. Not only was it easy to understand, it also cost much less.

Phone bills are the best example of things I don't understand, but not the only one. I work for an airline. I take luggage on and off airplanes. The airline I work for went bankrupt in 1985. They closed down for a while. Later they started flying again. I got called back to work and was happy to go, but my pay was about 20 percent less than it had been before. The courts had said the airline could cut wages while they were trying to reorganize.

I've been trying to look at this the way an economist would, and it seems to me that the distribution of certain costs and benefits in the economy has changed. People who make many long-distance calls are paying less. People who only make local calls pay more. Many airline workers have taken wage cuts, while passengers pay less to fly. Someone told me that these changes are partly the result of government attempts to maintain fair competition in these industries. I can see that trade-offs are being made. I feel bad because I believe I have paid more of the costs. Other people probably feel happy because they have received more of the benefits. I'm not really sure what's fair.

Discuss. How much market control is too much market control? For example, is it advisable to allow only two or three firms to supply the military with important weapons? What would be the cost of having more such firms?

I read a few years ago that General Electric has purchased the RCA corporation. RCA owns the NBC Television Network. The article said that General Electric is now the second biggest supplier to the military. The article said the firm was becoming a conglomerate by merging with other businesses. A conglomerate is a firm that is powerful in many different markets. The article went on to say that ownership of a television network could give General Electric power to influence public opinion on its work as a military contractor. I don't understand what it was all about, but the newspaper sure didn't think it was right.

There are so many things that go on that I don't understand. Sometimes I wonder if it makes much difference to me. Then I get my phone bill and I realize that these things do affect me whether I understand them or not.

Workable Competition and Antitrust Policy

The government of the United States has the responsibility to maintain a competitive market economy. It is impossible to have perfect competition, but we can have **workable competition.** Workable competition means that there is a reasonable balance between the benefits provided by large monopolistic firms and

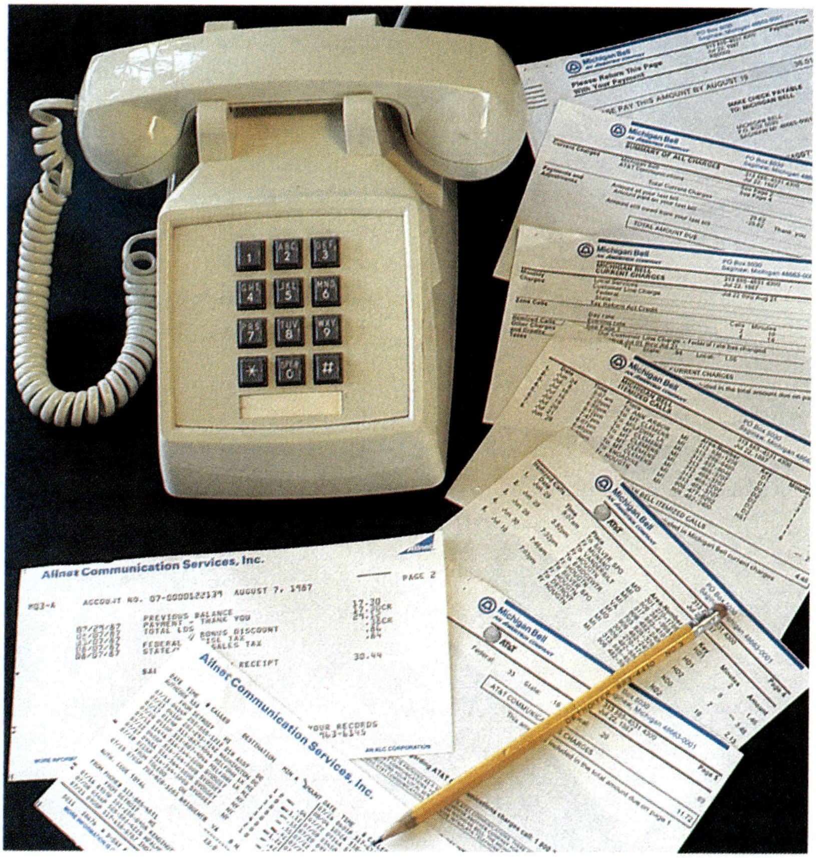

The break-up of AT&T was an example of government antitrust policy.The break-up had mixed results. What was once one phone company for the entire nation was broken into seven independent firms, each responsible for local service in its own area.

those provided by competition. The government tries to prevent firms from getting so large that they can abuse the public's interests. In cases where monopolies are necessary, the government regulates what the firms can charge.

Government efforts to maintain workable competition is called **antitrust policy.** Antitrust policy is the result of a number of laws. The most important antitrust law is the *Sherman Antitrust Act* of 1890. This law said that plans to restrain trade or attempts to monopolize production were against the law. Although this law has been amended over the years, it is still the basic rule in controlling the growth of monopolies in this country. A firm that is found guilty of violating antitrust laws can be fined or even broken up into smaller businesses.

Discuss. When monopolistic firms are broken up, their economies of scale, efficiency, and ability to compete in the world market may be harmed. If General Motors or Ford was broken into two or three firms, could they be as competitive as they are now?

In the early 1900s the government successfully took a number of large monopolistic firms, including Standard Oil, to court and forced them to be broken up into smaller businesses. The goal of this policy was to create more competition. Many economists doubt that these prosecutions accomplished very much for the average consumer.

In the past 20 years the government has often negotiated settlements with large, possibly monopolistic firms. The case of AT&T (the phone company) is a good example. In 1974 the Justice Department took AT&T to court, accusing the firm of monopolizing telephone service. The court case dragged on for years and cost billions of dollars. In August of 1981 the government asked that charges be dropped against AT&T. Federal Judge Harold H. Green refused to drop the charges and required AT&T to submit a plan for breaking up the phone system. A plan was eventually approved on August 5, 1983.

Note. In the past, AT&T had little competition in long distance service and was able to earn large profits from this business. These profits allowed the firm to charge relatively low prices for local services. When satellite communication made long distance competition possible, AT&T was no longer able to do this. Local phone companies now support their service from local revenues. This, at least in part, explains the increase in local phone rates.

This plan called for AT&T to "spin off" its local phone companies into seven new, independent firms. In exchange, AT&T (now 80 percent smaller) could move into the computer industry where it might compete with another monopoly, IBM. IBM was also being tried under antitrust laws at that time, but this case was eventually dropped by the government. AT&T also received the right to continue in long-distance communications. This agreement went into effect on January 1, 1984.

Each part of the country now has its own phone company, separate from AT&T. A survey reported that in the first two years of operation local phone companies averaged a 35 percent increase in their rates. This was at a time when inflation in general was about 4 percent a year. In these same years long-distance rates have declined. There is some question about whether or not local customers benefited from this agreement.

Government deregulation of the airlines greatly increased competition in that industry. More airlines, with more flights, entered the market place, and prices fell. There may have been trade-offs, however, in quality of service and in safety.

Another example of the effect of government regulation can be seen in the airline industry. Before 1978 the Civil Aeronautics Board regulated the number of airlines and flights that could serve any location in the United States. The Airline Deregulation Act of 1978 gradually reduced and eliminated most barriers to new airlines. Table 6–3 shows the growth in the number of U.S. airlines after deregulation.

Note. Another important consideration would be aircraft safety. Some people argue we have paid for lower air fares with people's lives.

Following deregulation, airline prices generally declined. In some cases they fell by more than 50 percent. The mid-1980s witnessed a number of airline mergers and a slight increase in prices. The market was doing its work, first correcting for regu-

Table 6–3
Number of Certified Air Route Carriers, 1975–1989
(passengers and revenues in millions)

Year	Number of Carriers	Number of Passengers	Revenues	Industry Profit or (Loss)
1975	35	205	$14,974	$ 134
1978	35	275	22,275	1,319
1980	72	297	32,947	(228)
1985	86	382	45,931	1,337
1988	66	455	63,589	3,446
1989	62	453	69,147	1,868

Source: *Statistical Abstract of the United States*, 1987, 1991.

lated prices that protected inefficient carriers. Later, it eliminated the inefficient firms and adjusted firm size to conform to economies of scale.

Where is Antitrust Policy Today?

For many years our country's antitrust policy reflected a suspicion that too much economic power can interfere with the democratic process by giving owners of large businesses political power. However, as competition from other countries has become stronger, our antitrust policy has shifted. This change has led to deregulation of some industries to allow more competition, and to ignoring size when it could result in improved efficiency. The major emphasis in antitrust policy today is to prevent price-fixing agreements.

Self-Check
1. Such a balance is called workable competition.
2. A firm that is found guilty of violating antitrust laws can be fined or broken up into smaller companies.
3. AT&T was accused of monopolizing telephone service.

Applying What You Have Learned
See Lesson Plans for Chapter 6, Section E, page T62.

Self-Check

1. What do economists call a reasonable balance between the benefits provided by large monopolistic firms and those provided by competition?
2. What can happen to a firm that is found guilty of violating antitrust laws?
3. Why was AT&T required to "spin off" its local phone companies before it could expand into the telecommunications and computer industries?

Applying What You Have Learned

In the Personal Narrative, a number of trade-offs were made. Describe three of these trade-offs. Then identify groups that benefited and those that paid a cost.

CURRENT CONSUMER ISSUES

Should Newspapers Be Allowed to Merge?

The table below demonstrates that the number of daily newspapers has been falling in recent years.

Year	1975	1980	1985	1989
Number of Daily Newspapers	1,819	1,744	1,701	1,626

You might think that the loss of 193 newspapers in 14 years is no problem. However, most of the decline happened in major cities. Most small town papers have stayed in business.

Many large cities now have only one newspaper. These newspapers have a form of monopoly-like power. They control much of the printed news and advertising consumers in their communities see. Newspapers that have no competition might choose not to cover controversial topics to avoid offending certain readers.

Some people have suggested that to guarantee consumer access to more than one paper, city newspapers should not be allowed to merge. In 1989 a court decision allowed the *Detroit Free Press* and the *Detroit News* to join their production and distribution operations. Both papers had been losing money. Both papers are now published under a degree of shared management, and they are smaller than they once were.

Although the merger probably saved several hundred jobs, some Detroit residents are upset. They believe they have less choice in what they read. The cost of newspaper advertising has increased, which may have caused businesses to increase consumer prices. Some people have suggested that Detroit's consumers have less access to advertisements that could help them make better consumer choices.

Do you believe this merger is a good idea? How would it affect you or your friends if you lived in Detroit?

Arguments in Favor of the Plan

1. It prevented the failure of a newspaper and saved jobs.
2. It allowed the owners to make a profit.
3. It assured consumers that they would have two papers.

Arguments Against the Plan

1. It created some monopoly-like power for the newspapers.
2. It resulted in higher advertising costs that may have been passed on to consumers in higher prices.
3. It reduced the advertising that Detroit's consumers see.

What Do You Think?

Consider the arguments for and against the merger. How would you protect the rights of consumers, advertisers, newspaper owners, and their employees?

Chapter 6 Review

What Have You Learned?

In this chapter you have learned the following important principles of economics.

- There are many different types of markets, ranging from *perfect competition* to *perfect monopoly*. The way in which these markets function determines their impact on the economic system.
- Firms in perfect competition have no control over market price because there are many businesses that supply the same product. Firms in perfect competition often try to improve their profitability by *diversifying* into other types of production. This may allow them to reduce their average fixed costs and enter into less competitive, and more profitable markets.
- Firms in perfect competition may earn profits that are relatively low. This may result in such firms being less able to invest in new and more efficient means of production. They may also be less able to withstand a downturn in the economy. For these reasons, some economists believe that it is possible to have too much competition.
- A firm that is a perfect monopoly is the only producer of a product that has no substitutes. Such a firm may set its prices at any level consumers are willing to pay. Perfect monopolies are likely to make a larger profit than more competitive firms.
- There are few or no perfect monopolies in the United States, but there are many firms that have some ability to set their own prices. Firms with some monopoly-like power have been classified into three groups. In *monopolistic competition* there are many producers of similar products that are differentiated through advertising. In *oligopoly* a few interdependent firms produce similar products. *Natural monopolies* are firms with such high fixed costs that it would be inefficient to have more than one in any area.
- Many large firms have been formed through combinations of smaller firms. *Horizontal combinations* are formed when firms that produce the same product join together. *Vertical combinations* are formed when firms that perform different steps in the process of producing a product join together. Many vertical combinations grew to have monopoly-like power because they were better able to control their costs of production.
- Large firms often have advantages over smaller firms in the same market. Such advantages are called *economies of scale*. In

Words and Terms

perfect competition (p. 143)
diversification (p. 144)
perfect monopoly (p. 147)
imperfect competition (p. 148)
monopolistic competition (p. 149)
oligopoly (p. 149)
natural monopoly (p. 150)
regulatory agency (p. 150)
horizontal combination (p. 156)
vertical combination (p. 156)
economies of scale (p. 159)
diseconomies of scale (p. 159)
workable competition (p. 163)
antitrust policy (p. 164)

See Chapter 6 Review Answers, page T63.

some cases small firms have advantages over larger firms in the same market. These are called *diseconomies of scale.*

- The government has taken an active role in controlling the growth of businesses with monopoly-like power. It has recognized that some large firms are necessary and tries to achieve *workable competition.* This is a trade-off between the advantages offered by competition and those offered by large size.
- The basic law used in government *antitrust policy* has been the *Sherman Antitrust Act* of 1890. Under this law, various firms have been broken up into smaller firms. The intent of this policy has been to ensure a reasonable level of competition and to prevent unnecessary monopolization of markets.
- In recent years the government's antitrust policy has allowed more U.S. firms to combine. One possible reason for this is the need for American firms to be large enough to compete successfully in international markets with large firms from other countries.

Building Your Vocabulary

On a separate piece of paper, write the vocabulary word or term that best completes each of the following statements.

1. A governmental organization that sets prices and quality standards for monopolistic firms is called a ______.
2. When firms that perform different steps in a process join together, it is called a ______.
3. Firms that have no control over the market price they can charge because many firms provide the same product are in ______.
4. An economic system that has a reasonable trade-off between the advantages of competition and large businesses is said to have ______.
5. An ______ exists where there are a few suppliers of the same kinds of products in the market, who may affect prices, production, or sales.
6. Government laws and decisions that are intended to control the power of monopolistic firms are part of ______.
7. Conditions that give a large firm an advantage over a smaller firm in the same market are called ______.
8. ______ exists when there are many firms that make similar products and that rely on advertising to attempt to convince customers that they offer a better product.
9. Many firms have tried to improve their profitability through ______ into other types of production.
10. When firms that produce the same good or service join together a ______ is formed.
11. A firm that is the only producer of a product that has no substitutes is an example of a ______.
12. Conditions that result in a large firm having a disadvantage compared to a small firm in the same market are ______.
13. A ______ exists when firms have very high fixed costs making it inefficient to have more than one in any area.
14. ______ exists when businesses are big enough to have some, but not complete, control over prices they can charge.

Understanding Economics

1. Explain why small stores that sell groceries often make very small profits. What does this have to do with their competition?
2. Many small stores that used to only sell groceries now sell hardware, sand-

Chapter 6 Review

wiches, and clothing too. Explain why they have diversified into these other markets.

3. Suppose you opened up a stationery store in your neighborhood and made very high profits. Describe what would probably happen over time that would force you to lower your prices and reduce your profitability.
4. List three different types of products that are sold in monopolistic competition. Describe how specific brands attempt to convince their customers that the products they sell are better than other similar products.
5. Most utilities are natural monopolies. Explain why it would make no sense to have more than one utility serve an area.
6. Describe the different types of firms that would have to join together to make a hamburger chain a vertical combination.
7. In 1987 the General Motors Corporation produced almost 50 percent of the cars manufactured in the United States. American Motors, going out of business, barely made .7 percent of our cars. Describe three different economies of scale that GM probably enjoyed over AMC.

Thinking Critically About Economics

1. Suppose that you own a business in a large shopping mall that sells clothing designed to be worn by young people. There are at least ten other stores in the mall that sell similar clothes. As things stand now, your store sells in an almost perfectly competitive market. Describe three different things you could do to try to improve your profits.
2. Almost all of the commercial aircraft used in the United States are manufactured by one of three firms: the Boeing Corporation, McDonnell Douglas, or the Lockheed Corporation. Explain why it is probable that this industry is an example of an oligopoly.
3. Suppose that the government decided that it would be good to have competition in the electric utility industry. With this in mind, all large electric companies would be broken up into smaller firms that often serve the same areas. Explain three different reasons why this would result in inefficient delivery of the product, electricity.
4. Many small farms have been bought out and joined into large farms in the last few years. This is an example of a horizontal combination. Describe three advantages that these larger farms could have over small farms that remain.

Thinking Critically About Economics
(1) evaluating alternatives; (2) analyzing cause and effect; (3) analyzing cause and effect; (4) predicting probable consequences.

Consumer Skills Project

1. Visit various stores that would have sold only one type of product in the past. Examples would be grocery, dry goods, sporting goods, or stationery stores. Make a list of products the stores now sell that are not related to their original market. Explain how consumers may be better served because these stores have diversified.
2. Go to a library and look up advertisements for air fares from 10 years ago. Find out what the current air fares are to the same locations. Write an essay that explains the effect these price changes may have had on consumers. What might they have to do with the deregulation of the airline industry?

Developing Your Economic Skills

Using a Table to Compare Prices

Skill: In this lesson you will use a table to compare prices charged by firms in a competitive situation with prices charged by firms in a monopoly-like situation. To complete this lesson, you'll follow these steps:

1. Determine the prices of the same products at convenience stores and at stores in a competitive environment (a shopping mall).
2. Use two columns in a table to compare prices from the two types of stores.
3. Use a third column to compute the amount of savings to be had by shopping at the more competitive stores.

Application: How much can I save if I go to the mall?

Jerry lives in a subdivision about five miles from a major shopping mall. There is one convenience store close to his home. Jerry always felt its prices were high, but he never bothered to figure out how high they were. Last week his teacher gave him an assignment to find out how much more convenience stores charge on an average than stores at the mall.

Jerry went to the nearby convenience store and found the prices of six items he buys. He then did the same for one of several department stores at a large mall. The items are listed on the left side. The next two columns are for the convenience store price and the mall price. The final column lists the differences between the two.

To find how much greater the convenience store's average price was than the mall store's average price, divide the total mall store price of $16.16 into the total savings of $3.74. The answer is .237, which is the same as 23.7 percent. On an average, the convenience store charged 23.7 percent, or almost one fourth, more than the mall store for the items Jerry buys.

Items Jerry Buys	Convenience Store Price	Mall Price	Savings
Model airplane glue	$ 1.29	$ .99	$ .30
A new baseball	$ 4.39	$ 3.69	$ .70
A box of candy	$ 5.25	$ 4.73	$ .52
A package of socks	$ 4.79	$ 3.47	$1.32
Batteries for a radio	$ 2.59	$ 1.99	$ .60
A box of hamster food	$ 1.59	$ 1.29	$ .30
Totals	$19.90	$16.16	$3.74

Why was there so much difference in prices between these stores? One possible reason the stores at the mall charge lower prices is that they are more competitive. If one mall store charged more than another, Jerry would choose to shop at the store that charged less.

Owners of convenience stores have some monopoly-like power. Their customers do not have an easy alternative to buying their products, because there are usually no other stores nearby. These stores can charge higher prices but only up to a point. If they charge too much, most people will choose to go to the mall.

Practice: Choose six items that you could buy at a nearby convenience store and in a shopping mall. Visit the stores and prepare a chart similar to the one above.

CHAPTER 7

Labor and the Economy: "I Built a Railroad, . . ."

Objectives

In the sections of this chapter, you will learn:

A

how labor fits into the *circular flow model,* how the principle of *diminishing marginal productivity* affects the demand for labor, and how the demand and supply of labor result in an *equilibrium wage rate;*

B

about the functions of *unions* in our economy and about laws intended to protect and to limit the rights of workers;

C

how the *collective bargaining* process works; and

D

why there is wide disagreement over *minimum wage laws.*

Introduction

Labor has a special place in a competitive market system. You learned in Chapter 1 that it is one of the four factors of production. However, labor has two roles in the economic system. It is part of the production process, but it is also the basic source of *demand.* Workers earn income. Income allows people to buy products. Every new job is a source of both production and demand. Lost jobs reduce production and workers' ability to consume.

Another important distinction is that labor is provided by the people that the economic system is intended to serve. Labor is not just a resource or the force that allows consumption. Serving people who provide labor is the central goal of the economy.

This chapter discusses how wages are determined. You will find that no firm willingly pays employees more than they are worth. Setting wage rates requires measurement of the value of labor. The value of labor is the price that the market sets. However, wages in the long run depend on businesses' ability to sell the products that are produced.

There is the possibility that workers could be paid less than they are worth. Many people believe that this has not only happened in the past but is also happening at the present. Labor unions were or-

Note. The line, "Once I built a railroad . . ." is from a song, *Buddy Can You Spare a Dime?*, that was popular in the Great Depression.

Like workers of today, the workers on this railroad at the turn of the century were providing labor. By doing so they earned income, which allowed them to buy goods and services.

Career. What reasons are there for working? Students may regard work only as a source of income. Discuss other things a job can provide, such as personal satisfaction or a means of self-expression.

Problem Solving. Have your students design and complete a survey of their beliefs about unions. Do the survey a second time at the end of the chapter. Discuss any changes in attitudes.

ganized in this country to protect workers and to improve their compensation. This chapter describes both union organizations and the relationship between unions and management.

The final section of the chapter deals with minimum wages. There is a difference of opinion between many economists, government officials, and labor leaders concerning the effects of minimum wages. Some people believe that these laws help the poor while others say they do more harm than good. You will study both sides of this debate.

There is a good chance that you will be personally involved with labor organizations in the future. The information in this chapter can help you understand what these organizations do and how they affect your life.

Section A How Wages Are Set

This section reviews the circular flow model as it relates to *derived demand* and supply for labor. It also presents the concepts of *diminishing returns* and the *equilibrium wage rate.*

Personal Narrative

Discuss. Many Americans believe that people who are out of work are responsible for their own problems. Help your students identify and discuss values associated with this point of view. Do they agree or disagree with it?

Sure I'd Like a Job, But How Much Will It Pay?

I'm 23 years old and I need a job. I've been out of work for almost six months. Soon my unemployment benefits will be used up. If I can't find work soon, I may have to go on welfare so my kids can eat.

I used to work at a factory that manufactures electric mixers. I didn't have a very exciting job. I put screws into a motor on an assembly line. On the other hand, it was a union job and paid well. I got over $10 an hour and had good fringe benefits. For someone with only a high school education, I thought I was doing well.

It didn't work out that way. The company's sales were down. They closed one production line and laid off everyone that had less than seven years in. I had just been hired. I was one of the first to go.

The company sent me an "informational" letter. It explained that foreign competition had forced them to lower the price of their mixers. They said the firm was in danger of going bankrupt. However, it suggested the possibility of new investments and calling back workers if the union would reopen their contract and discuss wage reductions. That was almost three months ago and nothing has happened yet.

Question. Would your students take a cut in pay to save someone else's job? To save their own jobs?

Whenever I apply for a job, they ask me what I can do. The fact is, I'm not trained to do much of anything. I can tighten screws or move boxes. I can't read a blueprint. I was never very good with numbers. I can drive a truck, but I've had a couple of accidents and speeding tickets. About the best thing I can say is that I get to work on time and I try hard. That doesn't seem to be enough to get a good job.

Discuss. Students might like a $6 an hour job when they are in high school. Would they want the same job at the same pay when they have a family to support?

I can find lousy jobs. If I was willing to take a job that paid five or six dollars an hour, I could be working now. The problem is that five or six dollars an hour is ten to twelve thousand dollars a year. There is no way I could support my family on that. If we went on welfare we could get over $8,000 a year in benefits. I wouldn't have to work or pay taxes. If I can't earn a reasonable wage, it makes more sense to me to just stay home.

The Circular Flow Revisited

Study the circular flow model in Figure 7–1. It is the same one you saw in Chapter 3, except that demand and supply curves have been added in the factor and product markets. This shows that the forces of demand and supply control prices in both of these markets.

Note. Another idea of the role of labor in the circular flow model is that if workers did not earn a wage in the factor market, they could not buy goods or services in the product market. Therefore, demand for finished products is derived from demand for labor.

Labor is sold for wages in the factor market. Money to pay these wages is earned by businesses in the product market. The amount of money that any firm can pay for resources (including labor) is determined by what it earns in the product market. The demand for any factor of production is called **derived demand.** This means that in the long run a firm will only buy (demand) a factor of production if there is demand for the firm's final product. Demand for factors of production is a derived demand because it comes from the demand for the final product.

The amount a firm is willing to pay for labor or any other factor of production depends on the price it is able to charge for its final product. In the preceding story, the electric mixer company was forced to lower the price of its product because of foreign competition. As a result, it was unwilling or unable to pay

Figure 7–1 *The Circular Flow Model with Demand and Supply Curves*

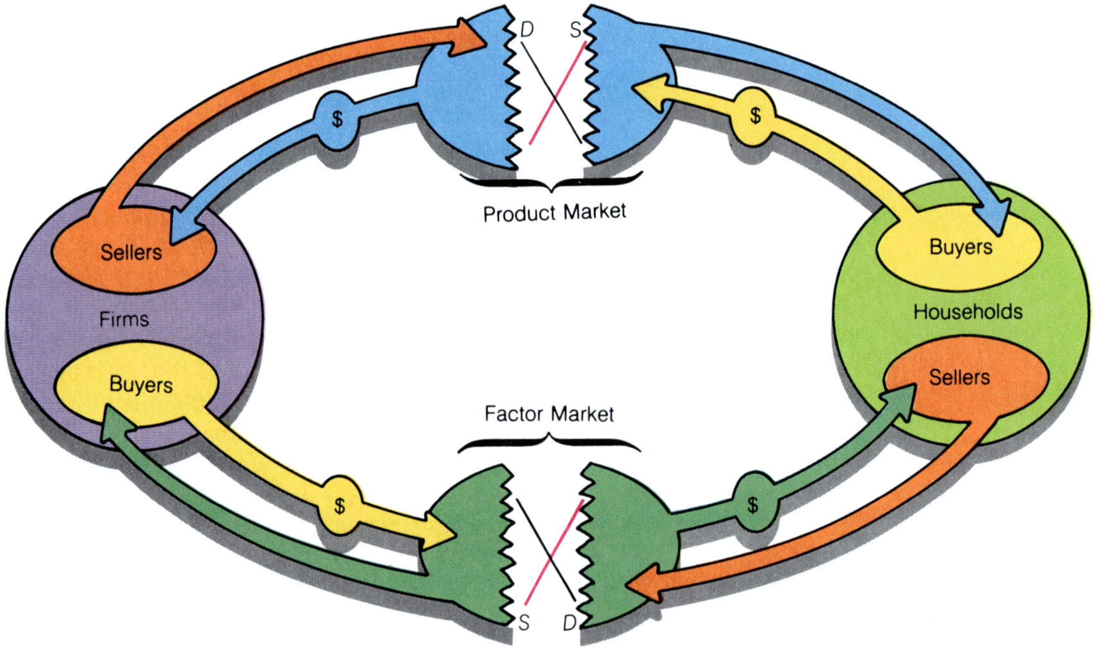

as many workers ten dollars per hour. No firm will pay a worker ten dollars an hour if the worker's labor is only worth five dollars an hour. If prices go up or down, the value of labor to the firm will also go up or down.

Diminishing Returns

Note. This example assumes a firm can produce more products by only adding more workers. This is *not* realistic, but it makes the example easier to work with.

Firms do not always have the time or ability to change their machines or the buildings in which they operate. Under these circumstances, they can only increase production by adding more workers and raw materials. When firms use this method, they find that the corresponding increase in production keeps getting smaller. The name for this is **diminishing returns.** It happens because there is a limit to how many workers can use a tool or a machine at a time. After some point, adding more workers or raw materials won't increase production because they will have no tools to use or space to work in.

Demand for Workers

As a firm hires its first workers, the amount of product they are able to produce increases, because some minimum number of workers are needed to run the firm's machinery. However, a point will be reached when each additional worker will add fewer additional products. This idea is called **diminishing marginal productivity** and it is a more specific example of diminishing returns. Studying Table 7–1 will help you understand diminishing marginal productivity.

Note. A real firm would not have this data worked out so exactly. Such tables are projections and subject to error. Still, a firm will not knowingly hire workers who cost more than they are worth.

Table 7–1

Number of Workers	Total Items Made	Additional Items Made (Marginal Physical Product)	Market Price	Value of Added Worker (Marginal Revenue Product P × MPP)
0	0	—	$50.00	—
1	5	5	$50.00	$250.00
2	11	6	$50.00	$300.00
3	16	5	$50.00	$250.00
4	20	4	$50.00	$200.00
5	23	3	$50.00	$150.00
6	25	2	$50.00	$100.00

With no workers, the firm was closed and nothing was sold. When the first worker was hired the firm was able to make five items a day. The addition of a second worker enabled the firm to use all of its machines and increased production by six items, which was more than the first worker. The number of additional units of product that are produced when another worker is hired is called the **marginal physical product,** or MPP. The MPP for the second worker was six items a day. As additional workers were hired, the MPP in column #3 on the table started to go down. This is an example of the principle of diminishing marginal productivity.

If the price of the product was $50 and labor was the only cost of production (this would be impossible, but it makes this example easier), the first worker would be worth $250 (in the table you will see that 5 items × $50 = $250). The second worker, who increased production by six items, was worth $300. The value of additional workers eventually went down because of diminishing marginal productivity.

Suppose you are worker number 6. What is your value to the business? Would the firm be willing to pay you $150? Workers will only be demanded by employers if they add more value to the firm's production than their cost. Since the value of the sixth worker shown on the table is only $100 the firm would not be willing to pay you $150.

The graph in Figure 7–2 has been drawn from Table 7–1. It shows the firm's demand curve for labor.

Figure 7–2 *Demand for Labor (value of added worker)*

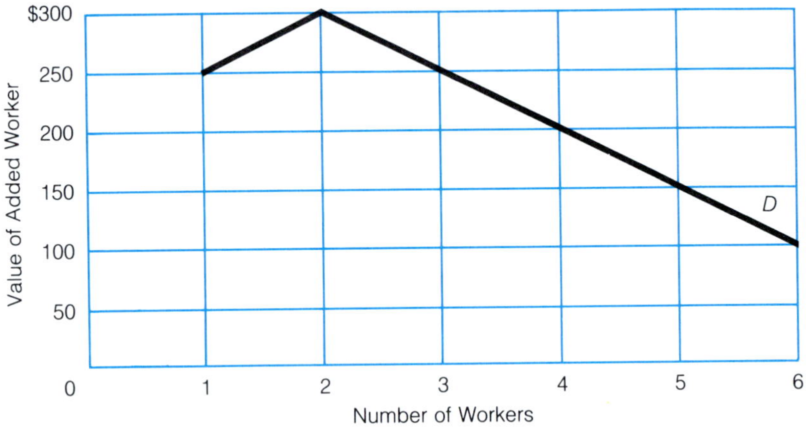

Note. The first part of the demand curve for labor slopes up. No firm would demand labor on this part of the curve because they could hire more labor at the same value to the right of the peak.

Supply of Workers

The number of people who are willing to work depends on the wage they can earn. The percentage of people 16 years of age or older who are either working or looking for work is called the

Note. Lower wage rates may increase the labor force participation rate. If a husband is laid off, it may force his wife to look for work too.

labor force participation rate. When wages are high, the number of people who look for work is greater than when wages are low. Suppose the table in Figure 7–3 shows the number of workers who would be willing to work for the firm above at different wage rates. The graph to the right is the firm's supply curve for labor.

Figure 7–3 *Supply of Workers*

Wage Rate	Number of Workers
$300	60
$250	50
$200	40
$150	30
$100	20
$ 50	10

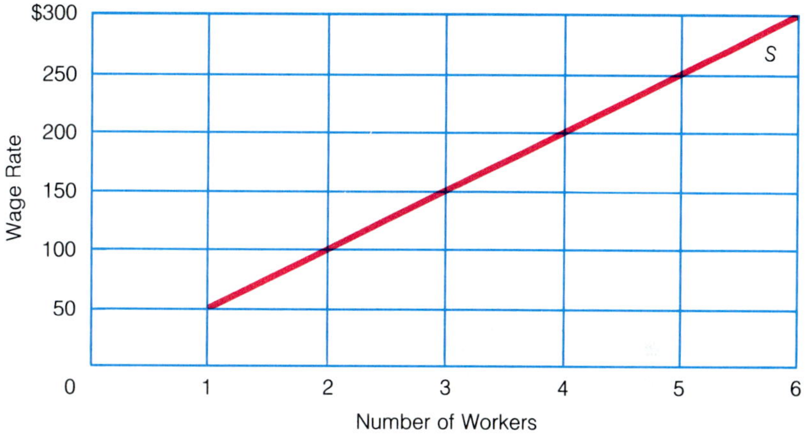

Equilibrium for Wages

It is possible to combine the two graphs from Figures 7–2 and 7–3 into one graph that shows the demand and supply for labor. This has been done in Figure 7–4. It results in an **equilibrium**

Note. The graph assumes all workers are equally skilled and motivated to work. In the real world, some workers are more skilled and motivated and therefore more productive than others.

Figure 7–4 *Demand and Supply for Labor*

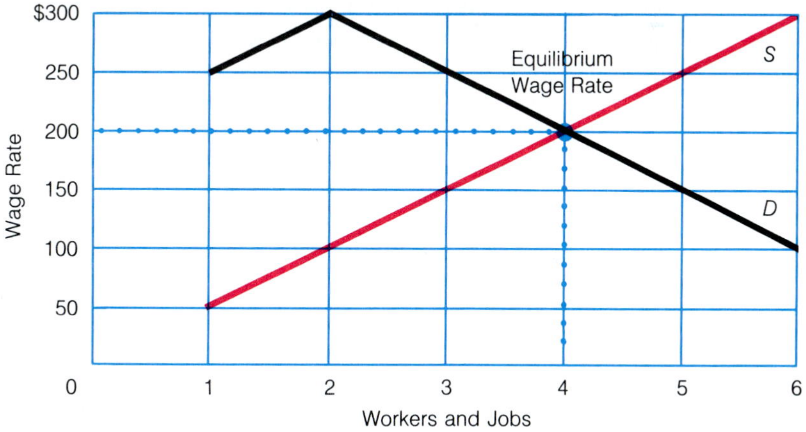

In the Great Depression, most businesses sold fewer products. As a result, the demand for labor fell, causing lower equilibrium wage rates. Many workers were unable to find a job at any wage rate. Businesses that could not sell products did not have sufficient reason or ability to hire workers.

wage rate, where the number of jobs and workers are exactly the same. In this example the equilibrium wage rate is $200 per week and the number of jobs is 4.

The Great Depression of the 1930s provided an example of changes in the equilibrium wage rate. Between 1929 and 1931 consumer prices fell by almost 27 percent. The value of retail sales fell by about half. One result of this was an increase in the unemployment rate from about 3 percent in 1929 to nearly 25 percent in 1933. Wage rates for industrial workers fell by about 22 percent between 1929 and 1933. Reduced prices and sales caused workers to be worth less to employers. Fewer workers could find jobs and those who did were paid less. However, because prices fell, each dollar a worker earned bought more products. Poverty in the Great Depression was more the result of not having a job than of receiving lower wage rates.

Note. In addition to unemployed workers, roughly 25 percent of the labor force was "underemployed" in 1933. They had jobs that required skills below their abilities and which paid relatively low wages.

When comparing wage rates over long periods of time, bear in mind the difference between *money wages* and *real wages.* The term **money wages** refers to the number of dollars workers re-

Note. Real values are discussed in Section B of Chapter 8.

ceive for their labor. The term **real wages** refers to how much the money wages will buy. Money wages were much higher in the early 1990s than they were in the late 1980s, but because of higher prices they bought less. This means that real wages had gone down.

Self-Check
1. Natural resources, labor, capital, and entrepreneurship are sold in the factor market.
2. Diminishing marginal productivity refers to the point where adding an additional worker will result in less additional products than the previous worker produced.
3. At a higher product price, a firm will be willing to hire more workers at the same wage rate.
4. As wage rates increase, more people should want to work.

Self-Check

1. What is the name of the market in which natural resources, labor, capital, and entrepreneurship are sold?
2. What is the meaning of the term *diminishing marginal productivity?*
3. If a firm is able to charge a higher price for its product, what will happen to the number of workers it is willing to employ at its current wage rate?
4. If wage rates increase, what should happen to the number of people who want to work?

Applying What You Have Learned
See Lesson Plans for Chapter 7, Section A, page T66.

Applying What You Have Learned

Answer the following questions from the graph below.

a. At a wage rate of $250, how many workers would want jobs?
b. At a wage rate of $250, how many jobs would be available?
c. At a wage rate of $250, would there be a surplus or shortage of workers?
d. At a wage rate of $250, how big would the surplus or shortage be?
e. What is the equilibrium wage rate in this example?

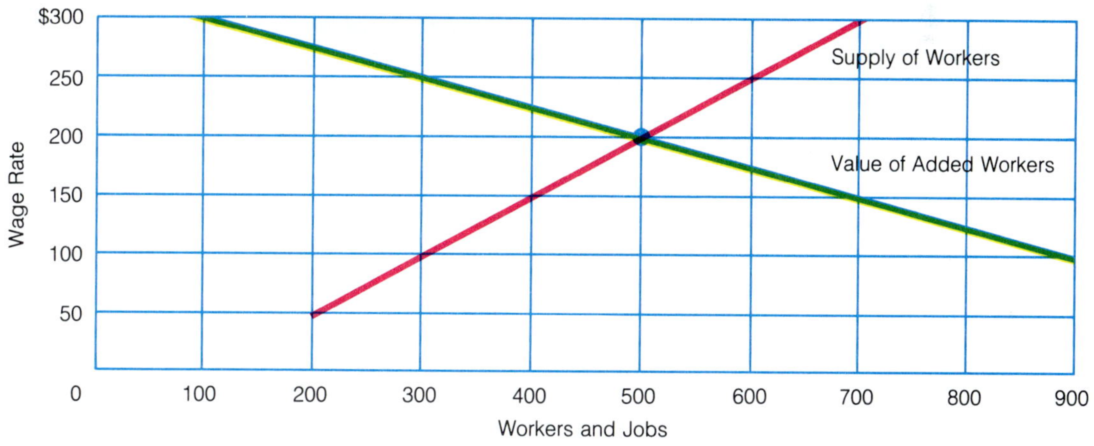

Section B Labor Unions in the Economy

This section will distinguish between *craft* and *industrial unions* and will introduce the terms *injunction, closed shop,* and *right-to-work law.*

Personal Narrative

I Want a Living Wage

No matter how many hours I put in at work, my paycheck isn't large enough for me to support my family. Even if I work fifteen hours of overtime I only earn $330 a week before taxes. Last year I earned just over $14,000 total.

My job is watching a machine stuff fruits or vegetables into cans at a local cannery. As long as the machine works, I have nothing to do. If it misses a can or jams, I have to shut the line down before it shoots food all over the place. The work is easy but boring. Did you ever watch peaches getting mushed into a can for eight or more hours a day? If you fall asleep you get fired. The foreman says he can get five people to replace any of us. He's probably right. I only get $5.27 an hour, but many people would be happy to get that.

Discuss. Do your students believe simple repetitive tasks make a good job because they require little thought, or are they bad because they are dull? What can be done to make production line work more interesting?

Note. Disability payments are a percentage of a person's former salary.

Note. Seasonal unemployment is discussed in Section A of Chapter 10.

Discuss. Unions helped many workers gain health insurance. What do people without jobs that provide insurance do when they get sick? Should the government provide health care for everyone? This question relates to public goods and services, which are discussed in Section A of Chapter 9.

The cannery isn't a very safe place to work. There are sharp pieces of metal all over the place and they cook the food with steam. If something goes wrong, people can get hurt. Last year a woman over in packing got her hand caught in a machine and lost three fingers. They gave her some sort of compensation, but not enough to live on. She can't get a different job because she can't use her hand. She supports her children through social security disability.

Another problem is the fact that they close down production at least four months every year when there is no fresh food to can. We can collect unemployment insurance while we are off work, but it just won't stretch far enough. That's why we all work extra hours when the factory is working. No one ever turns down overtime.

The company pays for medical insurance now, but ten years ago they didn't. A union tried to organize the workers. At about the same time we got a 5 percent raise and the medical insurance. They said there was no connection, but I think there was. The management didn't want a union. There were rumors all over the plant. One was that they would close down and move out of state if we voted for a union. When the vote came in, the union lost 87 to 52. I wonder if my life would be different today if we had joined that union.

What Are Labor Unions

Labor unions are organizations that attempt to improve the working conditions of their members through joint (collective) action. Through unions, workers are able to negotiate with man-

Explain. Before the 1840s there was little need for labor unions in the United States because there was a shortage of labor. Later this changed, largely due to immigration from Europe and Asia.

agement as a group instead of as individuals. The worker in the story above believed the possibility of a union being formed caused management to provide workers with medical insurance. Although she could be wrong, it is clear that unions have helped to improve working conditions, wages, and benefits for many Americans.

Types of Unions

Note. The largest industrial union of the late 1800s was the Knights of Labor. Led by Terrence Powderly, this organization suffered from disunity and the ease with which its largely unskilled membership could be replaced. It disbanded after a bombing in Chicago in 1886, for which some of its leaders were executed. The evidence against these men was not strong.

Labor unions can be divided into two basic types: *craft unions* and *industrial unions.* A **craft union** is sometimes called a *horizontal* union because it is made up of workers who all have the same skill. An example of a craft union would be one made up entirely of electricians. The American Federation of Labor (AFL) united various craft unions into a national organization in 1886. Since the late 1800s, craft unions have been reasonably successful in improving the compensation and working conditions of their members. It is possible that management may have been willing to cooperate with them because such skilled workers would have been difficult to replace.

Industrial unions, which are sometimes called *vertical* unions, are formed by all the workers who are employed in a particular industry. The United Mine Workers was an early example of an industrial union. Industrial unions organize skilled, semi-skilled, and unskilled workers. In the late 1800s and early

On many occasions, workers have formed labor organizations and chosen to go on strike in an attempt to improve their pay or working conditions. You can trace the history of some of the more noteworthy strikes in the United States through this illustration and those on the following pages.

In the Pullman Strike of 1894, the United States army was called in to prevent violence.

In the steel strike of 1919, management eventually was able to force workers to return to work on management's terms, and, to a large extent, to destroy the union organization.

The sitdown strikes of the 1930s led to the recognition of the United Auto Workers as a bargaining agent for workers in the U.S. automobile industry.

After World War II, a series of strikes led to the passage of the Taft-Hartley Act of 1947, which limited union powers.

Professional football players struck and eventually returned to work on management terms in 1987.

1900s, industrial unions had little success in improving the compensation or working conditions of their members. This may have been because most of their members were unskilled and easy to replace. In 1935 the Congress of Industrial Organizations (CIO) was formed to unite various industrial unions into a national organization. For the next 20 years there was competition between the AFL and the CIO for membership. This finally led to the joining of the two organizations in 1955 into the AFL-CIO.

Note. The success of the CIO was at least partially due to rights guaranteed in the National Labor Relations Act.

Labor Legislation

In the 1800s, state governments showed great hostility toward labor unions and took actions intended to limit the power of unions. The law that was used most effectively against union actions was the Sherman Antitrust Act. You will recall from Chapter 6 that this law said actions to restrain trade were illegal. Federal judges ruled that strikes were planned and intended to restrain trade. Strikes were therefore against the law. If a union went on strike, the management could use the Sherman Antitrust Act to request that a court issue an *injunction* against the strikers. An **injunction** is a court order to stop doing something. A person refusing to obey an injunction can be found in contempt of court and be fined, jailed or both.

Note. The military was used on a number of occasions to put down violence related to strikes, as in the Pullman Strike of 1894.

The use of the Sherman Act against strikes was stopped after the passage of the **Clayton Act** in 1914. This law said that it was not the intent of Congress to have the Sherman Act used against labor or farm organizations.

The **National Labor Relations Act,** or **Wagner Act,** of 1935 was intended to guarantee the right of workers to organize in unions and bargain collectively. Among other things, the law

Explain. Although the National Labor Relations Act outlaws actions against workers who organize unions, there is no guarantee that all employers respect this right. Each year, many cases are heard by the National Labor Relations Board, alleging such illegal actions.

said that employers could not discriminate against workers who tried to organize unions. It also required management to negotiate with any union that organized more than half of the firm's workers. The Wagner Act was upheld by the Supreme Court in 1937. A number of other laws that were also favorable to unions were passed under Franklin D. Roosevelt in the 1930s and in World War II. As a result, union membership grew rapidly.

Following World War II, the nation's economy was hurt by a series of crippling strikes. Public opinion turned against unions. Congress passed the **Taft-Hartley Act** over President Truman's veto. The purpose of this law was to limit the unions' ability to disrupt the economy. The law made it illegal for federal employees to strike. It outlawed *closed shops* for any firm that was involved in interstate commerce. A **closed shop** was one that required workers to join the union before they could be employed. States were allowed to pass **right-to-work laws,** which prevented workers from being forced to join or pay union dues. The most important part of the law was thought to be the power given to the President of the United States to seek court injunctions against strikes that harmed the national interest. This power has been used occasionally, with varying degrees of success.

Explain. The Taft-Hartley Act outlawed *closed shops*, but unions can negotiate for *union shops* in states that do not have right-to-work laws. In union shops, workers are required to join a union within some specific time after they are employed.

Union Membership

After 1935, union membership grew in this country, both in total number of workers organized and as a percentage of all workers. This growth continued until 1960. Since then, union membership has fallen. Table 7–2 will help you see how union membership has changed over the years.

Table 7–2

Labor Force and Union Membership, 1900–1990

(in thousands of workers)

Year	Labor Force	Union Membership	Union Membership as a Percentage of Labor Force
1900	27,640	791	2.9%
1920	40,282	5,034	12.5%
1930	47,404	3,632	7.7%
1940	53,299	8,944	16.8%
1950	60,054	15,000	25.0%
1960	72,100	23,600	32.7%
1970	82,800	22,600	27.3%
1980	106,900	20,900	19.6%
1985	115,500	20,800	18.0%
1990	124,787	20,465	16.4%

Sources: *Historical Abstract of the United States*, 1957, and *Statistical Abstract of the United States*, 1991.

An example of the difficulty of enforcing the Taft-Hartley Act injunction occurred in 1978. In December of 1977, 160,000 coal miners had gone out on strike, seeking both higher wages and protection of benefits for retired miners. The strike dragged on for almost 3 months with no sign of a settlement. On March 6, representatives of President Carter went to the Federal District Court in Washington, D.C., and requested a court order be issued requiring the miners to return to work. A temporary order was issued, which was to be effective on March 9. This order was to be transmitted to 1,400 officials in the labor union by U.S. Marshals. But because incorrect legal papers were filed, these orders were never delivered.

Explain. It is difficult to punish a large group for disobeying a court order. A small group of workers can be replaced, as in the air controllers' strike of 1981. But it was impossible to replace 160,000 coal miners in 1978. The government could not enforce the court order. What do your students think should be done in such cases? Can we allow any group to defy the law?

Fewer than 100 of the 160,000 miners ultimately returned to work as a result of the order. The District judge refused to make the return to work order permanent, because the government had failed to provide evidence that the strike would cause irreparable harm to the national health and safety. Non-union workers at some mines had kept coal production at about 50 percent of its normal level, and most areas of the country were suffering no bad effects from the strike.

The mine owners and union eventually settled for a 39% increase in compensation over three years. They did this without direct intervention by the government. However, the threat of a government takeover of the mines or of an imposed settlement may have speeded the agreement.

Self-Check

1. What are the two basic types of labor unions?
2. According to the National Labor Relations Act, when is management required to negotiate with a union?
3. What has happened to union membership as a percentage of the labor force since 1960?

Self-Check

1. The two basic types of labor unions are craft unions and industrial unions.
2. In accordance with the NLRB, management must negotiate with any union that has organized more than half of the firm's workers.
3. Union membership has fallen since 1960.

Applying What You Have Learned

1. Reread the Personal Narrative about the worker in a cannery. Describe at least five different problems the worker has that a union might be able to solve.
2. Now reconsider the problems mentioned above from the management's point of view. Describe what they would have to say about each problem.

Applying What You Have Learned

See Lesson Plans for Chapter 7, Section B, page T67.

Section C Labor-Management Relations

This section will introduce the process of *collective bargaining* and terms that are related to this process.

Personal Narrative

Daddy's out on Strike

My father is a member of the Oil, Chemical and Atomic Workers Union. When I was 8 years old, he had a job working for the BASF corporation in Geismar, Louisiana. We weren't getting rich, but he earned enough in his steady job that our family didn't have to worry about paying the bills. In 1984, when his union's old contract was almost over, the management locked the 1,200 union members out of the plant. The company managers ran the plant for a while and then hired new workers to replace the union members. Those were hard economic times and many people were willing to take these jobs even when it meant crossing union picket lines. BASF even said its old workers could come back to work if they would cross the picket lines. A few did, but most did not.

Note. BASF is a German business. Hourly wages and the cost of benefits in Germany were about 20% higher than in the United States in the 1980s. Union officials in the United States suggested that the firm's financial problems were more the result of poor management than of high wage rates.

Talks were held between the business and the union, but they went nowhere for many years. I remember my father telling me the union wasn't "going to take being walked on anymore." He said that he was willing to "stand up for what's right" even if he lost everything he had. I know he thought he was right, but my mother was awfully worried about how they were going to be able to feed us. Eventually she took a job as a waitress in a local restaurant. She didn't earn much, but we managed.

When the union leaders realized that they weren't succeeding at the bargaining table, they took their case to the press. They planted pickets in the community to tell people what had happened to them. Their story made the national news and even some international newspapers.

Discuss. Why do unions and management try to convince the public of their positions? How do unions and management get the media to pay attention to their arguments?

Finally in September of 1989, BASF invited the union to start negotiations again. After being locked out of the Geismar plant for more than five years, the union finally signed an agreement with BASF management. This might sound like it was the end to my father's troubles, but it wasn't. Each month, 10 union members were offered their jobs back. It took over a year before my father was offered his job back. By then he had been out of work for 6½ years. I'm not sure he showed the management that the union wouldn't be walked on anymore.

In 1986 and 1987 workers at United States Steel (USX) went on strike for job security. The company had cut back jobs because it was losing business to foreign steel competitors. In 1986 USX closed its plants in a lockout. The strike failed to achieve many of the workers' objectives.

Resolving Conflict

Unions are formed when workers join together in an organization that is intended to negotiate labor contracts with management. Unions attempt to improve the working conditions and pay of their members by negotiating as a group instead of as individuals.

Over the years, unions have negotiated improvements in working conditions, benefits, and wages for their members. Although such improvements are good for workers, they cause increased costs for employers. Some people suggest that high labor costs have reduced the ability of American firms to invest in new equipment. If this is true, it would at least partially explain why some American firms have not invested as much in new capital as their foreign competition. It is possible that high wages for workers at BASF may have contributed to union members losing their jobs.

Unions are supported through the dues paid by their members. Unions often negotiate for **union shops.** When there is a union shop, workers are required to join the union within some specific period of time after they are hired. Unions may negotiate for an **agency shop** as an alternative to the union shop. When there is an agency shop, workers must either join the union or pay an "agency fee" to the union, which is usually equal to the union dues. This fee supports the services that the union must legally provide to all workers in a union-protected group.

The Taft-Hartley Act of 1947 allowed states to choose to pass right-to-work laws. In the mostly non-industrial states that have these laws, workers cannot be required to join a union or pay a fee to a union if they don't want to. It is more difficult for a union to organize and bargain successfully in such states.

Collective Bargaining

Note. The power of collective action can be seen in the civil rights movement. If only one African American had chosen to boycott the bus system in Montgomery, Alabama, in 1955, there is little doubt that no one would have cared. However, when almost all African Americans stopped using buses in Montgomery, ridership fell by 60 percent. Then the city, state, and federal governments took notice.

Unions and management negotiate contracts through a process that is known as **collective bargaining.** This means that the union's elected representatives bargain for all the workers as a group instead of each worker bargaining as an individual.

In the collective bargaining process, each side has "weapons" they can use to try to gain their objectives. These weapons include the following:

Union Weapons

a. *Slowdowns*—employees do less work.
b. *Boycotts*—unions encourage members and the public not to buy the firm's products. *Secondary boycotts,* where unions ask the public not to buy from a firm's suppliers, are illegal.

In the late 1970s, Chrysler Corporation and the United Auto Workers reached an agreement through the process of collective bargaining.

Explain. Sit-down strikes were used effectively against the General Motors Corporation in 1937. This strike led to management recognition of the United Auto Workers as the bargaining agent for its workers.

Problem Solving. Ask students to survey their clothing to see how many have union labels. Can they find a relationship between union products and price? Would they pay more for a union product?

c. *Sit-down strikes*—union members occupy a plant to prevent other workers from taking their jobs.
d. *Strike*—workers withhold their labor from the firm. Strikes that are carried out without the approval of union leadership are called *wildcat strikes.*
e. *Picket lines*—union members march around plants to discourage other workers from entering to do the work.
f. *Union labels*—unions encourage the public to buy only products that were manufactured by union workers.
g. *Political action committees*—unions often form groups that are intended to put pressure on politicians to support union points of view in the government.

Management Weapons

a. *Injunctions*—the firm obtains a court order to stop striking or picketing.
b. *Lockouts*—the firm closes the plant to try to force the union to agree to its terms.
c. *Strikebreakers*—the firm hires other workers to take strikers' jobs.
d. *Relocation*—the firm moves the plant to another place where workers may agree to lower wages and benefits.

The objective of negotiations is a mutually acceptable agreement. No one "wins" when a dispute halts production.

Figure 7–5 shows the number of strikes involving 1,000 or more workers, and the number of work days lost in these strikes. Think how much these strikes cost the economy. In 1970 the average American worker earned about $30 a day. The 52.8 million lost days cost workers over one and one half billion dollars in lost wages. Owners lost profits, the government lost tax revenue, and all Americans lost the benefit they could have received from products that were not produced.

The Government's Role

Discuss. Many states have laws that make it illegal for public employees to strike. If a group is prevented from striking, has the government established unequal protection under the law? How can such laws be justified?

The government can assist in the negotiation process in an attempt to prevent or shorten strikes. There are several steps that can be taken by the government to help solve a labor dispute:

Government Tools

a. *Mediation*—an unbiased person (one who doesn't favor either side over the other) listens to each side and suggests a solution.

Figure 7–5 *Strikes and Total Days Lost, 1950–1989 (strikes involving 1,000 workers or more)*

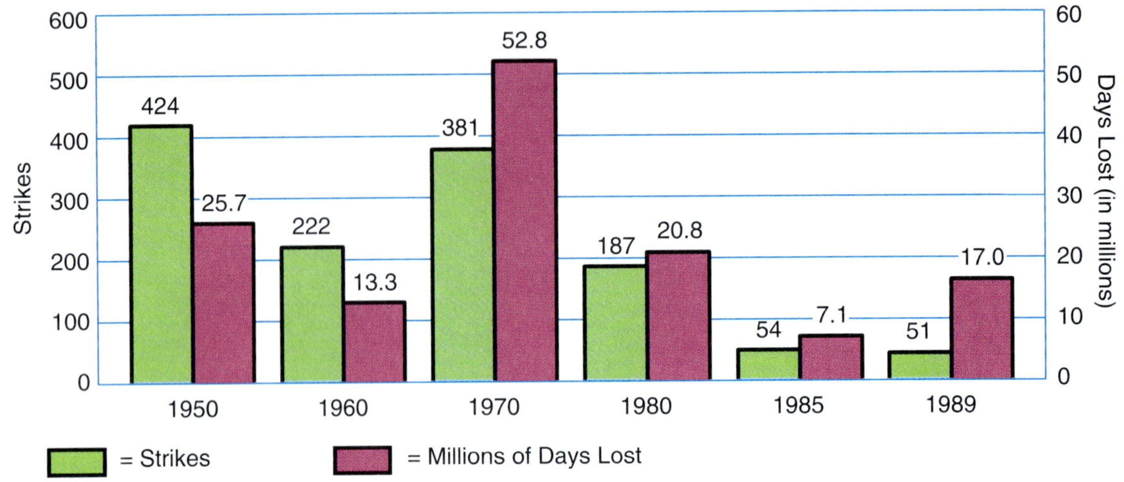

Source: *Statistical Abstract of the United States*, 1956-1991.

Note. The effectiveness of compulsory arbitration has been questioned. A settlement imposed on workers and management may cause workers not to do their best work and/or management to find other ways to cut labor costs.

Self-Check
1. Right-to-work laws say that workers cannot be required to join or pay a fee to a union if they don't want to.
2. Unions and management negotiate through the process of collective bargaining.
3. See Lesson Plans.

Applying What You Have Learned
See Lesson Plans for Chapter 7, Section C, page T69.

b. *Voluntary arbitration*—labor and management agree that an unbiased person should determine a solution.

c. *Compulsory arbitration*—the law *requires* that a solution be determined by an unbiased person. (This is done in several other countries and in some cases on a state level, but is not done on a national level in the United States.)

Self-Check

1. What does a right-to-work law say?
2. What is the process through which unions and management negotiate contracts called?
3. When there is a strike, what would each of the following groups stand to lose?

   a. workers b. management c. government d. consumers

Applying What You Have Learned

Many unions agreed to wage and benefit cuts in the early 1980s. In the mid-1980s they wanted to have these cuts restored. Many firms resisted this. Describe two arguments on this issue from the union's point of view and two from the management's point of view.

Section D Minimum Wages and Employment

This section will discuss the impact of the *minimum wage* on *marginal workers.*

Personal Narrative

I've Got Some Good News and Some Bad News

When I went back to work in 1992 I earned the minimum wage, $4.25 an hour. After one year I worked my way up to $4.75 an hour. Now there's talk of increasing the minimum to $4.75 or $5.00. If they do I doubt my boss would pay me any more than that. I would probably be back to earning the minimum wage again. I could look for a better job but I don't think I'd find one. I can only work a few hours in the middle of the day while my kids are in school.

I'm not sure what the minimum wage is intended to accomplish. There is no way a person could live on $4.25 an hour if they had no other source of income. Everyone who works here only plans to make a little extra money. Some of us are housewives, others are retired and on Social Security. Many of the workers are young and live at home with their parents. No one is the basic wage earner in their family.

Often I feel "used." I work just as hard as other employees. I'm smarter than most, yet I get paid a low wage. It doesn't seem fair. My neighbor is a baked goods clerk at the grocery store. They have a union. She earns $7.73 an hour and gets benefits. Her store put in new cash registers last year that read the item's product code. All she has to do is drag things across an electric eye while the machine does all the work. About the only thing she has to offer that I don't is that she can work nights. Her children are grown. I could go in nights too if my husband didn't work a swing-shift at his plant. We never know what his schedule is going to be.

If the government is going to increase the minimum wage, I wish they would make it high enough to do me some good. Why shouldn't it be $7.00 an hour? Then I would feel better about my job.

Note. Many studies have tried to measure the effect of unions on wage rates. Some have indicated that union workers in some industries have received higher wages than nonunion workers with similar jobs. If union members are paid more, why don't more workers join or form unions? Why has union membership fallen in recent years?

The Impact of Minimum Wages

The first federal **minimum wage** was established at 25 cents an hour in 1938 by the **Fair Labor Standards Act.** This rate was increased at various times over the years. It was raised to $4.25 an hour in 1991.

The woman in the story could not have supported herself on the minimum wage. Without her husband's income, she would have been forced to find a better paying job or to rely on government support. Some people believe the minimum wage provides little help for the working poor. Others argue that it prevents exploitation of those workers who often have no union to protect them.

Note. Organized labor now generally supports higher minimum wages. Some people suggest that this may be because higher minimum wages may increase the competitiveness of union firms that already pay wages higher than the minimum in the same markets. This could enhance job security for the union employees.

Minimum wages were originally opposed by the AFL because there was a fear that the minimum wage might also become the "maximum wage." Union leadership assumed that this law would eliminate normal wage increases. Although this has not happened, there are many different points of view concerning the success and impact of minimum wage laws.

An increase in the minimum wage increases costs of production for firms that pay this wage. Firms that pay wages that are already higher than the minimum wage are not affected directly by such increases. Firms with minimum wage employees could react to their increased cost in a number of ways. They could:

a. accept a smaller profit;
b. increase prices to their customers;
c. pay no more than the minimum wage;

Many young people work in jobs where they earn the minimum wage.

d. lay off some workers;
e. purchase labor-saving machines;
f. replace low-skill workers with higher-skilled workers who are more productive;
g. move the firm or some production to a low wage country;
h. close down.

The deciding factor for these firms is whether a worker's value is more or less than what the worker must be paid. If an employee adds four dollars an hour to the value of production, it makes little sense to pay him five dollars an hour. An increase in the minimum wage will cause fewer jobs that pay the minimum wage.

Discuss. Some people believe low minimum wages are not important because most people who earn the minimum wage do not support themselves solely from the minimum wage. What arguments can your students think of that would refute this point of view?

Most people who earn the minimum wage are called **marginal workers** by economists. This means that their wage is not their only means of support. Young people, retired workers, homemakers, and the poor who receive government aid can be marginal workers. The fact that such individuals have other sources of income does not make their jobs any less important to them. People who are willing to work for $4.25 an hour often need the money.

Minimum wages are paid most frequently to the young and the elderly. Table 7–3 demonstrates this.

Workers who earn the minimum wage and have other means of support in addition to their wages are known as marginal workers. Young people, people of retirement age, and the poor who receive government aid are often in this category.

Table 7–3

Age group	Percent of Group Who Earned Minimum Wage, 1990
16–19	18.9%
20–24	6.5%
25–64	3.1%
65 and over	9.1%

Source: *Bureau of Labor Statistics*, 1990, 1991.

People who earn the minimum wage tend to have less education than other workers. Some people believe higher minimum wages cause many who earn the minimum wage to be laid off. Table 7–4 tends to support this idea. It shows that unemployment rates in 1982 were higher for people with less education. An increase in the minimum wage of 25 cents an hour in 1981 may have contributed to this higher rate of unemployment.

Table 7–4

Years of Education	1982 Unemployment Rate
less than 12 years	12.5%
12 years	8.5%
college graduate	3.0%

Source: *Statistical Abstract of the United States*, 1991.

It is possible that higher minimum wages could do more harm than good if they increase unemployment among people with low incomes. They could also prevent young people from getting their first jobs and a chance for work experience.

Self-Check

1. Why aren't all firms affected equally by increases in the minimum wage?
2. What are marginal workers?
3. Why do some people feel higher minimum wages help the poor while others believe they harm the poor?

Applying What You Have Learned

1. The woman in the Personal Narrative suggested that the minimum wage should be increased to $7.00 an hour. Describe four possible negative results for workers if such a change took place. Explain why each might happen.
2. In the preceding section is a list of reactions a firm could have to higher minimum wages. Choose the three that you feel are most likely and explain why you feel this way.

Self-Check

1. Firms that pay wages that are already higher than the minimum wage are not directly affected by increases in the minimum wage.
2. People who earn the minimum wage and who usually have another means of support are called marginal workers.
3. Some people believe the minimum wage helps protect workers from exploitation, while others believe the minimum wage reduces employment opportunities for the poor.

Applying What You Have Learned

See Lesson Plans for Chapter 7, Section D, page T70.

CURRENT CONSUMER ISSUES

What Should You Look For in a Job?

Statistics show that more than half the students in the United States will hold one or more jobs before they graduate from high school. Although some students need to work to help support their families, the majority choose to take jobs for other reasons. Some are looking for spending money. Others want to save for a future goal.

Imagine that you are looking for work. You plan to save most of your earnings to pay your tuition to a business school you hope to attend after high school. Your career goal is to become a human resource manager for a large business because you like working with people. You also have an interest in protecting the environment and enjoy being outside as much as possible.

After applying to many businesses and having a number of interviews, you are offered two jobs. A fertilizer plant offers a beginning wage of $11.50 an hour with good benefits and regular raises. The job is unloading toxic materials. You would be required to wear special protective clothing and to have regular medical check-ups. The work would be outside, but you would have little opportunity to talk to other people.

In the other job you would work in the complaint and return department of a large garden equipment store. Your wage would be $5 an hour, and you would spend most of your time trying to make dissatisfied customers happy.

Although you don't think you would like the work at the fertilizer plant very much, you are tempted by the higher wage. Would you consider taking this job under these circumstances?

Arguments in Favor of Working at the Fertilizer Plant

1. It would pay more than twice as much as the other job.
2. It would allow you to save enough money to pay your tuition to a business school.
3. You would not need to keep it forever. You could look for a better job later.
4. There are good benefits and potential raises.

Arguments Against Working at the Fertilizer Plant

1. It has nothing to do with your career goal.
2. It may be dangerous to your health.
3. Working with people at the store would be better career experience.
4. It could involve you in putting toxic materials into the environment.

What Do You Think?

Almost all decisions we make involve trade-offs between costs and benefits. What would you include on a list of the arguments for and against taking the job at the garden equipment store?

Chapter 7 Review

What Have You Learned?

In this chapter you have learned the following important principles of economics.

- *Labor* is one of the factors of production, but it is different than the other factors. Labor not only helps to produce goods and services, it also provides the basis for consumption. Workers who earn wages buy products to provide a market for the goods and services they produce.
- Wage levels depend on the value the market places on an individual's labor. In the long run, labor's value is determined by the price of the product that it is used to make.
- As firms start making goods, additional workers result in increasing levels of production. But eventually a level of employment will be reached where additional workers create smaller amounts of additional goods. This idea is known as the principle of *diminishing marginal productivity*.
- The American labor movement developed as a means of improving working conditions through collective action. Labor organizations that began in the 1800s can be divided into two groups: *craft unions* and *industrial unions*. Members of craft unions all shared the same skill. Members of industrial unions were all employed in the same industry. Generally, craft unions were more successful in improving the compensation of their members, possibly because skilled workers were more difficult for employers to replace.
- Many laws have been passed that have affected the ability of labor organizations to function in the U.S. economy. They include the *Sherman Antitrust Act of 1890*, the *Clayton Act of 1914*, the *National Labor Relations Act of 1935*, and the *Taft-Hartley Act of 1947*.
- Labor organizations negotiate contracts with management through the *collective bargaining* process. In these negotiations, each side has "weapons" that they can use to attempt to achieve their objectives. Labor "weapons" have included slowdowns, use of union labels, boycotts, strikes, wildcat strikes, sit-down strikes, picket lines, and political action committees. Management "weapons" have included injunctions, lockouts, strikebreakers, and relocation.
- The government has frequently participated in settling labor disputes through methods that include mediation, voluntary arbitration, and, in some cases, compulsory arbitration.
- The first *minimum wage* was established under the *Fair Labor Standards Act of 1938*. There is a wide debate over the effect of minimum wages on this nation's poor. Some people feel higher minimum wages reduce the number of jobs poor people can find. Others believe that without minimum wages, poor people would be taken advantage of and be worse off than they are.

See Chapter 7 Review Answers, page T71.

Words and Terms

Sections A and B
derived demand (p. 176)
diminishing returns (p. 177)
diminishing marginal productivity (p. 177)
marginal physical product (p. 178)
labor force participation rate (p. 179)
equilibrium wage rate (p. 179)
money wages (p. 180)
real wages (p. 181)
labor unions (p. 182)
craft union (p. 183)
industrial union (p. 183)
injunction (p. 185)
Clayton Act (p. 185)
National Labor Relations Act (p. 185)
Taft-Hartley Act (p. 186)
closed shop (p. 186)
right-to-work law (p. 186)

Sections C and D
union shop (p. 189)
agency shop (p. 189)
collective bargaining (p. 190)
slowdown (p. 190)
boycott (p. 190)
sit-down strike (p. 191)
strike (p. 191)
wildcat strike (p. 191)
picket line (p. 191)
union label (p. 191)
political action committee (p. 191)
lockout (p. 191)
strikebreaker (p. 191)
relocation (p. 191)
mediation (p. 191)
voluntary arbitration (p. 192)
compulsory arbitration (p. 192)
minimum wage (p. 193)
Fair Labor Standards Act (p. 193)
marginal workers (p. 195)

Building Your Vocabulary

Sections A and B

1. An _______ is a court order to stop an activity.
2. If additional workers result in smaller amounts of added production, there is _______.
3. When a contract required workers to join a union before they could be employed, there was a _______.
4. The _______ guarantees workers the right to organize a union.
5. A _______ is a labor organization made up of workers who all have the same skill.
6. An _______ is a labor organization made up of workers who all work in the same industry.
7. The wage rate that results in the number of individuals who are willing to work being just equal to the number of jobs offered by firms is called the _______.
8. The _______ said that the Sherman Act was not to be used against labor organizations.
9. A _______ prevents workers from being required to join a union.
10. The demand for labor is a _______ because it depends on the demand for labor's final product.
11. The _______ gave the President of the United States the power to request a court order to force striking workers to return to work.
12. The term for the additional products produced when another worker is hired is the _______.

Chapter 7 Review

13. The percentage of people 16 years of age or older who are either working or looking for work is called the _______.
14. The number of dollars a worker earns is called _______.
15. The quantity of products workers are able to buy with the dollars they earn is called _______.
16. _______ explains why adding more workers and raw materials won't always increase production.
17. _______ are organizations that attempt to improve working conditions of their members through collective bargaining.

Sections C and D

18. If a firm closes to try to force a union to agree to its terms, there is a _______.
19. A _______ is when a union decides to withhold labor from a firm in an attempt to achieve a labor objective.
20. When a law requires an unbiased person to determine a solution to a labor dispute, the law provides for _______.
21. The _______ provided for the first minimum wage.
22. If union members occupy a plant to prevent other workers from taking their jobs, there is a _______.
23. Moving a plant to another place where workers may agree to lower wages and benefits is called _______.
24. _______ is when an unbiased person listens to each side in a labor dispute and suggests an answer.
25. If labor and management agree to allow an unbiased person to settle a labor dispute, they have agreed to _______.
26. If workers are required to pay a fee to a union they don't join, there is an _______.
27. When a union forms a group that puts political pressure on government officials, it is called a _______.
28. People who earn the minimum wage are generally _______.
29. A _______ happens when union members go out on strike without the approval of their union leaders.
30. A _______ is when employees do less work in a period of time to put economic pressure on management.
31. If union members march around a plant to discourage other workers from entering, they are in a _______.
32. Labor organizations use a _______ to encourage the public to buy products made by union members.
33. A worker who is hired to take the job of a striking worker is called a _______.
34. The lowest wage rate a person can be paid under the law is the _______.
35. When workers are required to join a union within a specific period of time after they are hired, there is a _______.
36. The process through which unions and management negotiate labor agreements is called _______.
37. A _______ is when a union encourages people not to buy a firm's products in an attempt to put economic pressure on the firm.

Understanding Economics

1. Suppose a firm has a large saw that needs two people to operate it. The first worker hired can cut only ten logs an hour. The second worker increases production to thirty logs an hour. Explain why hiring a third worker might add only five more logs per hour. What does

this have to do with diminishing marginal productivity?

2. A firm has been selling table lamps for $40 each. For some reason these lamps suddenly become very popular and the firm finds it can sell many of them for $50 each. Describe the effect this event would have on the number of workers the firm would like to hire and the wage rate it would be willing to pay.
3. Explain why a union formed by aircraft engineers would often be more successful than one formed by the workers at a car wash.
4. Suppose that the nation's railroad workers had been on strike for the last two months. The economy was suffering. Many factories had been closed down and thousands of workers had been laid off. Describe what the President could do through the Taft-Hartley Act to try to resolve the situation.
5. Assume that you have been given the job of mediating a strike between the workers in a grocery store and its management. Make a list of at least five things you would want to know before you suggested a solution.

Thinking Critically About Economics

1. A local firm spent $50 million on new computer-controlled production equipment, which will assemble cameras automatically. Make a list of the types of workers who would be harmed by this investment. Make a second list of those who would be helped.
2. In the early 1980s, many large unions agreed to what were called "concessionary contracts," in which they actually accepted lower rates of pay and benefits. Describe three different reasons they may have had for doing this.
3. Describe several problems that a "right-to-work law" might cause for a union that was trying to organize a new plant.
4. In 1960, union membership was more than 30 percent of the total labor force. In 1990 about 16 percent of all workers belonged to unions. Describe three different reasons that you believe could have helped cause this change.
5. In recent years a number of firms have chosen to lock their workers out when an old contract expired, rather than let them continue to work under the old contract. Explain what a firm could accomplish by doing such a thing.
6. Write an argument in favor of a lower minimum wage for young workers between 16 and 19 years of age. Write a second argument against such a minimum wage law.

Consumer Skills Projects

1. Take a survey of ten adults of various ages and economic situations. Ask if they make buying decisions based on whether products are made by union members. Do they feel union-made products have superior quality? Do they see anything wrong with buying products that were not made by union labor? Discuss your findings with your class.
2. Interview a local union leader. Discuss the goals and purposes he or she sees for the local union organization. Ask this person to explain how consumers benefit from buying union-made products. Discuss your interview with your class.
3. Interview the owner of a local business. Ask this person to describe his or her feelings toward union organizations. In what ways does this person feel unions have helped or harmed consumers? Discuss your interview with your class.

Thinking Critically About Economics
(1) comparison/contrast; (2) evaluating alternatives; (3) predicting probable consequences; (4) cause and effect; (5) cause and effect; (6) recognizing opinion.

Developing Your Economic Skills

Using Line Graphs to Compare Trends

Skill: In this lesson two line graphs will be drawn together to show changing trends. By studying the graphs you will be able to compare these trends. To complete this lesson, you'll follow these steps:

1. Identify the trends that are shown on the two graphs.
2. Study the graphs to see what has happened to each trend.
3. Compare the trends to each other.
4. Suggest possible reasons for changes in the trends.

Application: Has the minimum wage kept up with inflation?

Many young people earn the minimum wage when they take their first job. In 1992 the minimum wage was $4.25 an hour. Twenty-five years earlier the minimum wage was only $1.40 an hour. You might think the minimum wage was much smaller in 1967, but can you be sure? If you consider inflation, the 1992 minimum wage could have less purchasing power. The graph at right shows the long-term trend for changes in the minimum wage and prices.

On the graph, the percentage change in prices and the minimum wage between 1967 and 1992 is shown by a scale that appears on both vertical axes. The years are listed across the horizontal axis, from left to right. Growth in the minimum wage between 1967 and 1992 is shown with a green line, while the increase in prices is shown with a red line. (There are flat places on the graph of the minimum wage because there were many years in which it did not change. The minimum wage changes only by direct government decision, but inflation changes automatically in response to economic conditions.)

The graphs show you what the percentage increase in each value was in comparison to its level in 1967. For example, locate the year 1978 on the horizontal axis, and read directly up to locate the corresponding points on the two line graphs. You'll see that in 1978 prices had increased by about 95 percent from 1967, while the minimum wage had increased by a little less than 90 percent over the same years.

The graph shows you that the growth in the minimum wage roughly kept up with the increase in prices until the late 1970s. After 1979 the trend for prices went up much more rapidly than growth in the minimum wage. Between 1981 and 1989 there was no increase at all in the minimum wage.

What reasons can you think of that could explain this situation? Why didn't the growth in the minimum wage keep up with inflation in recent years? Could it have anything to do with the recession of 1981–82? Do you believe it might have something to do with the political party that held power in Congress or the White House?

Practice: Copy advertised prices for similar food items, building supplies, and apartment rent from a current newspaper, a ten-year-old paper, and a five-year-old paper at your library. What is the percentage of increase for each? (To get percent divide the amount of increase by the original price.) Build a simple graph that shows different rates of price increase for three items.

Inflation and Changes in the Minimum Wage (as a percentage of 1967)

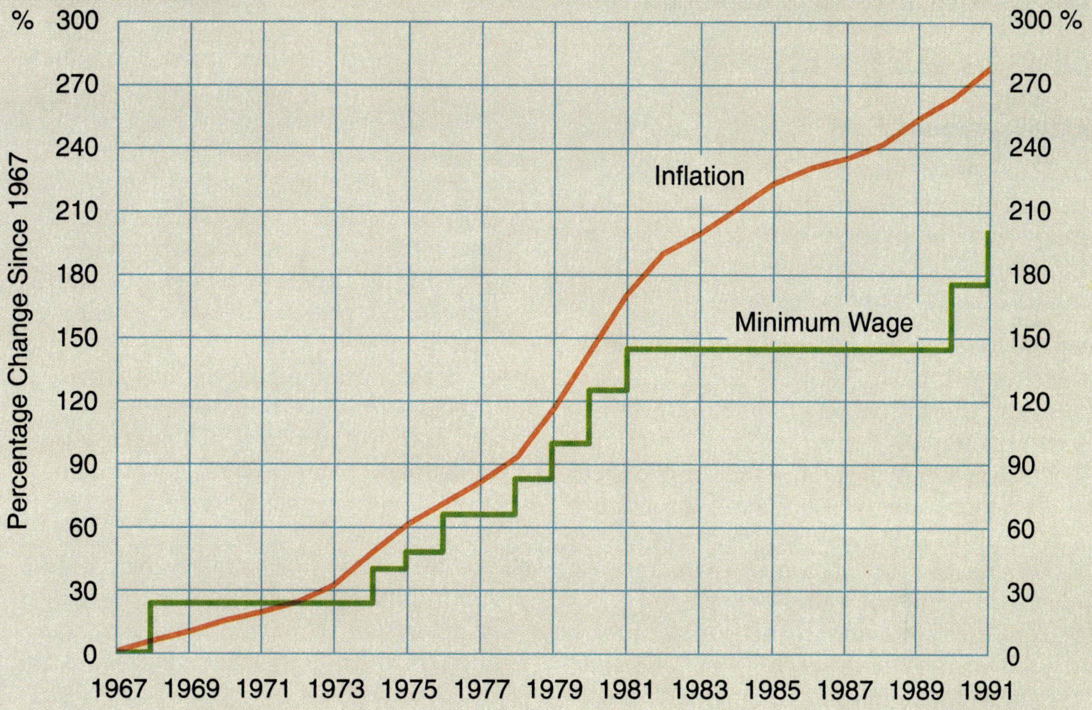

Part 2 Review

Summary of Major Economic Concepts

In Part 2 you have learned the following basic economic principles concerning the decision-making processes of businesses and individuals. These principles are part of what is called *microeconomics*.

- The *circular flow model* is used to demonstrate the flow of money, goods and services, and factors of production through the economy.
- *Demand* refers to the number of products that consumers will purchase throughout a range of prices, while *supply* is the number of products a firm is willing to sell throughout a range of prices.
- The forces of demand and supply interact with each other to reach a *point of equilibrium*, which indicates the market price and the quantity of a product that will be sold. In a competitive market, prices above equilibrium result in a *surplus*, which tends to force the price down. Prices below equilibrium cause a *shortage*, which tends to force the price up.
- The *elasticity* of demand is a measure of demand's responsiveness to a change in price. If the percentage change in the quantity of a product demanded is greater than the percentage change in price, the demand is *price elastic*. When the percentage change in quantity of a product demanded is smaller than the percentage change in price, the demand is *price inelastic*.
- As consumers buy more of a particular product, they experience *diminishing marginal utility*. This means that each additional unit of the product has less value to the consumer. Because of this, consumers distribute their purchases among many different goods and services.
- In *capitalism*, consumers control the products that are produced through what they buy. This idea is called *consumer sovereignty*. In their effort to serve their own interests, producers in capitalism are forced to supply products people want at competitive prices. This idea is called the *invisible hand*.
- As the American economy has grown, the need for government involvement and *consumer protection* has increased. Consumers pay a cost for government protection in higher prices and reduced competition.
- The three basic forms of business organization in the United States are the *single proprietorship*, *partnership*, and *corporation*. Each form has important advantages and disadvantages.
- All firms must take into consideration both *fixed* and *variable* costs of production. Businesses often increase production to reduce the *average fixed cost* per unit.
- Most businesses need to use capital that belongs to someone else. This leads firms to *rent* property or machines, and to borrow money from banks or through the sale of *bonds*. Corporations sell *stock*, or units of ownership, to raise money.
- There are many different types of markets, ranging from *perfect competition* to *perfect monopoly*. Firms in perfect competition have no control over the prices they can charge, while perfect monopolies set their own prices. Although there are few, if any, perfect monopolies in the United States, there are many firms that have some degree of monopoly-like power. These include firms engaged in *monopolis-*

See Part 2 Review Answers, page T73.

tic competition*, *oligopolies*, and *natural monopolies*.

- Large firms often have advantages over their smaller competition; these advantages are called *economies of scale*. In some cases the small firms have advantages over larger competitors; these advantages are called *diseconomies of scale*.
- Our government has used regulation and *antitrust policy* to try to achieve *workable competition*. This is a trade-off between the advantages offered by competition and those offered by large size.
- *Labor* is different from other factors of production because it also provides the basis for consumption. Workers who earn wages buy products to provide a market for the goods and services they produce.
- Wages depend on the value the market places on an individual's labor. As more workers are hired in a firm, a point will be reached where additional workers bring about smaller increases in production. This is called *diminishing marginal productivity*.
- The labor movement attempts to improve working conditions and compensation through *collective bargaining*. Labor organizations can be divided into *craft* and *industrial* unions. Workers in craft unions have the same skills, while members of industrial unions are employed in the same industry.
- Many laws have been passed that affect the labor movement. They include the *Sherman Antitrust Act of 1890*, the *Clayton Act of 1914*, the *National Labor Relations Act of 1935*, and the *Taft-Hartley Act of 1947*.
- Labor organizations and management have many tools that they use in the collective bargaining process. Our government often participates in this process through *mediation*, *fact-finding*, and *voluntary* and *compulsory arbitration*.
- The first minimum wage was established under the *Fair Labor Standards Act of 1938*. There is a wide debate over the effect of minimum wages on this nation's poor.

Understanding Economic Concepts

Each of the following questions emphasizes one or more of the important economic concepts you have learned in Part 2. The important concept is listed in parentheses after each question. Answer each question in complete sentences that *show you understand the meaning* of the concept. The first question has been answered for you as an example.

1. What figure do economists use to show the relationship between different markets in our economic system? (Discuss the *circular flow model*.) (*Answer:* Economists use the circular flow model to show the flow of money, goods and services, and factors of production through the product and factor markets.)
2. What should happen to the number of products a firm sells if similar products become more expensive? (Discuss *determinants of demand* and *substitute goods*.)
3. If a firm's workers receive a wage increase, what will happen to the number of products it is willing to sell? (Discuss *supply* and *costs of production*.)
4. If a firm produces more products than it can sell at its current price, what will it be forced to do? (Discuss *surplus* and *equilibrium*.)
5. Why do consumers distribute their spending among many different types of products? (Discuss *diminishing marginal utility*.)
6. What products do firms produce in capitalism? (Discuss *consumer sovereignty*.)

Part 2 Review

7. What is one reason for the increased government involvement in our economic system? (Discuss *consumer protection.*)
8. Why are most large firms organized as corporations? (Discuss *stocks* and *bonds.*)
9. Why do many firms want to increase their level of production? (Discuss *average fixed costs.*)
10. What are two ways for a person to earn money from owning stock? (Discuss *dividends* and *capital gain.*)
11. How have many of the larger firms been formed from smaller ones? (Discuss *horizontal combinations* and *vertical combinations.*)
12. Why is it necessary that certain types of firms have monopoly-like power? (Discuss *natural monopolies.*)
13. What does our government try to achieve through its regulation and antitrust policy? (Discuss *workable competition.*)
14. Why can't all workers make the same contribution to production? (Discuss *diminishing marginal productivity.*)
15. How has the government frequently participated in the collective bargaining process? (Discuss *mediation,* and *voluntary* and *compulsory arbitration.*)

Writing About Economics

Each of the questions below requires you to write a brief essay. Be sure to include *each* of the following in your answer:

- Demonstrate your understanding of the identified economic concept(s) in your essay.
- Explain how the economic concept(s) is involved in the situation.
- Describe how you would resolve the situation and on what basis you would make your decision.

1. Your shoe store has not been doing well lately. Although you stock quality products and sell them at low prices, you believe many people don't know your store exists. You would also like to increase sales so it would be easier to pay your rent. What should you do? (Discuss the *determinants of demand, informative advertising,* and *average fixed costs.)*
2. After seeing an advertisement for the "Handy Dandy Garden Tool" on television, you ordered one for $29.95 plus $4.95 shipping. The advertisement showed a beautiful woman digging in her garden with no effort at all. When you got the tool, it turned out to be much like an ordinary hoe that you could buy for about $10.00 in any hardware store. You are angry and feel you have been cheated. Why do you think you decided to buy the product? What should you do? What will eventually happen to the firm that sells the product? (Discuss *persuasive advertising, consumer protection,* and the *invisible hand.)*
3. You manufacture house paint. You have recently merged with a firm that discovered a new chemical that makes paint stick to wood for at least ten years. It has been patented by the government so no one else can use it. Although your paint is good, you know many other brands of paint are good too. How do you convince customers to buy your paint? (Discuss *monopolistic competition,* and *informative advertising.)*

Writing About Economics (1) evaluating alternatives; (2) identifying assumptions, predicting probable consequences, recognizing propaganda; (3) identifying alternatives; (4) assessing costs and benefits, predicting probable consequences.

4. You work as a lawyer for the government. Your job is to help make sure firms don't have too much monopoly-like power. A large chemical firm has asked permission to buy another large chemical producer. Although the new firm would control about 35 percent of the chemical market, you also believe that it would be quite efficient. Should you recommend approval of the merger? (Discuss *horizontal combination, antitrust policy, economies of scale,* and *workable competition.*)

Discussing Economics

The following paragraphs describe economic issues that have been the topic of recent public debate. In each situation, there is no one answer or point of view that all Americans can agree to. For each issue, decide whether you support or do not support the proposal, and think about how you would present your opinion to the rest of the class. When you present your opinion, be sure to

- identify and describe the issue
- explain what you would do
- explain why your choice is the best choice

1. In some states it is against the law to ride a motorcycle without a helmet. In others, wearing a helmet is a matter of personal choice. How can this be? Supporters of requiring helmets argue that accidents are more than a matter of individual choice. They point out that the government has been forced to pay for injuries resulting from motorcycle accidents. The government also has supported the families of accident victims. Taxpayers do pay a cost when people are injured in motorcycle accidents. If helmets reduce injuries, they would also reduce the burden on the taxpayers. Finally, insurance premiums seem to be higher in states with no helmet laws.

   People who feel helmets should be a matter of choice ask, "Where do you draw the line? There is some risk in everything we do. Should we pass a law that requires us all to walk because people are killed in automobile accidents? We can't eliminate risk, so why take away personal freedoms?"

   Do you believe the government should require motorcycle helmets?

2. In a number of states, large nuclear power projects have been started and then abandoned or converted to other types of fuel. This has occurred in the states of Washington, Michigan, and Illinois. The electric companies that started these projects have lost billions of dollars. They would like to pass their loss on to their customers in the form of higher prices. In many cases, state regulatory agencies have prevented them from recovering all of their loss in this way. This forces the firms to pay their costs in some other way. They can cut dividends to stockholders. They can reduce wages and benefits for employees. They can reduce spending for service and maintaining their equipment. Electric utility companies argue that these alternatives are unfair and will hurt ordinary people who live in the area, as well as the utility companies themselves.

   If you were in charge, would you allow electric utility firms to pass such costs on to their customers?

3. In some states it is against the law for public employees to go on strike. In other states such strikes are legal. Supporters of laws that outlaw public employee strikes believe that the services provided by public workers, such as po-

Discussing Economics (1) recognizing value orientations; distinguishing fact from opinion; (2) recognizing value orientations; identifying alternatives; (3) recognizing value orientations; predicting probable consequences.

Part 2 Review

licemen, firemen, teachers and sanitation workers, are so important that they should not be allowed to strike. Others wonder why doctors, nurses, and telephone workers are allowed to strike in these states. They ask, "Are these workers any less important to the public? Do such laws result in unequal rights?"

If you were in charge, would you allow public workers to go on strike?

Problem-Solving with Economics

Chapter 3

1. Below you will find a list of events. For each event, state whether the result would be an increase or decrease in demand for the particular product.
   a. demand for all products when taxes go up 10 percent
   b. demand for diapers when there is a baby boom
   c. demand for snow shovels at the start of December
   d. demand for popcorn at the theater when the price of peanuts goes up
   e. demand for hospital beds as people live longer
   f. demand for all products when many people get better jobs
   g. demand for fish nets at the start of a salmon run
   h. demand for canvas shoes when leather becomes very expensive
2. Consider the following list of events that would change a firm's costs of production. For each, decide whether the event would increase or decrease the cost of production and whether this would cause the firm's supply curve to move to the left or to the right over a period of time.
   a. The firm's workers are paid 10 percent more.
   b. The firm has to pay more for heat.
   c. The firm buys more efficient trucks.
   d. The firm installs pollution controls.
   e. The firm buys a computer system.
   f. The firm spends money on training.
3. Answer the questions based on the supply curve below:
   a. At $5.00 how many toys would be offered for sale?
   b. What price would result in twenty toys being offered for sale?
   c. If the price went from $3.00 to $5.00, would the number of toys supplied increase or decrease?
   d. If the price went from $3.00 to $5.00 how many more or fewer toys would be supplied?
   e. At $2.00 how many toys would be supplied?

Supply of Wooden Toys

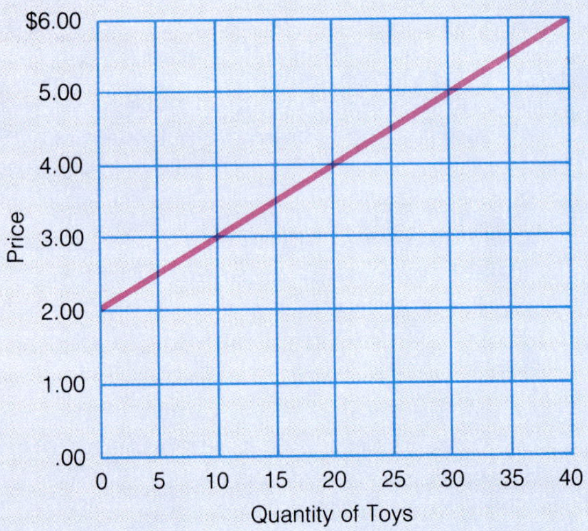

Problem-Solving with Economics
Chapter 3
(1) predicting probable consequences; (2) predicting probable consequences; (3) interpreting graphs, analyzing cause and effect; (4) analyzing cause and effect.

4. Below you will find a list of events. For each event state whether the result would increase or decrease the equilibrium price if nothing else changed.
   a. Consumer income goes up 10 percent.
   b. Labor costs increase by 10 percent.
   c. The cost of raw materials goes down by 10 percent.
   d. The product being sold becomes very popular.
   e. The government reports the product causes cancer.
   f. The product's raw materials become less expensive.
   g. The price of a product that could be used instead goes up.
   h. Other countries stop buying this product.

Chapter 4

1. Suppose you are going on a survival camping trip. The rules are that you can only take five items with you besides the clothes you wear. You may only take things you can carry ten miles into the forest *on your back.* (No cars, TV's, etc.) On a separate piece of paper, list the items you would take in order of their importance, most important first and so on. Briefly explain each choice.
2. The financial success of a professional sports team depends on its ability to please the fans. In many ways this concerns consumer sovereignty. List five different things management could do to encourage attendance at their games. You must be reasonable. They can't give away free tickets or beer or do anything else that would cost more than it could earn.
3. How could you explain the trends in advertising shown in the table below?

Advertising Expenditures for Newspapers and Television, 1950–89
(in millions of dollars)

	1950	1960	1970	1980	1989
Newspapers	2,076	3,703	5,745	14,794	32,368
% of total	36.3%	31.0%	29.3%	27.7%	26.1%
Television	171	1,590	3,596	11,366	26,891
% of total	3.0%	11.1%	18.3%	21.2%	21.7%

Chapter 5

1. Describe three different businesses. For each, identify the type of organization that would be best suited to the business and explain why. Provide one example each of a proprietorship, a partnership, and a corporation.
2. Assume that you are going to go into the bicycle manufacturing business. List five specific examples of fixed costs and five examples of variable costs you would need to pay.
3. It probably costs between $5,000 and $7,000 on an average to educate a student in your school district. In general it is less expensive to provide an education in large schools than in small ones. Explain what this has to do with average fixed costs.
4. In a number of foreign countries, workers are guaranteed a job and a wage by their employers no matter what. If these firms find that their products aren't selling, they may have to pay their workers for doing nothing. This means that labor can be a fixed cost to these firms. Explain why these firms could be willing to sell their products to the United States for less than it cost them to make them.
5. The following table shows the average interest rates paid by banks for large time deposits between 1980 and 1990.

Chapter 4
(1) identifying the problem; evaluating alternatives;
(2) identifying the problem; evaluating alternatives;
(3) analyzing cause and effect.

Chapter 5
(1) identifying the problem, evaluating alternatives;
(2) identifying the problem, evaluating alternatives;
(continues)

Part 2 Review

Study the table and then answer the questions that follow.

Year	Interest
1980	13.07%
1981	15.91%
1982	12.27%
1983	9.07%
1984	10.11%
1985	8.73%
1986	8.06%
1987	7.86%
1988	8.39%
1989	7.86%
1990	7.52%

a. Why did corporations have to promise higher dividends to sell new stock in 1981 than they did in 1990?
b. How would these higher dividends affect the ability of firms to invest in new equipment?
c. If the economy is doing poorly and many businesses do not want to expand or produce more products, what would probably happen to the demand for resources? What would probably happen to the amount of rent paid to use resources that belong to someone else?

Chapter 6

1. Competitive firms are "price takers." They can only charge what their competition charges.
   a. Describe an industry that is made up of firms in perfect or near perfect competition. Explain why each firm must charge the same price.
   b. If all the firms in a competitive market try to make as many products as they can, total production will grow. What is this likely to do to the market price in the industry?
   c. Why have some economists suggested that competitive firms are their own worst enemies?
2. Americans buy products from monopolistic and competitive firms every day. List two specific examples each of products that consumers buy from (a) competitive firms; (b) firms in monopolistic competition; (c) oligopolies; (d) natural monopolies.
3. Think of a local example of a large business. Make two lists. On one, list four advantages the firm has because it is large. On the other, list four disadvantages it may have because it is large. Be specific.
4. Many other countries have decided that their governments should own large firms that tend to be monopolistic. In Great Britain, for example, airlines, railroads, steel mills and power companies either belong to or have belonged to the government. Explain why you do or do not believe this would be a good idea for the United States.
5. Assume that there was only one firm that produced all of the soft drinks in the country. Suppose the government forced this one large firm to be broken up into at least ten smaller firms. Explain what would probably happen to each of the following:
   a. the number of workers in the industry
   b. the total cost of distribution and advertising

Chapter 5 (cont.)
(3) analyzing cause and effect; (4) analyzing cause and effect; (5) predicting probable consequences.
Chapter 6
(1) analyzing cause and effect; (2) classification; (3) comparison/contrast, assessing costs and benefits; (4) recognizing values, assessing costs and benefits; (5) predicting probable consequences.

c. the number of different soft drinks on the market
d. the market price of soft drinks
e. the quantity of soft drinks sold

Chapter 7

1. Each of the following events would tend to either increase or decrease wage rates. For each, tell which it would do and explain why.
   a. The entry of many new, young workers into the labor force would ______ wages because ______.
   b. An increase in the imports of inexpensive products from other countries would ______ wages because ______.
   c. Inflation would ______ wages because ______.
   d. An increase in government aid to the poor would ______ wages because ______.
2. Two arguments concerning unions are stated below. Evaluate each one. Explain why you feel the argument is right or wrong.
   a. Unions are bad for the economy. They cause higher wages, which lead to higher prices. Higher prices mean fewer people will be able to buy products, so there will be lower sales, fewer jobs, and less growth in the economy.
   b. Unions are necessary because they force wages up to a reasonable level. Reasonable wages mean workers can buy products. With no unions, businesses would pay low wages. Few people would have enough money to buy products. Sales would be low. Workers would be laid off and the economy would not grow.
3. Suppose that you represent a union involved in a contract dispute. Which labor "weapon" would you consider using first, and why? Suppose that you represent management involved in the same dispute, which management "weapon" would you consider using, and why? For both labor and management, what alternatives could you try before turning to any of the available "weapons"?
4. In 1983 President Reagan suggested that a lower minimum wage of $2.90 an hour be established for workers who are 16–19 years old. Give two arguments in favor of such a plan and two against it.

Chapter 7
(1) predicting probable consequences; (2) recognizing values, distinguishing fact from opinion;
(3) identifying the problem, evaluating alternatives;
(4) recognizing values, assessing costs and benefits.

Problem-Solving Chapter 4 activity 1 and Chapter 7 activity 3 may be an appropriate method of authentic assessment and may be placed in students' portfolios.

BANK OF AMERICA
BARKERS

P A R T

3

Understanding the Economy as a Whole

Part 3 will help you understand how the major parts of our economy fit together into a system. Economists call this *macroeconomics,* and it means you will be looking at the economy as a whole. In this part you will study several methods we use to measure the value of production. You will explore the role of the government in our economic system. You will grapple with the problems of inflation, unemployment, and poverty. You will learn about money, banking, and government regulation of the financial system. Finally, you will study government policies that are intended to help the economic system work and satisfy the needs of the people. Part 3 gives you an overall picture of the American economy.

Ethanol's Good for the
Economy and
GIVE 'EM AN
EARFUL

CHAPTER 8

Measuring the Economy: Made in America

Objectives

In the sections of this chapter, you will learn:

A

how the value of the *Gross Domestic Product* is measured through the *expenditure* and *income* approaches, and why the *underground economy* makes it hard to measure GDP;

B

the difference between *nominal, real,* and *per person* GDP, and why changes in GDP do not always result in similar changes in our standard of living;

C

how the *four phases* of the *business cycle* affect the sales of *durable* and *nondurable* goods, and how economists use *leading indicators* to try to predict the phases of the cycle.

You may use the *Nightly Business Report* videotape "New Years Day Special" with this chapter.

Introduction

"Have some wine," the March Hare said [to Alice] in an encouraging tone.

Alice looked all round the table, but there was nothing on it but tea. "I don't see any wine," she remarked.

"There isn't any," said the March Hare.

Lewis Carroll, *Alice in Wonderland*

In Wonderland, Alice discovered she couldn't have something that wasn't there. The same is true of the economic system. People can't have what isn't produced. Our material standard of living depends on our economy's productivity.

Economists, businesspeople, politicians, and many other people are concerned with what we are able to produce. In this chapter you will learn how we measure the value of our production and how productivity helps determine our standard of living. You will find that we use several different methods of measurement. There are problems with each method. The government must make an "educated guess" when it reports the value of production.

There are different opinions concerning how economic productivity relates to the quality of life. Remember, quantity and quality are not always the same thing. Having more goods and services will not do us much good if we are all sick from pollution.

Section A What Is the Gross Domestic Product?

This section will introduce the *Gross Domestic Product* and explain its measurement through the *expenditure* and *income* approaches.

Personal Narrative

More Is Better, Isn't It?

A door slams, "SMASH," feet run across the floor, "THUD, THUD, THUD," there is panting in the next room, "WHEEZE, WHEEZE." Someone is trying to get herself under control. The door slowly opens and your daughter Alison steps gracefully into the room. "Daddy," (you know you're in trouble) "Can you be a dear and *please* lend me $20 until next week? I found the most wonderful little top at the mall and it's on sale for 30 percent off." You know the chance of her ever paying you back is about as good as that of snow in July. You try to ignore her, but she pokes you in the ribs.

"You think I'm made of money! Last week it was new shoes, and the week before you had to have a bathing suit. You always want something and your closet is stuffed with things you never wear. You need to learn a little self control. When I was your age I didn't have more than two pairs of jeans to my name!"

Alison starts to pout. "Those old things are out of style. I can't wear them. Do you want everyone to laugh at me? I don't care about your stupid jeans. Those were the old days anyhow. You don't care about me at all!" She makes a snuffling noise and looks a little like your neighbor's basset hound.

Now she's gone too far. You're angry because she's trying to use you. You bellow, "Alison, go to your room and stay there until I tell you to come out!"

Alison disappears up the stairs. "WaaaaaaaaH!"

The next morning she is all smiles in her new top.

How to Compute the Gross Domestic Product

Like Alison, we would all like to have more things. However, there is a limit to what we are able to buy. Our nation's income is determined by the amount we produce. In the early 1990s the most frequently used measure of the value of production became the **Gross Domestic Product.** The GDP is defined as the retail market value of everything produced in the country in a year, regardless of who owns the firm that made the products.

Before 1991 the standard measure of production had been the Gross National Product (GNP). Slightly different than the Gross Domestic Product, the GNP includes interest and the dividends or profits of foreign firms received by residents of this country. The GDP excludes these payments. This may sound complicated, but it isn't really. Imagine you owned 100 shares of stock in a French corporation that paid you $500 last year in dividends. The value of this income would be included in the GNP, but not in the GDP because it was not the result of production and earnings that took place in the United States. Most economists believe that GDP is a better measure of production than GNP.

The government spends millions of dollars every year measuring the Gross Domestic Product. There are two basic methods that are used to calculate GDP. They are the *expenditure* approach and the *income* approach.

The Expenditure Approach

It is possible to compute the value of GDP by adding together all the spending for new goods and services produced in a year. This is called the **expenditure** approach. It is based on the fact that someone must pay for all new production. Therefore, it is possible to measure production by measuring spending. When Alison bought her new top, her spending became part of the measurement of GDP through the expenditure approach.

In the expenditure approach, spending is organized into four categories: (1) consumer or consumption spending, (2) government spending, (3) business spending, and (4) net spending by foreign purchasers.[1] The spending in all four categories is totaled to obtain the GDP. Figure 8–1 shows how GDP was distributed in these four categories in 1990.

Figure 8–1 *Distribution of Spending as a Percentage of GDP in 1990*

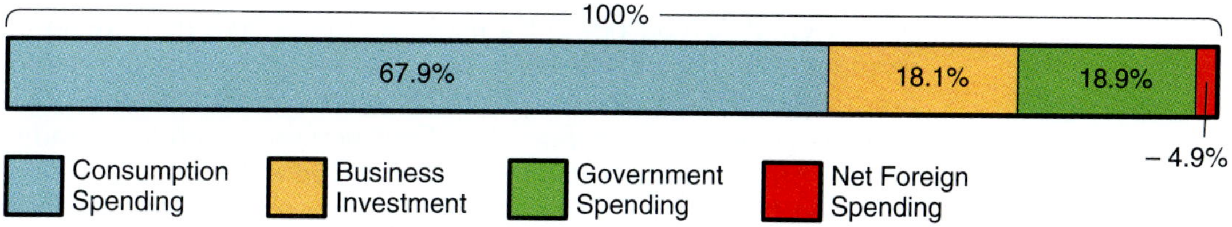

Source: *Economic Indicators*, January 1992.

[1]Net foreign spending is the difference between what foreigners buy from us and what we buy from them.

The 18.9 percent on this graph that shows government spending does not include all money the government controlled. Government transfer payments made to individuals for programs such as Social Security and welfare are included in "Consumption Spending."

The Income Approach

We can also calculate the GDP by counting all of the income earned in producing the GDP. As you might guess, this is called the **income** approach. The idea behind this method is that if income depends on the value of production, then it is possible to measure the value of production by measuring income. When Alison's father earned the money he gave her, this income became part of the measurement of GDP through the income approach.

The income approach is a relatively easy method of measuring GDP because most income is reported to the Internal Revenue Service. These values include wages, profits, rent, interest, some taxes, and the cost of wearing out capital (machinery). A problem with this method is the underground economy, which will be discussed later in this section.

Problems in Computing GDP

Example. Discuss added value. A firm that buys $5 worth of resources to produce a good it sells for $8 adds $3 to the value of the GDP. The other $5 was produced by the firms that sold the firm the resources for its product.

There are a number of problems that must be overcome to measure GDP. In several areas care must be taken to avoid including production that does not actually exist. **Double counting** is one danger. If a firm buys a wheel for $10, polishes it, and sells it for $12, it only added $2 worth of value. The government must be careful not to count the firm's contribution to GDP as $12. To do so would be double counting. Some other firm produced the wheel's first $10 of value. This value would already have been counted as part of GDP.

Spending for products produced in some other year is not part of GDP. If you bought a used car for $4,000, that spending would not be a part of GDP. The car was not part of this year's production. The same can be said for buying corporate stock that used to belong to someone else. One person's money is traded for the other person's stock. Although the value of the service provided by the broker is new production and part of GDP, the value of the stock itself is not.

Explain. Fees paid to a broker are counted as part of GDP because it is payment for a service provided in the current year.

Some areas of production are not included in the GDP. Only work that is paid is counted. When you paint your own house, no value is added to GDP. If you paint your neighbor's house for

$800 and report the payment to the government, it is counted as part of GDP. In both cases a house is painted, but the value of only one would be added to GDP. Homemakers create value every day, but it isn't figured into the GDP since they are not paid a wage.

The Underground Economy

One of the greatest problems in accurately measuring GDP is the **underground economy.** Many people work, produce value and are paid, but do not report their income to the government. This is often against the law, but it still happens. For example, if you pay your neighbor $100 to clean your garage but he does not report this income to the government, reported GDP will be less than real GDP. Underground production causes reported GDP to be smaller than actual production really is.

Note. Estimates of the value of the illegal drug trade ran as high as $50 billion in 1991.

Some production goes unreported because it is against the law. Some people earn income from selling drugs or from gambling. Although our government attempts to prevent such transactions, there is clearly demand and supply for these goods and

The income of illegal aliens is not likely to be reported to the government, and so is not included in the GDP.

Stress. The growth of government spending as a part of GDP does not include transfers. If transfers were included, the importance of the government share of GDP would be even greater.

services. Such production is not included in the GDP, but it is part of our economic system.

Why Measure GDP?

Some people believe that economists are inclined to measure nearly everything measurable. Measuring GDP, however, has practical value to the United States and the American people. By measuring the changes in the growth of GDP annually, economists are able to track the health of the economy. When the GDP fails to grow significantly, it is a sign that there may be underlying problems in the nation's economy. Then government officials may offer suggestions and take steps to influence the direction of the economy. If the overall GDP grows substantially, it indicates that economic policies do not need fixing. However, the relationship between GDP and our quality of life is not always clear or something we all agree on. In the next section, you will learn about methods of evaluating the meaning of the GDP.

Self-Check
1. The Gross Domestic Product is the retail market value of everything produced in the nation in a year.
2. The two methods used to measure GDP are the expenditure and the income approach.
3. The underground economy represents production that is not reported to the government.

Applying What You Have Learned
See Lesson Plans for Chapter 8, Section A, page T82.

Self-Check

1. What is the meaning of the term *Gross Domestic Product?*
2. What are the two methods used to measure the value of GDP?
3. How does the underground economy cause our measurements of GDP to be inaccurate?

Applying What You Have Learned

1. Identify each of the following as something that would or would not be considered in measuring the GDP.
   a. The narrator of the story above collects his week's pay.
   b. Alison buys a new top at the mall.
   c. John buys Frank's used car.
   d. John has aluminum siding put on the house.
   e. Sara deposits $110 in her bank account.
   f. Roger cuts his grass.
   g. Your teacher gives you a test.
   h. Your mother pays you $3 to clean your room.
2. It has been said that the "American Dream" is to see your children have a better life than you have. The idea of a better life for most people means having more things. List four things you would like to have in your life that your parents didn't have. Explain why each is important to you.

Section B What GDP Really Means

This section will discuss the difference between *real* and *nominal* values and the relationship of GDP per person to the quality of life.

Personal Narrative

If We're So Rich, Why Aren't We Happy?

When my father got a job as a draftsman in 1978, he earned $12,800 a year. He tells me that he was really happy at the time. The pay was enough to buy a house and a new car the next year. He couldn't pay cash, but he was able to borrow the money he needed. He got a mortgage for only 8 percent. Now he's a project leader and earns $35,500. He complains that he's poor all of the time.

Discuss. When would your students borrow money to buy something they otherwise could not afford? Under what circumstances should a person borrow?

Of course my father's life has changed. He got married and had three children. The old house was too small, so we moved into a four bedroom split-level in 1988. The new mortgage was at 12 percent. My brothers eat as much as an army (according to my mother). We're still paying on our minivan, which is three years old. Next week my brother has to go to the orthodontist for braces.

Note. You may want to discuss the possibility of refinancing this family's mortgage at a lower rate of interest.

My father's job has changed, too. There used to be nearly 30 people in his department. Now there are only twelve. The difference is that they have started to use computer-aided drafting. The computer does most of the work in less than half the time. They just don't need as many people. My father was smart. He went to school to learn how to use the new technology. That's why he's in charge of the department.

My parents are worried about how they're going to pay for my brothers' and my education. They can't save very much with all their payments. My mom says she'll try to find work in a year or two when my youngest brother is older. That isn't going to do me much good. In two years I'll already be in college.

Discuss. Material possessions are only one measure of standard of living. What other measures do your students regard as important?

Note. There is a discussion of poverty in Section C of Chapter 10.

For all of our problems, I know we are better off than many other people. We have a nice place to live, enough food, and my father's job is secure. Many of my friends at school are much worse off. Some of them have parents who have lost jobs. Others come from homes where there's only one parent to do everything. Some students wear nothing but hand-me-downs and secondhand clothes.

We know a lady named Mrs. Armstrong, who has a room above a fish store. She's a widow and has to live off her husband's Social Security. After she pays her rent and utilities, there's almost nothing left. When she was younger she used to do mending. That's how we got to know her. Now she doesn't see very well, so she has no extra income. Once a day a local church group brings her a warm meal. Her life must really be depressing.

On the other hand, my cousin Tara lives in a suburb about ten miles out of town. Her father is an "information systems director" for a local bank. He does something with computers that earns him a big salary. They just got back from Hawaii and are talking about an in-ground pool. They never worry about money.

Cutting GDP Down to Size

The American GDP in 1991 was more than twice as large as it was in 1975. For a number of reasons, this does not mean our standard of living was two times better. Like the family in the story, many Americans do not have as many things as they want, or even as many as they had in the past. Part of this may be the result of people wanting more goods and services than we can produce. It may also be the result of changes in who receives the products we produce. The distribution of income is related to this problem and will be discussed in Section C of Chapter 10.

Adjustments to the GDP

GDP is often reported in **nominal values.** This means it has not been adjusted for inflation. Between 1980 and 1991, consumer prices increased 50 percent. Therefore, a large part of the growth in GDP was the result of higher prices and not increased production.

The value of GDP can be adjusted for inflation. GDP increased 107 percent between 1980 and 1991. However, when inflation is taken into account, the **real value** growth in GDP was only about 50 percent.

This 50 percent can be adjusted again for population growth. Between 1980 and 1991, U.S. population increased by 12 percent. There may have been more production in 1991, but it had to be divided among more people. The real increase in GDP *per person* in these years was about 18 percent.

Discuss. Note the importance of military spending to our future. Many people base their opinions of military expenditures on emotions as much as on facts. Can your students give examples of normative and positive statements concerning the military?

GDP and the Quality of Life

Even this figure does not tell you how people lived. We need to know what kind of products were manufactured and who got them. For example, unadjusted military spending increased by over 130 percent between 1980 and 1991. This exceeded the rate of inflation in those years. Therefore, part of any real increase in production between 1980 and 1991 went to military spending.

Another important measure of the economy is the average wage workers earn per hour, adjusted for inflation. This is the **real hourly wage rate.** Between 1980 and 1991, this rate declined about 2 percent. This means that on an average, people had to work more hours in 1991 to buy the same products they could buy in 1980.

There is also a question of the type of additional consumer goods that were produced. Production of housing totaled over 12 million units between 1980 and 1990, but government-supported low-income housing increased by only 127,000 units in the same

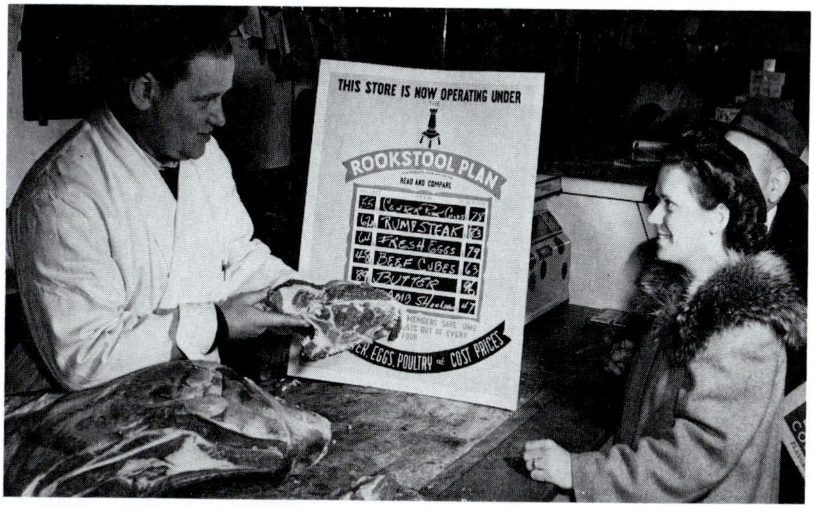

An apparent increase in the GDP can be caused by an increase in prices. To obtain the real value growth in the GDP, the figures must be adjusted for inflation.

years. Most of the new housing units that were built were for the rich and middle class. It is possible that poor people were able to move into the units that were vacated by higher income people. However, few lower income people were able to move into new housing units.

Another example is that there were billions of dollars worth of video games produced in these years. Some people probably believe that these games added little to our quality of life.

Income is not evenly distributed. Additional production is concentrated in the type of products that are sold to people who have the greatest income. People do not share equally in the benefits of increased productivity. The issue of whether or not our distribution of income and GDP is fair is something we are not all likely to agree on. It is certain that as you grow older you will be asked to help make decisions concerning government programs that redistribute income.

Self-Check
1. Real values have been adjusted for inflation, nominal values have not.
2. Real GDP *per person* includes adjustments for changes in the population.
3. The real GDP per person does not tell us the type of products that were produced, and this can have an effect on people's living conditions.

Applying What You Have Learned
See Lesson Plans for Chapter 8, Section B, page T83.

Self-Check

1. What is the difference between nominal and real values?
2. Why is there a difference between the rate of growth in real GDP and the rate of growth in real GDP *per person?*
3. What is one reason why we can't be sure people live better when the real GDP per person goes up?

Applying What You Have Learned

1. When additional products are made, how much do they add to the quality of life? Not everyone agrees on the value of different types of products. Below you will find a list of percentage increases in production or shipments of specific items in the United States between 1985 and 1989. Explain how much each added to the quality of life *in your opinion.*
   a. Color television shipments grew from 16,894,000 to 20,955,000 sets.
   b. Car telephone production grew from less than 10,000 to more than 1,081,000.
   c. Personal computer shipments grew from 4,025,000 to 4,737,000.
   d. Air conditioner shipments grew from 2.9 million to 4.9 million.
2. Make a list of four things that add to your quality of life but which do not involve money or goods and services. Explain why each is important to you.

Section C Life Within the Business Cycle

This section will introduce the ideas of the *business cycle* and of *leading indicators,* and will introduce the terms *durable goods* and *nondurable goods.*

Personal Narrative

I've Got a Job!

As long as I can remember, my parents have worried about my father getting laid off. It seemed to happen about every three or four years. He's employed by a firm that makes parts for semi-trucks. Whenever trucks sold, he worked long hours and we lived well. When trucks didn't sell, he got laid off. Then we did without many things. I understood why my father's job depended on how well trucks sold. What I didn't understand was why they sold well some years and poorly at other times.

Discuss. Assign students to ask their parents how they were affected by the recession of 1991–92. Have them report their findings and discuss them in class.

I learned some of the answers in school. Sometimes there are recessions in the economy. This is a period of time when sales are low, businesses make less profit, and there is unemployment. There are different theories about what causes recessions, but their result is clear. They make life much harder for many people.

When there is a recession, people and businesses are afraid to take risks. They would rather not buy things on credit. The possibility of not being able to make payments worries many people. Products that are expensive usually have to be bought on credit. As a result of this, fewer expensive items are sold in a recession. Inexpensive items are not affected as much because businesses and people do not have to borrow to buy them.

Semi-trucks are very expensive. When there is a recession, their sales go down and my father is laid off. I decided to get a job where this wouldn't happen. I figured that people would have to eat no matter what, so I decided to go into the food business. I went to school to learn retail management, and now I'm the assistant manager of a large grocery store. If there is a recession, I should still have my job.

Phases of the Business Cycle

Economists have studied changing trends in production for hundreds of years. They have identified a **business cycle** which they define as the repeated rise and fall of economic activity over time. The business cycle has been divided into four sections as shown in Figure 8–2: (1) *expansion,* (2) *peak,* (3) *contraction* and (4) *trough.* Recessions occur in the lower part of this cycle.

Not all sections of the economy are equally affected by the business cycle. Manufacturers of *durable goods* are hurt more by recessions than producers of consumer or *nondurable goods.* A **durable good** is a product that has an expected life span of several years and tends to be relatively expensive. When people or businesses are concerned about their economic future, they often put off the purchase of such items, in some cases by repairing old ones. Examples of durable goods include cars, refrigerators and furniture. The father in the story above helped to produce trucks, which are durable goods. When the economy went into a contraction, truck sales fell and he was laid off.

Figure 8–2 *Phases of the Business Cycle*

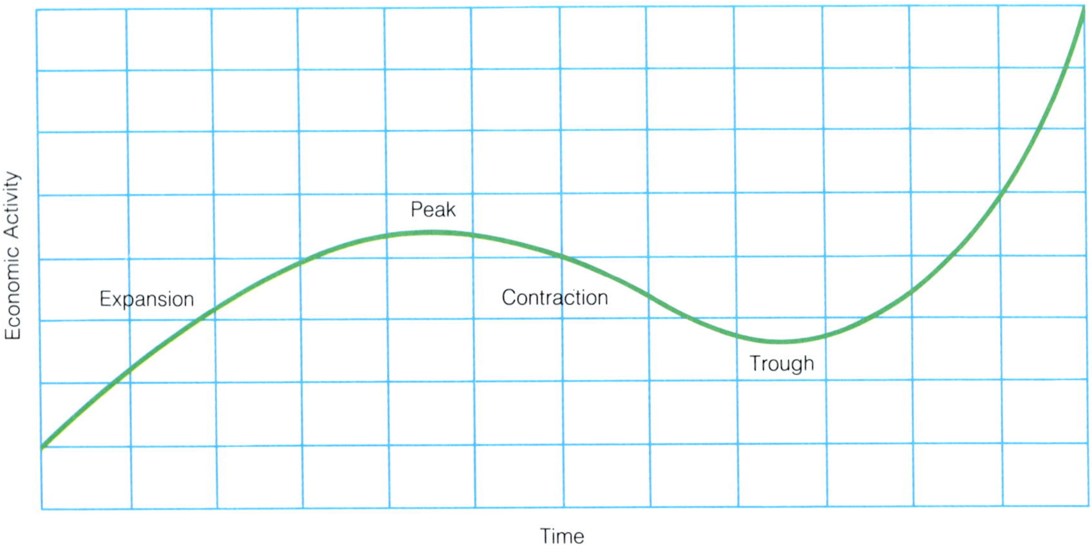

Nondurable goods—such as food or clothing—are intended for immediate use and are frequently less expensive. They are often purchased for cash instead of on credit. Sales of nondurable goods do not go down as much in a recession.

Forecasting

It is clear that businesses would benefit from knowing when a business cycle is going to come. This would help them plan their production and employment levels. The Department of Commerce reports what are called **leading indicators.** These are economic factors that usually change before the rest of the economy changes. These leading indicators include building permits, changes in inventories, and new orders for consumer goods. If inventories are falling, businesses will have to reorder new goods to replace those that have been sold. This would be a sign that the economy should improve. These and other indicators give us an idea of how the economy will be doing in the future.

Note. In 1991 there was a round of trade negotiations between the United States and Japan. Such negotiations can have important effects on the U.S. economy. There is no way leading indicators could predict these results.

There is no guarantee that leading indicators are always correct. They could not predict Iraq's invasion of Kuwait, which helped cause a recession in 1990. Still, they are more often right than wrong.

Businesses pay close attention to leading indicators. When they are down, businesses are less likely to invest or hire new workers. If they are up, businesses spend more. Later in this text you will see that government leaders also study the business cycle in their attempts to form good economic policies.

Figure 8–3 shows percentage changes in leading indicators and in the real GDP over ten years. By studying the indicators it is possible to estimate what will soon happen to production in the economy.

Building permits, which show how much new construction is about to take place, are one of the leading indicators.

Figure 8–3 *Changes in Leading Indicators and Real GDP, 1979-1989*

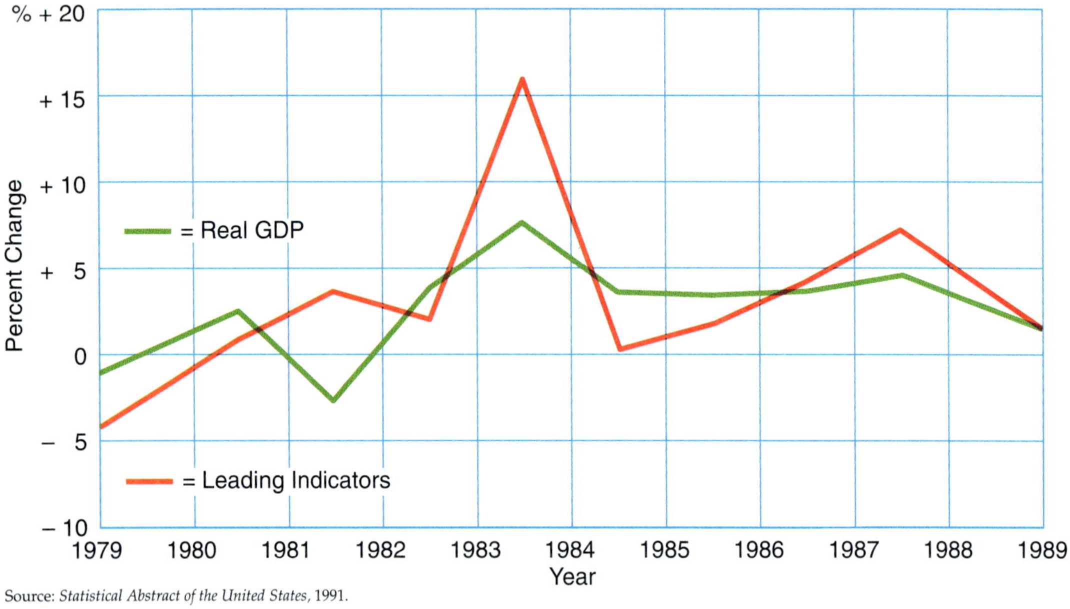

Source: *Statistical Abstract of the United States,* 1991.

Self-Check
1. The four phases of the business cycle are expansion, peak, contraction, and trough.
2. A *durable* good has a life span of several years and is likely to be expensive. *Nondurable* goods—such as food and clothing—are intended for immediate use and are likely to be less expensive.
3. Leading indicators help businesses decide whether to make additional investments.

Applying What You Have Learned
See Lesson Plans for Chapter 8, Section C, page T85.

Self-Check

1. What are the four phases of the business cycle?
2. What is the difference between durable and nondurable goods?
3. Why are businesses interested in leading indicators?

Applying What You Have Learned

In the Personal Narrative of this section, you read of the effects of a recession on a person employed in the manufacture of durable goods. Identify each of the following products as being a *durable* or *nondurable* good.

Item

a. refrigerator
b. shampoo
c. gasoline
d. shoes
e. television set
f. radio batteries

CURRENT ECONOMIC ISSUES

What Should Be Done About the Underground Economy?

The government loses billions of tax dollars each year from people who fail to report and pay taxes on all or part of their earnings. When some people cheat on their taxes, the rest of us pay more than our fair share.

What should be done about people who don't report their income? One suggestion has been to tax spending instead of earning. Then it would be harder to avoid taxes. Many European countries use *value-added* taxes to tax spending indirectly.

Value-added taxes require manufacturers to pay a tax on the products they produce. For example, if a firm made boats that sold for $1,000 from materials which cost $400, it would pay a tax on the $600 of value that it added.

Prices would be much higher if we had value-added taxes, because the tax would become part of the price of the products we buy. But with value-added taxes, people who do not report income would still pay taxes when they spend their earnings.

There could be some problems with a value-added tax. These taxes tend to be regressive because poor people have to spend a larger part of their income than rich people. Income that was saved or invested would not be taxed. Value-added taxes would be costly for firms due to extra bookkeeping expenses. Value-added taxes may discourage people from spending because of higher prices, reducing both sales and jobs.

How would a value-added tax affect you or your friends? What would be good or bad about the plan?

Arguments in Favor of the Plan

1. It would make it harder to avoid paying taxes.
2. It would reduce the tax burden on those of us who do not cheat.
3. It would encourage people to save and invest, which could cause growth in the economy.

Arguments Against the Plan

1. It could put more of a tax burden on the poor.
2. It would add to the cost of running a business.
3. It could discourage people from spending, which might reduce employment.

What Do You Think?

Consider the arguments for and against the plan. Do you believe the costs or benefits of the plan would be greater? What is the basis for your point of view? What other plans might discourage people from cheating on their taxes?

Chapter 8 Review

What Have You Learned?

In this chapter you've learned the following important principles of economics:

- The government uses different ways to measure the value of *Gross Domestic Product,* which include the *expenditures approach* and the *income approach.*
- The government's measurement of Gross Domestic Product is difficult because it must avoid *double counting* and take the *underground economy* into consideration.
- There is no general agreement over the relationship between the size of our Gross Domestic Product and the quality of life in the United States. Inflation, population growth, the type of products being made, and their distribution all affect this relationship.
- Our Gross Domestic Product is used as one measure of the *business cycle.* In the past, our economic system has experienced both *recessions* and periods of *expansion.* The business cycle does not affect all businesses equally. In general, businesses that produce *durable goods,* which are relatively expensive, will be affected more by a recession than businesses that produce less expensive *nondurable goods.*
- The government helps us to predict future economic trends by preparing *leading indicators.* These are factors that tend to change before the rest of the economic system changes. Although it is impossible to be accurate all of the time, generally the leading indicators have provided us with a reasonable picture of what will happen to the economic system in the near future.

Words and Terms

Gross Domestic Product (p. 216)
expenditure approach (p. 217)
income approach (p. 218)
double counting (p. 218)
underground economy (p. 219)
nominal values (p. 222)
real values (p. 222)
real hourly wage rate (p. 223)
business cycle (p. 225)
durable goods (p. 226)
nondurable goods (p. 226)
leading indicators (p. 226)

See Chapter 8 Review Answers, page T31.

Building Your Vocabulary

On a separate piece of paper, write the vocabulary word or term that best completes each of the following statements.

1. Economic activities that produce value that is not reported to the government are part of the ______.
2. Prices that are not adjusted for inflation are ______.
3. Prices that are adjusted for inflation are ______.
4. An economic factor that tends to change before the rest of the economic system changes could be used as a ______.
5. The method of measuring GDP that involves counting the value of all earnings is called the ______.
6. Fluctuations up and down in overall economic activity is called the ______.
7. The method of measuring GDP that involves counting the value of all expenditures is called the ______.
8. The retail market value of all goods and services produced in a year is called the ______.
9. Products that last for several years and tend to be expensive are called ______.
10. Products that are intended for immediate use and tend to be relatively inexpensive are called ______.
11. The average wage that workers earn per hour, adjusted for inflation is the ______.
12. If the full value of a tire is added to GDP by a firm that only markets the tire, they would have made the mistake of ______.

Understanding Economics

1. Explain why the purchase of a new machine for a factory would be included as a part of GDP while the purchase of a used car would not.
2. List and describe the four types of spending that make up the expenditure approach to measuring the value of GDP.
3. List and describe the types of earning mentioned in this chapter that make up the income approach to measuring the value of GDP.
4. Describe an example of how double counting might happen *other than the one which is described in this chapter.*
5. Explain why the underground economy represents a problem in measuring the GDP accurately.
6. Suppose you were told that you would earn $60,000 a year in 2008. Explain why this information would tell you little about the standard of living you might enjoy. What other information would you need to have before you could evaluate how well you could live in 2008?
7. Explain why we can't be sure that everyone will be better off if real GDP goes up 10 percent over the next five years.
8. Explain why durable goods industries are affected more by recessions than nondurable goods industries.
9. Explain why a firm might not choose to invest more money or hire more workers if the leading indicators were down for five months in a row.

Chapter 8 Review

Thinking Critically About Economics

1. Explain three different reasons why the GDP is not a perfect measure of the quality of life in the United States.
2. In 1991 the minimum wage was $4.25 an hour. In 1935 it was $0.25 per hour. Describe the information you would need to have before you could compare the minimum wages in these two years with accuracy.
3. Describe three different transactions that would be part of the underground economy.
4. In 1990 Congress approved legislation that provided $2.4 billion to fund an increased war on drugs in this country. Explain how such a use of GDP adds to the quality of our life.
5. In 1991–92 there was a recession in the United States. In this time the sales of new cars fell by 11.5 percent, while the sales of dairy products increased by 2.3 percent. Explain why this happened.
6. If business inventories are falling, the average hours worked per week is going up, and there is an increase in the number of new building permits, we would expect the economy to be in an expansion phase of the business cycle. Explain why each of these indicators would show that the economy would grow in the near future.

Consumer Skills Projects

1. Go to your library and ask the librarian to help you find a copy of a recent *Statistical Abstract of the United States* or a *World Almanac*. Look up the most recent GDP you can, and the GDP for ten years earlier (for example, 1992 and 1982). Draw one graph for each year that shows what part of the GDP went to these areas: (a) Personal Consumption Expenditures, (b) Gross Private Domestic Investment, (c) Net Export of Goods and Services, and (d) Government Purchase of Goods and Services. List any changes that have occurred in the distribution of GDP. Compare your results with the information in Figure 8–1.
2. Ask your parents or guardians how much they earned at their first jobs, what they did, when this was, and how old they were at the time. Many of you probably already have a job. Compare the wages paid for starting jobs now with the ones which your parents earned. Who was able to buy more with their income? Looking up the rate of inflation in a *Statistical Abstract of the United States* or *World Almanac* should help you complete this project.
3. You may remember the recession of 1991–92. If you do, you can answer these questions yourself. If you do not, ask your parents or other older relatives to answer them for you.
   a. Did anyone in your household lose or change their job in the recession?
   b. Was there anything that your family had to do without because of the recession? If so, what?
   c. Who did the members of your family feel was responsible for the recession? Why did they feel this way?
   d. When the recession was largely over, did your family live the same way they had before it began?

   When you have completed this, compare your answers with those of other students. What conclusions can your class draw from these results?

Thinking Critically About Economics
(1) cause and effect; (2) identifying the problem; (3) classification; (4) recognizing values; (5) cause and effect; (6) predicting consequences.

Developing Your Economic Skills

Using Dollar Values and Percentage Values in Graphs

Skill: This lesson will demonstrate that change measured in dollar amounts often does not provide the same meaning as change expressed as a percentage. To complete this lesson, follow these steps:

1. Study two graphs. One will show numeric change while the other will show percentage change.
2. Draw conclusions from each graph and compare these conclusions.
3. Consider how different conclusions can be reached from the same basic data.

Application: Do we save enough?

The part of Gross Domestic Product people have after they pay their taxes is called Disposable Personal Income (DPI). People may either spend or save this money. In recent years the part of DPI that people save has changed significantly. The bar graphs below demonstrate the change in savings.

The first graph shows how much Americans saved in each year. The amount of savings is listed on the vertical axis and the years appear on the horizontal axis. This graph shows you that Americans saved almost $80 billion more in 1990 than they did in 1970. You might conclude that we save more than we used to. In a way you would be right, because a larger number of dollars were saved. But did Americans save as large a part of their disposable income? The second graph answers this question.

The second graph lists the *percentage* of disposable income Americans saved in each year. Although both graphs are based on the same data, conclusions drawn from the second graph are likely to be quite different from those of the first. This graph shows we saved a smaller part of what we earned in 1990 than in 1970.

Which graph do you believe gives a more accurate picture of what has happened? Why is it easier to evaluate change that is expressed as a percentage?

Practice: Find five advertised items in a newspaper that give regular and sale prices for each. Prepare charts that compare percentages saved with dollars saved on each item.

Amount of Personal Savings, 1970-1990
(in billions of dollars)

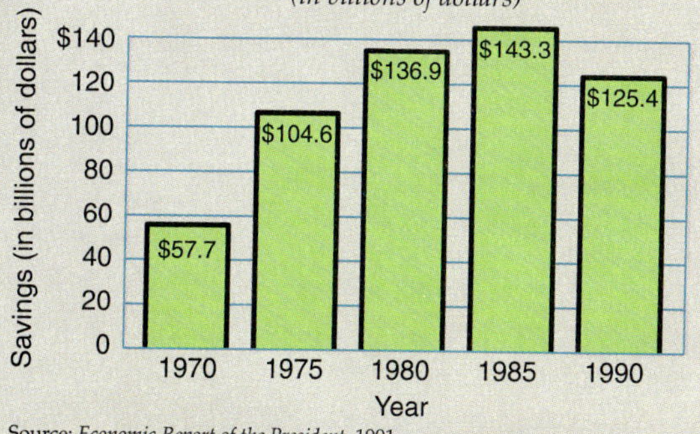

Source: *Economic Report of the President*, 1991.

Percentage of Disposable Income Saved, 1970-1990

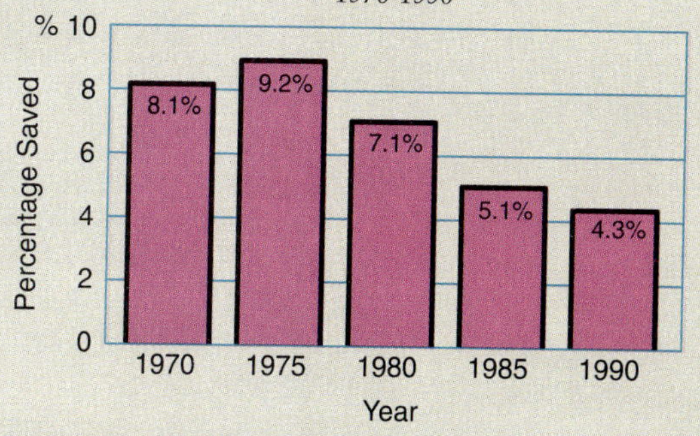

CHAPTER 9

Government's Role in the Economy

Objectives

In the sections of this chapter, you will learn:

A

why the government provides *public goods and services,* methods of correcting for *negative externalities,* and a mechanism for *redistribution of income;*

B

how taxes are selected according to basic *principles of taxation* and can be either *progressive, regressive,* or *proportional;*

C

how the government decides how to spend revenue; and

D

how government borrowing results in the *national debt.*

Introduction

If you don't own a car now, there is a good chance that you will in the next few years. Imagine what it would be like to own a car if there were no roads to drive on. You could not possibly afford to build your own roads. If the government did not build roads, your car would do you little good.

There are many goods and services people would not be able to afford if they were not provided by the government. These products are called *public goods.* Public goods and services include roads, schools, police and fire protection, and our national defense.

In this chapter you will learn about the differences between private goods and public goods. You will study the trade-offs that are made when we decide how much personal income to give up to support the production of public goods. You will discover that there is often disagreement over the kind and quantity of public goods that should be supplied by the government.

Public goods and services can only be provided if resources are allocated to them. This means there must be a way for the government to raise money to pay for these goods and services. In this chapter you will study how the government taxes and how it spends money.

Values. Government property belongs to everyone and is paid for through taxes. Do students see vandalism of school property as against their interests?

Government spending has a major impact on our lives. About one out of every three dollars spent each year passes through the government. What the government does with money is very important to the rest of the economy.

Discuss. Do your students feel resentment for the debt they will inherit from earlier generations? In 1992 the national debt was almost $16,000 for every person in the country.

The final section of this chapter deals with government borrowing. By 1992 the federal debt had grown to almost four trillion dollars. This was almost $16,000 for every man, woman, and child in the country. You will study the impact of this debt on our lives and evaluate its importance to your future.

There are many goods and services that people would not be able to afford if they were not furnished by the government. Goods and services that are provided to the people by government on an equal basis are called public goods and services.

Section A Public Goods and Services

This section will introduce the terms *public goods and services, private goods, principle of exclusion,* and *externality*. It will also describe our government's *redistribution of income.*

Personal Narrative

I Took a Bus to School This Morning

When I left for school this morning, my parents were arguing about taxes again. I could still hear my father when I got on the bus. It was a relief to be able to talk to my friends. The trip was slow and bumpy because the road was all torn up from construction. They are putting in sewers to the new waste treatment plant. At the corner of Main and Third the light was out, so a policeman directed traffic while some other men fixed it. We got to school late, but I didn't care. We were going on a field trip to traffic court that morning anyhow.

Every year the government classes have to go and see people get fined for speeding and stuff. We only stayed an hour. It was kind of interesting to hear all those stories about why they shouldn't have to pay their fines. We got back to school in time for lunch.

I ate with my best friend Mark. He gets his lunch free because his father is disabled and can't work. We don't talk about it much. He was all excited because his hockey team is going to play in the new municipal arena this year.

In sixth period a fire engine went roaring past the school. We all raced to the window to look. Actually we didn't care about the fire, it was just an excuse to stop doing our English assignment. Miss Gregg shouted at us. She told us to get back to work, but we managed to kill five minutes.

Our assignment was to write an essay about what our parents do for a living. My father is a civilian employee at the Air Force base outside of town. He works on jet engines. He used to be in the service, but he retired after 20 years. Now he gets a pension and earns a salary too. I don't know why he worries about taxes so much. He has plenty of money. I think the real problem is that he wants to buy a big expensive fishing boat. Now he puts our canoe in at the state park. If he gets a big boat, he'll have to rent a slip at the lake.

I wonder if they'll start arguing about taxes again when my father gets home.

The Need For Public Goods and Services

Discuss. What services can/should people provide for themselves? In some locations garbage is collected privately and in some the government provides this service. Garbage collection can be done privately, but would individual people be able to dispose of sewage properly in a major city?

Goods and services provided to the people by government on an equal basis are called **public goods and services.** Many of the events in the story above involved public goods and services.

When the American economy was starting to grow two hundred years ago, most people were farmers. They didn't need many things that they could not buy or make for themselves. However, as businesses grew, people often found they needed many things they could not afford. The need for inexpensive transportation is a good example of this. Farmers and businesses wanted canals and ports, but did not have the money to build them. The government recognized the need and provided these things as public goods.

In the early days of our nation's history, people could buy or make for themselves most of the things they needed. But as businesses and cities grew, many things were needed—for example, transportation systems—that could not be provided by individuals alone.

At one point early in our history, many families educated their own children. However, as specialization increased, so did the need for public schools, so that all children could get an education and contribute to society. Without public schools only the children of the rich could become educated. Such a situation would make it harder for many people to contribute as much as they could to production.

Explain. Public goods are not always free. Toll roads are public goods, but we must pay to use them. To be a public good or service, the thing must be provided by the government and available to all people on an equal (not necessarily free) basis.

The need for public goods and services has grown in many areas. The invention of the automobile led to the construction of the interstate highway system. In the past hundred years, many state and national parks have been established. Modern medicine has become so expensive that many people could not afford medical care unless the government helped them pay for it.

As production in the United States has become more specialized, it has become difficult for individuals to do many things for themselves. As a result, it has become necessary for the government to supply more goods and services. It is likely that this trend will continue into the future.

Characteristics of Public and Private Goods

Explain. Where there are public goods, there is always a problem concerning who should pay for them. Some people are likely to feel that they pay too much and that others pay too little.

Citizens can use most public goods on an equal basis. Even our military protects us equally whether we are rich or poor. Up to some point most public goods can be used by more people without additional cost to the government. A park will cost no more to have 100 people enjoy it than it would cost for 50. Public goods may not be free, but they are not subject to the **principle of exclusion.** When goods are not subject to the principle of exclusion, it means that no one can say, "It's mine, you can't use it." **Private goods,** on the other hand, are owned by individuals and *are* subject to the principle of exclusion. Owners of private goods have the right to prevent other people from using them.

Correcting for Externalities

It is possible for resources to be allocated improperly in a competitive economic system. When this happens, the government can take action to correct the problem. For example, businesses that are run to earn a profit can harm the environment. A factory may find it less expensive to dump wastes in a river than to provide proper disposal. Such an action would hurt people who live downstream of the factory. It would be a wasteful use of some of our resources.

Improper disposal of hazardous wastes is an example of a negative externality—in which people who neither use nor produce the product are hurt in some way by it.

Explain. Positive externalities are possible, although they are not common. A person who lives next to a theater may enjoy music each evening and derive a benefit (positive externality) not paid for.

Note. In theory, total costs to society do not change when the government corrects a negative externality. The costs are taken from the third party and assigned to the producer and/or consumer of the product.

This kind of a situation is called a **negative externality** by economists. It happens when someone who was neither the producer nor the consumer of a product pays a cost associated with the product. The people who live downstream of a polluting factory pay a cost in sickness or lost property values, even if they have nothing to do with the product itself. In recent years the government has forced many firms to reduce or eliminate their pollution of the environment. In doing so, the government is correcting a weakness in the economic system.

An example of how government can take action to protect citizens and to correct negative externalities occurred in Missouri in 1983.

Times Beach, Missouri, used to be the home of about 2,400 people. In December of 1982, the Centers for Disease Control recommended the evacuation of Times Beach because tests showed the presence of the chemical dioxin in the soil. The levels of dioxin were from 100 to 300 times the amount the government had set as the maximum safe level.

Investigations found that oil containing dioxin had been sprayed on roads in Times Beach in the early 1970s to keep down dust. The oil was purchased from a firm that had made chemicals for the U.S. government. That firm had gone out of business.

In January of 1983 the town was declared a federal disaster area. All homes were bought by the government at a total cost of $33,500,000. Local residents were given aid in relocating to other communities. 800 truckloads of debris were moved from the town and buried in a landfill.

The town of Times Beach, Missouri, was said to be contaminated with dangerous chemicals. To correct this negative externality, the federal government bought the homes and evacuated the people.

Example. A similar situation can be found involving U.S. nuclear testing. In the 1950s and 1960s, many atmospheric tests took place in Nevada. People who lived downwind of the tests were not warned of the potential danger from radiation. Many of these people filed suit against the U.S. government, alleging they became sick or that relatives died from the radiation. What do your students feel should be done in these kinds of situations?

Ten years after the evacuation scientists changed their minds. New research showed that levels of dioxin in Times Beach were not as dangerous as people had been told. The federal official who had ordered the evacuation said he should have told the Times Beach citizens, "we may be wrong."

The government decision to buy the homes in Times Beach corrected a negative externality regardless of whether anyone had been harmed. Residents had suffered at least a financial loss because the value of their homes had gone down. This loss was corrected by the government action.

Redistribution of Income

Most Americans share a set of values that are not part of the competitive market system. We agree that no one should be without basic food and shelter in this country. The government attempts to provide minimal support for Americans who are unable to support themselves. There is wide disagreement concerning how much help should be given, what form it should be in, and to which individuals it should go. However, there are few people who believe there should be no public support for the poor at all.

To meet basic needs the government provides welfare, unemployment compensation, and Social Security payments. These

Figure 9–1 *Federal Payments to Individuals, 1965–1990*

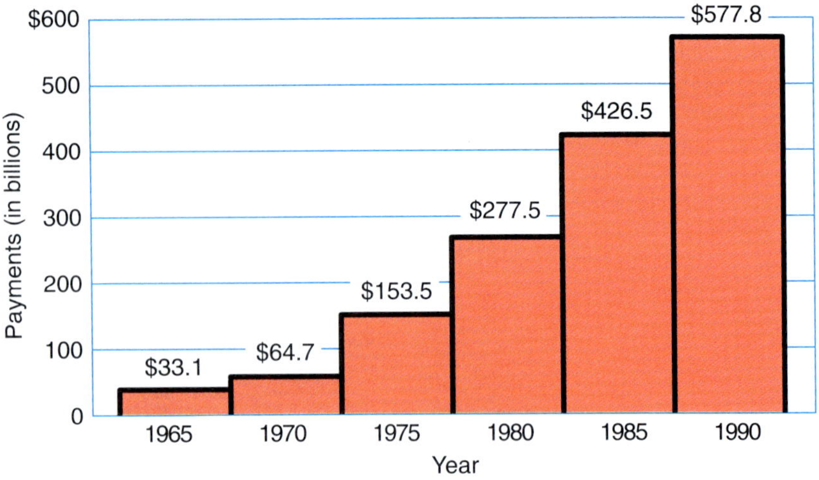

Source: *Statistical Abstract of the United States*, 1991.

are examples of the **redistribution of income** by the government. Income is taken from some people through taxes and given to others through **transfer payments** and **transfers in kind.** Transfer payments are payments in cash. Transfers in kind are nonmonetary payments. Transfers in kind include food stamps, free medical care, and low-cost housing.

Federal support for Social Security, welfare, and other similar programs is included in what is classified as Payments to Individuals in the federal budget. These payments grew more than 16 times between 1965 and 1990, as shown in Figure 9–1. This rate of growth was much larger than the increase in prices in those years. The federal government now spends the largest share of its budget on Payments to Individuals.

Explain. Most Americans benefit from government transfer payments. A person who owns a store benefits when a person on welfare or Social Security comes into his store to buy something.

Explain. These payments include all welfare, Social Security, unemployment compensation, and disability payments made by federal, state, and local governments.

Self-Check
See Lesson Plans for Chapter 9, Section A, page T89.

Applying What You Have Learned
See Lesson Plans for Chapter 9, Section A, page T89.

Self-Check

1. How is it possible to tell whether something is a public or a private good?
2. Why has the need for public goods and services increased over the past 200 years?
3. What is a negative externality?

Applying What You Have Learned

Make a list of at least six different public goods or public services that were referred to in the Personal Narrative for this section.

Section B Taxes and the Economy

This section discusses government taxes. It introduces the basic principles of taxation, and the concepts of *progressive, regressive,* and *proportional* taxes.

Personal Narrative

I Got My First Paycheck Today

Two weeks after I started work at my uncle's hamburger stand in 1992 I got my first paycheck. I had worked 28 hours at $4.25 per hour. I figured I'd get $119.00 or a few dollars less once they deducted taxes. Well, it was more than a few dollars. I had $9.10 taken out for Social Security, $5.56 for federal withholding, and another $2.94 for state income tax. That's $17.60 I didn't get. It may not seem like a lot of money, but to me it's important.

I borrowed my mother's car, took my $101.40 and went to buy a dress. I paid a 50 cent toll on the way to town. I parked in a municipal parking lot and put a quarter in the meter.

Explain. Fees are an important source of income for many state and local governments. Fees are usually regressive in nature. One common fee is the cost of registering a car. A registration fee of $50 is much more significant to a person who earns $15,000 a year than to someone who earns $50,000.

The dress I wanted was on sale, marked down from $100.00 to just $59.99, or at least that's what the tag said. I had to pay 8 percent sales tax, which brought the price to $64.79. Another $4.80 in tax down the drain.

When I got back to the car, the meter had expired and there was a $10.00 ticket on the windshield. It was not turning out to be my day. On the way home I put $5.00 worth of gas in the car to keep my mother happy. A sign on the pump said that federal and state taxes add 20 cents to the price of each gallon of gas.

At the end of the day there was just $25.11 left. I had my dress, but the government in one way or another had $33.90 of my pay. I got out my calculator and figured that this was about 28 percent of what I had earned. I know the government's important, but this just doesn't seem fair to me.

Principles of Taxation

Stress. The government cannot pay its bills by just printing money without causing inflation. The relationship between money, production, and prices is discussed in Section A of Chapter 11.

The government needs money to carry out its responsibilities. Most of the money governments spend is gathered through taxes. It is important that taxes be fair, easy to understand, easy to collect, and not harmful to the efficient operation of the economy.

Economists have identified two basic principles of taxation. Under the **benefits received principle,** taxes are paid by those who benefit from the government service supported by the tax.

Gasoline taxes are an example of the benefits-received principle. Drivers are the people who benefit from roads, and so they pay the gasoline sales tax that helps maintain roads.

Explain. Most benefits-received taxes do not pay the entire cost of the service they support. Entry fees to national parks do not cover the costs of the park system.

Explain. There is often controversy over what constitutes ability to pay. A person who earns a large income but has equally large expenses may feel unfairly taxed by the federal income tax. Those who have accumulated or inherited considerable wealth may pay little tax even though they have a large amount of money.

Example. Property taxes are often the exact opposite of a productivity principle tax. People who invest in their homes or businesses are assessed higher property taxes, while those who do not invest have relatively lower taxes.

For example, gasoline taxes are used to maintain our roads. If you drive on the roads, you buy gas and pay the tax.

The **ability-to-pay principle** is based on the belief that those who have the greatest income should pay the highest tax rates. Most income taxes are based on this principle. Individuals with more taxable income pay a higher tax rate. They should be better able to afford the tax.

In addition to these basic principles of taxation, two other characteristics of taxes are often found in our tax system. Some taxes are intended to encourage greater production and efficiency. They follow what is called the **productivity principle.** For example, in 1981 the federal government allowed firms that purchased new equipment to deduct 10 percent of the cost from their federal income tax. The purpose of this law was to encourage business investment and to improve the efficiency of production.

Another characteristic of many taxes has been called the **least-likely-to-offend principle.** Tax laws are passed by politicians who usually want to be reelected. When tax increases are needed, politicians may try to find a way to do it that voters won't notice. This can result in taxes that are not fair or efficient. Taxes on liquor and cigarettes, sometimes called "sin" taxes, may be examples of this type of law.

The Burden of Taxation

All taxes can be classified as either *progressive, regressive,* or *proportional.* The terms refer to the *percentage of income* paid by people at different income levels. In **progressive taxation,** people with *higher* incomes pay a greater percentage of their income in tax than do people with lower incomes. In **regressive taxation,** people with *lower* incomes pay a greater percentage of their income in tax than do people with higher incomes. In **proportional taxation,** all people pay the same percentage of their income in tax.

Federal, State, and Local Taxes

Federal Taxes

The **personal income tax** is the federal government's most important source of revenue. This tax is progressive, but less so than before the tax law was changed in 1990. There are now three personal income tax brackets—15 percent, 28 percent, and 31 percent. All taxpayers pay one of these three ratios. The rate paid depends largely on the amount of the taxpayer's taxable income. Those with the larger incomes pay the higher tax rates.

Social insurance taxes are the second greatest source of income for the federal government. These taxes are proportional for wage earners up to a maximum taxable income. After reaching this level they become regressive.

Corporate income taxes are paid at rates that range up to 36 percent of profit. They are the third most important source of tax revenue for the federal government.

Other sources of income for the federal government include excise taxes, tariffs, estate taxes, and borrowing.

EMPL. NO.	DATE	SALARY	TOTAL EARNINGS (GROSS PAY)	FEDERAL INCOME TAX	SOCIAL SECURITY TAX	STATE INCOME TAX
09706	9/10/92	$400.00	$400.00	$31.70	$30.60	$4.10

CHECK NO. 5139 NET PAY $333.60

EMPLOYEE ______________________

A paycheck stub shows two kinds of federal taxes—income tax and Social Security tax. Income tax is also deducted in many states.

Figure 9–2 *Sources of Federal, State, and Local Revenue, 1988*

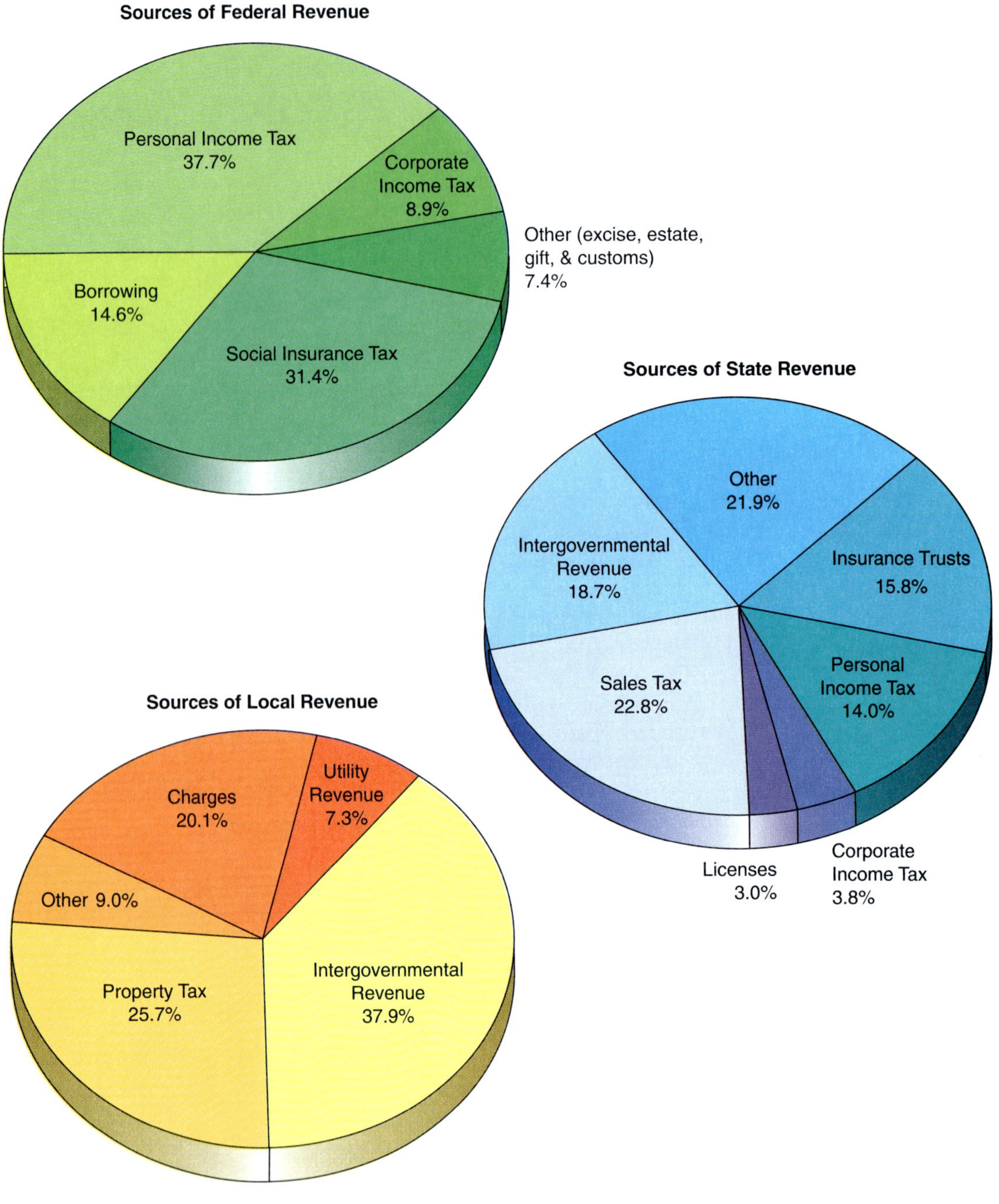

Source: *Statistical Abstract of the United States*, 1991.

State and Local Revenues

The greatest source of tax revenue for most state governments are **sales taxes.** The largest part of local tax revenue is made up of **property taxes.** Many state and a few local governments also have income taxes. These income taxes are progressive in most cases. However, most other state and local taxes are regressive.

Note. Although most state and local taxes tend to be regressive, the benefits they support flow largely to those with lower incomes.

For example, assume Joe earns $10,000 a year and pays $200 in sales tax, while his boss Steve earns $50,000 a year and pays sales taxes that total $750. Steve's sales tax is a lower percentage of his income because he spends a lower percentage on taxable items. The tax is regressive because Joe's tax is 2 percent of his income, while Steve's is only 1.5% of his.

An additional source of funds for state and local governments is **intergovernmental revenue.** Intergovernmental revenue is money paid by one level of government to another. Examples include state aid for local school districts, federal aid for roads, and payments received by local governments to help provide social services. The size and complexity of programs that make these payments can make it difficult to determine the original source of revenue for state and local governments.

The graphs in Figure 9–2 show the importance of different sources of revenue for the federal, state, and local governments.

Self-Check
See Lesson Plans for Chapter 9, Section B, page T90.

Applying What You Have Learned
See Lesson Plans for Chapter 9, Section B, page T91.

Self-Check

1. What are the two basic principles of taxation?
2. What is the difference between progressive and regressive taxes?
3. What is the most important source of tax revenue for the federal government, state governments, and local governments?

Applying What You Have Learned

Look back at the story at the beginning of this section, and find an example of a tax for each of the following principles or characteristics of taxation.

a. progressive tax
b. regressive tax
c. proportional tax
d. the benefits received principle
e. the ability-to-pay principle

Section C Government Spending

This section will discuss how the government chooses to spend money.

Personal Narrative

Explain. Remind your students of opportunity cost and how it applies to governments as well as to businesses and people.

Note. Many programs established by our government create unfunded future responsibilities. Examples include commitments to provide housing and health care to the poor on a state and local level. Unfunded pension responsibilities owed by the federal government to its civilian and military employees are of greater significance. The government requires private industry to set aside money to pay for worker pensions, but it does not do the same for its own employees. These responsibilities often make budget cuts very difficult to accomplish.

They Closed the City Swimming Pools

This has been the hottest summer in recorded history, or at least the radio announcer said so. I believe it. We've had 16 days in a row that were over 100 degrees. It hasn't rained for over three weeks. Sometimes I think I'm going to die. Some older people have. What has made it worse is the fact that the City Council couldn't afford to keep the municipal swimming pools open this summer.

There was a big debate over taxes and spending last winter when they were making up the budget. The city's expenses for various social programs had gone way up. They had to either increase taxes 28 percent or cut back on services. They ended up doing some of both. Taxes went up 21 percent and programs, including summer recreation, were cut.

I know something about this because I wrote a report for my economics class last year on how local governments spend their money. I was surprised to find how little spending they really have control over. The city government is required by the state to support both education and social programs. They have to pay interest on money they have borrowed. It could be dangerous to have less police or fire protection. When all is said and done, there is less than a third of the budget that could be cut. People wouldn't stand for all of these programs being eliminated. The city council had no choice but to raise taxes. I'm sorry the program they cut was one I would have used, but I understand why they did it.

I read in a newspaper that the government is giving away millions of dollars to foreign governments. I think it would be nice if they did the same to help local governments pay their bills.

Public Decision Making

It is important to understand that governments do not make decisions in the same way that businesses do. Governments do not exist to make a profit; their purpose is to serve the people. We have a representative form of government. Most government decisions are made by elected officials. Their purpose is often twofold. People who hold elective office generally want to do what is best for the country and for the people who elected them. Most of them also want to be reelected. One way for politicians to get reelected is to support government spending in the states or districts from which they are elected. Another way is to oppose tax increases even if they might be needed. What is good politically is not always good for the economy. It can sometimes be impossible for politicians to develop policies that are good both politically and economically.

Note. Government decision making is often slow. Economists have identified three lags in such decisions: (a) the time it takes the government to realize there is a problem; (b) the time it takes the government to decide what to do about the problem; (c) the time it takes the government decision to go into effect.

Discuss. Students often enjoy identifying government spending that they regard as wasteful. Ask them to explain why it is difficult to stop a government program once it has started. What does this have to do with vested interests?

Another problem common to government programs is that once they are begun it is often difficult to end them. When the objective of a government program is to provide money or benefits to people, it is very hard to measure its efficiency. A private business that is inefficient or wasteful will lose money and go out of business, but government programs that are inefficient and wasteful can just go on and on. Programs sometimes do not help the people they are intended to help. In those instances they may be a waste of money. What might the opportunity cost be for money spent on programs that do little to accomplish their basic purpose?

There Go My Consumer Dollars

In recent years, about one out of every five dollars of Gross Domestic Product has been spent by the federal, state, or local governments. Almost one more dollar out of five passed through the government to the people for transfer payments and transfers in kind. Government spending decisions have a great impact on what happens in our economic system.

Redistribution of Income

Federal spending can redistribute income not only from one person to another but from one part of the country to another. Federal taxes are collected primarily on the basis of income. Areas with the greatest income pay the most taxes. However, government spending can be concentrated in specific parts of the country, according to need. For example, the "War on Poverty" of the 1960s concentrated federal spending in Appalachia, a depressed area in the mountains of the central East Coast. Unfortunately, government spending can also be concentrated in the districts of members of Congress who have the most power.

Writing the Budget

The President prepares the federal budget and submits it to the House of Representatives and the Senate for their approval. Federal law requires a new budget to be passed by October 1 of each year. The federal government frequently misses this deadline, and often the budget that is finally approved by Congress bears little resemblance to the one originally submitted by the President.

The process of completing the federal budget has become more complicated since the federal **deficit** has become a major issue. In years when the government spends more than it collects in taxes, it must borrow money. The borrowed funds represent the deficit. Concerned by the rapid growth of the national debt, in 1985 the federal government passed a law to help reduce the deficit. Popularly known as Gramm-Rudman-Hollings after the Senators who designed it, the law required deep cuts in government spending if the President and Congress could not agree on a budget that met the law's spending target.

In 1990, despite amendments that set lower targets for deficit reduction, Congress and the President were unable to agree on a budget before the October 1 deadline. Although congressional leaders did meet the deadline with a tentative agreement, Congress rejected the agreement when it was put to a vote the following day. After this rejection Congress passed a series of stopgap measures to keep the government running for the next four weeks. Finally, the President and Congress reached an agreement that provided for some tax increases and spending cuts. It was supposed to reduce the budget deficit to about $100 billion in 1990-1991. The actual deficit in that year turned out to be about $270 billion.

Although a new budget was approved, the problem of how to write and approve a fair and realistic budget on time each year was not solved. The 1990 budget, for example, totally ignored the cost of the military buildup in the Persian Gulf that allowed the United Nations and the United States to wage war against Iraq. It cost about $90 billion.

The federal budget frequently contains many parts that have been called **pork barrel legislation.** Such legislation is passed to gain political support in the home district of a member of Congress, not because it is either necessary or even good for the country. It has been suggested that a large portion of money spent for the military and for government construction projects is carried out for this reason.

Figure 9–3 *Federal, State, and Local Expenditures, 1988*

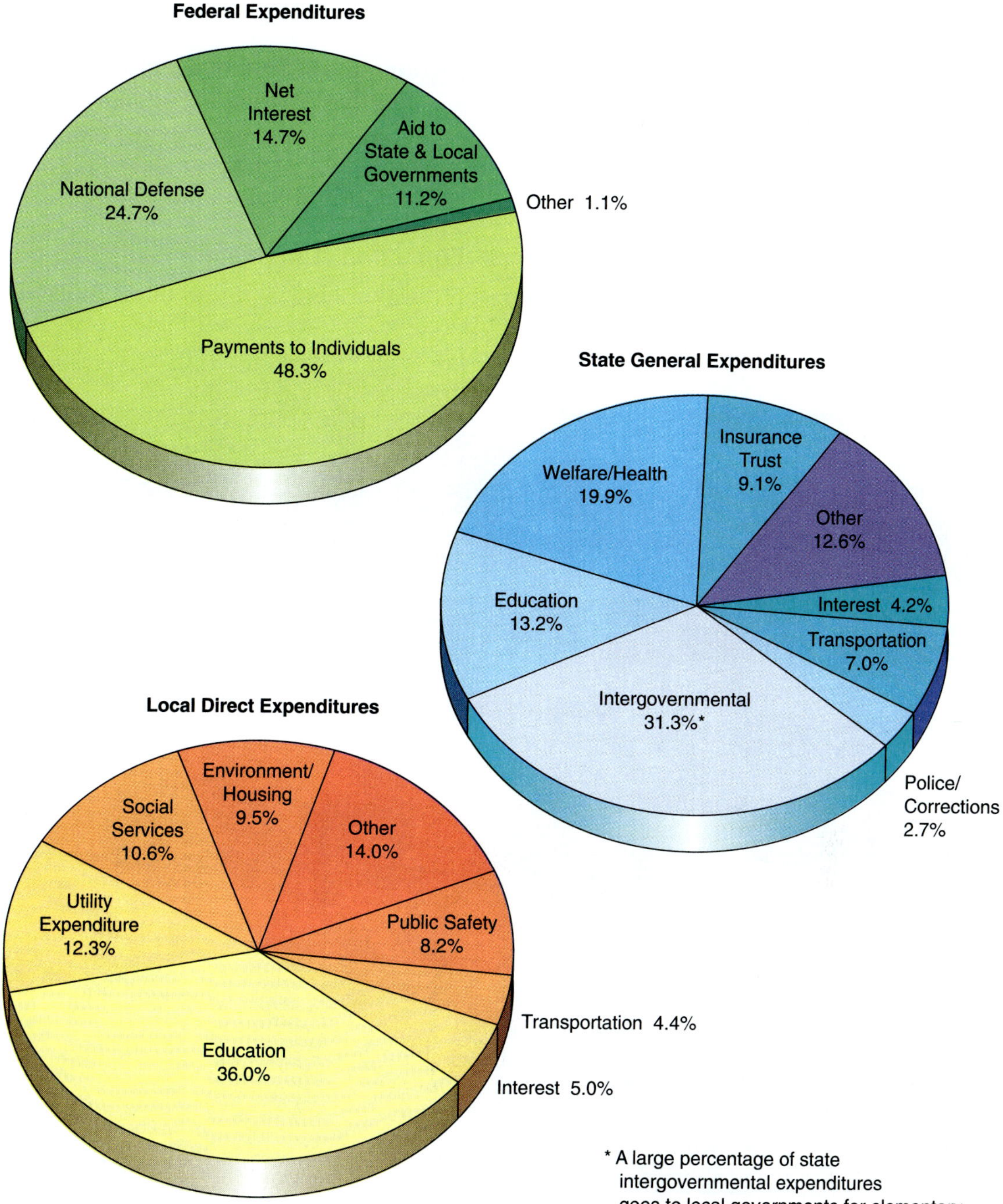

* A large percentage of state intergovernmental expenditures goes to local governments for elementary and secondary education and transportation.

Source: *Statistical Abstract of the United States*, 1991.

Self-Check
See Lesson Plans for Chapter 9, Section C, page T92.

Applying What You Have Learned
See Lesson Plans for Chapter 9, Section C, page T93.

Self-Check

1. How are public decisions made differently from business decisions?
2. Who is responsible for writing the federal budget?
3. What political body must approve the federal budget?
4. What is the most important type of spending for the federal government, for state governments, and for local governments?

Applying What You Have Learned

Examine the photograph below. Find at least three different types of government spending that are shown taking place (or that have already taken place) in the photograph.

Section D The Problem of the National Debt

This section will discuss the importance of the *national debt.*

Personal Narrative

Note. The national debt serves one purpose which many people are not aware of. The backing for most of the currency in circulation in the United States (Federal Reserve Notes) is federal government securities held by the Federal Reserve System. The law allows the Federal Reserve System to have money printed equal in value to the government securities it owns. Without a national debt, there would be no government securities to back Federal Reserve Notes. See Chapter 12 for more information on this topic.

Discuss. Many students' families have received unsolicited offers for credit. Do your students regard this as a proper thing for financial institutions to do? Are individual borrowers or our lending institutions more responsible for bankruptcies?

My Neighbor Didn't Pay His Bills

George is my neighbor. Yesterday they came and took his car away. He didn't pay his bills. George says he's going to file for bankruptcy before his creditors get everything he has. I don't understand how he could let this happen. I get nervous if I owe a library fine. We talked about his problems last week. George doesn't really think it's his fault. He blames the banks and finance companies.

George never tried to cheat anyone. About five years ago he got his first credit card, with a $500 line of credit. He used the card and paid his bills. After a while he noticed that the bank had raised his credit limit to $1,500. He thought, "Oh good, they trust me. Maybe I could use the card and buy that boat I've wanted."

George bought the boat. Soon other banks started sending him applications for their credit cards. They offered him "pre-approved" limits of one and two thousand dollars. George filled them out and sent them in. He took out credit cards from oil companies, department stores, and mail-order catalogs. At one point he had 23 different charge cards with a total credit limit of $41,000. George got to the point that he spent money with the cards without really thinking about it.

George owed everyone, at least it seemed that way. His minimum payment for all the loans came to over $800 a month. But after George paid his other bills, he only had $1,000 left a month for his loan payments and for his other living expenses. He went to a finance company and took out a "bill consolidation loan." This reduced his monthly payment a little, but the interest rate was 18 percent. It would have been seven years before he paid it all off.

Last month George's factory announced a six-week shutdown to reduce inventories. George hasn't been paid for three weeks. He missed his last two car payments and he couldn't pay this month either. The bank took his car and soon the mortgage company is going to try to take his house.

George says, "If the government can live on borrowed money, I don't understand why I can't too."

Individual consumers borrow money for personal consumption. The federal government borrows money to support programs that provide public goods and services. The total money the government has borrowed is called the national debt.

The Government's Debt

George is at least partially correct. The federal government does pay for some of its services with borrowed money. In 1992 the **national debt**—the total borrowing of the federal government—passed four trillion dollars. The importance of this debt is a subject of wide debate and disagreement among both economists and politicians.

Until recently the government borrowed almost all of this money from just four sources. It borrowed from:

Explain. Savings bonds are not the only type of security sold by the U.S. Treasury. Other types of government securities cannot be cashed in until they mature, but they can be sold to someone else. More information is provided on this subject in Chapter 12.

a. people who bought savings bonds. A savings bond is really just a loan to the federal government. When people buy bonds, they let the government use their money and in exchange they are paid interest;
b. banks and the Federal Reserve System, which buy large-denomination bonds with a specific date of maturity (you will learn more about this in Chapter 10);
c. businesses that buy the same type of bonds purchased by the Federal Reserve System and banks;
d. government trust funds that buy bonds with extra money. For example, if the Social Security System had extra money, it could purchase and hold federal bonds until it needed the funds it had loaned.

Note. In the past, payments of interest on the national debt did redistribute income from those who pay taxes to those who own government securities. However, the money stayed within the American economic system. As more of the debt is owned by foreign individuals or organizations, payments on the national debt may redistribute money out of this country.

In the last few years, a large part of the federal debt has been financed through the sale of government bonds to people and businesses in foreign nations. This is a significant change from the past. Until recent years, interest payments on the debt went to Americans or American organizations. Now a significant portion of the interest payment leaves the country.

Is the National Debt Bad?

Example. Ask students if they would rather be in debt $5,000 or $10,000 if they had to choose one or the other. Most will choose $5,000. Then tell them that if they choose $5,000 they are "on their own," but if they go into debt $10,000, you will see that they get a job that pays them $50,000 a year. Let them make the choice again. Most will choose $10,000. The point is that the size of a debt is not as important as the ability to pay the debt.

There are many different points of view concerning the importance of the national debt. Some people are upset by the size of the debt alone. They point out that the debt was over 15 times as large at the end of 1992 as it was in 1945. Other people argue that the debt should be evaluated in terms of our ability to carry or pay on the debt.

Suppose two people were in debt. Mr. *A* owed $20,000 while Ms. *B* owed $50,000. You might think that Ms. *B* was further in debt, but you might be wrong. If Mr. *A* earns $12,000 a year while Ms. *B* earns $100,000 a year, Ms. *B* is in a better position to pay her debt, even though she owes much more money.

The same argument can be made for the United States. In 1945 our debt of 230 billion dollars was more than our entire GDP. In 1991 the debt was about half of the GDP. From this point of view, the debt was less of a burden in 1991 than it was in 1945.

Some economists believe that the trend of the debt is more important than its size. Between 1945 and 1980 the GDP grew more rapidly than the debt. Therefore the debt seemed less important. But between 1980 and 1992 the debt grew more rapidly than GDP. It was therefore becoming more significant.

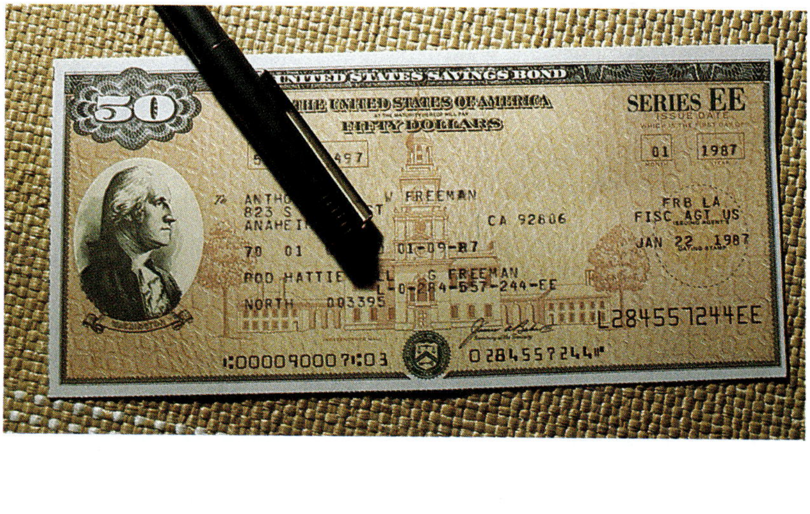

Part of the national debt represents borrowing from people who have bought savings bonds.

There is debate over the significance of the national debt. One important change in recent years is that now a significant portion of the debt is owed to people and businesses in foreign nations.

Others argue that the size of the payment is more important than the size of the debt. High interest rates in the early 1980s caused the payments on the debt to grow even more rapidly than the debt itself.

Still others suggest that the debt should be evaluated according to its effect on the rest of the economy. Borrowing comes from people's and organizations' savings. Large amounts of government borrowing could reduce the amount left over for people or businesses that also want to borrow. Some economists believe that deficit spending reduces the amount of spending people and businesses are able to do.

Note. Most economists probably believe that the debt as a percentage of GDP is the most significant measurement of the importance of the debt. The government is able to change the share of GDP it takes for its budget. It has less ability to control actual production or GDP.

Some people don't feel that the debt is as important as the government's responsibility to provide necessary services to the people. They may believe that there will be enough growth in the economy for the government to make its payments even if the debt does grow rapidly.

However, an important part of our debt payments are leaving the country. Many economists believe the debt held by foreign interests can harm us more than debt held by our citizens and businesses. One fact is clear: there is little agreement concerning the significance of the national debt.

Figure 9–4 shows a series of graphs concerning the national debt. Study them and try to decide which one gives you the most accurate picture of the debt between 1945 and 1990.

Figure 9–4 *Aspects of the National Debt*

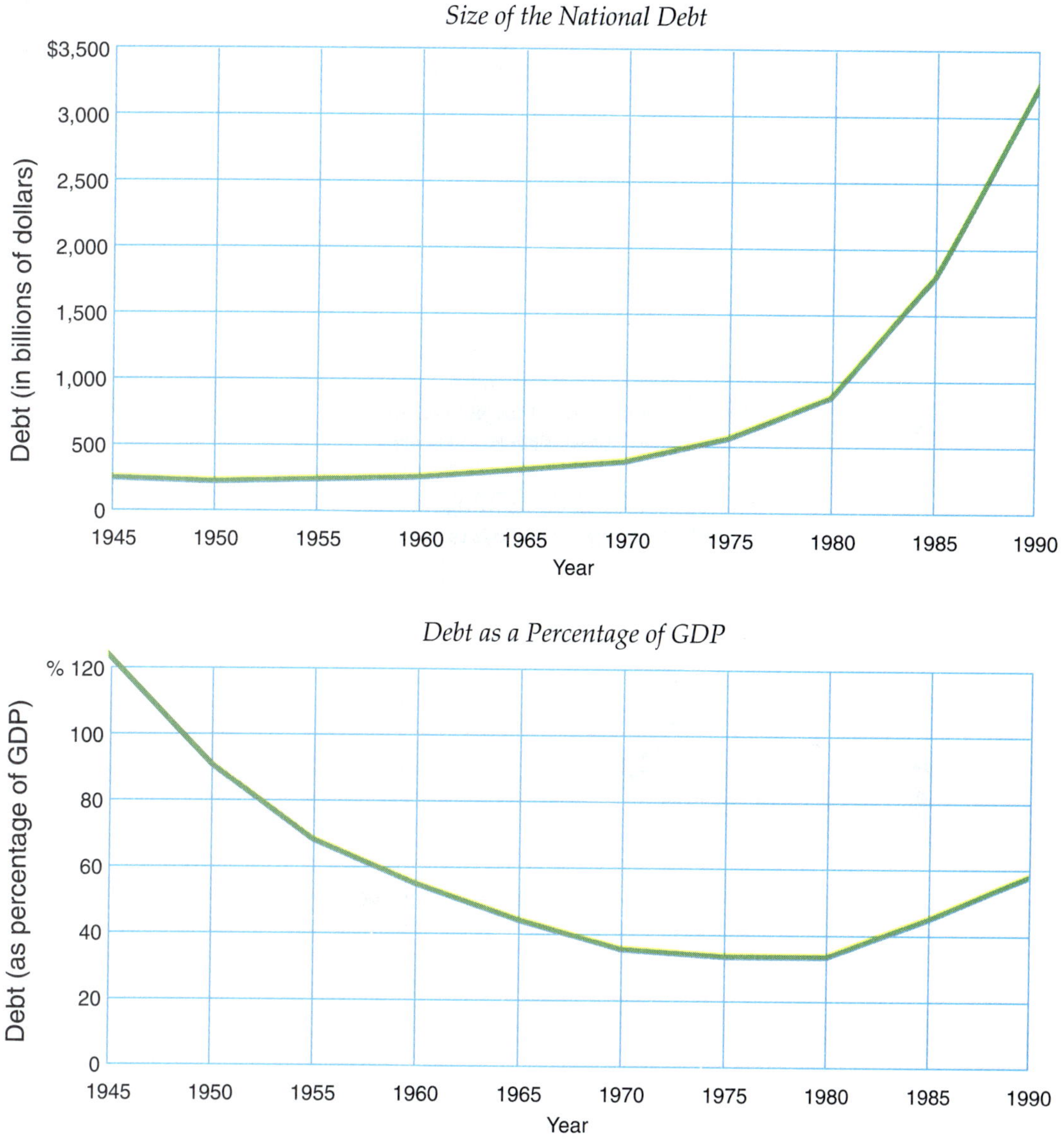

Source: *Economic Report of the President*, 1991.

Figure 9–4 (continued) *Aspects of the National Debt*

Payment on Debt as a Percentage of the Federal Budget

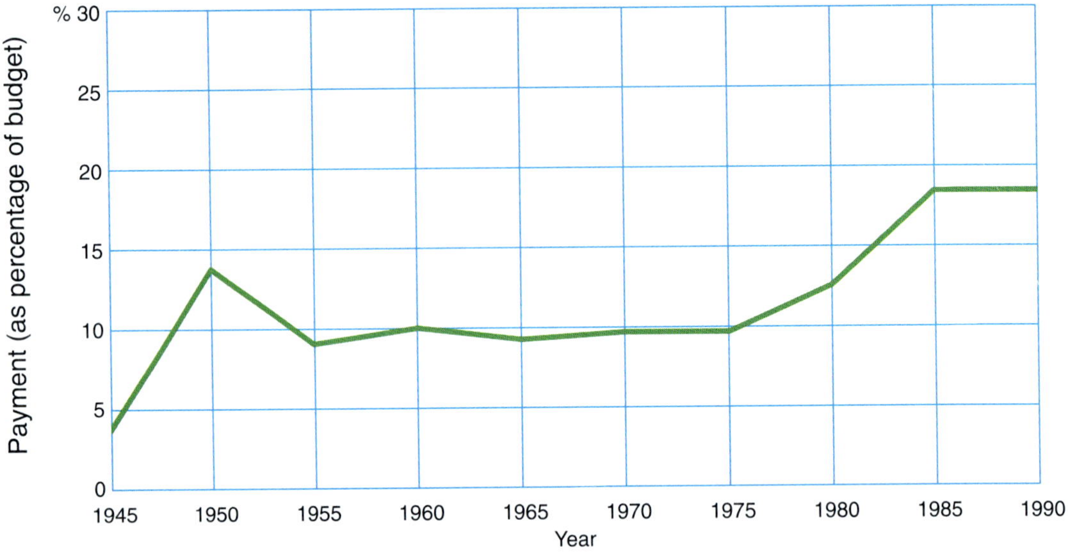

Source: *Economic Report of the President*, 1991.

Self-Check

1. What four sources of borrowing were used most frequently by the government until recently?
2. What new source of borrowing has been used by the government in recent years?
3. How much agreement is there over the importance of the national debt?

Applying What You Have Learned

1. Economists believe that George's debt and the national debt are different. George borrowed to buy things for himself. The government borrows to support programs that help us all. George must earn the money to pay back his loan himself. The U.S. Government has the entire economy to support its debt. Explain two others ways in which George's debt and the national debt are different.
2. In the preceding section, seven different points of view concerning the debt were described. Restate four of them in your own words. Identify the one which you feel is the best point of view and explain why you feel this way.

Self-Check

1. Four major sources of government borrowing: people buying savings bonds; banks and the Federal Reserve System buying bonds; businesses buying bonds; government trust funds buying bonds.
2. Recent borrowing has been through the sale of bonds to people and businesses in foreign nations.
3. There is little agreement over the importance of the national debt.

Applying What You Have Learned
See Lesson Plans for Chapter 9, Section D, page T94.

CURRENT CONSUMER ISSUES

When Should Consumers Borrow?

At one time or another most American adults have purchased consumer goods on credit. If you are like most Americans, sometime you will borrow money to buy goods or services you want.

A common decision consumers make is whether to borrow money for a new car, or to pay cash for a less expensive used one. In 1991 more than 80 percent of all new cars sold in the United States were financed. There are advantages to owning a new car, but there are also significant costs consumers should keep in mind when they make this decision.

Many people feel a new car is less likely to break down and is worth the extra cost. A new car is covered by a warranty that may last from three to seven years. New cars are more comfortable and easier to drive than older cars. Another reason to buy a new car is to get new safety features like anti-lock brakes.

Some people buy new cars for other reasons that may include impressing their friends or neighbors. Consumers may even be influenced by advertisements suggesting that members of the opposite sex are attracted to owners of certain new cars.

Probably the greatest cost of a new car is rapid depreciation. A general rule of thumb says a car will lose about a fifth of its value each year. This means that a typical $16,000 car would only be worth $12,800 after one year. The same car would lose another 20 percent, or $2,560, in its second year and so on. Used cars depreciate less each year because they are worth less in the first place.

The interest a consumer pays on a new car loan is a significant part of its cost. Insuring a new car costs more than insuring a used car because new cars are more likely to be stolen or vandalized. Finally, there is more sales tax to pay for a more costly new car.

Arguments in Favor of Borrowing to Buy a New Car

1. New cars are more reliable and covered by warranties.
2. New cars may impress other people.
3. New cars are usually more comfortable and easier to drive.

Arguments Against Borrowing to Buy a New Car

1. New cars depreciate more rapidly than used cars.
2. New cars cost more for insurance than used cars.
3. Consumers pay more interest and sales tax when they borrow to buy new cars.

What Do You Think?

If you were in the market for a car, would you buy a new or a used one? Why? What difference do you see between a consumer borrowing to buy a car and government borrowing to provide public goods and services?

Chapter 9 Review

What Have You Learned?

In this chapter you have learned the following important principles of economics:

- The government plays many roles in the economic system. It provides important *public goods and services* that most people could not afford as individuals. These include roads, military protection, schools, and parks. Public goods are not subject to the *principle of exclusion,* while *private goods* are.
- In some cases, a firm's activities can harm people who are neither producers nor consumers of the goods or services that the firm is producing. Such harm is called a *negative externality.* Our government tries to correct negative externalities. Anti-pollution laws are one type of corrective measure. Although most people believe this is an important job for the government, there is disagreement over how strict regulations should be.
- The government has taken on the responsibility of ensuring a minimal income for all Americans by *redistributing income.* The largest part of the federal budget is used to support payments to individuals through programs like Social Security, unemployment compensation, and welfare.
- Two principles of taxation are the *benefits received principle,* and the *ability-to-pay principle.* In addition, some taxes are based on two other ideas called the *productivity principle* or the *least-likely-to-offend principle.*
- Taxes may be *progressive, regressive,* or *proportional.* Progressive taxes increase as a percentage of income as income goes up. Regressive taxes decline as a percentage of income as income goes up. Proportional taxes tax all income at the same rate. Most state and local taxes are regressive, while the federal income tax is somewhat progressive for most people.
- Government decisions are often not made in the same way as decisions in private firms. Private firms make decisions that are intended to increase their profit. Government decisions are intended to help people by providing public goods and services. Many government decisions also serve the political interests of government leaders. Decisions that make political sense do not necessarily make economic sense. Decisions that help individual politicians through spending government funds in their elective districts are sometimes called *pork barrel legislation.*
- The *national debt* has often been the topic of public debate. Some people suggest that the debt is not a great problem. We have been able to support it in the past. Others believe that its rapid growth will lead to major economic problems in the future.
- In the past, money that was borrowed by the government came from people and businesses in the United States. However, since 1980 a growing part of this money has come from foreign nations. This means that an important part of our debt payments in the future will be leaving the country. Economists believe the debt held by foreign interests can harm us more than debt held by our citizens and businesses.

See Chapter 9 Review Answers, page T96.

Words and Terms

public goods and services (p. 238)
principle of exclusion (p. 239)
private goods (p. 239)
negative externality (p. 240)
redistribution of income (p. 242)
transfer payments (p. 242)
transfers in kind (p. 242)
benefits received principle (p. 243)
ability-to-pay principle (p. 244)
productivity principle (p. 244)
least-likely-to-offend principle (p. 244)
progressive taxation (p. 245)
regressive taxation (p. 245)
proportional taxation (p. 245)
personal income tax (p. 245)
social insurance tax (p. 245)
corporate income tax (p. 245)
sales tax (p. 247)
property tax (p. 247)
intergovernmental revenue (p. 247)
deficit (p. 250)
pork barrel legislation (p. 250)
national debt (p. 254)

Building Your Vocabulary

On a separate piece of paper, write the vocabulary word or term that best completes each of the following statements.

1. I can say, "It's mine. You can't have it" if the product is subject to the ______.
2. Taxes that encourage people and firms to make more goods and services are examples of the ______ of taxation.
3. Taxes on people who use the government service supported by that tax are examples of the ______ of taxation.
4. Taxes passed to increase government revenue without causing public protest are examples of the ______ of taxation.
5. Taxes that fall most heavily on the rich are examples of the ______ of taxation.
6. Products that are provided on an equal basis to the people by the government are generally ______.
7. Products that are owned by individuals are generally ______.
8. Laws that support spending that is intended to help politicians keep their jobs is often called ______.
9. ______ increase as a percentage of income as the taxpayer's income goes up.
10. ______ decrease as a percentage of income as the taxpayer's income goes up.
11. ______ tax everyone at the same percentage of their income.
12. When the government takes money from some individuals and uses it to pay for benefits given to others, it is involved in the ______.
13. A ______ occurs when a cost is paid by someone who is neither the producer nor the consumer of a product.
14. ______ occur when the government pays money to people for social programs, while ______ happen when the government provides goods or services.
15. Each federal budget ______ is borrowing that adds to the total ______.
16. Funds paid by one level of the government to another are called ______.
17. The second greatest source of revenue for the federal government is ______.
18. The ______ is progressive, but less so than before the tax changes in 1990.
19. The federal government's third most important tax is the ______.
20. Most state governments get most of their tax revenue from ______.
21. The largest part of local government tax revenue comes from ______.

Chapter 9 Review

Understanding Economics

1. Explain the difference between public and private goods.
2. Describe one example of a negative externality that you know about.
3. Explain one example of each of the four principles of taxation that were identified in Section B of this chapter.
4. If Joe pays $2,000 in taxes and Phil pays $4,000, what else would you need to know before you could say whether the taxes are progressive, regressive, or proportional?
5. Explain why decisions are made differently in government than they are in private businesses.
6. What are the four most important sources of borrowed money that the government used before the 1980s? What additional source is now used?

Thinking Critically About Economics

1. Identify five public goods or services that you often use. For each, explain how you would be affected if these things were not provided by the government.
2. In the 1980s, automobile manufacturers were required to install various pollution-control devices on all new cars. It has been estimated that this has increased the price of a new car by about $800. Explain what this law has to do with the government's responsibility to correct negative externalities.
3. Go back and study the graphs in Figures 9–2 and 9–3. Then answer the following questions.
   a. For each level of government, what type of tax brought in the greatest amount of revenue?
   b. For each level of government, what type of spending accounted for the largest part of total expenditures?
4. Explain why a decision to cut federal income taxes by 5 percent could not be an example of pork barrel legislation, while one to build a new seaport could be.
5. Explain why some economists are worried about the government borrowing from foreign sources.
6. What happened to the size of the national debt in relation to the value of GDP between 1945 and 1980? What happened to this relationship between 1980 and 1991?

Consumer Skills Projects

1. Suppose that to balance its budget your state government must cut spending by 7 percent. Of each dollar, your state spends 39 cents for education, 15 cents for welfare, 9 cents for health services, 5 cents for police and corrections, 12 cents for highways, and 3 cents for the environment. The remaining 17 cents is for state obligations such as interest that cannot be cut. Interview 5 adults and 5 students, asking each to choose how to divide the spending cuts. Record these responses and compare them with other class members' results.
2. Make a bulletin board that shows pictures of goods or services people in your community receive from the government. Discuss whether most consumers could afford these goods or services if they were not provided by the government. What part of our consumption is made possible by government spending?

Thinking Critically About Economics
(1) predicting probable consequences; (2) recognizing values; (3) interpreting graphs; (4) determining relevant information; (5) predicting probable consequences; (6) comparison/contrast.

Developing Your Economic Skills

Using a *Percent-of-Total* Graph

Skill: In this lesson you'll learn how to interpret a percent-of-total graph, showing the changing sources of federal tax revenue. To complete this lesson you'll follow these steps:

1. Examine the vertical and horizontal axes of the graph and understand what they represent.
2. Identify each of the four categories on the graph.
3. Interpret what the graph says about (a) how the percentage in one category compares to the percentage in another, and (b) how the percentages have changed over a period of years.

Application: The federal government has three major taxes which account for the bulk of its tax revenue. They are the *personal income tax* (PIT), the *social insurance tax* (SIT), and the *corporate income tax* (CIT). A fourth category, which we'll call "other," makes up the remainder of federal tax revenue, and includes tariffs, excise taxes, and estate taxes.

Suppose that you want to show what percentage of the federal government's tax revenue comes from each of these four categories. Suppose also that you want to see how these percentages may have changed over the years. Both of these types of information are shown on the graph to the right.

On the graph, the two vertical axes have been divided into percentage values from 0 percent through 100 percent. The years have been placed on the horizontal axis. You can see that personal income taxes (PIT) occupy the bottom area of the graph. The percentage of total tax revenue from the PIT is plotted for each year and connected with a line. The same has been done for each of the other four categories. Notice that each line represents the percentage for the *total of all the categories below it.* For example, read up from the year 1965 and you'll see that the PIT value for 1965 is about 42 percent. Read further up for the same year, and you'll find that PIT and SIT values together are about 61 percent. As you can see from the graph, most of that 61 percent comes from the PIT.

By looking at this graph, it is possible to quickly see what has happened to the sources of federal tax revenue. In 1985, the percentage from PITs was just slightly larger than it was in 1965. But the percentage from SITs has grown substantially. During the same time, the percentage from CITs has fallen by more than half. The share that comes from other taxes is also smaller as a percentage of the total. This information is clearer on a graph than it would be on a table.

Sources of Federal Tax Receipts as a Percent of Total, 1965–1985

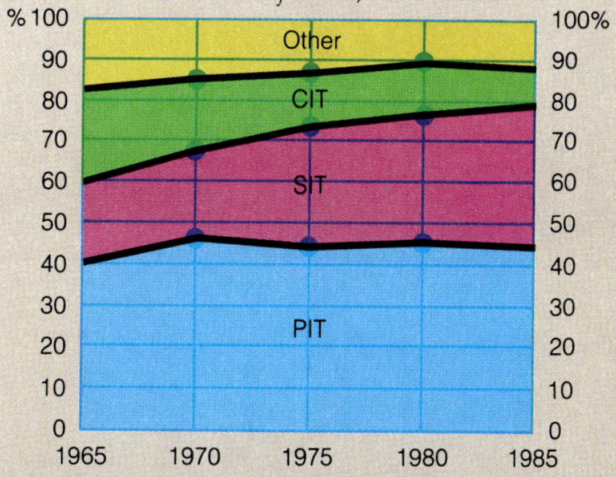

Source: *Statistical Abstract of the United States, 1987.*

Practice: Copy the graph on a separate sheet of paper and add 1990 figures. In 1990 PIT was 46%; PIT and SIT were 82%; and PIT, SIT, and CIT were 92% of the total.

CHAPTER 10

Inflation, Unemployment, and the Distribution of Income

Objectives

In the sections of this chapter, you will learn:

A

how unemployment has been classified by economists and why some types of unemployment create greater problems than others;

B

how inflation is measured through the consumer price index and how cost-push inflation and demand-pull inflation differ;

C

how the government defines poverty and how the distribution of income and wealth can be shown with a Lorenz Curve.

Introduction

Of all the problems faced by the American economy, unemployment, inflation, and poverty must be ranked among the most important. The burden of these problems is not shared equally by all Americans. A person who has a job might not worry about unemployment. Inflation is no problem if your income goes up with prices. Poverty has little impact on those who are wealthy. The people who suffer from these problems are often those who are least able to help themselves. The responsibility of finding fair and workable solutions falls to those who are less affected by the problems but who have power to do something about them.

In this chapter you will learn that there is more than one type of unemployment. Some types create greater problems than others. Policies to deal with unemployment need to vary depending on the situation.

You will discover that inflation can be the result of several different problems. Because there are different causes of inflation, there are also different ways to fight inflation.

Poverty is real, but it is difficult to define. Just how poor does a person have to be to deserve help from the government? How much and what type of help should be given? Most Americans agree that

Question. Discuss economic mobility in the United States. Can people move from the economic and social class in which they are born?

Values. Ask your students to explain the meaning of poverty before they learn about the way our government or economists define the term. Later, students can compare what they said with what the textbook says.

something should be done to help the poor. The problem is in agreeing on what to do.

As you study this chapter you will find that these problems are related to each other. People who are unemployed are often those who are hurt by inflation and end up living in poverty. When the government attempts to solve one problem, it can make others worse. You will learn that there are no easy answers. Finding solutions to these problems will take time, effort, cooperation, and understanding.

Unemployment, inflation, and poverty are important problems that confront the economy. The problems are related to each other. While most Americans are employed and enjoy a comfortable standard of living, some people live in poverty. Unemployment is a cause of poverty, and poverty can make it more difficult to acquire the training necessary to get and hold a good job. The problem is complicated by inflation, because payments to the poor through government social programs have frequently not kept up with increased price levels. This causes the poor to be hurt more by inflation than many other people. There continues to be much discussion on how to best deal with these problems.

Section A The Costs of Unemployment

This section will introduce the four types of unemployment identified by economists—*frictional, seasonal, cyclical,* and *structural.*

Personal Narrative

Note. Predictions forecast relatively low unemployment rates among young people in the late 1990s and thereafter because of demographic forces. The birthrate fell in the early 1970s and did not pick up again until the mid-1980s. This means there will be a relatively small number of people reaching maturity and entering the labor force in the next few years.

I Stood in Line All Day

Four people are standing in line at the State Employment Office. They are waiting to sign for their compensation checks. A conversation begins:

Jerry: "So how'd you lose your job?"

Tina: "I told my boss what I thought of my job so he fired me. I kept his books, typed his letters, and made his coffee for over three years. He only paid me $6.20 an hour. I know more about his business than he does. I wish I could be there when he tries to find something in his files. I'll get a better job soon."

Shawn: "You're lucky. I work on construction jobs and I haven't been able to find a job since last fall. Building slows down every winter. I have to wait until the spring. Then I'll be able to work again."

Tina: "If you know you are going to be laid off, why don't you save for it?"

Shawn: "I try to, but it isn't always possible. I only worked 30 weeks last year and my wife had another baby. We just couldn't save enough. Besides, it's hard for me to find other work because everyone knows I'll quit as soon as anything opens up in construction."

James: "At least you can look forward to getting your job back soon. I got laid off from my job at a tire factory because sales were so bad. The whole industry is in a recession. I'm number 381 on the recall list. I'll be lucky to get my job back even if business picks up next year. If I can't find a decent job soon, I'm going to have to go to work in my uncle's grocery store."

Jerry: "Yeah, but things could be worse. I got laid off because a robot took my job. I used to put motors together with 30 other workers on an assembly line. The firm bought machines that do it twice as fast as we can and never make a mistake. I worked that job for nearly 20 years. I never graduated from high school. There is no way I'm going to find a new job that pays anywhere near the $10.23 an hour I used to get. I don't know how I'm going to support my family."

James: "That's tough. How about going back to school?"

Jerry: "How am I going to do that? I've got a wife and three kids. There's the mortgage and the car payments. You think the bank's going to take my IOU? Besides, I'm 44 years old. I'm going to look pretty silly in a classroom."

The clerk says, "Next, please." Jerry steps up to sign for his check and the conversation ends.

Unemployment, What Kind?

Unemployment is measured through a scientific survey carried out by the Bureau of the Census. Roughly 50,000 households are questioned each month to determine employment and unemployment statistics. These homes are chosen from all geographic, ethnic, racial, and occupational groups to represent a cross-section of the American population. The result of this survey is then projected for the entire country.

Discuss. Many students know people who have been unemployed. Ask them to describe the situation and identify the type of unemployment represented in their example. What has happened to these individuals recently? Have they found satisfactory work? Why or why not?

In September of 1992 there were roughly 7.5 percent of Americans who were officially counted as unemployed. To be considered unemployed a person must be 16 years old or older and actively seeking work. There are different kinds of unemployment. Some types are a greater problem than others. Four specific types have been identified by economists. The types are *frictional, seasonal, cyclical,* and *structural* unemployment.

Frictional unemployment is made up of workers who are between jobs. These workers are short-term unemployed and will suffer little economic hardship from their lack of employment. Many chose to leave their old jobs to look for better work. Others, like Tina in the Personal Narrative above, have lost their jobs but will quickly find others.

Some frictional unemployment is the result of new people moving into the labor force. Unemployment of this nature is not a problem in the economy and cannot be eliminated. It is necessary for workers to be able to move to the jobs where they are most needed. Because of frictional unemployment, there will always be at least a 4 to 5 percent rate of unemployment.

Seasonal unemployment is made up of workers who have been laid off because their jobs exist only during certain parts of each year. Agricultural and construction workers, like Shawn, are often seasonally unemployed. Although this type of unemployment can be painful to the individual, it is at least expected and can be planned for.

Cyclical unemployment is made up of workers who have lost their jobs because of a recession or downturn in the economy.

These workers can be long-term unemployed and can go through great personal hardship. However, there is an expectation that eventually they will be called back to their jobs as the economy improves. In the Personal Narrative for this section, James was cyclically unemployed.

Structural unemployment is made up of workers whose skills or abilities are no longer in demand. This is the most serious type of unemployment, for both the individual workers and for the economy as a whole. Like Jerry in the Personal Narrative, these workers need retraining. They are often middle aged or older. Many of them have family responsibilities. The impact of their unemployment is often much more than economic; it can also be psychological and emotional. It can destroy families and lives.

Note. There is wide disagreement over how many discouraged workers there are. Measurement is done by a projection of interviews. People not looking for work may not be totally honest when asked if they would actually like to find a job. Estimates of the number of discouraged workers in 1992 ran from several hundred thousand to several million.

Structural unemployment can lead to a fifth type of unemployment that the government calls **the discouraged worker.** These are workers who have given up looking for a job. They are not counted as unemployed when labor statistics are gathered. There are many thousands of people in this country who are discouraged workers. They tend to be our least educated and least able workers. Some discouraged workers are homemakers who look for work from time to time but not on a regular basis. The

There are four types of unemployment. Frictional *unemployment is made up of workers who are between jobs, and who will quickly find new ones.* Seasonal *unemployment is made up of workers laid off because their jobs exist only during certain parts of the year.* Cyclical *unemployment is made up of workers who have lost their jobs because of a recession or a downturn in the economy.* Structural *unemployment—the most serious—is made up of workers whose skills are no longer in demand.*

fact that these people are not actively seeking work in no way means that they suffer less from unemployment than anyone else. However, they are less able to speak out for themselves and are more easily ignored than many other groups. These people truly need government help if they are ever to escape poverty.

The problems of unemployment do not affect all groups of workers equally. The chances of being unemployed vary greatly depending on a worker's sex, race, and age. Table 10–1 shows rates of unemployment for various groups.

Discuss. What are possible reasons for the different unemployment rates demonstrated in the table?

Table 10–1

Unemployment Rates for Various Groups, 1975–1991

	1975	1980	1985	1991*
All Workers	8.5%	7.1%	7.2%	6.7%
Male Workers	7.9%	6.9%	7.0%	7.2%
Female Workers	9.3%	7.4%	7.4%	6.1%
White Teenagers	17.9%	15.5%	15.7%	15.7%
Black Teenagers	39.5%	38.5%	40.2%	38.7%

Source: *Statistical Abstract of the United States,* 1991.
*June, 1991

Self-Check
1. Because of frictional unemployment—people moving within the work force—there will always be at least 4 to 5 percent unemployment.
2. Structural unemployment can have negative psychological and emotional as well as economic effects.
3. Discouraged workers are those who have given up looking for work.

Applying What You Have Learned
See Lesson Plans for Chapter 10, Section A, page T98.

Self-Check

1. Why will there always be at least 4 to 5 percent unemployment?
2. Why is structural unemployment the most serious type of unemployment?
3. What type of person does government call a discouraged worker?

Applying What You Have Learned

1. In the story above, each person was unemployed for a different reason. Identify the type of unemployment represented by each person (frictional, seasonal, cyclical, or structural).
   a. Jerry represented ______ unemployment.
   b. Tina represented ______ unemployment.
   c. Shawn represented ______ unemployment.
   d. James represented ______ unemployment.
2. Describe three steps you could take in preparing for a career that would reduce your chance of becoming cyclically or structurally unemployed in the future.

Section B Life With Inflation

This section discusses how *inflation* affects people. The discussion introduces the *consumer price index* and the terms *demand-pull* and *cost-push inflation*.

Personal Narrative

When I Was Your Age, I Earned a Dollar Forty an Hour

Explain. It is probable that students were affected more by inflation in the early 1990s than many adults. Prices of "big ticket items," and costs associated with housing, increased less rapidly than the prices of incidentals, clothing, and fast food, which might more often be purchased by younger consumers. Ask your students how they have been affected by inflation.

Yesterday evening I went to the show with three of my friends. We each took $8.00. We thought that would give us money for our tickets and popcorn. When we got there we found they had raised the price of a ticket from $6.00 to $7.00. We only had $4.00 left, so we shared two $2.00 boxes of popcorn. That worked out for us, but it would have been embarrassing if we hadn't brought extra money for food.

My friend Shelly works at the candy stand in the theater. I asked her why the price of tickets had gone up. She told me there were really three reasons. The rent on the theater had just been increased. The workers had been given a 5 percent raise. And finally, the manager was worried because attendance was down. He wanted to protect his profit.

On our way home we stopped by Jose's Burger Haven to see who was there. We didn't have any money left, but there's always the chance of seeing someone we know. We found Ted and Phil standing around outside the door. We could hear Phil complaining half a block away. He was saying, "Three fifty for a lousy hamburger? He has to be out of his mind!"

Ted mumbled something we couldn't hear, but it was clear he agreed with Phil. "What's happening?" I asked.

"All the prices at Jose's were raised," Ted answered. "You can't eat there for less than five or six dollars any more. What a rip-off!"

Explain. Firms are not all equally able to increase prices. If a firm is in a very competitive market, it may have to absorb cost increases by reducing profit margins. Firms that have monopoly-like powers are better able to pass cost increases on to their customers.

"But look at it!" I said. "There must be a hundred people waiting to get in. Those fools must not care about the price. Jose is making a fortune."

We all walked home wondering how we could be like Jose. The idea of making a fortune sounded pretty good, particularly with prices going up all the time.

When I walked in the door, I told my father I needed an increase in my allowance because prices were up. As soon as I said it I knew I had made a mistake. My father started, "When I was your age I earned my own spending money washing dishes and I only got paid a dollar forty an hour. If you want any more money you should look for a job."

What is Inflation?

Note. The method of measuring the consumer price index was adjusted in the spring of 1987 to reflect changes in how Americans spend their income. The share of the index attributed to housing was increased, while the part spent on food was slightly reduced. Such adjustments have been made roughly every ten years.

Note. Many students have difficulty reading indexes. Stress the distinction between the base year, which has a value of 100, and all the subsequent years. The index value compares each subsequent year to the *base* year—*not* subsequent years to each other. If an index increases from 220 in one year to 242 the following year, students may think there was a 22 percent increase. However, the increase was only 10 percent. The index change of 22 was 10 percent of the 220 index value from the previous year.

Economists define **inflation** as a general increase in the price level. This does not mean that all prices have to be going up. Some prices could be going down, but most are increasing. One of several methods of measuring inflation is the **consumer price index** (CPI). The CPI is found through a survey of several hundred goods sold in about 21,000 outlets. The prices for the goods and services are totaled and compared with their levels at an earlier point in time, called the **base year** (in 1992 the average for prices in 1982–1984). Base years are usually chosen because they are considered typical of most years. Some of the products are counted more than once, or *weighted,* because people buy them more often. Milk, for example, would be counted more times than radios because people buy milk more frequently.

Prices in the base year are given an index value of 100. Changes in price levels cause the index to either rise or fall. Although this may sound difficult, it is easy to work with. If the index for the current year is 140, it means that prices have gone up 40 percent since the base year (140 − 100 for the base year = 40 percent increase).

In Figure 10–1, Graph #1 shows the growth in the consumer price index from 1975 through 1991. Notice the rapid increase in the index in the late 1970s and early 1980s. Graph #2 shows the rate of inflation from 1975 through 1991.

The two graphs are based on the same data, but they do not look the same. Graph #1 does not show the sharp changes in the rate of inflation Graph #2 shows. That is because Graph #2 shows only the rate of inflation each year, while Graph #1 shows the cumulative effect of inflation on prices. Which graph provides the most accurate picture of inflation?

Types of Inflation

Explain. Demand-pull inflation is often associated with low rates of unemployment, as businesses expand production to try to keep up with growth in demand.

Like so many other things in economics, there is more than one type of inflation. One type is called **demand-pull inflation.** Demand-pull inflation is the result of demand for goods and services exceeding their supply. This type of inflation is often found in times of war. Shortages force prices up in demand-pull inflation.

A second type of inflation is called **cost-push inflation.** Cost-push inflation happens when prices go up because there has been an increase in the costs of production. This kind of inflation can be caused by increases in wages, rent, interest rates, or the

Figure 10–1 *Inflation and the Consumer Price Index*

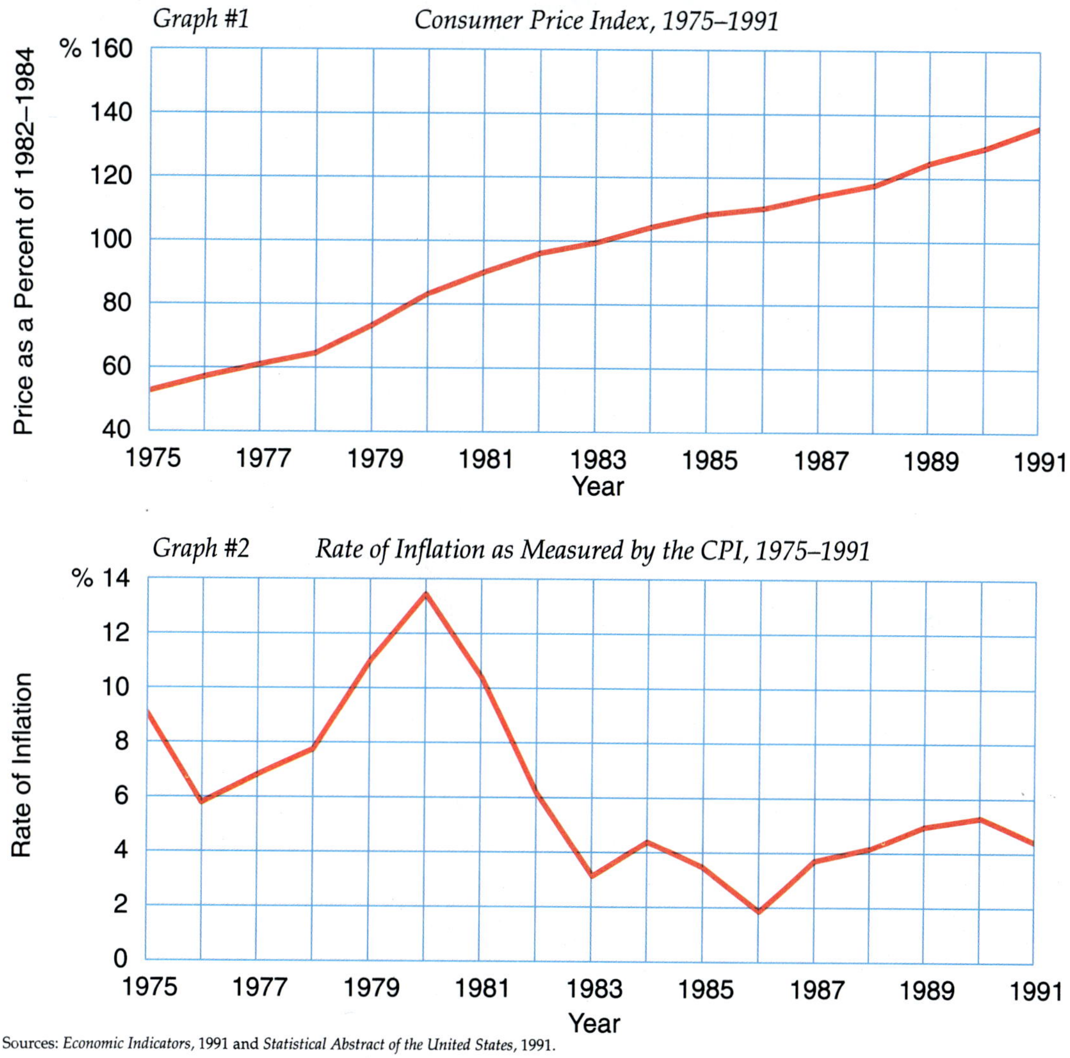

Sources: *Economic Indicators,* 1991 and *Statistical Abstract of the United States,* 1991.

costs of raw materials. Manufacturers attempt to pass their increased costs on to their customers in the form of higher prices.

The difference between these two types of inflation can be shown clearly on a set of graphs. Study the two graphs in Figure 10–2. Graph #1 shows *cost-push* inflation. Graph #2 shows *demand-pull* inflation. You can see that the equilibrium price and quantity for each product is the same at the start, which is represented by P^1 and Q^1.

Air travel is an industry where prices are subject to demand-pull inflation. In holiday seasons, when many people want to travel, fares are usually higher than in off-seasons, during which airlines often lower their fares.

Explain. Discuss the relationship between the price elasticity of demand for a product and the ability of producers to pass cost increases on to customers. Producers of price inelastic products can pass increased costs on to customers, because the demand for these products is not sensitive to changes in price. Producers of products that have price elastic demand cannot easily pass changes in costs on to customers, because their products *are* sensitive to changes in price.

On Graph #1, an increase in the cost of production shifts the supply curve to the left. This causes a new point of equilibrium and a higher market price (inflation), represented by P^2. However, production has fallen to Q^2. A sign of cost-push inflation is a shift of a product's supply curve to the left.

On Graph #2, the demand curve shifts to the right, showing an increase in demand. (This shift could have been caused by a change in any of the determinants of demand that were discussed in Section B of Chapter 3.) As a result, there is a new point of equilibrium with a higher market price (inflation), represented by P^2 on Graph #2. This time production has grown to Q^3. A sign of demand-pull inflation is a shift of a product's demand curve to the right.

Notice that the lower production shown on Graph #1 (showing cost-push inflation) will result in unemployment and a recession in the economy. The higher production on Graph #2 (showing demand-pull inflation) will cause an expansion in the economy and greater employment.

Who Wins? Who Loses?

Inflation hurts different people in different ways. Probably those who are hurt the most are those with fixed incomes. Many retired people are forced to stretch their incomes when prices go up. A second group of people who are hurt by inflation are *creditors*—people who have loaned money. If prices have gone up, the dollars with which they are repaid will buy less than those that they loaned out.

Figure 10–2 *Types of Inflation*

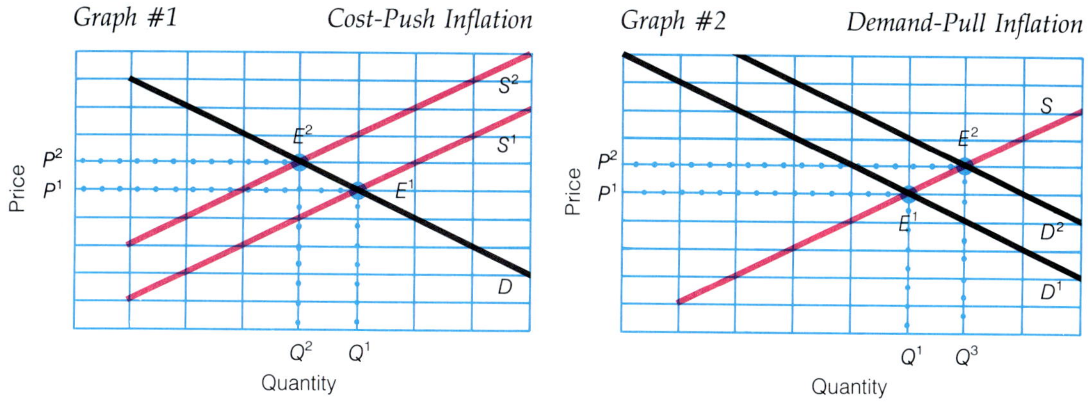

Debtors, who have borrowed money, can be helped by inflation. Higher prices often result in higher incomes, which make it easier for debtors to pay back their loans. The dollars they repay buy fewer products than those that they borrowed.

High rates of inflation can discourage business activity. When there is inflation, interest rates tend to increase. High interest rates discourage both businesses and individuals from borrowing and spending. This can lead to a recession. Most economists agree that rates of inflation that exceed 3 to 4 percent are too high.

The rate of inflation in the United States grew in the mid-1960s and again in the mid-1970s. The reasons for these two periods of inflation were very different. In the mid-1960s the United States was involved in the Vietnam War. Many billions of dollars were being spent to support the war effort. At the same time, the government was spending additional billions on expanding social programs in what President Johnson called "The War on Poverty." Unemployment was only slightly more than 4 percent in those years, so people had money to spend. The increase in prices in the 1960s was an example of demand-pull inflation.

In 1974 the Organization of Petroleum Exporting Countries (OPEC) increased the price of crude oil from about $2.60 a barrel to around $11.50. This caused the cost of all energy to increase. Firms found they had to pay more to manufacture goods and services, so they increased prices. This caused many unions to demand higher wages, which again increased the cost of production. A recession followed in 1975. The inflation of the mid-1970s was cost-push inflation.

Explain. Other groups affected by inflation are workers and owners of firms with long-term wage agreements. If workers accepted a 4 percent per year wage increase for three years, they would be hurt by unexpected inflation in excess of 4 percent. On the other hand, the firm could be hurt if inflation fell to 1 percent and prevented the firm from passing on increased labor costs to customers.

Note. Economists believe people who expect increased inflation spend more to avoid price increases. This growth in demand helps cause even more inflation, forcing people to reduce their spending, leading to a recession.

Gas prices today are considerably higher than they were in the 1960s. The increase is largely due to increases in the cost of crude oil, resulting in cost-push inflation.

Self-Check

1. How is the consumer price index found?
2. If there is cost-push inflation, is the supply or the demand curve likely to shift, and in which direction?
3. If there is demand-pull inflation, is the supply or the demand curve likely to shift, and in which direction?

Self-Check

1. The CPI is found through a survey of several hundred goods and services. The prices for the goods and services are totaled and compared with their levels at the base year.
2. Cost-push inflation will cause the supply curve to shift to the left.
3. Demand-pull inflation will cause the demand curve to shift to the right.

Applying What You Have Learned

Increases in the price of one product or service can sometimes cause increases in the prices of other products and services. In the Personal Narrative for this section, find at least one example where this occurs.

Applying What You Have Learned
See Lesson Plans for Chapter 10, Section B, page T101.

Section C The Distribution of Wealth and Income

This section will discuss problems that are related to the *distribution of income and wealth* and will introduce the *Lorenz Curve.*

Personal Narrative

Explain. Someone who won $10,000 might feel rich. But, if a third of the prize was paid in taxes, the remaining $6,667 would be only $18.27 a day for a year. This would be nice, but not enough to live on. Becoming wealthy usually requires a substantial income over an extended period of time.

Values. Although there are obvious advantages to having a large amount of wealth, there are also costs associated with it. What problems can your students think of that come with being wealthy?

I'd Like to Try Being Rich

When I'm out of school in the summer, I like to watch daytime quiz programs. It's fun seeing people win prizes. They always get excited and look foolish. I remember one woman who won a trip to a hunting lodge in Wyoming. She was about 25 years old and probably had no interest in hunting at all. I had to laugh when she tried to act really excited in front of the camera.

The host asked another contestant why he wanted to be on the show. The man said he had been laid off and his wife was sick. He wanted to win money to help with his bills. I felt sorry for him. They made him wear a clown suit and get hit with a pie. For his prize he got an electric golf cart. What could he do with it? Maybe they let him take cash instead. I wouldn't have been very excited if I had been him. He was all smiles while they wiped cream off his face.

It would be nice to win a prize, but unless you hit the lottery for a million dollars it wouldn't make any real difference in your life. A trip to Wyoming or a golf cart won't get you a good job, a nice home, or a big bank account. If I had my choice of prizes, I would take a job in a large corporation that paid a hundred thousand dollars a year. That would make a real difference.

Sometimes my family drives out to the beach. On the way we go through an area of estates. Most of them are so far back from the road that we can't see them. They have walls with gates. There are security patrols driving around to be sure that no one tries to get in. I wonder what it would be like to live like that. Those estates must be worth millions of dollars. The taxes and maintenance probably cost a hundred thousand dollars or more each year. I wonder how those people got to be so rich.

My family isn't poor, but I know people who are. Some students I go to school with don't know if there will be food at home for supper. A few of them come from families where their parents don't care about them. Others just seem to always have bad luck. It's hard to figure out why some people have so many things when others have so little. If I ever get rich I'm going to help the poor. If I could, I would just hand them all a lot of money. That would solve the problem.

What is Poverty?

Note. The official definition of poverty is measured by multiplying the cost of *feeding* a family by a factor of roughly 3 to cover other costs of living. Anyone earning less than this amount was officially designated as living in poverty. This method of measurement was developed in the early 1960s by Mollie Orshansky, and has not changed significantly since. Do your students feel this is a reasonable way to measure poverty? Some people suggest that increases in the cost of energy or medical care should have resulted in larger adjustments in the measure.

There are many different ideas about what poverty is and what causes it. **Poverty** is a relative term. That means poverty can be defined by comparing what poor people have with what other people have.

Poverty in the United States is not the same as poverty in many other places. In many parts of the world, poverty can mean starving to death. Although some Americans may suffer from a lack of proper nutrition, most people in the United States are not in any danger of starvation. Public and private programs supply at least a minimal diet for most of our poor.

Poverty for some Americans means not having enough money to buy a car or good furniture. Other Americans experience greater hardship when they are unable to pay for heat or electricity. The fact that few Americans go hungry does not mean we have no poverty. It shows us that our poverty is different from that found in many other nations.

The government has an official definition of poverty. In 1991 it was having an income of less than $13,924 for a family of four. This level is a government estimate of what is necessary to provide an adequate diet for a family of four living in the city.

The government's measurement of poverty is based only on money income. It does not reflect noncash benefits such as food stamps, Medicaid, and public housing. In 1991, 14.2 percent of all Americans were officially designated as living in poverty by the federal government. Some were just barely living in poverty. Others were far below the minimum poverty income level. The distribution of income is unequal even among the poor.

Income and Wealth

The government defines poverty in terms of income people receive and not in terms of what they have. This points out the difference between *income* and *wealth*. To an economist, **income** is a flow of value. It is what you receive over a period of time. **Wealth,** on the other hand, is an accumulation of value. It means that there has been saving from past income. The two terms are related, but they are not the same. It is possible for a person to have a house (wealth) but little income. It is also possible to have income but no wealth because all income is spent.

Income Distribution

Poverty is closely related to the distribution of income and wealth. Economists can show the distribution of income through a graph called the **Lorenz Curve,** such as the one shown in Figure 10–3.

Figure 10–3 *A Lorenz Curve*

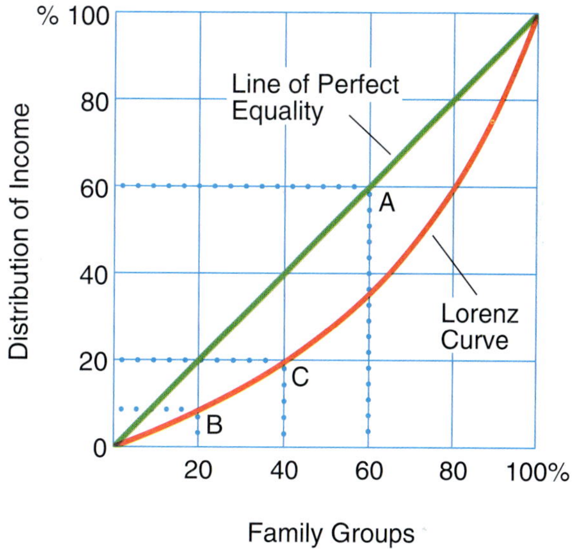

Note. The distribution of income and Lorenz Curves can be evaluated through the use of a mathematical relationship called the Gini Coefficient. This measure takes the area between the line of perfect equality and the Lorenz Curve and divides it by the total area below the line of perfect equality. This yields a value between zero and 1. The closer the Gini Coefficient is to zero, the more equal the distribution of income.

The vertical axis of the graph represents percent of income. The horizontal axis is for percent of family groups. The graph is split by a diagonal, called the *line of perfect equality.* At every point on this line, the horizontal percentage is exactly the same as the vertical percentage. Point *A,* for example, would show that 60 percent of the family groups got 60 percent of the income. *Please note that point 'A' is not on the Lorenz Curve.*

The Lorenz Curve falls below the line of perfect equality. To read a Lorenz Curve, find the percentage of family groups on the horizontal axis. From that point, go up to the Lorenz Curve and across to the vertical axis. The value on the vertical axis is the percentage of income going to these family groups. Point *B* shows that the 20 percent of family groups with the lowest income got 10 percent of the income. Point *C* shows that the 40 percent of family groups with the lowest income received about 20 percent of the income.

The closer a Lorenz Curve is to the line of perfect equality, the more equal the distribution of income. In a competitive economic system we do not want to have totally equal distribution of income. If everyone knew they would have the same income as everyone else no matter what they did, there would be little reason (incentive) to work hard. Businesspeople would not invest their time, money, and effort if they did not expect to earn more than people who did not do these things.

Explain. As countries develop, their distribution of income generally becomes more equal. Developing nations tend to have only the very poor and the very rich. More developed countries have a larger middle class.

Lorenz Curves do not always stay in the same location. In the 1920s the Lorenz Curve for the United States was further away from the line of perfect equality than it is now. Income distribution has become more equal. In the 1980s, however, 50 percent of added income went to the top 5 percent of family groups.

Figure 10–4 *Lorenz Curve, 1920/1990*

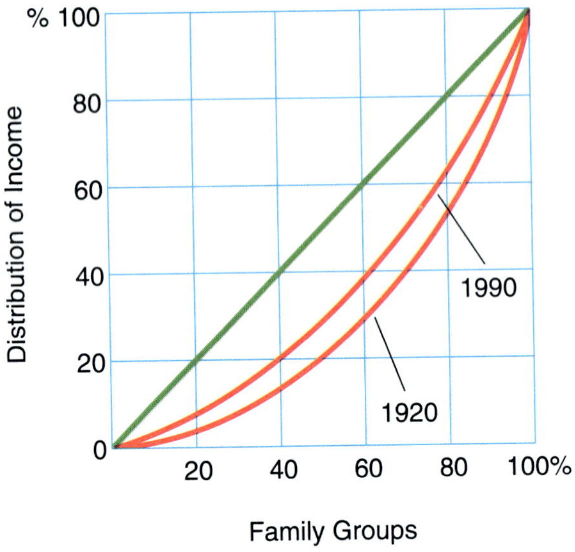

Lorenz Curves can also be used to show income distribution in different types of occupations. For example, the income distribution for teachers is quite equal while the amounts earned by lawyers vary widely. This fact can be seen on Figure 10–5.

We do not want a totally equal distribution of income; on the other hand, we do not want people to be starving in our streets either. We need to create a balance between encouraging people to work and being sure that others do not go hungry.

Figure 10–5 *Lorenz Curve, Teachers/Lawyers*

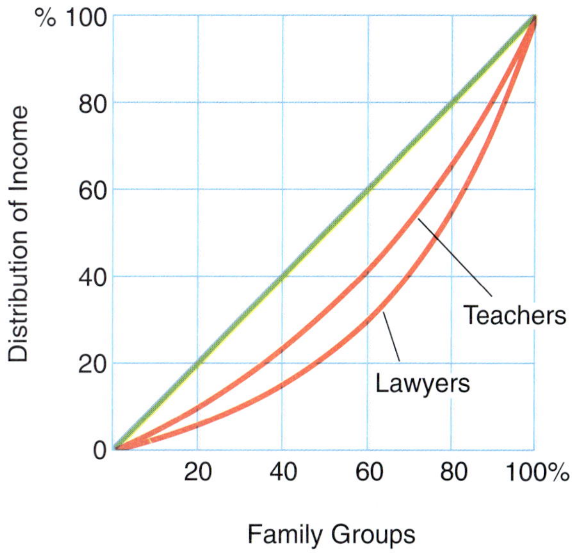

Capitalism could not work efficiently with a totally equal distribution of income. People in businesses would have little reason to produce goods and services if they did not expect that by doing so they would earn a larger income than people who did not produce as much. However, most Americans feel some help should be given to the poor. Study the photograph. Do you believe any Americans should have to live in such conditions? What steps can you think of that can reduce poverty without destroying our incentive to work and produce?

Question. What possible reasons can your students provide for the unequal distribution of poverty shown on this graph?

In Figure 10–6 you will find another graph that shows the percentage of various racial or ethnic groups that were officially designated as living in poverty in different years. Study the graph and think about its possible meanings.

Figure 10–4 *Percentage of Groups Below Poverty Level, 1976–1989*

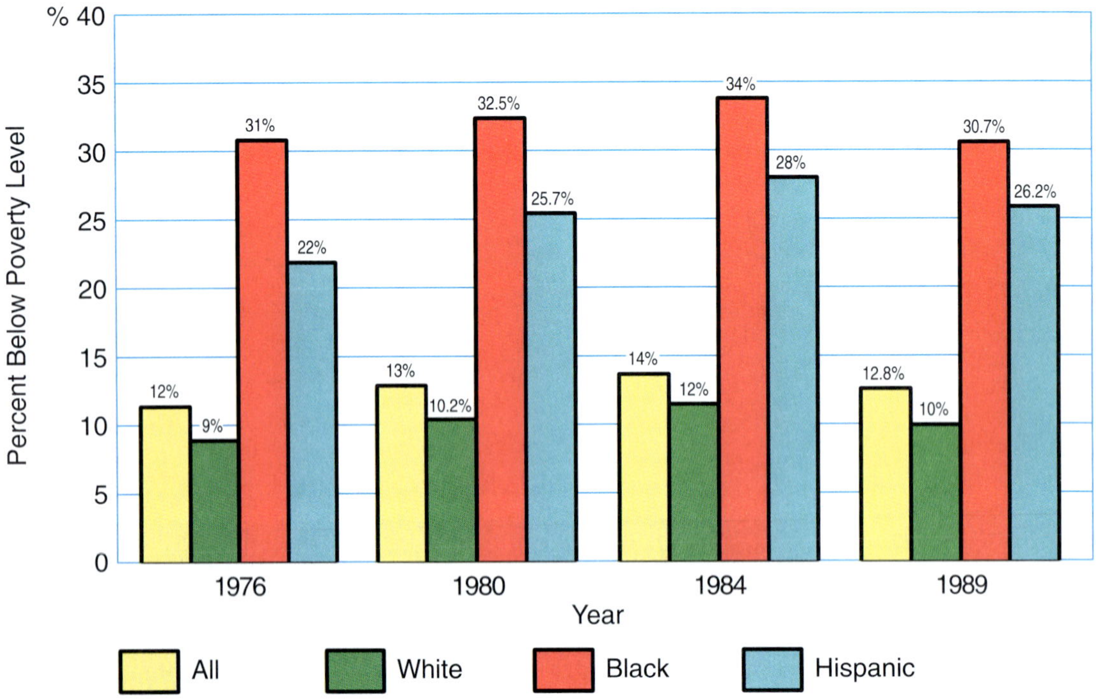

Source: *Statistical Abstract of the United States*, 1978–1991.

Self-Check
1. The government's definition of poverty is based on an estimate of what is necessary to provide an adequate diet for a family of four living in a city.
2. Income is a flow of value. Wealth is an accumulation of value.
3. A Lorenz Curve is used to show the distribution of income.

Applying What You Have Learned
See Lesson Plans for Chapter 10, Section C, page T102.

Self-Check

1. What cost does the federal government study when it defines poverty?
2. What is the difference between income and wealth?
3. What is a Lorenz Curve used to show?

Applying What You Have Learned

The person in the Personal Narrative for this section said that he would give money to the poor if he could. Would this solve all the problems that the poor have? Explain three different reasons why it would or would not.

CURRENT ECONOMIC ISSUES

Should Welfare Recipients Be Required to Train for Work?

In January 1992, Governor James Florio of New Jersey signed a bill into law that cut off benefits to mothers on welfare who refused to train for work or go to school. Under this law the state provides day care for children while mothers attend classes. The New Jersey welfare program pays for tuition, fees, and cost of books. The mothers in the program are required to attend class regularly and to make satisfactory academic effort. They are not required to achieve passing grades.

The purpose of the law is to force welfare recipients to obtain skills that will allow them to become self-supporting. Under the law mothers who complete their education and take jobs may earn up to 50 percent of their benefits without having their welfare payments cut. Governor Florio stated that this law will help people escape a system that "entraps our children in a cradle-to-grave cycle of dependency." However, not everyone believes it is a real solution to the problem.

Some people have stated that the new law will cost too much money. They also argued that welfare mothers may train for jobs that do not exist, and that they do not need to succeed, but only participate to keep receiving benefits. One political leader suggested that the most effective solution would be to reduce welfare benefits for women who have more children.

Is requiring welfare mothers to train for a job a good idea? Consider the following arguments.

Arguments in Favor of the Plan

1. It forces welfare mothers to attend classes and learn a skill.
2. It may eventually reduce the number of people who receive welfare and the cost of the welfare program.
3. It may break the cycle of welfare that some people believe goes from generation to generation.

Arguments Against the Plan

1. It has a high cost at the present.
2. It does not require welfare mothers to succeed in their studies or guarantee that they will find a job.
3. It takes welfare mothers away from their children while they are attending school.

What Do You Think?

What are the costs and benefits of this plan for welfare mothers and their children? Do you believe welfare recipients should be forced to train for a job? What other suggestions would you make for ways to reduce our nation's welfare burden?

Chapter 10 Review

What Have You Learned?

In this chapter you have learned the following important principles of economics:

- There are different types of unemployment, which affect people differently. People who are between jobs are *frictionally* unemployed. People who have jobs that exist only during certain parts of each year are often *seasonally* unemployed. People who are laid off because of a recession are *cyclically* unemployed. The most serious type of unemployment is *structural,* because these people do not possess skills that businesses need. They must be trained before they can get what most people would regard as a good job.
- People who have given up looking for work but who would like a job are called *discouraged workers.*
- *Inflation* is a general increase in the price level. One measure of inflation is the *consumer price index,* which is based on the prices of typical products consumers buy.
- Economists have identified two basic types of inflation. *Demand-pull* inflation happens when prices go up because the quantity demanded exceeds the quantity supplied. *Cost-push* inflation is the result of an increase in the costs of production being passed on to customers in the form of higher prices. Both types of inflation can be shown on a graph of demand and supply.
- Not all people are affected equally by inflation. People who live on a fixed income are hurt the most. Individuals or organizations who have loaned money are also hurt by inflation because the dollars repaid to them buy less than those they loaned out.
- *Poverty* is defined in terms of the economic and social conditions in each country. In the United States poverty is closely related to unemployment, inflation, and the distribution of income.
- The desire to earn money is the basic incentive to produce under capitalism. It is therefore necessary for income and wealth to be distributed unequally for our economic system to work. However, it is also important that we assure a minimum standard of living for all Americans. There is a trade-off between our need for an economic incentive and our desire to treat people fairly.
- Our distribution of income can be demonstrated through a *Lorenz Curve.* When this curve moves closer to its line of perfect equality, it shows that income is being more equally distributed. Between 1920 and 1990 the distribution of income became more equal in the United States. Even so, in 1991 the government classified more than 14.2 percent of our population as living in poverty.

See Chapter 10 Review Answers, page T103.

Words and Terms

frictional unemployment (p. 268)
seasonal unemployment (p. 268)
cyclical unemployment (p. 268)
structural unemployment (p. 269)
discouraged worker (p. 269)
inflation (p. 272)
consumer price index (p. 272)
base year (p. 272)
demand-pull inflation (p. 272)
cost-push inflation (p. 272)
poverty (p. 278)
income (p. 278)
wealth (p. 278)
Lorenz Curve (p. 279)

Building Your Vocabulary

On a separate piece of paper, write the vocabulary word or term that best completes each of the following statements in the appropriate place on your answer sheet.

1. A general increase in the price level is referred to as ______.
2. The most common measure of inflation used in the United States is called the ______.
3. ______ occurs when prices go up because of an increase in the costs of production.
4. ______ occurs when prices go up because the demand for goods and services exceeds their supply.
5. Economists say ______ represents a flow of value, while ______ is an accumulation of value.
6. The consumer price index measures percentage increases from a ______, which is given a value of 100.
7. People who are briefly unemployed as they change jobs are part of ______.
8. People who require training to be employed are classified under ______.
9. People who have been laid off due to a recession are victims of ______.
10. Economists call people who have given up looking for a job ______.
11. People who regularly lose their jobs during a part of the year are subject to ______.
12. The ______ is a graph that shows the distribution of income.
13. ______ is a term that can mean different things in different countries depending on social values and economic conditions.

Understanding Economics

1. Describe a specific example of each of the following (do not use any of the examples from this text):
   a. frictional unemployment
   b. seasonal unemployment
   c. cyclical unemployment
   d. structural unemployment
2. Explain what the difference is between a person who is designated as *unemployed* by the government and someone who is a *discouraged worker*.
3. Describe two things that could cause a supply curve to shift to the left. What type of inflation would this cause?
4. Describe two things that could cause a demand curve to shift to the right. What type of inflation would this cause?
5. In your own words, describe how the consumer price index is found.
6. Explain why people who lend money can be hurt by inflation.
7. Explain how poverty in the United States is different from poverty in many other countries.
8. Explain the difference between income and wealth.

Chapter 10 Review

Thinking Critically About Economics

1. Explain why structural unemployment is worse for the economy and for individual workers than other types of unemployment.
2. Make a list of three reasons that could cause a person to become a discouraged worker.
3. Explain three different reasons that might explain why different groups of workers in Figure 10–6 have different unemployment rates.
4. In 1974 the price of crude oil increased from about $2.60 per barrel to $11.50. What type of inflation did this cause? Explain how you know this.
5. Everyone seems to believe that inflation is bad. Describe four specific things that inflation does that hurt people.
6. Explain what might happen to the economy if the government decided to redistribute income so that everyone had about the same standard of living.
7. Describe what you think living in poverty in the United States means.

Consumer Skills Projects

1. Interview someone who has been unemployed for an extended period of time (at least 10 weeks). Ask how the person's life changed when he or she became unemployed. Does the person look at life differently now? If so, what has changed? Classify the person's unemployment as being frictional, seasonal, cyclical, or structural.
2. Go to a library and ask for help to find a copy of a newspaper from ten years ago. Make a list of ten different prices of common household items from advertisements in the newspaper. Find the current prices for the same items now. Measure the rate of inflation for these items over the past ten years. Make a table of your findings and present it to your class.
3. Make a copy of a Lorenz Curve using data from the most recent edition of the *Statistical Abstract of the United States.* Compare your results with Figure 10–4 in this text. Have there been any important changes since 1990? How can you explain these changes or lack of change?

Thinking Critically About Economics
(1) identifying the problem; (2) analyzing cause and effect; (3) determining relevant information; (4) analyzing cause and effect; (5) assessing costs and benefits; (6) predicting probable consequences; (7) recognizing values.

Developing Your Economic Skills

Constructing an Index

Skill: This lesson will show you how an index can be constructed from the prices of specific products purchased in different years. You'll follow these steps:

1. List the prices of products commonly purchased in two different years.
2. Multiply these prices by the number of times you usually purchase each item in a year.
3. Total the spending in each year and divide the value from the first year into the value for the second year.
4. Multiply the result by 100 to obtain the index value.
5. Interpret the index value.

Application: How does an index work?

You have read about the consumer price index in this chapter. This example shows how to create an index.

Suppose you want to compare your cost of living two years ago with your cost of living today. You can't possibly compare the costs of *all* the items you purchased then with those you purchase now. So you'll make a list of only the more common items.

Use the list as the left-hand column of a table. Next to each entry you'll list its price two years ago. Multiply each of these prices by how many times you buy that type of item each year. This gives you the amount you spent on each type of item. Add these values together to reach the total you spent on *all* of the items two years ago. Follow the same procedure for the items at their current prices. These totals provide you with the information you need to figure a price index.

Use these steps to find the index value:

1. Divide the total spent on the items from the current year by the amount from two years ago. This gives you the value 1.233. — $\frac{\$252.66}{\$204.86} =$ 1.233
2. Multiply this value by 100. This assigns a value of 100 to the first year and moves the decimal two places to the right. — 1.233 becomes an index value of 123.3

To interpret this index value, it's helpful to convert the number to a percentage. To do this, subtract 100 (the value assigned to the first year) from the index value. This gives you the percentage increase (23.3%) in your cost of living between the base year and the current year.

Practice: Find prices for five similar items in the current year and in a prior year. Follow the above example to construct a price index and to find the index value.

Item Often Purchased	Price Two Years Ago		Number Bought		Value Spent	Price Now		Number Bought		Value Spent
Hamburgers	$ .85	X	80	=	$ 68.00	$1.10	×	80	=	$ 88.00
Batteries	$ .79	X	10	=	$ 7.90	$ .99	×	10	=	$ 9.90
Hair spray	$2.49	X	4	=	$ 9.96	$3.19	×	4	=	$ 12.76
Candy bars	$ .35	X	100	=	$ 35.00	$ .40	×	100	=	$ 40.00
Movie tickets	$3.50	X	24	=	$ 84.00	$4.25	×	24	=	$102.00
					Total $204.86					Total $252.66

IN GOD WE TRUST

CHAPTER 11

Money and the Economy

Objectives

In the sections of this chapter, you will learn:

A

how money functions in the economy;

B

how banks *expand* the money supply through checking accounts and loans;

C

how banks earn profit; and

D

how the Federal Reserve System can take actions to affect the money supply.

Introduction

What is it like to be rich? You probably believe that having lots of money would be wonderful. You might be right, but you could be wrong. Fifty million dollars is a lot of money, but it would do you very little good if you were marooned on a desert island. Money has little usefulness of its own. It makes people rich only because of the things it allows them to buy. These goods and services are what people really want from money. Any value money has is the result of what it can buy.

Money can be studied from several points of view. In this chapter you will learn about the functions of money and what its characteristics are, and you will investigate its role in our economic system.

In Section A of this chapter you will learn what makes money what it is and how it contributes to the production of goods and services. You will find that there are several different functions for money within the economic system. Then you'll explore the relationship between money, prices, employment, and economic growth.

In Sections B and C of this chapter you will examine the American banking system and its relationship to the economy. Banks are businesses. Their owners intend to make a profit. At the same time, banks

Note. Discuss alternative forms of money. In prisons, cigarettes often serve as a medium of exchange. Native Americans have used animal hides or shells for money.

In the Personal Narrative for this section, a young man inherits a watch from his grandfather. What reasons can you think of for the young man treating the watch differently than he would a gift of money?

have a vital role to play in helping other businesses succeed. It is important that banks balance their own needs for profit and security with the need of the economic system for a reliable source of credit.

Note. Study of the workings of the Federal Reserve System can be fairly complex. The important point is that students be aware that the Federal Reserve System has powers that influence interest rates and credit.

Section D of this chapter discusses the Federal Reserve System. This is an agency of the federal government that was established to oversee the operation of the American banking system. It has been given the job of controlling the supply of money in the economy. The Federal Reserve System also regulates banks and has the power to influence interest rates. Although many people do not understand the Federal Reserve System, it is one of the most powerful parts of our government. It affects all of us in many important ways.

There is some mathematics in this chapter. If you follow directions carefully, none of it should be a problem to you.

Section A What Money Is and Where It Came From

This section defines *money,* explains the functions of money within our economy, and describes the characteristics of money. It also explains the relationship between prices and the *money supply.*

Personal Narrative

I Don't Know Much About Money, But I'd Like Some On-The-Job Training

My grandfather Amos died last year. Amos was very special to me. He was a friend. Every time I got in trouble with my parents or things went wrong at school, I could talk to Amos and he'd understand. I know he wasn't always pleased with what I did, but I don't think he ever yelled at me.

Discuss. Many things have value but are not money because their value is not uniformly accepted. The watch in the narrative has value, but its value is not generally agreed to. Therefore, it could not function as money. What other items can your students think of that have value but could not function as money?

Amos didn't have much money. He lived with us for as long as I can remember. He gave my parents the little income he got from his pension. When he died, he left me a gold watch that had belonged to his father. I was happy with it because it had been his and I knew how much he cared about it. Some of my friends said I should be happy because it was old and probably worth a lot of money. They convinced me to take it to an antique shop and have it appraised.

The first man I took it to wanted to buy it for $20. I knew he was trying to rip me off. I finally found someone who I think was honest. He said the watch was probably worth between $500 and $800 but I would have to find a collector who wanted to buy it. He offered me $300 if I needed money in a hurry. I thanked him and left.

Knowing how much the watch was worth kind of frightened me. I was afraid I'd lose it or someone would rob me. I also was tempted by the money I could sell it for. I would have liked to sell just part of it for $80 so I could order a new jacket I had seen in a catalog.

If the man had offered me $800 right away, I might have taken it. I'm glad I didn't now. I would have spent the money on clothes or something. Soon it would have been gone and I wouldn't have anything to remember my grandfather by.

I talked with my neighbor about the watch. He was interested and asked to see it. It really impressed him. He wanted to buy it. I told him "no." Then he offered to trade me his canoe for it. I like to fish and it sounded good. I almost agreed before I realized that the canoe was worth much less than $800 and I had no way to get it to the lake. My parents don't own a car and I couldn't take it on the bus. I thanked him for the offer but told him to forget it.

I've still got the watch and I guess I'll keep it. My father said it will probably grow in value over the years. Maybe when I'm old I'll give it to my grandson.

What is Money?

The young man in the story would probably have acted differently if he had been left money instead of a watch. How is money different from the watch? They both have value but they aren't the same type of thing. Economists view **money** as a *claim* on something that has value. Money usually has little value of its own, but it *represents* value. People must agree that something is money. In some places, beads or special rocks are money because the people there accept them as representing value.

Money in the United States is **fiat money.** This means that it is money because the government says it is. Look at any dollar bill. To the left of George Washington's picture you will find a statement that the bill is "legal tender." This means that it must be accepted to satisfy a debt.

Explain. The difference between the functions and characteristics of money may be easier to understand if students think of functions as answering the question, "What does it do?" while characteristics answer the question, "What is it like?" or "What can be done to it?"

The Functions of Money

Economists have identified the following functions of money in our economic system:

- **Money is a medium of exchange.** This means that most sales or exchanges are carried out with money. For example, if you buy your lunch at school, you pay with money.
- **Money is a measure of value.** This means that we can compare the value of different products by studying their prices. If you have $20 you might be able to buy one shirt or ten pairs of socks. This would show you that the shirt is worth ten times as much as a pair of socks.
- **Money is a store of value.** This means that money can be accumulated and saved, hopefully without losing value. If there were no inflation, the value of a dollar today would be the same as its value was five years ago.

The Characteristics of Money

For money to perform its functions in the economy, it must have the following characteristics.

- **Money must be accepted.** This means that everyone within the economic system must agree that the money has value and be willing to take it as payment for debts.

This piece of Yapese stone money has all the functions in that society that money has in ours: it is a medium of exchange, a measure of value, and a store of value.

Although Yapese stone money fulfills the functions of money, it lacks some of the usual characteristics. You can see, for example, that it is not divisible. Small transactions on Yap take place with other units of money, which include beads of various colors and sizes. As you would imagine, these stones are not portable. But this is not a problem on Yap, because the island is small. Each piece of money is named and its ownership can be transferred without actually moving the stone.

Note. The value of Yapese stone money is very stable, because there are a limited number of stones and no more will be made. They were mined and transported by canoe from another island (Palau) over 200 miles away. Yapese money works because it serves the most important function—it is accepted.

- **Money must be divisible.** This means that units of money can be divided into smaller units without losing their relative value. For example, the value of ten dimes is the same as one dollar.
- **Money must be portable.** This means that it must be possible to move the money from one place to another with ease. One reason we use more paper money than coins is the fact that it would be difficult to carry large quantities of coins from place to place. Think of trying to buy a new car with the coins we now use.
- **Money must have a reasonably stable value.** This means that a person will be able to buy about the same number or value of products with an amount of money today, next week, or next year.

Money in the United States is made up of currency (coins and paper money), and of checking deposits. A check is a call on money that is deposited in a checking account. Although checks are not legal tender (that is, a person is not necessarily obligated to accept a check as payment for a debt), most large transactions in the United States are carried out through checks. Checks are safer than cash and provide a record of the transactions in which they are used.

Money and Prices

The amount of money that consumers, businesses, and the government have available to spend is closely related to prices. This amount of money to be spent is called the **money supply.** It is important to keep the money supply under control. Rapid changes in the money supply can cause inflation or deflation and other problems for the economy.

Inflation and Deflation

Note. Changes in velocity or speed of circulation of money may also cause changes in price. If the same number of dollars circulates more rapidly, when there is not change in the number of products offered for sale, it causes inflation.

Study Figure 11–1. Suppose that the total money supply at the start of each example is represented by the solid box on the left. The solid box on the right represents production—the amount of goods and services available to buy. In example A there is no change in either the money supply on the left, or the amount of production on the right. Therefore, prices stay the same.

In example B, the money supply on the left and the amount of production on the right both grow the same amount, and again prices stay the same.

In example C, the money supply on the left increases while the amount of production on the right stays the same. There is more money trying to buy the same amount of production, so prices go up. This is **inflation.** More dollars are chasing too few goods and services.

Note. The Civil War example (in the text below) refers to a time when the U.S. dollar was backed by gold. It no longer is. There was an official value for the dollar in terms of gold in 1987 ($42.22 = 1 ounce of gold); however, the government would not exchange dollars for gold. Before 1933, individuals could exchange dollars for gold. After 1933 and until 1968, foreign governments could cash dollars in for gold. Now dollars can only buy gold on the free market. An ounce of gold was worth roughly $350 in the spring of 1992.

In example D, the money supply remains the same but production grows. The same amount of money must be used to buy more products, so prices will go down. This is **deflation.** Less dollars are chasing more goods and services.

Later you will learn how the Federal Reserve System tries to keep the amount of money in circulation from changing very rapidly. This helps to reduce the chances of having either inflation or deflation and helps to stabilize the economy.

The relationship between the amount of money in circulation and prices was demonstrated by events in the American Civil War. At that time our country was on a gold standard. That meant holders of dollars could exchange them for gold. However, from 1862 through 1864 the U.S. government issued 450 million dollars worth of paper money, called greenbacks, to help

Figure 11-1 *The Money Supply, Production, and Prices*

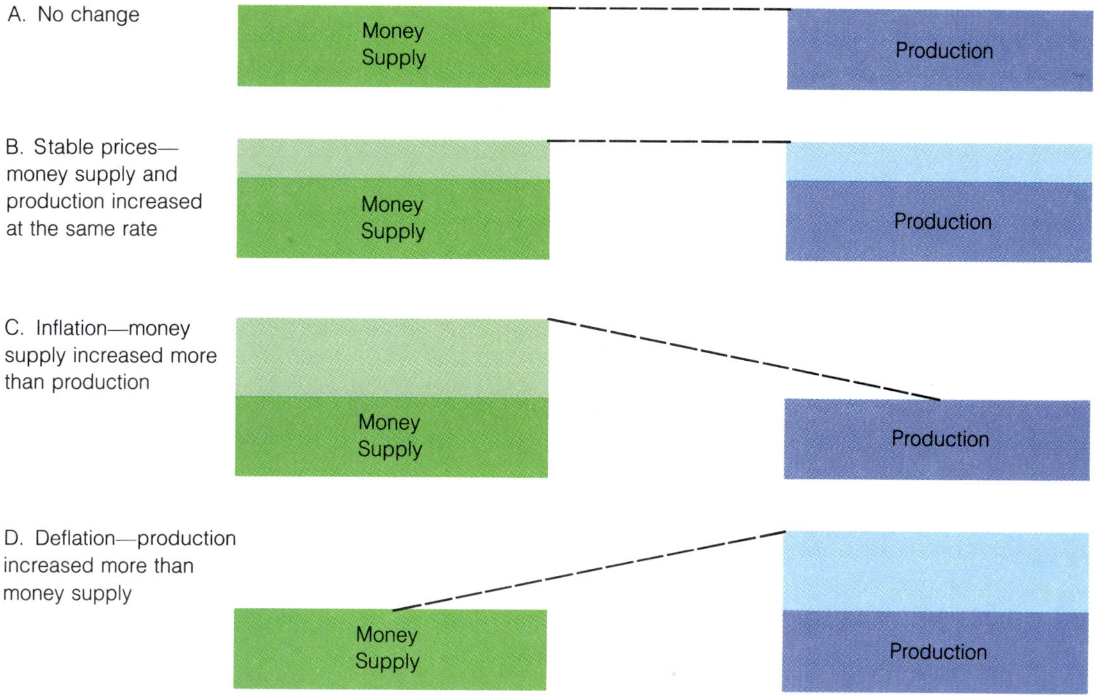

pay for the war. This money could not be converted into gold. The resulting increase in the supply of money contributed to inflation. Also contributing to this inflation was the fact that much of our production was devoted to making military goods. This meant that the box representing money was increased, while the box for production that civilians could purchase was reduced.

When more money is spent on the same number of products, prices go up. Between 1860 and 1865 the price of meat, fuel, and rents increased over 50 percent, the price of flour doubled, and the price of textiles quadrupled. As more and more greenbacks were put into circulation, their value fell. At one point in 1864, the value of a greenback was only 39 percent of a gold or silver dollar.

Explain. Between late 1976 and mid-1979, the money supply grew at an average 8.2% annual rate. In these years, real GDP increased by roughly 2.5% a year. The higher rate of growth in the money supply may have contributed to inflation in these years.

A more recent example of inflation is illustrated in Figure 11–2. Many economists believe inflation between 1970 and 1990 was partially caused by growth of the money supply. Between 1970 and 1990, production grew by 55 percent, but the money supply increased by 249 percent. Because the money supply grew more rapidly, there were more dollars to buy each product.

Figure 11–2 *Percentage of Growth in the Money Supply, Production, and Inflation, 1970–1990*

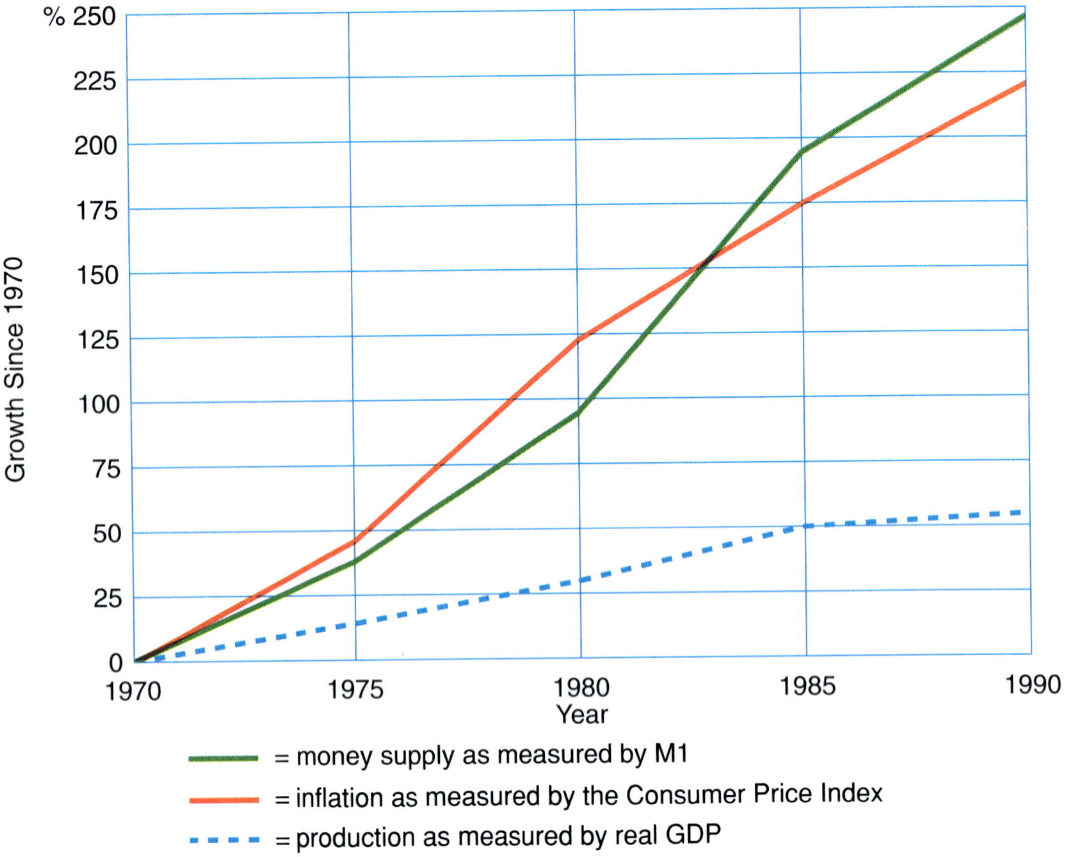

Source: *Statistical Abstract of the United States*, 1991.

Self-Check
1. Money is a claim on something that has value; it represents value, but usually has little value of its own.
2. A medium of exchange, a measure of value, and a store of value.
3. When more money is trying to buy the same amount of goods and services, prices go up, and inflation exists.

Applying What You Have Learned
See Lesson Plans for Chapter 11, Section A, page T106.

Self-Check

1. How do economists define money?
2. What were two of the three functions of money identified in this section?
3. If the supply of money grows more rapidly than the number of goods and services that are offered for sale, what will probably happen to prices?

Applying What You Have Learned

Identify and describe four specific problems the young man in the story would have had trying to use his watch as money.

Section B Checks, Money, and the Economy

This section will explain the process through which banks *expand* the money supply and will introduce the *reserve requirement*.

Personal Narrative

My Father Paid the Bills Today

I learned long ago that it is best not to be home when my father pays the bills. Once a month he goes into his study and starts writing checks. He never stays there very long. Soon he is out asking my mother what this bill is and what we needed that for. If any kids are around, he's sure to tell us how much easier we've got things than he did as a child. His other speech is about how we're going to go to the poor house. Then, after he's had his say, my dad always calms down—at least until next month's bills.

Stress. The importance of checks in the economy. Although purchases students make are likely to be for cash, almost all large transactions are carried out through checks.

When I was young I didn't understand about checks. I thought all you had to do was write them. I couldn't figure out why my father got so upset. If he was short on cash, why not just write a bigger check? I thought it was easy.

Later I found out you had to deposit money in the bank before you could write checks. I wondered what would happen if the bank gave our money to someone else instead. When my father told me that is exactly what they do, I got really worried. I imagined the bank running out of money just when we had to pay our mortgage or something. My father laughed when I told him what I thought.

Note. Banks in the United States run on the *fractional reserve system*, which requires them to maintain a set percentage of their deposits on reserve.

Eventually I discovered that banks are required to keep money in reserve for people who want to make withdrawals or write checks. They can also borrow cash from the Federal Reserve System if they run short. That made me feel better, but I still didn't understand how checks worked.

I understood more after I got a job. I work as a general helper at a shoe store. Two of my jobs are to take the mail to the post office and to make deposits at the bank. I put checks in the mail to our suppliers and deposit checks from our customers. For all the money that goes through the store, we handle very little cash. Any cash that we do receive we deposit at the end of the day. It seems to me that cash spends most of its time in one bank or another. Even my pay is in the form of a check, which I usually put in my savings account.

If the government wants to control the economy, it will have to control checking first.

Checking Accounts and the Supply of Money

Most spending in the American economy is done through checking accounts. (Cash transactions are more frequent, but they tend to be small.) More than half of the value of all spending is done through checks. You can follow the path of a check through the economy by studying Figure 11–3.

Figure 11–3 *A Check's Path Through the Economy*

(1) Mary writes a check on her account in the State Bank of Mt. Pleasant to Mo's Garage for $56.25 for fixing her car.

(2) Mo receives Mary's check for $56.25 and deposits it in his account at the First Bank of Mt. Pleasant.

(3) The First Bank of Mt. Pleasant credits Mo's account for $56.25 and deposits the check in its account in the Federal Reserve Bank of Chicago.

(4) The Federal Reserve Bank of Chicago credits the account of the First Bank of Mt. Pleasant with $56.25. It also debits (charges) the State Bank of Mt. Pleasant's account for $56.25 and sends it Mary's check.

(5) The State Bank of Mt. Pleasant receives Mary's check from the Federal Reserve Bank of Chicago. It debits Mary's checking account for $56.25 and returns the canceled check to Mary.

People and businesses deposit money in banks for many different reasons. Deposits in checking accounts are frequently spent quickly. Savings deposits are usually left in banks for longer periods of time. Some deposits, called certificates of deposit, are placed in banks for a specific period of time, such as six months or a year. Banks pay higher rates of interest on these deposits, because they know how long they will have the use of the money and because they are not required to maintain as large a reserve for such deposits. All deposits serve the purpose of enabling banks to make loans to their customers, which increases our ability to buy goods and services.

To measure the amount of money in circulation, it is necessary to measure the flow of money through checking accounts. For the same reason, regulating the amount of money in circulation requires control over these accounts.

The Expansion of Money

Banks have the ability in effect to allow more than one person to spend the same money. They do this by approving loans from money deposited in checking accounts. Economists call this process the **expansion** of money. The expansion process is described below. Study Figure 11–4 while you read the explanation.

a. Suppose a new deposit of $1,000 is made in a checking account at a bank. This deposit is shown in yellow on row 1 of the figure.

b. The bank has a **reserve requirement** that it must meet. This is the percentage of the deposit which the law says the bank must keep on reserve. The reserve requirement for the checking deposits of most banks was 10 percent in 1992. 10 percent of $1,000 is $100. The bank must keep $100 on reserve and can lend the remaining $900 to someone else. The amount kept on reserve in row 1 is shown in blue, while the amount loaned out is shown in green.

c. Money the bank lends out is almost always spent. Therefore, someone else receives it and probably deposits it somewhere in the checking system. This is another new deposit, which becomes the basis for additional loans and spending. This process can be seen in rows 2 and 3 of Figure 11–4. Each time a loan is made on the right side of the figure, it is spent and becomes a new deposit on the left side of the figure. This new deposit allows more money to be held on reserve and still more money to be loaned out. By studying the figure you can see how this expansion process allows total

Figure 11–4 *The Expansion of Money*

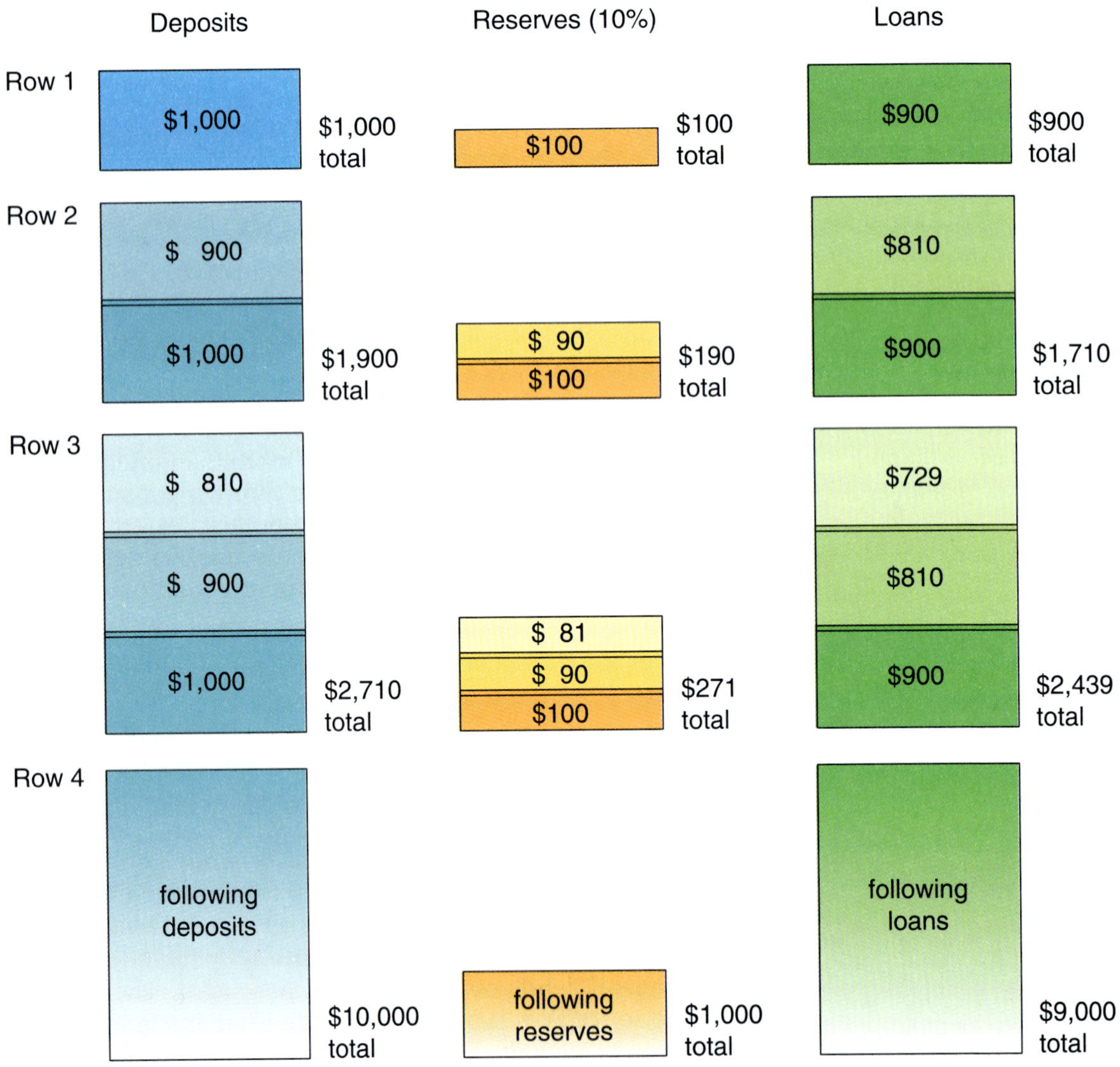

deposits, loans, and spending to grow far beyond the original deposit of $1,000.

d. Although only three steps of the expansion process are shown on the figure, you should realize that it goes on and on. The total expansion of money can be found by using what is called an *expansion multiplier*. This is found by dividing the reserve requirement of 10 percent into 1. The result is a value of 10. When this value is multiplied times the original new deposits of $1,000, the total "following deposits" figure of $10,000 is found. Likewise, multiplying the value of 10 times the amount held on reserve ($100) and the original loan ($900) completes these totals in row 4. If every possible step in the expansion process took place, the totals in row 4 would be reached. (The scale on the graph in row 4 is smaller than the scale on the other rows.)

Note. See Section D of this chapter for more information on the expansion multiplier.

What Limits and Controls the Expansion Process?

A number of factors limit the expansion process. One factor is that banks normally keep more money in reserve than is required. This provides the banks with a sort of "safety margin," which prevents them from falling below their reserve requirement if deposits are withdrawn. Banks may also choose to invest in other securities rather than make loans.

Another limit on expansion is the fact that people hold cash. People keep some money to pay for things they intend to buy. In addition, some people save cash at home rather than depositing it in a bank. Money that is not put into circulation either by banks or by people cannot become part of the expansion process.

Actions of the Federal Reserve System may also limit the expansion of money. These will be discussed in Section D of this chapter.

Self-Check

1. About what part of spending is done with checks?
2. What is the meaning of the reserve requirement?
3. What two factors limit the expansion of money?

Self-Check
1. More than half of all spending is done with checks.
2. It is the percentage of deposits that the law says a bank must keep on reserve.
3. Banks normally keep more money in reserve than is required, and people hold cash.

Applying What You Have Learned

Since most money is spent in the form of checks, there must be important advantages to this form of spending. List and describe three such advantages. It may help to consider the characteristics of money that were explained to you in Section A.

Applying What You Have Learned
See Lesson Plans for Chapter 11, Section B, page T108.

Section C Banks Are in Business to Make a Profit

This section will introduce the FDIC and will discuss how banks operate as businesses, with *assets* and *liabilities.*

Personal Narrative

If You Really Need a Loan, the Bank Won't Give You One

My father works as a gardener for several local businesses. His job is to make sure that the trees and flowers outside their buildings look good. Up until this year he did pretty well. We weren't getting rich, but we could pay our bills. Last spring the city's dam broke and we've had a water shortage ever since. The new dam won't be done until fall. The city council passed an ordinance against watering anything. Have you ever tried to grow flowers without water? It can't be done. Most of my father's customers decided not to have flowers at all. Some of them stuck plastic plants in the ground. My father hasn't had much work this year.

Last year my father bought a new truck with spraying equipment for his business. It cost over $25,000. Every month his payments are almost $700. With our mortgage and other expenses, he owes at least $2,500 a month. He hasn't been able to earn much more than seven or eight hundred dollars from his work and doing odd jobs. My mother took a job as a waitress, but they are still short several hundred dollars. We really need some help to get through this year.

My parents applied for a loan at the bank, but didn't get one. The loan officer said we weren't a good risk. Used trucks aren't worth much. We have little value built up in our house. We don't own anything else to use for collateral. The loan officer said there is no guarantee my father's customers will hire him back even after the dam is fixed. She said she couldn't risk the depositors' money.

Critical Thinking. The importance of banks is measured in terms of their function within the economy. For example, banks' ability to loan money helps other firms produce goods and services. Ask your students to list and discuss the contributions banks make to our economic system.

I can understand the bank's point of view, but it doesn't seem fair. When my father was doing well, they were happy to lend him money and take his interest payments.

My father finally borrowed $5,000 from a doctor he works for. The doctor loaned him the money mostly as a favor. Still, my father has to pay him 10 percent interest on the loan. The doctor's going to make money.

Banks as Businesses

Comparison. Do students set different standards for their own financial dealings than those set by banks? Ask your students what factors they would consider if a relative asked to borrow $500 from them. Are the factors a bank considers before making a loan the same, or different? Why?

Banks are businesses. They are in business to make a profit by providing services to their customers. Two of their primary services are to provide safety and interest income for their depositors' money. Another major service is to provide a source of loans for individuals and businesses that need to borrow money.

The money on deposit in a bank is the merchandise the bank has to sell. Banks earn their profit by charging borrowers a higher rate of interest than they pay their depositors. There is usually a difference, or "spread," of four to five percent between what a bank pays its depositors and what it earns from its loans. Banks are hesitant to make risky loans. One bad loan can wipe out the profits from many good loans.

Economists believe that banks would act in a **pro-cyclical** way if the government allowed them to. *Pro-cyclical* means that their policies would increase any existing economic trends. For example, if the economy were doing well, businesses would make good profits and the banks would be willing to make more loans. More loans would cause the economy to grow even faster, possibly causing inflation.

Banks are able to compete with each other by offering different rates of interest to depositors. Therefore, it is important to determine what interest rates are paid at different banks before making a deposit. The difference in what the savings will earn over several years can be substantial.

If the economy were in a recession, businesses would make little profit. Banks would have a difficult time making profits from loans. Fewer loans would result in less spending and a deeper recession.

In other words, without government intervention bank policies would make expansions larger and recessions deeper. These would be pro-cyclical policies. **Countercyclical** policies, however, are policies that *reverse* trends in the economy. Depending on the circumstances, countercyclical policies are usually better for the economy than pro-cyclical ones.

In Section D of this chapter you will learn about Federal Reserve policies that attempt to stabilize the economy or to prevent pro-cyclical actions by banks.

Insuring Depositors

In the past there were times when people lost confidence in banks. Mass withdrawals, or runs on banks, accompanied the Great Depression in 1932. The government established the **Federal Deposit Insurance Corporation** (FDIC) in 1935 to raise confidence in banks by insuring deposits. In 1992 the FDIC

The Federal Deposit Insurance Corporation was established in 1935, to prevent the kinds of mass withdrawals that occurred in 1932 during the Great Depression. The FDIC insures savings, thereby maintaining depositors' confidence in their banks.

insured deposits up to a maximum of $100,000 per depositor.

New government regulations in the 1970s and 1980s increased competition among banks and reduced their profits. The new rules also encouraged banks to make higher-risk investments. As a result, bank failures increased dramatically in the late 1980s. In 1991 the federal government arranged a new source of funds for the FDIC, so that it could pay depositors of failed banks.

Savings and loan associations (S&Ls) work much like banks today, but they were quite different in the past. These institutions expanded in the 1930s to give small savers a place to deposit their money and to provide home loans at low interest rates. The government created the Federal Savings and Loan Insurance Corporation (FSLIC) to protect depositors.

S&Ls made billions of dollars of long-term loans at low fixed interest rates in the 1950s and 1960s. High inflation in the 1970s forced S&Ls to pay higher interest on deposits. Most S&L income, however, came from previous low-interest rate mortgages. S&Ls were not competitive.

In 1982 Congress decided to allow the S&Ls to make higher-risk loans and investments. When these investments went bad, hundreds of S&Ls failed in the late 1980s and early 1990s. The Federal Savings and Loan Insurance Corporation ran out of funds. Congress created the Resolution Trust Corporation (RTC) in 1989 to take over the failed S&Ls and sell off their property. The FSLIC was replaced with the Savings Association Insurance Fund (SAIF). Some economists estimated that the S&L disaster would cost taxpayers a half trillion dollars.

Self-Check
1. Banks earn a profit by charging their borrowers a higher interest rate than they pay their depositors.
2. Pro-cyclical refers to policies that would increase any existing economic trends.
3. The FDIC insures deposits in order to maintain confidence in banks.

Applying What You Have Learned
See Lesson Plan for Chapter 11, Section C, page T111.

Self-Check

1. How do banks earn a profit?
2. What does "pro-cyclical" mean?
3. What was the reason for the creation of the Federal Deposit Insurance Corporation?

Applying What You Have Learned

List and explain three different reasons why the man in the Personal Narrative was not a good risk for a loan.

Section D What the Federal Reserve System Does

This section will explain the role of the *Federal Reserve System* (the Fed) in our economic system.

Personal Narrative

Give Me the Sports Section, You Can Have the Rest

Whenever I bring in the paper, my family splits it. My mother takes the front page, my sister reads the clothing ads, my little brother finds the comics, and I get the sports section. My father takes what's left. No one wants the financial pages.

Earlier this year I was assigned to read and cut out articles from the business section. One article I read was about the Federal Reserve System and interest rates. It said that the amount of money in circulation was growing faster than the Federal Reserve System wanted it to. Market analysts thought that the Federal Reserve System would slow the growth of the money supply, which would force interest rates up. There was some fear that this could contribute to a downturn in the economy. A discussion of how this would affect attempts to reduce the federal debt followed. I copied over some of the things that I read and handed it in. My teacher gave me a *B* on my paper. To be honest, I didn't understand more than two words I wrote.

Explain. Interest rates are very important. A 2% increase in interest rates would increase the cost of a $10,000 loan by roughly $1,000 over ten years. Each monthly payment would be about $8.50 higher. Consider the cost of a new house and the fact that interest rates on mortgages have fluctuated between 7% and 16% in recent years.

We have been thinking of moving to a new house this year. We put our home on the market three months ago. At least one hundred people have come to see it. Some of them came back two or three times. We have had offers, but none my parents were willing to accept. The real estate agent said that interest rates have gone up lately and people are putting off buying a home until interest rates go down.

My father sees the same problem at work. He is an industrial architect. His business has been slow recently because there has been less construction. He believes his customers have been cutting back on new building because of the high interest rates. If the Federal Reserve System slows the growth of the money supply, Dad says interest rates may go up even more.

When I studied the Federal Reserve System, my teacher said that money acts just like anything else people want. If the supply is reduced when people want the same amount, prices will go up. The price of borrowed money is the interest rate. If interest rates go up even more, I wonder what will happen to my father's job.

I realize that the Federal Reserve System is important. Its actions have a major effect on businesses and people, but I don't really understand how it works.

The History of the Federal Reserve System

Explain. Prior to 1935, each of the Federal Reserve System's 12 district banks were free to make their own decisions. The creation of the Board of Governors in 1935 provided leadership and coordination for the Fed's powers.

Note. In the 1970s, a number of state-chartered banks chose to leave the Federal Reserve System. This caused Congress and the Federal Reserve System to be concerned about the ability of the Fed to regulate the banking system. The Banking Act of 1980 was intended to maintain this control by forcing all financial institutions to meet reserve requirements set by the Fed, regardless of whether or not they belonged to the Federal Reserve System.

Following a run on banks in 1907, the **Federal Reserve System** (also known as "the Fed") was created to oversee banking in this country in 1913. Since then its powers have grown to the point that it now has the ability to influence the entire economic system.

In 1935 Congress established a Board of Governors for the Federal Reserve System. The seven members of this board set Federal Reserve policies. Each member is appointed by the President and approved by the Senate to serve a 14-year term of office. These appointments are staggered, so that there are always experienced people on the board.

Individual banks may or may not belong to the Federal Reserve System. Banks that have been chartered (given the right to operate) by the national government *must* belong. Those chartered by state governments have the choice to belong or not. Generally, larger banks have chosen to belong and smaller ones have not.

In the past, member banks were required to follow rules set by the Federal Reserve System while nonmember banks were not. Since the passage and implementation of the Banking Act of 1980 (Depository Institutions Deregulation and Monetary Control Act), there has been little difference between banks that choose to belong and those that do not. All depository institutions, including banks, saving banks, and savings and loan associations, must now meet reserve requirements set by the Fed.

Tools of the Fed

The most important job of the Federal Reserve System is to maintain a stable supply of money for the economy. There are three basic tools the Fed has to carry out this responsibility: the *reserve requirement*, the *discount rate*, and *open market operations*.

The Reserve Requirement

The *most powerful tool* the Fed has is the power to change the reserve requirement on demand deposits to any value between 3 and 14 percent. A change in the reserve requirement would have a large effect on the expansion of money that was described in Section B of this chapter, and on the economy in general. If the reserve requirement is lowered, more money becomes available for loans. If the requirement is raised, less money becomes available. For example, if the Fed sets the reserve requirement at 12½ percent, the expansion multiplier would be 8. However, if the Fed sets the reserve requirement at 10 percent, the expansion multiplier would be 10. With a lower reserve requirement, the expansion multiplier becomes greater—and the amount of money in circulation increases.

The Fed has not used this power very often. Between 1980 and 1992, the reserve requirement on checking deposits remained at 12 percent. The Fed lowered it to 10 percent in May 1992 to encourage lending.

Note. Some economists believe the Fed does not carry out policy by adjusting the discount rate but only follows changes that have already occurred in the economy. They point to the drop in interest rates in the mid-1980s, and say that other interest rates went down before the discount rate was lowered by the Fed.

The Discount Rate

The Fed has the power to change the **discount rate.** This is the rate of interest the Fed charges banks to which it lends money. Private individuals and businesses cannot borrow from the Fed. Banks can, and frequently do. If the discount rate goes up, fewer banks will want to borrow from the Fed. This will reduce the amount of money these banks have available to loan to their customers and will force interest rates up. Changes in the discount rate usually result in similar changes in other interest rates.

Open Market Operations

The *most important tool* the Fed has is **open market operations.** To understand how this works you need to know that there is a market for previously owned government securities in New York City. Every business day millions of dollars worth of "used" securities are bought and sold. By buying and selling government securities in this open market, the Fed exercises control over the money supply.

Explain. In theory, the Federal Reserve System can buy any quantity of government securities that exist. The Fed can have money printed equal in value to the government securities it owns. Each time the Fed buys a government security it could have money printed to buy another security.

The Fed is the largest single owner of government securities in the country. It also buys and sells more securities than anyone else. When the Fed buys securities from banks, businesses, or individuals, it puts money into the banking system in exchange for the securities that it buys. When it sells securities, it takes money out of circulation.

Table 11-2 will help you understand how this works. In example 1, the Fed *buys* a government security from Joe. The Fed pays money to Joe, and Joe will deposit the money in the banking system. This will be a new deposit, which can be expanded. There will be additional money in circulation. This should make it easier for people or businesses to borrow money.

In example 2, the Fed *sells* a government security to Frank. Frank will pay with money he withdraws from the banking system. This will reduce the amount of money banks have to expand. There will be less money in circulation. This should make it more difficult for people or businesses to borrow money.

In this way the Fed regulates the amount of money available for new deposits in the expansion process. The Federal Reserve System carries out most of its responsibility to control the money supply through open market operations.

Monetary Policy

Federal Reserve actions that are intended to stabilize the economic system make up what is called **monetary policy.** The Fed uses open market operations most frequently to carry out monetary policy. For example, if the Fed wanted banks to have more money to lend, it would buy government securities. This would add more money to the expansion process and increase the ability of banks to make loans.

The Fed does change the discount rate from time to time. In the early 1990s the discount rate was lowered from 7 percent to just 3½ percent in 1992. This drop may have encouraged banks to borrow from the Fed to make loans. It allowed them to reduce the interest they charged their customers, which would encourage businesses and consumers to borrow.

On a few occasions the Fed has changed the reserve requirement. The results of these changes on the economy have been so great that it is doubtful such changes will be made frequently in the future.

Note. Between 1936 and 1937, the Fed increased the reserve requirement for checking deposits to 20 percent. (The maximum percentage has been lowered by Congress to 14 percent since the 1930s.) The result was a drop in the number of loans made by banks and a deepening of the Depression.

Over the past 50 years the Fed has had different objectives for its monetary policy. In World War II it tried to keep interest rates low to help the government pay for the war. In the mid-1960s it tried to reduce the amount of money banks had available to loan in order to fight inflation. In the early 1980s Federal Reserve actions helped force interest rates to very high levels. These high interest rates contributed to the recession of 1981–82, but

Table 11-2

Example 1. The Federal Reserve Buys a Security

Federal Reserve System	Joe	Joe's Bank
The Federal Reserve buys a government security from Joe. The Fed receives the security and pays Joe.	Joe sells his government security and is paid by the Fed. Joe puts the money in his bank.	With Joe's deposit, the bank now has additional money to make more loans.

Example 2. The Federal Reserve Sells a Security

Federal Reserve System	Frank	Frank's Bank
The Federal Reserve sells a government security to Frank. The Fed receives a check from Frank. The Fed sends the check to Frank's bank for payment.	Frank buys a government security from the Fed. He writes a check to pay for it, so money comes out of his bank and flows to the Fed.	Frank's bank pays the Fed on Frank's check and reduces Frank's balance in his account. Since the bank now has less money on deposit, it is able to make fewer loans.

Note. Milton Friedman (see Biographical Sketch in Chapter 12) feels the Fed should not try to adjust the economy by changing the money supply because the Fed cannot react quickly enough to changing economic conditions. He would have the Fed increase the money supply at a constant rate of 3% to 5% each year, no matter what.

eventually helped to reduce the high rate of inflation. Figure 11-5 shows the levels of prime interest rate (the rate that banks charge their best customers) for the years 1977–1990.

Some politicians and economists feel that the Fed has made many mistakes. Others feel that it has done a good job most of the time. It is clear at least that the Federal Reserve is an important power in our economic system.

Figure 11–5 *Average Prime Interest Rates, 1977–1990*

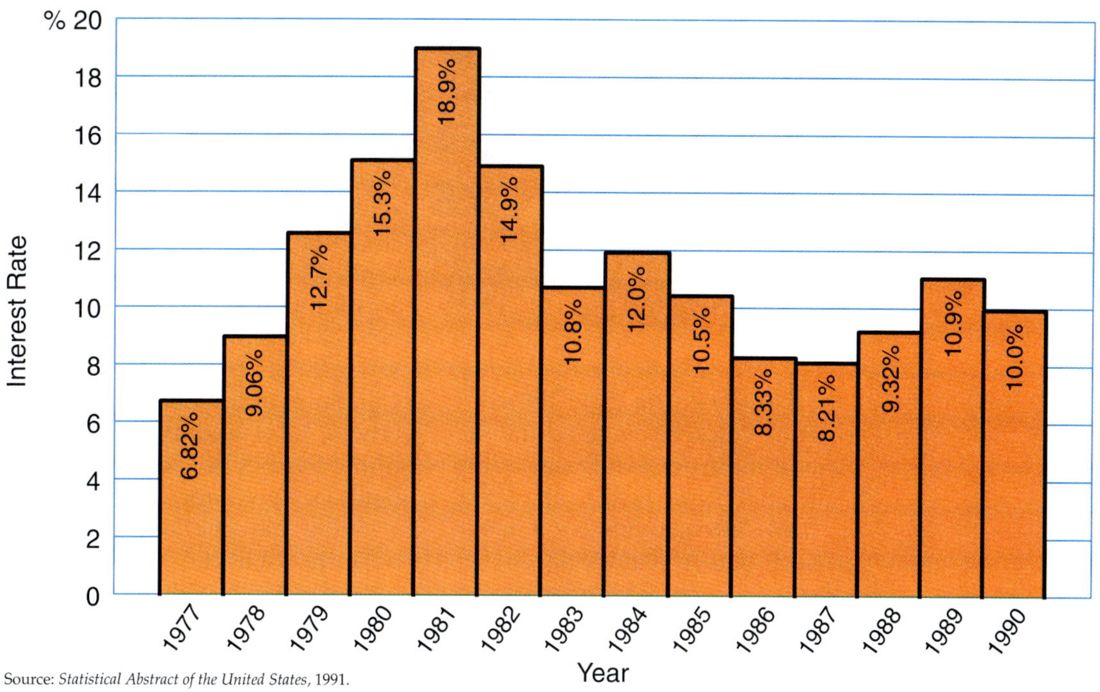

Source: *Statistical Abstract of the United States*, 1991.

Self-Check
1. The most important job of the Federal Reserve is to maintain a stable supply of money.
2. A change in the reserve requirement would have a very large effect on the economy.
3. The Fed uses monetary policy to stabilize the economy.

Applying What You Have Learned
See Lesson Plans for Chapter 11, Section D, page T113.

Self-Check

1. What is the most important job of the Federal Reserve System?
2. Why hasn't the Federal Reserve's Board of Governors changed the reserve requirement very often?
3. What is the purpose of monetary policy?

Applying What You Have Learned

There is a list of possible Federal Reserve actions below. In each case the action is intended to either increase or decrease the amount of money in circulation. Identify the purpose of each action.

a. The Fed increases the discount rate.
b. The Fed lowers the reserve requirement.
c. The Fed buys government securities.
d. The Fed sells government securities.
e. The Fed raises the reserve requirement.
f. The Fed lowers the discount rate.

PROFILE

Paul Volcker
(1927–)

In a survey of national leaders made in the early 1980s, Paul Volcker was rated the second most powerful man in the United States next to the President. What could give a man such power? Paul Volcker served as the Chairman of the Board of Governors of the Federal Reserve System at a time when monetary policy squeezed inflation from 13.5 percent in 1980 to 3.3 percent in 1985. During this time our country went through the worst recession since the Great Depression, and experienced unemployment of nearly 10 percent. In 1981–1982 real GDP actually declined 2.5 percent.

Paul Volcker was appointed Chairman of the Board of Governors in 1979 by President Carter and was later reappointed by President Reagan. He left the Board in 1987.

He brought a wide and impressive background with him to the job. He was a brilliant student at Princeton, Harvard, and at the London School of Economics. He held several important banking positions before accepting the post of Undersecretary for Monetary Affairs for the Department of the Treasury. While holding this position he was influential in establishing a new system for setting exchange rates. Before being appointed Chairman of the Board of Governors, he served as President of the District Federal Reserve Bank in New York.

How did Volcker accomplish the "miracle" of whipping inflation? He had the Fed sell government securities to reduce the money supply. At the same time the discount rate was increased to an unprecedented 14 percent. These actions forced interest rates above 20 percent for car loans, mortgages, and businesses. Sales of these items fell, leading to a recession. Many people called for Volcker to resign. He seemed to be winning the battle to reduce inflation, but at what cost? Was it worth having nearly 11 million people unemployed? In the latter part of 1982 the Fed allowed the money supply to grow more rapidly. This gradually brought down interest rates and helped the economy recover without a return to inflation.

CURRENT ECONOMIC ISSUES

Should Controls Be Placed on the Powers of the Federal Reserve System?

Although there are effective checks-and-balances on powers held by the Congress and the President, there are few checks on the monetary power of the Federal Reserve System's Board of Governors. Under current law, the Board of Governors is free to act within broad limits established by Congress and the President. Actions taken by the Fed are important to the success of government economic policy, yet there is no guarantee that members of the Board of Governors will cooperate with Congress and the President in implementing economic plans. Some political leaders have suggested that the powers of the Fed's Board of Governors should be limited, or that they should be made responsible to the President.

Supporters of controlling the Fed believe such a policy would assure the country of a unified economic policy. Some argue that it is wrong for people with so much power not to be elected by the people.

Other people are against the plan because it would allow the Fed's powers to be used for political reasons instead of the good of our economic system. They argue that politicians would be too slow to act, that decisions would be made to help people get elected, and that politicians would probably put too much money into circulation to keep interest rates low and make voters happy. There is a fear that this would lead to inflation.

How would putting the Fed under the control of the President affect you or your friends? What would be good or bad about this idea?

Arguments in Favor of the Idea

1. It would lead to a more unified government economic policy.
2. It would give voters a choice in who carried out monetary policy.
3. It would prevent the Board of Governors from making important decisions with no checks.

Arguments Against the Idea

1. It would make monetary policy subject to political pressure.
2. It would make monetary policy very slow to react to change.
3. It could lead to more money being put into circulation and result in inflation.

What Do You Think?

Consider the arguments for and against this idea. Do you believe it is a good idea? Do you feel politicians would be able to regulate our banking system properly? What might happen if they made mistakes?

Chapter 11 Review

What Have You Learned?

In this chapter you've learned the following important principles of economics:

- Money plays many important roles in our economic system. Money serves as a *medium of exchange*, a *measure of value*, and a *store of value*. To carry out its economic functions, money must be acceptable, divisible, portable, and stable in value.
- The amount of money in circulation is closely related to prices. When more money becomes necessary to buy the same number of goods and services, there will be *inflation*. On the other hand, if the same amount of money is used to buy more products, there will be *deflation*.
- The largest part of spending in this country is done with checks. It is necessary to control checking to control the money supply. When banks loan money, the banking system is *expanding* the money supply. This is accomplished by a series of deposits and loans that pass through checking accounts.
- Money that is withdrawn from accounts and not redeposited, or that is deposited but not loaned out by the bank, reduces the expansion process.
- The *Federal Reserve System* was established in 1913 to oversee the American banking system. It is now administered by a seven-member Board of Governors. These governors set what is known as *monetary policy*. Monetary policy is intended to help keep our economic system from going into a recession or from having inflation. It does this by ensuring a reliable banking system and supply of money.
- The *Federal Reserve System* can control the expansion process and the supply of money by adjusting banks' *reserve requirement*, by buying and selling government securities in the open market, or by changing the *discount rate* to affect bank borrowing from the Federal Reserve System. These tools make up the Fed's monetary policy. In recent years the Fed has been hesitant to change the reserve requirement on checking deposits and has relied on *open market operations* most of the time.
- In trying to earn a profit, banks would run in a *pro-cyclical* way if they were able to. In bad times they would find it hard to make as many safe loans. In good times they would make many loans. This would tend to make expansions greater and recessions deeper. The Federal Reserve System takes actions to influence banks to run counter to the business cycle.
- In 1935 the *Federal Deposit Insurance Corporation* was established to insure deposits in our banks. This organization has faced challenges because of increased bank failures in recent years.
- There is often disagreement over the proper role of the Federal Reserve System. Some people feel the Board of Governors has made too many mistakes. Still, it is clear that the Fed has an important function to carry out in our economic system.

Words and Terms

money (p. 292)
fiat money (p. 292)
functions of money (p. 292)
characteristics of money (p. 292)
money supply (p. 294)
inflation (p. 294)
deflation (p. 294)
expansion of money (p. 299)
reserve requirement (p. 299)
pro-cyclical (p. 303)
countercyclical (p. 304)
Federal Deposit Insurance Corporation (p. 304)
savings and loan associations (p. 305)
Federal Reserve System (p. 307)
discount rate (p. 308)
open market operations (p. 308)
monetary policy (p. 309)

See Chapter 11 Review Answers, page T115.

Building Your Vocabulary

On a separate piece of paper, write the vocabulary word or term that best completes each of the following statements.

1. The ______ was established to build trust in the banking system by insuring bank deposits.
2. ______ were institutions that expanded in the 1930s to provide small savers a place to deposit their money and that could offer home loans at low interest rates.
3. An increase in the average price level is called ______.
4. The process that allows banks to increase the amount of money in circulation through checking accounts is called the ______.
5. Economists define ______ as a claim on something of value.
6. The ______ include medium of exchange, measure of value, and store of value.
7. The ______ include acceptability, divisibility, portability, and stability of value.
8. A decrease in the average price level is called ______.
9. Something that is money because a government has said that it is money is called ______.
10. The part of a deposit that a bank is required to keep on hand is called the ______.
11. The interest that a bank must pay when it borrows from the Federal Reserve System is called the ______.
12. The ______ was established in 1913 to oversee banking in the United States.
13. ______ policies make expansions greater and recessions deeper.
14. ______ policies make expansions smaller and recessions less severe.
15. The Federal Reserve carries out ______ to try to maintain a steady supply of money in this country.
16. When the Federal Reserve System buys and sells government securities, it is carrying out ______.
17. The amount of money in circulation is called the ______.

Chapter 11 Review

Understanding Economics

1. Explain why a valuable watch or gold ring would not make good money. Explain what this has to do with the functions of money.
2. Describe what would probably happen to prices if the amount of money in circulation increased by half. Explain why this would happen.
3. If you deposited $100 in a checking account when the reserve requirement was 10 percent, how many dollars would the bank have to keep and how much could it loan out?
4. If the bank loaned this money out (from question 3), describe how it would be expanded through the banking system.
5. What are the two ways that the expansion process can be controlled?
6. Explain why banks would tend to act in a pro-cyclical way if they could.
7. Describe what the Federal Deposit Insurance Corporation does and why it is important to the banking system.
8. Identify the group that makes decisions for the Federal Reserve System.
9. Describe each of the three tools that the Fed has for carrying out monetary policy.

Thinking Critically About Economics

1. Suppose you inherited a piece of land in the country. You want to use it to pay your tuition at school next year. Describe the problems you would have if you couldn't sell the land for money.
2. Draw your own table to show the relationship between the money supply, products for sale, and prices. Use Figure 11–1 to give you ideas, but don't just copy it.
3. Explain how a deposit of $500 in a checking account could be expanded into a total increase in deposits of thousands of dollars.
4. Describe what would happen to the expansion of money if the Federal Reserve System increased the reserve requirement for checking deposits from 10 percent to 12 percent.
5. Explain why the Federal Deposit Insurance Corporation is important to our banking system.
6. Describe what would probably happen if the Federal Reserve System increased the discount rate to 6 percent from 3½ percent.

Consumer Skills Projects

1. Go to various local banks and find out what interest rates they are offering for deposits. Make a large chart that shows these different rates. Show it to your class. Try to think of several reasons that could explain any differences in interest rates. You could do the same project for interest rates on loans.
2. Interview a person who makes loans for a bank. Ask this person about the things a young person could do to establish a good credit rating. Report your findings to your class.

Thinking Critically About Economics
(1) identifying the problem; (2) using graphic displays; (3) cause and effect; (4) predicting probable consequences; (5) cause and effect; (6) predicting probable consequences.

Developing Your Economic Skills

Using Tables to Compare Interest Costs

Skill: This lesson will show you how to use two types of tables to evaluate the cost of borrowing money. To complete this lesson you'll follow these steps:

1. Study the two tables and identify specific values on each.
2. Consider why the two tables could lead people to different decisions.
3. Evaluate the meaning of each table.

Application: How important are interest rates?

Many people who borrow money are only interested in knowing their monthly payments. They ignore the interest rate and the total interest cost of their loan. This may be a costly mistake. Low monthly payments can hide high interest costs when loans are spread out over many years. The tables below demonstrate this fact.

The first table lists the term of the loan (the number of years over which it must be paid off) on the left side and various interest rates across its top, and shows the monthly payment for each possible combination. The second table is set up the same way, but instead of showing the monthly payment, it shows the total interest paid. Loan officers at banks have tables similar to these.

Interest Cost of a $1,000 Loan at Different Rates, Over Different Terms

Term of Loan (in years)	Interest Rate/Monthly Payment		
	12%	14%	16%
1	$88.85	$89.79	$90.73
2	$47.07	$48.01	$48.96
3	<u>$33.21</u>	$34.18	$35.16
4	$26.33	$27.33	<u>$28.34</u>
5	$22.24	$23.27	$24.32

If you looked at the first table without really thinking about what it means, you might conclude that a 3-year loan at 12 percent was more expensive than a 4-year loan at 16 percent. The monthly payment for the 3-year loan is $33.21, while the 4-year loan at a higher interest rate has a payment of only $28.34 (find these values, underlined on the table). Your conclusion would be wrong. The interest expense would be much greater with the higher interest rate loan. The next table demonstrates this fact.

Total Interest Paid at Different Rates

Term of Loan (in years)	Interest Rate		
	12%	14%	16%
1	$ 66.19	$ 77.45	$ 88.77
2	$129.76	$152.31	$175.12
3	<u>$195.71</u>	$230.40	$265.65
4	$264.02	$311.67	<u>$360.33</u>
5	$334.67	$396.10	$459.08

This table shows you that the total interest you would pay on the 4-year loan at 16 percent would be $360.33, while the 3-year loan at 12 percent would cost only $195.71.

Which of the two tables do you believe provides more important and useful information?

Practice: A customer wants to borrow $1,000 for 2 years with monthly payments of $47.07. Determine how much more interest the lender could earn by offering a lower monthly payment of only $27.33 on a $1,000 loan at 14% interest for 4 years. If you were the customer, would you accept the offer?

CHAPTER 12

Government Decisions and Economic Success

Objectives

In the sections of this chapter, you will learn:

A

how the government uses *fiscal policy* to attempt to promote employment, production, and purchasing power, and how Classical economists and Keynesian economists disagree about using fiscal policy;

B

how government price controls and supply-side policies have been used in an attempt to control inflation and unemployment, and why they have met with only limited success;

C

how the ability to regulate our economy is limited by the global nature of our economy; and

D

about programs that are intended to guarantee a minimum level of economic security for all Americans.

Introduction

The Declaration of Independence states that governments are created to secure the rights of "life, liberty and the pursuit of happiness." We believe that our government exists to serve the people. Among other things, our government assures us an opportunity to earn a decent living. To carry out this responsibility the government must be involved in our economic system.

The Laissez-Faire System

In the early days of the United States, the government played a relatively small part in the economic system. The role of the government was limited to protecting property rights, making sure that contracts were carried out, establishing a fair civil code (laws dealing with business transactions), and enforcing general rules for how businesses could operate. In general, the government stayed out of the everyday affairs of individual firms. There was a **laissez-faire** economic policy. This means that the government tried to let the economic system run on its own with as little government involvement as possible.

In a laissez-faire economy (also known as a *free-market* economy) the forces of demand and supply are allowed to make the basic economic decisions of *what, how,* and *for whom*. People who favored this type of

In the early days of the United States, the government played a very limited role and attempted to let the economy operate on its own. This was known as a laissez-faire, or free-market economy. But over the years, as businesses and society have become more complex, it has been necessary for the government to play a greater role in the economic system.

Explain. One principle of Classical economics was to have the government balance its budget. When the Great Depression started, President Hoover tried to balance the budget by reducing government spending, making the Depression worse instead of helping to end it.

economy were called **Classical economists.** The Classical theory said the economic system would take care of itself and that unnecessary government intervention could only cause problems. Classical economists believed that if the government made too many decisions in the economic system, the result would be inefficient use of the factors of production (land, labor, capital, and entrepreneurship).

The Role of Government

However, over the years it has become necessary for our government to play a greater role in our economic system. Most businesses and products were relatively simple 200 or more years ago.

There were few big monopolies and practically no labor unions. Today we have giant firms that negotiate contracts with powerful unions and sell complex products in monopolistic markets. Individual consumers are no longer able to protect themselves from economic abuse. As our economic system has grown and become more complicated, our government has taken on more responsibilities.

This chapter will discuss problems regarding the role of the government in today's economy. Unlike businesses, the federal government is not run to make a profit. Its purpose is to provide services to the people (you read about some of these services in Chapter 9).

A relatively new service of the government is its attempt to provide economic stability. Because of its immense size and power, the government is able to influence economic conditions in many areas. It can create more jobs by cutting taxes or increasing its spending. It can carry out policies that encourage investment or reduce inflation. And government decisions can increase or decrease our trade with other countries.

Stress. A decision to do nothing is an important decision. The government allocates every third dollar in the U.S. economy. It will have a major impact on the economy and people's lives, whether or not it establishes objectives.

Although the government plays a vital role in our economic system, there is often disagreement over how the government can best use its powers. There are several general areas of disagreement concerning government economic policy. One is a lack of agreement over what our economic objectives should be. However, even if we could agree on our objectives, we would still have a second problem. We would have to set priorities—that is, we would have to decide which goals to try to achieve first. It is impossible to deal with all problems at the same time.

Important questions need to be answered. Is it more important to reduce poverty or to increase investment? If unemployment and inflation are both too high, which should we work on first? What is the best trade-off between individual freedom and government protection? It is difficult to set government economic policy until we agree on what we want to achieve.

Question. Ask your students how the discussion of the problem of agreeing on objectives relates to the difference between positive and normative statements in Section E of Chapter 1.

Another problem is that even if we do agree on our objectives, we still need to choose the policies that can best achieve our goals. Is it better to reduce unemployment by giving a tax cut to businesses or to individuals? Should inflation be fought through increased production or through reduced demand? What effect will attempts to control the size of the federal deficit have on the rest of the economy? There is widespread disagreement over the specific policies that would be most effective in achieving our objectives.

In this chapter you will study the debate over our economic objectives. The basic ideas of several economic theories will be outlined for you. You will learn about what the government tries to do, and why there is so much disagreement over government policies.

Section A Government Spending and Jobs

This section will discuss the role our government plays in creating jobs for American workers.

Personal Narrative

Note. Economists define the "natural rate of unemployment" as those who are unemployed and don't really want to work, or who would lose government transfer payments if they took a job. It has been suggested that employment could be increased by reducing government transfers, or by not cutting benefits for poor people who do work.

Discuss. Ask your students to relate experiences their relatives or friends have had with government training programs. What do they think was accomplished by the program(s)?

My Mother Got a Job with the County

About two years ago my mother lost her job when the shirt factory shut down. There used to be lots of mills and clothing factories in this area, but they were hurt by imported goods. Now most of them are closed.

Mom had supported four kids on her salary. (My father died about the same time my little sister Jessica was born.) We have been through some hard times. For years we lived on welfare in a government low-income housing project. Food stamps helped, but there never seemed to be enough to eat. My mother couldn't take a part-time job. She said it would cost us more in lost benefits than she could earn. We all did what we could. I delivered newspapers and my older sister did babysitting in the evening. Mom wouldn't let us quit school to find work.

Finally last month things began to look up. The government has set up a program to retrain workers. My mother knows how to type and keep records. She got a job working for the county in the retraining program. She helps people fill out applications and keeps files up to date. They are teaching her how to prepare reports for the federal government. She earns almost as much now as she did when she worked in the factory, and she likes her work. Mom isn't worried about being unemployed any more. She is learning skills that will help her get a better job in the future.

We've been lucky, but I wonder about all the other local people who are out of work. They are supposed to be training for new jobs, but there aren't any jobs around here for them to take. I think most of them will have to move if their training is going to do them any good. Many people won't want to do that. They have families, friends, and homes here. I think most of them will stay and remain unemployed.

Our representative visited town last week to talk about getting "high-tech" firms to move into the old mill buildings. He said something about giving tax breaks to encourage them to move here. That sounds good, but I doubt it would help people who live here now. We don't have "high-tech" skills. The businesses would probably bring people in from outside for most of the jobs. Any work we could get would probably pay minimum wage.

My social studies teacher said there was a tax cut a few years ago. It was supposed to get the economy moving again. Last year

Problem Solving. Assign your students to review a local spending plan that is controversial. Do they believe the project is worthwhile? Ask them to explain their reasoning.

my family's income was almost nothing. We paid no income tax at all. Reducing taxes did not help us very much.

There is a debate in Congress over ways to balance the federal budget. They talk about increasing taxes or cutting aid for the poor. One suggestion was to get rid of the program that pays for my mother's job. If they cut her job, we might have to go back on welfare. The government would end up supporting us, but they would get no work from my mother in return. It desn't sound like a very efficient way to save money to me.

Theories of Government Involvement in the Economy

Discuss. 'The composition of people who must find jobs to achieve full employment today is not the same as 30 years ago. More women, minorities, and young people are looking for work today. These groups have experienced greater difficulty in finding employment than the adult white males who made up most of the labor force in the past. Do your students feel there is an important difference between past and present unemployment rates? Does it hurt less to be unemployed if you are a minority, female, or young?

The **Employment Act of 1946** stated that it is the responsibility of the government to promote employment, production, and purchasing power. This law said the government should take actions that would help people find work. The law stopped short of guaranteeing everyone a job, but it did say the government should help achieve full employment.

Although full employment is a goal that most people could agree with, there are many different ideas about what the best way is to achieve it. In the preceding story you saw several examples of things the government can do to try to affect the economy and increase employment. There is disagreement over which actions the government should take. There has also been disagreement over how much government involvement there should be. Two important schools of thought have been the *Classical theory* and the *Keynesian theory*.

The Classical Theory

Explain. Classical economists saw recessions as a means to "weed out" inefficient businesses. Weak businesses would fail in the recession, leaving only the strong and efficient firms to grow and prosper after the recession ended.

Before the Great Depression of the 1930s, most economists thought that the economy did not require government involvement. **John Baptiste Say,** a Classical economist who wrote in the early 1800s, believed that a market economic system would naturally have full employment. He suggested that if there was a recession, the market would quickly bring it to an end by lowering prices, interest rates, and wages. He said that unemployed workers would accept lower wages, which would encourage employers to hire them. Banks would reduce interest rates to encourage borrowing, and firms would lower their prices so they could sell their products. The result would be that the market, through the forces of demand and supply, would adjust the economy and bring the recession to an end. Classical economists believed there was no need for government intervention in the economy. But when the Great Depression did not automatically

John Baptiste Say (top left), a Classical economist, believed that the economy worked best without government involvement.

When the Great Depression failed to come to an end of its own accord, attention focused on the theories of John Maynard Keynes (top right). Keynes said that capitalist market economies are not self-regulating. He believed the government should take the responsibility for seeing that there is full employment and economic stability. Keynes said that governments could encourage spending and increase employment in a recession by having a deficit budget; that is, by spending more than it took in from tax revenues.

come to an end, it became clear that other theories would have to be found to explain how the economy worked.

The Keynesian Theory

Note. The idea that spending creates jobs can be related to the circular flow model. This argument asserts that demand for labor and other factors of production in the factor market is the result of demand for products in the product market.

An alternative theory was suggested by an English economist, **John Maynard Keynes.** Keynes believed that economic activity and jobs depend on the rate of *spending* in the economy. Keynes said that there were three types of spending—spending by *people* (for personal consumption), spending by *businesses* (for investment), and spending by the *government* (to provide goods and services for the people). In a recession, people and businesses become worried and cut back on consumer spending and investment. This results in lower sales, unemployment, and lower production.

Increased government spending for services is one example of Keynesian policies to end a recession. If government spending increases and taxes stay the same, more money is introduced into the economy. An alternative Keynesian approach is lowering taxes without decreasing the current level of spending. Either policy could cause a budget deficit.

Note. Keynes did not believe government borrowing would have much of an effect on interest rates, wages, or prices in a recession, because there was so much "slack" in the economy. Banks, firms, and people in general would be glad for the business, and not consider increasing interest rates, wages, or prices very much.

Keynes believed that in a recession, the third spending group (the government) should try to make up for the decreased spending from consumers and businesses. The government should help the market along by spending more than it took in from tax revenues. This could be accomplished in two ways. The government could cut taxes without changing its spending. This would give households more disposable income (income after taxes) to increase their spending. An alternative would be for the government to increase its own spending without changing taxes. For example, building roads or providing more services would create more jobs. It would also be possible for the government to do some of each of these policies.

If the economy was expanding too rapidly, Keynes believed the government should take the opposite actions and increase taxes and/or reduce its own spending. This would decrease total spending and reduce the possibility of having inflation.

According to Keynes, ensuring full employment would require continual adjustment of government spending and taxing to achieve the correct level of total spending. This amount of spending would create enough jobs for everyone who wants to work.

During the past several decades, Keynesian economic policy has been used in varying degrees by the federal government. Presidents Kennedy and Johnson, in particular, relied on Keynesian ideas to "fine tune" the economy.

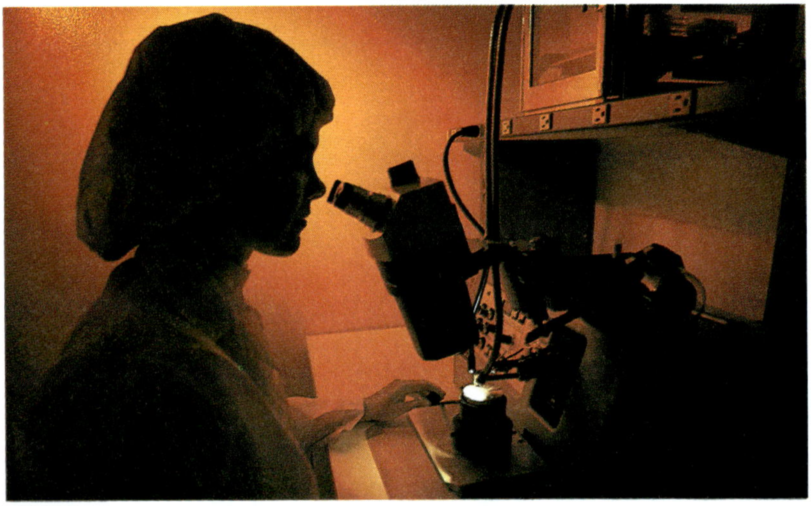

The types of products needed and produced in our society have changed dramatically in recent years. In a number of cases, the government has stepped in to help businesses and workers whose livelihoods were threatened by changes in technology. Special tax breaks for businesses, and training programs for workers, have allowed some factories that were closed to reopen and produce in high-tech fields.

Fiscal Policy

Economists call the federal government's attempt to stabilize the economy through taxing and government spending **fiscal policy**. Fiscal policy involves planning a budget that has either surpluses or deficits that are intended to maintain a steady level of total spending in the economy. Fiscal policy can be either *discretionary* or *automatic*.

Explain. All Keynesian policy is fiscal policy; however, *not all fiscal policy* is Keynesian. Some tax cuts and spending decisions made by our government to carry out "supply-side" policies (see Section B) would not have been supported by Keynes.

Discretionary fiscal policy is policy that someone must *choose* to implement. It requires an action by either the Congress and the President, or by an agency of the government, to take effect. For example, in 1964 there was a tax cut to encourage economic expansion. Four years later, in 1968, there was a tax increase to reduce inflation. In 1992 the economy was in a period of slow growth. Candidates in the 1992 presidential campaign debated whether or not to lower taxes to encourage investment.

Individual government departments have the ability to either speed up or slow down their spending. An advantage of discretionary fiscal policy is the fact that it can be targeted to specific areas of the country that have special problems. For example, in the 1960s large amounts of money were spent in depressed areas in the eastern part of our nation. In the early 1980s, President Reagan frequently suggested that "urban development zones" be identified in depressed areas of our cities. His plan called for reduced taxes and special aid for firms that moved into or expanded in such areas.

Explain. The fact that fiscal policy can be targeted also means it can be subject to political pressures. (See pork barrel spending in Section C of Chapter 9.)

Fiscal policy that reacts automatically (referred to as **automatic stabilization**) is different from discretionary fiscal policy in that it does not require new or special action to go into effect. It reacts automatically when the economy changes. Several examples of automatic stabilization are welfare, unemployment compensation, and income taxes. To see how automatic stabilization works, consider what happens to these examples in a recession.

When the economy goes into a recession, additional people automatically become eligible for government transfer programs. As a result, government expenditures to support welfare and unemployment compensation automatically increase. Neither Congress, the President, nor any government agency has to make a new decision in order for this to happen. This automatic increase in expenditures injects more money into the economy.

At the same time, people who become unemployed in a recession would pay less income tax. This results from people falling into lower tax brackets as well as from people paying taxes on lower incomes. This also puts more money into the economy. When the economy recovers, the opposite events would take place, automatically reducing the amount of money going into the economy. Generally, automatic stabilization goes into effect much more rapidly than discretionary fiscal policy. On the other hand, it is more difficult to target specific problems with automatic stabilization.

Classical economists would say that the free market, through changing wages, prices, and interest rates, is all the automatic policy that is needed. Keynesian economists answer that the market needs help from the government because it works too slowly.

Weaknesses in Keynesian Theory

Note. Milton Friedman is a leading spokesman for those economists who oppose the use of discretionary fiscal and monetary policies. He suggests that the time lags in putting such policies into effect are both long and variable, and that it would be better to allow the market to regulate the economy.

There are several limitations on the effectiveness of Keynesian economic policy. One problem is the difficulty the government has in predicting what the economy is going to do in the future. It is hard to formulate policies to deal with problems if you don't know what the problems will be.

Another limitation on Keynesian policy is that discretionary policy—an important tool in the Keynesian approach—takes a long time to put into effect. Some economists believe that the "lags" between the beginning of a problem and the government's taking action are so long that we would be better off if the government did not try to use discretionary fiscal policy.

Discretionary policy may not only be slow, it may also be misguided. In the Personal Narrative for this section, the government was training workers for jobs that did not exist in their local area. The young man believed most of the workers being trained would have to move to find jobs. It is also possible for jobs to be brought to an area which has few qualified workers. The tax breaks for "high-tech" firms supported by the member of Congress in the narrative would be an example of this problem. Spending money to create jobs does not guarantee that the money will be well spent.

A third problem is the fact that Keynesian policy cannot fight both inflation and unemployment at the same time. Keynes believed that the government should deal with inflation by cutting spending and/or increasing taxes.* He said it should fight unemployment by increasing government spending and/or cutting taxes. The government can't follow both of these policies at the same time.

Finally, there is the problem called the "**crowding-out effect**." This idea states that government borrowing to support Keynesian policy in a recession could force interest rates up. Higher interest rates would discourage consumers and businesses from borrowing and spending. Therefore, extra government spending could cause lower private spending, so that total spending might not change much. Government borrowing could crowd consumers and businesses out of the credit market.

The crowding-out effect can be seen in Figure 12-1. Suppose that the demand curve, D^1, is for money that people, businesses, and the government want to borrow. The supply curve, *S*, is for money that is available to be loaned. If the government decided to borrow \$100 billion more, D^1 would shift to the right to D^2. This would result in the interest rate (vertical axis) at the equilibrium point going from 8 to 10 percent. The higher interest rate would discourage people and businesses from borrowing and spending. Although the government increased its borrowing by \$100 billion, the amount of money loaned (the horizontal axis) would go up by only \$50 billion, from \$150 to \$200 billion. This would happen because higher interest rates would cause people and businesses not to borrow and spend \$50 billion that they otherwise would have.

---

*It is also possible to use monetary policy to encourage investment and spending, by increasing the money supply and causing interest rates to decrease. See Section C of Chapter 10.

Figure 12-1 *Private and Public Demand and Supply for Loanable Funds*

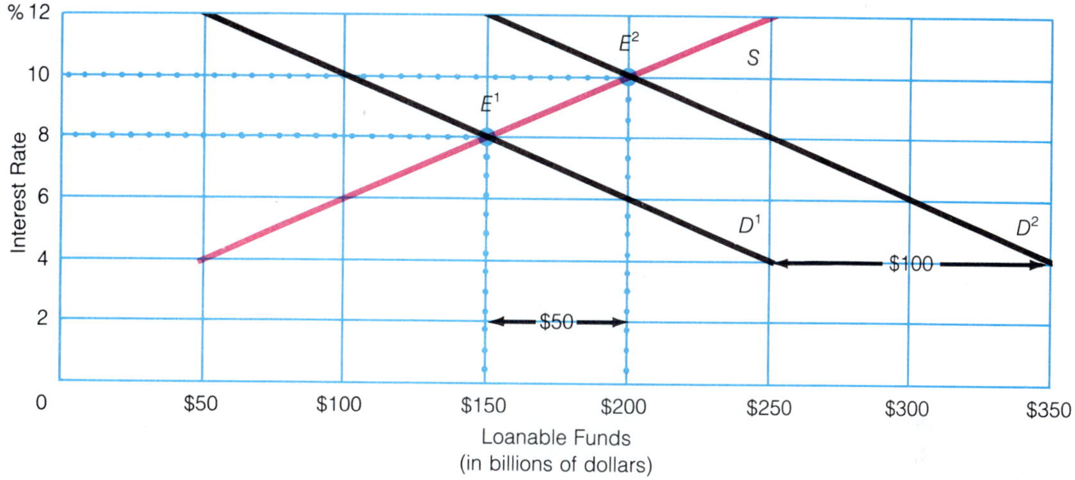

In spite of such problems, there are many economists (called *neo-Keynesians*) and politicians who believe in a modified Keynesian approach as a basis for the best government economic policy.

Keynes supported the idea of helping unemployed people through government job programs. One example of such a program was the Comprehensive Employment and Training Act of 1973 (CETA). This law was enacted to provide training and job opportunities for America's "hard-core" unemployed. The program grew from a budget of just over $2 billion in 1974 to almost $12 billion in 1979. The program was specifically directed to help "offenders (of the law), persons of limited English language proficiency, handicapped, women, single parents, displaced homemakers, youths, older workers and people who lack education." At its peak, CETA provided 725,000 public service jobs.

Explain. Many policies of the Carter administration in the late 1970s were Keynesian. By employing and training many thousands of people in the CETA program, the government attempted to reduce unemployment and increase total spending. Some economists believe this contributed to high rates of inflation in these years.

On the other hand, many people believe that CETA wasted a great deal of the people's money. The dropout rate from many CETA training programs ranged up to 50 percent. Frequently people were trained for jobs that did not exist. One example of this problem involved 2,000 classroom aides who completed CETA training in 1976. Of this group, only about half found jobs in the fields they had been trained for.

Many local governments found that they could pay for their ordinary employees out of CETA funds. In 1979, New York City paid for 20,000 of its 200,000 municipal employees through the

Keynes supported the idea of government spending to provide training and job opportunities for the unemployed. The CETA programs of the 1970s were an example of this, as were public works programs of the 1930s.

program. Cleveland, Washington, D.C., Detroit, Miami, and many other cities did the same. Relatively few of the nation's poorest people were helped through the program.

CETA was gradually eliminated under the Reagan administration.

Self-Check
1. They believed the market economy would end a recession by lowering prices, interest rates, and wages.
2. Keynes believed that in a recession, the government should help the market along by spending more than it took in from tax revenues.
3. Discretionary policy requires a choice of specific action to go into effect; automatic policy does not.
4. The action chosen may take place too long after the economic event.

Applying What You Have Learned
See Lesson Plan for Chapter 12, Section A, page T119.

Self-Check

1. What did Classical economists, like John Baptiste Say, believe would happen when there was a recession?
2. What did John Maynard Keynes believe the government should do if people and businesses reduced spending in a recession?
3. What is the difference between automatic and discretionary fiscal policy?
4. Why do some economists believe that "lags" make discretionary fiscal policy ineffective?

Applying What You Have Learned

The young man's mother in the Personal Narrative worked for a government-sponsored job training program. Such a program would be created through discretionary fiscal policy. Identify and describe two things the program did that were good for the people of her community. Then, identify and describe two specific weaknesses in the program.

PROFILE

John Maynard Keynes
(1883–1946)

Most economists would rate John Maynard Keynes as the most influential contributor to economic theory in the twentieth century. Born in England and educated at Cambridge, Keynes had a wide variety of famous friends in music, literature, the dance, and government. He worked for his government in several ways including the settling of England's debts with France. He became very wealthy by trading currencies on the foreign exchange market and spent many years editing the *Economic Journal.*

Keynes used his knowledge of economics to help his government, his college, and himself. He developed many important ideas concerning macroeconomic theory, which he explained in his book, *The General Theory of Employment, Interest, and Money.* This book was published in 1936 during the Great Depression. It provided an explanation of what had caused the Depression and proposals for bringing it to an end.

Keynes believed that the forces of demand and supply in the market would not always bring about full employment and stable prices. He said that total spending of consumers, business investment, and government spending might not produce enough total demand to provide jobs for everyone who wanted to work. Government could regulate total spending through its taxes and spending. By creating a budget deficit, it could stimulate the economy to provide more jobs in a recession. In times of inflation, the government could reduce total spending by having a budget surplus. Keynesian policy was most successfully used in the first half of the 1960s, when taxes were cut for the purpose of increasing jobs.

Although John Maynard Keynes called for limited government action to help market forces create full employment, he did not believe in central planning.

Keynes led a full life. He accomplished most of his personal objectives, helped his government, and gave the world a better understanding of economics.

Section B Government Policies and Inflation

This section will discuss government policies intended to limit inflation.

Personal Narrative

Values. How good were the "good old days"? Being elderly and retired before 1935 often meant real poverty, because there was no Social Security program. Elderly people had to rely on savings or on their family for support. Ask your students if they expect to take care of older relatives and how they feel about such an idea.

Discuss. Tuition at most colleges has been increasing more rapidly than the rate of inflation. One reason is the high cost of staying up-to-date with technological advances. Another problem is keeping qualified teachers, who could earn more in private business. Do your students feel the cost of college is justified? Do they believe college would be a worthwhile investment for themselves? How may education be considered human capital?

Why Don't They Do Something About Prices?

My grandmother talks about the "good old days." She remembers when bread cost 10 cents a loaf and eggs were 20 cents a dozen. She believes that life was better then. Maybe she's right. Prices certainly were lower.

Prices are a real concern for Grandma. She lives on Social Security and a small pension. Social Security payments have increased over the years, but her pension is the same as it was ten years ago. Rent for her apartment cost $95 a month when she first moved in. Now it's $380 and she thinks they are going to raise it again next year.

Grandma can't drive anymore, so she takes the bus. She likes to go downtown to shop or see a show. She can get into senior citizen bargain matinees for $2.00, where she meets her "boyfriend." Often they go out for something to eat after the show. The city gave Grandma a special card so she can ride the bus for half price. Even with the discount, she thinks about the 1950s when she took the bus to work for a dime. Grandma doesn't think older people should have to pay the higher prices.

Grandma isn't the only person who is affected by higher prices. I'm going to attend a junior college about 20 miles from here next year. The school sent me a letter saying the tuition had been raised by $200 a semester. I've been told to expect to spend about $200 to $250 on books. My father was not happy to hear this news.

I needed to buy a car to get back and forth to school. My father and I went to look at new cars. I thought he was going to have a heart attack right there in the showroom. It's practically impossible to buy a new car for less than $9,000. I had to listen to him talk about his first car that cost less than $2,000 in 1966. We finally agreed on a small used car for $4,500. I hope nothing goes wrong with it.

When we got home from buying my car, Dad opened the mail. There was a letter from the school district, explaining why our school taxes had to go up 12 percent this year. It was not a good day for my father. I wish the government would do something about inflation.

Controlling Inflation Through Fiscal Policy

Explain. Inflation is closely related to expectations. When workers and businesses expect prices and costs to be higher, they attempt to protect their own income by seeking increases in wages and profits. These increases force prices up if there isn't an equal increase in productivity. The expectation of price increases can cause inflation.

The federal government does take steps to try to control inflation. These steps can be part of the fiscal policy that you learned about in Section A of this chapter. Keynes believed that the government could limit inflation by reducing demand. He said that higher taxes, or reduced government spending, or any combination of the two that would result in a government budget surplus, could reduce the total demand for goods and services. He believed this would lead to a lower rate of inflation or even to stable prices. Most economists agree that in cases of demand-pull inflation, such a policy should succeed in reducing price increases (see Chapter 10). However, it would not be effective against cost-push inflation.

In cost-push inflation, prices go up because of higher costs of production. This type of inflation is caused by increases in the cost of labor or raw materials, not by increased demands. Steps to reduce demand probably will not eliminate this type of inflation, but they are likely to cause more unemployment. What can the government do to reduce cost-push inflation?

Price Controls

Note. The Cost of Living Council was divided into two parts: the Wage Board and the Price Board. All businesses were classified into one of three groups depending on the number of workers they employed. Large firms (over 3,000 workers) had to ask permission to make price or wage changes. Medium firms (100 to 3,000 workers) could make changes, but were required to report them for approval. Small firms (under 100 workers) could make changes, but were asked to keep within guidelines set by the government.

On a number of occasions the government has tried to reduce inflation by regulating prices. In World Wars I and II there were price controls and rationing of many products. A more recent example came between 1971 and 1974, when the federal government attempted to control inflation through price and wage regulation.

On August 15, 1971, President Nixon announced a 90-day price and wage freeze. During this time it was against the law to increase either prices or wages for any product other than agricultural production. At the end of the 90 days, a program called **Phase II** was established. Its purpose was to keep price and wage increases within reasonable levels. An organization known as the "Cost-of-Living Council" was given the job of making sure that increases were not excessive. Although this program lasted for more than a year, its success was questioned by many economists. Some people felt it gave the government too much power. It was gradually eliminated between 1972 and 1974.

Any time the government sets an artificially low price for a product, it increases the possibility of a shortage of that product. The graph in Figure 12–2 demonstrates this problem. When the

Figure 12-2 *Effects of Price Regulation on Production*

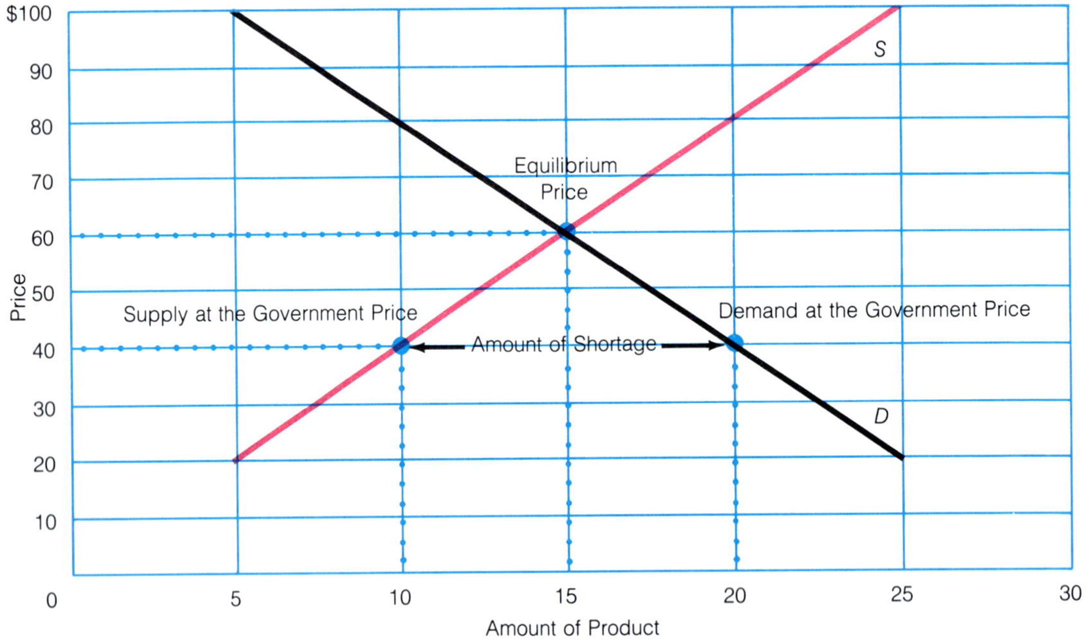

This graph shows the demand and supply curves for a product. These curves intersect at a point of equilibrium that indicates a price of $60 and a quantity of 15. If the government decided that $40 was the highest price a firm could charge, producers would be discouraged from making any more than 10 units of the item. However, the lower price would cause customers to want to buy 20 units. The result would be a shortage of the product, equal to the difference between the demand (20 units) and the supply (10 units).

Explain. The U.S. government has also established price floors. For example, price supports for agricultural products have encouraged farmers to expand production beyond demand, resulting in vast surpluses.

government set the maximum price below the equilibrium price, customers demanded more items than producers were willing to supply. The result of government price control was a shortage of the product.

In general, since the 1970s there has been less pressure on the government to regulate prices. Most economists seem to doubt that such plans work very well.

A Policy for Unemployment and Inflation?

It is difficult for either monetary policy or fiscal policy to deal with the twin problems of inflation and unemployment at the same time. (You learned about monetary policy in Section D of Chapter 11.) The government cannot raise taxes to fight inflation

In 1971, President Nixon announced a 90-day price and wage freeze. The freeze was followed by Phase II, during which wage and price increases were restricted. Phase II lasted more than a year, and it may have contributed to a reduced rate of inflation in 1972. However, many people felt the system was unfair, that it did not allow the market system to operate efficiently, and that it would eventually result in shortages and the misallocation of resources. Phase II was eliminated in January of 1973.

THE DAILY CHIEF-UNION

A Wyandot County Newspaper For Wyandot County People

NEWSPAPERS ARE BETTER THAN EVER

UPPER SANDUSKY, OHIO, MONDAY, AUGUST 16, 1971

-DAY WAGE-PRICE CURBS IN EFFECT

ECONOMISTS REACT OVER NIXON PLAN

Disagree Widely Over How Program Will Affect Country

LOCAL RESIDENT CLAIMED SUNDAY

Devaluation Of Dollar Sought In Normal Trade Under Nixon's Proposal

6,000 ATTEND WHARTON PARADE

Nixon May Speak At VFW Session

A. E. HOUGENDOBLER SUCCUMBS TODAY

DEAN NYE DIES SUNDAY MORNING

DEVALUATION NOT

and at the same time lower taxes to fight unemployment. Nor can the Federal Reserve System take steps to increase interest rates to fight inflation at the same time it is lowering interest rates to fight unemployment. Is there a way to deal with these two problems at the same time? In the 1980s a group of people who were known as "supply-side economists" thought they had found the answer.

Supply-side economics says that the best way to fight unemployment combined with inflation is to reduce the costs of production. The reasoning is that if it costs businesses less to produce their products, they will not need to raise prices (less inflation) and they will sell more products. Selling more products, they will need more workers to make more goods and services (less unemployment). Supply-side economists argue that the objective of government policy should be to help businesses reduce their costs and therefore increase **productivity.** Productivity is a measure of the value of products that can be created from a quantity of factors of production. When a firm becomes more efficient, its productivity improves and its costs of production are lowered. An improvement in productivity should increase the supply of products manufactured and offered for sale. This is why people are called supply-side economists.

In recent years, many American businesses have invested in new, more efficient machinery. As a result, many workers who lack the training to run new machines have lost their jobs. These investments have caused a dilemma for the American economy. We need to use new technology to keep our businesses competitive in a world economy. However, in doing this, we may be creating a class of people who cannot keep their old jobs and are not qualified for the new ones being created.

Although there were a number of ways that supply-side economists thought the government could help businesses reduce costs of production, the most important method was to encourage investment in new, more efficient technology. Supply-side economists reasoned that if businesses bought more efficient machines they could reduce their labor costs and their consumption of energy, therefore becoming more productive. Many of the policies of the Reagan administration from 1981 to 1989 were basically supply-side economics.

From 1981 through 1983 federal income tax rates were reduced by 25 percent. One reason for this reduction was to encourage people to work harder and produce more because they would be able to keep a larger part of the money they earned. At the same time businesses were allowed to reduce their taxes if they bought new machinery. People were encouraged to invest when taxes were reduced for capital gains. Provisions were made that allowed people to put off paying taxes for money they saved in special individual retirement accounts (**IRA**s). All of these changes were intended to increase investment and therefore productivity.

There is little evidence that these policies actually resulted in much greater investment or productivity. They were criticized because they provided more benefits to people who were wealthy than those who were not. For these and other reasons, most of the supply-side policies passed in the early 1980s were eliminated when federal tax laws were reformed in 1986.

Table 12–1
Measurements of Economic Growth, 1981–1986

Year	GDP in billions of constant (1982) dollars	Gross Private Saving (billions of dollars)	Percent of GDP saved
1981	$3,249	$550.5	16.0%
1982	$3,166	$557.1	17.6%
1983	$3,279	$592.2	18.1%
1984	$3,501	$673.5	19.2%
1985	$3,619	$665.3	18.4%
1986	$3,722	$681.6	18.3%

Source: *Statistical Abstract of the United States*, 1989.

Some people believed that the government had not passed laws that would make supply-side theories work. One of President Clinton's priorities was tax credits for industries that invested in new technologies—a plan that served the goal of supply-side economics.

Self-Check
1. Fiscal policy is thought to be effective mainly with demand-pull inflation.
2. Price regulation can result in product shortages.
3. Businesses must be encouraged to invest in more efficient means of production.

Applying What You Have Learned
See Lesson Plan for Chapter 12, Section B, page T121.

Self-Check

1. Do most economists feel fiscal policy would be more effective in controlling demand-pull or cost-push inflation?
2. What problem may result from government price controls?
3. What do supply-side economists believe must be done to fight inflation and unemployment at the same time?

Applying What You Have Learned

In the Personal Narrative, "Grandma" thinks older people shouldn't have to pay higher prices. Suppose the government passed a law that made it illegal to charge people over 65 higher prices. Describe three different problems that would result.

Section C Government Policy in a Global Economy

This section will introduce the effect of the global economy on the financial policies of individual nations.

Personal Narrative

Discuss. How could a slowdown of new housing construction have a ripple effect on other sectors of the economy? What other industries would be affected?

When Iraq Invaded Kuwait I Lost My Job

In 1990 I was 19 years old and had a job making plastic counter tops that were used in new homes. My wage rate was more than $11 an hour. My employer gave me health insurance and other benefits. I borrowed $14,000 to buy a new car and was planning a skiing trip to Colorado in the coming winter. Everything looked fine to me. I could never have dreamed the leader of Iraq, Saddam Hussein, could do anything that would matter much to me. I was wrong.

After Saddam's forces invaded Kuwait on August 4th, the price of oil shot up from about $17 a barrel to nearly $30 in only a few weeks. Oil was the basic raw material that was used to make the plastic for our counter tops. Only a few weeks after the invasion, my employer had to pay almost twice as much for the plastic we used. He raised the price of our products 20 percent and sales began to fall. But the problem was larger than that. Lots of people who had been thinking of buying homes got worried about the war in the Middle East and put off making any purchases. Many new housing developments were stopped and others slowed down. With fewer homes being built there was less demand for our products. Our sales fell almost 50 percent.

After the invasion, President Bush sent American soldiers to Saudi Arabia and other countries as part of the U.N. forces. There was talk of a war that would go on for months or even years. Estimates of its costs were as high as several hundred billion dollars. At the time I paid little attention to these events. I put in my time on the job and took long drives in the country. The only thing I noticed was that the price of gasoline was about 25 cents a gallon higher. Then I got my pink slip.

My employer laid off more than 40 percent of the factory's workers. I received a letter with my pink slip that explained why the layoffs were necessary, but it didn't make me feel any better. Without a job, I couldn't make the payments on my car. I had to sell it to pay off the loan. Then I started taking the bus to look for a new job. Eventually, I found one as a shoe salesperson, but I only earned $7 an hour. I bought a used car for $4,000 and forgot about my plans for a trip to Colorado.

Explain. After the United States and its allies defeated Iraq in the Persian Gulf War in 1991, oil prices fell to prewar levels.

I never did get called back to the factory. The managers bought new equipment from a company in France that required fewer workers, and they laid off even more employees. I still sell shoes for a living. I enjoy the work, but I feel poor. The government spent a lot of time and money protecting Kuwait. I wonder why the government doesn't do more to help people like me.

What the Government Can't Do

The individual in the story above wonders why the government did not prevent or solve the economic problems that resulted from the invasion of Kuwait in 1990. The answer is, once the invasion began there was very little that the government could have done to help. The United States is part of a global economy. Events that take place in other parts of the world often impact the American economy. There are limits to what the government can do with its economic policies to prevent these events from affecting Americans. For example, in 1990 Saddam Hussein did not care what interest rates were in the United States, or whether the U.S. government's taxes or spending changed. His invasion of neighboring Kuwait and the resulting economic events would have taken place no matter what internal economic policies the U.S. government had. With the invasion, there was nothing our government could have done to stop the price of crude oil in world markets from increasing. The effects of the price increase were dramatic in the United States because of our dependence on foreign oil. As long as the United States imports more than half of the oil we use, we must pay the world's prices.

Similar events had happened in the 1970s when tension and wars in the Middle East affected oil supplies. Trouble in the Middle East caused shortages of imported oil in the United States. This drove up prices for gasoline and most consumer goods, affecting the whole American economy. There is no reason to believe that these types of events will not take place in the future, with the same results. One cost of living in a global economy is the risk of experiencing economic problems that are beyond our control.

The Reduced Power of the Federal Reserve

Thirty years ago interest rates in the United States were largely determined by actions of the Federal Reserve System. This is much less true today. Our interest rates are more likely to be affected by the rates of other nations. This is because the United States government finances part of the federal deficit by borrowing funds from other nations. It does this by selling bonds. In the 1980s and 1990s the United States government and

Note. The unification of East and West Germany in 1990 contributed to higher interest rates throughout the world. West Germany promised to invest 60 billion marks in what was East Germany to help rebuild houses, roads, the telephone system, and factories. It also promised to pay the Soviet Union to help resettle soldiers as they were withdrawn from East Germany. Most of the money to pay for these promises was borrowed. This forced interest rates up in Germany and in other nations as well.

U.S. businesses sold more that $1 trillion worth of bonds to people in other countries. To attract foreign investors the United States must pay interest rates that are at least as high as those offered in other countries. We cannot expect German or Japanese investors to buy United States bonds if our bonds pay less than those sold in Germany or Japan. Therefore, when interest rates go up in Germany or Japan, they are likely to increase in the United States as well.

Many economists believe that the Fed has less power over the United States economy than it had in the past. This is in part the result of global influences on the United States economy. An example of the effect of foreign interest rates on the United States rates happened in 1990. That year the Fed took steps to try to force interest rates down in the United States. However, interest rates were going up in other nations at that time. As a result, interest rates went up in the United States too, despite the actions of the Fed.

Another reason that the Fed may exercise less control over interest rates is the attitudes of its own board members. In the early 1990s, the Fed concluded that it was not very effective in controlling short-term economic conditions, especially interest rates and unemployment. Instead, the Fed aimed at the long-term objectives of price stability and steady, low interest rates. When the economy is sluggish, rather than trying to stimulate growth quickly through inflationary policies, the Fed may decide to move cautiously. Rather than seeing itself as the cure-all for economic ills, sometimes the Fed tries to avoid being the source of economic disturbances.

Economic Conditions Flow from Nation to Nation

Different economic systems (including that of the United States) are no longer immune from problems that happen in other countries. A good example occurred in October 1987 when the United States stock market crashed, losing about one-third of its value in just several weeks. The fall in the U.S. stock market was mirrored in other stock markets throughout the world. It is difficult to tell which fall started the worldwide slide, but it is clear that when American investors read that the London stock market fell 18 percent, they were influenced to sell their stocks too.

Economic changes in one nation do not always influence every other nation as directly as the above examples. Changes in a small economy such as that of Bolivia may have little impact on the global economy. Changes in the economy of a major power

Note. The "Group of Seven" (United States, Canada, Great Britain, France, Italy, Germany, and Japan) now meet regularly to try to coordinate economic policy in the world.

such as the United States are more likely to be felt throughout the world. Sometimes even economists, however, cannot predict the effect that changes in one major economy may have on that of another nation. For example, in the spring of 1992 the American stock market hit a series of all-time highs. At the same time the Tokyo stock market hit a five-year low. Still, Americans worried that the problems in Japan would affect the United States market. At the time, however, foreign investors controlled only 4 percent of the Japanese stock market and only 6 percent of U.S. stocks. Investors realize that as international investing increases the effects of changes in one market will be more likely to cross national boundaries.

Economists continue to study the effect of the global economy on individual nations. In some instances international financial changes clearly have influenced the individual nations' financial markets. In other cases, the connection is not so clear. For example, U.S. interest rates did not rise or fall with foreign rates in 1989. Beginning in 1990, however, U.S. rates did seem to do so. Economists who wanted to find out how closely interest rates in different economies were linked could create a graph showing two nations' interest rate changes over a period of time. The following graph shows U.S. and Japanese interest rates over an 18-month period.

Figure 12–3 *Interest Rates of United States and Japan, 1989–1990*

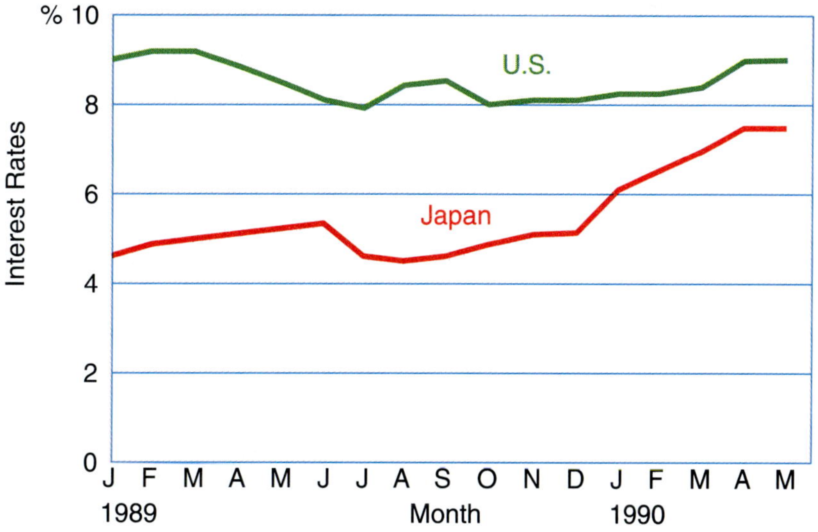

The graph on the previous page shows that Japanese and United States interest rates did not move in the same direction during most of 1989. Beginning in the first half of 1990, they did move in the same direction. To provide a clearer answer as to how interest rates in one nation's economy affect interest rates in another nation's economy, an economist might track rates in both economies over a longer period.

The International Economy

Many of the reasons that the United States economy is becoming more international in nature will be discussed in Chapter 13. Two important aspects of the global economy are international trade and the growth of multinational corporations. There are important benefits that the United States receives from international trade as well as from having multinational corporations. There are also costs that we must pay. As we have learned in this chapter, one of the costs of playing a major role in the international economy may be the loss of some of our ability to control our own economic climate.

Self-Check
1. More than half of the oil we consume is imported.
2. To compete with Germans for borrowed money we need to pay similar interest rates.
3. If stock prices fall in London, it may worry American investors, causing them to sell their stock.
4. The Fed may have less power because of global influences on the American economy and because the Fed may not try to control short-term economic conditions.

Applying What You Have Learned
See Lesson Plan for Chapter 12, Section C, page T123.

Self-Check

1. Why can't the U.S. government control the price of oil sold in the United States?
2. Why should Americans care if interest rates go up in Germany or Japan?
3. How may an American investor be affected by a fall in the value of stock on the London market?
4. What are two reasons why the Fed may have less power over the United States economy than it has had in the past?

Applying What You Have Learned

Many people tend to think of the negative things that happen as a result of the global nature of our economy. Perhaps this is because negative news, being more dramatic, captures more headlines. When a large factory closes down, it is big news. If several small new firms each hire 50 people, it is not such big news. Can you find positive news related to the global nature of our economy? Search through newspapers and magazines to find examples of international events that have helped American consumers or workers. Summarize each news article by writing a positive statement about its effect on the United States economy.

Section D Government Social Programs

This section will discuss the role of the government in providing a minimum standard of living for all Americans.

Personal Narrative

Dignity at the City Mission

I belong to a youth group at my church. One of the projects we work on is taking food to the poor. Each Saturday morning we all get together in the church kitchen and cook. We don't make anything fancy, but we make well-balanced meals. We take some of the food to shut-ins, and the rest goes to the city mission. I usually ride in the van to the mission.

I live in the suburbs. My family seems to have enough money to take care of our needs. The first time I went to the mission I got a real education. I knew that there were poor people, but I didn't know any myself. I thought only drunks or drug addicts were poor. So far as I was concerned, their poverty was their own fault because of the way they lived. I found that although I was right in some cases, for most poor people I was wrong.

Discuss. What is society's responsibility to the mentally disabled? In recent years many people who are not able to care for themselves have been released from institutions. Should these people be left to take care of themselves? Why do your students believe they were released? Was it an attempt to protect their rights, save money, or something else? How much would your students be willing to pay to help these people?

Many of the poor people at the mission are mentally or emotionally disabled. They are people who would have been in an institution 30 years ago. The government decided that they should be returned to the community, but there were few programs set up to help them after they were released. Many of them are unable to care for themselves. They go to the mission because they have nowhere else to go.

Another large group at the mission is made up of the elderly. They come for a free meal because they can't afford to feed themselves. Many receive welfare and use food stamps, but they still can't afford enough food. They have a particularly hard time in the winter when heating bills are high. They need to be warm, but often must live in old places that are not well insulated. Some of them use up almost all their income on their heating bills.

Note. In the mid-1980s, a group called the "new poor" developed. They have been compared with displaced people in the Great Depression. See John Steinbeck's *Grapes of Wrath*.

I was told that in the last few years entire families have started coming to the mission. In most cases the parents of these families have been out of work for months. They have run out of unemployment compensation benefits. Often they have no place else to go. I met one family that slept in their car. It's true that many of these people are not well educated, but they want a chance in life just as much as anyone else.

Each Saturday I help serve over 500 people. They are always polite and say, "Thank you." It makes me feel kind of strange. I have never done anything to earn my standard of living. I live well because my father has a good job. I wonder what my life would have been like if I had been born in a poor family. When I'm at the mission I know that in a few hours I will be home with plenty to eat. But these people will still be at the mission with nowhere to go. I wonder why the government doesn't do more to help them.

Searching for Security

The **Social Security Act** of 1935 started the federal government on the road toward helping the nation's poor. This law included the foundations for today's Social Security program, unemployment insurance, and welfare. Although these programs have been expanded over the years, many of their basic concepts still come from the original Act.

Social Security covers about 90 percent of the workers in the United States. The only major group that is excluded are federal government workers who were hired before 1984 and some state government employees. These workers are covered by other retirement programs.

Among the important programs that stem from the Social Security Act are *retirement benefits* (including Medicare), *unemployment insurance*, and *welfare*.

Retirement Benefits

Decision. One way to reduce Social Security taxes would be to eliminate benefits for people who have saved enough for their own retirement. Others say these people have paid into the system and therefore deserve benefits, and that such a policy could discourage people from saving. Do your students think this would be a good idea?

To be eligible for retirement benefits under the federal program, an employee must have paid into the system through a withholding tax over a number of years. Employee withholding is matched by employers. Self-employed people must make their own payments into the system at a higher rate than employees because their payments are not matched. People with low incomes pay a greater percentage of their income than the wealthy. However, social security benefits are more important to people with low incomes. As the system exists today, people who live for a reasonable length of time after they retire will receive more from the system than they paid in. Since 1972, benefits have been **indexed**—that is, adjusted upward to keep pace with rising inflation. A 1965 amendment to the Social Security Act created the Medicare program. Medicare provides basic medical insurance to retired people in the Social Security program.

It is often pointed out that it is difficult to live on Social Security benefits. There is little doubt that this is true. However,

Although the Social Security system was established only to supplement *private savings, many Americans rely on this program for all or most of their support. Some elderly people may not have saved for their retirement through lack of planning. Others may not have earned enough income to save. For whatever reason, society is now faced with the responsibility of caring for a growing number of people who are not financially able to support themselves.*

the original intent of the law was to supplement private savings, not to provide total retirement needs. People are still expected to save for their own retirement.

The trend toward smaller families and longer life has put financial pressure on the Social Security system. In the future we will have more beneficiaries and fewer employed people who will work to pay the bills. It is probable that either increased taxes or decreased benefits will become necessary in the future.

Unemployment Insurance

Explain. Unemployment compensation helps people who keep working by allowing those who are unemployed to continue buying goods and services. Without these payments, the unemployed would consume fewer products, sales would decline, and other workers would be laid off.

The Social Security Act provided a federal mechanism to help states set up unemployment compensation programs, but each state has its own program. Therefore, programs and benefits vary widely from one state to another. All benefits are paid for by taxing employers. There is a federal minimum tax of 3.9 percent on wages paid, but states can tax firms at higher rates. States that tax more are able to pay greater benefits. Recipients are paid up to half of their former weekly earnings for as long as 26 weeks. In 1989 the average weekly benefit for the nation was $152. The lowest payments were in Louisiana, with an average of $105. The highest were in Massachusetts, which paid a weekly average of $212.

The inequality in payments and taxes in different states may cause both firms and workers to move from one state to another. Businesses might move to low-tax states, while workers might migrate to states with higher benefits. It is clear that there is inequality in the burden and benefits of the unemployment insurance program.

Welfare

Millions of Americans receive unemployment compensation, but even more are given some form of welfare. In 1989, roughly 11 million Americans received cash assistance through the welfare system. More than two-thirds of these individuals benefited from Aid to Families With Dependent Children **(AFDC)**. Other groups to receive benefits were the aged, disabled, and the blind.

Welfare programs, like unemployment insurance, are set up by each individual state. Welfare benefits vary from state to state. In 1989 the benefit for an average family in Mississippi was just over $1,400 a year, while a California family received over $7,400. Again, there are many questions of fairness and equity in the nation's welfare system. Table 12–3 shows the differences in payments among states.

Values. Do your students feel welfare recipients should have different rights than other people? Should they have to report how they live and who they live with to the government?

Although there is aid available to the nation's poor, there is serious doubt about whether the welfare system is run efficiently or if its benefits are distributed equitably. There are many states where the poor have to eat in city missions or other private establishments because their aid from the government will not support them at even a minimum standard of living.

Table 12-3
Average Aid to Families with Dependent Children, 1989

State	Average Payment per Month	Total Recipients
California	$620	1,833,000
Connecticut	$534	117,000
New York	$530	964,000
Rhode Island	$483	44,000
Ohio	$314	623,000
West Virginia	$253	109,000
South Carolina	$208	105,000
Texas	$168	581,000
Mississippi	$118	178,000
Alabama	$114	130,000

Source: *Statistical Abstract of the United States*, 1991.

This table shows the average aid paid to families with dependent children in various states. What factors might explain the differences in aid among states?

Millions of children are supported on welfare. Some people worry that children who have grown up in families that depend on welfare will come to accept it as a way of life. They argue that such children may lack self-respect and a belief in their ability to succeed. Others feel that children who have lived on welfare will desire better things for themselves and be willing to work for them. Do you believe that being raised in a family that depends on welfare would change a child's outlook on life?

In recent years there has been a significant increase in people who have been called the "new poor." These are people who have recently become poor because of changes in the economy, social conditions, or government programs. A large part of this group is made up of households headed by women and their children. Some of these households have fallen into poverty because they receive less support from the government. Others are poor because of separation or divorce. Regardless of the reason, there are many new poor in the United States who need help.

Discuss. Prior to 1935, our government supplied little or no help for the poor. Do your students feel that private help could take the place of government transfer programs today? What changes have occurred in the past 50 years that would make government help more necessary or less necessary?

In 1985, private help for the nation's poor was organized through the "Hands Across America" program. Almost five and a half million Americans joined hands in one long chain from New York City to Long Beach, California. Each participant collected an average of $35 in pledges, bringing the total raised to almost $200 million. Although this seems like a large sum of money, it is only about $13 for every person living in the United States who is designated as living in poverty by the government.

Private aid of this nature helps, but the problem of hunger is so great that many people doubt there can be a solution without more government support.

Self-Check

1. What are three social programs that were started under the Social Security Act of 1935?
2. What has the trend toward smaller families and longer lives done to the Social Security system?
3. Name two programs described in this section that are administered by state governments and two that are run by the federal government.

Self-Check
1. The Social Security Act created programs for retirement benefits, unemployment insurance, and welfare.
2. The trend toward smaller families and longer life has put financial pressure on the Social Security system.
3. Federally administered: retirement benefits, Social Security, and Medicare. State administered: unemployment insurance and welfare.

Applying What You Have Learned

Over 70 percent of the people who receive welfare are either children, aged, or disabled. Another 20 percent have either part-time or full-time jobs. With this fact in mind, answer the questions below. Explain your answers.

a. Would it be useful to make recipients work for their benefits?
b. How much would cuts in welfare benefits affect the number of recipients who are looking for work?
c. What type of people would be most affected by cuts in welfare benefits?

Applying What You Have Learned
See Lesson Plan for Chapter 12, Section D, page T125.

PROFILE

Paul Samuelson
(1915–)

Do we need to tinker with the market to make the economy run well? Two economists of powerful reputation answer the question differently. Paul Samuelson, the best known and most influential Keynesian economist in the United States, would say, "Yes." Milton Friedman, America's most famous conservative economist, would say, "No."

Paul Samuelson

Paul Samuelson, the first American to win the Nobel Prize in Economics and author of the most successful college economics textbook in this country, believes that it would be a waste of resources to wait for the market to adjust production when unemployment is high. He suggests that by using countercyclical fiscal policy to create temporary budget deficits, total spending can be increased to create needed jobs. When inflation is a problem, he would create a budget surplus through increased taxes, reduced government spending, or a combination of these actions. Total spending should be reduced, resulting in lower prices.

Samuelson recognizes the importance of controlling the money supply, but he feels it works more slowly than fiscal policy.

Many economists have improved their understanding of and ability to analyze the economy by studying Samuelson's book, *Foundations of Economic Analysis.* The public has come to know his ideas through his journalistic writings on current economic problems. Presidents and the Congress have often asked his advice, although he has never taken a government post. No economist questions Samuelson's knowledge and skill, but conservative economists find fault in his approach to economic problems.

Milton Friedman

Like Paul Samuelson, Milton Friedman has been awarded the Nobel Prize in Economics. But unlike Samuelson, Friedman believes the market should be left alone.

Continued on page 350.

PROFILE (Continued)

Milton Friedman
(1912–)

Friedman is best known among economists for the book he coauthored with Anna Schwartz, *A Monetary History of the United States, 1867–1960.* His stand against government involvement in the economy and against Federal Reserve countercyclical adjustments in the money supply assures him a large audience whenever he speaks.

Friedman believes nothing regulates the economy better than the free market. Like Adam Smith, he respects the ability of individual consumers, workers, and businesspersons to decide what is in their own best interest. This self-interest is shown in consumer demand and businesses' willingness to supply products to satisfy this demand. These forces interact in the market to determine prices, wages, and profits. Resources will be allocated most efficiently when the government does not interfere in the market.

Friedman has shocked liberals with his opposition to almost all existing social welfare programs. He would provide help for the poor through a negative income tax, a direct payment to the poor to supplement their income. He would allow the poor to decide how to spend the money they receive, rather than give food stamps or subsidized low-income housing.

As a monetarist, Friedman would have the Federal Reserve System increase the money supply between three and five percent per year, or at about the same rate as the increase in production. His studies have shown the Federal Reserve to have such a poor record of implementing monetary policy that he feels we would be better off not letting them adjust the money supply other than at a constant annual rate.

Friedman taught for many years at the University of Chicago. He and his colleagues made that university famous for its conservative economic position. Samuelson of the Massachusetts Institute of Technology, and Alvin Hansen and John Kenneth Galbraith at Harvard, made their respective institutions famous for a liberal economic point of view.

CURRENT ECONOMIC ISSUES

Has Tax Reform Been Fair for All Americans?

In 1986 and again in 1990 the structure of federal income taxes was changed. The intent of the changes was to create a tax system that was more fair. To accomplish this, the amount of the exemption that could be subtracted from taxpayer income for each person supported was increased to $2,000. The standard deduction that could be subtracted was raised to $5,000. These amounts were increased each year after 1988 according to the rate of inflation. As a result, a married couple with two children could earn $14,300 in 1991 before they had to pay any federal income tax. The new rates reduced the number of taxpaying Americans by more than 10,000,000 people.

The number of different tax rates was also reduced from 14 to only 3. The maximum rate that had been 50 percent in 1985 became 31 percent in 1991. After 1988, the federal income tax rate for most taxpayers was 15 percent.

How could the government give so many tax breaks? This was done by getting rid of "loopholes" or deductions that had allowed people to reduce their taxable income in the past. Deductions for sales taxes, medical expenses, losses, business expenses, and many types of investments were reduced or eliminated. As a result, the government collected about the same amount of money that would have been taken in under the old laws.

The reforms did reduce tax rates for many. However, the law increased taxes on investments and may have discouraged businesses from investing in new factories that would have created jobs. Also the law did not seem to benefit middle income taxpayers as much as those with lower and higher incomes. How have these tax changes affected your family?

Arguments in Favor of the Reforms

1. They eliminated taxes for many low-income Americans.
2. They made it difficult to avoid paying taxes.
3. They were intended to make the tax laws easier to understand.

Arguments Against the Reforms

1. They did not eliminate all tax loopholes.
2. They did not eliminate the growth of the national debt.
3. They may have discouraged people from investing in the economy to create more jobs.

What Do You Think?

Consider the arguments for and against the reforms. What information can you find that shows how they have worked? Is the tax system more fair because of the changes introduced in these reforms? Do they appear to have helped the country or harmed it?

Chapter 12 Review

What Have You Learned?

In this chapter you've learned the following important principles of economics:

- The government's role in the economy has grown over the past 200 years.
- *Classical* economists believed the natural state of the economy was full employment.
- The Great Depression of the 1930s showed the ideas of Classical economists were wrong, and an alternative theory was offered by *John Maynard Keynes*.
- Keynes believed the government should implement policies to stabilize the amount of total spending so that there would be jobs for all people who want to work.
- Although Keynes's ideas have been widely accepted, there are problems with his theory. These include our limited ability to predict the future, the time it takes the government to make policy changes, its inability to fight inflation and unemployment at the same time, and the effect government borrowing may have on interest rates.
- Government attempts to limit inflation through price controls have often led to shortages and have met with only limited success.
- In recent years a theory called *supply-side economics* has been accepted by some economists. This theory suggests that policies to encourage business investment should be carried out by the government. Supply-side economists believe these policies will result in economic growth, greater production, and more jobs.
- The global nature of our economic system has limited the ability of the United States government to regulate our economy through fiscal and monetary policy.
- Although we have attempted to provide jobs and limit inflation, there are still many people in the United States who live in poverty. Our government has established a number of programs which are intended to help these people.
- The foundations for our Social Security, unemployment compensation, and welfare programs were established by the Social Security Act of 1935. Although unemployment compensation and welfare programs exist in all states, differences cause inequity in taxes and benefits from state to state.

Words and Terms

laissez-faire (p. 319)
Classical economics (p. 320)
Employment Act of 1946 (p. 323)
John Baptiste Say (p. 323)
John Maynard Keynes (p. 324)
fiscal policy (p. 326)
discretionary fiscal policy (p. 326)
automatic stabilization (p. 327)
crowding-out effect (p. 328)
Phase II (p. 333)
supply-side economics (p. 335)
productivity (p. 335)
IRA (p. 337)
Social Security Act (p. 344)
indexed (p. 344)
AFDC (p. 346)

See Chapter 12 Review Answers, page T126.

Building Your Vocabulary

Answer each of the following by placing the word or term which best completes each of the following sentences in the appropriate space on a separate answer sheet.

1. The idea that additional government borrowing will lead to reduced consumer spending and business investment is called the ______.
2. The largest number of people who receive welfare are mothers and children who are paid ______ benefits.
3. Welfare, Social Security, and unemployment compensation were all started by the ______ of 1935.
4. Social Security benefits have been adjusted for inflation, or ______ , since 1972.
5. If the government does not become involved in the economic system, it is following a ______ economic policy.
6. ______ was an economist who believed that prices, interest rates, and wages would fall to end any recession.
7. ______ was an economist who believed that it was necessary to regulate total spending for economic success. He also felt that governments should either adjust taxes or their own spending, or a combination of both, to achieve the correct amount of total spending.
8. ______ was a system for government regulation of prices established by President Nixon in 1971.
9. When a firm's costs of production fall, its ______ will increase.
10. The attempt of the Congress and the President to stabilize the economy through taxing and government spending is called ______.
11. Before the Great Depression of the 1930s, many people believed in ______, which stated that the economic system would regulate itself and that the government should stay out of the system to the greatest extent possible.
12. An ______ is a special type of savings account that allows depositors to put off paying tax on the part of their income they save.
13. ______ suggests that it is possible to fight both inflation and unemployment by lowering the cost of production.
14. ______ will go into effect without any new action by either the President or the Congress or a government agency.
15. ______ requires the action of either the President or the Congress or a government agency to go into effect.
16. After World War II, Congress passed the ______, which placed a responsibility on the government to carry out policies that would promote full employment.

Understanding Economics

1. According to Classical economists, what three things would happen in a recession that would lead to economic recovery?
2. What were the three sources of spending that Keynes identified?
3. According to Keynes, what are two ways the government could achieve higher levels of spending in a recession?
4. Explain the difference between automatic and discretionary fiscal policy. Give an example of each.
5. If the government tries to fight unemployment by increasing spending, what is this policy likely to do to the rate of inflation?

Chapter 12 Review

6. If the government tries to fight inflation by cutting spending, what is this policy likely to do to the rate of unemployment?
7. Explain why many people were opposed to President Nixon's Phase II policy of the early 1970s.
8. Supply-side economists want the government to have policies that would encourage businesses to produce more goods and services. What are two results they believe would come from such policies?
9. Explain why the price of oil cannot be controlled through fiscal and monetary policy.
10. Describe why welfare and unemployment compensation programs may have caused people to move from state to state.
11. Explain why many people feel private programs are not able to do an adequate job of helping the poor in the United States.

Thinking Critically About Economics

1. When this country was originally formed in the 1700s, our government had a relatively small role in our economic system. Describe three things that have changed to cause our government to take a larger role in our economic system.
2. Suppose there was a recession in the United States. Describe the policies a *Classical* economist would want the government to follow. Do the same for a *Keynesian* economist and a *supply-side* economist.
3. In 1981–82 there was a recession in the U.S. economy. In November of 1982, Congress passed a five cent per gallon increase in the tax on gasoline. The increase took effect on April 1, 1983. The money was to be used to provide needed jobs by rebuilding the nation's roads. It was late summer of 1983 before any contracts were awarded with this money. Construction actually began at the end of 1983. Describe what this shows you about fiscal policy that involves government spending and the time it can take to implement it. Would a tax cut work more quickly? Explain why or why not.
4. Suppose the government borrows and spends large amounts of money to carry out Keynesian economic programs. Some people believe a result of such a policy would be to reduce consumer and investment spending. Explain why they believe this.

Consumer Skills Projects

Go to a local social services office. Obtain copies of the forms that have to be filled out to qualify for welfare in your state. Show them in class. Discuss whether the questions the forms ask are reasonable. Be sure to address the question of whether people who receive aid from the government should have the same rights to privacy and individual choice as people who are able to support themselves.

Thinking Critically About Economics
(1) analyzing cause and effect; (2) comparison/contrast; (3) identifying the problem; (4) predicting probable consequences.

Developing Your Economic Skills

Interpreting Pie Graphs

Skill: A pie graph is especially useful for showing how the parts of a whole amount (the pie) are divided. In addition, two or more pie graphs can be compared to show how a whole amount—for example, total expenditures—has changed over time.

In this lesson you'll look at pie graphs to see how total payments for social service programs have grown and how proportions of the payments are divided between federal, and state and local governments. To complete this lesson, you'll follow these steps:

- Compare the total sizes of the three graphs to see how total spending for social services has grown.
- Examine the sections within each individual graph to see how the expenditures for that year were divided between federal, and state and local governments.
- Compare the sections between the three graphs to see how the distribution of the spending has changed.

Application: How are social service benefits paid for?

Social programs supported by the federal, state, and local governments have grown dramatically in recent years. In 1970 a total of $146 billion was spent by all levels of government for social programs. By 1988 this spending had grown to $887 billion. The graphs below illustrate this.

The increasing size of the graphs from left to right shows growth in total spending of all governments.

Each graph is divided into two sections. The orange section represents spending that was supported by the federal government. The blue section is for spending supported by state and local governments. By studying these graphs, you can see that the share supported by the federal government grew between 1970 and 1980, but fell between 1980 and 1990.

Practice: These graphs allow you to see both the total spending and the distribution of support for that spending. How would you determine whether total federal spending increased or decreased between 1980 and 1990? Why do you think the share of spending supported by the federal government fell in the 1980s?

Spending on Social Service Programs by Federal, and State and Local Governments, 1970/1980/1990

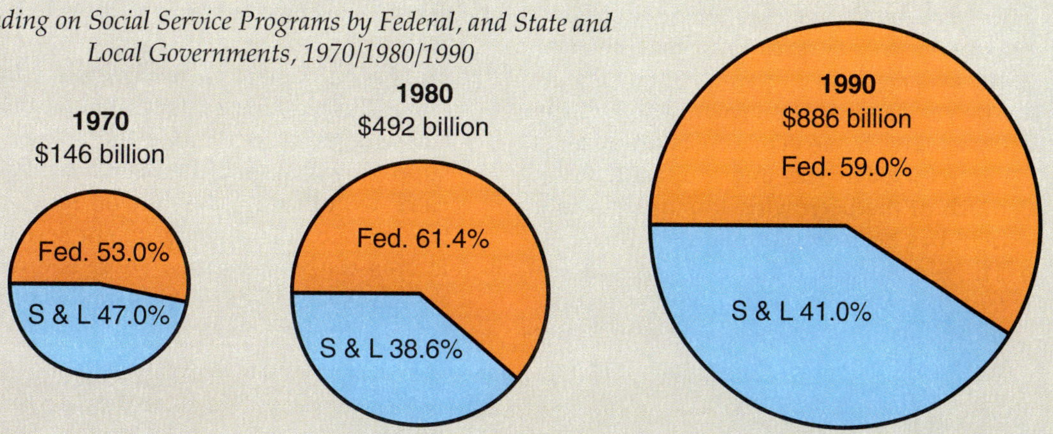

Part 3 Review

Summary of Major Economic Principles

In Part 3 you have learned the following basic economic principles concerning the function of our economic system and concerning government involvement in the economy. These principles are part of what is called *Macroeconomics*.

- The basic measure of production in the United States is the *gross domestic product*, which is measured through the expenditure and income approaches by our government.
- The GDP is used as a measure of the *business cycle*, which changes over time from *expansion* to *recession*. The business cycle can be predicted through the use of *leading indicators*.
- Our government provides *public goods* and *services* that most people could not afford as individuals. It also tries to correct *negative externalities* and to assure all Americans a minimal income by *redistribution of income*.
- Taxes may be based on the *benefits-received principle*, the *ability-to-pay principle*, the *productivity principle*, or on the *least-likely-to-offend principle*, and may be *progressive*, *regressive*, or *proportional*.
- The *national debt* has grown rapidly in recent years. Some economists are concerned over its size and the fact that much of the borrowing to support the debt has been from foreign sources.
- The several types of unemployment are *frictional*, *seasonal*, *cyclical*, and *structural unemployment*. People who give up hunting work are called *discouraged workers*.
- *Inflation* is a sustained general increase in prices. *Demand-pull* inflation is the result of demand that exceeds supply. *Cost-push* inflation happens when producers pass increased costs of production on to customers in higher prices.
- People are not hurt equally by inflation. Those who live on fixed incomes or who have made loans are likely to be hurt the most by inflation.
- *Poverty* is defined in terms of economic and social conditions in each country. In the United States, poverty is associated with unemployment, inflation, and the distribution of income. In 1989 more than 12 percent of our population were identified as living in poverty.
- Money serves as a *medium of exchange*, a *measure of value*, and a *store of value*.
- If the money in circulation grows more rapidly than the supply of products offered for sale, there will be inflation. If the supply of products offered for sale grows more rapidly than the supply of money, there will be deflation.
- Most spending in the United States is done through checks. Banks have the ability to *expand* the money supply through a process that involves checking deposits and loans made in repeated cycles.
- The *Federal Reserve System* oversees the American banking system. It also sets *monetary policy*, regulating the money supply by changing the *reserve requirement*, by adjusting the *discount rate*, or by buying and selling government securities in *open market operations*. There is often disagreement over the proper role of the Federal Reserve System and the actions of its Board of Governors.

See Part 3 Review Answers, page T127.

- The role of the government in the economy has increased during the past 200 years. *Classical economists* believed the economy would regulate itself and the government should not attempt to interfere with it. This policy did not work in the Great Depression.
- *John Maynard Keynes* developed a new theory that said the government should implement policies to stabilize the amount of total spending, so that there would be jobs for all people who want to work. Although his ideas have been widely accepted, there also have been problems in using his theory to form government policy.
- In some cases, the government has tried to limit inflation with price controls. This policy has often led to shortages. There has been less pressure on the government to use price controls in recent years.
- A theory called *supply-side* economics was used as the basis for many government decisions in the 1980s. Supply-side economists believe policies that encourage investment will result in economic growth, greater production, and more jobs.
- Although we have attempted to provide jobs and limit inflation, there are many people in the United States who live in poverty. Our government has established programs that are intended to help these people. They include Social Security, unemployment compensation, and welfare.

Understanding Economic Concepts

Each of the following questions emphasizes one or more of the important economic concepts you have learned in Part 3. The important concept is listed in parentheses after each question. Answer the questions in complete sentences that *show you understand the meaning* of the concepts. The first question has been answered for you as an example.

1. What are the two methods used by the federal government to measure the gross domestic product? (Discuss the *expenditure* approach and the *income* approach.)
   (*Answer*: In the expenditure approach, the government measures GDP by counting all spending on new products. In the income approach, the government counts all earnings.)
2. What is the most important problem in accurately measuring GDP? (Discuss the *underground economy*.)
3. The producers of what type of goods will be affected most by a recession? (Discuss *durable goods*.)
4. How can businesses predict economic conditions in the near future? (Discuss *leading indicators*.)
5. Why is it necessary for governments to supply many things to its citizens? (Discuss *public goods and services*.)
6. When the government requires a firm to stop polluting a river, what economic problem is it trying to resolve? (Discuss *negative externality*.)
7. What are the two basic principles of taxation? (Discuss the *benefits-received* principle and the *ability-to-pay* principle.)
8. What name has been given to parts of many government spending bills? (Discuss *pork barrel legislation*.)
9. What is an important difference between most state and local taxes and the federal income tax? (Discuss *regressive* and *progressive* taxation.)
10. What are the basic types of unemployment? (Discuss *frictional, seasonal, cyclical*, and *structural* unemployment.)
11. What is the difference between the two basic types of inflation? (Discuss *de-*

Part 3 Review

mand-pull inflation and *cost-push* inflation.)

12. What is often associated with unemployment, inflation, and the distribution of income in this country? (Discuss *poverty*.)
13. What are the three functions of money in our economic system? (Discuss *medium of exchange*, *measure of value*, and *store of value*.)
14. What process do banks participate in when they make loans based on money deposited in checking accounts? (Discuss the *expansion process*.)
15. What is the name of the policy the Federal Reserve System carries out? (Discuss *monetary policy*.)
16. What are the three things the Fed can do to affect the amount of money in circulation? (Discuss the *reserve requirement*, the *discount rate*, and *open market operations*.)
17. How would banks act if they were allowed to? (Discuss *pro-cyclical*.)
18. How was confidence in the banking system restored in the Great Depression? (Discuss the *Federal Deposit Insurance Corporation*.)
19. What is a description of the economic theory that supported government involvement in the economy? (Discuss *Keynesian* economic theory.)
20. Why does the global nature of our economy limit the government's ability to regulate the United States economy? (Discuss *fiscal* and *monetary policy*.)

Writing About Economics

Each of the questions below requires you to write a brief essay. Follow these steps:

- Demonstrate your understanding of the identified economic concept(s) in your essay.
- Explain how the economic concept(s) is involved in the situation.
- Describe how you would resolve the situation and on what basis you would make your decision.

1. Pretend you have a pen pal named Helga who lives in Norway. She writes you that she has been assigned to do a report for her social studies class on the economy of the United States. She would like you to explain how production is measured in the United States economy. Write Helga a letter that answers her question. (Discuss *gross domestic product*, the *income* approach, and the *expenditure* approach.)
2. You have been employed as an advisor to your city's mayor. She wants to attract more businesses to the area. Members of the city council have presented her with three ideas (listed below) on how this could be done. Your job is to write a report that identifies the best plan and explains why it is better than the others. You may also reject all of the plans, but you must explain why. (Discuss the *ability-to-pay* principle, the *productivity* principle, and *negative externalities*.)

   The plans are:

   - Reduce property taxes on new businesses or on new investments made by existing businesses. Increase the sales tax to make up for lost property taxes.
   - Reduce all property taxes and cut back on public services such as schools,

Writing About Economics
(1) classification; (2) identifying the problem, analyzing cause and effect; (3) predicting probable consequences.

roads, and police protection, so that the city government can still balance its budget.

- Let new factories bury their waste on city land if they agree to provide jobs to local people.

3. Suppose you are a newspaper reporter. A local politician is running for Congress. You are assigned to listen to a speech he gives to a group of local businessmen. In his speech he makes these points:

   - He wants to reduce taxes for businesses that invest or hire more workers.
   - He wants to reduce taxes on money that is saved.
   - He wants to reduce public service programs to encourage more people to find work.

   Your job is to write an article for your newspaper that explains what he wants to accomplish and what problems might result if his ideas are put into use. (Discuss *supply-side economics*.)

Discussing Economics

The following paragraphs describe economic proposals that have been the topic of recent public debate. For each issue, decide whether you support or do not support the proposal, and think about how you would present your opinion to the rest of the class. When you present your opinion to the class, follow these steps:

- Identify and describe the controversial issues of the proposal.
- Clearly state the decision you have reached.
- Explain why you think your choice is the best one.

1. Some people believe a law should be passed that would prevent the government from increasing tax rates unless the people vote to approve the tax increase. Supporters of this idea argue that the government is too large and that we could prevent it from getting larger if politicians could not increase tax rates by themselves.

   Other people say such a law would make it impossible for the government to provide necessary public goods and services. They argue that few people would vote to increase their own taxes even if an increase was needed. Such a law would probably hurt the poor and elderly the most.

   Would you support such a law? On what basis would you make your decision?

2. According to our government, there are slightly over 30 million people in the United States who live in poverty. It would cost the government between $80 and $100 billion dollars more than it now spends to give these people enough money to escape poverty. Some people say the United States is rich enough to do this. They feel no American should have to live in poverty.

   Other people disagree. They suggest that giving people so much money would destroy their desire to work. They argue that if it cost $80 billion to get rid of poverty this year, it would cost much more in the future because many poor people would give up working. They also point out that the extra benefits would probably be paid for through taxes on people who are working to escape poverty through their own effort.

Discussing Economics
(1, 2, and 3) recognizing values, predicting probable consequences.

Writing About Economics activities 1-3 may be an appropriate method of authentic assessment and may be placed in students' portfolios.

Part 3 Review

Would you support such a law? On what basis would you make your decision?

3. Some people believe that all banks should be required to make loans to small firms or minority-owned businesses that would not otherwise be able to get loans. They argue that banks earn money from the entire community and should therefore have to make loans to all parts of the community. If banks only make loans to people and businesses that are already successful, then few new people will have a chance to succeed.

   Other people disagree. They say that banks must protect their depositors. Making risky loans to new or small businesses could hurt these people and force the cost of banking up. They argue that such a law would treat people unequally. Banks could end up looking for small or minority-owned businesses to make loans just to abide by the law. This could make less money available for slightly larger businesses to borrow.

   Would you support such a law? On what basis would you make your decision?

Problem-Solving in Economics

Chapter 8

1. It has been said that the "American Dream" is to see your children have a better life than you have. To most people, the idea of a better life means having more things. List four things you would like to have in your life that your parents didn't have. Explain why each is important to you.
2. Make a list of four things that add to your quality of life but that do not involve money or goods and services. Explain why each is important to you.
3. When additional products are made and sold, how much do they add to the add to the quality of life? Not everyone agrees on the value of different products. Below you will find a list of percentage increases in sales of certain items between 1989 and 1990 in the United States. Explain how much each added to the quality of life, *in your opinion*.
   a. Sales of bottled water increased by 13 percent.
   b. Sales of cosmetics increased by 6.5 percent.
   c. Sales of snack foods increased 2.8 percent.
   d. Sales of soap beauty-bars increased 7 percent.
   e. Sales of antacids increased 3 percent.
4. Explain whether each of the following would indicate that the economy would expand or contract soon.
   a. New building permits are down.
   b. Interest rates are down.
   c. Employees are working more hours.
   d. It takes longer to get deliveries.
   e. People are saving less of their income.
   f. Few new businesses are being started.

Chapter 9

1. Suppose you are on the town board. There is a suggestion to build a new harbor on a river that flows through the town. If the project is completed it should increase tourism, but it will re-

Problem-Solving in Economics
Chapter 8
(1, 2, and 3) recognizing values; (4) predicting probable consequences.

quire a 10 percent increase in property taxes to pay for it. Explain how—and why—each of the following people would react to the plan.
   a. a person who owns land on the river
   b. a person who has a farm on the other side of town
   c. a person who owns a bait shop
   d. a person who owns a house on the river and likes peace and quiet
   e. a person who owns a factory along the river

2. Below you will find a bar graph showing how the federal government spent its money in 1970, 1980, and 1990. You will notice that the percentage of spending in some categories increased over these years, while the percentage of spending in other categories decreased. Study the graph and answer the following questions. (Your answers from the graph do not have to be exact, but try to make them as close as possible.)
   a. What percentage of federal spending went to payments to individuals in 1970?
   b. What percentage of federal spending went to payments to individuals in 1990?
   c. What percentage of federal spending went to national defense in 1970?
   d. What percentage of federal spending went to national defense in 1990?
   e. Describe the change in emphasis for federal spending between 1970 and 1990 that is shown by the answers to questions *a* through *d*.
   f. What has happened to the importance of the federal government's interest payment between 1970 and 1990?

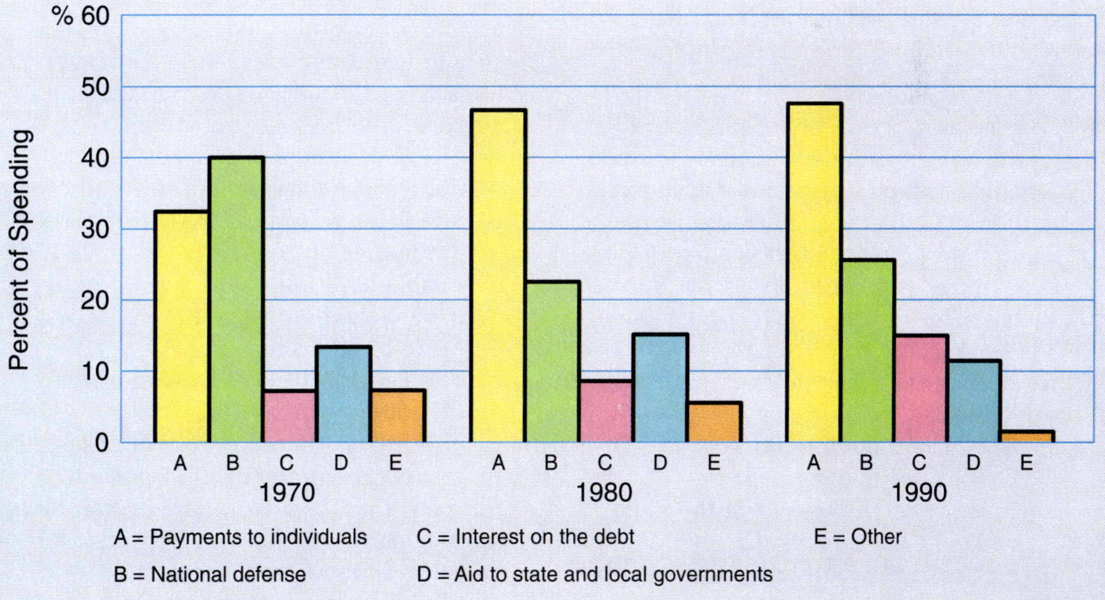

Source: *Statistical Abstract of the United States*, 1991.

Chapter 9
(1) predicting probable consequences; (2) interpreting graphs.

Part 3 Review

Chapter 10

1. Identify the type of unemployment described in each of the following examples (frictional, seasonal, cyclical, or structural). In each instance, think of at least one action that the person could have taken in advance to help avoid a lengthy period of unemployment.
   a. Joe loses his job when inventories grow too large.
   b. Max quits his job to look for a better one.
   c. Jan loses her job after the Christmas sales rush.
   d. Sue loses her job when a new computer is installed.
   e. Ted is replaced on his job by a college graduate.
2. Unemployment can cause many problems other than economic hardships. Describe three different problems that could result from long-term unemployment. Be specific.
3. People can react to higher prices in different ways. Suppose you really wanted a particular type of car and you found that its price had just increased from $12,000 to $15,000. There is a list of possible things you could do below. Rank each action from 1 to 5 (1 is most likely, 5 is least likely), according to which you would be most likely to do. Then explain each ranking.
   a. Give up on buying the car.
   b. Buy a used one instead.
   c. Save longer and buy it at the higher price.
   d. Buy one, but with fewer options than you had wanted.
   e. Try to find someone to share the car and cost with.
4. Identify what you consider to be one of the major causes of poverty. Suggest at least one action that you think could be taken to help eliminate that cause.

Chapter 11

1. Identify each of the situations below as an example of one of the functions of money—as a medium of exchange, as a measure of value, or as a store of value. Then explain your answer.
   a. Your little brother puts money in his piggy bank to save for a pair of roller skates.
   b. You pay for your milk with a dollar bill.
   c. Your mother shops where the prices are lowest.
   d. A firm borrows $50,000 from a bank to pay for a new machine.
2. Decide whether each of the following actions would *increase* or *decrease* the amount of money in circulation.
   a. The Federal Reserve System lowers the reserve requirement to 10 percent.
   b. The Federal Reserve System reduces the money supply.
   c. People hold less cash, deposit more.
   d. Banks decide to hold more cash and make fewer loans.
   e. The Federal Reserve System increases the money supply.
   f. The Federal Reserve System raises the reserve requirement to 14 percent.
3. Suppose that your aunt has several thousand dollars that she wants to lend out as an investment, and she asks you how she should go about finding someone to

Chapter 10
(1) analyzing cause and effect; (2) predicting probable consequences; (3) decision-making; (4) analyzing cause and effect.

Chapter 11
(1) classification; (2) predicting probable consequences; (3) identifying the problem; (4) analyzing cause and effect.

lend it to. What qualifications for a borrower would you suggest, and why?

4. In the end, the Fed has only the power to make it easier or more difficult to borrow money. It does this by increasing or decreasing the money supply. With this in mind, answer each of the following questions.
   a. If there is inflation, would the Fed probably try to increase or to decrease the amount of money in circulation to reduce demand?
   b. If there is unemployment, would the Fed probably try to increase or to decrease the amount of money in circulation to increase sales and jobs?
   c. Study your answers to questions *a* and *b* above. If there is both unemployment and inflation, can the Fed attack both of them at the same time?
   d. If prices go up because of an increase in the price of imported raw materials (such as oil), will monetary policy solve the problem? (Hint: think of what type of inflation this might cause.)
   e. In a recession, people and businesses are often worried about being able to pay their bills. What effect would lower interest rates probably have on people's willingness to borrow and spend?
   f. Describe the three limitations on monetary policy that you have learned about in answering the preceding questions.

Chapter 12

1. It has been suggested that jobs created by the government only last as long as the government is willing to pay for them. Almost everyone knows of a relative or an individual who has been unemployed. Briefly describe one such person you know of. What type of work did he or she have? How did he or she become unemployed? What hardships has the person experienced, and what prospects does he or she have for the future? Describe at least two actions you believe the government should take to help people like this. Be realistic by considering the political and economic consequences of your suggestions.
2. Suppose that you own your own business. Inflation in general has been 6 percent. The cost of your raw materials has gone up 10 percent in the past year. You are negotiating with your workers for a new contract. They want a 9 percent pay increase and you are convinced that they will go on strike if they don't get it. You have seen your profit margin fall from over 12 percent to just 3 percent in the last year. Most of your competitors have increased their prices more than you have.

   The government has sent you a letter asking you to limit your price increases to no more than 4 percent this year. Write a letter back to the government telling them what you plan to do and why you intend to do it. Include at least three specific reasons for your plan.
3. Programs to help the poor, retired, and unemployed also help those who have jobs. If there were a recession and these programs did not exist, what would the answers to the following questions be?
   a. What would happen to the number of products that could be purchased by the poor?
   b. What would happen to the number of foreclosures and repossessions?
   c. What would happen to the number of jobs in the economy?
   d. How do programs to help the poor help those who keep their jobs?

Chapter 12
(1) analyzing cause and effect; (2) identifying the problem; (3) predicting probable consequences.

JAWI

P A R T

4

Understanding International Economics

Part 4 will help you understand how the American economy fits into and has become part of the world economy. In Chapter 13 you will learn why nations trade and why they limit trade. Problems related to international payments and exchange rates will be discussed. You will then examine multinational corporations and see what part they may play in bringing national economies closer together. In Chapter 14 you will study developing nations and the difficulties they have producing enough to satisfy their people's needs. You will evaluate the arguments for and against industrialized countries providing aid to developing nations. Finally, in Chapter 15 you will look at different ways of answering the basic economic questions in other countries. Part 4 will help you understand how the world's economy has become interrelated and global.

RIO MAGDALENA
TEXLON
TEXLON

CHAPTER 13

Why Countries Trade

Objectives

In the sections of this chapter, you will learn:

A

why countries trade according to the theories of *absolute advantage* and *comparative advantage*, and why countries try to restrict trade through tariffs, quotas, and other methods; and how there are costs and benefits to both *positive* and *negative* balances of trade;

B

how the *exchange rates* for the dollar affect the U.S. economy and are related to the balance of trade; and

C

why corporations become multinational, and how they affect jobs and trade.

Introduction

The economic system of the United States is just one part of the world economy. Like all other countries, we depend on international trade. Each year we export and import hundreds of billions of dollars worth of goods and services. As we have already learned, specialization allows us to produce products of better quality and lower prices. Florida and California produce oranges in exchange for Idaho potatoes and corn from the Midwest. Specialization in international trade is merely an extension of the same principle. We import fuel, bananas, and textiles and export grains, airplanes, and computers. We must import some products, such as coffee, aluminum ore, and sugar. Without our wheat, selected medicines, and coal, however, other countries would have a lower standard of living.

We not only need to buy products from other countries, but other nations provide markets for many of the goods we produce. It has been estimated that more than 10 million jobs are created by our exports.

Although we need and benefit from trade, there are problems associated with it. Money spent on imported goods is money that cannot be spent on American products. Importing too many foreign products can reduce the demand for prod-

Trade—both importing and exporting of goods—is essential to our economy. But there are trade-offs in importing goods from foreign nations. Different people have different viewpoints on the costs and benefits of importing foreign-made cars and other products.

Explain. The relation of the U.S. economy to world trade can be seen in price fluctuations in the commodities market. When Brazil had bad coffee crops in the mid-1980s, coffee prices increased to almost $3.00 a pound. Predictions of a good crop in 1987 forced the price as low as $1.00 a pound. Sugar, cotton, cocoa, lumber, copper, and other prices depend on production in other countries.

ucts that are made in this country. This can cause unemployment in some industries in the United States.

In this chapter you will study the trade-off between using foreign goods and domestic goods. Buying foreign goods, which are often less expensive, can help keep inflation under control. On the other hand, purchases of domestic goods create jobs for Americans. There is something to be gained and something to be lost with either course of action.

Another problem you will investigate is the fluctuation in U.S. exports. In the early 1980s, American producers found it increasingly difficult to sell their products to other countries. At least part of this problem was the result of the high value of our dollar. To buy American products, foreign nations must trade their currency for dollars. When the dollar's value is high, foreign nations receive fewer dollars in exchange for their money. Beginning in 1986 the value of the dollar declined in relation to foreign currencies. That was like putting American products on sale to foreign buyers. U.S. exports increased sharply.

This chapter will show you how Americans are affected by trade, and how it helps most of us.

Section A The Benefits of Trade

In this section you will learn about the theories of *absolute advantage* and *comparative advantage* and why nations trade. You will then explore why nations sometimes use *tariffs* and *quotas* as barriers against trade.

Personal Narrative

My Father Sells Nissans For a Living

My father has always earned his living selling cars. He started in 1973, selling Chryslers. In 1979, when Chrysler almost went bankrupt, he took a job selling Nissans. Now he says he likes his job more than before, because he believes in the product he sells.

According to my father, you can't be a good salesperson unless you're excited about what you're selling. Customers sense how you feel, and are more likely to buy because of it. My father thinks Nissans are great. He says they are well designed, carefully assembled, efficient, and reliable. He feels good when someone buys one of his cars. He must believe in his product; he's won sales awards in each of the last four years.

Discuss. Do your students believe there is anything "wrong" with buying imported goods? How would they evaluate these arguments?

Some of my friends at school think what my father does for a living is wrong. They say Americans should buy only products that were made in the United States. My father has heard this argument many times and has several answers for it. They are:

a. Americans believe in freedom. They should be free to buy the best products at the lowest prices, no matter where the products were made.

b. American firms used to be too lazy. They had years to improve their efficiency and quality, but they didn't really try until there was foreign competition. Foreign imports have forced American firms to produce better products.

c. Many parts in American cars are made in other countries. U.S. manufacturers have found that foreign parts are inexpensive and have high quality. Today many products that are called "American Made" have parts that were produced in other countries.

d. Many Americans are employed selling and servicing foreign products that are sold in the United States. There are salespeople, mechanics, distributors, and people in advertising who earn their livings because of imports. If we didn't buy imports, these people would have to find other jobs.

Discuss. Trade may benefit a nation as a whole, while hurting individuals. What trade-off should be made between the interests of the few and those of the group?

e. If we didn't buy foreign products, foreigners would not have money to buy from us. Many Americans earn their living by producing goods and services that are sold abroad.

When I try to explain these arguments at school, most of my friends don't listen. I can understand why. There is a big General Motors plant near town that has laid off many workers in recent years. If my father had lost his job because of imported cars, I probably wouldn't want to hear these arguments either.

Why Trade?

No country in the free world is forced to trade, yet all countries import and export goods. If no country is forced to trade, only one conclusion makes sense: countries trade because they want to.

Discuss. The theory of absolute advantage says that if your take-home pay is greater than the cost for hiring a gardener you should pay someone else to care for your lawn. Why do so few people hire gardeners or lawn services?

Economists have developed two theories to explain why countries trade. They are called the theories of *absolute advantage* and *comparative advantage*. Both of these theories state that countries should specialize in making products that they are most efficient at and trade for products that they do not make as well. If this were done, all countries would make the things they do best, causing total production to increase. These theories say that after trade, all countries would have more products.

An example that demonstrates the theory of **absolute advantage** would be U.S. trade with Central American countries for bananas. The United States could never produce bananas efficiently. It would be a waste of our time to try. On the other hand, we do manufacture machinery more efficiently than most Central American nations. Therefore, it makes sense for the U.S. to buy bananas from these countries and to sell them our machinery. We both benefit from the exchange because we each have a type of production that we do best.

Explain. Specializing in the production of raw materials rather than final products usually results in lower earnings and fewer high-paying jobs. Many developing nations have attempted to specialize in technologically advanced production to speed their economic growth. However, this policy has often led to waste and inefficiency.

Should a country trade even if it is better at all types of production than other countries? The theory of **comparative advantage** says yes. Suppose that an executive who earns $50 an hour can type better than her secretary, who is paid $7 an hour. It would be inefficient for the executive to do her own typing, because she has more important things to do. Even if the secretary took twice as long as the executive to do the work, it would still be less expensive for the secretary to do it. The same is true of countries. Suppose that the United States produces both airplanes and watches cheaper than does Switzerland. However, its relative efficiency in airplanes is 3 to 1 (one-third the cost of Swiss airplanes), while its relative efficiency in watches is 2 to 1 (one-half the cost of Swiss watches). Both the U.S. and Switzerland would be richer if they specialized, the U.S. in airplanes and Switzerland in watches, and traded with each other.

Barriers to Trade

Note. Any barrier to trade will have the effect of reducing the total supply of products and increasing the price of imported and domestically produced goods. Tariffs and quotas require a trade-off between higher prices for the present and various other benefits, some of which are discussed below.

Discuss. A tariff on imported oil has been suggested as a way to help balance the federal budget and to reduce our dependency on imported energy. However, such a tax would increase the costs of production in the United States and make it more difficult to sell our products to other nations.

Although countries benefit from trade, they also want to control their imports and exports. This can be done through *tariffs, quotas,* or other types of restrictions.

Tariffs

A **tariff** is a tax on an import. Tariffs make imports more expensive and therefore less attractive to consumers. Tariffs can be used to reduce a nation's imports, as well as to provide revenue for government expenditures.

There are three major types of tariffs, classified according to their main purposes. The three types are *revenue, protective,* and *restrictive.*

Revenue tariffs are intended to raise money to run the government. Many U.S. tariffs in the 1800s were of this type.

Protective tariffs are intended to increase the price of imported products to a competitive level with products made in the country that sets the tariff. Tariffs on imported cars and steel are examples of this sort of tax.

Restrictive tariffs are intended to reduce or eliminate the flow of a particular type of product into a country. Tariffs on luxury goods imported into many poorer nations are examples of this type of tax.

Quotas

A **quota** is a limit on the amount of a product a nation will allow to be imported. The United States uses both tariffs and quotas to control imports.

U.S. Trade Policy

From its beginnings until the mid-1860s the United States encouraged trade with other nations, protecting only a few industries from foreign competition. We encouraged the world to buy American agricultural products and traded for manufactured goods. Beginning in the 1860s, Northern industrial interests in control of the government passed high protective tariffs to prevent foreign competition from threatening our young industries. With some fluctuations, these tariffs remained high until the 1930s. President Franklin Roosevelt tried to increase trade by lowering tariffs and encouraging our trading partners to do the same. That policy of encouraging free trade has remained, only recently encountering any serious opposition.

When World War II ended, the U.S. knew it would be necessary to help Europe rebuild its economy. The government did this through the Marshall Plan, which provided the resources needed to reconstruct European economies. Along with other nations, the U.S. set up a World Bank for Reconstruction and Development from which all nations could borrow. We also led in the development of the International Monetary Fund, so that nations could borrow foreign currencies in short-term loans in order to trade. Finally, the U.S. helped organize the General Agreement on Tariffs and Trade (GATT). Under this agreement nations meet regularly to discuss mutual tariff policies. Each of these meetings, called "rounds," has resulted in the removal of many trade barriers. In short, the U.S. has been responsible for much of the increase in world trade, as you can see in Figure 13-1.

Note. In 1967 Western European nations formed the European Community to achieve economic unity. The EC set out to remove barriers to trade and permit workers, capital, goods, and services to move freely throughout member nations. In the 1980s and 1990s Japan moved to strengthen trade by agreements with nations of the Pacific Rim, and the United States negotiated with Canada and Mexico to establish a North American Free Trade Zone.

Figure 13–1 *U.S. Merchandise Exports and Imports, 1950–1991 (billions of dollars) and Total Merchandise Trade as a Percentage of Gross Domestic Product*

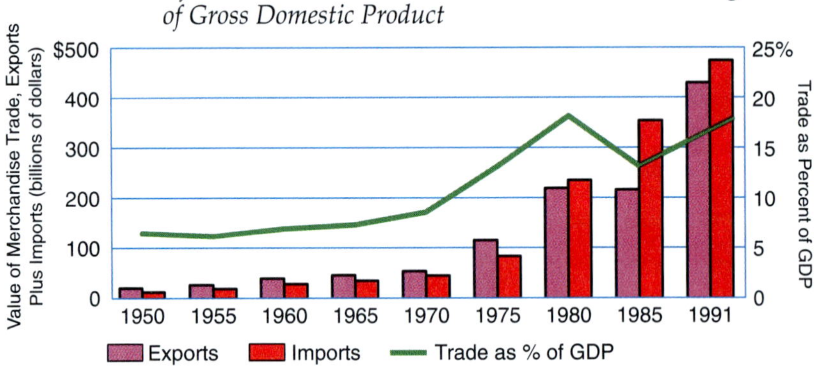

Source: *Office of Trade and Investment Analysis, U.S. Department of Commerce.*

The best measure of how important trade has become to the U.S. economy is the line showing trade as a percentage of the nation's GDP. From 1950 to 1965 it averaged about 6.5 percent. From 1980 to the present it has averaged about 15 percent.

Voluntary Export Restraints (VER)

Because import quotas are no longer permitted under GATT, exporting countries may be induced by special agreements to limit shipments of specific goods to an importing country. The most well-known of these was Japan's agreement to limit exporting automobiles to the United States. The announced reason was to save American jobs. The trade-off was that the American consumer had to pay a higher price for an automobile. Hundreds of other items have been placed on VER lists.

Discuss. How well are plans for trading blocs in Europe, the Pacific Rim, and North America developing? Have students check newspapers and recent magazine articles under "European Community," "free trade agreements," "Pacific Rim."

Regulations and Certification

Most nations have import restrictions that are supposed to protect the safety and health of their citizens. In some instances, imported products must be certified for standards of quality. In reality, these often turn out to be devices for keeping out foreign goods and protecting home industries. The European Community barred imported American beef because it was treated with hormones. The United States bars tomatoes unless they are a certain size, which hurts Mexican exports. Japan requires foreign firms to team up with Japanese firms in order to do business there. Brazil requires all imported cars to have a certain percentage of their value produced in Brazil. These are some of the many restrictions that countries use to protect their own producers but which cost their own consumers millions to billions of dollars.

The Costs and Benefits of Trade Barriers

Why Restrict Trade?

Explain. A problem with the infant industry argument is the possibility it offers firms to remain inefficient. If tariffs eliminate meaningful competition from imports, domestic firms may have less of an incentive to invest and become efficient.

Although the theories of absolute advantage and comparative advantage tell us that as countries trade more they will become better off, all countries have some barriers to trade. Some people believe barriers to trade are able to *protect infant industries,* to *improve national security,* to *protect domestic jobs,* and to *maintain economic stability.*

a. The **infant industry** argument states that countries should protect new industries with tariffs. An infant industry is one that is just starting out. Such an industry won't be as efficient as established industries in other countries. If it is not protected, it may fail. For example, when India started to manufacture steel in the 1950s, it put high tariffs on imported steel. This allowed its new firms to compete successfully against cheaper foreign steel.

Explain. A problem with the national security argument is the possibility that in attempting to provide military equipment for itself, a country may fall behind its potential enemies. The costs of research and development may prevent small countries from staying up-to-date, regardless of their commitment to military self-sufficiency.

b. The **national security** argument states that a country should produce vital military products for itself, even when they can be purchased for less in other countries. A country would not want to depend on others to supply weapons that it needs to defend itself. For example, France, at great expense, has chosen to build its own nuclear weapons rather than rely on the United States for its defense.

c. The **protection of domestic jobs** argument points out that many foreign workers are paid much lower wages than

Explain. A problem with the protection of domestic jobs argument is the possibility that tariffs may lead to retaliation from other countries in the form of higher tariffs that could prevent American firms from selling to other countries.

Explain. A problem with the maintaining economic stability argument is that it assumes countries can afford to diversify their production to a point where they can supply many of their own needs. The cost of such diversification has forced many developing nations into debt that may be beyond their ability to pay.

American workers. Because of the lower wages, foreign producers are able to charge lower prices and increase their sales in the U.S. Tariffs would increase the price of foreign goods to levels that U.S. products can compete with.

d. The **maintaining economic stability** argument states that nations that depend on trade are more likely to be hurt by disruptions in trade. An example of this problem came in 1973 when Arab countries cut off exports of oil to the United States. If we relied less on imported energy we would be less vulnerable to actions of this nature.

Keeping Trade Balanced

Turn back to Figure 13-1. You can see that before 1980 U.S. exports were greater than imports. The difference between the value of exports and of imports is called the balance of trade. From 1950 to the 1970s our merchandise exports were greater than our imports, and we had a favorable or **positive balance of trade.** In 1980 that balance was negative—called an unfavorable or **negative balance of trade.**

The advantages of a positive balance of trade include (1) greater employment, (2) higher profitability, (3) increased economic growth, (4) larger income for the government to tax, and (5) the ability to buy things from other nations.

Unfortunately, if some countries have positive balances of trade, then other countries have negative balances of trade. They import more than they export. The disadvantages of a negative balance of trade are the opposite of those above. Negative balances of trade tend to (1) reduce employment, (2) decrease profitability, (3) slow economic growth, (4) reduce taxable incomes, and (5) make it more difficult to buy things from other nations.

Not all effects of a negative balance of trade are bad. For example, less expensive imports help keep inflation under control. Many economists believe that having more goods and services enter instead of leave the country is better for the economy. However, most people believe the benefits of a positive balance of trade are much better than those of a negative balance.

In the 1980s Presidents Ronald Reagan and George Bush vetoed legislation that would restrict trade, because they both believed in free trade. The United States opened talks with Canada and Mexico to eliminate trade restrictions. In 1991 Congress authorized President Bush to begin negotiating a North American Free Trade Agreement (NAFTA) that would link the three nations in a trading bloc. The federal government earlier had taken steps to help individuals who had been hurt by trade. For ex-

In the early 1980s, foreign production of some parts for electronic goods became so inexpensive that American firms gave up making them in this country. Some Americans asked whether Japan was competing fairly.

ample, the Trade Adjustment Assistance program was established in 1974 to help workers who lost their jobs because of imported goods. The program paid extended unemployment benefits and helped with the cost of retraining.

Protectionism and Politics

In the 1980s many advocates of free trade changed their position to support "fair trade." They pointed out that U.S. trade policy had far fewer restrictions than many of its trading partners. Political pressure led to the passage of the Omnibus Trade and Competitiveness Act of 1988. Much of the act supported free trade, giving the President authority to negotiate reductions and even elimination of trade barriers on dozens of products. Nearly $1 billion was made available to retrain workers who were displaced because of imports. In addition, the so-called "super 301" provision required the administration to list the names of all countries that practiced "unfair trade," and to negotiate the removal of these practices. In May 1989 the first listing designated Japan, Brazil, and India as having unfair trade practices. Negotiations have resulted in Japan and Brazil being removed from the list, but the threat of retaliation by the United States remains.

Discuss. Is losing a job to foreign competition different than losing a job to domestic competition? For example, in 1963 the Studebaker corporation stopped producing automobiles, costing thousands of workers their jobs. Their employer was driven out of business by American competition. Do your students feel that situation was different from the one in the early 1980s, when thousands of automobile workers lost their jobs due to foreign competition? If so, in what ways was it different?

One practice the government tries to prevent is **dumping** of products. Economists define dumping as selling goods in foreign markets for less than they are sold in the producing nation. Most countries agree that this practice is unfair competition. The United States imposes special taxes on a country found guilty of dumping. This policy is not often needed, because actual cases of dumping are relatively few.

Pressure to keep out foreign competition grew even stronger as the recession of 1990 to 1992 caused the closing of many automobile plants. Presidential candidates ran on platforms of America first. It became popular to blame the Japanese for our foreign trade troubles. While the United States was still the most efficient overall producer in the world, other nations were improving efficiency. American producers sought protection on products that others produced more efficiently.

Protection is an expensive and inefficient way to save jobs, however. Economists have estimated that Americans have spent more than $20 billion in higher prices on automobiles because of restrictive policies. To save one job in some industries, it is estimated that consumers have had to pay $250,000 in higher prices. When consumers pay higher prices they cannot afford to save and invest as much. This, in turn, reduces funds for business expansion and new jobs.

Self-Check
See Lesson Plan for Chapter 13, Section A, page T134.

Self-Check

1. What do the theories of absolute advantage and comparative advantage state countries should do?
2. What is the difference between a tariff, a quota, and voluntary export restraints?
3. According to the infant industry argument, why should developing countries establish tariffs?
4. What are the benefits and the costs to countries from a favorable (positive) balance of trade? From an unfavorable (negative) balance of trade?
5. Explain how American trade policy has fluctuated. Explain why.

Applying What You Have Learned
See Lesson Plan for Chapter 13, Section A, page T134.

Applying What You Have Learned

In the Personal Narrative for this section, five arguments were given that favored free trade. State an answer to three of these arguments that could be given by someone who was against free trade.

Section B The Value of The Dollar and Trade

This section will discuss the relationship between the value of the U.S. dollar and our balance of trade.

Personal Narrative

Sometimes Business Conditions Are Beyond Our Control

My father used to work for a firm that manufactured high-quality machine parts, almost half of which were exported. For the first 15 years he worked for Mert's Machine Parts his employer's business grew steadily. Mert's profits increased and Dad's income gave us a good living. During the recession of 1980-1982, Mert's sales fell. Everyone thought business would improve when the recession ended, but it didn't. The problem was that after 1983 Mert's sold almost nothing to foreign nations.

I remember one evening in 1986 when Dad called a family meeting. His expression told me he was worried. He said his manager had announced that all hourly employees would only be allowed to work 30 hours a week until Mert's business improved. Dad explained that the value of the American dollar had almost doubled in relation to some other types of currency. Although Mert's prices had not changed very much in dollars, it could cost foreigners twice as much of their money to trade for the dollars they needed to buy Mert's products. Most of them could buy similar products from other countries for less. Mert's tried to keep its customers by cutting costs and lowering profits, but there was a limit to what they could do. The only real solution was a lower value for the dollar. In the meantime Dad said we all had to cut back on our spending.

About a month after our family meeting, I read a newspaper article that described an agreement between leaders of industrialized nations to lower the value of the dollar. It said the American balance of trade was getting worse each year. The article explained that the high value of the dollar allowed Americans to buy more yen, francs, and marks, encouraging imports and discouraging exports. I realized this was bad for American businesses that depended on exports.

Explain. Before 1971 the U.S. dollar was defined in terms of gold, and currency exchange rates were fixed. In 1971 President Nixon announced the U.S. would no longer define dollars for gold. The forces of supply and demand now establish the value of one country's currency in terms of other countries' currencies.

About two years later the value of the dollar was lower and Dad was back working full-time. The value of the dollar had fallen to about the same level it was in 1980, making Mert's products less expensive to foreigners. I guess the value of the dollar in the foreign exchange market makes a big difference.

Exchange Rates

Note. The current method of setting exchange rates, called the "floating" exchange rate system, was established in 1973. Exchange rates are set by international financial institutions according to the demand and supply for each type of currency. We have a "dirty float" rather than a "free float" because governments buy and sell currencies in a counter-cyclical way to try to make changes more gradual. Although this policy may reduce short-term fluctuations in exchange rates, it cannot stop a major trend up or down over time.

Foreign trade requires converting one type of money for another. The price of an imported good depends on the **exchange rate** between the American dollar and the money of the country that manufactured the product. Exchange rates are set in an international market according to the demand and supply for different types of money.

For example, if German prices were very low, many Americans would want to buy German products but few Germans would want to buy American products. Once again we can apply our simple model of demand and supply. As Americans went to banks to trade their dollars for German marks, the banks would find that they had an increasingly large supply of dollars and a deepening shortage of marks. The banks would react by making Americans pay more dollars for German marks. Economists would call this increase in the value of the mark **appreciation.** The decrease in the value of the dollar would be a **depreciation.** German prices would seem more expensive to Americans because it would take more dollars to get the marks to buy the German products. On the other hand, American prices would appear lower to Germans because they could get more dollars for their marks. Fewer Americans would buy German products and more Germans would buy American products. If prices were the only things that affected exchange rates, the system would work more easily. Unfortunately, many other things can affect exchange rates.

Causes of Changing Rates

Note. The purchase of U.S. government securities by foreigners (see Section D of Chapter 9) increased the demand for U.S. dollars and helped to cause the appreciation of the dollar in the early 1980s. If foreigners sell their securities and exchange the dollars they receive for other types of currency, it will cause the value of the dollar to fall.

Anything that causes people to trade one type of money for another will affect exchange rates. In the early 1980s, many foreigners traded their money for dollars for reasons that had little to do with trade or prices.

American interest rates were higher than interest rates in other countries in the early 1980s. Many foreigners traded their money for dollars so they could invest in U.S. banks or buy U.S. securities to earn these higher interest rates. Demand for dollars increased and the value of the dollar went up.

At the same time, there were many political and economic problems in other parts of the world. Wealthy individuals and firms wanted to put their money where it would be safe. Many of them bought dollars and invested in United States firms because they were secure. Again, the demand for U.S. dollars increased.

A final reason for the appreciation of the dollar was the early recovery of the U.S. economy from the recession of 1981–1982. Our economic problems started to improve before most other countries. As a result, many foreigners invested in U.S. businesses. This required them to convert their money into dollars.

For these reasons the value of the dollar went up more than 50 percent on an average between 1980 and 1985. After 1985, the trend has reversed itself. By 1992 the dollar had declined to about the same value it had in 1981 against other currencies.

This reversal was at least in part the result of actions taken by the governments of the United States and other countries. In January of 1986 a meeting was held in London to discuss steps that could be taken to reduce the value of the dollar. Although no public announcement was made concerning any agreements, it seems that the foundations for international cooperation were laid there. In 1986 interest rates fell in the United States. The U.S. economy slowed its expansion and economic conditions improved in other nations. These factors combined to reduce the value of the dollar. Figure 13-2 shows the sharp upturn in U.S. exports when the dollar began to decrease in value. As foreign buyers received more dollars in exchange for their own currencies, they bought more American products. American consumers bought less foreign goods, because they received less yen, less francs, and less marks for their dollars.

Explain. A positive result of the depreciation of the dollar became apparent in the first quarter of 1987, when the size of the U.S. trade imbalance began to fall.

From 1987 to 1991 the U.S. unfavorable balance of trade dropped sharply. The change in the value of the dollar accounts for only part of the change in the balance of trade, however. A recession also slowed American purchases of foreign products, while American businesses increased their exports.

Figure 13–2 *Value of U.S. Merchandise Exports and Fluctuations of the Dollar in Relationship to Currencies of U.S. Trading Nations*

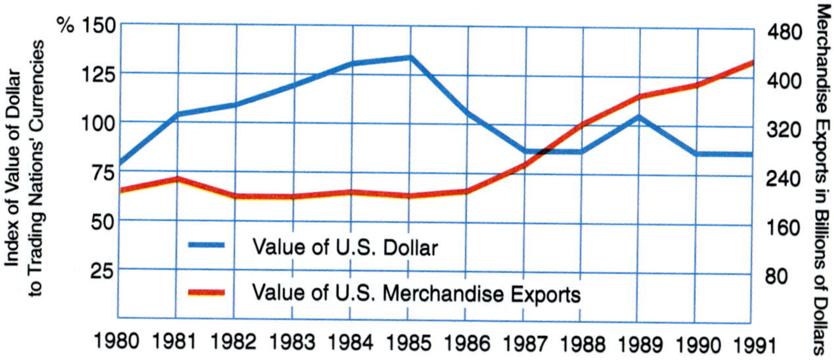

Basic Solution

The Omnibus Trade and Competitiveness Act of 1988 allowed the U.S. government to restrict imports from nations we believed were not practicing "fair trade." It also gave aid to firms hurt by imports through worker retraining and other programs. Motorcycle producer Harley Davidson and many U.S. steel companies took advantage of this act to improve competitiveness in the world market.

A study of U.S. imports and exports shows that most of our negative balance of trade is caused by imports of oil and automobiles. Foreign nations have had both absolute and comparative advantages in supplying these products. Some people suggest the solution to our trade problem is simply to stop buying as many foreign products. A better answer is to improve our productivity and increase our exports. Lower costs allow businesses to reduce prices and increase sales. American producers can become more productive by improving education and technology.

Self-Check

1. How and where are exchange rates set?
2. What is the relationship between the value of the dollar and foreign trade?
3. What factors besides trade influence the value of currencies?
4. How can the U.S. increase its productivity and be more competitive in the world market?

Self-Check

1. Exchange rates are set in an international market according to the demand and supply for different types of money.
2. A declining dollar usually increases exports and decreases imports.
3. High interest and political stability.
4. Through better education, research, and improved technology.

Applying What You Have Learned

In each of the cases below, you are asked to use the changing value of foreign currency (or of the dollar) to find an answer to buying or selling decisions.

a. If you wished to buy a specific Japanese camera whose price in Japan stayed the same, which would have been the better year to buy it, 1985 when the dollar was worth 238.5 yen or 1992 when the dollar was worth 133 yen?

b. In 1989 the Italian lira was worth $.00073 and a dollar would buy 1372 lira. In 1992 the lira was worth $.0008 and a dollar would buy 1250 lira. Which would have been the better year to buy Italian shoes?

c. Would you have been better off buying or selling Swiss francs in 1992? A franc was worth $.70 in 1990, $.69 in 1991, and $.67 in 1992.

Applying What You Have Learned
See Lesson Plan for Chapter 13, Section B, page T136.

Section C Multinational Corporations

This section will define and show the growth of multinational corporations. It will explain why they have spread throughout the world and point out their contributions and the harm they may cause both the parent and host countries.

Personal Narrative

What's American?

There is a business in town that makes auto parts. A few weeks ago the owner had a big sign installed in front of his building that read, "Only American Cars Allowed in This Parking Lot!" I wonder what the owner thinks an American car is.

My Uncle Bob works in Ohio making Honda Accords. At a Chrysler dealership my father sells Plymouth Colts and Dodge Stealths that are made in Japan. In the same area there are dealers who sell Jaguars produced by a factory owned by Ford in Great Britain, Geo Prizms manufactured by General Motors and Toyota in California, and Mercury Grand Marquis that are assembled in Canada. Even cars produced by American-owned firms in the United States have many parts that were made in other countries.

I have a friend whose father is a stockbroker. He told me that most of the big corporations in the world are multinationals, doing business in many different nations. Businesses become multinationals to improve their ability to compete in the world market. He said that Tropicana Orange Juice, for example, used to be restricted in the types and amounts of juice it could sell in Japan. By agreeing to allow a Japanese company to buy a portion of Tropicana, their quota was increased and they were allowed to export all types of orange juice to Japan. He said we have similar rules in the United States.

This information left me a little confused. Is it good for the United States to have a Honda factory in Ohio or an IBM factory in Japan? Is my father taking away American jobs when he sells cars that were made in Japan? Would it make any difference whether I took a job working for SONY or for RCA in this country?

Multinational Corporations

Any business that is headquartered in one country but carries on business activities in one or more foreign countries is a **multinational corporation.** With the great expansion of trade after World

Explain. The largest investors in the U.S. economy are the British.

Note. More money is invested by foreign investors in U.S. companies than U.S. companies have invested abroad.

War II and the increase in sales by U.S. businesses abroad, firms like Ford, ITT, General Electric, and IBM set up plants in other countries. They did so for many reasons. Sometimes it was to avoid the high cost of labor here, sometimes to avoid quotas and tariffs. Coca-Cola did it to expand the market size. Encouraging foreigners to invest in their company was a reason for some.

While the largest U.S. firms started the trend, it soon spread. Today there are more than 10,000 large multinationals with more than 90,000 subsidiaries in different nations.

Types of Organizations

Multinationals may be organized in several different ways. Most started out with control by the parent corporation over the branches (subsidiaries) in other countries. Later, many subsidiaries were given more decision-making power. In some corporations, such as IBM, more than half of the company's income is now generated by its foreign operations.

Note. A parent country is where a multinational has its headquarters. Host countries are where multinationals set up subsidiaries.

Explain. Low labor costs in a host country may be offset by poor workmanship.

Some companies have *joint ventures* involving mergers of corporations from different countries. Car manufacturers and electronics firms have many such arrangements. Firms which take minerals from the earth, usually from developing countries, often have a partnership with the host country's government.

Hiring employees from the labor force of the host country depends on the types of skills needed and those that are available. Usually managers and technicians are sent abroad to start production and train local workers.

What Are the Benefits of Multinationals?

Explain. Host countries are given royalties on the minerals extracted by multinationals.

Corporations choose to operate outside the borders of their own countries to take advantage of opportunities in other nations or to maintain their competitive position in the market. Originally most multinationals were involved in extracting oil, minerals, or other natural resources. Their investments helped develop the resources of developing countries and provided jobs, education, capital, and taxes to the host countries. Their motivation may have been to earn a profit for their owners, but the results provided benefits to citizens of the host nations as well.

Explain. A growing number of small firms are going multinational.

Explain. Many foreign companies invest in the U.S. because of its political stability.

Recently, multinationals have more often been involved in exporting more efficient methods of production. U.S. cars have better quality today in part because of new technology that was developed in other countries and brought to the United States.

Multinational corporations may provide another benefit that is not directly economic. With the nations of the world becoming so intertwined in their economic interests, there may be a greater opportunity for understanding and world peace.

What Harm May Multinationals Cause?

Note. Attempts to formulate universal guidelines for multinationals in dealing with host countries have failed.

While more U.S. jobs may be created when multinationals move into the American economy, U.S. corporations often take away jobs when they move production to other countries. Frequently this results in exploiting cheap foreign labor. This can cause bad feelings toward the United States in other countries, and resentment of foreign workers by Americans who have lost their jobs. Critics can also cite examples of U.S firms that have interfered in the internal affairs of host countries.

There is also a real question as to whether or not these firms pay their fair share of taxes. While some profits made by a foreign multinational may stay in the host country, much of it will return to the parent country. This often contributes to trade and financial problems of the host country. Most economists, however, welcome the low-cost production and quality that competition in our global economy brings. They also believe a greater use of research and new technology will raise the standard of living for all people.

Multinationals may cause short-term upheavals that force some people to lose their jobs and businesses to fail as our economy changes. It is difficult to think of the benefits of multinationals when you are out of work and are in danger of losing your possessions. Another problem is finding a way to control the power of multinational corporations when their interests are in conflict with those of the host nations.

Self-Check

1. Companies go multinational to avoid high labor costs, avoid quotas and tariffs, expand market size, and encourage foreign investment.
2. Multinationals help develop resources and provide jobs, education, capital, and taxes to host countries.
3. Developing countries may fear multinationals because they exploit cheap labor, interfere in the countries' internal affairs, and drain off profits to the parent country.

Self-Check

1. What reasons are there for a company to go multinational?
2. What advantages may a multinational bring to a host nation?
3. Many developing countries fear multinationals. Why?

Applying What You Have Learned

See Lesson Plan for Chapter 13, Section C, page T138.

Applying What You Have Learned

In the Personal Narrative these questions are raised: 1) What is an American company? and 2) Who benefits from multinationals?

CURRENT CONSUMER ISSUES

Should the United States Use Trade Barriers to Help Its Industries?

The traditional argument for protecting businesses with tariffs has been to give *new* industries a chance to become more efficient so they can compete with foreign industries at home and in the global market. Should tariffs be used to protect *established* U.S. firms that have not kept up with foreign competition? Should the American consumer be asked to pay the costs for trade protection? The problems of the American steel industry illustrate this controversy.

In the 1950s and early 1960s the United States dominated the world steel market. However, construction of new facilities in other countries left our steel industry in a noncompetitive position by the 1980s. The United States imported millions of tons of steel, while American plants closed. Leaders of U.S. steel firms pleaded for tariffs or quotas that would give them a chance to improve their productivity.

During the next ten years U.S. steel firms closed inefficient plants, improved production methods, and reduced hourly wages. The number of worker-hours required to produce a ton of steel fell from 10.5 in 1980 to just 5.3 in 1990. This improvement was made possible at least in part by trade protection. This trade protection cost roughly $175,000 for each job that was saved.

Was this policy inconsistent with an earlier agreement? The United States helped establish the General Agreement on Tariffs and Trade (GATT) in 1947. Objectives of GATT included the reduction of tariffs and elimination of quotas among participating nations. Had the United States disregarded the rules for trade that it had helped create?

Arguments in Favor of Protection

1. It helped the U.S. steel industry recover.
2. It protected many American jobs.
3. It reduced the United States's dependence on other nations for a basic product.

Arguments Against Protection

1. It cost American consumers billions of dollars.
2. It may have diverted American investments into a business that had little comparative advantage.
3. It may have cost the United States some respect in the GATT organization.

What Do You Think?

Do you believe the government should protect other industries from foreign competition in the future?

Chapter 13 Review

What Have You Learned?

In this chapter you have learned the following important principles of economics:

- The United States trades because our benefits from trade exceed our costs. The theory of *absolute advantage* states that countries should specialize in products they produce most efficiently and trade for products they produce less efficiently. *Comparative advantage* differs by saying countries should specialize in producing things in which they have the greatest relative efficiency and trade for things in which they are relatively least efficient.
- U.S. trade policy began with *revenue tariffs,* shifted to moderately *protective tariffs,* and then became very protective from the Civil War to the 1930s. Since then the U.S. has led the world in trying to end trade restrictions. This has led to a boom in world trade. Trade is a significant share of U.S. GDP.
- Although theories suggest countries should have free trade, there are reasons that cause nations to impose tariffs, quotas, and other measures to restrict trade. Four such reasons are the *infant industry* argument, the *national security* argument, the *protection of domestic jobs* argument, and the *maintaining economic stability* argument.
- In general, countries prefer to have a *positive balance* rather than a *negative balance of trade.* A positive balance of trade contributes to a nation's employment, economic growth, and taxable income.
- Some steps have been taken to help those who have been hurt by foreign competition. The Omnibus Trade and Competitiveness Act provided help for those who lost their jobs. Rules have been made against *dumping.*
- The price of imported products is partially the result of *exchange rates.* Part of the reason for the U.S. negative balance of trade in the early 1980s was the increased value of the dollar. Our high interest rates, political and economic problems in other parts of the world, and our early recovery from the recession of 1981–1982 all contributed to the dollar's rise in value. When the dollar declined beginning in 1985, U.S. exports increased sharply.
- U.S. businesses were the first to start the trend toward *multinational corporations.*

Words and Terms

absolute advantage (p. 370)
comparative advantage (p. 370)
tariff (p. 371)
revenue tariff (p. 371)
protective tariff (p. 371)
restrictive tariff (p. 371)
quota (p. 371)
infant industry (p. 373)
national security (p. 373)
protection of domestic jobs (p. 373)
maintaining economic stability (p. 374)
positive balance of trade (p. 374)
negative balance of trade (p. 374)
dumping (p. 376)
exchange rate (p. 378)
appreciation (p. 378)
depreciation (p. 378)
multinational corporation (p. 381)

Chapter 13 Review

See Chapter 13 Review Answers, page T139.

These giants operate outside the borders of their parent countries providing jobs, education, capital, and taxes to host countries. Their power can also cause problems in the host countries.

Building Your Vocabulary

On a separate piece of paper, write the vocabulary word or term that best completes each of the following statements.

1. When the value of a country's money increases in comparison to other types of currency, it is called ______.
2. When the value of a country's money decreases in comparison to other types of currency, it is called ______.
3. A ______ is a tax on an imported good.
4. The theory of ______ states that a country should specialize and trade even if it is better at doing everything than other nations.
5. The theory of ______ states that each country should specialize in making the products that they are most efficient in producing and should trade for other products they do not make as well.
6. A ______ is an upper limit on the quantity of a good that can be imported into a country.
7. A tariff intended to increase the price of imported products to a competitive level with domestic products is a ______.
8. The ______ argument states that countries should limit trade to help control unemployment.
9. The ______ argument states that countries should limit trade to avoid being too dependent on other nations for important goods.
10. The ______ argument states that countries should limit trade to allow their new industries to grow and become efficient.
11. The ______ argument states that countries should limit trade so that they do not become too dependent on only a few types of production.
12. A tariff intended to reduce or eliminate the flow of a particular type of product into a country is a ______.
13. A ______ is a firm that is headquartered in a parent country with branches in host countries.
14. The value of different types of currency in terms of each other is called ______.
15. A ______ will tend to increase employment, economic growth, and business profitability.
16. A ______ will tend to decrease employment, economic growth, and business profitability.
17. ______ happens when a nation sells its products to other countries for a lower price than it charges its own people.
18. A tariff intended to raise money to run the government is a ______.

Understanding Economics

1. What do countries need to do in order to follow the theories of comparative advantage and absolute advantage? Explain how they should benefit from this.
2. Explain why many countries that are not advanced technically choose to place tariffs on imported goods.

3. Many countries choose to manufacture their own military equipment when they could buy these products from the other countries for less money. Explain why they do this.
4. Describe three advantages a country would enjoy if it had a positive balance of trade.
5. Many Americans benefit from lower prices and better quality that can result from imported goods. However, the costs of trade are not paid equally by all Americans. Explain why this is true.
6. Explain why some Americans were hurt by the decline of oil prices in the mid-1980s.
7. Describe the results of the voluntary limit Japan put on its exports of cars in the early 1980s.
8. Explain what it means when we say, "Between 1980 and early 1985 the U.S. dollar appreciated about 40 percent."
9. Describe three reasons for the increase in the value of the U.S. dollar in the early 1980s *that were not directly related to trade.*
10. Why did the U.S. dollar decrease in value after 1985? Explain the consequences.
11. Why do corporations go multinational? What undesirable results might occur?
12. What are the benefits to the host country of having a multinational corporation? What might be the costs?

Thinking Critically About Economics

1. Suppose you have been placed in charge of setting tariffs for a country that has high rates of unemployment and inflation. Explain why it will be very difficult for you to please everyone.
2. Some economists believe that foreign competition will be good for U.S. industries because it will force them to invest in new equipment and become more efficient. They point to the new factories that have been built by U.S. automakers to support this idea. Explain why you either agree or disagree with this argument.
3. Is the Omnibus Trade and Competitiveness Act of 1988 the work of protectionists, free traders, or a compromise to help the United States deal with an economic problem? Explain your answer.
4. "Dumping" is selling products to foreign countries for less than the price charged in your own country. Describe what a country could gain from doing this.
5. If interest rates go down in the United States, the value of the U.S. dollar should go down or depreciate (assuming nothing else changes). Explain why this might happen.
6. Explain why it is becoming increasingly difficult to identify an American product or company. Do foreign multinationals in the United States help or hurt our economy? Explain.

Thinking Critically About Economics
(1) recognizing values; (2) identifying the problem; (3) predicting probable consequences; (4) identifying the problem; (5) analyzing cause and effect; (6) recognizing values.

Consumer Skills Projects

1. Take a survey of the kinds of cars that are owned by students (and parents) in your class. What are the reasons for purchasing these particular cars? Do students' reasons differ from parents' reasons?
2. Bring a month-old issue and a current issue of *The Wall Street Journal* to class. Look up exchange rates under the title "Foreign Exchange." Find out whether the value of the dollar is going up or down in terms of other currencies. What generalizations can you make from the changing value of the dollar?

Developing Your Economic Skills

Positive and Negative Values on a Line Graph

Skill: In this lesson you will learn how to draw a line graph that includes both positive and negative numbers. This graph will plot information that shows a change in the financial position of the United States in relation to other countries. To complete this lesson, follow these steps:

- Study a table that shows the U.S. international investment position, over a period of years.
- Plot a graph of this information, in which positive amounts are shown above the horizontal axis and negative amounts are shown below it.
- Evaluate the importance of the information provided on the graph.

Application: Is the United States a debtor nation?

Americans conduct many financial transactions with other nations. International trade, travel, and investments represent huge dollar transactions each year. Governments loan to each other; banks loan to businesses in other countries; people buy securities (stocks and bonds) issued by foreign businesses or governments. For many years the results of these exchanges made the United States a creditor nation. This means that each year our investments abroad were greater than foreign investments in the United States.

In the 1980s this changed. The United States developed large trade deficits as Americans bought more goods and services from other countries than we sold to them. Many dollars returned to the United States in the form of foreign investments in American business and foreign purchases of U.S. government securities. Our international investment position changed from being a creditor nation to being a debtor nation. By 1987 the balance of U.S. foreign investment debt was greater than that of any other country, and still growing.

The following table shows the change in the U.S. financial position. **Balance** indicates the difference between U.S. investments abroad and foreign investments here.

United States Net International Investment Position 1980-1990
(in billions of dollars)

Year	Balance	Year	Balance
1980	$392.5	1986	$ 18.7
1981	$374.3	1987	$- 26.6
1982	$378.9	1988	$-183.8
1983	$337.4	1989	$-312.3
1984	$232.9	1990	$-294.8
1985	$139.0	1991	$-361.5

Source: *Survey of Current Business*, June 1992.

Practice: Plot these values on a line graph to show the trend more clearly. Make a copy of the following graph, with numbers on the vertical axis running from a positive value of 400 to a negative value of 400. A positive number represents a *surplus* U.S. investment position; a negative number represents a *debt* position.

The great size of this debt is causing economic problems for the U.S. economy, and could cause greater problems in the future. For example, payments made on this debt in the form of interest and other earnings send money out of the United States and reduce our purchasing power. Foreign companies are able to expand in the United States, while domestic firms lay off workers. How does the visual help you understand the trend in the U.S. international investment position? What might reverse this trend?

A United States International Investment Position at Year End, 1980–1990

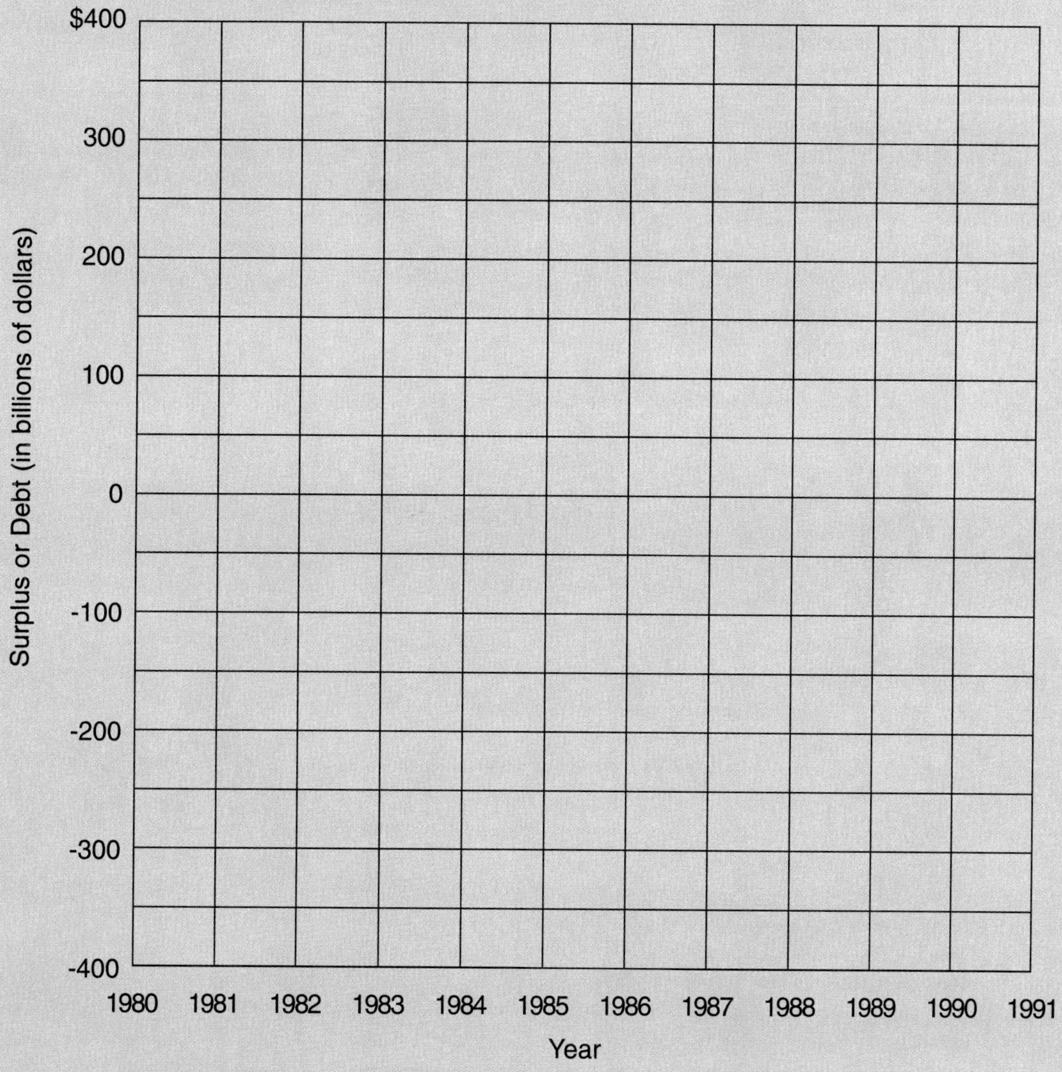

CHAPTER 14

Developing Nations, Growth, and Population

Objectives

In the sections of this chapter, you will learn:

A

what is meant by *developing nations,* what hampers their growth, and what is needed by these nations to speed development;

B

what type of aid is available, the controversy over whether aid should be given, and, if so, what type of aid; and

C

why many developing nations also have a problem with *population,* and how economic growth is linked to control of population growth.

Introduction

Most Americans have at least an adequate standard of living. They eat regularly, have clothing to wear, and a place they can call home. Many of us have a great deal more than just enough. This cannot be said of many other people in the world. There are nations in which the majority of people do not have even a minimal standard of living. Over the years these nations have been called "less developed," "underdeveloped," "emerging," or "disadvantaged countries." In this text they will be referred to as **developing nations.** All of these countries have at least one thing in common—low average incomes. The term **developed nations** will refer to industrialized countries like the United States, Germany, and Japan. The term **newly developed nations** will mean those middle-income countries with some developed industry, such as Poland, Mexico, and South Korea.

Average per capita income shows vast differences among the peoples of the world. The average personal income in the United States was about $20,000 in 1992. The World Bank lists 56 countries whose per capita income is below $1,000 per year. More than half of these countries had incomes of less than $500, and 350 million people living in 14 countries had incomes no higher than $250 per year.

Discuss. Review the discussion of poverty in Section C of Chapter 10.

The people of Ethiopia, Zaire, Kenya, and some other developing nations have experienced repeated famines in recent years. In many cases, there were steps that could have been taken to reduce or solve this problem. Unfortunately, internal conflicts prevented people from helping themselves and stopped outside aid from achieving its intended effect on development.

Explain. When a developed nation tries to help a developing nation, values frequently come into conflict. For example, many Americans value individual initiative and assertiveness. In some developing nations, a person who displayed these characteristics could suffer from social ostracism.

In this chapter you will learn some of the reasons for poverty in other nations as well as suggested solutions for increasing growth. The United States, other developed nations, and multinational corporations have attempted to help developing nations, with varying degrees of success. Nations and businesses that offer aid usually want some control over that aid. The developing nations, however, want freedom to do what they choose with the money. The cultural values of developing nations, their internal political instability, insufficient capital for investment, and lack of adequate educational systems often prevent developing nations from making economic progress. In some developing nations less than half the people can read, and rapid population growth strains already scarce resources.

The last section of the chapter will deal with population growth. Countries with the highest rates of population increase are often those that are least able to support and feed more people. Projections of future population trends offer little hope for the future in some parts of the world. Demands for help are likely to be made on wealthy nations by the people of less fortunate nations. The time may come when you will be asked to help make decisions that are related to this problem.

Section A The Problems of Developing Nations

This section will discuss problems that are faced by developing countries in their attempts to improve their standards of living.

Personal Narrative

Why Don't They Help Themselves?

My ancestors came to North America from Africa some time around 1750. There is no way to know exactly when they came, or where they came from, because they were black and brought here as slaves. I have never been to Africa and I probably never will go. I would know nothing about the language or customs there. But I feel a kinship for people who live in Africa. I know that I might be living there if history had been different.

I learned about problems in Africa from watching TV. I saw Africans starving on the news. It bothered me more than other problems that were reported. I was upset because I knew it could have been me. I wanted to know why they had these problems and what could be done to help them.

On one television program, I saw a reporter interview an expert on the economic problems of Africa. She explained several reasons for the problems she studies. One of the most important she mentioned is that many people in Africa do not know how to take care of their land and its resources. They often waste things that should be saved and cared for. Many Africans do not have the basic tools for farming or the skills to use tools they have been given. It is difficult to teach new skills because most African countries have limited funds to spend on education. Another important problem is fighting that has gone on in many parts of Africa. There are many cases where land and crops have been destroyed for political reasons. These, and other problems, have combined to make life almost impossible in many parts of Africa.

Values. Why do nations like the United States have vast food surpluses while people are starving? Discuss the impact of giving food to people who would otherwise be customers of farmers in developing nations. If we give away food, how will these farmers earn a living? How do economic and moral values conflict in this situation?

My church collected money to buy food for people in Ethiopia. I gave what I could. It made me feel a little better to be doing something, but I knew that it wasn't going to solve the real problems in Africa.

What Are the Problems?

Growing food requires more than seeds and rain. It requires tools and fertilizer—and most of all, knowledge. Farmers in many parts of the world learn what they know about farming from their relatives, and not in schools or from books. As a result, their farming methods almost never change.

A Traditional Economy

Explain. There are traditions and values associated with a capitalistic economic system. We could consider our conception of private property, profit, or the value we place on individual achievement as our traditions. Some people suggest that these traditions prevent us from cooperating with each other and can lead to economic inefficiency.

Traditions play a role in all economic systems, but they play a larger role in some countries than in others. In Medieval Europe, 900 years ago, there was an economic system called *feudalism*, which was based on tradition. In that system, everyone was expected to do the same job as their parents. All the land belonged to a king, a feudal lord, or to the church. The peasants farmed it and got to keep part of what they grew. This system went on for several hundred years with almost no social or economic change. We can find similar situations in regions of many developing nations today.

Even in the United States, what we consider right and wrong depends on what we were taught by our parents and families. However, we also learn from schools, books, and through other institutions in our society. In many countries most people learn almost everything they believe in from their families. These countries have what are called **traditional economies.** It is very difficult to bring about change in such economic systems.

Explain. Most Americans regard the word *new* as similar to *better.* This can be seen in our advertising of "new" products. In many countries, *new* is assumed to be bad and something to be avoided.

If your father fed cattle in a drought by cutting down trees to get the leaves, you would do the same. You would not realize that you were destroying the environmental balance of the land. If your mother told you that a sign of power and status was a large family and lots of cows, you would believe this was true. The problem is that when everyone believes this, the number of cattle and people can grow beyond the ability of the land to support the population.

This is what has happened in large parts of Africa. The people could solve some of their own problems if they knew how, but they don't. Trying to teach new methods to people who have done things the same way for generations is not an easy task.

What is Needed for Change?

There is general agreement among economists that in order for developing nations to improve their economies they need to better educate their people, to increase their capital, to improve their management, and to have stable governments that other people and governments can trust.

Investment capital usually comes from savings, but how can poor people save? When capital becomes available, it may be invested in industries such as steel that offer prestige but little economic value to the nation. Management is frequently placed in

Although enrollment in schools and the literacy rate are improving in developing nations, many classrooms lack the basic educational tools that most schools in developed nations take for granted.

Discuss. Can the dislocation of American workers from jobs in basic industries like steel or automobiles be compared with the dislocation of farmers in developing nations? In both cases, a way of life is being changed by economic forces beyond the control of the individuals involved.

Question. The political systems in many developing nations have been inherited from former colonial powers and are not suited to the needs of the people in these countries. It could be argued that a parliamentary form of government is not the best form of government for nations populated by uneducated peasant farmers. On the other hand, do totalitarian forms of government have much to offer as an alternative?

the hands of the politically powerful or inherited by the upper class instead of entrusted to the best trained and hardest-working people. Governments may hold power by favoring the few and controlling the army. Much of the money taken in may be used to put down rebellions and uphold the ruling powers.

If people know how to read, they can learn how to improve their health, develop skills, and better their living conditions. Unfortunately, only a little more than half of the children in developing nations attend primary school, and in most poorer nations less than ten percent attend high school. The ratio of teachers to pupils is more than double that of high-income countries. Books, chalkboards, desks, and even pencils and paper are scarce. Learning skills by example is useful, but few volunteers are willing to leave their own comfortable environments to provide such needed service.

Another problem of many developing nations is a lack of **infrastructure.** Infrastructure refers to the physical developments necessary for efficient production and distribution of goods and services. Such things as roads, ports, electric generators, telephones, and sewers are considered infrastructure. Without these things, it is difficult for an economic system to function efficently. The lack of infrastructure makes it impossible for such countries to compete successfully with more developed nations. Building an infrastructure is very expensive. Many developing nations cannot afford to invest in these improvements.

The following table compares six nations in some key areas of infrastructure and of secondary school enrollment.

Roads are an example of infrastructure—the physical developments necessary for efficient production and distribution of goods and services. A major problem for many developing nations is that they cannot afford the investment necessary to create enough infrastructure to become competitive with the more developed nations.

Table 14–1

Infrastructure and Secondary School Enrollment for Various Nations

Nation	Km Roads per sq. Km*	Km RR Tracks in Thousands of Miles**	Percent of Adults Enrolled in Secondary School	Energy Production Per Person in Kg of Coal Equivalents
United States	.68	225.4	98	9,542
Japan	2.93	19.9	95	3,741
Brazil	.20	22.1	38	767
Thailand	.15	3.7	28	493
Nigeria	.01	3.5	29	166

*Generally, more densely populated nations have more roads, but all countries need roads to develop resources.
**Geographically larger countries are more likely to have more Km of railroad tracks. The United States is about 18 times as large as Thailand, but has 80 times as many miles of track.

What Has Happened to Growth in Developing Nations?

Table 14.2 shows the average annual percentage changes in GDP per capita in industrial and developing nations for three groups of years. It also gives World Bank projected growth for the 1990s. Both for the industrialized countries and all of the developing nations, with the exceptions of East and South Asia, growth rates have declined or remained at a plateau from 1965 to 1989. With a few exceptions, the poorest countries are part of the

Sub-Saharan or Latin American and Caribbean regions. Both of these show negative growth for the decade of the 1980s. They also have negative projections for the 1990s. Compare these figures with those of East Asia and South Asia. What are the reasons for growth in Asia?

Table 14–2

Growth of real GDP per capita, 1965–2000 (average annual percentage change, unless noted)

Group	Population, 1989 (millions)	1965–73	1973–80	1980–89	Projection for 1990s[a]
Developed countries	773	3.7	2.3	2.3	1.8–2.5
Developing countries	4,053	3.9	2.5	1.6	2.2–2.9
Sub-Saharan Africa	480	2.1	0.4	−1.2	0.3–0.5
East Asia	1,552	5.3	4.9	6.2	4.2–5.3
South Asia	1,131	1.2	1.7	3.0	2.1–2.6
Europe, Middle East, and North Africa	433	5.8	1.9	0.4	1.4–1.8
Latin America and the Caribbean	421	3.8	2.5	−0.4	1.3–2.0

Sources: World Bank data and World Bank 1991[a].

Taiwan, South Korea, Hong Kong, and Singapore, sometimes called newly developed nations, have had the fastest growth rates in the world. They have also had fairly stable governments, have provided good education for their people, and have high savings and investment rates. In the poorest Sub-Saharan and Latin American and Caribbean nations, political unrest has kept the economies from growing. There the rich have spent a high portion of their income on luxuries and have invested in other countries. Meanwhile, these governments have spent little for education and the work force is discouraged, with little hope of improving its income or position.

Self-Check
1. Traditional economies resist change.
2. Training, capital, management, and a stable government are needed.
3. South Asian countries have grown most rapidly, while Sub-Saharan Africa and Latin America have slow growth.

Applying What You Have Learned
Student answers will vary but should consider education, infrastructure, farming, and basic industry needs.

Self-Check

1. How is a traditional economy hampered in its growth?
2. What are the major factors necessary for growth in developing nations?
3. Which regions of the world recently have the best record of growth? Which have the poorest?

Applying What You Have Learned

If you were in charge of economic growth in a developing nation and the United States gave your country $30 million as a development gift, how would you spend it? Explain why.

PROFILE

Sir William Arthur Lewis
(1915-)

Sir William Arthur Lewis is one of the rare individuals to have succeeded in combining a life of scholarship, teaching, and doing. He was honored with the Nobel Prize in Economics in 1979 for his work on theories of economic development. He has been a Professor of Economics at Princeton and at the University of Manchester in London. He was also made an Honorary Fellow of the Weitzman Institute and the President of the American Economic Association.

At the same time that Lewis was accumulating these impressive academic achievements, he was also working with a United Nations group on developing countries, was a consultant to the governments of the Gold Coast and Western Nigeria, and was an economic advisor to the Prime Minister of Ghana.

Lewis's keen interest in human problems brought him into the service of developing nations. His studies of the policies that worked and that failed in such nations led him to write his most important publication, *Theory of Economic Growth.* In it, Lewis explained his belief that developing nations must recognize the importance of agriculture and develop their industrial sectors slowly. Too often, poor countries pour resources into industrialization, only to find them wasted for a lack of a trained work force. The key to success, Lewis thought, was to be found in dual economies that have a large farm sector and a small industrialized urban sector. The small industrialized sector should make use of the surplus labor from the agricultural sector. Lewis believed that the wages of factory workers could not go up until surplus labor from rural areas was entirely employed. Although not all economists agree with his model, the foundations for much of our economic development theory were laid by Lewis.

Lewis served as an administrator in several Caribbean universities and was knighted by the British Government in 1963. He also founded the Caribbean Development Bank of Barbados. Few scholars have devoted as much time or effort to the problems of the poor as Sir William Arthur Lewis.

Section B The Relationship Between "Have" and "Have Not" Nations

This section will discuss the role of the United States and other developed countries in assisting developing nations.

Personal Narrative

Explain. Sending food to developing nations will not solve their long-term shortage problem. Free food will not increase their ability to grow crops and may discourage local farmers from trying to increase their production.

Discuss. In many nations, bribes are an economic and political fact of life. Often business and government officials are paid so little that this source of income is regarded as necessary. Do your students believe the United States should participate in such systems by paying the bribes, or should we refuse? What would the consequences of either action be?

Is There Anything We Could Do?

Students at my school earned money to pay for sending food to people in Africa last year. We sold candy door-to-door. Some other schools in town held paper drives or collected soda bottles to turn in for money. My homeroom won a free pizza party for earning the most money. The total for all the schools in town was almost $7,000. The president of our student council, and a bunch of other students, got their picture in the paper giving the money to leaders of the Red Cross. They said our money would save hundreds of lives. It made us feel good to know we had helped, but I know our money only made a small dent in the problem of world hunger.

I read that it would take billions of dollars to solve the problems of poverty and hunger in the world. I doubt that anyone except the government could afford to do it. We had a debate in English class about how much aid the government should give to other countries. I was surprised to find that many students were against the government giving anything at all.

I remember one student who said she was more worried about poverty in the United States than in other countries. She thought the government should spend its money here until all Americans had a "decent" standard of living. Many other students seemed to agree with her.

My teacher thought that sending aid might be a waste of our money because many developing nations aren't able or willing to deliver the aid to the people who need it. He said he had read about thousands of tons of food rotting in ships that were waiting to be unloaded. He also thought that dishonest government officials in some countries might steal the aid for their own use. He said we should only send aid if we were sure it would be used to help people who were really in need.

One of my friends believes that we should only send tools, seed, fertilizer, and educational aid. She said that sending food to developing nations will discourage them from learning to help

Discuss. If the United States withholds aid from nations that do not support our political point of view, the people of that country will suffer from the lack of help, while their leaders may feel no effect. Do your students feel that poor and often powerless people should be made to suffer for the policies of their government officials? Would the answers be different if the question read, "Should the United States give aid to countries that do not respect our political objectives?"

themselves. Free food from developed nations would compete with food grown by local farmers. This would make it more difficult for farmers to succeed and therefore for the nation to ever be able to feed itself.

Another student said he thought we should only send aid to countries that supported our foreign policy and political ideas. He said that many countries take our aid and then accuse the United States of trying to tell them what to do. For example, he thought we should "cut off" any country that voted against our point of view at the United Nations.

A final idea was that we should only help countries that had a chance to escape poverty. One student said that some countries have so many people and are so poor that there is nothing we could do to solve their problems. He said our aid would only make it take longer for people to starve to death. He wanted to help the countries that were already making progress. He said aid sent to really poor countries was a waste of money and resources.

When the debate was over, I don't think anyone had changed their mind. I hadn't. I think we should all send something, even if it isn't enough to solve the world's problems. The government has more money than we do. I think it should do its part, too.

The Changing Nature of Aid

During the 1950s foreign aid from industrialized countries was considered absolutely necessary for the economic growth of developing nations. European countries and Japan, just beginning to recover from the massive destruction of World War II, were unable to provide aid during that period. The United States, which had helped with Japan's and Europe's recovery, provided the largest share of aid to developing nations during that decade. When Europe and Japan became richer, the distribution burden shifted. From 1960 to 1990 the United States's percentage of total aid supplied by the Western nations to developing countries dropped from 60 percent to 17 percent. Japan became the largest donor, and many European and Arab states provided a larger percentage of their GDP in aid than did the United States.

Total aid to developing nations more than doubled during the 1980s, but the needs of these nations increased even faster. This was a period when recessions hurt developing nations even more than industrialized countries because of the severe drop in the price of basic **commodities,** or products of agriculture or mining. These products made up most of developing countries' exports. Because of the apparent lack of progress in many devel-

When developed nations sent food to Ethiopia and other African nations in recent years, they prevented the deaths of many thousands of people. But many of these nations still have traditional economies, with few tools and a shortage of trained people. Unless these and other problems can be solved, they are likely to experience periods of famine again in the future.

oping nations, people in developed nations questioned whether aid could ever solve the world's economic problems.

The early 1990s brought the collapse of the Soviet Union and the end of its dominant influence in many nations. The former communist nations asked for immediate aid from the wealthy industrialized West. Without such aid, many feared that these nations might return to some form of communism. The industrialized nations estimated that $24 billion worth of aid would be needed. At that time the United States government's budget deficit was reaching record levels, however. Americans questioned raising the level of foreign aid.

Other Sources of Aid

Many private organizations and individuals send aid to both governments and foreign citizens to ease their burdens. In some cases, such as aid to India and China, the sum of such aid is fairly large. Emergency relief and United Nations related organizations ease suffering, but this aid has little to do with development.

Commercial banks grant loans that are important sources of investment capital to developing nations. Many of the nations that ask for such loans have had good growth records or possess mineral deposits that are in demand. Commercial banks charge high interest rates for such loans, making them financially profitable. There is a risk that a developing nation may not pay back its loans. However, the risk is offset by the hope that the United States government would come to the rescue if American banks faced large losses.

Multinational corporations are another source of investment capital for developing nations. As we studied in Chapter 13, multinationals can be very helpful to developing nations' economies, or they can attempt to get what profits they can without really contributing much to growth and development. Negotiations between multinationals and developing nations largely determine how much each will benefit.

The Debt Crisis

Note. In 1987 Brazil suspended payments on part of its debt to foreign banks. Although this situation did not cause an immediate international banking crisis, many economists believed that the potential for such a crisis existed. An agreement to refinance Brazil's debt was reached in 1992, allowing that nation to make payments over a longer term.

A number of factors brought on a debt crisis for many developing nations in the 1980s. The value of many of their exports, including oil, dropped sharply. Many loans had to be paid back in dollars at a time when the value of the dollar was increasing. Economic growth slowed, and poor management and inflation contributed to doubling the size of developing nations' debt compared to their GDP. By 1990 the accumulated international debt of developing nations was $1.3 trillion.

In the early 1990s interest fell to the lowest rates in many years. Lenders seemed more willing to renegotiate developing nations' loans. The alternative, in some instances, was to lose most of the money they had loaned. The International Monetary Fund and the World Bank played key roles in setting up new terms for payments and requiring the developing nations to discipline themselves in spending, saving, and moving toward free trade. These actions seemed to help developing nations with their debt problems.

Whose Attitude Is Right?

Developing nations are sometimes called the "have nots." They fear and resent being told what they can and cannot do by foreign nations, multinational corporations, or international organizations. They often feel that rich countries are trying to exploit them. Wealthy nations do see advantages in helping poorer nations develop. Developing nations can be sources of good quality products, inexpensive suppliers of raw materials, and good cus-

Investments in training, tools, and new seeds and fertilizer helped India develop from an importer of food in the 1970s to an exporter of food in the 1980s. Aid that promotes self-help is essential if developing countries are to overcome their problems.

tomers for industrialized nations' merchandise. However, multinationals will not risk their stockholders' money unless there are safeguards against losses. Regional and international agencies acting as neutral overseers may be able to establish ground rules acceptable to both developing nations and multinational corporations.

Self-Check
1. It became a smaller part of total aid provided to developing nations.
2. A larger part of aid is now the result of bank loans and investments by multinational corporations.
3. Lower prices for developing nations' exports and higher interest rates caused the debt crisis.

Applying What You Have Learned
See Lesson Plan for Chapter 14, Section B, page T144.

Self-Check

1. What has happened to United States aid to developing nations in the last 40 years?
2. How has the source of international aid changed in recent years?
3. What world events caused the developing nations' debt crisis?

Applying What You Have Learned

Reread the Personal Narrative and explain why you believe aid should continue or stop to developing nations during a recession in the United States.

Section C The Population Explosion

This section will discuss problems related to population growth in developing nations.

Personal Narrative

Will There Be Enough Resources for Tomorrow?

I like people. I enjoy talking with my friends. Crowded dances are fun. Being at a concert when everyone is excited makes me feel alive. I think New Year's Eve with crowds of people is the best night of the year. But, as much as I like people, sometimes I want to be alone. I believe that most people need a place of their own. It doesn't have to be big or luxurious, it just has to be a place where you can think in peace with no one else to bother you. When I look at newscasts about poor people in Africa or Asia, I wonder how they can stand to be so poor and so crowded together with nothing of their own. I also wonder if they did this to themselves.

I ask questions that aren't very popular. I can't help myself, I need to ask them. For example, if there are hundreds of millions of people in the world who are starving, doesn't it mean that millions of people had babies they couldn't support? When people can't educate their children, why do they have more of them? Does it make sense to have more children if your house is already too crowded? When I ask these questions at school, lots of people get mad at me, but others agree with my point of view. Few people are able to answer my questions.

Discuss. What are the economics of having children? Some of your students may already be parents. What insights do they have into the costs of raising children and what it does to their individual standard of living? What differences and similarities are there between having children in the United States and in developing nations?

I remember watching a news special on the famine in Africa. There were pictures of hundreds of thousands of people living in tents or out in the open. Most of them were starving. There were flies and garbage everywhere. The people were too weak to do anything for themselves. A reporter said that for every person in the camp there were probably five or six more back in their villages who were also starving.

I felt sorry for the kids, but not for the adults. Didn't they know what they were doing to themselves? How could a person bring children into a life like that? I don't understand it.

Poverty and Population Control

Many countries that have high rates of population growth are the same countries that are least able to support more people. To understand why poor people have large families, you need to know about their values and social systems.

Developing countries with high rates of population growth face great difficulty in trying to improve their standards of living. In such countries, most increases in production are used to support new children as they are born. Many economists believe these nations will not be able to achieve economic growth until they control their birthrates.

Explain. The Social Security System and other government transfer programs have reduced the need Americans had in the past for large families. We no longer have to worry as much about who will care for us when we are old. This is not true of most people in developing nations.

Truly poor people have few or no possessions. Their countries can't afford to pay them social security or pension benefits. Any economic security they have must be provided for by their families. If you expect your children to support you in your old age, it makes sense to have many children. One of them may do well and be able to take care of you.

Conflicts in Values

Most poor people are also poorly educated. They often do not know how to limit their family size. Attempts to educate people in methods of family planning have met with limited success in many developing nations. Some leaders in developed countries feel that family planning is not an appropriate answer to the problems of the developing countries, or that it is something that developed countries should not be involved in.

Explain. Inadequate nutrition can cause reduced mental ability. It is possible that millions of hungry children today will grow up to be mentally deficient adults. Malnutrition has long-term as well as short-term costs to both individuals and society.

In the past, population growth was often limited by sickness. For example, the **mortality rate** (average number of deaths per thousand people per year) in Egypt was over 16 as recently as 1960. Advancements in medicine reduced this number to 10 by 1991. Health programs supported by the United States and other developed nations have helped people live longer, but in doing so they have made the population problem worse.

Effects of Growing Population

Population growth in many developing nations has made economic growth almost impossible. Countries that have population growth rates of 2 to 3 percent per year will double their population every 30 years. If these nations can't increase their production at an equal or faster rate, their standard of living will go down.

Discussion. Do your students feel that the benefits offered by reduced population growth justify limiting individual rights to have any size of family they want? Does the need for reduced population growth justify authoritarian forms of government?

High population growth rates mean that there will be more children to take care of. Children do not contribute to production for at least the first few years of their lives. They also create a greater need for schools. When young workers do join the labor force, they may be less productive than more experienced older workers. Countries with high birthrates are likely to be less productive than those with lower birthrates (see Table 14–3).

Some countries have reduced their poverty in recent years. Most of these countries have first reduced their population growth rate. This has often been accomplished through harsh regulations on family size. An example of this happened in the People's Republic of China during the 1970s and 1980s.

The government of China took strong steps to encourage smaller families in recent years. They tried to convince their people that having fewer children is good for both social and economic reasons. Their government used schools, printed materials, and public advertising to make this point. To a large extent, they have succeeded.

Table 14–3
Population Growth Rates and Per Capita GDP for Various Nations

Country	Population Growth Rate (Average for 1980–1989)	GDP Per Capita (1989)
United States	1.0%	$20,910
West Germany	.0%	$20,440
France	.4%	$17,820
Argentina	1.4%	$ 2,160
Pakistan	3.2%	$ 370
Kenya	3.9%	$ 360

Source: *Statistical Abstract of the United States*, 1991.

In the 1950s, China's population was growing more than 3 percent per year. By 1990 this rate had fallen to 1.4 percent. At the same time, GDP per person in China increased from less than $100 to about $350 per person. To accomplish this, the Chinese government attempted to set a limit of one child per family. There has been resistance to this program, particularly in the countryside, where large families were important to farmers. Nevertheless, the Chinese population problem has become much less severe in recent years.

Self-Check
See Lesson Plan for Chapter 14, Section C, page T146.

Applying What You Have Learned
See Lesson Plan for Chapter 14, Section C, page T146.

Self-Check

1. What is one reason that people in developing nations often want a large family?
2. How has a reduced mortality rate added to the population problems of many developing nations?
3. What special demands does a high birthrate put on a nation's economy?

Applying What You Have Learned

Make a list of three advantages and three disadvantages to having a large family in the United States. For each one, explain why the problem would be either more or less important in a poor country.

CURRENT ECONOMIC ISSUES

Should the United States Increase Its Aid to Developing Nations?

In 1964 the United Nations Conference on Trade and Development was created largely through the efforts of developing nations. This agreement established guidelines to govern the relations between rich and poor nations. Later the developing nations signed the New International Economic Order, calling on rich nations to favor poorer countries in purchasing their products, to increase aid and loans with no strings attached, to help raise commodity prices, and to allow host nations to buy foreign property holdings in their countries at fair prices. While the developed countries agreed to a few requests, they rejected ideas that would have changed the world economic order at their expense.

Businesses in industrial nations do see the potential of large markets for exports in developing nations. However, in the United States support for granting aid to developing nations has weakened in recent years. Many Americans believe that the United States should solve some of its own economic problems before extending more aid to other nations. In addition to this argument, Economic growth has been slow in developed countries, and recessions have hurt their economies. Few nations have been willing to increase their foreign aid, because many are not satisfied with the results. Do you believe rich nations should increase aid to developing nations?

Arguments in Favor of More Aid

1. Developing nations can become markets for developed nations' exports.
2. Economic growth helps developing nations pay back their loans.
3. Unlike private investments, aid may be used for improvements in education, health, infrastructure, and agriculture.

Arguments Against Aid

1. The United States should reduce its federal deficit and its negative balance of trade, and help its own poor before aiding developing nations.
2. Much aid winds up in the pockets of politicians or is wasted on projects never completed.
3. Many developing nations that the United States aids do not support our positions when important issues come before the United Nations.

What Do You Think?

Consider the arguments for and against giving aid to developing nations What personal factors might influence your position? If you were older, owned a business, or worked in an exporting company, how might your position change?

Chapter 14 Review

What Have You Learned?

In this chapter you have learned the following important principles of economics:

- *Developing countries* have many special problems that make it hard for them to increase their production and the standard of living of their people.
- Developing nations often have *traditional* economic systems that are difficult to change. They often are unable to provide an adequate education to their people.
- Developing nations generally do not have an adequate *infrastructure* of roads, electrical generating facilities, water, sewage systems, or other capital improvements to allow efficient production.
- Developing nations often have political problems with origins that can be traced to times when they were colonies of other nations.
- When developed nations try to help developing nations, they must deal with many different problems at the same time.
- In the past 40 years the share of aid given by the United States has declined. Recently, developing nations have benefited from bank loans and investments by multinationals.
- In the 1980s many developing nations experienced a debt crisis as the prices of their exports fell and interest rates on their loans increased.
- Many developing nations have a population problem. Social values in many of these nations encourage people to have many children. High population growth rates require even higher rates of growth in production if people are to live better.
- In general, the developing nations that have been most successful in improving their standard of living have been those that were willing and able to place limits on family size.
- The problems of developing nations are so great and complicated that it is unlikely that any amount of aid would solve all their problems. Developing nations will have to do much of the work for themselves.

Words and Terms

developing nations (p. 391)
developed nations (p. 391)
newly developed nations (p. 391)
traditional economy (p. 394)
infrastructure (p. 395)
mortality rate (p. 405)

Chapter 14 Review

See Chapter 14 Review Answers, page T147.

Building Your Vocabulary

On a separate piece of paper, write the word or term that best completes each of the following statements.

1. The United States, Japan, Germany, and many other industrialized countries are often referred to as ______.
2. While economic growth has slowed in much of the world, some of the ______, especially in South Asia and East Asia, have experienced impressive rates of growth in recent years.
3. In a ______ people learn most of what they know from their relatives rather than in school or from books.
4. A lower ______, made possible through advancements in medicine, has contributed to the rate of population growth in many developing nations.
5. Many developing countries lack an adequate ______, or roads, electric power systems, schools, and other physical improvements necessary for economic growth.
6. Nations in which the majority of people do not have even a minimal standard of living are called ______.

Understanding Economics

1. Explain why it would probably be more difficult to bring about change in a traditional economic system than in a developed country like the United States.
2. Describe why a lack of infrastructure makes it difficult for developing nations to produce goods efficiently or to increase their economic growth rates.
3. Identify two reasons why international economic conditions caused many developing nations to experience a debt crisis in the 1980s.
4. It is possible that some U.S. aid has been wasted by developing nations because their people did not know how to use the aid that was given. Explain why sending tools to these nations is not enough to ensure economic growth.
5. Summarize the arguments for and against investments by multinational corporations in developing nations.
6. Explain why countries with high rates of population growth tend to have difficulty in achieving economic growth.
7. Explain why many people believe that a strong government is needed to reduce the rate of population growth.

Thinking Critically About Economics

1. Make a list of five important things you know about that you would not understand if you only knew what you had learned in your home.
2. Suppose that someone suggested the countries in Africa be joined together into one big nation to make it easier to assist their development. Explain why this would not be a good idea.
3. If you wanted to open a large paper mill in a South American rain forest, what problems would you have to overcome to achieve your goal?
4. Suppose that you are in charge of educating people in a developing nation. What sort of education would you emphasize? Explain why you would do this.

Thinking Critically About Economics
(1) classification; (2) predicting probable consequences; (3) identifying the problem; (4) identifying the problem; (5) recognizing values; (6) recognizing values; (7) analyzing cause and effect.

5. Why do you believe many foreign banks have been willing to allow developing nations to renegotiate their loans and reduce their payments?
6. Do you believe that most Americans would be willing to give more aid to developing nations? Would *you* be willing to give more aid? Explain why you feel the way you do.
7. Suppose that you are in charge of improving the standard of living in a developing nation. Although the production of goods and services has been increasing by 2 percent a year, your nation's population has been growing at 3 percent a year. Your people are worse off today than they were five years ago. Describe two realistic steps that could be taken to solve the problem.

Consumer Skills Projects

1. Interview ten adults. Ask each of the first five whether they would support giving more aid to developing nations. Tabulate their answers. Ask the next five if they would support sending more tools to poor countries to help them feed themselves. Tabulate their answers. Identify any differences between the answers from the two groups of adults. Try to explain these differences.
2. Look at a map of your neighborhood. Identify as many examples of infrastructure as you can on the map. Explain how these things help local firms compete to sell their products.
3. Take a poll of the students in your class, asking how many children there are in each of their families. Also find out how many brothers and sisters each student's parents and grandparents had. Using this information, find the average size of the family for today's students, for their parents, and for their grandparents. Has this average increased or decreased? What reasons could explain this change? Try to explain what this has to do with social and economic changes.

Developing Your Economic Skills

Interpreting Economic Data on Maps

Skill: In this lesson you will learn how to use a map to compare data about different nations.

Maps can enable a reader to easily relate economic data to geographic and political areas. Economists often make use of political maps (showing boundaries of nations) and adapt them to show economic data. In this lesson you will study a map of South America that shows levels of per capital Gross Domestic Product (GDP) in different nations. The map will allow you to make general comparisons of the probable standards of living in these nations. To complete this lesson, you will follow these steps:

- Look at the map to see what types of areas are represented.
- Study the key to determine what kind of information is being shown and how it is being presented on the map.
- Examine the map and relate it to the key.

Application: Every map contains a *key* (or *legend*) that shows you how to interpret the map. When you study the key for this map, you will see that each color shown on the key represents a different level of per capita GDP. By matching each nation with a color shown on the key, you can determine the level of per capita GDP for that nation. Notice that the levels are broadly drawn. A country that falls in the second level, for example, can have a per capita GDP of any amount between $500 and $1499.

When you study this map, you will see that there is some variation among the per capita GDPs of different South American countries. There is much greater variation, however, between these countries and the United States and Canada, both of which have per capita GDPs greater than $20,000.

Practice: List the names of all South American countries in four sets, from the highest GDP per capita to the lowest.

South America, Per Capita GDP

Source: *Economic and Social Progress of Latin America,* 1991 report.

Валентина

CHAPTER 15

Alternative Economic Systems

Objectives

In the sections of this chapter, you will learn:

A

how different economic systems may be identified and evaluated;

B

about differences between theories and the realities of how different types of economic systems work; and

C

how the values and cultures of different nations are reflected in the economic systems they use.

Introduction

In Chapter 2 you learned about differences between market and command economies. In this chapter you will look more closely at a variety of ways nations choose to answer the basic economic questions *what, how,* and *for whom.* You will discover that the way different nations answer these questions is closely related to their political systems, their values, and cultures.

Economic systems are often said to be based on economic theories or models. As you read about the systems that exist in various nations, you will realize that the way they work in reality is not exactly like the theories economists have developed. These theories have value, however, because they may be used as guides to help you understand real economic systems more easily. As you learned in Chapter 2, economic models provide a foundation on which students of economics may build a better understanding of the way economics works in the real world.

Studying a nation's economic system tells you a great deal about that nation's goals, values, and human relations. This will be clearly demonstrated when we compare the differences between the capitalistic economies of Japan and the United States in Section C.

Section A A Variety of Economic Systems

This section will identify different economic theories and explain differences between these theories and real economic systems that exist or have existed in the world.

Personal Narrative

Note. Much of the cultural life of a kibbutz is provided by its own members. Kibbutz actors, musicians, dancers, and painters are supported by the community. They don't have to be concerned with the commercial success of their work.

An Island of Socialism

My name is David Goldberg. I am 17 years old. Last summer my parents sent me to Israel to live and to work on a **kibbutz.** They said they wanted me to "get in touch with our people," and to learn about "life." When I left I didn't really know what they meant. After spending two months living in what often seemed to be a dream world, I think I understand why they sent me.

A kibbutz seemed like a combination of a community and a family to me. The 270 or so kibbutzim (plural) in Israel are villages in which all residents work together for their common good. No one owns private property except for a few personal possessions. All the buildings, tools, cars, trucks, land, and other resources are owned collectively by the community. Like most others, the kibbutz where I stayed was largely involved in farming. It had orange groves, a fish farm, and a recently built small factory where it assembled parts for computers. In many ways the kibbutz was self-sufficient. The people who lived there grew almost all of their own food, built their own buildings, and produced many of their own clothes.

At the kibbutz I was assigned a place to live with many other young men. We all received work clothes and shared a telephone, TV, radio, and bathroom. We all ate in a community dining hall. None of us had any real privacy. We were assigned jobs by the Work Coordinator, who tried her best to give us jobs we liked. However, disagreeable jobs, like cleaning toilets, were shared by all. What really surprised me was how hard everyone worked in spite of the fact that no one got any more for their work than anyone else. In fact, the only money we received was just enough to buy candy or a few souvenirs to take home.

At first I wondered why everyone worked so hard. What was the point, if no one could earn much money or own cars or houses of their own? I discovered that many members of the kibbutz wanted the praise and admiration they received from others when they worked hard. The few people who did not seem to do their share were not respected in the community. I learned that a few had even left. I found that the kibbutz would pay for its members' college educations and support them in their old age. So, people worked because they wanted to be respected by other members of their community, and because it gave them a sense of security.

Explain. Kibbutz children live away from their parents, with many other children of their same age. In the evenings parents and children get together to visit, play, or just talk.

The kibbutz was run by an elected General Assembly, which chose officers and an Economic Committee. The Committee made the basic economic decisions of what, how, and for whom. I soon realized that the kibbutz was really an example of a small command economy like the ones I had learned about in school. Most economic decisions were made by a small group that told the others how to use the community's resources.

Almost everyone seemed happy at the kibbutz. Anyone who became dissatisfied had the right to leave. There were a few specialists who worked in the computer parts factory who were not members but were hired for their special skills. They received a salary like workers in capitalism. They preferred the individualism, personal income, and private property that are found in most of the Israeli economy.

At the end of the summer I was invited to come back again next year. This made me feel good because it showed I had been accepted. I have decided not to return but to take a job in my uncle's store, where I will earn almost $2,000. I guess having my own TV in my own bedroom and only having to share a bathroom with one sister may have something to do with my decision. I don't regret having visited Israel; I just like our system better.

Some societies do not value individualism as highly as the United States. Instead, they emphasize a spirit of community. Many workers in Japan begin the day with 10 minutes of group exercise.

Answering the Basic Questions

Discuss. The larger the planned economy, the more difficult is the task of planning. Planning for a kibbutz is much simpler than directing the resources of a country of several million people. Why is this so?

You learned in Chapter 1 that all nations face the same basic economic problem of having limited resources and unlimited wants. They try to choose the economic system that will provide them with the greatest satisfaction possible, given the limited resources they have. All nations must answer the basic economic questions of what to produce, how to produce, and for whom the production is created.

The model shown in Figure 15-1 illustrates a range of ways that these key questions may be answered. On the far left is a command economy where the *what, how,* and *for whom* are decided by a central planning agency. This was the approach used by the former Soviet Union and that is being used by the Economic Committee of the kibbutz in the Personal Narrative. In a command economy productive resources are owned collectively by all, and a planning agency determines how the resources will be used. Individuals have little voice in making the basic economic decisions.

On the far right side of the model is a market economy where the basic economic questions are answered by individuals through the forces of demand and supply. In a market economy resources are owned by individuals, who determine how they will be used.

Figure 15–1 *The Range of Economic Systems*

Command Communism	— Socialism	— Welfare Capitalism	— Industrial Capitalism	— Market Capitalism
North Korea China	Cuba	Sweden United Kingdom	Germany Japan	Singapore United States

In the range between the two extremes of the model are communism, socialism, welfare capitalism, industrial capitalism, and capitalism. Each of these systems has different degrees of government ownership and control over the system's productive resources. No country fits either extreme of the model perfectly. All nations have mixed economies that range from near capitalism to near communism. The position of the countries listed below the range of systems shows about where the economic systems of these nations were located in 1993. One way to place a country on this range is to find what share of total spending is carried out by the nation's government. The larger the share, the farther to the left the country is likely to be.

The Importance of Political Systems

Trying to classify countries strictly by their economic systems does not provide an accurate picture of how they work. We should also consider their political systems. In all countries there is a division of political power between the people and the government. In some countries people hold most of the power, in others the power belongs largely to political leaders. How this power is distributed provides a clue to how the system works.

Any country that has a command economy must tolerate a strong government role in its system. In these countries political leaders are likely to hold more power. In market economies most economic decisions are made by individuals who own and control the productive resources. Less government intervention in the economy is needed or tolerated. In such nations more of the political power is likely to be held by the people.

Note. People tend to give more power to government or remove power from government during periods of economic stress. Compare the direction taken by the United States in the 1930s with that of the Eastern European nations in the 1980s and 1990s.

The balance of power between people and their political leaders is likely to change over time. As societies become more complex, the need for government power tends to increase. As the economic system of the United States developed, the country found a need for social security, public schools, government transfers for welfare and medical care—the list goes on and on. These additional government programs required giving both more political and economic power to the government. In the twentieth century the United States economic system took on more characteristics of a command economy and increased the power of the central (federal) government and its influence over the individual's life.

Economists, politicians, and citizens have debated the issue of how power should be divided between the people and the government. Under President Franklin Roosevelt, government economic powers grew rapidly. Many government agencies were established that limited the economic rights of businesses and people. Minimum wage laws replaced negotiations over wages in some industries. Fifty years later, under President Ronald Reagan, attempts were made to reduce the power of the government in the economy. Tax rates were lowered and some government regulations were eliminated.

Look at Figure 15-2. It shows a relationship between the political and economic systems that are likely to be associated with each other in a nation. In the left column more of the economic and political power is given to the government and less to the people. In the right column the opposite is true—more power is in the hands of the people and less power belongs to the government. There are costs and benefits associated with each distribution of power. The left column represents a system that provides greater security and less individual opportunity for a nation's citizens. The right column shows a nation that provides its people with greater individual opportunity but less security.

Figure 15–2

The Distribution of Political and Economic Powers

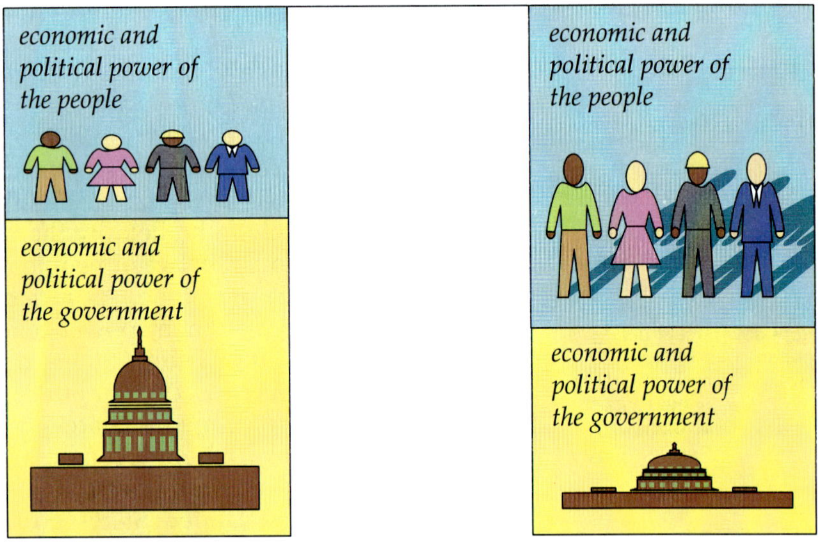

More reliance on central political control and a command economy

More reliance on individual political choice and a market economy

Self-Check

1. Where should a kibbutz be placed on the range in Figure 15-1?
2. Why do countries have mixed economic systems?
3. Why do countries with centrally controlled economic systems usually have governments with strong political powers?

Applying What You Have Learned

Identify a current debate over government spending in your community. Describe how this debate is related to the role of government in the economy of your community and its ability to use its political power.

Self-Check

1. A kibbutz as a command economy should be placed far to the left on the range in Figure 15–1.
2. Countries have mixed economic systems because neither pure market nor pure command economies work efficiently.
3. Nations that have central control over most of the basic economic decisions generally need strong political powers to enforce their decisions.

Applying What You Have Learned

See Lesson Plan for Chapter 15, Section A, page T151.

Section B Economic Theory vs. Economic Reality

This section will explain the ideas of Karl Marx and discuss differences between economic theories and the mixed economic systems that exist in nations today.

Personal Narrative

Note. The American Communist party has had very little influence in United States politics. Some estimate that it had about 100,000 members during the Great Depression of the 1930s. By the early 1980s, its own leaders claimed only 20,000 members in the United States.

The Theory and the Reality

Yesterday I saw an old movie of a news program from 1960 in my economics class. At first I thought I was going to be bored, but it turned out to be interesting even if the sound wasn't too clear. The subject of the movie was an interview with a man named Gus Hall, who was introduced as a leader of the American Communist party.

I learned from the film that in 1960 there was a recession in the United States economy. That was the year John Kennedy and Richard Nixon were running against each other to be President. The film showed Mr. Hall saying neither of these men had an answer to the people's problems. He told the interviewer the real problem was America's capitalist businesses that were only run to earn profits for their owners. According to him, the owners didn't care about consumers or workers. They charged the highest possible prices and paid the lowest possible wages. Mr. Hall said capitalists were exploiting American workers as well as people in other countries. He said business owners were getting richer, while workers were becoming poorer. The answer to our economic problems, according to Mr. Hall, was to get rid of the capitalists and their economic system. Then, he said, we could produce the products ordinary people needed and everyone would have a fair share of our nation's wealth and income. The whole idea seemed strange to me, but I think Gus Hall really believed what he was saying.

Yesterday evening when I talked about the movie at supper, my father became really angry. He said, "Don't you know that communism stuff is dead? It was nothing but a bunch of ideas that didn't work. Even the Russians got rid of it when the Soviet Union broke up. People didn't work in communism, because they had nothing to work for. The few products they produced fell apart. Most of the time people couldn't find anything to buy at all. The only people who gained in communism were the leaders who told everyone else what to do. That Hall guy was just plain crazy and I don't want to hear any more about him!" I think my father reacted too strongly, but I understand. I told him it was just a history lesson and excused myself from the table as quickly as I could.

Communism: The Theory

Note. Karl Marx's revolutionary ideas were feared by European governments. Marx moved from country to country during the 1840s under pressure from several governments, and finally settled in London, England.

Only a handful of people through history have had as much influence on people's lives as Karl Marx (see his Profile on page 427). Through most of the twentieth century hundreds of millions of people lived in countries that had economic and political systems based on his ideas.

Marx believed history is mostly the story of the struggle between capitalists, who owned the means of production (land, factories, machines, etc.) and other people, who owned little and usually worked for the capitalists. During the industrial revolution, according to Marx, the means of production became too large and expensive for most people to own. Fewer and fewer capitalists earned increasingly larger profits by exploiting workers who received less and less wages. When workers became unable to buy the products they made, there was overproduction that caused recessions and widespread misery. Marx predicted that when conditions became intolerable, the workers would revolt and take over the means of production from the capitalists. Then, he said, the workers would join together in a spirit of brotherhood to produce the products that were needed by all and share the fruits of their labor equally—a system called **communism**. Although the revolution Marx predicted never happened in the way he thought it would, his ideas had a strong influence on many people in the twentieth century.

Communism: The Reality

Explain. Marx believed that society was divided into social classes that fought against each other. He said that workers would form a **dictatorship of the proletariat** (workers) to direct the evolution from socialism to communism.

Karl Marx never laid out careful plans for how a communist economic system should be set up or controlled. Therefore, when a revolution in Russia made that nation the world's first communist country (the Soviet Union) in 1917, no one knew how to run its economic system. Between late 1917 and 1924 Nikolai Lenin was the leader of the Soviet Union. He tried to start a system of complete government ownership and control of the means of production, but his attempt was a dismal failure. There was economic chaos and little production. Lenin revised his system to mix government ownership with a degree of private ownership of farms and smaller businesses. Although this mixed system worked reasonably well, after 1928 it was replaced with almost total government ownership and control by Joseph Stalin.

Under Stalin's leadership private ownership of the means of production was eliminated and the basic economic choices of *what, how,* and *for whom* were made by a government planning agency. The government set wages and prices and determined how resources would be allocated. The result was shortages of

The basic theory of communism was developed by Karl Marx in the late 1840s. Although Marx laid the foundations for modern communism, many of his ideas have been changed to fit the needs of communist countries in the world today.

Discuss. Marx believed communist government officials would be less self-centered and motivated by greed than owners of private business. Do your students feel this was a reasonable belief?

many consumer products at the same time there were surpluses of other goods that often had low quality or that no one wanted.

Many of Stalin's goals for the Soviet Union were achieved. In the 1930s the Soviet Union (Union of Soviet Socialist Republics, or USSR) became a major military power. Basic industries were established and thousands of miles of railroad tracks were built. These accomplishments came at the price of great human suffering. Under Stalin, the government forced workers to work through fear. When the government eased its oppressive policies under later leaders, workers were left with little **incentive,** or motivation, to work hard. The standard of living for most people in the Soviet Union was very low. The central planning agency set production goals, but plant managers chose to produce the quantity of goods demanded by sacrificing the quality of the goods. Millions of people, without incentives, seemed only to be "putting in time" on their jobs. This inefficient economic system remained essentially the same until the late 1980s. Then it collapsed because it could not provide basic necessities. This was perhaps the greatest cause for the breakup of the Soviet Union.

Many Eastern European nations were close allies of the Soviet Union. For many years they also attempted to make communist economic systems work. More recently, these nations have tried varying mixtures of socialism and capitalism as their economic systems. The People's Republic of China remains as the largest nation that continues to use the communist model. Even China, however, has opened up part of its economy to private ownership, using the **profit motive** as an incentive to en-

Which is more productive, a command economy or a market economy? Hoping to improve productivity, some socialist governments in Europe have returned some government-owned industries to private business.

courage greater production. Communism in theory supported a democratic state, but in reality communism has never existed in a democracy. When the people have political power they are not likely to allow any government to have so much control over their economic choices.

Socialism: The Reality

Both communism and **socialism** trace their main ideas to the thinking of Karl Marx. However, socialists did not predict a revolution by workers against owners. Various forms of socialism developed in democratic nations, especially in Europe. Although communism seems to have failed as a political and economic system, various mixtures of socialism still exist in many countries. Several nations of Western Europe have relied on socialist ideas including government ownership of large industries and utilities. Some prices have been set and many resources were allocated by government agencies. Incomes in these nations were more equal and tax rates higher. People in these nations have enjoyed personal security through extensive social programs provided by their governments. Some economic systems have been called **welfare capitalism** because of these benefits. In exchange for security, the people have given up a degree of individual economic freedom.

In the past several years most countries have reduced the amount of socialism they mix into their economic systems. They have turned more toward capitalism, mainly to encourage greater productivity. In France, for example, a socialist president sold some government-owned industries to private businesses and reduced government regulation of the economy. Similar steps have been taken in Scandinavian countries that have reduced benefits of government social programs and lowered tax rates. Even in the United States many local governments have stopped providing services like garbage collection and public transportation. They let private businesses sell these services in their communities.

Capitalism: The Reality

Note. European countries have returned some basic industries to private ownership. By providing incentives for greater production, this may boost a nation's total GDP and thus improve its competitive position in world markets.

According to the theory of capitalism, private individuals have the right to use resources they own to produce the goods and services they believe will earn them the greatest profit. The basic economic questions of *what, how,* and *for whom* are answered by people making individual economic choices. The problem of allocating resources is not centralized in government but **decentralized** in the market. The government's role in this system is limited to setting and enforcing basic rules for how businesses are organized. In such a system the government collects and spends a very small portion of the total national income.

If a country chooses to become less capitalistic, the government's role in the economy grows along with the share of income it collects and spends. One simple way to measure the degree of capitalism or socialism that exists in a nation's economy is to look at the share of national income that is spent by its government. Using this method, we can see that the United States is far from pure capitalism. In the United States government support for education, welfare, health services, retirement programs, and many other services takes up nearly one-third of the income earned in this country. In most European economies the share of income spent by the government is even larger. In these nations people have given up some individual economic freedom to gain a degree of economic security and equality for all.

Note. In 1927 federal government spending was about 3 percent of GDP. In 1991 the federal government spent about 20 percent of GDP.

Table 15–1
Tax Revenues of Selected Countries, 1988

Country	Tax Revenue as Percent of GDP
United States	29.8
Japan	31.3
United Kingdom	37.3
France	44.4
Sweden	55.3

Present and Future Systems

We live in a world that has steadily become more complex and interdependent. Many nations have moved away from pure market or pure command economies in an attempt to provide the best features of both capitalist and socialist systems. There is little reason to believe current economic systems will remain the same over time. As long as people have the right and power to control their governments there will be changes in the mixtures of economic systems.

In this chapter we have compared economic theory with reality. Theories are important because they provide direction. If one change does not work, a theory may suggest another approach. For most of the twentieth century the United States experienced a gradual growth of government involvement in its economic system. Much of this government involvement came in reaction to abuses that many people believed had developed because government had been reluctant to change the economic system. This trend reversed in the 1980s and 1990s. Many people in the United States and in other nations believed government had become too powerful. They felt it was time to return to greater individual economic freedom. How long will this most recent trend last? No one knows. However, we can say with a reasonable amount of certainty that the exact mix of market and command economies in the United States will continue to change throughout our lives.

Self-Check
1. A government planning agency decided what products should be produced, how they would be made, and to whom they would be distributed, based on its understanding of what was best for the nation.
2. Our social security and welfare programs, progressive income taxes, and public ownership of utilities are socialist in nature.
3. Many nations have chosen to use less socialism to try to increase people's incentive to work, invest, and be more productive.

Applying What You Have Learned
See Lesson Plan for Chapter 15, Section B, page T153.

Self-Check

1. How did the economic system in the former Soviet Union answer the basic economic questions of *what, how,* and *for whom?*
2. What are several characteristics of the United States economic system that are more socialist in nature than capitalist?
3. Why have many countries chosen to change the mix of economics in their systems to less socialism and more capitalism in recent years?

Applying What You Have Learned

Investigate the economic statements of politicians running for a government office in a recent or a coming election. Which of these candidates seems to favor more government control? Which would have less? What reasons does each candidate provide to justify his or her point of view?

PROFILE

Karl Marx
(1818–1883)
and
Joseph Alois Schumpeter
(1883–1950)

Karl Marx

Few people in history are as closely identified with revolution and economic struggle as Karl Marx. In *Das Kapital,* he interpreted the history of capitalism through his economic and social theories. He also wrote *The Communist Manifesto,* with Frederick Engels, in which he said that capitalism would fall and that communism would triumph.

Marx believed that history showed a never-ending class struggle between those who owned capital (machines, buildings, etc.) and those who had to work for the capitalists. He thought capitalism was a necessary evil that enabled society to create the tools of production. However, he believed that firms in capitalism were run only to earn a profit for the owners, and not to produce what people needed. Marx said that capitalists earned a profit by paying workers less than the value of their labor. As a result, capitalists grew richer while workers got poorer.

Marx believed that as time went by, there would be more poor people and fewer rich people. At some point the workers would revolt, seize control of the means of production, and establish a dictatorship of the proletariat (the workers).

While Marx never explained exactly how a communist country should be run, countries that called themselves communist lagged far behind more capitalistic countries in terms of their ability to produce goods and services. Marx's predictions seem far from the way the real world turned out.

Joseph Alois Schumpeter

Born in 1883, the same year that Karl Marx died, Joseph Schumpeter believed that capitalism would lay the seeds for its own destruction through its success rather than through its failure. Schumpeter was born and educated in Austria and later taught at Harvard.

In his book *Capitalism, Socialism and Democracy,* Schumpeter started with his economic hero, the entrepreneur. Business owners were anxious to produce goods and services so that they might earn large profits. These risk-taking capitalists would bring prosperity to themselves as well as to society.

However, at a certain point in their success, firms would become overly cautious. The spirit of the risk-taking entrepreneurs would give way to bureaucracy and socialism. In Schumpeter's view, capitalism and the economic advantages it offered would decline, and the world would be poorer, not richer, when capitalism disappeared.

Section C Different Kinds of Capitalism

This section will compare the different types of capitalism that are practiced in the United States and Japan.

Personal Narrative

Discuss. Studies show that most Americans will change jobs several times during their working careers. This is partly because of new kinds of opportunities that develop in a changing economy. How might a system that keeps a person in one job for life affect this kind of change?

Two Views of Japan's Economy

Last week a new student named Eric registered in my economics class. He had just returned from spending a year living with his father, who works for the Motorola Corporation in Japan. My teacher asked him to tell us about his experience there. Some of the things he said surprised me, some made me angry, and others made me worried.

Eric told us that the economic system in Japan is a different form of capitalism than we have in the United States. Although their businesses are owned by people, there are different rules for what these firms may do and how they treat their workers. Probably the thing that surprised me most was that many Japanese workers are hired for life by their employers. Employees agree not to work for any other firm, and the employer guarantees them a job until they retire. It sounded like a really good deal to me. My father had worked making electronic parts for automobiles for almost 20 years. Then he was laid off because his employer started buying electronic parts from Japan. They gave my father a couple of months of salary and advised him to train to be a computer operator, and that was just about it. Now both my parents work in retail stores, so we can make ends meet.

When Eric lived in Japan he spent a day at a factory that produced VCRs. He said everyone started the day with 10 minutes of exercise. Workers were divided into groups that were allowed to decide how to do assigned tasks. Managers walked around the factory asking questions and talking to workers as if they were equals. The tour guide told Eric that the difference between workers' and managers' salaries is not too large. Eric learned that unemployment and inflation in Japan are very low. The rate of economic growth has been roughly 50 percent faster than that of the United States in the past 20 years. They have earned hundreds of billions of dollars from exports and have invested in other nations' businesses. He made it sound like everything in Japan was great. I felt really depressed.

I guess our teacher was concerned about the reaction of the class. The next day she invited an American of Japanese heritage to speak to us about another side of the Japanese economy. Mr. Shento told us that the United States is still the most productive country in the world. Production per worker in the United States is

$55,300 compared to only $38,800 in Japan. Mr. Shento praised Japan for the economic progress they have made, but he also pointed out that most Americans have better material lives than the Japanese. He said housing costs in Japan are almost twice as high as they are in the United States. An imported melon can cost $60 in Japan. I felt a little better, but I am still worried about my father finding a good job.

Testing for Capitalism

Note. In the United States debate has often centered around the dangers that could result from the government allowing business interests to combine in monopolistic ways that would go against the public interest. What potential dangers could result from a close cooperation between business and government, as in Japan?

There are several tests that may be used to determine the degree of capitalism that exists in an economic system. One is whether people own the means of production. Another is if resources are allocated according to profits or controlled by the government. A third method that was discussed earlier in this chapter is the share of national income that is spent by the government. In the United States and Japan government spending is a much smaller share of the national income than in many more socialistic nations.

Market forces determine most resource allocation in the United States. Different businesses buy resources based on their profitability. The Japanese government, on the other hand, takes a leading role in allocating resources. In the Japanese economy businesses and government cooperate to direct resources to firms that are expected to be most successful in producing and exporting goods. Some 700 large corporations have organized into the Federation of Economic Organization, whose chief executive officer is sometimes called the "prime minister of Japanese industry." In the United States such an organization of producers working together would be challenged and broken up under the government's antitrust laws.

Different Trade Responsibilities for the Government

The United States Commerce Department tries to help American firms compete in world markets by providing them with information and advice. However, it tries to show no favoritism to any particular industry or firm.

This is not the case in Japan. The Japanese Ministry of International Trade and Industry (MITI) picks industries that it believes will be successful in international competition. It helps these industries by providing low-cost loans, research grants, tax breaks, and advice. Also, restrictions on how goods may be imported put foreign producers at a disadvantage competing in Japanese markets. This type of economic system is sometimes called **industrial capitalism.**

Different Labor-Management Relations

In the United States labor and management are usually on opposing sides. The U.S. government has passed laws to protect the rights of workers. These laws include minimum wages, rights of unions to negotiate collectively, protection against discrimination, and safety regulations. The U.S. government avoids becoming involved in labor-management relations most of the time. Although the United States has a National Labor Relations Board, more than 95 percent of labor disputes are settled without government intervention.

Japanese workers treat some firms almost as if they were part of the family. They see the firm's success as their personal responsibility and sacrifice their needs for those of the group. This is only a part of the picture, however. Only about 30 percent of the labor force in Japan has this type of lifetime worker-employer relationship. The other 70 percent are either self-employed or work for firms that do not provide guaranteed jobs with good benefits. Many Japanese workers have no job security. Social benefits provided by the Japanese government are less extensive than those of the United States. Workers who retire without a pension in Japan often must rely on the support of their children in their old age.

Other Differences

Many economists believe the most important factor in Japan's economic success is that country's high saving and investing

Japanese culture places more value on conformity than does American culture. Children learn some cultural values in school.

rates. Japanese people save a share of their income that is about twice as large as Americans save. This may be caused by their different values or by the fact that their government provides smaller retirement benefits. Japanese firms pay lower dividends than American corporations, investing a larger share of their profits back into their businesses. The Japanese devote more of their income to education for both children and adults. Japanese culture places a value on conformity and not showing emotion. These and other social values may contribute to Japan's productivity. On the other hand, many people suggest that the desire for conformity reduces creativity. The Japanese government and some businesses have experienced cases of corruption that some say surpass the U.S. Savings and Loan disaster. As in all nations, there are both good and bad aspects of the Japanese economy.

Self-Check

1. Two possible advantages of working for a Japanese firm are greater job security and relatively good wages. Two possible disadvantages of working for a Japanese firm are fewer opportunities to be creative and less chance to change your job if you are dissatisfied.
2. The economies of both the United States and Japan are capitalist because they have private ownership of the means of production, and because their governments spend a much smaller part of national income than the more socialistic economies of Scandinavian countries.
3. Some Japanese firms are identified by their government to receive low-interest rate loans, research grants, and special aid in marketing their goods in other countries that may give them an unfair advantage over American firms they compete with.

Applying What You Have Learned

See Lesson Plan for Chapter 15, Section C, page T155.

Defending Japan

Another factor that may have aided Japan's economic growth is the national defense provided by the United States for many years. United States defense efforts directed toward keeping peace around the world have cost an average of about 8 percent of its U.S. GDP since World War II. The Japanese have spent less than an average of 2 percent of their GDP for defense. This has left Japan with more resources to devote to investment and production. Japan also benefited from U.S. investment and technical help immediately after World War II. Today and in the future the United States and other nations expect Japan to contribute more to world security and growth.

Self-Check

1. Explain whether you would want to work for a Japanese corporation based on Eric's report in the Personal Narrative.
2. Why can we say that both Japanese and American economies are capitalistic, while those of Scandinavian countries are more socialistic?
3. What types of help do Japanese businesses receive from their government that cause many Americans to feel that they have unfair advantages over competing American firms?

Applying What You Have Learned

"The world would be a better place if the Japanese worked less and consumed more." What do you think this statement means? Is it consistent with the principles of economics? Explain.

CURRENT CONSUMER ISSUES

Should Our Government Provide Medical Insurance for All Americans?

At the time of the 1992 presidential campaign more than 35 million Americans had no medical insurance. Millions more had inadequate coverage. Members of both major political parties supported government intervention to assure all Americans a minimum amount of medical insurance. However, each party had a different plan. Americans heard the candidates explain their differing approaches to providing medical insurance in the campaign.

President George Bush suggested that the government should issue vouchers to low-income Americans. These papers could be used by consumers to buy insurance coverage of their own choice, at the government's expense. Under this plan middle-income people would benefit by being able to deduct their insurance payments from their taxes. The main point was that consumers could buy their own insurance from private companies.

Democrats argued that some people would not buy insurance under President Bush's plan. President Bill Clinton came into office with a different plan. The government would be the provider for those workers whose employers did not provide a health plan. Employers would have to pay into a government insurance fund for these employees. People without jobs would receive a tax subsidy to help pay the premium for a basic package of health benefits.

Which plan do you believe was best?

Arguments in Favor of President Bush's Plan

1. It would allow individual consumers to choose their own insurance coverage.
2. Middle-income people would be allowed to deduct their insurance payments from their taxes.
3. It would limit the involvement of the government in determining the type of insurance people have.

Arguments in Favor of President Clinton's Plan

1. It would cover all people, regardless of their income.
2. People without jobs would receive government tax subsidies to help pay their premiums.
3. It would eliminate the need for inefficient private insurance programs.

What Do You Think?

Are all Americans qualified to choose their own insurance? Could the government run a large insurance program efficiently?

Chapter 15 Review

What Have You Learned?

In this chapter you have learned the following important principles of economics:

- Many types of mixed economic systems exist between the extremes of command and market economies. Although there are differences between these systems they must all answer the basic economic questions of *what, how,* and *for whom.* They must also have a way to allocate scarce resources. All economic systems are mixed, having a combination of central control and individual freedom that suits their values and political system.
- People who live in economic systems that rely more on a central authority trade a degree of economic freedom for more security. Other people who live in nations that rely more on the market system enjoy more personal freedom and less economic security. As always, there is a trade-off when economic choices are made.
- One way to judge the degree of central control in an economic system is by studying the share of national income that is spent by the government. Countries with a higher percentage of government spending tend to also have more central control. These nations are also likely to have government leaders with greater political power.
- Communism is an economic system that has both centralized control of the means of production and of the political system. The theory for this system was developed by Karl Marx in the mid-1800s. Communist theory suggests that once workers are given the opportunity to work together for their common good they will enjoy peace and prosperity. In reality communism proved inefficient and restrictive of people's rights. Most nations that have had communist systems have replaced them with various forms of market economies.
- Many countries, including the United States, have some characteristics of socialism mixed into their economic systems. The nations of Western Europe and Scandinavia have used extensive government ownership and control of resources for many years. Their governments commonly spend 40 percent or more of their national income. In recent years most nations have reduced the amount of central control over their economies in an attempt to improve their productivity.
- Both Japan and the United States have economic systems that are forms of capitalism. However, the ways each of these nations uses capitalism are quite different. The government of the United States allows most economic decisions and the allocation of resources to be accomplished through decisions made by indi-

Words and Terms

kibbutz (p. 416)
communism (p. 422)
incentive (p. 423)
profit motive (p. 423)
socialism (p. 424)
decentralized (p. 425)
welfare capitalism (p. 424)
industrial capitalism (p. 429)

See Chapter 15 Review Answers, page T156.

viduals. The Japanese government takes a more active role in deciding which businesses will receive resources and how investments will be made. Japanese firms are often encouraged to work together to develop new products and export goods to other countries.

- There are advantages and disadvantages to the Japanese brand of capitalism. Although some Japanese workers have guaranteed jobs and many benefits, others lack these advantages. The Japanese economy has grown rapidly for many reasons that may include their greater rates of saving and investing, a closer relationship between their workers and employers, and the fact that Japan has been spared the cost of maintaining a large military to defend itself. Some people believe that a Japanese desire for conformity stifles creativity in that nation. Japan's growth and production will force it to take a larger role in world affairs in the future.

Building Your Vocabulary

On a separate piece of paper, write the vocabulary word or term that best completes each of the following statements.

1. _______ is an economic system that relies on centralized control over a nation's productive resources and political system.
2. The basic _______ to run a business in capitalism is the desire entrepreneurs have to earn a profit.
3. The _______ is an incentive that encourages greater production in capitalism.
4. In _______ the government assures all citizens a basic standard of living by providing extensive social programs that are paid for through relatively high taxes.
5. In capitalism most of the power to make economic decisions is _______.
6. A _______ is a community in Israel that has a command economy which makes most of the basic economic decisions.
7. In _______ the government helps businesses work together and often takes part in the allocation of resources to encourage greater productivity.
8. Generally the greater the share of national income that is spent by a country's government, the more _______ is mixed into its economic system.

Understanding Economics

1. What types of rewards are supposed to give people an incentive to work in command economies?
2. What does it mean to say that all countries have mixed economic systems?
3. If a nation's government is taking and spending a growing share of national income, what is probably happening to the mixture of capitalism and socialism in its economic system?
4. What types of governments are most often found in nations that have strong central control over their economic systems?
5. Why did Karl Marx think workers would revolt and replace capitalism with communism?
6. What are three economic problems that were experienced by nations that had communist systems before the 1990s?
7. Why have most nations reduced the amount of socialism mixed into their economic systems in recent years?

8. What are three measures that are often used to tell if a nation's economy is a form of capitalism?
9. What type of help is provided to Japanese businesses by their government that the American government does not give to its businesses?
10. What are three possible reasons for the rapid growth of the Japanese economy in the past 20 years?

Thinking Critically About Economics

1. Suppose that you visited a kibbutz and were asked the following questions by children in one of their schools. How would you answer each question?
   a. Why are there many poor people in a nation that is as wealthy as the United States?
   b. What is the purpose of the billions of dollars your businesses spend on advertising each year?
   c. Why are so many schools in the United States in need of repair?
   d. When so many people compete against each other in the United States, how can you expect people to live together in peace and harmony?
2. Make a list of four questions you would ask a student who lives on a kibbutz about his or her life.
3. Suppose you run a business that employs several hundred workers who build public housing projects in large cities. List and describe four different ways that the government would limit your freedom to run your firm as you see fit. How does this demonstrate our mixed economic system?
4. Explain why firms in the former Soviet Union could make low-quality products and continue to exist year after year. What would happen to such a firm in the United States economy?
5. Explain why many people believe the extensive social programs in nations with socialist economic systems reduced the incentive people felt to work hard.
6. What reasons may Japanese managers have to work hard when the salaries they receive are not much more than ordinary workers are paid?

Consumer Skills Projects

1. Interview five adults. Ask each to explain reasons for the changes that took place in the economic systems of nations in Eastern Europe and the former Soviet Union in the early 1990s. Record their answers and report them to your class. What conclusions can you draw about the knowledge many adults have about the events in these nations?
2. American consumers purchase auto insurance under the market system. Imagine how auto insurance might be provided in a command economy. Describe the advantages and disadvantages of such a system.

Thinking Critically About Economics
(1, 2) recognizing value orientations, determining relevant information; (3) assessing costs and benefits; (4) analyzing cause and effect; (5) assessing costs and benefits; (6) recognizing value orientations.

Developing Your Economic Skills

Interpreting a Bar Graph To Compare Related Information

Skill: In this lesson you will learn how to interpret a bar graph that is used to compare information that is different but may be related. In this example the rates of inflation and changes in production in Japan and the United States will be compared. Some economists believe inflation may sometimes cause increased production. They feel businesses may respond to increased demand and higher prices by producing more goods and services. This graph may be used to evaluate this belief. To complete this lesson, you'll follow these steps:

1. Examine the vertical and horizontal axes of the graph to see what kind of information they show.
2. Examine the types of bars on the graph to see what they compare.
3. Evaluate the significance of the information provided on the graph.

Application: What were the rates of inflation and growth in real (adjusted for inflation) GDP in the United States and Japan in 1990 and 1991?

On this graph the percent of change in prices (inflation) and in real production (measured by GDP) appear on the vertical axis. The graph's horizontal axis shows various categories that include the years 1990 and 1991, which country is being considered, and the type of change that is being measured.

When you compare the bars you will notice that the United States had almost no change in its real GDP in both 1990 and 1991. However, the American economy did experience inflation that was greater than 5 percent in 1990 and more than 4 percent in 1991. Inflation did not seem to encourage more production in the United States in these years. In both 1990 and 1991 Japan had a real rate of growth in its GDP of over 5 percent. Although Japan also experienced inflation its rates were lower than those in the United States. Japan experienced a growth in production although it had a relatively low rate of inflation. The information provided on this graph does not seem to support the idea that inflation causes growth in production.

Inflation and Rates of Change in Real GDP in the United States and Japan, 1990 & 1991

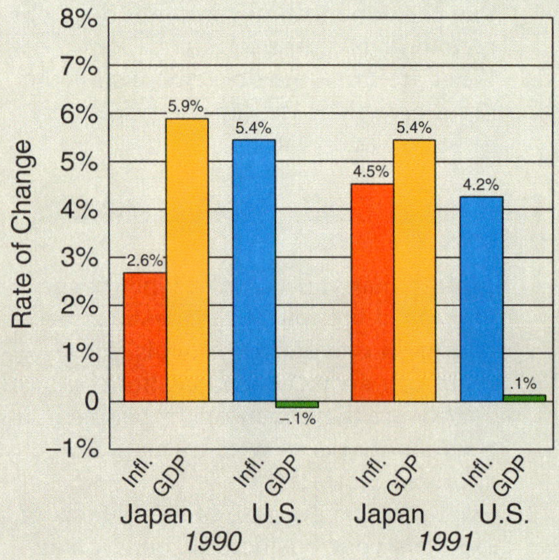

Sources: *Economic Indicators*, April 1992; *Economic Trends*, Federal Reserve Bank of Cleveland, November 1991.

Practice: Is this explanation correct, or may other factors explain the growth in production in Japan and the lack of growth in the United States? To further test this explanation, prepare a graph that shows the relationship between inflation and changes in production in the United States over a longer period of time or in more countries.

Part 4 Review

Summary of Major Economic Concepts

In Part 4 you have learned the following basic economic principles concerning relationships between the economy of the United States and those of other nations.

- The United States and other countries trade because the benefits of trade exceed the costs. The theories of absolute and comparative advantage state that countries should specialize in making the goods they produce most efficiently and trade for others they produce less efficiently.
- Countries may limit trade with tariffs, quotas, or standards imported products are not likely to meet. This is done to protect industries and domestic jobs, and to maintain national security and economic stability.
- Countries prefer to have a positive balance of trade, which contributes to employment, growth, and taxable income.
- Multinational corporations have been taking an increasingly important role in the world economy. Although countries benefit from the increased trade, employment, and investment these organizations bring, they may also cause problems. Multinationals may not pay their fair share of taxes, and they may interfere in a nation's internal affairs.
- The United States had a negative balance of trade through most of the 1980s and into the 1990s. This was caused by many factors that included an increased value of the U.S. dollar, inflation, and a desire of some Americans to buy foreign products they believed had high quality. When the value of the dollar fell in the late 1980s the U.S. balance of trade improved but remained negative.
- Developing nations have special problems that make it difficult for them to improve the standard of living of their people. These problems include economic systems that resist change, inadequate educational systems, a lack of infrastructure, rapid population growth, and political instability.
- In recent years, the share of foreign aid given to developing countries by the United States has fallen. However, developing countries have benefited from bank loans and investments made by American businesses.
- Many types of mixed economic systems exist between the extremes of command market economies. Although there are differences between these systems they must all answer the basic economic questions of *what*, *how*, and *for whom*.
- Many countries, including the United States, have characteristics of socialism mixed into their economic systems. Many nations of Europe in recent years have reduced the amount of central control over their economies in an attempt to improve their productivity.
- Both Japan and the United States have economic systems that are forms of capitalism. However, the ways each of these nations uses capitalism are quite different. The government of the United States allows most economic decisions to be made by individuals. The Japanese government takes a more active role in deciding which businesses will receive resources and how investments will be made.
- The Japanese brand of capitalism has advantages and disadvantages. Although

Part 4 Review

See Part 4 Review Answers, page T157.

some Japanese workers have guaranteed jobs and many benefits, others lack these advantages. The Japanese economy has grown rapidly for many reasons that may include greater rates of saving and investing, a closer relationship between workers and employers, and the fact that Japan has spent little for military defense. Japan's growth will force it to take a larger role in world affairs in the future.

Understanding Economic Concepts

Each of the following questions emphasizes one or more economic concepts or terms from Part 4. The concept is listed in parentheses after each question. Answer in complete sentences that show you understand the concept. The first question has been answered for you as an example.

1. What theories tell us which products countries should produce and which products they should trade for? (Discuss *absolute* and *comparative advantage*.) (Answer: The theory of absolute advantage says countries should produce goods they can make most efficiently and trade for other goods. Comparative advantage emphasizes *relative* efficiency.)
2. What three types of barriers to trade may countries establish? (Discuss *tariffs*, *quotas*, and *standards that discourage trade*.)
3. Why do many developing nations have high tariffs? (Discuss the *infant industry argument*.)
4. Why would countries prefer to export a greater value of goods and services than they import? (Discuss *positive balance of trade*.)
5. What was one important reason for the U.S. negative balance of trade in the 1980s? (Discuss the *exchange rate* for the U.S. dollar.)
6. How have large firms that do business in many nations helped and hurt different nations? (Discuss *multinational corporations*.)
7. Why is it often difficult to bring about change in developing nations? (Discuss *traditional economic systems*.)
8. What is one important form of capital that many developing nations lack? (Discuss *infrastructure*.)
9. Why doesn't sending tools to developing nations guarantee that they will be used effectively to increase production? (Discuss *inadequate education systems*.)
10. What is one important change that has contributed to population growth in developing nations in the past 40 years? (Discuss reduced *mortality rates*.)
11. What basic characteristics are found in different types of command economies? (Discuss *communism* and *socialism*.)
12. What reason probably contributed to the low worker productivity that existed in many communist countries in the past? (Discuss the *incentive* people feel to work.)
13. What advantages are provided to Japanese businesses by their government? (Discuss *industrial capitalism*.)

Writing About Economics

Each of the questions below requires you to write a brief essay. Follow these steps:

- Demonstrate your understanding of the identified economic concept(s) in your essay.

Writing About Economics activities 1-3 may be an appropriate method of authentic assessment and may be placed in students' portfolios.

Writing About Economics
(1) determining relevant information; (2) analyzing cause and effect; (3) comparing and contrasting.

- Explain how the economic concept(s) is involved in the situation.
- Describe the choice you would make in the situation and on what basis you would make this decision.

1. A politician is going to visit your school to talk about foreign trade. You know from what you have read that she is in favor of reducing tariffs. Write three different questions to ask her, and explain why each is an important question. (Discuss the *protecting domestic jobs argument*, *dumping*, and *negative balance of trade*.)
2. Pretend you have helped organize a drive to raise money to pay for tools, seed, and training for poor South American farmers. You are going to a meeting at a local church to ask for contributions. You are sure you will be asked to explain why people in developing nations need help from people in the United States. Prepare a written answer. (Discuss *traditional economic systems*, *infrastructure*, and *inadequate education systems*.)
3. Suppose there is an exchange student from Japan visiting your school. One day he asks you to explain what you believe are the most important differences between the U.S. economic system and the economic system of Japan. Write an answer to his question. (Discuss differences between the *industrial capitalism* found in Japan and the *mixed capitalism* of the United States.)

Discussing Economics

The following paragraphs describe economic issues that have been topics of recent public debate. For each issue, decide whether you support or oppose the proposal, and how you would present your opinion to the class. When you present your opinion, follow these steps:

Discussing Economics
(1) identifying alternatives; (2) predicting probable consequences.

- Identify and describe the controversial issues of the proposal.
- Clearly state your decision.
- Explain why you think your choice is the best one.

1. There is evidence that American automobile firms have been harmed by imports from other nations. Suppose a bill was introduced in Congress that would require that at least 80 percent of the parts in all cars sold in the United States be made in this country. This law would force foreign producers to make or buy many parts for their cars in the United States, or else stop selling them here. Those who support the bill believe it would increase the number of jobs in this country. Opponents of the bill say it would make our cars much more expensive. What action do you recommend to your congressional representative?
2. Some Americans have become concerned about the large loans that many American banks have made to developing countries. They are afraid that these loans may not be repaid and that U.S. taxpayers will be forced to "bail out" U.S. banks when these loans go bad. They want a law passed that would prevent banks from making loans to developing nations. Other people say such a law would go against the economic principles of our capitalistic system and would harm developing nations that need our loans. Which side of this debate would you support?

Problem-Solving with Economics

Chapter 13

1. Suppose you could afford and wanted to buy each of the products listed below. For each, indicate whether you would

Problem-Solving in Economics
Chapter 13
(1) evaluating alternatives; (2) assessing costs and benefits.

Part 4 Review

expect to buy an American or foreign-made product, and explain the reasons for your belief.

a. VCR
b. home computer
c. automobile
d. suit

2. A number of suggestions have been made for things that could be done to help people who are hurt by imported goods. Describe the costs and benefits that would result from each of the following suggestions. (In considering costs, remember that government programs are paid for by the taxpayers.)
   a. Limit the amount of goods that may be imported.
   b. Increase tariffs on imported goods.
   c. Extend unemployment benefits by two years for people who lose their jobs due to imported goods.
   d. Provide government retraining programs for anyone who loses a job because of imported goods.
   e. Give government jobs to anyone who is unemployed because of imported goods.

Chapter 14

1. Suppose you are in charge of a developing nation. You know that in order to grow, a country must invest in tools and factories, in education and training, and in infrastructure. You have the resources to work on these areas, but not all equally. Explain which type of investments you would concentrate your resources in and why you would do this.
2. Suppose that the following ideas were suggested to help the world's poor people. Explain how well you believe each would work and why.
   a. Have U.S. government pay tuition of foreign students to study in the United States to learn how to help their people.
   b. Encourage U.S. businesses to invest in developing nations by giving them tax breaks if they do.
   c. Send U.S citizens to developing nations to show people how to be more productive.
3. Suppose you are the director of the ministry of health in a developing nation. You learn that a developed nation has recently marketed a vaccine that will prevent a disease that has been a major cause of death in your nation. You also realize that lowering the death rate will cause rapid population growth that will slow economic growth and could later result in famine. Should you recommend that the government purchase the vaccine?

Chapter 15

1. Suppose you live in a command economy and want to achieve economic growth. Describe three steps you might take that would be different than steps you would take in a market economy. Would the steps in the command economy be as likely to increase productivity as those in a market economy? Explain why or why not.
2. The kind of person who is a good business manager is not always the same kind of person who can win an election. Describe the personal traits that would make a good manager. Do the same for a person who could win elections. Use these lists to explain why nations with socialist systems and democratic governments may have economic problems (in these nations elected officials often make basic economic decisions).

Chapter 14
(1) identifying alternatives; (2) evaluating alternatives; (3) identifying the problem.

Chapter 15
(1) cause and effect; (2) comparing and contrasting.

CAREERS AND EMPLOYMENT OPPORTUNITIES

Some of you are working now, some of you will start work when you are graduated from high school, and still others of you will delay work until you leave college. Almost everyone who looks for work can find something somewhere, at least part-time. But most people have in common a desire to find a full-time job that will pay an adequate income now and hold good promise for the future. We look for jobs that have the potential for advancement, with additional responsibilities, greater authority, better job security and more money. We would all like to enjoy our work and be successful at it. Finding such a job is not easy. But you can improve your chances by carefully exploring different job opportunities and by learning about your own abilities.

Every year, the U.S. Bureau of Labor Statistics publishes the *Occupational Outlook Handbook* (OOH). Information about almost all occupations is listed. For each occupation, the Handbook describes working conditions, employment training, qualifications, advancement opportunities, job outlook, and current and expected earnings. It also covers related occupations and provides sources for additional information, career counseling, and financial aid for education and training.

Anyone looking for a job or considering training for a career should consult the latest edition of the *Occupational Outlook Handbook*. This source and other valuable career planning guides can be found in most libraries.

What Is the Job Market?

Like all markets, the job market is made up of buyers and sellers. The buyers are businesses, governments, and consumers who need people to work for them. The sellers are the labor force: all persons sixteen years or older who are working or looking for work. Of the 250 million people in the United States in 1992, about 128 million were in the labor force. They represent supply. Those who hire workers represent demand. The total job market is the sum of many smaller job markets, and it involves individual decisions by millions of people.

In the early 1990s, an average of 93 percent of those in the labor force had jobs. But the job market is much tougher on new job entrants than on experienced workers. New entrants into the work force can improve their chances with more education, additional skills, training, and any work-related experience they can acquire.

What Are the Employment Trends?

Although the total number of people in the labor force continues to grow, the number of new people entering the labor force has slowed in recent years. For the high school or college graduate looking for an entry-level position, it's encouraging to know that not as many new workers are now competing for those positions. However, the growing total number of people in the work force means job advancements might be slow.

In 1948, manufacturing accounted for 27 percent of civilian employment, while workers in services and trades combined made up 25 percent. By 1992, manufacturing had dropped to 20 percent, while services and trades jumped to 57 percent. Manufacturing clearly offers less job security to new entries than do services and trades.

What Are the Occupational Trends?

Almost all occupations will need new workers in the 1990s, even if it is just to replace retiring workers. But some areas will be growing rapidly, some slowly, and still others will be declining.

The health-care field, for example, will expand, because of the increase in the number of elderly. Advancing technology will increase opportunities in some fields, but decrease opportunities in others. Occupations related to computers, word-processing equipment, and industrial robots will expand. But employment of statistical clerks, stenographers, and welders will decrease. Despite these changes, office clerical workers will likely remain the largest major occupational group.

Below are listed (in alphabetical order) some occupations expected to grow rapidly and those headed for decline.

Fastest-Growing Occupations
Accountants and auditors
Computer programmers
Corrections officers
Data processing equipment repairers
Electrical and electronics technicians
Employment interviewers
Lawyers
Mechanical engineers
Medical assistants
Paramedical personnel
Physical therapists
Registered nurses
Securities and finance sales workers
Travel agents

Fastest-Declining Occupations
Central office operators
College and university faculty
Farm management advisers
Farm workers
Furnace operators
Machinery maintenance mechanics
Postal service workers
Railroad brake signal operators
Sewing machine operators
Shoe and leather workers
Statistical clerks
Stenographers
Textile workers
Tractor operators

Making a Personal Choice

While it is important to know as much as you can about the careers you are thinking about, the choice must be a personal one. The market will determine the present and future demand for workers in a particular occupation and the degree of competition. You have no control over the market other than to accept or reject what it offers. What you do have control over is determining your own career goals. In determining a career path, you need to assess your own abilities and evaluate the sacrifices necessary to achieve different possible goals. You need to consider which career paths will likely bring the rewards that will be worth your total investment in money and time.

It is difficult to make such choices without adequate information. Take the time to consult sources such as the *Occupational Outlook Handbook* and seek the advice of a career counselor. Finally, there is a good chance you will be in the work force for about 40 years. If you are like most people, you will change careers, perhaps more than once in your lifetime.

Selected Job Categories

This section contains samplings of the kinds of information that you should consider when you think about your career choices. In the space of this book it is only possible to present a few job categories. There are many other career fields that you can explore. Detailed information about most types of jobs can be found in the *Occupational Outlook Handbook* and in other sources.

The OOH provides earnings information for many job categories in terms of the "middle range." To find this range all people employed in a job category are ranked according to their annual earnings. The highest paid 25 percent and the lowest paid 25 percent of the category are not considered. The range of income of the middle half is reported in the OOH.

Accountant

Nature of the Work

Most people think of accountants as preparers of income taxes. While that is certainly an important task, it is but one of their many responsibilities. Their major purpose is to prepare, analyze, and verify financial reports that furnish information to management in both the public and private sectors.

The four major fields in accounting are public, management, government, and internal auditing. *Public accountants* serve the general public (not government) in privately owned firms. They check clients' financial records, seeing to it that they conform to standard procedures for reporting. They give advice on tax advantages and disadvantages, on setting up an accounting system and on managing cash resources, and they prepare income tax statements.

The largest group are *management accountants.* They usually work for larger businesses in such areas as budgeting, investment, and taxation. The financial information they provide helps management make decisions.

Government accountants are employed at all levels of government. Some deal with the financial management of government agencies and operations, including the preparation of budgets, while others (such as those working for the IRS) examine tax returns.

Internal auditors are hired by a company as full-time employees to audit that company's records. This field is growing faster than the other areas of accounting, as the demands for management to account for their actions increase. Internal auditors approach their examination of records with an attitude of "what can I find that is wrong or wasteful."

Working conditions for accountants are generally pleasant, and hours are frequently regular, with the exception of tax season.

Education and Training

Most firms and government agencies require applicants to have a bachelor's degree in accounting or some closely related field. More selective employers prefer those with a master's degree and who are familiar with computers. Those planning to become accountants must be good at mathematics, be able to compare, analyze and interpret numbers and facts, to make sound judgments, and to communicate well. Patience and accuracy are essential.

Job Outlook

There are approximately 1 million accountants. About 300,000 are Certified Public Accountants (CPAs), which gives professional recognition. About 10 percent are self-employed. Very few accountants work part-time.

The job outlook for accountants is very good, because of increasing demands made on management and by government. Turnover and firings due to decline in business conditions are low. Starting salaries for those with bachelor's degrees average $25,300. For those with experience, salaries average $33,500, while chief accountants or those with supervisory duties average $53,300. Some CPAs earn over $100,000.

Automotive Mechanic

Nature of the Work

Automotive mechanics repair and service automobiles and trucks. When repairs are required, the mechanic must first diagnose the problem, and then make the necessary repair or replacement. Preventive maintenance during routine servicing is considered equally important to treating breakdowns.

Larger shops, particularly automotive dealers, have specialists. These include mechanics for automatic transmissions, tune-up, front end, air conditioning, brakes, radiator, and electrical systems. Mechanics use a variety of tools, both power and hand, some of which they own personally. Machine tools, such as lathes, jacks and hoists, infrared engine analyzers, diagnostic devices, and welding and flame-cutting equipment are usually furnished by the employer.

Working conditions for automotive mechanics depend on the conditions in the garages where they work. These may be fairly pleasant, or they may be noisy, poorly lit, too cold (or hot), or poorly ventilated. Many jobs are greasy and dirty and may require working in awkward positions. Lifting heavy parts and receiving cuts and bruises is commonplace.

Education and Training

Automotive mechanics get their training through apprenticeships, formal schooling, or a combination of both. However, fewer employers are willing to hire people with no formal classroom work in automotive technology. Programs are offered in high school, public and private vocational and technical schools, and in community colleges. Instruction may be concentrated in six months or be extended over two years at a community college where academic courses are combined with automotive training. Employees, particularly at new dealerships, may be sent to factory training centers to learn about new models and to receive specialized training in one of eight different specialized areas. Achievement is recognized by certification from the National Institute for Automotive Service Excellence for having two years experience and passing a written test in each of the eight different service areas.

Job Outlook

In 1988 there were 771,000 automotive mechanics. Most worked for dealers, repair shops, gasoline service stations, and supply stores. Many others worked for organizations that had fleets of cars, such as governments, large companies, taxicabs and automobile leasing firms. Some worked for motor vehicle manufacturers. About 20 percent were self-employed.

The job outlook for those with some formal training is better than average because of an expected increase in the number of motor vehicles and the need to replace experienced workers who move on to other occupations or retire. Earnings for skilled mechanics who are employed by a dealer average $17.40 an hour; less skilled workers average $8.70 an hour. Most mechanics work about 40 to 48 hours per week.

Computer Systems Analyst

Nature of the Work

If a retail chain wants to computerize its inventory or if a research organization wants to improve its efficiency, each will need a computer systems analyst. Some computer systems analysts plan and develop computer "networks" for businesses. These networks connect all the computers in an individual office, department, or building. This allows all the users of microcomputers on the system to retrieve data from a mainframe computer and use it at their workstation machines.

Analysts usually begin an assignment by discussing the needs of the organization with managers or specialists. They define the goals of the system and then use models to develop a plan that meets these needs. They may also prepare a cost-benefit analysis to help management decide whether the proposed system is satisfactory. If a system is accepted, the analyst may determine what specific computer hardware and software will be needed to set it up. They may also prepare specifications for computer programmers to follow or work with programmers to eliminate errors from the system.

The possible uses of computers are varied and complex. Analysts usually specialize in either business, scientific, or engineering applications. They may need training in the field for which they develop the computer systems. Some analysts improve systems already in place or adapt them to handle more tasks.

Systems analysts work in offices. Their work week is usually the same as other professionals and office workers. At times, however, evening or weekend work is necessary. For example, they may have to make changes in a system when system users are not at work.

Education and Training

The qualifications of a systems analyst vary because they depend on the preferences of employers. Many employers, however, expect the analysts to have a college degree in computer science. The college degree indicates that the analyst is familiar with programming languages, computer concepts, systems analysis, and data base management.

A background in accounting or business management is important for a computer systems analyst who wants to work in a business environment. Scientific organizations prefer analysts with a background in science, applied mathematics, or engineering.

Prior work experience is important. Most people entering this field transfer from occupations such as engineer, manager, or computer programmer. The titles Certified Data Processor and Certified Systems Professional are conferred by the Institute for Certification of Computer Professionals. Candidates for certification passed a general test and a specific two-part examination.

Job Outlook

Demand for computer systems analysts will increase with the advancing technology that leads to new applications for computers. There were more than 463,000 people employed as computer systems analysts in 1990 and median annual income was about $38,700. The range of income was fairly broad. The lowest 10 percent of systems analysts earned less than $23,000. The highest 10 percent earned more than $62,000.

Cosmetologist

Nature of the Work

Beauticians or hairstylists are common names to describe cosmetologists. They also may give manicures, clean and style wigs, give scalp and facial treatments, and provide make-up analysis for women.

Working conditions are generally pleasant. However, most cosmetologists must be on their feet for hours at a time. Full-time workers usually have a 40-hour week, but some work in the evenings and on weekends and holidays, when beauty salons are busiest.

While there were 649,000 cosmetologists working in the late 1980s, about 40 percent worked part-time. Most are employed in beauty salons, some in "unisex" salons, barber shops, department stores, hospitals, and hotels. A few leading cosmetologists in large cities set fashion trends.

Those wishing to become cosmetologists should have finger dexterity, a sense of beauty, and should enjoy working with people. They should be able to carry out the instructions of their customers, and should keep up with current hairstyles, so as to offer suggestions when asked. They should expect to begin their first jobs doing simple tasks such as shampooing and gradually increase their responsibilities.

Education and Training

All states require cosmetologists to be licensed, although the qualifications vary. Most states require graduation from a state-approved school, a physical examination, and that the person be at least 16 years old. A few require high school diplomas.

Training is offered in public and private vocational schools and in the evening as well as the day. Attending school full time requires from six months to one year to complete the program. Many high schools offer a course of study along with the usual academic subjects. Much of the program centers around demonstrations and practical experience.

Job Outlook

Job opportunities are expected to be plentiful, at least through the mid-1990s. Most openings will be replacements, because there is a fast turnover as workers seek better-paying jobs. Opportunities for part-time work are excellent.

Average weekly earnings for the middle range are between $175 and $320. The size, location, and reputation of the salon will be most important in determining wages.

Dental Hygienist

Nature of the Work

A dentist is able to expand his or her services with the help of a dental hygienist. Working under the direction of a dentist, a hygienist cleans teeth, takes and develops X-ray films of the teeth, applies topical fluoride to prevent tooth decay, makes impressions of teeth for study models, and performs other services as an assistant to a dentist. State laws control how far a dental hygienist may go in patient care and how closely the dentist must supervise the hygienist's activities.

In school systems, hygienists may examine children's teeth and educate youngsters on good oral hygiene. For those with advanced training, positions in dental hygiene are plentiful.

Working conditions are pleasant, usually in a comfortable office surrounded by professionals. Most hygienists work less than a 35-hour week. Many will hold more than one job. There could be danger of overexposure to diseases or radiation if proper procedures are not followed.

Education and Training

All states require dental hygienists to be licensed. Requirements include graduation from an accredited dental hygienist school and passing both a written and clinical examination. Most programs are for two years and offer an associate degree. There are four-year programs leading to a bachelor's degree. Many taking the four-year program obtain jobs with school systems. Six schools offer master's degrees. Admission to any of the 200 schools requires a high school diploma. The curriculum includes subjects in the liberal arts as well as basic, clinical, and dental sciences. Those working to become dental hygienists should have manual dexterity, be neat, in good health, and should enjoy working with others.

Job Outlook

There are about 75,000 jobs in dental hygiene, but the number of jobs is greater than the number of people who want to fill them. This is because most hygienists are hired to work only two or three times a week. While most work in private dental offices, many work in clinics, public health agencies, hospitals, and large businesses.

The job outlook is somewhat better than average as the demand for dental care rises. Also, the change to group practices should add more jobs. The factors that may change this increasing demand are the greater supply of dentists and the improvement of dental care as a result of fluoridation.

Earnings vary with training. The average yearly earnings in the late 1980s were $15,000 to $20,000 for the middle range.

Drafter

Nature of the Work

Drafters provide a necessary step between those who create ideas for making objects (such as equipment and buildings) and the actual construction of those things. They prepare detailed drawings from rough sketches made by engineers, scientists, and architects. These include specifications, views from different positions, and any other information needed to carry out the project. Their tools include compasses, dividers, protractors, rulers, triangles, technical handbooks, tables, and calculators. Drafters are also increasingly using computer assisted design (CAD) systems. These systems, which are slowly changing the field, allow the preparation of a design and the change of that design with a minimum of routine work. While CAD can produce designs more quickly, accurately, and thoroughly, it has made only a small dent in the traditional approach used by drafters.

Working conditions are usually pleasant, but sitting for long periods of time can produce eyestrain and be boring. Those thinking of becoming drafters should have good eyesight, patience, and manual dexterity. They should be able to draw freehand three-dimensional objects and do detailed work with accuracy and neatness.

Education and Training

While college training is not a prerequisite, more than 40 percent of recent employees have had some post high-school training, usually at a community college or technical institute. The curriculum usually includes courses in structural design, architectural drawing, engineering, and industrial technology.

Learning how to use computer aided design (CAD) equipment is helpful. However, employers frequently prefer to teach their drafters how to use the company's own CAD system, because not all CAD systems are compatible.

Job Outlook

There were 319,000 working drafters in 1988. About one third worked in manufacturing firms that produced machinery, electrical equipment, and fabricated metals. Another third worked for engineering and architectural businesses. About 16,000 worked for governments, primarily state and local.

The expected impact of CAD on future jobs has not been great. There will be some increase in jobs, but most openings will result from replacement of existing drafters. Job security is less than average because the industries in which drafters are employed are sensitive to economic recessions.

Average earnings for drafters in the late 1980s was $24,000. The middle range was $17,700 to $30,000. A few drafters will continue their studies and go on to study architecture, engineering, landscape architecture, and surveying.

Elementary School Teacher

Nature of the Work

To many, there is no greater calling than to help shape the lives of young children. Elementary school teachers introduce youngsters to the basics of primary skills: mathematics, languages, social studies, and science. Equally important, they try to instill an appreciation for learning. They observe and evaluate both the performance and potential of their students and take steps to overcome weaknesses. They observe the development of their children's health and social behavior and work with parents and school officials to improve each.

Elementary school teachers usually instruct their students in a number of subjects, although specialization is common in art, music, and physical education. Some teachers are trained to offer remedial work, or to deal with emotionally or physically disabled children.

Only a part of a teacher's work takes place in the classroom. Lessons have to be prepared, papers graded, and faculty and committee meetings attended. Teachers are expected to keep up to date on educational materials and subject matter through reading and attendance at workshops. The demands of clerical work and supervision of lunchrooms and playgrounds are sometimes lessened with the help of teacher aides.

The working conditions of teachers vary considerably with the grade level and nature of the class. Attending to children's physical needs are greatest at the lower grades, while coping with those who are disrespectful and emotionally volatile may be more difficult at upper grades. Most elementary school teachers have a nine or ten-month schedule, with week-long or greater breaks in the fall and spring. School days range from 175 to 205, with 184 as an average. After a trial period of about three years, a teacher can be granted tenure, which provides greater job security than in most employment. Not all teachers are given tenure.

Education and Training

All states require public school teachers to be certified, and most states require the same for private schools. Typically, certification will be for early childhood (nursery school through third grade), elementary grades (one through eight), or special education or reading. While requirements vary by states, all now require a bachelor's degree from a college with an approved teacher training program. Course work includes specific subject matter as well as professional education. Information about special state requirements may be obtained by writing the state education department. Teachers should like being with children, and they should be creative, dependable, and patient.

Job Outlook

There presently are about 1.4 million teachers of elementary school. About 85 percent work in public schools, the rest in private schools. Enrollments in elementary school are expected to grow rapidly until the mid-1990s. This will increase demand. Supply, however, is not as predictable. It will depend largely on salaries and the priorities and prestige afforded teachers. Earnings (for both new and experienced teachers as a group) average $28,900 with slightly higher salaries in the Mid-Atlantic and western states and lower salaries in the South.

Hotel Manager

Nature of the Work

Hotel managers are responsible for the successful operation of their establishments. The manager is in charge of all aspects of the hotel (or motel), including marketing and sales, accounting, food service, housekeeping, recreation, personnel, security and maintenance, guest satisfaction, and just about any problem that might arise. In small establishments, the manager may have to supervise all these operations. In large chains, many of these functions are centralized.

Working conditions will vary depending on the circumstances. Because hotels/motels operate around the clock, managers may be on call at all times if emergencies arise. Some managers live on the premises, which in itself can be tiring. Stress may build in dealing with angry guests. Problems with low-paid help may be frequent. Managers should have dispositions that are not easily ruffled.

In larger hotels and motels, the general manager may coordinate the operations of the front desk manager, food and beverage manager, accounts manager, and so on. Frequently these functional managers will rise to become general managers.

Education and Training

Most hotel managers rise to their positions through experience in this and related businesses. More recently, however, employers are seeking people with college training in hotel management. More than one hundred colleges and universities offer four-year programs in this field, and an even greater number are offered in two-year colleges. Typical courses include accounting, economics, marketing, computer science, food service management, and others related to operating a business. Large hotel and motel chains may offer their own courses, with many opportunities for advancement.

Job Outlook

There are currently about 96,000 hotel/motel managers, plus an additional number of owner/managers. The job outlook is better than average, as more hotels and motels are built, tourism expands, and people now in the field retire.

Salaries vary, depending on experience and responsibilities. Front-office managers average $30,000, while general managers average above $53,000. Liberal fringe benefits are given and bonuses are not uncommon. Managers generally receive paid vacations, life insurance, medical benefits, and pension plans. Some earn bonuses up to 15 percent of their basic salaries. Experience and training in hotel and motel management are easily carried over to managing apartment buildings, stores, and offices.

Insurance Sales Worker

Nature of the Work

The purpose of insurance is to protect individuals, families, and businesses from financial loss. Three basic categories of policies are life, property-liability (which includes automobile insurance), and health. There are many specific types of policies within these categories. Insurance sales workers offer professional advice in helping to find the right policy for the circumstances. Some sales workers sell insurance in all three major categories; others specialize in certain fields, such as life insurance. Some workers specialize in group policies that employees or members of organizations may buy at lower prices.

Hours for insurance sales workers are frequently irregular, with evening and weekend appointments commonplace. Long work-weeks and a great deal of local travel may be drawbacks, but insurance sales workers have some control in arranging their hours. About a third of all sales people work for themselves. Most beginners usually need income from some other job until they can get enough clients.

Education and Training

A college degree is not necessary for most insurance sales jobs, although most firms prefer their people to have some college work. Many people enter the field from other occupations, which results in older entrants. Many colleges have courses in insurance and a few have insurance programs leading to a bachelor's degree. In addition, several different insurance associations offer conferences, seminars, and courses. After passing an examination, each offers appropriate designations of achievement that are prized in the industry. These achievement designations go well beyond the required licensing examination that each state requires.

Job Outlook

There were 423,000 insurance sales workers in 1988, many of whom were part-time. The job outlook is for comparatively slow expansion. This is because insurance sales workers are now using more productive methods, even though the amount of insurance sold continues to increase. Most openings will come from high turnovers, since many people find they cannot make a good living in insurance sales.

When new sales workers join a firm, the company will frequently pay them about $1,200 a month. This is a subsidy while they are learning. Most sales workers are paid on a commission. They earn a higher commission on a new policy than on a renewal. The median income after five years is $30,400, after ten years $50,300, and many very experienced sales workers, particularly in casualty insurance, earn more than $100,000.

Lawyer

Nature of the Work

In a nation ruled by law, all of us are affected by laws in most aspects of our lives. Lawyers (or *attorneys*) help connect our system of laws with our actions as individuals, in groups, and as a part of government. Lawyers may act as counselors, advising their clients of the potential legal consequences of their actions, and examining and writing legal contracts and other documents. They may act as advocates, representing their clients in a court of law. Some lawyers perform all of these functions. Some lawyers thrive on trial practice, and some rarely see the inside of a courtroom.

Lawyers frequently specialize in certain areas of law, such as taxes, real estate, administrative law, or personal injury law. Some lawyers specialize in civil cases, where one party sues another. Others deal in criminal cases, where the government brings actions for crimes against society. A few defend the poor in legal aid societies, some teach, and still others have found their training useful in businesses not directly related to the law.

Most frequently, lawyers work in offices, law libraries, and courtrooms. Those who work for government or corporations are likely to have regular hours, while those in law firms or in business for themselves go through periods of great pressure.

Education and Training

Most states require lawyers to pass their bar examination. Educational preparation is usually four years of undergraduate college and three years of law school. Some states accept the results of passing the bar in another state. While there is no national licensing, all but four states require a Multi-state Bar Examination along with the state examination. A few states still permit candidates to take their examinations without formal college and law school training.

Job Outlook

There are about 582,000 lawyers employed in this country. Almost 460,000 are in private practice with most of the remaining working in government, particularly local government.

The job outlook for lawyers reflects an increase in both demand and supply. Increases in laws and litigation in many fields, including consumer protection, environment, and safety, have created a need for more legal services, and this has been matched by a doubling of law school graduates in the last ten years. Job turnover is not frequent, perhaps because income tends to be high. First-time jobs usually begin at $34,000 or more; average salaries for experienced lawyers are above $80,000 and much higher than that in private industry.

Medical Record Technician

Nature of the Work

Doctors and hospitals set up permanent record files for each patient they treat. These files include the patient's medical history, results of physical examinations, laboratory tests, diagnosis and treatment plans, and doctors' and nurses' notes. Medical record technicians work together with other medical record professionals to manage the records system. This management is important because it must meet strict medical, administrative, ethical, and legal requirements. Recent changes in the way hospitals are paid for their services have made medical records even more significant. Medical record administrators are key members of the hospital management team.

Medical record technicians organize and evaluate records for completeness and accuracy. They ensure that all forms are present and properly identified and signed. Increasingly, this task is done on computers. Each technician has a computer terminal that can retrieve information from the patient's files in the hospital's mainframe computer.

Technicians also assist hospital administrative staff in tabulating and analyzing data from medical records. This statistical information can be studied to determine such things as occurrences of disease by type and length of hospital stay. Technicians may also assemble information in response to inquiries from law firms, insurance companies, government agencies, or researchers.

Medical record personnel usually work a 40-hour week. In hospitals where medical record departments are open 18 to 24 hours a day, technicians may work day, evening, or night shifts.

Education and Training

To gain a credential as an Accredited Record Technician, a person must pass a written examination given by the American Medical Record Association (AMRA). The examination is given to persons who have graduated from an AMRA accredited 2-year associate degree program or who have graduated from the Independent Study Program in Medical Record Technology and have also obtained 30 semester hours of prescribed academic credit. Courses include biological sciences, medical terminology, medical record science, business management, legal aspects, and computer data processing.

Job Outlook

Three out of five medical record technician jobs are in hospitals. In addition, public health departments, insurance firms, nursing homes, clinics, accounting firms, and law firms hire medical record technicians. A change in Medicare reimbursement in 1990 increased the need for detailed records in doctors' offices. Demand for experienced or credentialed technicians as well as for recent graduates is strong. More than 52,000 technician jobs were held in 1990. The average fulltime technician employed by a private hospital earned $9.70 per hour in 1991. Because of overtime pay, average yearly wages approached $25,000.

Photographer and Camera Operator

Nature of the Work

The objective of photographers and camera operators is to capture the visual image and emotion of people, places, and events. Still photography, such as taking portraits, is quite different from camera operation for either video or film. Most photographers specialize in a particular field, because specific skills are required for achieving different effects. Specialization in scientific photography may reveal images not seen by the naked eye. Advertising and industrial photography require taking pictures of a wide range of subjects. The results must be attractive to be effective in newspaper and magazine advertising or in catalogs. Camera operators are employed by television and movie studios.

Both still photographers and camera operators use a wide variety of cameras, with numerous accessories to meet different circumstances. Some operators develop their own films, others use a laboratory.

Photographers employed by government and commercial enterprises usually have regular hours. Those who work freelance and for the news media may be subject to immediate call and the necessity of traveling. Those who freelance are under pressure to solicit clients.

Education and Training

Formal education is not always required to go into photography, although a good understanding of the technical aspects of equipment is needed. Imagination, creativity, and timing are all important. For specialized photography, some knowledge of the subject matter may be required.

Many colleges and universities offer programs in photography and cinematography, leading to a bachelor's degree. Two-year colleges have programs with associate degrees. Art and design schools usually have classes in photography.

A type of apprenticeship in a studio is a frequent way of moving into the field. Typically the trainee will start in a darkroom, mixing chemicals and developing film. Responsibilities will gradually be increased.

Job Outlook

Slightly more than 105,000 jobs are held by photographers and camera operators. Half of this number are salaried, working in photographic or commercial studios or for the news media. The remainder are self-employed. Photographers are employed almost everywhere, while camera operators, found mainly in television broadcasting and motion pictures, are usually in metropolitan areas.

Job opportunities in photography are expected to grow faster than the average for all occupations until the mid-1990s. Demand continues to grow as businesses rely more on visual aids for both learning and advertising. Demand for camera operators is also expected to grow, but the excitement and glamour of the field will probably attract more applicants than the jobs available.

New and relatively inexperienced photographers average $21,000 a year; those with greater experience usually earn in the range of $24,600 to $33,800, and those most experienced or doing more difficult work average close to $40,000. Camera operators may earn even more than this.

Police Officer

Nature of the Work

Police work can range from keeping order in public places and investigating crimes to controlling traffic and lecturing the public on safety. In small communities, officers may be called on to do all these things. In large cities, work may be highly specialized, including chemical and firearms analysis, fingerprint identification, harbor and border patrol, and work with the canine corps and even helicopters.

All levels of government need law enforcement officers. There are related jobs, such as security guards with private companies. Most police recruits begin with patrol, on foot or riding in a police vehicle. They are expected to be alert to anything that could be dangerous to people and to react appropriately.

Working conditions will vary with particular assignments. Most officers work a 40-hour week, but many must work nights, weekends, and holidays because of the demands of protecting the public. Even when police are off duty, they are subject to immediate call. Such challenges as working long hours outside in severe weather, risking a high injury rate, taking the chances involved in pursuing speeding motorists and apprehending criminals, all demand dedication to the job.

Education and Training

Most police jobs are covered by civil service regulations. Usually candidates must be at least 21 years old and U.S. citizens. Competitive tests are given to determine physical fitness and personal qualifications. Both written tests and interviews are given to determine the candidates' honesty, good judgment, and sense of responsibility. Most jobs require a high school education or more. The more specialized jobs require college training.

Some large cities hire civilian police cadets or trainees right out of high school. They perform clerical jobs and take classroom instruction in job-related areas. This procedure helps select the best candidates for officers.

Job Outlook

Approximately 575,000 men and women are employed as police or detectives. Most work in local government with about ten percent in state agencies and five percent at the federal level.

The job employment outlook through the 1990s is above average. Most openings will come from retirees. Transfer to other jobs is small.

The average starting salary was $20,600 and the average maximum $26,700 a year in 1988. Sergeants, detectives, and lieutenants can expect an average of $4,500 more. Maximums with experience are frequently above $35,000. These low salaries are usually offset by very liberal benefits, including education, vacations, and a retirement pension at half pay after 20 or 25 years.

Registered Nurse

Nature of the Work

Registered nurses (R.N.s) deal with health and illness. Their concern is with the entire person, for whom they observe, assess, record symptoms, and administer care.

More than two-thirds of all nurses work in hospitals or similar health institutions. There they provide skilled bedside care and carry out the physicians' orders. Some nurses specialize in such fields as surgery or psychiatric care.

For patients who need constant care, there are private duty nurses. Office nurses assist physicians in the maintenance of their practice. Occupational health and industrial nurses work for governments or businesses. They treat minor injuries, offer health counseling, give health examinations, and arrange for further medical care. Community health nurses care for patients in clinics, retirement homes, and other community settings.

While most nurses work in good facilities, the physical demands of patient care can be very strenuous. Coping with human suffering and frequent emergencies requires emotional stability. Working at night, during holidays, and on weekends is not unusual, because patients demand constant care.

Education and Training

Programs for nursing vary in length from two to five years after graduation from high school. There were almost 1,500 training programs in the United States in 1988. Programs taken at two-year colleges offer an associate degree. At hospitals, where three years are required, a diploma is given. At colleges and universities the four-to-five-year program leads to a bachelor's degree. Some schools offer masters and doctoral programs. All graduates become eligible to take the national licensing examination, leading to the R.N. Supervisory or administrative positions require a minimum of a bachelor's degree.

All nursing education programs include classroom instruction as well as clinical (practical "hands on") experience.

Job Outlook

There were about 1.6 million nurses in the late 1980s, but about 30 percent were part-time.

Those interested in a career in nursing must be able to show sympathy, accept responsibility, and follow orders. There are numerous opportunities for advancement. These include specializing in some branch of medicine, or becoming a nurse practitioner or a physician's associate. Secretarial, computer, and management skills increase the opportunities and the earnings of nurses.

The job outlook for nurses is excellent, with opportunities in many settings. The shortage in the late 1980s has raised the middle range of annual salaries to about $23,100. The top ten percent make over $32,100.

Retail Sales Worker

Nature of the Work

The primary purpose of a retail sales worker is to interest customers in the merchandise. How successful an establishment is depends in large part on how efficient and courteous its sales force is. The worker should know the product and its construction and design, and the competitors' products. Being able to demonstrate the use of the product, when appropriate, is also important. For those selling complex items such as computers, knowing special features and what they can do is essential.

Retail sales workers are also called on to make out sales slips, receive and record payments, handle exchanges, and help make or keep the sales area attractive.

The working conditions are generally pleasant. However, during sales and holiday seasons the demands on a sales worker can cause stress. Some must stand for long periods of time, while others may have to travel to customers' homes. Many stores are open evenings and weekends. Some workers may have to put in long hours.

In the late 1980s, there were about four million jobs in retail sales. The largest employers are department stores; general merchandise, apparel and accessories stores; drug, food, and furniture stores; and car dealers. Sales workers who sell expensive items are likely to be employed full-time. Almost 60 percent of the others are likely to be part-time.

Education and Training

Employees are expected to be neat and pleasant and to communicate easily. Most people who enter the field have no experience. Usually their main objective is to earn immediate income rather than start a career in selling. Employers generally prefer to hire high school graduates for full-time positions, but high school students are sometimes employed on a part-time basis. Stores may have a training program, or may assign the new employee to work with an experienced sales worker. When employees perform well, they generally are switched to selling more expensive items.

Management positions have sometimes come from the ranks without a college education. However, more stores are turning to college graduates who enter a management training program.

Job Outlook

While sales are expected to grow, so are the number of self-service areas. Therefore, the number of jobs should grow at about an average rate. Opportunities in retail sales will continue to be numerous because of the size of the work force and the rate of turnover.

Average weekly earnings in 1988 for retail workers were about $320. Sales people in motor vehicles and appliances averaged $439, while those in apparel and shoes averaged below $207. Workers may be paid a salary, a commission, or some combination of the two. Fringe benefits for full-time workers are usually generous.

GLOSSARY

This Glossary defines terms that are important in the study of economics. The number in parentheses after each definition indicates the page in the textbook where the term is introduced.

A

ability-to-pay principle: A belief that those with the greatest income should pay the highest tax rates. (p. 244)

absolute advantage: A theory that countries should specialize in producing those products or services that they are most efficient in and trade their surplus for goods and services they produce with less efficiency. (p. 370)

advertising: Attempts by businesses to *inform* and *persuade* consumers to buy their product. (p. 106)

agency shop: An arrangement in which all employees are required to pay union dues whether they join the union or not. (p. 189)

Aid to Families with Dependent Children (AFDC): Government cash assistance (welfare) to families with children 18 or under. (p.346)

allocation of resources: The problem of how to distribute scarce resources given unlimited wants. (p. 45)

antitrust policy: Government policy to enforce competition and stop monopolistic practices. (p. 164)

appreciation: An increase in the value of a nation's money in relation to other types of money. (p. 378)

arbitration: A manner of settling a labor-management dispute by submitting disagreements to a third party for a decision. If a labor contract or law requires all disagreements to be settled this way and both parties must accept the decision, it is compulsory arbitration; otherwise, it is voluntary arbitration. (p. 192)

automatic stabilization: Items in the budget, such as income taxes and transfer payments, that change when the economy changes. Designed to keep the economy stable through countercyclical policy that requires no action by government in order to operate.(p. 327)

average fixed cost: The total costs divided by the number of units produced. (p. 125)

B

balance of trade: The difference between the total value of goods and services exported to other countries and the total value of goods and services imported. (p. 375)

barriers to trade: Obstacles, such as tariffs and quotas, designed to discourage trade, particularly imports. (See *tariff* and *quota*.)

base year: A past year used to compare other years in a variety of economic measurements, such as the consumer price index. (pp. 272, 287)

benefits received principle: The belief that taxes should be paid by those who use the services supported by the tax. The gasoline tax is a good example. (p. 243)

bond: A security representing a debt owed by a borrower to a lender, which pays a fixed rate of interest. Businesses usually issue bonds in $1,000 denominations. Government bonds are issued in many different amounts. (p. 132)

boycott: A group decision designed to put pressure on another group. Usually a union urging its members and others not to buy from an employer in order to make the employer come to terms. (p. 190)

business cycle: The expansion and contraction of business activity in four fairly regular periods—expansion, peak, contraction, and trough. (p. 225)

C

capital: A factor of production used by labor in making products; a man-made instrument of production such as a tool, machine, or sheet metal. (p. 15)

capital gain: Occurs when stock can be sold for more than it originally cost to buy. (p. 132)

capitalism: An economic system in which production and the means to produce are owned and controlled by private individuals or groups. Government plays a very small role. The market determines how resources are distributed. (p. 34)

central problem: In economics, how to distribute production when resources are scarce and wants are unlimited. (See *scarcity*.)

characteristics of money: For money to perform its functions in the economy, it must be accepted as payments, be divisible, portable, and have a reasonably stable value. (p. 292)

checking deposits: Money in a bank or thrift institution that may be withdrawn at any time by writing a check or similar instrument. (p. 298)

circular flow model: A simplified diagram of the economy, showing the product market (production flows from businesses to consumers and dollars flow in the opposite direction) and the factor market (households sell their factors to businesses in return for dollars). (p. 65)

classical economist: One who believes that the interaction of demand and supply in the market with no government interference will produce the best economic system. (p. 320)

Clayton Act: Antitrust legislation passed in 1914 that closed some of the loopholes left by the Sherman Antitrust Act, and said that antitrust legislation did not apply to labor unions. (p. 185)

closed shop: A union contract in which the business can only hire union members. Currently, this is illegal. (p. 186)

collective bargaining: A method for reaching agreement on wages, hours, and conditions of work where representatives of workers and representatives of business discuss changes for all. (p. 190)

command economy: An economic system in which decisions on the questions of *what*, *how*, and *for whom* are made by the government. (p. 34)

communism: An economic system in which goods, particularly capital goods, are owned collectively and payment is made according to need. In practice, decisions are made centrally and the individual has little freedom. (p. 422)

comparative advantage: A theory that states all nations will have more goods if they specialize in producing those items in which they have the greatest relative efficiency and import those things in which they have the least relative efficiency. (p. 370)

complementary good: A good that is used with another good, such as a bow is to an arrow. (p. 72)

compulsory arbitration: The law *requires* that a solution be determined by an unbiased person. (p. 192)

Consumer Price Index: The most commonly used measurement of inflation. (pp. 272, 287)

consumer protection: When government intervenes in the market to protect consumers from harmful products. (p. 103)

consumer sovereignty: The idea that customers determine what products will be produced by showing demand in the market. Also, the belief that competition in the market protects the consumer. (p. 98)

corporate income tax: The third most important source of tax revenue for the federal government (p. 245)

corporation: A form of business organization requiring a government charter granting the company specific powers separate from those of the individuals who own the firm. These include the right to sue and be sued and to issue stock. (p. 117)

cost-push inflation: An increase in prices caused by an increase in the cost of production, such as higher oil prices. (p. 272)

countercyclical: An economic policy that is aimed at changing the direction of the business cycle, such as stimulating the economy when it is contracting and slowing it down when it is expanding. (p. 304)

craft union: An organization of workers who have similar skills (also called *horizontal* union). (p. 183)

crowding-out effect: When government borrows heavily, the additional demand increases interest rates, thus discouraging businesses and consumers from borrowing and spending. (p. 328)

cyclical unemployment: Job layoffs caused by a decline in business conditions. (p. 268)

D

decentralized: Economic questions, *what, how,* and *for whom* are answered by individuals in the market, rather than by centralized government. (p. 425)

deficit spending: It happens when government spends more than it takes in. This may be useful if done when the economy needs to expand in order to increase employment. (p. 256)

deflation: A general decline in the price level. (p. 294)

demand: The willingness on the part of people to buy certain quantities of a product at different price levels. (p. 69)

demand curve: A graphic representation of a demand schedule. It generally slopes downward from left to right. This shows the lower the price, the more people are likely to buy. (p. 70)

demand-pull inflation: When prices rise because there is a greater demand than there is a supply; too many dollars are chasing too few goods. (p. 272)

demand schedule: A table that shows how many products people will buy at various prices. (p. 70)

demand-side economics: The Keynesian idea that total spending, the sum of consumers, businesses and government, will determine the GDP. (See *John Maynard Keynes*.)

depreciation: A decrease in the value of a nation's money in relation to other types of money. (p. 378)

deregulation: The act of reducing the amount of government controls over the economy. (p. 165)

derived demand: The demand for factors of production that results from the demand for a product or service. (p. 176)

determinants of demand: The things that cause demand to change: for example, consumer taste, income, price of substitutes and complementary goods, and a change in the number of potential customers. (p. 71)

developed nation: A country such as the United States which is highly industrialized (p. 391)

developing nation: A nation in which the majority of people do not have a minimal standard of living. (p. 391)

diminishing marginal productivity: At a certain point, adding another worker (or other factor of production) does not increase production as much as the preceding additions of workers. (See also *diminishing returns*.) (p. 177)

diminishing marginal utility: Each additional unit of a product is less valuable than the one that came before it. (p. 94)

diminishing returns: At a certain level of production, the cost per unit of producing additional units increases. This occurs because when one factor of production increases but other factors are held constant, a point is reached where the additional inputs will add less production than the preceding inputs. (pp. 73, 177)

discount rate: The rate of interest the Federal Reserve Bank charges banks that borrow money from it. (p. 308)

discouraged worker: A worker who has given up looking for a job. (p. 269)

discretionary fiscal policy: An economic policy that requires a person or agency to take some action. It can be fiscal (budget changes) or monetary (changing the money supply). (p. 326)

diseconomies of scale: A diseconomy of scale exists whenever the per unit costs increase as production increases. The larger the production, the less efficient the operation of that business. (p. 159)

disposable personal income: That income that is left to consumers after they have paid their personal taxes. Some of it will be spent and some saved. (p. 325)

diversification: When a business increases the types of products it sells in order to lower its fixed costs and take advantage of less competitive market conditions. (p. 144)

dividend: That share of the corporation's profit that is distributed to stockholders. (p. 132)

division of labor: Dividing production up into specific tasks in order to increase efficiency and to lower costs. (p. 36)

double counting: Occurs when the value of a contributor is counted more than once when determining GDP using the income approach. (p. 218)

dumping: Selling goods to other countries at below cost to get rid of surpluses or to hurt foreign competition. (p. 376)

durable goods: Goods that do not need to be replaced every year, such as cars and appliances. (p. 226)

E

economics: The study of how people produce, distribute, and consume resources in order to satisfy their wants, and of how people make choices in trying to satisfy their wants with limited resources. (p. 5)

economic system: A set of rules by which a nation answers the basic questions of *what, how,* and *for whom*; how it decides to distribute its resources to satisfy its peoples' wants. (p. 33)

economies of scale: The things that make a large firm more efficient than a small firm. As production increases, unit costs decrease; the larger the production, the more efficient the operation of the business. (p. 159)

elasticity: The effect that a change in price has on demand. (p. 81)

Employment Act of 1946: Law that required the President of the United States to make annual reports to the nation on the condition of the economy and to recommend economic policy, if needed. It established the Council of Economic Advisers and abandoned *laissez faire*. (p. 323)

entrepreneurship: The factor of production that takes the risks and responsibilities of starting a business; an organization that combines the other factors of production. (p. 15)

equilibrium: When economic forces are balanced. If the economic forces of demand and supply are equal, the price will be at equilibrium. (p. 78)

equilibrium wage rate: The wage level that will provide the same number of workers as jobs available. (p. 179)

exchange rate: The value of one nation's currency in relation to other nation's currency. (p. 378)

expansion multiplier: The amount that a dollar of reserves will support in checkable deposits in the bank. (p. 301)

expansion of money: Process by which the granting of credit (loans) by banks results in an increase in the money supply. (p. 299)

expenditure approach: One of three methods for determining GDP. Add consumer spending, plus government spending, plus business spending, plus net spending by foreign purchasers to determine GDP. (p. 217)

externality: When someone who is neither the producer nor consumer of a product pays a cost or receives a benefit from its production. (p. 237)

F

factor market: Where businesses buy natural resources, labor, and capital needed to produce their goods and services. (pp. 65, 176)

factors of production: The inputs used in the production process, including natural resources, entrepreneurship, labor, and capital. (p. 15)

Fair Labor Standards Act: A law passed in 1938 that determined the minimum wage that a worker could be paid. (p. 193)

Federal Deposit Insurance Corporation (FDIC): A government agency that insures deposits up to a certain amount in a bank that is covered if that bank should fail. (p. 304)

Federal Reserve System: An agency created in 1913 to oversee banking and which can influence the economy. (pp. 290, 307)

fiat money: Money that has value because the government orders that it be accepted for payment of debts. (p. 292)

fiscal policy: Planning a federal budget that has either surpluses or deficits intended to maintain a steady level of total spending in the economy. (p. 326)

fixed costs: Production costs that remain the same regardless of the number of units produced. (p. 123)

for whom: One of three major economic questions every economic system must answer. Asks *for whom* is the production meant or what is the method for distribution. (p. 41)

free market economy: An economic system in which individuals and businesses own the factors of production and basic economic decisions are determined by the interaction of demand and supply. (p. 319)

frictional unemployment: Short-term unemployment caused by workers changing jobs. (p. 268)

full employment: A condition in which anyone who wishes to work can. Usually set at 94 to 96 percent of the labor force, or 4 to 6 percent unemployment rate. (See *frictional unemployment.*)

functions of money: Money can be used as a medium of exchange, as a measure of value, and as a store of value. (p. 292)

G

goods: Tangible (physical, touchable) things that satisfy human wants and needs. (p. 5)

Gross Domestic Product (GDP): The retail value of all final products produced in a nation in a given year. (p. 216)

H

horizontal combination: A merger of companies in the same business; occurs when firms that do the same thing join together. (p. 156)

how: One of three basic questions any economic system must answer; namely, *how* goods and services will be produced. (p. 41)

I

imperfect competition: A market condition in which an individual or a group of sellers and buyers is large enough to influence price. It includes natural monopoly, oligopoly, and monopolistic competition. (p. 148)

incentive: An inducement to do something or not do something. In capitalism, profits influence people to produce; higher wages influence workers to work overtime. (p. 423)

income: A flow of value; what you receive over a period of time. (p. 278)

income approach: A method of calculating GDP; total of income, including wages, profits, rent, interest, some taxes, and the cost of wearing out capital (machinery). (p. 218)

indexed: Adjusted income that overcomes the decline in the value of money through inflation. (p. 344)

individual retirement account (IRA): A retirement plan that allows individuals to put off paying taxes on money they save. (p. 337)

industrial capitalism: An economic system that relies on the market to make most decisions but allows the government to allocate some resources to some firms. (p. 429)

industrial union: A union in which all workers in an industry belong to the same union regardless of their job (also called *vertical union*). (p. 183)

infant industry: An argument used to justify a temporary tariff to allow new industries to learn how to produce more efficiently. (p. 373)

inflation: A general increase in the price level resulting from a decline in the value of money. (pp. 272, 294)

informative advertising: Advertising that is intended to inform. (p. 108)

infrastructure: Facilities such as roads, water systems, communications, etc., that help a nation to produce and distribute production. (p. 395)

injunction: A court order to stop some kind of action. (pp. 185, 191)

interest: Payment for the use of money. (p. 130)

intergovernmental revenue: Revenue paid by one agency or level of government to another. (p. 247)

invisible hand: Business owners serving the interests of society when they attempt to serve their own self-interests. (p. 100)

K

Keynes, John Maynard: An English economist who believed that economic activity and jobs depended on the rate of spending in the economy. (p. 324)

kibbutz: A community in Israel that has a command economy. (p. 416)

L

labor: A factor of production contributing human effort in the production process. (p. 15)

labor force participation rate: The percentage of people, 16 years of age or older who could work, who are either working or looking for work. (p. 179)

labor union: An organization of workers formed to give them greater bargaining power, that attempt to improve their wages and working conditions through collective action. (p. 182)

laissez faire: A policy that believes government should not intervene in the economy. (p. 319)

law of demand: States that people will buy more of a product at a lower price than at a higher price, if nothing else changes. (p. 69)

law of supply: At higher prices producers are willing to offer more products for sale than at lower prices. (p. 74)

leading indicator: A measurement that anticipates changes in the direction of the economy. (p. 226)

least-likely-to-offend principle: In evaluating taxes, politicians frequently choose those which will offend their voters least. Taxes on liquor and cigarettes are the best examples. (p. 244)

limited liability: The legal doctrine that protects stockholders in corporations from losing more than the money they invested. (p. 119)

limited life: The condition that proprietorship and partnerships cease upon the death of an owner. Corporations have unlimited life. (p. 117)

lockout: When management closes the work place to prevent unionized employees from working. (p. 191)

Lorenz Curve: A graphic method of showing the inequality in the distribution of income. (p. 279)

M

macroeconomics: The study of the economy as a whole. (p. 213)

maintaining economic stability: An argument which states that nations that depend on trade are more likely to be hurt by disruptions in trade. (p. 374)

marginal physical product: The amount of additional product that is added to the total when an additional factor (such as another worker) is added. (p. 178)

marginal revenue product: Same as marginal physical product, but converted to the money value of the additional product. (p. 177)

marginal worker: Generally, workers who are hired last because they are least qualified. Usually such workers earn the minimum wage and have other means of support. (p. 195)

mediation: A method for settling a labor dispute in which a third party helps union and management arrive at an acceptable compromise. (p. 191)

microeconomics: The study of how decisions are made by individual parts of the economy, such as businesses and consumers. (p. 61)

minimum wage: A law setting the lowest wage that may be paid to a worker. (p. 193)

model: A tool used by economists to show how different factors act and react on each other, such as a demand and supply graph; a simplified picture of the real world. (p. 17)

monetary policy: Actions to control the money supply by the Federal Reserve system to achieve full-employment, stable prices, and economic growth. (p. 309)

money: Medium of exchange that is accepted for payment of debts; a claim on something that has value. (p. 292)

money supply: The amount of money that is available to be spent in the economy. (p. 294)

money wages: The number of dollars workers receive for their labor (as opposed to *real wages*). (p. 180)

monopolistic competition: Imperfect competition in which there are many firms selling similar products; the seller tries to make his/her product appear different from others. (p. 149)

mortality rate: The average number of deaths per thousand people per year. (p. 405)

multinational corporation: Any business that is headquartered in one country but carries on business activities in one or more foreign countries. (p. 381)

N

national debt: The amount of money the federal government owes. (p. 254)

National Labor Relations Act: Legislation passed in 1935, which recognizes labor's right to bargain collectively as a union. (p. 185)

national security: Used to justify trade barriers against military products, on the grounds that the country should not depend on another nation for such items. (p. 373)

natural monopoly: When an industry requires such large capital investments that it would be inefficient to have more than one firm in that area. (p. 150)

natural resources: A factor of production that has not been changed by people. Also called *land*. (p. 15)

negative balance of trade: When the value of a nation's imports is greater than the value of its exports. (p. 374)

negative externality: Occurs when someone who is neither the producer nor the consumer of a product pays a cost associated with the product. (p. 240)

newly developed nation: A country that has experienced rapid economic growth in recent years. (p. 391)

nominal values: The numbered value of measurements in the economy such as GDP, prices, and wages. Not adjusted for inflation, in contrast to *real values*. (p. 222)

nondurable goods: Those goods that need to be replaced frequently, such as food and clothing. (p. 226)

normative statement: A statement involving value judgments as opposed to a purely objective, factual statement. (p. 22)

O

oligopoly: An imperfect market in which a few firms dominate. (p. 149)

open market operations: Buying and selling of U.S. Government securities by the Federal Reserve Bank in order to control the money supply. (p. 308)

opportunity cost: The value of the second choice that is given up when the first choice is taken. (p. 11)

P

partnership: A form of business organization with two or more owners, having limited life and unlimited liability. (p. 117)

perfect competition: A market in which there are numerous buyers and sellers seeking to trade a similar product. There is easy movement in and out of the market and no seller can control the price. (p. 143)

perfect monopoly: A market in which there is only one producer, thus offering some control over price. (p. 147)

personal income tax: The federal governments most important source of revenue. (p. 245)

persuasive advertising: Advertising that is intended to persuade. (p. 108)

Phase II: The attempt by government in 1971–1973 to keep price and wage increases within reasonable levels after a 90-day price and wage freeze. (p. 333)

picket line: A union weapon in which striking workers walk in line carrying placards which express their grievances. (p. 191)

point of equilibrium: The intersection of the demand and supply curves, indicating the price and quantity at which a product will be sold in the market. (p. 78)

political action committees: Groups that intend to put pressure on politicians to support their points of view. (p. 191)

pork barrel legislation: Laws passed by Congress to gain political support in the home district of a member of Congress, not because it is either necessary or even good for the country. (p. 250)

positive balance of trade: When the value of a nation's exports is greater than the value of its imports. (p. 374)

positive statement: A statement of fact, as opposed to a statement of personal values. (p. 21)

poverty: A relative term; defined by the U.S. government in 1991 as an income of less than $13,924 for a family of four living in the city. (p. 278)

price control: A policy that prevents prices of designated items from going above or below a specified level. (p. 333)

price elastic demand: A change in price causes a change in the quantity sold. Demand for luxuries is elastic. (p. 82)

price inelastic demand: People want the same amount no matter what the price. Demand for necessities is inelastic. (p. 81)

prime rate: The lowest interest rate that banks charge their best customers. (p. 131)

principle of exclusion: A claim of sole use of a product. (p. 239)

private goods: Goods owned by individuals and subject to the principle of exclusion. (p. 239)

pro-cyclical: Economic policies that increase the direction in which the economy is moving. (p. 303)

production: The creation of various kinds of goods and services. (p. 14)

production possibilities frontier: A graph showing different attainable combinations of two possible outputs that a given amount of resources (inputs) can produce. (p. 25)

product market: Sales of consumer products; the final goods and services that are bought by households. (p. 65)

productivity: The measure of the value of products that can be created from a quantity of factors of production. (p. 335)

productivity principle: A tax incentive given to business to encourage greater productivity and efficiency. (p. 224)

profit: The basic incentive for operating a business in capitalism, consisting of the amount of money left over after all costs are paid. (p. 44)

profit motive: The incentive that causes people to work hard to make money because they know they can retain the profit. (p. 423)

progressive taxation: A tax in which the tax rate increases with the tax base (higher incomes pay a higher percentage of income). (p. 245)

proletariat: A term used by Karl Marx and his communist followers, meaning *workers*. (p. 423)

property tax: A local tax on buildings and land. (p. 247)

proportional taxation: A tax in which the tax rate stays the same regardless of the tax base. (p. 245)

protection of domestic jobs: An argument to increase tariffs on lower priced foreign goods to make U.S. products more competitive with foreign products. (p. 373)

protective tariff: A tax placed on foreign goods, meant to discourage their being imported and to protect home producers. (p. 371)

public goods and services: Goods and services provided to the public by the government. (p. 238)

Q

quota: A limit placed on the amount of imports or exports. (p. 371)

R

rational choice: Decisions made on the basis of selecting things with greater value in return for giving up things with lesser value. (p. 20)

real GDP: The retail value of a nation's annual output stated in constant dollars. Converts nominal or current dollar GDP into constant dollars using the purchasing power of a given base year. (p. 222)

real hourly wage rate: Hourly earnings as adjusted for inflation. (p. 223)

real values: Stating wages, interest rates, income, or other measurements in constant dollars in order to correct for the changing value of money. (p. 222)

real wages: How much can actually be bought with the wages paid (as opposed to *money wages*). (p. 181)

recession: The contracting portion of a business cycle, when output declines and unemployment increases. The opposite of recovery. (p. 226)

recovery: The expanding portion of a business cycle, when output is increasing and unemployment is decreasing. (p. 226)

redistribution of income: Changing the income of households by the way government taxes and spends. Generally, it reduces the income of those having high income and increases the income of those with low income. (p. 242)

regressive taxation: A tax in which the tax rate declines as the tax base increases (lower incomes pay a greater percentage of income). It hurts the poor in favor of the rich. (p. 245)

regulatory agency: A board appointed by the executives of a state which sets rates that natural monopolies can charge. (p. 150)

relocation: A firm moves the plant to another place where wages, taxes, or other costs may be lower, making profits greater. (p. 191)

rent: Payment for the use of a natural resource. (p. 130)

reserve requirement: The percentage of a deposit that a bank must put aside and not use for loans. It is determined by the Federal Reserve Bank. When stated as a fraction, it is the reserve ratio. (p. 299)

resources: All the things that are necessary for production. (p. 14)

restrictive tariff: A tariff designed to reduce the flow of a particular kind of product into a country. (p. 371)

revenue: The income of a business or government. (p. 247)

revenue tariffs: Tariffs intended to produce revenue for the government. (p. 371)

right-to-work laws: State laws that make contracts requiring employees to join a union as a condition of work illegal. (p. 186)

S

sales tax: A tax on retail products made at the time of purchase. (p. 247)

savings: The part of disposable income that is not spent. (p. 233)

Say, John Baptiste: A French classical economist who believed that the production of goods and services (supply) would create enough demand so they would be bought. (p. 323)

scarcity: The condition in the economy where wants are greater than the resources to satisfy them. The central problem in economics. (p. 9)

seasonal unemployment: Decline in employment due to seasonal conditions, such as lay-offs in outdoor construction in the North in the winter. (p. 268)

secondary boycott: Where unions encourage the public not to buy from a firm's suppliers. Now illegal. (p. 190)

services: Intangible things that satisfy human wants or needs. (p. 5)

Sherman Antitrust Act of 1890: Said that plans to restrain trade, or to monopolize or attempt to monopolize production, were against the law. (p. 164)

shortage: When the equilibrium price is below the offered price, a shortage develops. At that price, the quantity demanded is greater than the quantity supplied. (p. 79)

single proprietorship: Form of business organization that places full responsibility on a single owner. (p. 117)

sit-down strike: When workers refuse to leave the plant which is being struck. (p. 191)

slowdown: An organized attempt by workers to slow down their production in order to put pressure on the company to meet workers' demands. (p. 190)

social insurance tax: Taxes used to support Social Security programs. (p. 245)

socialism: An economic system in which most of the means of production are owned by government and in which there is much central planning. (p. 424)

Social Security Act: A 1935 act which established the Social Security program, unemployment insurance, and welfare. (p. 344)

specialization: Concentrating a person's labor (or other function of production) on a single task in order to increase efficiency. (p. 36)

specialized capital: Tools designed to increase the efficiency of a particular task in production. (p. 36)

stock: Ownership in a corporation, expressed as shares. (p. 132)

strike: When workers withhold their services in order to pressure management to yield to the workers' demands. (p. 191)

strike breakers: Workers called in by a firm to replace workers who are out on strike. (p. 191)

structural unemployment: Loss of jobs for workers whose skills are no longer in demand; caused by changes in consumer tastes or in technology. The skills of workers looking for jobs do not match the skills employers are looking for. (p. 269)

substitute good: A good that is interchangeable with another, such as butter and margarine. (p. 71)

supply: The quantity of goods and services that sellers will offer at various prices during a given time and place. (p. 73)

supply curve: A graph of a supply schedule, showing the relationship between price and quantity. (p. 75)

supply schedule: A table showing the relationship of price and the quantity sellers will offer in the market. (p. 74)

supply-side economics: The theory, associated with President Reagan, that emphasizes increasing supply, in contrast to Keynesian economics where aggregate demand is stressed. (p. 335)

surplus: When the equilibrium price is above the intersection of supply and demand, a surplus remains. At that price the quantity demanded is less than the quantity supplied. (p. 79)

T

Taft-Hartley Act: Legislation passed in 1947 that outlawed the closed shop, prohibited federal employees from striking, permitted the President to seek an injunction delaying strikes that harm the national interest, and permitted state "right-to-work" laws. (p. 186)

tariff: A tax on an item that is imported. (p. 371)

tax: A charge made by government on individuals and businesses, usually for the purpose of shifting resources from the private to the public sector. (p. 243)

tax base: The value of what is being taxed; for example, the value of a person's taxable income. (p. 245)

tax rate: The percentage of the tax base (for example, a person's taxable income) that is taxed. (pp. 244, 245)

trade-offs: Choices between alternatives

with the understanding that using resources for one purpose must be at the expense of another purpose. (p. 11)

traditional economy: An economic system in which the basic questions of *what, how,* and *for whom* are decided by custom (doing things the way they were done in the past). (pp. 34, 394)

transfer in kind: Redistribution of income through non-cash payments such as food stamps, medical care, or low-income housing. (p. 242)

transfer payment: Redistribution of income through the payment of cash, such as welfare payments or unemployment compensation. (p. 242)

U

underground economy: The unreported economic activity, sometimes illegal, that is never reported. Results in large losses in government revenue, and causes reported GDP to be smaller than actual production. (p. 219)

unemployment rate: The percentage of those in the labor force who are not working but who are actively looking for work. (p. 270)

union label: By sewing a union label into garments, unions try to encourage the public to buy only products that were manufactured by union workers. (p. 191)

union shop: An agreement between labor and management that all workers must join the union after they have been hired. (p. 189)

unlimited liability: If an unincorporated business (proprietorship or partnership) goes bankrupt, much of the owners' personal property may be taken over by creditors. (p. 117)

unlimited life: A condition that allows a corporation to continue doing business even after the death of its owner. (p. 119)

V

value judgment: Decision-making based on personal values rather than on facts. (p. 6)

variable costs: Costs that increase as production increases. (p. 123)

vertical combination: A merger of businesses that perform different stages of production. (p. 156)

voluntary arbitration: An agreement between labor and management that a labor dispute be settled by an unbiased person. (p. 192)

W

wages: Payment for labor. (p. 181)

wealth: The total value of accumulated goods and services. (pp. 37, 278)

welfare capitalism: An economic system that relies on the market to make most economic decisions but which provides many benefits paid for by relatively high taxes. (p. 424)

what: One of the three major questions every economic system has to answer, namely, *what* to produce. (p. 41)

wildcat strike: When workers strike without approval of the union. (p. 191)

workable competition: Sufficient competitiveness so that consumer interests are protected, but where the economic advantages of large scale production are recognized. (p. 163)

INDEX

Page numbers in *italics* refer to figures in the text.

D

E

F

Photography

Cover, Will Shively.

iii, Dan DeWilde; iv, Mike Yamashita/Woodfin Camp & Associates; v, Robert Brenner; vi, © Nobiru Kimine 1987/Photo Researchers; vii, © Jeffrey A. Rycus, courtesy City Center Mall, Columbus OH; viii, Boroff\TexaStock; ix, courtesy NY Convention & Visitors Bureau; x, Glennon P. Donahue; xi, Frank Wing; xiii, Eastcott-Momatiuk/Woodfin Camp & Associates; xiv, Frank Wing; xv, David Zalaznik of the Peoria Journal-Star; xvi, George Hall/Woodfin Camp & Associates; xvii, Michael D. Sullivan/TexaStock; xviii, Frank Wing; xix, Susan Friedman; xxi, Adam Woolfitt/Woodfin Camp & Associates; xxii, Sepp Seit/Woodfin Camp & Associates; xxiii, Karen Rantzman; xxiv, Adam Woolfitt/Woodfin Camp & Associates; xxv, Tom Craig/FPG; xxvi, Jeff Bates; 2-3, Dan DeWilde; 4, Mike Yamashita/Woodfin Camp & Associates; 6, © Don & Pat Valenti/Tony Stone Worldwide; 7, clockwise from top: Christopher B. Kuhn/TexaStock, Sepp Seitz/Woodfin Camp & Associates, AP/Wide World Photos, Dan DeWilde; 10, U.S. Air Force Photo; 12, Tony Freeman; 16, NASA; 18, Jeff Bates; 21, Barrera/TexaStock; 22, Patricia Fox-Smith/TexaStock; 23, Elliot Varner Smith; 25, Paul Light/Lightwave; 32, Robert Brenner; 38, courtesy The Ford Archives, Henry Ford Museum, Dearborn, MI; 39, (t) Terry Wild Studio, (b) courtesy Caterpillar Inc., Peoria, IL; 42, (t, bl) David E. Kennedy/TexaStock, (br) William Rogers; 45, O. Abolafia/Gamma-Liaison; 46, Gene Fitzer; 48, © Nobiru Kimine 1987/Photo Researchers; 60-61, © Jeffrey A. Rycus, courtesy City Center Mall, Columbus OH; 62, Boroff/TexaStock; 67, Alec Duncan; 68, Bettmann Archive; 71, Grant Heilman Photography; 74, Frank Cezus; 85, Gene Fitzer 86; 92, courtesy NY Convention & Visitors Bureau; 95, Robert Brenner/PhotoEdit; 96, George Hall/Woodfin Camp & Associates; 99, Susan Friedman; 100, David R. Frazier Photolibrary; 103, Susan Friedman; 105, James M. Mejuto; 107, (t) courtesy Microsoft Corp., (b) Dennis Monarchy Photography, courtesy Nike Inc.; 114, Glennon P. Donahue; 118, (t) Joseph A. DiChello Jr., (c) Elliot Varner Smith, (b) Michael L. Abramson/Woodfin Camp & Associates; 123, Patricia Fox-Smith/TexaStock; 126, © Bob Daemmrich/Tony Stone Worldwide; 127, 131, Susan Friedman; 140, Frank Wing; 142, (t) David E. Kennedy/TexaStock, (b) Michael D. Sullivan/TexaStock; 144, Kolvoord/TexaStock; 146, Susan Friedman; 148, Dennis Barnes; 149, Bill Gallery/Stock Boston; 150, PhotoEdit; 152, Arthur Grace/NYT Pictures; 154, Jim West; 155, Tony Freeman; 157, courtesy Chevron Corporation, San Francisco, CA; 159, Tom Pantages; 160, Al Levy; 163, Jim West; 165, Susan Friedman; 172, Eastcott-Momatiuk/Woodfin Camp & Associates; 174, Bettmann Archive; 180, Library of Congress; 183, Bettmann Archive; 184, (all) UPI/Bettmann Newsphotos; 185, AP/Wide World Photos; 189, 190, UPI/Bettmann Newsphotos; 194, Paul Light/Lightwave; 195, © Ann States/Saba Press Photos; 212-213, Frank Wing; 214, David Zalaznik of the Peoria Star-Journal; 219, David E. Kennedy/TexaStock; 223, (t) AP/Wide World Photos, (b) Susan Friedman; 227, Barbara Filet; 234, George Hall/Woodfin Camp & Associates; 236, (t) Dale Ahearn/TexaStock, (b) James M. Mejuto; 238, (t) Bettmann Archive, (b) Gene Fitzer; 240, Dennis Barnes; 241, AP/Wide World Photos; 244, Aaron Haupt; 252, 254, 255, Tony Freeman; 256, © Gordon/R.E.A./Saba Press Photos; 264, Michael D. Sullivan/TexaStock; 266, (t) Michael D. Sullivan/TexaStock, (b) Susan Friedman; 269, Alon Reininger/Contact Press/Woodfin Camp & Associates; 274, Lorraine Parrow/First Light; 276, courtesy Chevron Corporation, San Francisco, CA; 281, David E. Kennedy/TexaStock; 288, Frank Wing; 290, Gene Fitzer; 293, Wolfgang Kaehler; 299, Blair Seitz/Photo Researchers; 303, Aaron Haupt; 304, Dennis Barnes; 312, AP/Wide World Photos; 318, Susan Friedman; 320, (t) courtesy the Historical Society of PA, (b) James Wilson/Woodfin Camp & Associates; 324, (l) Historical Pictures/Stock Montage, (r) Bettmann Archive; 325, Steve Allen/Peter Arnold, Inc.; 326, Chuck O'Rear/Woodfin Camp & Associates; 330, Michal Heron/Woodfin Camp & Associates; 331, AP/Wide World Photos; 335, Dennis Barnes; 336, (t) Michael L. Abramson/Woodfin Camp & Associates, (b) Dwight Cendrowski; 345, (all) Barrera/TexaStock; 347, Barbara Laing/TexaStock; 349, 350, AP/Wide World Photos; 364-365, Adam Woolfit/Woodfin Camp & Associates; 366, Sepp Seitz/Woodfin Camp & Associates; 368, © John A. Giordano/Saba Press Photos; 375, Gene Fitzer; 390, Karen Rantzman; 392, David Burnett/Contact Press/Woodfin Camp & Associates; 395, © Marion Patterson/Photo Researchers; 396, Alan Oddie/PhotoEdit; 398, AP/Wide World Photos; 401, Korma Puusa/Woodfin Camp & Associates; 403, Marc & Evelyne Bernheim/Woodfin Camp & Associates; 405, Gianfranco Gorgoni/Contact Press/Woodfin Camp & Associates; 406, Alon Reininger/Contact Press/Woodfin Camp & Associates; 414, Adam Woolfit/Woodfin Camp & Associates; 417, © Fujifotos/The Image Works; 423, AP/Wide World Photos; 424, Tom Craig/FPG; 430, © 1989 Jean Kugler/FPG.

Illustrations

Tom Kennedy; Randy Miyake (technical); Mary Moye-Rowley